POCKETFUL OF ROCKETS

POCKETFUL OF ROCKETS

History And Stories Behind
White Sands Missile Range

BY

JIM ECKLES

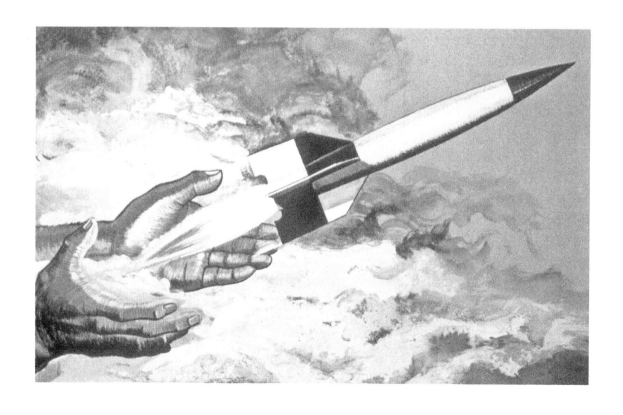

ISBN-13: 978-1492773504
ISBN-10: 1492773506

Published by the Fiddlebike Partnership
Las Cruces, New Mexico 88011

For all the thousands of men and women who
have quietly worked and served at White Sands.

Contents

Preface

First of all, just so there is no misunderstanding, this book is NOT about White Sands National Monument and all those white gypsum dunes. This book is about White Sands Missile Range and all of its sand dunes.

When I went to work in the White Sands Missile Range Public Affairs Office in 1977, I certainly had no intention of writing a book. All I knew was that it was a huge place and I didn't have to wear a coat and tie to work every day - in fact, almost never.

Right away, my job demanded that I learn as much about the missile range as possible. I needed to be able to explain how the range operated, what technologies White Sands used to collect information about a test, how tests were conducted safely, what the different weapon systems were all about, how the past influenced current events, and how all the pieces fit together. An interest in history quickly led to looking under the rocks for those Wild West stories, how Native Americans lived off the apparent barren desert, and how missile range pioneers built the foundation for what happens today at all the military's test ranges.

It was a lot to learn. It took years before I was comfortable explaining much of it. When I added the history, it was readily apparent I couldn't learn it all. The volume was overwhelming.

One reason I needed this kind of background on White Sands was for dealing with reporters, a major part of my job. I quickly learned that most reporters have no background or education in science and technology, the military or big government. Put those three areas together and you have a White Sands Missile Range. In fact, about the only thing they knew to ask about was the price tag. Ho-hum.

Because of this disconnect, almost every encounter with a reporter turned into a bit of a teaching ses-

sion. I had to be prepared to provide the background to make sense of many stories.

During my 30 years on the Range, I found that people enjoyed hearing some of the stories I stockpiled. An added bonus was that I liked telling them. The obvious next step was to summarize what was floating around in my head and make it easily available in a book.

It took years to write this because I never let it get in the way of vacation trips (although I'm not sure you get a "vacation" during retirement), good books, a long bike ride, golf outings, and all the other distractions that pop up in retirement. I've always thought "carpe diem" was an excellent motto to live by as long as you don't do anything stupid. You've always heard the cliche that the best education is learning from one's mistakes. In reality, that is just someone not paying attention in school or not learning the lessons brought to us every night on the news. A much better way to learn is to take advantage of all those mistakes already made by other people and move on. Repeating their foolishness only brings pain and delay.

I thought about calling the book "Everything I Know About White Sands Missile Range," but that would be either a lie or an exaggeration. First of all, there is a whole bunch of information I've simply forgotten. Then there is the vetting process of deciding what to put in and what to leave out. A lot has been left still floating in my head.

The decision-making process of what I chose to keep didn't have a precise set of rules. However, doing tours of the missile range, talking to folks downtown, and answering emails, I found people were really interested in places like Trinity Site and Victorio Peak, seeing wildlife from the roads, asking where the alien bodies were kept in freezers, and where did

Albert Fountain die. There were some who asked about a particular weapon system because of its gee-whiz aspects. Then it might be a year or two before anyone showed any interest in the Range's capabilities to run the testing mission.

That pretty much outlines my approach to this book. First of all, it is not an academic history of White Sands. I have a few important dates but who cares, after all, when the Range went from being a Class IV facility to a Class II? (If you really want to know, it was in Army General Order Number 59, dated Sept. 8, 1948.)

Nor is it a listing of all of the weapon systems tested at WSMR. A huge number of tests were for vehicles and systems that simply faded away or evolved into something else that was actually used. We'd need several volumes to cover it all.

Finally, many of the technical folks may be disappointed there isn't a whole chapter or two on the history of radar, optics or other technologies used at White Sands. At the same time, those looking for information about the Apache and Hembrillo Battlefield may find the few paragraphs on the FPS-16 radar a bit tedious. In the end it was my decision on how to balance these ends of the continuum. It is what it is.

Then there are stories that just don't fit into a book like this. An example is the WSMR float. Did you know the missile range once had a parade float? For instance, in 1968 range employees built one for the Sun Bowl Parade. It was covered with thousands of computer punch cards that the workers dyed different colors. They covered the float with cards the same way the floats are covered with flowers for the Rose Bowl Parade.

When I arrived at White Sands, the Public Affairs Office was in charge of the float. It was about 30 feet long, just small enough to fit on a flatbed trailer so the thing could be hauled to El Paso, Las Cruces, Truth or Consequences, Alamogordo and Deming.

One of my first jobs was to accompany the truck and float to Deming where Jim Bryant and I would unload it and drive it in the 4th of July parade.

The float had a mountain on the back that we mounted a skier on. Up front was a picnic table with an umbrella of small missiles protecting all the people seated around the table. The float's theme was the Department of Defense protecting the American way of life.

Going through Las Cruces, the rockets in the umbrella (they were little Loki rockets) caught in the big tree overhanging Picacho Ave. at Alameda. In fact, one of the rockets was bent up into a vertical position instead of the horizontal. That rocket then hit the stoplight at Alameda as the truck driver went on.

The stoplight bounced around wildly and went black. I was following in my car and signaled for the driver to stop. Not long after, a policeman showed up who just happened to be a Vietnam Vet. He warned us to be careful, told us he'd call some folks about the light, and sent us on our way.

In Deming Jim Bryant grabbed onto the errant rocket and tried to pull it back down into position. Didn't work. He then tried hanging on the rocket. No go. Then, I put my arms around Jim and pulled. It started to move and when I lifted my feet off the ground it slowly came down into the correct position. The next day the parade was a great success.

Putting the next float together fell into my lap. I spent hours covering all the plywood surfaces with vividly colored plastic sheeting. Thank god, that was the last of the WSMR floats.

Mostly I had a great time at my job. Having a series of open-minded bosses really helped. Larry Furrow, the last of that line, always used to tell me that if my activities uprange and downtown were supporting WSMR and the Public Affairs mission of communication and outreach, have at it.

In addition to Larry, I need to thank all of my mates in Public Affairs, especially Debbie Bingham and Monte Marlin. Indirectly, they made this book possible. I should also single out Lisa Blevins, who took my office slot after I retired in 2007. She has badgered me about this book for years. Lisa - here it is.

Also, I need to thank Robb Hermes, Vickie Reynolds, Karl Laumbach, Patrick Romero, J.P. Moore, Patrick Morrow, and Mara Weisenberger, who all took the time to read some portion of the book and provide their comments.

Finally, a big thanks to my wife Debbie for her patience during this process. Much house maintenance and many chores have been delayed long enough. Also, she helped with the editing and always provided sound judgement about many aspects of the book.

Jim Eckles

The official caption for this photo reads "603rd Engineers camouflage area surrounding Corporal missile." There is some basic information stenciled on the side of the missile to include "Flight No. 1567." Also, up high near the nose, are the names, "Barbara, Nancy and Alexis." I'm pretty sure that is not standard information. Unfortunately we don't know who they were or why the men painted their names there. If we could find the missile guys for this test, there just might be a great story waiting to be told. Corporal was America's first ballistic missile and was capable of carrying a nuclear warhead. It was designed by the Jet Propulsion Laboratory (JPL) and inherited some design characteristics found in the WAC Corporal, an earlier JPL rocket. WSMR photo.

Aerial Orientation

A VIP's View Of White Sands Missile Range

At 3,200 square miles, White Sands Missile Range is as large as Yellowstone National Park or, as we liked to say in Public Affairs, as large as Rhode Island and Delaware combined. It is a big Western landscape with a rich natural and cultural history.

Interesting people have walked that ground for thousands of years now. It started with early hunter-gatherer peoples who moved around harvesting their meals from the deserts and mountains. Eventually, the land was a backdrop for outlaws and lawmen with ranchers on the sidelines trying to eke out a living. Then there were the giants at the end of World War II who launched the Space Age and Nuclear Age on what was to become the largest military installation in the country.

Since 1942, most of that land has been restricted by the military and very few members of the public have seen it. For many, the missile range and its property are a bit of a tantalizing mystery, something they'd like to know more about.

Before jumping into the range's past, I think it would be helpful to get a sense of the place by flying a large counterclockwise orientation loop over it. This is something I did many times while working in the Public Affairs Office. It was a valuable tool for showing outsiders the sheer size and unique geography of White Sands. Also, we'll get a quick look at many places covered in more detail later in the book.

During our helicopter trips, we usually covered the two separate mountain ranges, prehistoric lakebeds, very recent lava flows, oryx, horses, forests of piñon, and a few skimpy water sources. Imposed on the natural landscape are many ranching structures as well as the late 20th century military facilities. It includes everything from Trinity Site to the latest laser testing range. I loved flying those trips as a tour guide since they were so much more satisfying than pushing paper from my government desk or attending another of the endless meetings.

For decades, the tours were conducted using old Vietnam era helicopters better known as Hueys. Of course, the current Hueys are not really relics from the 1960s. They have repeatedly been rebuilt, upgraded and improved. Not much of the original helicopter is there.

A typical flight would take about three hours to go up one side of the range and come back down the other after refueling at Stallion Range Center. When the weather was warm, we flew with the doors locked open to provide ventilation – actually it was stronger than ventilation as the air whipped through the open cabin. As the guide, I had to have the microphone for the intercom almost in my mouth for the others to hear me.

Flying with the doors open also provided spectacular views out either side of the Huey. Those sitting next to the doors had the extra advantage of being able to lean a little to the side and look straight down under the helicopter.

Depending on the individual or group in the helicopter, we would overfly specific places of interest. We even went so far as putting guests on the ground so they could see things first hand. When the command was requesting money to fix roads literally falling apart, we put influential visitors from Washington, D.C. in cars to drive sections of a road with the excuse that the chopper needed to get fuel. This cautious drive on roads with minefields of potholes usually jarred some money loose to fix a few more miles of paving, leaving another road section to the next VIP.

This may sound trivial, but when you use the roads to transport very sensitive optical instruments worth millions of dollars and equipped with precisely aligned lenses and mirrors, it is best not to bang them about on a road that could easily be fixed.

The shape of the place is basically a large rectangle measuring about 100 miles south to north and 40 miles east to west. At first glance you might say, "Wait a second, that should be 4,000 square miles, not 3,200." There are some oddities in the rectangle that reduce the Army's share of it.

First of all, the boundaries are not nice straight lines. There are many cutouts that make small intrusions into the range. For instance, when the boundaries were drawn, there were a few cases where the line was allowed to deviate so a spring or well would remain outside White Sands, allowing the local rancher access to the site. Also, at the south end, the corners zig and zag as needed to work around other landowners.

However, these don't account for most of the 800-square-mile difference. The main reason is the land inside the missile range that belongs to someone else. White Sands National Monument and the San Andres National Wildlife Refuge are both islands in the sea that is the missile range. The monument belongs to the National Park Service and the refuge to the U.S. Fish and Wildlife Service.

Looking at the land and its ownership, as looking at a paper map, only gives a two-dimensional picture of White Sands. There is a third dimension to the missile range as well. White Sands controls the airspace overhead all the way into Space.

So, in addition to fences and gates marking the boundaries on the ground, White Sands has invisible walls around it. Since it is three-dimensional, the airspace is often spoken of as a volume, a chimney rising from the ground. Only with the permission of the Air Force controllers (who have the job of managing the airspace) do private and commercial aircraft cruise overhead – which isn't very often.

Our tour helicopter will lift off from one of several landing spots on the main post. In addition to tours, the helicopter's cab can be used to retrieve missile and rocket debris, carry countermeasures for tests, and conduct wildlife surveys.

The main post at White Sands, where most of the thousands of employees work, is in the southwest corner of the range - out of harm's way. More than 45,000 rockets and missiles have been tested at the missile range since 1945. They haven't all performed as predicted. Being tucked away allows the rest of the missile range to act as the safety area for the tests.

Looking Out the Doors

Lifting off from one of the heliports on the main post, there are manmade and natural sites to see in all directions. To the south is Fort Bliss. The boundary with Bliss runs from Texas Canyon in the Organ Mountains all the way east across the Tularosa Basin. Very few people, even those from Fort Bliss, realize the old fort extends well into the Organ Mountains and gathers in Granite and Organ Peaks.

To the west is private land belonging to the Cox family and public land administered by the Bureau of Land Management. This includes the Organ Mountains with majestic Sugarloaf Peak and the jagged Needles looming right out the window. The high point is Organ Needle at 9,000 ft., almost a mile higher than our takeoff point.

To the north, across U.S. Highway 70, is the southern tip of the San Andres Mountains that extend for 80 miles along the west boundary of White Sands. The dividing point between the Organs and the San Andres is an area just north of San Augustin Pass where the different kinds of rock smashed into each other and created metamorphic rock deposits.

Far to the east about 35 miles across the relatively flat Tularosa Basin, the Sacramento Mountains are visible as a dark ridge on the skyline. A few days every year, when smog blows up from the El Paso/Juarez metro area, the mountain ridge is not visible from the post.

In the winter, Sierra Blanca, a 12,000-foot peak some 75 miles away at the north end of the Sacramentos, is often blanketed with a thin covering of snow and it glistens in the morning sun.

From the main post the ground slopes down into the Tularosa Basin, a huge bathtub of a basin running north and south in between the San Andres and Organs complex on the west and the Sacramentos on the east. Out in the middle, there are a few small buttes jutting up here and there and lots of playas (low spots) that are normally dry unless there is exceptional rain. For centuries, spring winds have

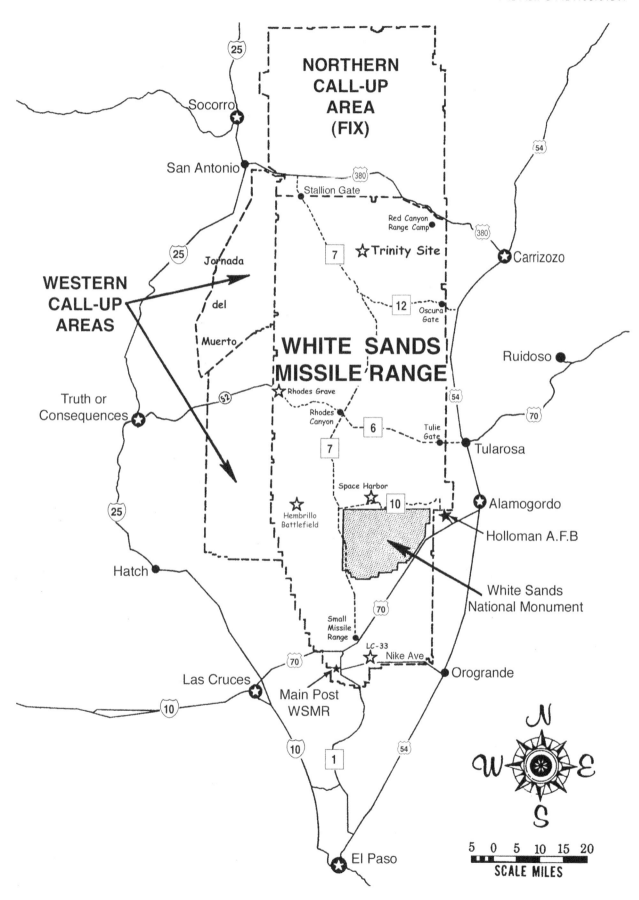

NORTHERN
CALL-UP
AREA
(FIX)

WESTERN
CALL-UP
AREAS

WHITE SANDS
MISSILE RANGE

Socorro

San Antonio

Stallion Gate

Red Canyon
Range Camp

Trinity Site

Carrizozo

Jornada

del

Muerto

Oscura
Gate

Ruidoso

Truth or
Consequences

Rhodes Grave

Rhodes
Canyon

Tulie
Gate

Tularosa

Hembrillo
Battlefield

Space Harbor

Alamogordo

Holloman A.F.B

White Sands
National Monument

Hatch

Small
Missile
Range

LC-33

Nike Ave

Orogrande

Las Cruces

Main Post
WSMR

El Paso

SCALE MILES

5 0 5 10 15 20

raced across the basin moving enough sand to create dune fields in many places.

Terrain and Its Impact

I don't want to try a Michener-like exploration of the distant past, but it is necessary to explain the current terrain and how it works. The surrounding landscape is not just something to look at. Here it shapes the weather, it determines where water can be found, where to look for prehistoric dwellings, where and how hard the wind will blow, and where to place cutting-edge instrumentation sites.

An excellent example is the summer thunderstorm dynamic. Warm, moist air blows across the desert from the southwest in the summer. It gets pushed up thousands of feet to cross the Organ Mountains that tower right above the range's main post. As the air rises, it cools and the water vapor condenses to form clouds.

If the conditions are right, the clouds can build into thunderstorms in just a matter of hours. Little or big, these storms dump most of their rain on the Organ Mountains or, as the winds push from the west, on the eastern slopes of the mountains. If the clouds are large enough, they may continue to rain as they push across the Tularosa Basin.

This means the annual rainfall for the desert varies greatly depending on the local terrain. The main post gets much more rain each year than the west side of the Organs or areas out in the middle of the Tularosa Basin.

This rain is absolutely necessary to bring any life to the surrounding desert, but sometimes it turns deadly. If the thunderstorms don't move much and continue to build one after another in one spot, tremendous amounts of water can be dropped in a small area. That happened over the Organs on an August night in 1978. It rained hard for a couple of hours, and there was no way for the rocky slopes to retain it. That night the Cox family, just west of the main post, recorded 10 inches of rain in their government rain gauge. That is about the yearly average.

The water came gushing downhill, flooding all the drainages through and around the main post. On the approach road from U.S Highway 70 to the north, there is a large concrete culvert under the road. The buildup of the roadway here effectively acts as a six-foot-tall earthen dam across the arroyo with one hole to drain water through it.

In the early days of the range, the road simply dropped down into the arroyos. Old-timers talk about being stuck on post many afternoons in the summer waiting for the water from a local thunderstorm to finish running across the road. The large culvert/bridge eliminated the need to wait around as it handled the storm waters quite well – until 1978.

On the night of Aug. 19, witnesses reported water collecting, forming a large lake west of the road, because the culvert couldn't handle it. Eventually, water started to wash over the road surface. Air Force dentist Captain James Maret, Jr with his wife and two children tried to drive through the flood. The car stalled. Private First Class Marvin Owen, a young military policeman, saw the Maret car start to float away and drove his pickup truck into the flood to assist them.

As he got to them, a wall of water reportedly 10 feet high struck the vehicles and washed them out into the desert. All five people were killed. The MPs truck was found two miles east of the road.

The access road was renamed Owen Road in 1979 to honor the young policeman.

In addition to the deaths, water rushed through the main post flooding houses and mission-related buildings. A few had basements that filled up. The damage was estimated in the millions. One result was the construction of the dike on the west side of the post to channel water around and away from the main post.

The various mountain ranges one can see from any location on White Sands got their start millions of years ago. When the supercontinent Pangaea was formed, this part of it was submerged under a shallow sea. Sediments were laid down over hundreds of millions of years on top of a bed of granite. The material became rock over time, mostly limestone, but also there are layers of gypsum, sandstone and shale.

As Pangaea broke apart and the current continents drifted away, tectonic forces squeezed North and South America and pushed the West up to the point where the rocks were thousands of feet above sea level. Running north and south through the region now occupied by White Sands was a large dome or ridge. Some have described it as a meatloaf of rock.

In addition to the tectonic action pushing everything up, just over 30 million years ago lava ballooned up through this sedimentary rock coming close to the surface on the western edge of the meatloaf-bulge. Although some of the lava flowed out onto the surface, most of it remained below. That pocket of cooled lava, now granite, is called a batholith.

The big transformation in the landscape we still clearly see took place about 10 million years ago – give or take a year or two. The center of the north-south ridge slowly sank. The edges were left standing when it was done.

What was left was a tremendous hole, shaped something like a graben or grave, with nearly vertical walls on the east and west. That is why the Sacramento Mountains and San Andres Mountains have cliff faces on the edges of the Tularosa Basin and more gentle slopes on the other side.

Since then nature has been at work. Erosion has exposed and eroded a large area of the granite batholith to give us the Organ Mountains. Erosion from the Sacramento and San Andres Mountains has washed and blown debris into the Tularosa Basin, leveling its surface.

In fact, the fill material in the basin is thousands of feet thick. Whatever was in the mountains, some of it ended up in the basin. A lot of it is sand and gravel. In 1967, the missile range had a borehole drilled in the basin to find its bottom. They quit at 6,015 feet down and never hit bedrock.

The nature of this fill material makes it a lot like a sponge. That means most of the water entering the Tularosa Basin from rain and snowmelt in the mountains or falling directly in the basin is absorbed. On the other hand, there are areas where there is a great deal of clay on or near the surface that acts as a barrier to the water. There are places in the Tularosa where a little rainfall creates nasty mud – the kind that makes you taller and taller and heavier and heavier with every step.

Since the Tularosa Basin is a bolson, meaning it has no outflow, it has literally been collecting a sea of water underground for all these millions of years. During this time there were some very wet periods in the region and the spongy fill material drank the water in, creating a large aquifer. In some places the water table is close to the surface and can be tapped with just a shovel to dig a hole a few feet deep.

This sounds like great news for communities like Alamogordo that have always been strapped for potable water. Unfortunately, most of the basin water contains more salts than ocean water. It is pretty nasty stuff and requires processing through a desalinization plant before it can be used for anything.

The water at Pellman Ranch was sort of drinkable if you got used to it – at least the owner used it. The ranch was located along the old road from Las Cruces to Tularosa – now U.S. Highway 70.

The water from the well was probably "perched" water meaning that it hit a barrier like a layer of clay when it soaked into the ground and didn't pick up as much mineral material as the main body of water.

When I was taking George McNew around looking at the places where his father Bill McNew ranched and the spots associated with the Albert Fountain murder, George said as a child he drank some of the water at Pellman.

McNew said not long afterward he developed cramps and went outside to relieve himself. The adults all had a good laugh when the panicked youth came rushing inside to announce he thought he was dying. Apparently, his stool was black because drinking the water was like taking a large dose of Epsom salts. It had quite a laxative effect. He was assured he was fine and did grow up to enjoy a successful academic career.

If the water in the basin is so salty, where does the missile range's water come from? Again, the terrain plays into the story as most of it comes from wells right around the main post. Additional wells are near the mouth of Soledad Canyon just south of the main post but on Fort Bliss.

Unlike the vile basin waster, this is good stuff even though it is only a stone's throw away. John Hyndman, the WSMR hydrologist in 1982, told me it was good enough to pipe directly to buildings. However, to meet state and federal regulations, the water had to be chlorinated before it could be used. Now the water is filtered for sediments and fluoride is added as well.

It turns out that water percolating down through the alluvial fans and the canyons in the Organ Mountains doesn't pick up many minerals. To top it off, that potable water sits underground as a tidy little pocket or pool floating atop the salt water down in the basin.

The two bodies of water press against each other with equal pressure, so there is very little mingling except at the contact site. Because of this the missile range has to be very careful. If the range pumps too much water from an area near the contact point, the fresh water pressure will be diminished. That would allow the salt water to push into and contaminate part of the potable pool. The trick is to pump equally from all wells so there is no decrease in pressure.

As one can imagine, water withdrawals for the main post and the areas fed by the well field, to include all the launch complexes and Orogrande Range Camp, grew steadily and rapidly in the first two decades of the missile range's existence. In 1959, the range erected the first of its large water towers west of the housing area. This tank is 80 feet in diameter and holds a million gallons of water. When it is full there are 4,000 tons of water held over 100 feet above the ground.

By the 1970s, the amount of water used stabilized at around 670 million gallons a year. Since then, water usage has declined and by 1992 it was averaging 620 million gallons a year.

No matter how you cut it though, the amount of water being pumped by White Sands is going to run the supply dry eventually. In 1992, the Corps of Engineers reported "natural recharge of the potable water aquifer is at 38% of the annual withdrawal." To compound the problem, WSMR has been suffering through drought conditions so the amount of recharge from rainfall and snowmelt has to be even less.

Flying Away

Leaving the main post, we'll follow the highway to El Paso for a couple of miles, then swing east and back north to pick up Nike Ave. Along the road to the El Paso gate are the static test stands nestled up against the Organs. *(See Chapter 11)* Also, just before the gate is the Nuclear Effects Laboratory (NEL) where equipment can be exposed to any of the individual effects found on the nuclear battlefield. *(See Chapter 8)*

A little east of the El Paso gate is Condron Field. It sits in a playa area that once was used by the Mogollon people centuries ago. When the field was being developed by White Sands, the adobe walls to a pueblo were found there.

A little north of the airfield is another playa that held water for most of the year after the big rain in 1978. On the eastern side of this playa are sand dunes and a pueblo that was burned; at least, the wooden supports uncovered by archaeologists in one area were scorched. In this area, it is impossible to walk without stepping on the carpet of pottery sherds.

The airfield is named after Second Lieutenant Max Condron, 21, who died trying to make an emergency landing on the old dirt strip in 1942. During World War II, the desert flats to the east and north were used by Fort Bliss for training anti-aircraft gunnery crews.

Initially, White Sands used the field to house a number of small aircraft used to search for missile impacts immediately following a test. These pilots, with their spotters, would be directed uprange to probable impact areas based on radar data. When they found the site, they in turn guided the ground recovery crews to the wreckage.

Eventually, aircraft were moved to Holloman where the facilities were much improved and the necessary maintenance support was readily available. Condron started out with two runways. The north/south one has been removed, leaving 09/27, an east/west, paved runway, 6,100 feet long. It is still used by a variety of planes, helicopters and drone vehicles.

Early in the 1950s, White Sands had a flying club that stored their aircraft at the strip and used it for training personnel to get their private pilot's license. By February 1963, the club was boasting 100 members and had just acquired a twin-engine C-45 at no cost. At the time, the club owned eight other airplanes – everything from a 90-horsepower Piper Cub trainer to a five-seat-Cessna 195.

Between the El Paso gate and Nike Avenue are a number of support facilities and buildings. For instance, the igloos for storing explosives stand very isolated in one area. The sewage treatment plant sits just as much alone and down the slope from the main post. Also, there are many buildings used by various WSMR organizations and the missile programs testing on range. Buildings are often reused repeatedly by different customers as they come and go.

Nike Avenue

Nike Avenue is the main east-west road at the south end of White Sands and is just north of the boundary with Fort Bliss. It starts at the headquarters building on the main post and leaves the missile range at the Orogrande Gate where it continues past the Jarilla Mountains to the little village of Orogrande, New Mexico on U.S. Highway 54.

Orogrande sprang up because of mining in the Jarilla's but quickly shrank to just a pit stop on the highway. However, around 1980, Wood Johnson thought up some promotional activities. Johnson ran the Oro Chico hamburger joint in Orogrande. For instance, residents erected signs designating the town's one tree the "Orogrande National Forest" and one street next to the gas station the "Orogrande International Airport." The airport idea came about when a Border Patrol plane made an emergency landing on one of the town's vacated streets.

Originally, in 1945, Nike ended at the Army Launch Area now called Launch Complex 33 or LC-33. When a second Army launch complex was added, numbers were tacked on to distinguish them. The first one was ALA-1 and the later one became ALA-2. When the Navy added their launch area it was simply the Navy Launch Area.

The main attractions along Nike are the launch complexes. But before getting to them, let's talk about some support facilities. For instance, the Temperature Test Facility (TTF), built in the early 1980s, is on the south side of the road.

This place is part of the environmental testing done at White Sands. The missile range quickly grew from a place to fire missiles into a huge laboratory for fully testing a missile and its support system. A missile's flight usually only takes a few seconds, but the things that can degrade its ability to hit a target start adding up hours, days, weeks and months beforehand. It is absolutely necessary to tests for these factors as well.

One of the more important aspects of environmental testing is related to weather. If your missile system requires hydraulics to elevate the launcher for firing, will it function if the temperature is zero or lower? Or your missile program might be challenged to answer whether or not the missile will launch from its tube if it has been baking in the Middle Eastern sun for days with the temperature inside the container reaching 150 degrees.

In the TTF, items can be baked, frozen, rained on, sleeted on, covered with ice from freezing rain, shrouded with salt fog, and subjected to steamy jungle humidity. Using heat lamps they can make the sun shine and fans can simulate the wind. One of the few things they can't do in the facility is make it snow. That is still reserved for Mother Nature.

Originally, climatic chambers were built in the Tech Area of the main post. Since they were right in the heart of the post with people all around, testing

of missiles with explosives or live motors was impossible. The TTF was built two miles east of the post and can safely handle explosives.

The smaller chambers were always good to show TV reporters when they were doing a story on White Sands. We would put a reporter in a parka and have him stand in a chamber with icicles hanging down from the ceiling. You could see his breath when he spoke. It was impressive in July.

The TTF has three chambers with the largest one able to handle a whole missile system. In other words, the old Pershing II missile and its support equipment could be put in the chamber, then frozen, heated, rained on and tested to see if everything worked as ordered. The ceiling was high enough, they could even erect the missile on the launch trailer.

Further east on Nike are more buildings from the past. There is a liquid propellant storage yard where tanks of chemicals were housed. Nearby is a building with a tower on it. The tower was used to spin liquid-fueled rockets to make sure they were still balanced before taking them to the launcher. Right beside the road in this area is a large wash facility where vehicles could be washed down if there was a propellant spill.

Eventually, we get to Launch Complex 32, the first place most people would recognize as a launch area because of the pads, rails, blockhouse and other items for support.

During my time at White Sands, this area was used mostly for air defense firings. For instance, I watched HAWK and Chaparral launches there. However, the 1968 guidebook to White Sands states LC-32 was being used for Sergeant launches at the time. Replacing the Corporal, Sergeant was the Army's second-generation ballistic missile capable of carrying a small nuclear warhead. Also it was the first missile fired from a location away from White Sands (Plains of San Augustin) back onto the missile range. *(See Chapter 16)*

One obvious question here is why do the current launch complex numbers start at 32? I looked for that answer in many places over the years but never found an official document explaining the change in labeling. I saw an article in the post newspaper from the early 1960s stating that the numbers were changed but no reason was given.

An explanation given by many old-timers has to do with the missile range's competition with Cape Canaveral at the time over space launches. During the 50s and 60s, as the birthplace of America's space activities, White Sands officials and workers always felt NASA should be based in New Mexico and not Florida.

The strongest points in support of White Sands were the dry weather with no corrosive salt air, low population density, and an altitude of 4,000 feet above sea level. The added altitude meant a space vehicle was closer to the stars and would need less energy to get to orbit. In turn, less fuel and its associated weight would be involved.

According to the old-timers, when White Sands went to meetings back East to give their pitch, they would have to refer to Army Launch Area 1 and 2, etc. Cape Canaveral came in with dozens of launch areas. It sounded more impressive. So, the solution was to redo the numbering system and start with 32.

This doesn't sound like a very realistic explanation given the nature of the men running White Sands. But who knows, the history of the place is riddled with slightly cockeyed experiments.

After LC-32 is, of course, LC-33, the original Army launch complex. This is where the very first rockets, the WAC Corporals, were fired in the fall of 1945 followed by V-2s in 1946. Over the years it has been used for all kinds of tests, both ground-to-ground and air defense launches. *(See Chapter 9)*

Rockets like the V-2s launched at LC-33 were the first steps taken in exploring Space. Because of that early work, the launch complex was designated a National Historic Landmark by the National Park Service in October 1985. Major General Niles Fulwyler, range commander then, had us search the mountainside to find a large rock on which we could mount a couple of bronze plaques.

We found a huge boulder near the main post at the base of the Organ Mountains and took the general out to personally approve it. The engineers then moved it to the entrance of LC-33 and mounted two plaques on it: a small one from the Park Service about the designation and a large one created by Fulwyler.

The large one reads: "Launch Complex 33, Birthplace of America's Missile and Space Activity: It was from this site that rocket and missile pioneers took the first fledgling steps which were to free man from earth's bonds and take him into the last frontier of space, to the moon and the planets beyond. Here began space travel and exploration in man's eternal quest for greater knowledge of his universe."

On May 27, 1986, White Sands held a dedication ceremony for the new historical designation.

Just over three miles directly south of LC-33 is C Station. This is where the original range control building was located. Like so many structures on the range, it has seen several lives since then. Nearby are the old buildings that housed the first radars. Since the rockets and missiles were fired from the north side of Nike, being south several miles was considered safe.

The next launch complex, LC-34, was originally built for Mauler support. This was a very ambitious air-defense weapon. When it floundered in the early 60s, it was replaced by the Chaparral. The launch complex simply shifted gears to support the new system.

Next are the two Navy complexes. LC-35 is where the USS Desert Ship is located. Early Navy missiles such as Talos, Terrier and Tartar were tested here. Today, the Navy can test all versions of its Standard Missile out of its Vertical Launch Assembly. *(See Chapter 11)*

Before the missile testing began, the site was home to the Navy's sounding rocket efforts. Just to the east of the Desert Ship is the original Navy blockhouse. Vikings and Aerobees were launched here.

The Navy also owns LC-36 where it currently conducts NASA sounding rocket launches. Just north of Nike, on the road into the site, is an assembly building where scientists put together their payloads. Further north is a blockhouse, an old enclosed launch tower, and a couple of current environmental shrouds used for assembling and launching rockets.

The eastern shroud covers an old Athena launch rail that was brought down from Green River, Utah long after the site closed. It is now put to good use launching sounding rockets.

The site started life as a launch area for the Redstone missile. By today's standards, the Redstone was a monstrous missile for such a short range. But when it was first proposed in the early 50s, it was supposed to carry a sizeable nuclear warhead which was quite heavy back then.

The Redstone was 70 feet tall and about six feet in diameter. With a range of just over 200 miles, it was not a great fit for White Sands.

An area north of the current Navy buildings was used for Redstone launches from 1958 to 1962. There were never more than five firings in a year.

The area then transitioned to NASA for their Little Joe II launches before being taken over by the Navy. *(See Chapter 25)*

Launch Complex 37 was originally Army Launch Area 3 and was developed for testing Nike Ajax and Nike Hercules air-defense systems after initial R&D firings at LC-33. According to the White Sands Museum website, "Several thousand Nike Ajax and Hercules missiles were fired from 6 launch sections" at LC-37.

Launch Complex 38 is a major facility with all kinds of buildings and bunkers. Originally called Army Launch Area 5, the site was developed for testing the Nike Zeus anti-ballistic missile system, America's first attempt to build an ICBM interceptor.

In the early 60s, the system morphed into a national system called Nike X during development and then Safeguard in the end. The system used two missiles – a modified Zeus dubbed Spartan for killing incoming warheads outside the atmosphere, and a new missile called Sprint for destroying targets much closer, those that got through the net of Spartans.

It was a complicated system with big radars and big computers to discriminate targets and figure trajectories. The huge MAR site (Multi-function Array Radar) up north of U.S. Highway 70 was part of the system.

Spartan firings were from LC-38 while Sprint missiles were fired from silos at Launch Complex 50, out in the no-man's land between Nike and U.S. Highway 70. Sprint was designed to be stored in a protective silo and then fired from there when needed. Since they couldn't put a silo in the desert floor because of the close water table - there is that landscape affecting things again - a large mound was built and the three silos dug into the artificial hill. Officials called them test cells.

In 1966, during the third launch of a Sprint at WSMR, a system malfunction caused the first stage to explode while the missile was still in the silo. No one was injured but the silo was shattered in the explosion.

Sprint missile was the fastest thing ever seen at the time. It reportedly accelerated at 100 Gs and reached a speed of Mach 10 in only five seconds after both stages were burned out. That is easily eight times faster than a bullet fired from a .45-caliber pistol. Old-timers at White Sands use to say that, "if you blinked at launch, you missed the show."

Soon, the Safeguard anti-ballistic missile system was negotiated away with the Soviets to preserve the Cold War principle of Mutual Assured Destruction (MAD). The idea behind MAD was that both sides had enough nuclear firepower to utterly destroy each other. If one side attacked, the other would surely strike back with equal ferocity and both would cease to exist. Therefore, neither side risked attacking the other because it would be suicide.

A new system, SAM-D, was eventually given LC-38. When I got to WSMR in 1977, this air defense system was in the early stages of development as SAM-D. Eventually, it was renamed and is today called Patriot. It has been at White Sands for decades during which time the system was given the additional capability of destroying medium-range ballistic missiles.

In the end, a battlefield commander can use Patriot to shoot down fighter jets, bombers and Scud-like missiles. *(See Chapter 16)*

Before heading north, note the Orogrande Range Camp just outside the east WSMR gate on Nike. The camp belongs to Fort Bliss and was a boomtown in the 50s and 60s. This is where the Fort Bliss troops lived while firing Nike missiles from LC-37.

Between LC-38 and the Orogrande Gate, about two miles north of Nike, is a cluster of buildings erected for a Star Wars project. When President Reagan proposed the Strategic Defense Initiative in 1983, one of the laser programs put into play was the Ground-Based, Free-Electron Laser (GBFEL) system. Some folks stuck "technology integration experiment" or TIE on the end of it. *(See Chapter 28)*

Heading North – what are those things?

Flying north from Nike Avenue, there are a few structures scattered throughout the boondocks that are readily visible from U.S. Highway 70 and raise questions for travelers. They are unusual in shape and are obviously not buildings. Visitors and community members often ask what they are looking at.

First of all, for those unfamiliar with southern New Mexico, "boondocks" are the many fields of mesquite-anchored sand dunes. When a mesquite bush starts to gain some size, it acts as a slight shelter when the spring winds blow the fine sand across the desert flats. The gusting wind is slowed down just enough as it pushes through the bush that some of the grains of sand drop out of the air into the bush.

Soon the sand starts to accumulate and build a mound around the bush. Year after year, as the sand accumulates, the bush has to grow to keep up or be buried. Eventually, these boondocks grow to be taller than a man and are sometimes over 10 feet tall. They make ground navigation through an area difficult because the traveler must constantly zigzag to avoid the obstacles and can never see far ahead. From the helicopter they don't look like much.

One of the visible oddities is only a mile or two south of the highway and appears to be a tallish, dark, pillar-like object. It is very clear to drivers coming down from San Augustin Pass. Some have suggested it might be the black monolith from Arthur C. Clarke's *2001: A Space Odyssey.*

Unfortunately, it is nothing so exotic. This is a cluster of large wooden telephone poles set very close together in a huge block of concrete. According to John Hyndman, who worked in the Facility Engineering Directorate at the time the structure was built, it was simply meant to be a rock-solid mount for a laser target.

The idea was that the target at the top of this structure couldn't sway in the wind or move for any reason except maybe an earthquake. So the poles are mounted in something like 150 yards of concrete and the whole monolith is as solid as the earth itself.

The other two items are much further to the east, right along the range's eastern border, and are sometimes referred to as the elephant fences. When you get close enough, the things do look like gigantic pens.

These are the clutter fences for huge radars (RAM and AMRAD) used back in the 1960s and early 70s in association with the Air Force's Athena launches from Green River, Utah. The fences stand over 100 feet tall and prevent reflections of radar signals back from nearby buildings, hills and mountains that might garble the data from tracking the real targets as they dive to the ground. *(See Chapter 17)*

It seems silly, but these fences have generated a myth that is posted on the internet. I found one website correctly explaining the fences were connected with powerful radars used to track missiles. However, the site's author claims the radars were so powerful they would "kill people on Highway 70, some 12 miles away" without the fencing to block the low angle signals. I chuckled over that one for days. Since the RAM fence was erected in December 1969,

I have wondered how many thousands of motorists were fried as they drove by the national monument.

Some of these myths are so good I still snicker years after first seeing the story. Another good one came from an eBay seller years ago who was auctioning a postcard of the dunes at White Sands National Monument. He said the sand was white because it was bleached by the first atomic bomb test at Trinity Site.

Roadblocks

Heading north, the next item of interest is U.S. Highway 70 as it crosses the Tularosa Basin on a diagonal line from the base of the Organ Mountains to Alamogordo. Since the highway crosses in front of all those launch complexes just behind us to the south, White Sands has been in the business of closing the highway for short periods since the 1940s. Permission to close the road is granted by the State of New Mexico.

At the height of the Cold War, when WSMR's airspace was filled with missiles and targets, roadblocks on Highway 70 were pretty much a daily routine with many days punctuated by several. Because surrounding communities cooperate with White Sands to announce the roadblocks in advance, travelers are not inconvenienced anymore than can be helped. People still forget to check or miss the announcements and the blocks often have over a hundred cars in them.

Over the years the system has developed to reduce roadblock times as much as possible. Instead of simply stopping traffic at the east and west boundaries of White Sands, a number of roadblock points have been developed. At these points the road has been widened to provide parking for all the vehicles, and toilets are permanently on site.

In a nutshell, every missile test has a safety footprint and roadblocks are set in response to that area. A system like Patriot with its long-range, air defense missiles requires a big footprint, especially when it is firing at a radio-controlled supersonic jet fighter. For such a test, a block might be set at the western-most spot, San Augustin Pass, and the eastern-most spot which is just west of the White Sands National Monument Visitors Center.

For a small missile that is intended to simply go in a straight line, the roadblock points can be much closer together. For eastbound traffic they might be set at a point, just west of the Otero/Dona Ana

County line. Westbound traffic might be stopped at a point about eight miles west of the monument.

All of these roadblock points are color coded so everyone knows which is which. San Augustin Pass is Red and White Sands National Monument is Yellow. In between there are Blue, Black and Brown. The color codes continue up on U.S. Highway 380 connecting Carrizozo with San Antonio, New Mexico. There, the block points are Silver and Gold.

White Gypsum Dunes

Crossing the highway near the range's east boundary takes us into the dune field at White Sands National Monument, near the monument visitors center. The monument was created in 1933 after much pushing by Alamogordo booster Tom Charles. The monument takes up about 225 square miles of the basin and is completely surrounded by the military in the form of White Sands Missile Range on three sides and Holloman AFB to the east.

If you climb high over this part of the basin, you see a large, dry lakebed to the west of the dunes and extending north just over 20 miles. On maps this large area is called Alkali Flats, but at the end of the last Ice Age it was a shallow, swampy lake covering a few hundred square miles. Scientists now call the playa Lake Otero. Whether or not you could have water skied on it is a subject for debate.

Water has been draining out of the mountains into the lakebed for a long time. When there is enough moisture, the water dissolves the gypsum in the sedimentary layers of the mountains. When that mineral-laden water pools in the lake, it quickly dries up but leaves behind its load of gypsum.

In damp conditions, gypsum has the ability to grow into crystals. Called selenite, the crystals can grow to be many feet long. The monument visitors center has some fine examples on display.

On the lakebed, erosion breaks the crystals down into smaller and smaller sizes until they are like grains of sand. Springs winds, which are typically out of the west, blow these crystals to the east, across Lake Otero. On the eastside they have piled up to form dunes. Occasionally, the wind has a north or southerly slant to it, so there are dunes to the southeast and northeast of the lakebed. A total area of about 275 square miles is covered with these white piles of sand.

A missile range Huey flying over the white gypsum dunes found in White Sands National Monument and White Sands Missile Range. The helicopter's paint scheme is typical for the test ranges and is made up of blocks of white, red and black so it is as visible as possible both in the air and on the ground. WSMR photo.

The dunes are not made of typical silica-based sand like those on a beach or in the Great Sand Dunes National Park in Colorado. Also, gypsum crystals are typically clear but can have other shades depending on the impurities from the ground in which they grow. As the crystals blow across the ground and rub against each other, they are scratched which gives them a white color. That is why the monument dunes glisten in the sun and appear to be like snow. Sometimes snow falls on the dunes and it becomes evident they aren't quite pure white.

The national monument was created to preserve and protect a portion of this, the world's largest surface deposit of gypsum. But it only encompasses the south end of the system to include some of Lake Otero and its southernmost tip, an area called Lake Lucero. A little over half of the old lake and its dune fields are part of the missile range.

As in most things, the science of dune fields can be quite detailed. For instance, the basin doesn't simply have gypsum dunes. There are "dome" dunes, "transverse" dunes, "barchan" dunes, and "parabolic" dunes – all based on their shapes.

The western half of the national monument, to include Lake Lucero, is part of a "Zone of Cooperative Use." It is an area where the missile range can freely fly aircraft and missiles overhead but not deliberately drop things on the ground. The monument runs monthly trips to Lake Lucero with the cooperation of the missile range as the car convoy must drive through military property to get there.

Because of its location, the monument experiences the missile range all the time. In fact, the range sometimes needs to have the monument delay opening on some mornings so there is no one inside the dune area on the picnic loop. This is because the safety footprint for a particular test reaches out to include that area. When this happens the picnic loop opens just 60 to 90 minutes late.

Although the missile range does not plan to drop any debris in the monument, it does happen. In my time at the missile range, I remember two very distinct incidents. In one accident, a remotely controlled F-100 jet fighter being flown as a target went out of control and, by sheer dumb luck, landed itself

near Lake Lucero. It came down at a very shallow angle and low speed, skidded across a playa area and stopped. It was almost undamaged.

The monument staff was notified and a ranger was put onboard an Army helicopter to look at the site. Because the jet was too heavy for WSMR's small choppers to airlift it from the scene, a ground recovery effort was organized. I went along to take pictures as a monument ranger carefully drove to the site followed by a small caravan of missile range vehicles. All the vehicles had to enter and then exit carefully driving in the ranger's tire tracks.

A crane was used to put the jet on a flat bed truck and within an hour we were gone, making as little impact as possible.

In another incident, a missile came down pointy end first in a playa area and buried itself dozens of feet in the mud. When the missile range and Park

An F-100 droned target being recovered from inside White Sands National Monument. The fighter basically landed itself on the old lakebed and stayed remarkably intact. Photo by the author.

Service discussed the options for digging the missile out of the muck, the Dept. of Interior decided the least intrusive thing to do was fill in the small surface hole and just leave it.

The relationship between the monument and the missile range has never been very warm nor has it been overtly hostile. The monument sees itself as being there first and sees the military infringing on its mission and principles of preservation and protection. For instance, many on the monument staff are not happy about airplane and helicopter overflights. The Park Service staff sees them as intrusive noise, spoiling the desert experience for some of the 600,000 annual visitors.

The missile range often sees the monument as a pain in the neck because it is in the way and missions often require special arrangements because it is there. In the early days, there is evidence the Army simply did what it wanted on and over the monument because officials viewed the military mission as trumping the Park Service's. Sometimes it was just ignorance as soldiers came in and didn't know there was a national monument next door or had no idea what the rules were.

On a staff level, the relationship between the two organizations was good. I got along well with everyone I worked with during my 30 years. There was one person who disliked having anything to do with the military. I could tell he disliked working on any project involving the range, but he was professional enough to not let his feelings affect the work. We always got that tour or special visitor taken care of.

Lately the monument has had a different kind of interference – from local residents. In 2007, the monument staff was notified they were being considered as a World Heritage Site in the natural category. The program of recognition was started in the 1970s with the United States as one of the principal designers of it.

There are close to a thousand World Heritage Sites around the world (in over 140 countries) categorized as either natural or cultural. For instance, on the "natural" list there are places such as the Grand Canyon, Yellowstone National Park, Redwoods National Park, the Galapagos Islands, a chunk of the Swiss Alps, Carlsbad Caverns, the Great Barrier Reef, and all of Canada's Rocky Mountain National Parks.

On the cultural side are places like Mesa Verde National Park, the Statue of Liberty, Chaco Canyon, Stonehenge, the Tower of London, the Acropolis in Athens, the Cathedral of Notre Dame in Paris, and the whole historic center of Rome.

So the staff at the monument was honored and sought help from the local community to support their rise to the main list. By joining the main list, they would move in with some very elite places on the planet and, probably, draw more visitors. They thought everyone would be happy, especially with the potential for added tourist dollars.

The monument superintendent received letters of endorsement from New Mexico's two U.S. senators and many others, including the commander of White Sands Missile Range. However, the local congressman balked. He claimed that such recognition would hamper future Holloman and WSMR activities and that somehow the United Nations would come calling to spy on the nearby military activities.

One citizen in Alamogordo voiced fears that the U.N. would come in to steal the precious water found beneath the national monument. Considering that water is at least as salty as ocean water, one has to wonder about the logic. Surely it would be easier for the U.N. to just pump water out of the Atlantic or Pacific where there is a largish supply. Why come to New Mexico for salt water?

Some local residents joined the congressman's paranoia and signed a petition to demand the monument not be put on the list of World Heritage sites. The Otero County Commissioners even passed a resolution in opposition to the designation.

As of early 2013, White Sands National Monument was still on the tentative list.

Holloman Air Force Base

East of White Sands National Monument is Holloman Air Force Base. Holloman started life during World War II, June 1942, as the Alamogordo Bombing Range (ABR). Most of the lands inside the missile range came from the old bombing range. B-17, B-24 and later B-29 crews were trained here during the war.

After the war Holloman just about shrank away to nothing but was resurrected in 1947 as the Air Force's Missile Development Center. During this time, Holloman controlled the east side of the missile range as the area into which they would fire their missiles. That was changed in 1952 when the "integrated range" was established with the Army totally in charge of the real estate.

One of the first rockets fired at the new facility was a Boeing product called Ground to Air Pilotless Aircraft (GAPA). Some old-timers told me the first GAPA was a telephone pole with JATO bottles and some fins attached. It fired out of its launcher fine but when it hit the ground the pole was shattered into splinters. They said they dubbed the GAPA the "toothpick maker."

It is true there is a photo of a GAPA taken after a test that shows part of it being splintered wood, but this was a serious development program with Boeing looking at various kinds of rocket engines, staging and guidance systems. Probably the engineers used wood to simulate the nosecone or some other part early in testing, and that little kernel was twisted into a good story at the Air Force's expense.

As we fly over the base, you see all the typical things on any Air Force base. On the north side of the runways, however, is an area related to White Sands Missile Range. The outdated jet fighters that have been remotely piloted over WSMR for decades come out of a facility here. The jets are launched from Holloman and then flown by pilots or a computer system over in Range Control on WSMR's main post.

Next door is the Army Air facility. The missile range's aircraft, both helicopters and fixed wing, have flown from here for 50 years. In fact, they occupy one of the oldest buildings on Holloman, an old wooden hanger, circa World War II.

Further north are a few facilities used by the missile range to house communications and range instrumentation. It is easier to deploy to the east side of the range from there than back on the main post.

Then as we fly near Lost River, a small stream flowing west and disappearing in the dunes at the monument, there are several blockhouses and other structures relating to those days in the 1950s when the Air Force regularly tested missiles from Holloman. Lost River is one of the places where the famous pupfish can be found. *(See Chapter 23)*

Today, Holloman doesn't fire missiles and rockets from ground locations, but Air Force missile and bomb tests using aircraft as launch platforms often stage from there.

Like many Air Force bases, Holloman's mission has changed several times. At the end of the 60s, Holloman was transformed into a fighter pilot training base, first with the F-4 then the F-15, F-16, F-117 (Stealth Fighter) and most recently the F-22. Pilots train in the airspace over WSMR when missile testing isn't underway.

It is probably unfair to include the F-117 in the list as a "fighter" since it had no guns or missiles for air-to-air combat. It was a small stealthy bomber.

When I visited Holloman in the 1970s and early 80s, the main street from the U.S. Highway 70 gate was lined with targets and test vehicles from the mis-sile development days. It was quite a sight. I guess the Air Force decided the display was inappropriate since the mission had changed because all the vehicles have been removed.

In 1996, the German Air Force took up residence at Holloman by establishing its own tactical training center on the base. The Germans fly the F-4 and Tornado in training in the skies of southern New Mexico.

At the very north edge of Holloman and right up against the eastern edge of the gypsum dunes is the 10-mile-long rocket sled track. Called the High Speed Test Track, it is used to propel vehicles to high speeds, some approaching Mach 10, in an effort to test a plethora of items.

Opened in 1954, John Stapp immediately made it famous by riding a rocket-propelled sled down the track accelerated to a speed of 632 miles per hour and then coming to a complete stop in 1.4 seconds. He was testing new restraint systems for jet aircraft pilots. *(See Chapter 26)*

Whole cockpits from jets have been mounted on sleds and rocketed down the track. Every ejection system in the Air Force's inventory since the 1950s has reportedly been tested in this way.

To test ballistic missile re-entry vehicles, much higher speeds have been used. For instance, the nosecones to missiles have been sent down the track at realistic speeds well beyond a thousand miles per hour and run through a sprinkler system. The sprinklers simulate an encounter with rain.

At very high speeds, even something as inconsequential as a raindrop can do damage, especially if there are hundreds of strikes. In touring the facility, the engineers like to show a few items that were on sleds that hit birds. It is very impressive to see a thick plate of steel with a deep dimple in it from striking a small bird.

During the first war with Iraq after they invaded Kuwait, commanders wanted a bunker buster bomb capable of destroying deeply buried command and control facilities. In response the GBU-28 was put together and tested in a matter of weeks in February 1991.

The casing for the bomb was made from excess 8-inch artillery tubes to which fins and guidance equipment were attached. To test its penetrating capability, one of the bombs was run down the north end of the Holloman track at the same speed it would hit the ground if dropped from an F-111. At the end of the track the sled was stopped, but the bomb was not attached so it flew straight ahead into a series of huge concrete blocks.

The slow-motion video of the test was quite impressive. No explosives were involved but the bomb cleanly cut through more than 20 feet of concrete and exited intact on the backside.

Operation Desert Storm ended so quickly, only two of these bombs were used in the conflict.

At the south end of the sled track is a paved road going west into the gypsum dune field. This is Range Road 10 and before drivers hit the dunes, they enter White Sands Missile Range. The road was built to get Air Force employees out to their Radar Target Scatter (RATSCAT) facility out on the missile range.

Along this route is where the missile range allowed Michael Bay and his film crew to film scenes for the first two *Transformer* movies. Since they also filmed on Holloman, it was very convenient for the crews. *(See Chapter 18)*

RATSCAT was opened in 1963 and is located on the Alkali Flats just west of the dune field. It is there to take advantage of the extremely flat ground and the isolation from any potential prying eyes. Testers can light up scale models or real pieces of military hardware with radars to study their profile. Everything from real tanks and small aircraft to scale models of bombers can be examined. They have a fantastic model-building facility where exact, and I mean exact, copies are made.

Because the facility is very sensitive as far as outsiders knowing what is actually under test, they work outdoors mostly at night. One can assume they look at models of aircraft from potential enemies. Although they are usually mum on the issue, it seems likely our own advanced vehicles are tested here in efforts to make them more stealthy.

The facility is now called the National Radar Cross Section (RCS) Test Facility (NRTF).

North of Holloman and scattered all the way to the north end of the range are a number of Air Force Askania sites that date back to the base's missile development days. Each site has a square building several stories high with a metal pyramid roof.

Scientists like Ralph Steinhoff, a member of the original German V-2 Paperclip crew, understood how heat waves rising off the ground can greatly distort what we see and photograph. After his days with Wernher von Braun, Steinhoff went to Holloman as their chief scientist.

To avoid this ground-effects problem with photography, the Air Force erected buildings to elevate their recording cameras well off the desert floor. However, looking at the buildings, one might wonder how they used cameras in them.

The roof was split down each of the four sides. When it came time for a mission, the corners of the roof were lowered down to the sides of the building leaving a flat surface on top and a mount for placing the camera.

This design had the advantage of being high off the ground and providing the photographers with a full 360-degree view of the area. To help shelter the camera and operator, one or more corners could be left up to provide a little shade and wind protection. However, when this was done, the roof pieces restricted the operator's view if the action took an unpredictable turn and ended up on the other side of the shelter.

So the system had a number of disadvantages. Open the roof completely and it left the camera and operator fully exposed to the sun, wind and anything else the atmosphere wanted to throw at them. Partially close the roof and if something unpredicted happened the operator might not be able to track the new flight path of the missile – the roof would be in the way.

Now, the optical instruments are mounted inside the kind of domes used by astronomers. The dome has a narrow slit that slides open. The camera peeks out the slot in the roof. As the camera moves one way or the other, the roof moves at the same time so the lens always has a clear view. This arrangement protects operators and equipment, plus it can track a complete circle.

Grasslands and Lava

Flying just a bit north of RATSCAT is the old White Sands Space Harbor. This is where the space shuttle Columbia landed on March 30, 1982 and shuttle pilots trained for decades. *(See Chapter 25)*

Off to the west are the camel and mammoth pedestalled footprints. To the north are the bluffs marking the end of the lakebed. On the bluffs scientists have found the bones and teeth from some of the now extinct Pleistocene animals that used the lake. *(See Chapter 23)*

As we fly off the Lake Otero playas, we cross from barren flats almost completely devoid of any vegetation to desert grasslands. There is one large drainage cutting down through these flats to the old lake. This is Salt Creek and its water rarely reaches the lakebed except after good rains when the stream is flooded with runoff.

Soon we come to Range Road 6, a paved road running east and west. Many people call it old state "highway" 52.

Using the word "highway" probably connotes visions of a nice paved road. That may be why New Mexico state officials very clearly used only the term "road" in their 1978 study on reopening the route to the public. Some of it is a far cry from any kind of civilized highway. *(See Chapter 19)*

On the east, the old highway exits through the Tularosa gate and heads into the village of Tularosa. Just west of the old gate is the Tula-G launch area. This is where the fabled adobe Bismarck battleship target is located. *(See Chapter 22)*

Hot Target Areas

North of Range Road 6 are a number of hot target areas that have been used for decades by White Sands. By "hot" we mean real warheads or small explosives used on the weapons fired into these areas. In fact, the MLRS rockets fired from Tula-G used these.

The missile range calls them "Warhead Impact Target" (WIT) areas. There is a string of them just northeast of the Small Missile Range, the ones north of Tula-G, and two up near Trinity Site. They tend to be circles with the ones used for live ordnance fenced off to keep humans and wildlife out.

There are two categories of WITs – those that allow live explosives and those that don't. The ones allowing it are Stallion, Rhodes and Denver WITs. The others can have fusing detonators but that is all.

Inside a WIT, which can be almost two miles in diameter, there will be a target. In the old days, a grid using string was laid out to measure where each bomblet or submunition landed when it hit the ground. This was necessary to compare the planned accuracy with reality. Eventually, the grid was replaced with survey methods and can now be done more quickly and more cheaply using sensitive GPS equipment.

In the hot WITs, duds (explosives that didn't explode and still might) are destroyed in place so the area can be used again and again without anyone getting hurt. WITs are obviously very dangerous area and safety precautions are very strict. Anyone entering, even project personnel, must be escorted by an unexploded ordnance technician.

As we fly north, the first WIT is ABC-1, an area where real ground targets such as tanks can be placed as static or moving targets. Next are the Rhodes and Denver WITs with PUP WIT further north.

For the MLRS firings from Tula-G, the project was probably using one of the hot WITs. The original MLRS peeled open over its target area and spun to flip out 644 small bomblets designed to explode on impact. They were and are useful against personnel and small vehicles.

By using one of the WITs, project personnel could go in and see if the rocket was on target and if the dispersion pattern of the bomblets was as advertised. They could also count the number of duds in the round.

Flying further north over the eastern half of WSMR, we come to the Malpais, the black lava flow easily seen from Space. The flow is only a few thousand years old and originates off the missile range. It is jet black and from high altitude is quite a contrast to the stark white of Lake Otero and its dunes just to the south.

In fact, shuttle astronauts commented that because of these features, the White Sands Space Harbor was the only landing site they could see while in orbit.

At the southwest corner of the lava flow is Malpais Spring gushing water onto the desert floor. Just north of it a few miles is a series of springs, dead and alive, that formed small hills. Generally they are known as Mound Springs with their little craters of water. They show up very well on satellite images and many observers probably assume they are bomb craters. *(See Chapter 23)*

Continuing north we see the Oscura Mountains looming ahead. They run from the south to the north, ending at U.S. Highway 380, a distance of about 30 miles. Also, the mountain ridge splits the north end of White Sands into an eastern third and a western two-thirds.

The Oscuras are like the Sacramento Mountains in that the east side is a natural slope while the west side is a cliff face sheered by faulting. The east slopes are covered in piñon and juniper trees giving the mountains a dark shade when seen from a distance. "Oscura" is Spanish for dark.

As we fly into the northeast corner of White Sands, we pass the Oscura Range Camp. This was an outpost for the first few decades of the missile range where various range organizations had a presence so they could support missions at the north end. This is where the Air Force and FAA conducted one of their sonic boom tests in 1964 and 1965. *(See Chapter 27)*

There isn't much activity in Oscura today. The range road that crosses the lava flow here and exits the range no longer has a manned gate. Like many others it is padlocked and requires the combination to get through. The road ends up on U.S. Highway 54 at a little community called Oscuro.

Just north of Oscura Range Camp is one of the range's surveillance radars. There are three of these radars to provide aerial surveillance of the whole missile range. Air Force controllers use the information from them to monitor the airspace and direct air traffic.

Many people think the Army is ready to shoot down private aircraft that trespass into the restricted missile range airspace. That is not true. The air traffic controllers will try to contact the plane to get it to turn around. If they can't communicate with the errant pilot, they can track the plane using the radars and pass along the information to the FAA. The FAA can then pull the pilot's license if needed.

Just north of Range Road 12, which crosses this area from east to west, is the Air Force's Oscura Bombing Range. To the bombing range's west is Estey City, the only real ghost town on White Sands. It was a boomtown for a very short time at the beginning of the 20th century complete with its own post office. *(See Chapter 20)*

North of the bombing range is a broad valley with high ridges to the east and west. During the 1980s, this was a busy area for some interesting tests of air-defense weapons designed to provide close-in support for troops, tanks and other equipment moving forward.

At that time, military leaders around the world were struggling with what approach to use in providing close-in air defense support. The traditional method was to use guns that could put a lot of lead into the air very quickly. With technological advances, the new systems used radar and fast computers to train the guns on the target. In fact, they were talk-ing about having the guns go to an automatic mode where the gun would find the target and fire long before human beings could do the job.

On the other hand, some leaders were looking at replacing guns with smart missiles. The idea was instead of firing hundreds of shells at the target and hoping for a hit, a single missile could easily do the job. One shot, one kill was attractive.

Before 1980, the United States was using a combination of missiles and guns in the form of the Vulcan gun and the Chaparral missile. The Army decided to lean heavily to the gun side. It contracted with Ford Aerospace in 1981 to build a fancy gun-based defense that would mount on the old M-48 tank chassis. The system's two 40-mm canons were to use radar and computers to automatically fire at low-level targets like helicopters and jets.

It turned into a fiasco with the system rarely working well. There were stories of the system's radar locking on a latrine's exhaust fan and tests that were so dumbed down, one pundit said it was like asking a bloodhound to find someone standing in the middle of an empty parking lot with steaks tied to his body.

By 1985, the gun system had been named the Sergeant York and was receiving fire from all angles. There were a few supporters who, unable to point to glowing test results, resorted to questioning the patriotism and loyalty of the critics. However, not even that time-honored ploy could prevent the gun from sinking fast into failure.

Finally, "Follow-on-Evaluation" tests were ordered for the Sergeant York by the Department of Defense. The firing tests took place in our little corner of the missile range. Because of mechanical, radar, computer and other problems, the weapon was only available for actual firing at targets 33 percent of the time. Saying the tests didn't go well was an understatement. Secretary of Defense Caspar Weinberger killed the weapon in August 1985.

That left a bit of a hole in the Army's planned defense. Army planners didn't flinch a bit. Instead of looking for a simple replacement, they came up with a system approach – a bunch of weapons tied together on a state-of-the-art network. It was called FAADS for "Forward Area Air Defense System." According to officials at Fort Bliss, FAADS was "a system of four weapons components and a command, control and intelligence structure."

The *Army Times* reported the Army had spent $1.8 billion over seven years on the Sergeant York. The same article, on March 16, 1987, put the price tag for the new FAADS approach at a whopping $6.9 billion.

One of the four weapons to be used was something called "line-of-sight, forward heavy." This was a major weapon that normally would have taken years to develop and test. At this point, the Army took a shortcut and announced it would seriously consider a ready-to-go foreign-designed weapon. The idea was to find something suitable and simply buy it.

Four foreign companies partnered with four U.S. companies to demonstrate their solution to the problem. For the Advanced Rapier, British Aerospace hooked up with United Technologies. For the Paladin, Euromissile partnered with Hughes. The ADATS was presented by Oerlikon Aerospace and Martin Marietta. Finally, the Liberty came from Thomson CSF and LTV Missiles and Electronics.

Highly publicized live-fire testing for the systems took place in what became known as "FAADS Valley" on White Sands in 1987. Free-flying targets and static ones were employed. Some of the stands for mounting static targets were still visible in the area years later.

When the dust settled, the contract was awarded to ADATS, the Swiss entry. During the shootout at FAADS Valley, we had a press day and I was able to take photos of the four systems. Interestingly, the ADATS was the only one with a gun paired with its missiles.

The system was never fielded, as it was decided that without the Cold War the demand for such a weapon was very limited. The contract was cancelled in the early 1990s.

Northeast of FAADs Valley, in the very northeast corner of the missile range, is Red Canyon Range Camp, the Fort Bliss facility from the 1950s where thousands of Nike Ajax missiles were fired. The concrete foundations to many of the buildings are still

> *Pop-Up: During the FAADS shootout in 1987, a missile firing started a grass and brush fire in the hills east of the Oscuras. Black Hills Aviation out of Alamogordo was called on to drop slurry on the fire. On Sept. 10 the plane carrying Nathan Kolb and Woodard Miller crashed into a ridge near the fire and both men were killed instantly. Witnesses said it looked like the plane just flew right into the ground.*
>
> *Kolb's father, the owner of Black Hills Aviation, sued White Sands and the Army, accusing them of shooting down the airplane with a missile. There was no evidence to support his claim.*

there along with a couple of the streets. They are very visible along Range Road 11 in Google Maps or Google Earth. *(See Chapter 15)*

West of Red Canyon is a bombing and gunnery range called Red Rio. It is hilly country with several valleys. The area has a fake runway with obsolete aircraft around. There are defensive missile emplacements and various ground vehicles, all in an effort to provide realism. In one spot there is a convoy of old trucks that look like they are headed into the mountain – maybe into a tunnel.

I drove through Red Rio once years ago and found the vehicles were used for gunnery practice. Most looked like Swiss cheese.

Because of the unexploded ordnance, the area is considered quite dangerous and requires an escort now.

Red Rio is another area discovered by people sitting at their computers, searching through satellite images. Some refuse to ask the missile range what the place is or then refuse to believe the explanation when one is provided. Instead, they make up their own and then feed off of each other, sometimes piling speculation on top of other speculation. Most of these stories concern a secret base under the mountain as evidenced by the trucks driving into the mountain.

NOP

Turning west now, we fly right at the massive ridge that is the Oscura Mountains, heading to North Oscura Peak (NOP). Still in the foothills, we fly over the old Ozanne Stage Station. The stone building once served as a stop for the stage line connecting San Antonio, New Mexico and the mining community of White Oaks in the late 1880s. *(See Chapter 5)*

Climbing quickly as we fly west, the slopes are densely covered with trees and brush. In an opening near the top is a two-story, cinderblock building with a parking lot on one side. Built in the 1950s, this was home to military personnel who operated and maintained the many sites on top of the mountain.

According to Jim Andress, who was a civilian in the White Sands Signal Agency in 1958-59, "The main mission of NOP was to provide radar support in the north range, as well as general communications support for the J-10 telemetry station. There was also a small frequency monitoring station, along with relay facilities for mission aircraft, mobile radio nets, and the new microwave radio relay for traffic in the Stallion area." In other words, there was a lot of tube-driven technology in place on the 8,000-foot peak that needed a lot of tender loving care to keep it going day after day.

The barracks building has a kitchen and dining room on the first floor along with a recreation area. The second floor has the bedrooms. It has been used off and on over the decades. For instance, when it was being used by Air Force personnel and contractors working at the Airborne Laser research facility on NOP, we fed the range's guests for "Rancher's Day" in the dining and recreation area.

The Airborne Laser was an outgrowth of the Star Wars programs in the 1980s. The idea here was to put a powerful chemical laser on board a Boeing 747 and use it to shoot down enemy ballistic missiles in their boost phase. This meant the airplane had to be fairly close to the launch points in order to put photons on the missiles while their rocket motors were burning – not a long time.

This was a difficult assignment because the 747 and the target would both be moving and jumping around as they were buffeted by winds. That made it hard to keep the laser energy focused on one spot long enough to burn a hole in the skin of the missile so it would blow up.

At White Sands, researchers were working on just part of the puzzle – sensors, tracking the target, and compensating for atmospheric distortion of the beam. Our tour of the facility was impressive, especially with the strides they had made in overcoming some of their difficulties. For instance, the head of the facility explained they were getting very good at keeping the laser beam focused on one spot on the moving target. He used this analogy: if you were several miles away and running through the desert with a quarter held overhead, the weapon system could keep the laser beam focused on the coin.

Apparently it wasn't enough, or maybe it didn't work all the time, because in early 2012 Secretary of Defense Robert Gates pulled the plug on the whole program. Reasons sited included the expense (billions), so-so test results, and the realization that keeping 747s flying 24/7 just off the borders of Iran and North Korea probably wasn't very practical.

The test vehicle the Air Force built was put into storage at Davis Monthan Air Force Base in Tucson.

At one point there were as many as 40 soldiers assigned to NOP. They kept a bobcat as a mascot and called it Kilowatt. The post newspaper jokingly reported in June 1959 that Kilowatt had passed his test to see how long it would take him to open his cage by lifting the latch from the inside. One night the sly cat figured it out and simply walked away into the night. Later the men captured another bobcat kitten and named it Kilowatt 2.

In addition to soldiers maintaining the old equipment on NOP in the 50s and 60s, some would be on station for tests. One old-timer told me he was sent to NOP to maintain a radar used as a target.

There have been a number of missiles designed to home in on radar signals. They are called anti-radiation weapons.

According to the old-timer, he and another soldier had their radar way south of NOP but on top of the ridge. It was near Jim Peak. They were to make sure the radar was running until they received word via radio that the missile had been launched. Then they were supposed to run over the edge of the ridge and hunker down in a bunker.

Jim Andress, in his recollections of the NOP barracks, remembers the mess hall being run by an experienced sergeant who catered to the few personnel on site. He fixed great tasting and generous meals for the men.

Andress also remembers picking up old automobile tires when driving along the public highways on his way to NOP. He said he would take them up to the edge of the escarpment on NOP and roll them off the edge. They would free fall, bounce and bound as gravity pulled them down the 2,000-foot cliff face.

When we flew from the barracks on to the top of NOP, the pilot usually stayed close to the tree tops so the view ahead was nothing but forest. Then as we got to the top of the ridge, I would stop speaking and just let the next few seconds happen.

As we got to the top, we would burst past the last line of trees and fly off the edge of the cliff. In an instant we would go from having trees right below us to having 2,000 feet of air there. Most visitors loved it, although some said their hearts jumped into their throats at the unexpected change.

The views from NOP are terrific. You can see the Black Range, the San Mateo and Magdalena Mountains to the west, and Taylor Peak to the northwest. Such clear line-of-sight to the west and northwest made NOP important for communications in the days of missile firings from Fort Wingate and Green River, Utah. *(See Chapter 16)*

As we fly away from the cliff, right down below is Trinity Site where the first atomic bomb was exploded on July 16, 1945. A circle of different-colored vegetation is visible. It is the area that was burned off by the heat of the explosion. It has come back covered in grass that is a stark contrast to the mostly darker creosote and mesquite vegetation around it. *(See Chapter 7)*

To the immediate west and south of Trinity are test beds used for decades by the Defense Nuclear Agency, now called the Defense Threat Reduction Agency. Most of the bunkers, equipment and other facilities seen around Trinity belong to this Department of Defense agency. *(See Chapter 24)*

The organization once provided huge test beds at WSMR for all the military services and U.S. allies to use during simulated nuclear explosions. In 1998 the organization's name and focus changed. Now the agency is the DoD's agency to counter weapons of mass destruction.

Just to the south of Trinity Site is the Aerial Cable Test Range. This facility takes advantage of the Oscura Mountains escarpment and the little valley separating it from a minor ridge called the Little Burros. The Little Burros sit in the gap between the north end of the San Andres Mountains to the west and the Oscuras. The low pass between the Little Burros and the San Andres is called Mockingbird Gap.

Opened in 1994, the cable takes much of the expense and guesswork out of air-defense missile testing. For decades, White Sands conducted air-defense tests against free-flying aircraft and helicopters (very expensive) or against aircraft fixed atop poles or towers (not very realistic). The cable provides a cheap, safe, and fairly realistic way to engage targets. Another plus is the quality of the data because everything takes place in a small engagement box.

The Aerial Cable is simplicity itself. A three-mile-long Kevlar cable or "rope" was strung from an anchor on Jim Peak in the Osuras to a huge take-up reel at the north end of the Little Burros. The cable hangs from its high point on Jim Peak down to the Burros. It is not stretched tight but hangs slack so it is not a straight line but has a sagging curve to it.

Using the big reel, much like a fishing reel, cable can be let out so it actually comes down to the valley floor. This is done so it is not a hazard to Air Force pilots when they are training in the WSMR airspace. At 2.5 inches in diameter, the cable is very difficult to see.

Also, the cable is lowered to mount targets on it. When the cable is raised above the valley floor by reeling in the west end, the target can then be hoisted uphill to the east using a pulley and cable system.

To conduct the test, the target can be released and then allowed to accelerate down the cable using gravity, or a rocket booster can be used to get it going even faster. Then it is a matter for the missile testers to fire at the moving target.

When using a heat-seeking or infrared-based missile system, the target is equipped with an appropriate heat source to simulate the aircraft. When the facility first opened, these heaters were very specialized and vey expensive. The problem was the missiles usually destroyed them after just one use.

Range employees quickly discovered they could use the heating elements found in the common kitchen stove. As long as the heat source created the correct heat signature, it didn't matter if the source was some specially constructed device or an off-the-shelf element from Sears. They saved a lot of money.

However, showing high-ranking officials and congressmen film of a missile destroying a stove coil isn't very impressive. To make a more lasting impression, projects would sometimes want to shoot at a realistic target like a real jet or helicopter. The facility has a junkyard of old helicopters with all the innards removed to save weight so a real chopper can be run down the cable and impress the folks who control the purse strings.

Kevlar is used for the cable because, according to the facility's engineers, steel won't support its weight on such a span. Also, being non-metallic, the Kevlar doesn't influence electronic testing. Kevlar is an amazing material, very soft to the touch, but when stretched across the valley it compresses down into a steel-hard line that rings if you hit it with something.

Also, Kevlar is expensive. The cable does occasionally break and it can't be spliced back together. It costs something close to a million dollars to put in a replacement cable.

The Northern Boundary

Next we head north toward the Hansonberg Hills in the distance and on our right. The hills are a low ridge at the base of the Oscuras and are riddled with prospect holes and small mines.

Soon, we approach Mine Site, an instrumentation site. Off to the left is ZURF Site, once used to launch targets south to be engaged by the Nike Zeus. Just off of Range Road 24, running east and west from Mine Site to Stallion Range Center, a young man was tragically killed on Sept. 28, 1998.

The victim was Airman Marcus Zaharko, only 19, who was waiting at a roadblock along this road. His team was going to set up sensors for an Air Force test but had to wait while another project used the area.

They got out of their vehicle and Zaharko wandered out into the desert. He found an interesting object, picked it up (it looked something like a can with a parachute attached) and then dropped it. That is when the little bomb exploded. We know what happened because Zaharko told his sergeant as he lay bleeding to death.

Zaharko died on the ambulance ride to the hospital over 30 miles away in Socorro.

This was the first and only death, so far, caused by an encounter with "unexploded ordnance" (UXO) at White Sands. Even though the range has tried to restrict live munitions to the WITs, there have been many cases where weapons have gone astray and the duds and other material never recovered. Basically, it is possible to encounter something from a test almost anywhere on White Sands.

When I took people out on the range, I always warned visitors about the dangers, especially the bomblets that look like baseballs or softballs. They are something any kid would be tempted to pick up.

My warnings paid off on one trip near the Malpais when a photographer brought his son along on a photo shoot there. The young boy, probably only 9 or 10, came to me to say he thought he'd seen one of the bombs. He took me over by the lava and sure enough there was a silver ball with small ridges on it. The ridges spun the ball as it exited the mother ship and activated it so it would explode on impact.

I thanked him and we quickly moved away. After

all, the spinning may have failed to activate the bomblet, but the impact on the ground may have done so. The next movement might have set it off.

After Zaharko's death, a UXO warning was required for anyone going uprange. Employees had to receive training, and visitors were required to view a briefing video that warned them of some of the possible UXO dangers – and there are a lot of them. Of course, the lawyers had a lot to say about wording the warning and the acknowledgement each person must sign. Many glance over it and jokingly say they assume the paper means they are agreeing that if they blow themselves up, it is their own fault.

Long before this, there was an incident out at the High Energy Laser Systems Test Facility (HELSTF). Some range guys who had equipment near the facility were hanging around with nothing much to do before a test. This has been true of instrument operators for decades – hurry up and prepare followed by lots of downtime.

These guys, in wandering around the desert, found a flare dispenser. This box-like item was once mounted in an airplane or helicopter so the pilot could shoot out white-hot flares as decoys to distract any heat-seeking missiles shot his way. The military term for such a setup is "countermeasures."

The container was partially used and thus was no longer safe to have onboard for a landing back at Holloman so it was ejected. In my time on the missile range, I often saw jets dispensing these flares while pilots engaged in mock dogfights as part of their training.

The two inquisitive technicians took the dispenser back to their trailer and proceeded to try and take it apart. You guessed it. One of the flares ignited in the box and set the others off.

These flares reach thousands of degrees almost instantly. In this case, the guy who ignited the flare dispenser received some fairly serious burns on his face and hands. The other guy was unharmed. Their trailer, however quickly went up in smoke.

Stallion Range Center

Continuing west we break our flight at the Stallion Range Center, the northern-most facility on WSMR. Range Road 7, the range's main north/south road, exits here and continues to U.S. Highway 380 just 12 miles east of San Antonio. By internal roads it is about 118 miles from the main post to Stallion.

In the 1950s and 60s, Stallion was a mini-post with barracks buildings, a mess hall, a small post exchange, and its own swimming pool. An Army officer was assigned to command the post.

Since it is so far from the main post, many of the range organizations maintained offices, shops and equipment at Stallion. The cadre of military personnel lived on site; the civilians lived in small towns like Socorro and commuted back and forth. The civilians that man the site today still do the same thing.

In June 1960, Stallion hosted its own open house for the public. At the time there were about 200 personnel working out of the site.

With so many buildings and activities, Stallion has its own infrastructure for such things as water, sewage treatment, streets, security, fire protection, and a fueling station. But the shrinkage of the range's activities, the automation of equipment, and budget cuts, Stallion is just a shadow of what it was. The barracks buildings have been turned into administrative space or are standing empty.

Water here has always been pretty salty, much like the stuff found in the Tularosa Basin. Potable water for Stallion was originally pumped from a well in Mockingbird Gap and hauled by truck here and there. A 750-foot well was dug at Stallion in 1960 but only provided non-potable water.

In the summer of 1967, the well in Mockingbird suddenly went sour. For two years, WSMR hauled about 200,000 gallons of potable water a month from a well on the Bosque del Apache National Wildlife Refuge.

In 1969, the money and planning finally came together for the range to put down another well at Stallion and build a desalination plant to purify water from the two wells on site. According to the Missile Ranger newspaper, the project included pumps, a water tower, chlorination equipment, and distribution system. The cost was reportedly $532,000.

The salts are still removed from the water in an electro-dialysis system. The principle is based on the fact that the dissolved salts are usually either positively or negatively charged. By running the water past electrodes mounted in the stream, the salts will be attracted to the oppositely charged electrode.

The result is potable water coming out and occasional cleanup to remove accumulated minerals from the electrode material.

During my time, the mess hall did function for a few years as a place to get breakfast and lunch – a snack bar. It was called the "Munch Box" or "Goldie's" after the lady who managed it for a long time. On an aerial tour we would stop for fuel for the chopper and ourselves.

The big deal, especially for those visiting from back East, was to get a green chile cheeseburger. Some employees and our visitors often raved about these burgers as if they were something really, really special.

When we had a big group, I sometimes helped serve the food to speed up our turnaround time. In the kitchen, I saw the burgers were simply those machine-made patties that come frozen in a huge box from a big national distributor. They were fried on a griddle with the cheese added at the end. Then, a dollop of chopped green chile was spooned on top. That was all there was to these gourmet burgers.

This probably demonstrated how your eating experience may be more tied to the hype and your hunger than to the food itself. For most of our visitors, the lunch was just wrapped up into the same package as the aerial tour. It was something very special and the enthusiasm rubbed off on the food.

Up the hill, on the edge of Stallion, stands GEODSS. This is my favorite WSMR acronym ever. Years after retirement, I can still recite what it stands for: Ground-Based, Electro-Optical, Deep Space Surveillance.

This is an Air Force satellite tracking facility that is just about impossible to get into. Completed in 1982, the observation site was the first of four. The others were built in South Korea and on the islands of Diego Garcia and Maui. The Korean site has since closed because the air quality is not suitable for looking into Space with telescopes.

The one on Maui is probably the most accessible – at least anyone can easily see it. It is up on the edge of Haleakala Crater at the end of the road.

These sites are each equipped with three telescopes capable of tracking an object as small as a basketball at 20,000 miles in Space. They only work at night.

A very sophisticated computer system has the telescopes move at the same rate the earth is turning, so the stars on the video stay locked as solid spots of light. Most everything else, at least in the 3,000 to 20,000-mile range, is a manmade object and leaves a slight streak of light on the images.

The site's observations are reported to the 21ˢᵗ Space Wing at Peterson Air Force Base in Colorado Springs.

I said "most everything else" is manmade. Lincoln Labs from MIT developed this system for the Air Force. They have been allowed to use a GEODSS telescope mounted next to the site at WSMR to track asteroids. The system works well for finding objects out there never detected before.

Given what we know now about the extinction of the dinosaurs from an asteroid impact, everyone is pretty serious about the threat big rocks pose to our future existence. Dubbed LINEAR for "Lincoln Near Earth Asteroid Research," the civilian searchers have now found hundred of NEOs – Near Earth Objects.

At one point, when this all became public, there was a great demand by reporters and documentary filmmakers to visit the Lincoln Labs site at Stallion GEODSS. If the Lab's astronomers were willing to talk to the writers and television crews, my office got involved because we had to escort the individuals and film crews. If you want a boring task, sit around while a crew films shot after shot of computers and a telescope. It really is like watching paint dry.

Eventually, the media grew tired of hyping the extinction possibilities of asteroids after nothing happened for a few years. They moved on to other calamities.

Heading South

After taking off from the landing strip at Stallion we head south. Immediately we pass the Large Blast Thermal Simulator, one of the white elephants on WSMR. *(See Chapter 24)*

Off to the west boundary is the Navy's Sulf Site. The small launch complex has been used frequently to launch targets to be engaged mid-range with the interceptors coming from the south. For instance obsolete Navy Talos missiles were refurbished and fired from Sulf to be killed by the Navy Standard missile and the laser at HELSTF. The targets were called Vandals. Also, two-stage Storm targets have been launched from Sulf.

This area of the missile range is relatively flat. On the western boundary is a lava flow three-quarters of a million years old and covering about 170 square miles. This one has blown sand covering parts of it and several big tubes. The lava tubes are home to large populations of bats.

According to some geologists, the lava flow may have blocked the Rio Grande for a time. To the west of the lava flow is the Jornada del Muerto – the road of the dead. *(See Chapter 7)*

Next are two WIT areas with the graded Stallion WIT often mistaken by airline passengers as the Trinity Site ground zero.

Ahead is the northern tip of the San Andres Mountains. They taper from their widest, where Salinas Peak juts out into the Tularosa. to this narrow ridge often called the Mockingbird Mountains. On the east is Mockingbird Gap and the Little Burros while on the west is a broad plain.

South of Stallion WIT is the old Dave McDonald Ranch, a place now called Pond Site by the missile range. *(See Chapters 5, 6 & 7)* This McDonald Ranch is where the Trinity Site base camp was located. In addition, Dave played a very public role in the controversy about how the government acquired the ranch lands now in White Sands.

Zumwalt Test Track and BATS

Just south of the Dave McDonald Ranch is the Zumwalt track. It is named for Glyn Zumwalt who was the manager of facilities engineering at Stallion during the time of its construction.

This road network was built in the 1990s in response to new weapons needing to be tested at White Sands. It is a highly instrumented area with several roads where the missile range can remotely run one or two vehicles or a whole column of tanks, whatever the customer wants.

Since weapons developers would be trying to kill the vehicles, the vehicles and many of the instruments must be controlled from somewhere else, miles away. That sounds simple but what happens if the third tank in a column of 15 suddenly dies? This is not a far-out scenario when using obsolete equipment for targets.

White Sands had to develop the necessary sensors and software so the system would see the stalled vehicle and then initiate a drive-around maneuver in the following tanks. This would allow the test to continue, just short one tank. Yes, this also means the computer is driving the tanks, not a roomful of tank drivers using joysticks.

One of the more remarkable weapons to use the track was the Brilliant Anti-Armor Submunition (BAT). Although BAT has been turned into an acronym, the word was used originally to refer to the small mammals that fly out at night and feed off insects. Developers did this because, like the bat that uses acoustic sensing to find its way, this weapon used acoustic sensors to find targets. *(See Chapter 8)*

The BATs were relatively small at 44 lbs. and 36 inches long. They were designed to be delivered to a target area by a mother-ship missile like the Army Tactical Missile and deployed in a cluster. The Army TACMS could carry 13 BATs.

Once deployed, the projectiles extended fins and wings and started their search for a suitable target. They were equipped with acoustic sensors to listen for the clinking, clanking sound of tanks and other vehicles moving about. Each BAT's onboard computer could distinguish the sounds and single out the most valuable targets – like a tank versus a jeep.

Once the munitions found the column of tanks, they "talked" to each other so they didn't all home in on the same tank. Also, for the final plunge to attack the top of the tanks and armored vehicles, the BATs switched to infrared mode and focused on the heat signature for each vehicle, a well-proven method of guiding bombs and missiles to targets.

Each BAT was equipped with an armor-penetrating warhead for taking out the target. The term "brilliant" was used in association with the BAT because of the great deal of autonomy built into it.

Initially, BATs were simply dropped from airplanes in early testing at the Zumwalt track. Later, Army TACMS missiles delivered the BATs from 75 miles away, with launches from south White Sands or McGregor Range on north Fort Bliss.

The Army TACMS had a long history of testing at White Sands. Initially, it was built to deliver close to a thousand bomblets onto a target area. These little bombs were relatively large and could take out soft targets like anti-aircraft missile sites and observation posts.

The first firings were in the late 1980s with one test in 1989 impacting the intended target on a ranch in the FIX, the range's northern call-up area. *(See Chapter 16)*

This first version of Army TACMS was called Block I and could reach out 100 miles. To extend the range to 185 miles, the program reduced the weight by cutting the number of bomblets to 300. This missile was called Block IA and was equipped with a GPS system to make it more accurate.

The Block II version had a range of 90 miles and could carry the BATs.

On Feb. 12, 1995, White Sands assisted the program and the Navy in the first 'at-sea' launch of an Army TACMS missile. For this test an Army M270 launcher was fastened to the deck of the U.S.S. Mount Vernon (a dock landing ship with a large helicopter area perfect for mounting a tracked vehicle) and the Block IA missile launched off the coast of California. The missile flew 86 miles to the intended target on San Clemente Island.

According to the White Sands BAT Office, "A total of 35 White Sands Missile Range personnel supported the 'at

An Army TACMS missile launch. WSMR photo.

sea' launch in California." The range provided the launcher, vans, and people supporting preparations, launcher instrumentation, software analysis, and flight safety engineering assistance. This was on-board the Mount Vernon, while others were in the target area helping with optics and measuring the bomblet dispersion pattern.

Down the San Andres

Climbing a couple of thousand feet above the track, we can fly over to the Mockingbird Mountains and head south on the spine of the range. Just out to the left is the northwest corner of the Tularosa Basin; to the right we can see out to the Rio Grande. Between the chopper and the river is a little bump of ridges called Poison Hills. *(See Chapter 5)*

The Mockingbirds quickly peter out. To the south is Capitol Peak and the Defense Threat Reduction Agency's tunnel complex. *(See Chapter 20)*

Just southwest of Capitol Peak, across Thurgood Canyon, is Sheep Mountain. In the narrowest part of the canyon is a spot called Lava Gap. This is an area where the pinkish granite basement rock is exposed with the gray limestone sitting on top. It is one of the places on the range where you can take a billion-year step from one kind of rock to another.

Here we usually fly over the top of Sheep Mountain so people can see the very isolated line cabin built by the Greer family. *(See Chapter 5)*

Out to the east in the Tularosa Basin is the ranch of Jim Gililland, the man accused by many as the killer of the famous Las Cruces lawyer and politician Albert Fountain and his eight-year-old son Henry. Gililland stood trial with Oliver Lee for the murders but was found not guilty. Interestingly, descendants in the Gililland line say it was Bill McNew who slit the throat of the boy and that Lee shot the father.

Even in 2013, people were pursuing leads to the murders and trying to find the location of Gililland's ranch so they might find the graves. *(See Chapter 4)*

Heading southwest a bit we fly by Silver Top Mountain and toward the west side of Salinas Peak. Several miles out west of Silver Top is the Dick Gililland Ranch. Dick was Jim Gililland's brother, but he was a respected family man. *(See Chapters 4 & 5)*

Salinas Peak

Salinas Peak dominates our view to the south. This huge domed peak is the highest mountain on the missile range at 8,965 feet. It stands well over 4,000 feet above the Tularosa Basin and is visible from anywhere in the basin. From the top of Salinas nothing blocks your view – except for the range facilities perched there.

Because of this prominence, Salinas grew into a major communications site for WSMR. Radio signals from the launch complexes can hit Salinas and then be relayed on north or vice versa. Commands to destroy straying missiles can be routed to Salinas Peak and broadcast to cover most of the range.

That communications capability requires a great deal of equipment. In fact, there is a large communications building on the peak filled with equipment that used to be manned by personnel on regular shifts. Most drove down from Stallion.

All of this development on the peak got started in the late 1950s. Jim Andress, who was with the White Sands Signal Agency, wrote about the beginnings of the buildup in a May 2007 article for the *Hands Across History* newsletter.

Andress said the initial push was to put radio equipment on the peak in 1958 to support the military police who were going to be conducting deer hunts in the mountains that fall. At the time, there was no road and helicopters were impractical for getting some of the heavy equipment to 9,000 feet.

The agency personnel transported all their equipment to a basecamp at an old mining development on the northwest corner of the peak. According to Andress, this was as far as they could take their trucks. They then used a D-8 Caterpillar bulldozer to tow a trailer filled with equipment up the peak.

Andress wrote, "This was a big dozer but was needed for its stabilizing weight as well as the power to climb steep terrain that was almost 45 degrees at times." The trip "was slow and dusty as the bulldozer slipped, spun and labored up the rocky trail, pushing rocks and small trees out of the way."

For the personnel, they either walked which Andress said was quite a challenge, or rode on the trailer tailgate, which wasn't much better. Then, at the top, prolonged physical exertion was difficult because of the thin air.

When it was done, Andress and the others put in travel vouchers because they had to camp overnight at their basecamp. Even though they were still on White Sands, they had been issued travel orders as if they were going to Washington, D.C. They checked out sleeping bags from Special Services and bought groceries at the commissary for the trip.

When their vouchers were initially submitted, the finance folks reduced the amount of payment because they assumed anyone staying on White Sands was being housed in "government quarters." After some discussions at higher levels, it was determined that laying in a sleeping bag in the back of a pickup truck was "inadequate" government quarters. They received the full travel amount.

In 1959, a permanent road was constructed to the top and the large commo building erected.

The peak has been convenient for other uses as well. The Air Force's Airborne Laser project had a small building with line-of-sight to the main research facility on North Oscura Peak. More recently, the Navy was testing a new radar installed on the peak.

On the south side of Salinas is a small shelf that looks like a park compared to all the modern construction at the very tip of the peak. This shelf has a stand of ponderosa pine trees, the only large quantity of these trees on the missile range.

One biologist I talked to said that at the end of the last ice age, the area was much wetter and ponderosa pines were probably found throughout the San Andres and Oscura Mountains. However, as things dried out and naturally occurring fires scoured most of the lower ridges, the ponderosas disappeared to be replaced by piñon and juniper.

He said Salinas was so high, often creating it own weather, it remained cool and wet enough to support the trees.

Salinas Peak also figures into Apache cosmology. In my time in Public Affairs, we received a few requests from the Mescalero Apache to visit Salinas Peak or gather certain plants there. We were told the mountain is sacred to the Apache because it is one of the four peaks that hold up the sky.

Flying to the southwest from Salinas puts us over the widest section of the San Andres Mountains. A variety of goat and cattle ranches are found in the canyons and valleys.

Rhodes Canyon

Soon we come to Rhodes Canyon, a major west-to-east drainage that old New Mexico Route 52 followed. At the top of the canyon is Rhodes Pass and the Hardin and Miller Ranches. Just to the west of the ranches on the north side of the road is the Eu-

gene Manlove Rhodes gravesite. In the 1930s New Mexico State University was charged by the state legislature with maintaining the grave. *(See Chapter 4)*

This is beautiful country below us with thick growths of juniper and piñon. In the heart of Rhodes Canyon, the missile range's Morale, Welfare and Recreation organization used to hold a mountain bicycle ride open to the public. I found them a route that allowed riders to traverse a large loop that included Rhodes, Bear Den and Bosque Canyons. Riders found themselves in the mountains that only hunters were allowed to roam.

Out at the east mouth of Rhodes Canyon stands the Air Force's RAMs Facility. This site is complimentary to the RATSCAT radar imagining facility. RAMS is short for RATSCAT Advanced Measurement System.

At the west end of the site is a large array of different radar antennas. Down the slope from them is a blacktopped runway-like area over a mile long. This flat surface reduces the number of spurious return signals when a target is illuminated with the radar.

This is another item that intrigues Google Earth searchers. They assume it is some sort of runway just because it is long, rectangular and paved. Since it is not listed anywhere as a runway (because it isn't one), they assume some cover-up is underway to hide a secret facility. The work done there is sensitive and officials are very secretive about it. However, the facility itself, like so many on the White Sands complex, advertises for business.

At the bottom of the hill are most of the support structures. Buried in a silo is a tall support pylon on which targets are placed. Putting the target, which can weigh up to 30,000 lbs., on the pylon can be done indoors, completely out of sight.

For a test, the top to the silo is opened and the pylon raised. The target can be positioned at the same level as the runway or higher. The target can then be rotated or tipped to see what kind of a signature shows up on the different kinds of radar.

Just a few miles east of RAMS is the old Rhodes Canyon Range Center. This was once a busy village of support organizations that included Communications, Logistics and Engineers.

Now most of the buildings have been abandoned and removed. There is still a Commo building but the equipment is automated. Also, there is an automated gas station for personnel to get fuel without having to return to the main post.

Not long after I arrived at White Sands in 1977, I was sent uprange to interview some folks and write a story. I checked out a pickup truck from the motor pool and headed north. I needed a pickup because I was headed into the mountains on the primitive roads and needed the clearance.

Partway to Rhodes Canyon I had a blowout that completely shredded the tire. I changed it and then stopped at the Logistics shop at Rhodes Canyon Range Center. Since the truck was pretty standard for WSMR, they had an appropriate tire for my rim and I was able to continue knowing I had a spare tire again. I wasn't even late for the meeting.

That capability disappeared decades ago.

More Mountains

This west side of the missile range is mostly more mountains, although the chain will get thinner, east to west, as we continue south. From Rhodes Canyon, we pass over an area called the Hard Scrabble Mountains.

It really isn't a separate mountain range but is a subset of hills and ridges. It is more of the same, as far as terrain, except for the tunnel. The tale I heard from a few treasure-hunter types was of a deep, fabulous tunnel in the Hard Scrabble Mountains that leads all the way under the Jornada del Muerto and exits near the Rio Grande. The interesting part of this magical story is that whoever explored it long ago thought it was not natural but was hand hewn in many places. Start the Twilight Zone music.

On the west side of the Hard Scrabble area is the old Woolf Ranch with one of the nicest houses on White Sands. Further south are the two Crockett ranches. One is near the top end of Sulfur Canyon and was near the area Captain Henry Carroll passed on April 6, 1880 on his way to battle Chief Victorio in Hembrillo Basin. *(See Chapter 4)*

Hembrillo Basin and Canyon are just south of Sulfur Canyon and are the most interesting historical places on White Sands. In the canyon are several locations for Apache and Mogollon rock art images. The basin is the site of the last battle in the U.S. between Victorio's Warm Springs Apache and the Army's Buffalo Soldiers. Also in the basin is Victorio Peak, still hiding its legendary 100 tons of gold bars. *(See Chapter 21)*

In addition, there are the remains of Henderson and Ritch Ranching activities up and down the canyon. Finally, at the east end of the canyon is the old Sierra Talc Mine. *(See Chapters 5 & 21)*

Next are Lost Man and Dead Man Canyons, home to the Andregg Ranches. *(See Chapter 2)*

Gardner Peak is the next large peak and it marks the north end of the San Andres National Wildlife Refuge. *(See Chapter 23)* Within the boundaries of the refuge on top of San Andres Peak is the old White Sands optics site located by Clyde Tombaugh, the astronomer who discovered the planet Pluto – now considered a dwarf planet. Tombaugh worked for White Sands from 1946 to 1955 directing the development of optical instrumentation. *(See Chapter 10)*

This part of the refuge and missile range has seen a number of visits from the public. In the 1990s, I received many requests from the El Paso chapter of the Sierra Club to hike in the refuge. After coordinating with the refuge manager and WSMR organizations, we took hikes to many places within the refuge.

There were no trails for these trips, as hiking has never been recognized as recreational activity at White Sands. So the hikes were often difficult trudges through brush. They were so bad because the canyons at the south end of the San Andres range have springs spilling enough water for it to flow downstream. Where there is water, there is thick vegetation.

San Andres Canyon has such a spring. When we visited water flowed on the surface for hundreds of yards. The bottom was choked with reeds and brush so walking on the banks of the drainage was easier. By getting 20 to 30 feet away from the stream, we were faced with the normal cactus and catclaw found in the desert.

On the south end of San Andres Peak is Ash Canyon, a place we visited several times. This is one of the nicest places on the refuge or the whole missile range. On the backside of the mountain water freely flows over short waterfalls into pools of crystal-clear water. Ash trees and other large plants line the banks of this short steam. It is a true desert oasis.

Once, we climbed San Andres Peak going up from Ropes Springs on the west side. Basically, we followed the Army tram that used to carry photography personnel to the top of the peak to film V-2 launches. *(See Chapter 10)*

One other spot we hiked was up Little San Nicholas Canyon, south of Ash Canyon. Again, deep in the canyon is water flowing over small falls, creating shallow pools.

To the east of this area, out on the basin, is Lake Lucero. The national monument takes visitors on tours to the lake on a monthly basis. For a few years, we took special groups to the lake by bicycle.

These requests were from the El Paso Bicycle Club. They arranged with the missile range and the national monument to ride their bikes from the Small Missile Range out to the lake. Once there, a Park Service ranger would walk everyone to the lake and give the standard briefing. Afterward, we would all ride back to the gate.

In this area are the two ranches belonging to the Lucero brothers, Jose and Felipe. When Pat Garrett was killed outside Las Cruces, Wayne Brazel surrendered to Felipe who was serving as deputy sheriff at the time. Just west of Felipe's ranch is the San Nicholas Spring that provided the water he used to irrigate his orchard. *(See Chapter 5)*

A little further south at the base of Goat Mountain is Cedar Site. This is where the Precision Guided Munitions viewing site was located for the press show in December 1978. *(See Chapter 18)*

At the point where the San Andres Mountains end and Range Road 7 runs into U.S. Highway 70 is the Small Missile Range (SMR). This facility was built in the 1950s to get the testing of smaller weapons onto the north side of U.S. Highway 70. This frees up the large launch complexes along Nike Avenue and greatly reduces the number of roadblocks required on the public highway.

The SMR is equipped with a number of launch points, support buildings and target areas. Over the years it has been used for numerous missile and artillery tests ranging from the Little John, Mauler, and Redeye to the Copperhead and Hypervelocity Missile. This is just a tiny list but does represent some of the diverse systems tested at SMR.

Little John was a smaller version of the Honest John, a surface-to-surface rocket. Weighing less than 800 pounds, the Little John could deliver a conventional or small nuclear warhead up to 10 miles away. It was easily airlifted by helicopter.

Starting in 1956, hundreds of these missiles were fired at White Sands.

Mauler launches at SMR began in 1960. This was an air-defense system. Only some early launches would have taken place at SMR, as the system fired mostly from Launch Complex 34. The system was cancelled in 1965 before moving into production.

The Redeye was a very portable shoulder-fired anti-aircraft missile. The thing weighed only 30 pounds, so an individual could tote one around the battlefield and effectively bring down a close-in airplane.

The missile used an infrared seeker to lock onto the exhaust of the jet. It had a range of just over two miles. Launches at White Sands were in the mid 60s.

The Copperhead was something from the 1970s and was completely different because it employed a laser guidance system. This was an artillery projectile fired from a 155mm canon and had one-shot, one-kill accuracy. *(See Chapter 28)*

The Air Force's Hypervelocity Missile (HVM) was a very short-lived program in the early 1980s, but there were five firings at SMR. The tests were conducted to validate the concept of using a laser guidance unit onboard the launch vehicle to send course correction information to the missile as it flew to the target.

It was designed to be a small, low-cost weapon to use against elements of armored assault forces. The HVM was to use its accuracy and its velocity of five times the speed of sound for kinetic energy kills of armor. It didn't require an expensive or complex warhead or a sophisticated, stand-alone guidance package.

The missiles were only four inches in diameter and weighed less than 50 pounds. Theoretically, the Air Force claimed, a single A-10 could engage a column of vehicles and take them all out on one pass because the plane could carry lots of these little missiles. The system was supposed to be quick enough to simultaneously guide many missiles to their targets.

One has to wonder how well the course correction signals from the laser penetrated the smoke and fire coming out of the missile's back end. The Air Force didn't proceed with developmental testing.

Then there is the Loki, an excellent example of a spinoff. Loki was a development by the Army around 1950 to create a small barrage rocket for air defense. The idea was to launch dozens of these rockets at planes in a shotgun effect and hope one would explode near the enemy plane. It was based on a German World War II idea but was abandoned.

However, someone in the Navy cleverly came up

with the idea of substituting chaff for the warhead. The Loki could reach altitudes of up to 50 miles. At the rocket's apogee, the chaff was dispensed to be tracked with radar. The resulting information was used to determine upper wind direction and speed, something valuable when launching bigger items to those altitudes.

This idea of collecting weather data using a cheap, small rocket was soon grabbed by researchers all over the world. Eventually, a variety of small weather instruments could be placed atop Loki in a "dart."

At White Sands such wind and temperature information was needed on a daily basis. For decades, the Atmospheric Sciences Lab at WSMR launched a couple of Loki's each day to collect the data. Since it was not classified equipment or information, the lab was very generous with making the launches available as a scientific demonstration. My office frequently took school groups to these launches. The technicians usually let one of the students or the teacher push the button to launch the rocket.

Eventually, using rockets to collect weather information was replaced by Doppler radar and other technologies. The daily launches died.

In reality, SMR itself looks pretty dead when you drive by. The so-called "tank farm" is the most active facility there now. *(See Chapter 18)*

Up the slope to the west of SMR and north of Highway 70 is the range's Hazardous Test Area (HTA) and Electromagnetic Radiation Effects (EMRE) facility. The HTA was used for years to store explosives and destroy them as well. The EMRE is where large items like tanks and helicopters can be subjected to the electromagnetic effects of a nuclear explosion.

Unfortunately, phosphates from the burning of explosives in the burn pit at HTA over the decades have leeched into the soil. A number of monitoring wells now dot the hillside as the water is sampled to see if the pollution spreads.

On the south side of the road to EMRE is the ruin of Hal Cox's ranch. Just to the northeast of EMRE are Alamo Spring and the small dugout lived in by W.W. Cox and his family. To the west of EMRE is Pat Garrett's ranch – where he was living when he was shot and killed outside of Las Cruces in 1906. Finally, south of Garrett's place and at the west base of Mineral Hill is the Lena Cox Ranch. Lena was W.W. and Margaret Cox's oldest child. *(See Chapter 3)*

Crossing Highway 70 we can see the main post at the base of the Organ Mountains. If we had more time we could fly west toward San Augustin Pass and then south along the eastern front of the Organs. It is impressive looking straight out the door and seeing the tips of the Needles. The cliff faces are hundreds of feet of sheer granite that look like they would be a challenge for any rock climber.

Instead, we usually followed Owen Road right to the Las Cruces gate and landed where we began the tour. Sometimes, getting to this point was a relief. People getting airsick on the flight was always a possibility. If they made it this far, they were certainly going to make it home.

My boss, Larry Furrow, had a passenger vomit on his leg on one of these flights. Larry, a former Army pilot, was not happy.

I was more lucky. Those few who threw up on my tours got to the barf bags in time and quietly puked into one of them. This is obviously another good reason for flying with the doors wide open.

On landing, it was always pleasant to leave the chopper, stretch one's legs and get away from the constant roar of the Huey's turbine engine.

There is much to be said for simple quiet and solid land underfoot – the sensation of constant vibration slowly fades away.

Early People

Making A Living In A Barren Land

For centuries people have been attracted to southern New Mexico by the promise of land, minerals, independence, a nice dry climate, religious freedom and a bit of adventure. On the other hand, others have seen this chunk of Chihuahuan desert as a hellhole with lots of burning sand, screaming winds and choking dust.

One popular anecdote about the Southwest involves famous Civil War General William Tecumseh Sherman when he was a young officer. At the end of the Mexican-American War in 1848, Sherman was sent to the Southwest to survey just what the United States had won.

When he returned to Washington, he reported to President Zachary Taylor. The President asked him about the region. Sherman supposedly responded, "Sir, I think we'll have to go to war with Mexico again."

Taylor was surprised and asked him for an explanation. Sherman said, "To make them take the damned place back."

I ran into a similar attitude on Oct. 29, 1984, when I accompanied a couple of generations of the Baber family to their old ranch on the north end of the missile range.

I had received a call from Dru Jones who explained her father, Charles Edward Baber, was born on the ranch on March 7, 1911. She said she wanted to take her kids out to the old ranch and have Charles tell them all what it was like way back then.

Once I found the place, I arranged to take the family to a site clearly visible from Range Road 7 and only a couple of miles from Trinity Site. It turned out brothers George and Bill Baber homesteaded right next to each other. Charles was the son of George.

When we got to the ranch, we found the walls to the house still standing along with part of a wooden windmill to the east and a large concrete cistern near the house. Charles proceeded to tell the kids about the house with its adobe walls and how vigas and latillas held up the dirt roof. He explained that his mother tacked cheesecloth across the latillas to keep the scorpions and spiders from dropping down on them.

He said the well was hand dug with salty water at the bottom. The cistern was used to store whatever fresh water they could collect. One of his jobs as a kid was to go out immediately after any rain and scoop water off the flat areas. The muddy water was dumped into the cistern where the sand would settle out, leaving better water than what came out of the well.

Toward the end of our visit, I stood beside him near the house and we talked about the barren landscape. From the ranch you can see for miles in every direction. Mostly you see creosote and mesquite bushes with gaps of naked sand in between. There isn't a single tree anywhere in view.

After a while, Charles turned to me and said, "You know the best decision my dad ever made was to leave this place in 1920."

Native Americans

We know Native Americans used the plains and mountains for centuries on what is now White Sands. They left a lot of evidence. Their rock art, both pictographs and petroglyphs, can be found in many of the mountain canyons. Then there are places near old water sources where you cannot walk without stepping on pieces of ancient pottery. It literally covers the ground.

Initially the Native Americans who roamed southern New Mexico were hunter-gatherers. This area around the missile range, southeastern Arizona and northern Mexico provided them with a regular supermarket of food sources. They moved around between the deserts and mountains harvesting both plants and animals as dictated by the seasons and annual rainfall.

Terrain elevations vary from 3,000 to 12,000 feet above sea level, which provides for a huge variety in flora and fauna. Even when snow covered the high mountains, they could live in the deserts harvesting mesquite beans and grass seeds and hunting ubiquitous jackrabbits and occasional quail. During the summers they could move higher to hunt elk, deer and beaver while harvesting piñon nuts and fruits that thrived on the higher moisture levels and cooler temperatures in the high country.

About 3,000 years ago, they began to supplement their diets with a little agriculture. Corn has been found in area shelters dating to that time.

Over the centuries their use of agriculture matured and their society changed along with it. Pithouses were built around watered areas where corn, beans and squash were grown. These shelters were fairly simple to make. They dug a shallow hole and, with a few strategically placed poles, covered it with layers of branches and grass. This was capped with mud to provide a tight little shelter for a family.

These places are still being discovered on the range. Out near the east boundary of White Sands,

near the Orogrande Gate, archeologists excavated several clusters of pit houses in early 2013. The excavations were done as a mitigation process to clear the sites. The idea was to gather important artifacts, document everything and learn as much as possible before turning it over to the military for use as a training site.

These pit houses dated to about 1,100 to 1,500 years ago. One area was dated to the time of Christ.

In excavating one site, the archeologists found the bones from more than a whopping 500 individual rabbits. The bones were cracked and crushed, so when cooked in a stew with the meat the nutritious marrow was released for consumption. These people obviously extracted evey calorie of energy they could exploit.

By a thousand years ago, the Mogollon were very proficient at growing corn, and by 700 years ago they were building large adobe pueblos for the substantial populations supported by the crops. Scientists sometimes compare the diets of Native Americans with Europeans from this time and find Americans had much healthier food with the vegetables and meats.

We have no idea what they called themselves, so scientists have labeled them as the Jornada branch of the Mogollon culture. Scientists suggest they are related to the Mogollon Pueblo people of Southwestern New Mexico who were named after the Mogollon Mountains near the Arizona border.

People living and working around the main post at White Sands have been finding evidence of these people for decades - right in their backyards. In the April 9, 1952 issue of the *Wind and Sand*, the official missile range newspaper, a front-page story an-

---

Pop-Up: *A pictograph is an image painted on the rock. The paints consisted of smashed and pulverized minerals like hematite that produced a red color. Then they used a variety of materials as binders to hold the minerals together. Eggs, blood and plant resins were organic materials sometimes used for this purpose.*

Petroglyphs are images that are pecked into the patina or varnish of the rock. For instance, many rocks oxidize and darken when exposed to the air. The patinas vary in color depending on the kind of rock but some are black on much lighter rock. Also, as water oozes through porous rock, minerals end up being deposited on the surface when the water evaporates. By pecking through that varnish the artist reveals lighter colors and can easily create an image or symbol. Being made from the rock itself, a petroglyph can last centuries whereas rain and wind can destroy pictographs fairly quickly.

Pictographs have bigger problems than the weather today. People are fascinated by them and flock to see them. Simply touching them and leaving an oily residue behind can lead to destruction just as much as the occasional vandal who spray-paints an image.

nounced that F.W. Thompson had uncovered "the foundations of 15 Indian dwellings."

Thompson was running heavy equipment in road construction on the base and accidentally dug up the ruin. The article stated, "A well preserved skeleton, measuring almost seven feet in length, was found buried beneath a mud slab floor of one of the rectangular huts." Other bones and skeletons were supposedly found in the other ruins. A photo of Thompson ran along with the article that showed him holding the skull at the spot he found it.

Thompson described himself as an "amateur archeologist" and the newspaper simply printed what he told the staff about the site. Apparently there was quite a bit of loot in the ruins and Thompson collected it.

The writer said, "At one spot that might have been an altar, Mr. Thompson recovered large and small shell and bone pendants, bracelets and beads."

The article concluded with, "Collecting Indian

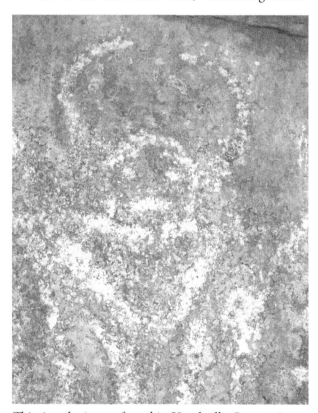

This Apache image found in Hembrillo Canyon is both pecked into the rock and has painted highlights. Being Apache, it is rather rare. In fact, a National Geographic photographer once visited just to photograph this mountain spirit and others on the canyon walls near Rock Art Spring. Photo by the author.

relics is a hobby with Mr. Thompson. Within the White Sands Proving Grounds in the past two years he has accumulated several hundred arrowheads, ornaments and other paraphernalia used by early man." Sounds like a whole museum exited White Sands when Thompson left.

But that isn't the only example. In the May 31, 1957 issue of the *Wind and Sand*, photos and an article showed off the huge Indian artifact collection of Mr. and Mrs. A.G. Devirian.

The article stated the couple came to White Sands in 1952, and early in their residency they found an arrowhead in the main post area. They were bitten by the collecting bug and started gathering everything they could find.

It appears from the article that some of their "relics" were collected from other areas, but most of it came from White Sands. The writer says, "From all appearances, most of the items are El Paso Polychrome, artifacts of a prehistoric people who lived in the El Paso area."

The Devirians said their oldest pieces were Sandia points. Next they said they had eight Folsom points, around 10,000 years old, that they found within 10 miles of the main post.

They found pottery bowls and dishes, in pieces, that they glued together to make them whole. One photo of the couple's collection points out "a pottery dish found in the Wherry Housing area."

Other items listed in the collection were a stone pipe, weaving disks, a water olla, different colored minerals used as body paint and for pottery, clay dishes, over 1,000 arrowheads, strings of beads, carved shells, and burned ears of corn. The photo in the paper shows most of it laid out on a large dining table.

At the end of the article, the reporter says, "The Devirians are planning to take their artifacts with them to Pasadena when they leave the proving ground. Devirian, a field test coordinator with Jet Propulsion Laboratory, is being transferred back to the California office."

Those are just two examples of collectors that we know about. One can only guess at the thousands upon thousands of artifacts that have probably been relocated from White Sands. The sheer plenty of artifacts hints at how many people may have lived in the area a thousand years ago.

A large segment of today's society understands it

is illegal and unethical to take away prehistoric and historical artifacts from government lands. However, during our tours out onto the missile range it was always surprising how many people still did not have a clue.

When I've talked to others about these collectors from the 1950s, most believe it was legal to pick up artifacts then. They assume the antiquities laws are fairly recent.

Actually, the first Antiquities Act was passed and signed in 1906 by President Teddy Roosevelt. The law is very short, only a half page, but gave government officials a powerful tool in trying to preserve America's heritage.

The first part of the law is pretty straight forward and states, "That any person who shall appropriate, excavate, injure, or destroy any historic or prehistoric ruin or monument, or any object of antiquity, situated on lands owned or controlled by the Government of the United States, without permission of the Secretary of the Department of the Government having jurisdiction over the lands on which said antiquities are situated, shall, upon conviction, be fined a sum of not more than five hundred dollars or be imprisoned for a period of not more than ninety days, or shall suffer both fine and imprisonment, in the discretion of the court."

That's pretty clear. Folks collecting artifacts on White Sands in the 1950s were clearly in violation of federal law unless they had permission of the Secretary of the Army.

Did they have permission? Absolutely not. The law goes on to say that the various departments (it specifically mentions the Department of War) can allow collection if the work is "undertaken for the benefit of reputable museums, universities, colleges or other recognized scientific or educational institutions." A personal collection certainly doesn't qualify.

So what was going on? The government, in the form of management at White Sands Proving Ground, didn't object and even gushed about the collections with articles in the post newspaper.

I suspect most didn't know it was against the law and, if they did, they didn't care. They figured it didn't affect the military mission and was irrelevant.

Pop-Up: Is a piece of broken pottery a shard or a sherd? Basically the words mean the same thing with archaeologists often preferring sherd. This is probably because it comes from "potsherd," a centuries-old term for broken bits of pottery.

The funny thing is that it still happens today. Whenever we took very important visitors to Trinity Site, high-ranking civilian and military escorts usually went out of their way to find pieces of Trinitite to give to the visitor. I'm sure they reasoned that there is so much of it, no one will miss a few pieces. Also, it seems to be part of human nature to want to ingratiate yourself with a prominent person by providing something very rare and very special. Unfortunately, it's illegal and the material will eventually become even scarcer.

There are the remains of several pit houses just southeast of the main post at White Sands. They are very near an arroyo that drains a large area of the Organ Mountains. With large snowfalls in the mountains or big rainfalls, this arroyo may have contained flowing water for several months each year.

When the small airfield, now called Condron Field, was being built several miles southeast of the post, construction workers uncovered pueblo walls. In 1962, White Sands had its own soldier archaeologist to excavate the site. He was Specialist 4 Laurens (Larry) Hammack and he came to WSMR with a degree in anthropology from the University of New Mexico. He had been drafted and trained to be a military policeman.

According to the *Wind and Sand* newspaper, because of his educational background and with the backing of the White Sands Command, Hammack received permission from both the State of New Mexico and the federal government to conduct digs on the missile range. At Condron, he and a group of volunteers uncovered a seven-room structure estimated to have been occupied around 1250 to 1350 A.D. One of his enthusiastic volunteers was Brigadier General Shinkle, the White Sands commander.

In the ruins they found over 7,000 pieces of pottery and a cache of 99 beads buried in one spot. In another area they found the remnants of burned corncobs indicating the owners were farmers. In the corner of one room they found a complete skeleton that Hammack said was a middle-aged adult.

After his stint with the Army, Hammack went to work for the Museum of New Mexico doing archaeological work.

The airfield sits next to a large playa that is

formed by the slope from the mountains finally flattening out. The big flood of 1978 filled this playa with water that was there for more than a year. Employees brought canoes and rowboats to work to paddle about on the small lake.

On the east side of the playa, in a dune field, researchers found another pueblo. The area is partially covered with sand dunes and mesquite bushes, but between them Mogollon pottery can be found. It is like someone smashed up a bunch of pots and then walked through throwing handfuls of sherds randomly on the ground. They are everywhere.

No excavations have been done here, but in a few places you see evidence of the walls that once stood on this high ground overlooking the playa.

It is probable these playas and elsewhere held water most of the year and maybe year round. In addition, there is evidence of water control features such as reservoirs and spreader dams that allowed these early farmers to better irrigate their crops.

That water allowed the locals to shift from a hunter-gatherer society to the more leisurely life of farming. Using the water in the playas, Mogollon farmers could have irrigated corn, beans and squash. If harvests were good, they would have stockpiled the excess in clay pots and used it all during the year.

Staying in one place for long periods and not constantly looking for the next meal allowed these farmers more time for creative pursuits. Initial Mogollon pottery, starting about 1,800 years ago, was plain stuff that would be described as utilitarian. Many of the pottery sherds found near the missile range main post are painted, and there is evidence some pieces had handles. Instead of just making a vessel to hold food or water, they were taking the time to decorate the items. Each jar or pot became an artist's canvas for the maker to express himself.

All of what I have described is on or very near the main post at White Sands. Today, kids skateboarding to school and parents driving to work in air-conditioned cars have no idea they live in a thousand-year-old ghost town that once housed families also trying to make ends meet.

This shift to full-bore farming and building projects was not confined to the eastern slopes of the Organ Mountains. Evidence is seen all along the Organ and San Andres Mountains. North of U.S. Highway 70, on the western edge of White Sands National Monument, is Lake Lucero. It is a playa that periodically holds a great deal of water.

Along the western shore of this playa there may have been another pueblo. Here, large areas of desert are covered with pottery sherds. Decades ago, I was in the area with a monument park ranger and he found a mano and metate. Nearby, erosion has exposed several burial sites probably associated with this pueblo.

The erosion was caused by the missile range's Range Road 7 located along the western edge of White Sands National Monument. The road is elevated through the area, so it acts as a small check dam for all the water running down from the mountain slopes. The water hits the roadway and is channeled to a few culverts to continue on to the east. This rearranging of the water flow gradually swept away the grave's cover sand and left bones exposed to the sun.

Further uprange, near the Space Harbor, is another pueblo site where people flourished and left evidence of their being there. It sits on the western shore of old Lake Otero and is called the Huntington Site.

The lowest flat or playa in this area is called Lake Otero because 10,000 years ago, at the end of the last ice age, hundreds of square miles of the Tularosa Basin held a shallow lake. The lake is long gone, but the

> **Pop-Up:** *Manos and metates were used in pairs. The metate is the bottom stone that is usually cupped to hold the ground grain once it is crushed by pounding or sliding the mano (another but smaller rock) over it.*
>
> *The missile range is also home to another form of grinding mechanism that is akin to the modern mortar and pestle. It is called a "bedrock mortar." In this case the mortar or bowl is formed in a boulder or the bedrock itself. Many of these are several inches and in some cases at least a foot deep. The constant grinding of seeds and corn in these depressions eroded the rock, making each mortar hole deeper and deeper. The pestles would have been other rocks or branches.*
>
> *There are many bedrock mortars on the slopes east of the Organ Mountains and north of U.S. Highway 70 providing more evidence large populations may have lived in the area 800 years ago.*

old flat lakebed provided an excellent material for the missile range's space shuttle landing strips.

In 1914, Elsworth Huntington described the pueblo site as a fan of "gravel and other alluvium" extending onto the lakebed. He wrote, "The ancient village covered an area about half a mile in diameter, thickly inhabited in the middle, and with a gradually decreasing number of houses toward the edges. In two distinct central areas pottery is so thickly strewn that one crushes it at every step; in places it is literally so thick that it is impossible to put one's foot down without touching it."

Now, big rainstorms turn parts of the lake into huge, shallow water puddles that hold water for days and sometimes weeks at a time.

One story I heard from old-timers about early Indian activities just west of the Huntington site in the San Andres Mountains centered on Indian volunteer corn still growing north of the Andregg ranch. There is a spring in a bit of a depression, just over a low ridge from the house. The idea is that the corn plants harvested by the Indians 600 years ago have continued to thrive near the constant source of water.

It is an intriguing story that has never been verified. One fact that adds to the story is the wall of partial pictographs in a side canyon just north of Dead Man Canyon. When I visited the site in the 1990s, bits of mineral paint were still visible in many places on the rock wall. It was obvious most of the images had disappeared because of weathering – the wall is not well protected and probably gets washed with wind and rain during most thunderstorms. Hundreds of years ago, the rock must of looked like a billboard.

Other sites exist on the west side of the San Andres Mountains. One spot has a pueblo with more than a hundred rooms. It straddles the boundary with White Sands and Bureau of Land Management (BLM) property and has suffered greatly at the hands of pothunters.

I saw a looted site on the missile range's west boundary in the mid 1980s. Major General Niles Fulwyler, who was commander then, and I flew in a helicopter to look at the area around Cottonwood Spring.

We found the place had been graded with some sort of vehicle. Apparently the looters were looking for graves and structures that might have been buried in the sand. As we walked around, the archaeologist pointed out a few beads of turquoise and shell as well as pieces of pottery that were strewn on the ground by the grading.

The missile range's cultural resources people, with support from Public Affairs, have been working hard to educate employees and visitors about the value of artifacts and the stories they can tell. Employees and visitors are encouraged to note artifacts but leave them in place. It has already paid off.

In January 2001, an oryx hunter in the northeast area of White Sands came across a black on white water jug or "olla" buried in a sand dune. The pot was partially exposed. He knew enough to leave it alone, mark its location, and then call missile range authorities.

White Sands archaeologist Bob Burton went to the site, carefully uncovered the rest of the pot, and extracted it. Burton said it was probably Mogollon in origin and used around 1300 A.D. He found a patched hole in the bottom and speculated it may have been abandoned because of the leak.

The pot is now on display in the missile range museum. It has a graceful short neck and large lip with one handle. The decoration consists of black rings around the jar with geometric figures in black frames around the bowl section.

This olla was found in a desolate sand dune area and may have been left there by a traveler. With people successfully living in many locations all across Southern New Mexico, it makes sense that they traded goods back and forth. Maybe they traded ideas too.

In addition to the pottery, mortars, structural ruins, and other remnants of everyday life, the Mogollon people left behind a great deal of rock art. At the mouth of Rhodes Canyon are some intriguing masks painted in red and yellow. There are a couple of large, very well-executed faces and a few small incomplete ones lower on the rock wall.

To a layperson like myself, the panel looks like an adult painted the big faces and the children were allowed to doodle lower down. What these masks represent or mean is unknown. I have taken a lot of visitors and experts there and heard a plethora of opinions.

One archaeologist thinks the paintings may be the result of a vision quest. This is a rite of passage for a young male who goes off by himself to discover what his place will be in his group. He would starve himself and pray for several days. Eventually, because of the lack of food, he would probably have hallucinations. His people called them visions.

To help himself and others remember what he saw, he might have painted it on the rock as a reminder or reference point.

An anthropologist I escorted to the site said the faces were very similar to images from Central America where they represented deities. She said we know the Mogollon and Anasazi in what is New Mexico today traded goods with their neighbors to the south. For example, turquoise went south to adorn temples, and parrots came north. When Chaco Canyon, in northwest New Mexico, was excavated the scientists found mummified parrots.

The anthropologist went on to say ideas probably were exchanged as well. People were obviously interacting, as they do now, and someone locally may have been intrigued by this particular spirit and decided to leave the icon as some sort of tribute. Or, it is possible a religious follower came north and left

his mark much the way a Christian missionary might have painted or chiseled a cross on a rock.

Another archaeologist on one of our tours to the site refused to get sucked into the speculation. She said we'll never know exactly what the faces represent, since we know so little about their culture. We have no context for them and our speculation is a bit pointless. Instead, she said we should enjoy them and appreciate they were made by fellow human beings hundreds of years ago. That they still exist is a marvel and a gift.

Rock art is typically abstract or representational. Abstract images are usually lines and designs that don't seem to portray anything real. Representational images look like something. The masks in Rhodes Canyon look like stylized human faces.

Many pictographs and some petroglyphs can be found in the heart of Hembrillo Canyon. There is a beautiful spot in the canyon where old cottonwood trees thrive because of the underground water feeding a spring that has been dubbed "Rock Art Spring."

This face or mask is a pictograph found in the lower end of Rhodes Canyon. It is Mogollon so it has survived hundreds of years on the rough rock. It and a few others are accessible enough that we frequently took buses of WSMR visitors to see them. It was an opportunity to educate large numbers of people about the local history and warn them to never touch - so they remain for centuries more. Photo by the author.

On the canyon wall above the spring are several panels of Indian rock art.

Both Apache and Mogollon cultures are represented on the rocks and most of it is representational. The Mogollon images are small animal figures painted on with a red pigment. Some are obvious like a mountain lion and a bighorn sheep, but others take some imagination to see what they symbolize. Next to the animals are some petroglyphs carved into the limestone. They are typical spirals that are found all over the Southwest.

Only a few hundred feet away are Apache pictographs and petroglyphs. We know they are Apache images instead of Mogollon because at least one figure is mounted on a horse. Of course, horses were not available to Native Americans in New Mexico until well after the Spanish arrived in the 1500s. The Mogollon people were long gone by then.

We also know the images are Apache because visiting Mescalero Apache told us so. They indicated that a couple of the figures are clearly mountain spirits, and the Mescalero still dress in similar costumes during their ceremonial dances.

When you show these images to enough people, you eventually run into someone with a loose screw. During tours in the canyon, some people sidled up to tell me the images were produced by Vikings who traveled from the East coast to the Southwest. Others want to believe the markings were made by the Spaniards and are directions to a gold mine or a hidden treasure.

Of course, these proposed interpretations could be just as correct as others presented by scientists. What should give one pause is the certainty of the individuals advancing them. I have talked to lots of scientists and very studious amateurs. They are unanimous about the images – we just don't have the cultural context to really understand what most of them are about. If someone tells you they are sure, it is probably time to run away.

While these are all known Native American sites, there may be hundreds more undiscovered sites ranging from campsites to places where small groups of people lived together. Bob Burton, the first full-time archaeologist at White Sands, told me he thought there may have been thousands of Mogollon people living in the immediate area about 700-800 years ago.

And then they were gone. They disappeared at about that same general time the Ancient Pueblo people left Mesa Verde and Chaco Canyon. Could the two groups have merged and dispersed? Maybe some of them became what we call the Apache today. Some say the Apache pushed them out. Will we ever know what happened to these people? Hopefully there is enough information still hidden away at places like White Sands to get us a satisfying answer.

The Apache

After the Mogollon people disappeared, the Apache moved into the Southwest. The Apache were a different kind of "hunter gatherer." As evidenced by their encounters with the Spanish and later Mexican and American settlers, they tended to hunt other people's stuff and then gather it up.

They didn't leave much behind on the missile range to indicate what their culture was like. The rock art in Hembrillo provides a few insights but doesn't say much about everyday life.

Another artifact of Apache life associated with Hembrillo Canyon is an agave-roasting pit at the mouth of the canyon. By roasting agave bulbs, Apache turned the spiky plants into a nutritious food source.

By "agave" we are usually talking about Palmer's century plant, although there are several others. It is a native succulent found throughout southern New Mexico at elevations between three and six thousand feet.

It is basically a bulb with short, plump, grayish green leaves radiating from the core. The leaves are tipped with needle-sharp spikes that are best to avoid. At some point, when temperatures and moisture conditions are right, a mature plant sends up a tall flowering stalk in a matter of days. These stalks can be 20 feet high.

Once the seeds are produced and scattered in the wind, the whole plant dies. The myth is that this happens after a hundred years. On the contrary, the plants usually bloom somewhere between five and 25 years of age.

To push up the stalk and then produce flowers and seeds, the plant must store up a great deal of energy. According to Mescalero Apaches who have visited Hembrillo, they hunt for century plants that are just ready to send the stalk up in late spring. At that point the plant is at its maximum sugar load and is primed to expend it all in an attempt to reproduce.

The Mescalero ought to know as they cooperate with the Living Desert Museum in Carlsbad, New Mexico to roast agave, also called "mescal," at an annual event in spring.

In 2003, Human Systems Research, a non-profit corporation providing archaeological and historical support to White Sands, excavated the Hembrillo agave pit. The effort was led by archaeologist Karl Laumbach who has decades of experience studying missile range sites.

The mound is actually a mass of rock with a pit in the middle. In the pit the Apache would build a large fire to heat the rock walls.

They then collected agave bulbs, cut off the leaves, piled them into the hot pit, and covered them with stone and dirt. In other words, it was a crude but effective oven to roast the bulbs for days.

Once they were cooked, the bulbs could be cut up and the fibrous material stored or carried along on trips. To use it, you simply chewed on a piece to extract the sugary pulp. Once you sucked all of the goodies out of it, you spit out the inedible fiber.

One Mescalero told us they had an incident some years ago at the annual roasting ceremony in Carlsbad. He said a visitor tried to swallow the fiber and it got caught in his throat. He started choking and they almost had to perform the Heimlich maneuver to save him.

Laumbach and his crew measured the mound of rock at 35 feet in diameter and just over four feet high. They found a few artifacts like projectile points and sherds of pottery.

They extracted several samples of charcoal from the pit, and from the radiocarbon dates they estimated the pit was used between 1450 and 1650 A.D. It doesn't seem to have been used continuously. Instead, the users may have had to wait for the agave to reestablish itself in the area after a big harvest. It would have taken years each time.

Hembrillo Battlefield

When I started work at White Sands in 1977, I was told by many old-timers about an 1880 battle fought in Hembrillo Canyon between the Warm Springs Apache and several companies of Buffalo soldiers. Like any word-of-mouth story, every teller had a little different take on the details.

In short, the story was that the soldiers drank salty water at Malpais Spring in the Tularosa Basin and lamely stumbled into Hembrillo Canyon looking for good water. There, they ran into Chief Victorio's Apache camp and found themselves quickly surrounded. Luckily for them, Apache scouts and U.S. soldiers came from the west to rescue the poor Buffalo soldiers. The storytellers usually added that a number of the soldiers were killed and buried at the site.

It is amazing what a little science and good research can do. Thanks to the efforts of Karl Laumbach and others in the 1990s, the popular good-old-boy story proved to be mostly myth. It turns out the truth is much more interesting.

In southwest New Mexico, the dominant Apache group was the Chihenne or "Red Paint People." For years they were pushed, shoved and forced from place to place by the influx of Europeans in the middle of the 19th century. They ended up at Warm Springs and the name "Warm Springs Apache" was tacked on to further muddy the water.

Warm Springs or "Ojo Caliente" is a mountainous spot northwest of present-day Truth or Consequences with plentiful water and game. A natural hot spring forms a pool on one side of the canyon and water tumbles out of it to join cooler water coming from other springs.

The Warm Springs area was established as a reservation for the Red Paint People by President Ulysses S. Grant in 1874. It didn't last long, however, as the country's Indian policy became one of concentrating natives on a few far-flung reservations. This was probably seen as a way to save money and be more efficient. Handily, it also removed Indians from better lands that white miners, ranchers, farmers and other businessmen wanted to exploit.

For the Warm Springs Apache, who were led by Chief Victorio, consolidation meant a move to the San Carlos reservation in Arizona. The Warm Springs group hated it, and after a short time Victorio led them back to New Mexico. Another move prompted Victorio to say that if he had to move again, he would never surrender to the soldiers.

In 1879, Victorio and his followers were offered space at the Mescalero reservation in the Ruidoso, New Mexico area. Local Army officers were sympathetic to Victorio's plight and tried to get the Warm Springs reservation back for them. Their letters up the chain of command received local support but were rebuffed in Washington.

Colonel Edward Hatch, the commander of the Army in the District of New Mexico, reportedly met with Victorio and asked him not to leave the Mescalero reservation.

Later in 1879, Victorio and his people fled Mescalero. Apparently they were not treated fairly by the white administrators running the reservation. In turn, Hatch was ordered to return them to the reservation or kill them.

In the spring of 1880, Hatch received intelligence that Victorio was camped in Hembrillo Basin in the heart of the San Andres Mountains. He devised a strategy to confront Victorio and end the matter one way or another. His plan involved bringing three forces into the mountains from three different directions to surround Victorio and finish him one way or another.

One of Hatch's forces was on the east side of the San Andres Mountains. It was led by Captain Henry Carroll from Fort Stanton which is northeast of present-day Ruidoso. He commanded four companies of Buffalo soldiers, about 140 men, from the 9th Cavalry. Carroll and two companies of soldiers ended up surrounded by Apaches late on April 6, 1880, and were in need of rescue the next morning.

In the late 1980s, people were scratching their heads wondering where the battlefield was located, what might still be there, and what actually happened there. In 1989, White Sands archaeologist Bob Burton led a small group of personnel to include Karl Laumbach and myself into Hembrillo Basin to have a look around.

The basin is at the west end of Hembrillo Canyon and sits below Hembrillo Pass which crosses a high ridge on the west. That ridge and others form a bit of a bowl with the drain being on the east side. Water falling into the bowl flows east out into the Tularosa Basin. For reference, Hembrillo Basin is bisected by the Dona Ana and Sierra county boundary.

Also, almost in the middle of the basin sits a knob on the end of a ridge from the south rim that just happens to be Victorio Peak. It is a very prominent feature in the basin and this is where Doc Noss supposedly discovered 100 tons of gold in 1937.

As we walked around a hillside near the jeep road that goes through the basin, someone found an old rifle cartridge. In just a few minutes others found cartridges as well. Then near a small wall of rocks, probably five or six stacked to make a breastwork or a shooter's shelter, someone found a .45-caliber cartridge with the lead slug or bullet still intact.

It was a red-letter day as Burton and Laumbach both felt this could be part of the battlefield. Adding to the developing picture was evidence from Harold Mounce who first entered the basin in 1950 when his father worked for Ova Noss digging in nearby Victorio Peak. Mounce was able to produce more cartridges and photographs all pointing to the ridges just north of Victorio Peak as a place where "something" had happened.

Like many government officials, Burton didn't get to participate much in the fun part of the resulting battlefield research – like getting dirty, scratched by catclaw and sunburned. He had too many other projects and programs on his plate. But he made sure the research was done. Because of Burton the money kept flowing year to year as Laumbach and Human Systems Research carried out a thorough investigation of the area.

To find out how extensive the spread of cartridges and other artifacts might be, Laumbach gathered dozens of volunteer metal detectors. These diligent folks spent hours going over 900 acres of rough terrain covered with catclaw and mesquite bushes.

Catclaw or "wait-a-minute bush" is covered with tiny thorns that tear your skin like kitten claws. One of workers said , "Blood was shed doing the research."

In the end, they found a thousand artifacts. Most of the objects were rifle and pistol cartridges left behind from the battle.

To make the material useful, Laumbach and the other scientists needed to know exactly where every artifact was located in the landscape. To accomplish that, Jim Wakeman recorded each discovery spot using a precision global positioning system device with accuracies of just a few inches. Also, he created a detailed three-dimensional computer map of the battlefield on which to place every artifact.

Next, all the rifle and pistol cartridges were sent to Doug Scott, an archaeologist for the National Park Service, who volunteered to perform a forensic analysis. He looked at each cartridge and came back with the make and model of rifle or pistol each cartridge was used in.

Since each gun leaves unique scratches and firing pin marks on the cartridges, Scott was able to sort out how many guns were represented and match each cartridge to an individual gun. In the end,

Laumbach's volunteers picked up cartridges from 145 different rifles and 39 different pistols.

Many cartridges disappeared long ago in the pockets of various collectors while many are still hidden under dense bushes. Laumbach assumes there were many more weapons on the battlefield. But what he was able to gather was enough to develop a good sketch of what happened.

The cartridges found in Apache positions revealed how slow moving this battle may have been. A number of Indians were using .44-caliber Henry rifles. Much of their ammunition must have been old or damaged. Scott found that 21 of these cartridges had failed on the first attempt to fire them and had to be retried.

This meant the rifle breech had to be opened and the cartridge rotated just a bit. The user could then cock it and try again. If he was lucky it would fire. One cartridge Scott examined required 27 tries before it worked. That means there was a very patient Apache with the time to fiddle around for just one shot.

Since each cartridge was clearly mapped, it became obvious where Captain Carroll and his two companies of men spent the night. On a shelf or a step-up on the ridge just west of the Hembrillo road were clusters of .45-55 caliber cartridges consistent with the carbines used by the cavalry. Also, along one side of the ridge were neat little piles of .45-caliber pistol cartridges.

At the time, the cavalry was using a carbine and the infantry used a rifle. They were basically the same .45-caliber weapon except the carbine had a shorter barrel for use on horseback.

The cartridges for the two weapons were the same size and look the same. However, the carbine had a smaller load of powder and those cartridges were designated .45-55-caliber casing. The infantry's rifles used a longer-range cartridge with more powder, and it was designated a .45-70-caliber casing.

On the ridge to the east and a variety of other points in the basin, the volunteers found all kinds of ammunition. It was consistent with what the Apache would have used – basically anything they could get their hands on. The searchers found cartridges from .50- and .45-caliber Springfields, Remingtons, Sharps and other weapons all in the same area.

Near a spring at the base of Victorio Ridge, southwest of the cavalry position, they found cartridges from 15 different .44-40-caliber 1873 Winchester repeating rifles. These rifles were held by the Apaches and provided much more firepower than the soldiers possessed. They allowed the Apache to protect the spring and prevent the soldiers from rounding the west edge of the ridge and walking into their camp.

Once all this work was complete with a database of all the cartridges, researchers suddenly had a very useful tool. For instance, if you wanted to know

These .45-caliber cartridges were found on the battlefield during a visit by military personnel long after the initial survey. These are unusual because they are intact - obviously never fired. Karl Laumbach, who conducted the battleground survey, feels many cartridges were overlooked because of the plethora of catclaw and mesquite on the hills. Photo by the author.

where all cartridges from .50-caliber Sharps rifles were found, you could query the database and have the spots displayed on the computer map. You can do the same thing with a request for a single rifle. In this case you can see if the person using the rifle moved around leaving cartridges in several locations.

With cavalry and Indian positions clearly mapped on the ground, Laumbach needed additional information to paint a more complete picture of what happened on April 6 and 7. With the help of others, Laumbach uncovered a number of documents that helped clarify the history.

One of the most important was a published article by John Conline. Conline was a first lieutenant under Captain Carroll and commanded Company A. His piece was published in 1903 in *The Order of Palestine Bulletin* and recounted his role in the battle.

First of all, he reported all four companies camped at Malpais Spring on April 4, 1880.

Malpais Spring is a lovely area at the edge of the southwest corner of the Carrizozo lava flow on the eastern boundary of White Sands Missile Range. At the spring, water gurgles out of the ground with flows of over 700 gallons per minute and spreads out over the basin floor to form a grassy marsh for hundreds of yards.

Conline wrote that on April 5, he led two scouts and 29 troopers southwest to the mouth of Hembrillo Canyon. There they found horse and cattle tracks in the gravel and followed them west into the canyon. At one point late in the afternoon, Conline stopped and deployed his men across the canyon floor and up the sides in a defensive position.

He stated he didn't see anything at first but said, "I felt morally certain, however, that Indians were in the neighborhood. After all preparations had been made for an attack, and to prevent a surprise by the Indians, in accordance with my usual habit, I made a careful examination of the canon in every direction through a powerful pair of field glasses, and a little before 5 p.m., I saw up the canon, first two Indians, and upon turning the glasses to the right, I discovered about 35 to 50 more Indians coming down the hillside into the canon on the run."

They exchanged gunfire with the Apache beginning at 5:30 for about two hours until it got dark. Conline then withdrew and rode north to link up with Carroll.

Laumbach was not able to find Carroll's actual orders, but the evidence points to Carroll being the net on the east side of the mountains. His job was to scoop up any Apaches trying to flee back to Mescalero when Colonel Hatch and his units confronted Victorio.

Once Conline reported his skirmish and that he thought Victorio himself was directing the Indians, Carroll was faced with an important decision. It was now obvious Victorio knew the Army was in the area. What if Victorio went back to his camp and evacuated the day before Hatch and the main force could get there? The whole plan might fall apart.

Carroll chose a decisive course of action. On the morning of April 6, he sent two companies of soldiers south to look for a way into the mountains bypassing Hembrillo Canyon. He led the other two companies north looking for the same thing. A few miles north he came upon Sulphur Canyon running to the west.

When it became obvious this was a major canyon that would take them into the heart of the mountains, Carroll sent a courier to tell the other two companies to turn around and follow him.

One document Laumbach found stated the troopers had to leave some men behind to guard their water wagon. It is now obvious the old story of Carroll bumbling into the canyon looking for water is bogus. He had water and he wasn't blindly going into the mountains. By all the evidence, he knew generally where Victorio was located and was trying to find and engage him.

Carroll rode several miles west into the canyon and then southwest up to the rim of the canyon with companies "D" and "F" – around 70 men. From the rim he could look south into Hembrillo Basin and easily see Victorio Peak and the various ridges. However, from this position he probably could not see the Apache camp as it was hidden behind Victorio Ridge jutting into the basin.

Knowing he had another 70 well-armed men somewhere behind him, he led his troopers into what may have appeared to be an empty basin. As he got down to the present-day road, the Apache opened fire from ridges to the east (Apache Ridge) and west of Carroll who was in the bottom of the basin. Carroll and his men charged a low ridge on the west, displaced the few Apache there, and dismounted to set up a defensive position.

Initially this attack was interpreted as a planned surprise attack with the soldiers caught in a crossfire. I agree with Ron Burkett that it may not have been a classic, well-planned trap but instead a makeshift response to an enemy force riding toward their camp.

Burkett served as the Director of the White Sands Museum at the time of Laumbach's research. Before that he served in the Army in Special Forces and knows something about guerilla warfare.

Basically, we see Victorio's actions as reactive. After the skirmish with Conline's patrol, Victorio sent his warriors down Hembrillo Canyon expecting the soldiers to come up the canyon in pursuit.

Instead, Carroll surprised the Apache by circling around to the north. When Carroll entered the basin, the Apache had to scramble to meet the threat. A few warriors went to the west side of the drainage but most, coming up the canyon from the east, ended up on a high ridge on the east side of the route Carroll took.

The distribution of cartridges from several dozen rifles on that eastern ridge is consistent with the Apache rushing back up the canyon toward their camp and taking high ground from which to engage Carroll. The only problem for them was the distance to Carroll's position across the arroyo and to the west. It was too far to actually hit what they were aiming at. On the other hand, if they lobbed enough shots, eventually they would get lucky and hit something beside rocks and bushes.

Also, there were large numbers of Apache cartridges found southeast of Carroll's position from warriors trying to block Carroll's advance down the drainage. Since the battle took place over an entire night, some of these cartridges could also be from warriors trying to sneak closer to Carroll during the night.

When Carroll took the little ridge he must have felt fairly secure. He was higher than the warriors to his south and most of the higher ridges were far away. Of course, planning on holding the spot may have depended on the hope that the other two companies of cavalry would arrive sooner rather than later.

Carroll arrived at this position late in the day on the sixth. Within a couple of hours, the sun went down and brought on a very dark night. According to Laumbach's research, the moon didn't come up until 4:30 a.m. and was only a sliver. So there was little light for the Apache to maneuver and attack during the night. According to Laumbach, this fact probably saved Carroll from becoming the Custer of the Apache wars.

That and the fact that early the next morning, Carroll's other two companies of Buffalo soldiers rode into the basin to reinforce his position. That alone probably would have driven Victorio from the basin. At that point the number of combatants would have been about equal and typical guerrilla forces usually don't stand to fight in such situations. They have limited numbers of people and supplies so they cannot afford the potential losses of such a battle. As Burkett has pointed out, they wanted to strike quickly with overwhelming force and then escape.

The clincher for Victorio was the almost simultaneous arrival that morning of some of Hatch's forces from the west. They came over the western rim of the basin and also engaged the Apache. At one point they mistook Carroll's late-arriving companies for the enemy and fired down on them. No men were hurt and one mule suffered a bullet to the knee.

With Carroll saved, the rest of April 7 was taken up with chasing Victorio. During the day, Victorio fought a brilliant retreat action from ridge to ridge that allowed all of his women, children and elderly followers to escape to the south.

Laumbach noted that Second Lieutenant Thomas Cruse, from the 6th Cavalry, was part of the chase. Laumbach wrote, "He (Cruse) reported that initially he was excited by the situation until a few bullets hit close to him and he realized they were shooting at him. He further noted that he knew he did not kill any Apache because he did not see any Apache. All he saw was a long ridge from which came smoke and bullets."

Laumbach found that two Buffalo soldiers, Issac James and William Saunders, later died of their wounds at the hospital at Fort Stanton. In 2009, Laumbach found more records indicating that another soldier died from his wounds in the battle.

Carroll himself was wounded. No one knows about Apache injuries or deaths.

According to Laumbach, the Hembrillo battle was the largest battle in the Victorio War. It was also the beginning of the end for Victorio. In October 1880, Victorio and what was left of his band were slaughtered at Tres Castillos by Mexican troops.

With his archaeological and historical research, Laumbach has managed to rewrite and correct the old accounts of this battle. The black soldiers fought bravely and were led by a decisive commander who dared to try and save Hatch's original plan. There was no stumbling around looking for water.

At the same time, it may show that Victorio was not as infallible in battle as is often portrayed. On the other hand, he clearly saved his group from a superior force on April 7 when all the Army units arrived.

Laumbach often concludes his talks about the battle saying it was fought by a lot of people who didn't really want to be there. The Apache just wanted their homeland back and the soldiers, mostly former slaves or their descendants, were following orders.

In his research, Laumbach found a letter from Second Lieutenant Walter Finley to his mother that summarizes the situation. Finley wrote:

It is the old story, unjust treatment of the Indians by the Govt., treaties broken, promises violated and the Indians moved from one reservation to another against their will, until finally they break out and go on the warpath and the Army is called in to kill them. It is hard to fight against and shoot men down when you know they are in the right and are really doing what our fathers did in the Revolution, fighting for their country.

When the basic research was complete, the missile range held a ceremony at the battlefield on April 24, 1999. Laumbach provided a historical overview that was later turned into a Public Affairs fact sheet. Apache and Buffalo soldier representatives attended as well as a few reporters. At the end of the ceremony, an interpretive sign was unveiled on the ridge west of Carroll's position. For visitors, the sign's maps and photos make some sense of the whole battlefield that is visible down below. The view also vividly shows how exposed the soldiers were on the ledge.

Today the missile range's Public Affairs Office takes tour groups into the site. The groups have to be really motivated to go. The site is an hour's drive north of Highway 70. The last eight miles require a high clearance vehicle when the road has been graded and four-wheel-drive vehicles the rest of the year. Shovels and picks are sometimes handy to have as well.

Visitors have included New Mexico State University ROTC students and young Army officers from Fort Bliss and White Sands who were interested in studying a battle in their own backyard. These "staff rides" are interesting because the personnel come from all kinds of backgrounds and offer differing points of view.

The tours now include a stop at Conline's April 5th skirmish site at the east end of the canyon. Laumbach again led efforts to find this site and was successful in recovering a number of rifle cartridges defining cavalry and Indian positions.

Over the years since research began, Laumbach

Karl Laumbach, the archaeologist who wrote the book on Hembrillo Battlefield, briefs ROTC cadets from New Mexico State University as they explore the cavalry and Indian positions. The staff ride to the battlefield gives future combat leaders a look at guerilla warfare as fought in the 19th century. Photo by the author.

has been interviewed by a number of print and video outlets about the battle. He also escorted world-famous military artist Don Stivers to the site. Stivers then created a painting depicting Buffalos soldiers discovering the rock art in Hembrillo Canyon after the battle. It is titled *The Discovery*.

The Spanish

The first Europeans to set foot on what is now White Sands Missile Range had to be the Spanish when they conquered the Southwest. Although nothing on the missile range stands out as being Spanish in nature, there are many tantalizing stories.

Some enthusiasts claim that the early explorer Cabeza de Vaca may have passed through the Tularosa Basin and over San Augustin Pass in the 1530s. He was one of the few survivors from a group that landed in Florida in 1528. Using rafts they then sailed west and eventually landed near Galveston Island in Texas.

For years Cabeza de Vaca wandered across what is now northern Mexico and the Southwest looking for rescue in the Spanish settlements in Mexico. At times he was enslaved by Native Americans and at other times he actively traded with them. Eventually, he gathered a following of natives who viewed him as a healer.

He was finally rescued in 1537 when he found his way to Mexico's Culiacan and then Mexico City.

There is no evidence he came anywhere near the Tularosa Basin. But it is such a great survival story people want their area to be part of it. It is probably similar to all the "Washington Slept Here" claims back East.

We do know the Spanish were in the Southwest during the 17th and 18th centuries and probably wandered through the San Andres Mountains and Tularosa Basin. By 1610, their Camino Real, or Royal Road, traversed a course just a few miles west of the present-day missile range.

The road connected Mexico City with their northern capital of Santa Fe. From Paso del Norte (El Paso), the road followed the Rio Grande up through present-day Las Cruces to Dona Ana. Then, due to canyons, it left the river to cross the plains between the Rio Grande and the San Andres Mountains

We know Coronado and others came north into New Mexico looking for the legendary seven cities of gold. It stands to reason other Spaniards explored the mountains searching for gold and silver. Some of the prospect holes found in the mountains may be Spanish in origin, but since they are just shallow holes it is impossible to tell.

Near the Cox ranch headquarters, just west of the White Sands main post, are various ruins. Some are early 19th century but the family and others believe some might be Spanish in origin.

General Hugh Milton II, president of New Mexico State University from 1938 to 1947, dictated a history of the Cox ranch in 1976. In it, he said the spring below the Cox house was called "El Ojo del Espiritu" (Spirit Springs) by the Spanish. He said the Mexicans and the Spanish before them probably used the spring on their travels to and from the salt beds further north in the flats east of Salinas Peak.

Also, Milton said early entrepreneurs like Bull and Shedd, who cut lumber and herded sheep before the Coxes settled the area, saw ruins and had no idea who built the original structures.

I have heard of two instances where 20th century residents found artifacts that might have come from the early Spanish. In Texas Canyon, behind the missile range's main post, miner Fred Schneider found a dagger at the mouth of the canyon. According to the family, the knife was very old and had Moorish symbols on its handle. They thought it might have been lost by a Spanish miner working in the canyon.

Texas Canyon is just southeast of the ruins at the Cox ranch headquarters.

Another story comes from the Andregg family who herded goats in Dead Man Canyon of the San Andres Mountains. The story came to light during the collection of oral histories from ranch families by Human Systems Research under contract to the missile range.

The researchers met with family members of many of the former ranch owners and asked them to recall life before the missile range. Part of the process usually included a trip back to the ranch to help jog memories. I helped escort many of these trips and listened in.

The Andregg family was represented by Verena Andregg Mahaney on one of these trips. She recounted living in the canyon as a child and all the fun things they did. She said one favorite pastime was to hike up Dead Man Canyon after a big rain. Apparently the water would roar down the drainage and rearrange everything. On one trip up the canyon she said they found a gold Spanish coin that had been uncovered by the flood.

The coin could have been lost by a prospector searching for ore deposits in the hills, or it could have been dropped by an American much later - maybe even someone from the 20th century. We'll never know for sure because the coin itself has disappeared.

Highlights from the oral history program were published by Human Systems Research in two infromative volumes. The first was called *Homes on the Range* and the second was *School Days*. The books were edited by Peter Eidenbach, Beth Morgan and Linda Hart.

In the end, it is a harsh and hostile landscape. But for those brave enough and strong enough, the land has given ample nourishment to sustain human habitation. It has done so for several thousand years. In fact, at times the area has been so bountiful, the human residents have been able to free their creative urges and express themselves in their art.

This sign was created by Human Systems Research after they completed the Hembrillo Battlefield survey and report. Looking down over the sign gives visitors a bird's-eye view of Captain Carroll's position on the night of April 6, 1880. Visible in the bottom of the arroyo is a Suburban which is probably about where Carroll was when his troops were attacked. He led his men uphill toward the sign and established a perimeter on the step between the Suburban and the sign. The V-shaped gap on the horizon is the end of Hembrillo Canyon as it spills out into the Tularosa Basin. Photo by the author.

In The Cox's Backyard

3

With the Apache basically subdued in 1880, the great Tularosa Basin and surrounding mountains were wide open for exploration and exploitation. In 1878, members of the government's Wheeler Mapping Expedition set the stage when they made it into southern New Mexico to survey the Tularosa Basin and surrounding mountains. Under the leadership of Lieutenant Eugene Griffin, the small group did more than simply map the mountains and plains. Griffin wrote there were two industries suitable for such country – grazing and mining.

It didn't take long for the Texans, with their cattle, and others to move in. When they got to the Tularosa they found cowboy heaven. Most historians report the Texans found grass that tickled the bellies of their horses.

Unbeknownst to these early ranchers, they entered the area during a fluke of nature. Rainfalls were regular and above average. The extra moisture produced extraordinary grass that early settlers thought was the norm. Later, reality would catch up with those expectations.

The Cox family was here early and is still here. They have owned the San Augustine Ranch for more than a century and have experienced some amazing events. Family members rubbed shoulders with Pat Garrett in the Wild West, watched from their porch as missiles and rockets have streaked into the sky, and hosted generals and bigwig officials from all over.

Rob Cox owned and lived at the famous San Augustine Ranch just west of the missile range's headquarters during my 30 years at White Sands. He often commented that it didn't make too much sense to try and ranch in the deserts of southern New Mexico.

Water was the key to all agriculture in southern New Mexico and there has never been much.

During dry years Cox pointed out how marginal it was to try and raise cattle when there was no rain to grow grass. The typical rancher would be faced with three choices, none of which helped the bottom line. One choice would be to buy supplemental feed for the cattle. Another would be to ship them to leased greener pastures. Finally, selling the livestock was an option but could be a disaster if prices were low.

William W. Cox, Rob's grandfather, was one of those Texans who moved into the Tularosa Basin. Better know as "W.W.," he arrived in the Tularosa Basin in 1888 right in the middle of the colorful old West – some call it the "Wild West." He was originally from the San Antonio area but fled a violent situation that killed his father and threatened him.

Working as a foreman for Myer Halff, a rich businessman from San Antonio, Cox moved west, scouting grazing lands for his employer. His relationship with Halff developed into a life-long friendship. When W.W. started a family, he named his oldest son to reach adulthood Reily Halff Cox (he called himself Hal) in honor of the man who helped get him started.

Two other sons, Frank and William Hester, died within weeks of birth.

W.W. was on this scouting mission when he entered the Tularosa Basin with his wife, Margaret (maiden name Margaret Zerilda Rhode), their first daughter Lena and Margaret's sister, Winnie Pocohontas Rhode. Winnie was only 13 years old when they arrived but would later marry Oliver Lee, the prosperous rancher from the east side of the Tularosa

Basin. Lee's ranch headquarters is now Oliver Lee State Park at the mouth of Dog Canyon below the Sacramento Mountains.

The Cox family ended up living in very primitive conditions for a couple of years. While Myer Halff lived the good life in San Antonio, W.W. basically camped below Alamo Spring at the foot of Black Mountain in the San Andres. It is an isolated area a few miles north of U.S. Highway 70 and a couple of miles northeast of the missile range's EMRE (Electromagnetic Radiation Effects) facility.

There they lived in a dugout. It was simply a hole dug into the side of the arroyo wall. Years ago I visited the dugout with Rob, and he explained they stretched a tarp out over the entrance to provide a small porch and shelter for cooking. Water was piped down from Alamo Spring.

Another daughter, Laura Ann, was born there.

Some feel the choice of a dugout may have been driven by fears that trouble might follow W.W. from Texas and this was a way to lay low for a while. Whatever the case, the important thing was that it was next to the San Augustine ranch, owned by Julia Davies at the time. Living next door, W.W. got a

Rob Cox standing at the entrance to the dugout near Alamo Spring where his grandfather's family lived in 1888. Photo by the author.

good look at the property and liked what he saw.

After enduring the extended campout below Alamo Spring, W.W. moved his family west to a ranch near Deming. In 1893, he learned the San Augustine ranch was for sale and he was able to gather enough capital to purchase it. The family returned to the Tularosa Basin and much better digs.

The San Augustine ranch is very appealing for two reasons, both relating to water. The first reason is the natural springs that give the ranch its name. Water pops out of the ground, just east of the house, on a fault line that runs across the alluvial fan the ranch headquarters sits on.

According to geologists, the land on the lower side of this fault sank almost 30 feet while the ground on the other side of the line remained in place. That means there is a big step up from one side to the other. This action probably happened in just the last 5,000 years and is why the drop-off is still so prominent. Erosion hasn't had time to even out the slope.

The drop interrupted the normal underground flow of water near the surface, so it just flowed out onto the desert. By collecting and storing this precious commodity, early settlers were assured of a constant water source. To get even more water, the Coxes dug a well or two and equipped them with windmills. Using large storage tanks, they were always assured of plenty of water.

The other part of the water equation is rain. At nine thousand feet, the Organ Mountains protrude enough to create thunderstorms overhead on many normal summer days. Hot humid air is forced up above the peaks and condenses in the cooler air above. If conditions are right, this condensation can quickly build into a cloud formation ready to drop rain.

The thunderheads, even small ones, have a tendency to drift to the east and drop their rain on the slopes below. In just a few miles, the smaller storms are usually wrung out in the process, and the Tularosa Basin might get nothing. It follows that if there is going to be rain, San Augustine ranch gets more than places out in the flats.

Even with those advantages, the weather can still be a problem. As Rob Cox pointed out to me, the desert can be brutal for ranching.

For example, in 1976 General Hugh Milton, former president of New Mexico State University and great friend to Hal Cox, interviewed Hal about San

Augustine Ranch. Hal related that in 1906 the ranch was hit by extreme drought. At a cost of thousands of dollars they moved their cattle to another location for grazing.

This was a case where the springs supplied plenty of drinking water for the cattle but no rain meant there was no grass. Without grass, keeping cattle from starving was the challenge.

The house W.W. moved into in 1893 was a legendary fortress. There was an outer patio wall 14 feet tall. In earlier days, a ladder was required to get in and out. The walls of the house are several feet thick and had no exterior windows at the time. As the threat of Indian attack and bandit raids disappeared, the Coxes cut holes in the adobe walls for entrances and windows.

According to Milton's history of the ranch, Thomas Bull was the first operator in the San Augustine area. In addition to working livestock, in the 1850s he had a contract with the Army to supply lumber for building Fort Filmore, south of Las Cruces.

In his interview with Milton, Hal said there used to be two huge wheels over 10 feet in diameter with an axle between them still up in one of the mountain canyons. He said he always thought the contraption was used in hauling trees down the slopes for Bull's operation.

After Bull, Warren T. Shedd moved into San Augustine and set about developing it. Initially he built a small inn and commissary. As business picked up he built a real hotel and stage station with good corrals.

In Milton's summary, the place attracted tired travelers and more than a few unsavory characters. Drinking and gambling led to several shootings at the hotel. Supposedly a number of bodies are buried in unmarked graves on the property.

Shedd then sold the property to Benjamin Davies because he "feared for his life." In 1880, Bertha Wales Davies, the 4-year-old daughter of Ben and Julia Davies, was bit by a rattlesnake. She died on July 19 and is buried in one of the corrals at San Augustine. A tombstone marks the grave and a fence protects it from livestock.

Davies then suffered terrible losses to his herds during incredible winter conditions in 1890-91. Later in the year, he died and left his wife with a mountain of debt. This was followed by two summers of

drought that opened the door for W.W. to purchase the place when she had to sell.

When W.W. bought San Augustine he probably thought he had found the place to put down permanent roots. On Oct. 7, 1899 the Wild West intruded and threatened the safety of his family.

It was a Saturday and Dona Ana County Sheriff Pat Garrett, along with his deputy, tried to arrest a man in the Cox house. It went badly and the deputy shot and killed the suspect.

The victim, Billy Reed – also known as Norman Newman, was a fugitive from Oklahoma where he had killed his partner. Like many of these stories, one version has Newman murdering his partner for the money; another version has Newman defending himself from his thieving partner.

Newman ended up on the Cox ranch looking for work. He called himself Billy Reed. Cox put him to work doing household chores. Margaret Cox was pregnant and needed help in the kitchen and around the house.

Sheriff George Blalock, from Greer County, Oklahoma, tracked him to the San Augustine ranch and properly went to Sheriff Garrett to obtain a warrant for the man's arrest. Garrett and his deputy Espalin accompanied Blalock to the ranch.

Garrett and Espalin entered the house's open door and confronted Reed. As Garrett tried to put handcuffs on him, Reed struck out at Garrett and tried to flee. As he got to an outer door where he could get to a pistol, Reed was shot and killed by Espalin who fired two shots. One missed with the bullet lodging in the wall. The other hit Reed and passed through his heart, killing him instantly.

This took place with Margaret Cox nearby and 4-year-old son Jim in the house as well. W.W. was not pleased there was gunplay in his home with women and children present. However, W.W. didn't seem to hold it against Garrett personally. He would later lend money to Garrett.

Decades later when Rob Cox gave tours of his famous house, he would pull out the bullet that lodged in the wall and show it to his visitors. Rob and his father Jim didn't seem to have much use for Garrett whenever they talked about him. For them the incident in the house was inexcusable.

In the November 1998 issue of *New Mexico Stockman* magazine, Rob Cox said W.W. started off raising sheep. However, he quickly sold them and imported some of the first registered Herefords to southern New Mexico. The Herefords have been a mainstay at San Augustine ever since.

W.W. and Margaret went on to raise eight children at the ranch. They were – oldest to youngest: Lena, Laura Ann, Blanche, Reily Halff, Jim, Albert Bascom or A.B., Bonnie, and Emma Lou.

When Hugh Milton asked Hal about going to school, Hal replied, "Well, I didn't go very much, but we went to the school at our home ranch. Dad always had a governess come in there and they weren't these pretty girls. They were old, homely, old maids."

In addition to the spring below the house, for decades the Coxes had a stream running down from the mountains past the house. According to Hal, it was there as long as he could remember. He used to shoot ducks that would land on the few puddles it created.

In Hal's lifetime the stream diminished and by 1976 he said it was flowing only occasionally. He blamed it on the lowering of the water table because of the massive pumping done near Organ to keep the various mines dry and workable.

Over the years the Cox ranch grew to be around 150,000 acres or 235 square miles. It radiated out to the east into the bottom of the Tularosa Basin.

In 1919, in an attempt to broaden his business base, W.W. went looking for oil on his property. He had an exploratory well drilled in the basin southeast of the house but nothing was found.

W.W. died on the last day of 1923. Apparently, all the children shared the inheritance and the ranch ran as an estate for three years. Then in 1926, brothers James, A.B., and Hal and brother-in-law John Stablein (Laura Ann's husband) banded together to form Cox Brothers, Inc. and bought out the other heirs.

Ten years later, the partnership was dissolved with Hal taking one quarter of the ranch, the area north of U.S. Highway 70. In the process Hal bought Lena's ranch on the northwest corner of Mineral Hill which gave him everything north of the highway from San Augustin Peak down east into the basin. Jim bought out the other partners and moved into the main house on the south side of the highway.

Hal and his wife, Alyce Lee, took up residence at what they called the "steam pump ranch." It acquired the name because they used a steam engine to pump water out of the 35-foot-deep, hand-dug well into a large holding tank. The tank was up the hill from the house and the corrals so they always had plenty of water with gravity to pull it toward them.

On May 25, 1990 I escorted a film crew to the old place so they could interview Alyce Lee about what it was like living there in the 1930s. During camera set-ups, she and I talked. She told me when she first married Hal they lived in the old main house at San Augustine.

She recalled Jim and A.B. were also married but their wives were living in town while the men tended the ranch. She was the only in-law at the ranch.

One night she woke up to strange noises. She reached out for Hal but he was gone. Curious, she got up and followed the noise to the outdoors. There she saw Hal, Jim, A.B. and some of the cowboys whooping and hollering and dancing around. Why so happy? It was raining. They were smack in the middle of a drought and it was the first rain in months. Again, we see the preciousness of a little water in this dry country.

Alyce Lee said when she went back to bed, "I wondered if mother's warning about marrying Hal might be right."

The use of the steam pump to move water was an indicator of Hal's viewpoint on innovation and trying new things. To produce more income, Hal and Alyce Lee added a "dude ranch" activity to their operation.

They built five rooms for guests and hung a sign down on the highway. Alyce Lee said she did all the cooking and cleaning. Eventually business was good enough to hire some help.

As we talked, Alyce Lee complained she baked fresh biscuits and bread everyday, seven days a week, for family, guests and cowboys. They also served beans, lots of beef, tea and coffee. Pie was a mainstay as well and she was expert at putting peach pies together.

One of Hal's innovations helped Alyce Lee in the kitchen. He installed a wind generator so they would have electricity on the ranch. It was used for lighting, but they had enough batteries so they could run a small freezer as well. This allowed Alyce Lee to freeze pies and other foods so she didn't have to bake and cook at full speed every day. Also, it allowed them to buy ice cream in town and eat it over several days instead of wolfing it down as soon as they got it home.

Hal and Alyce Lee liked to dance. When Hal had a garage built, he made sure its concrete floor was finished as smooth as possible. Also, on two walls he had a bench made from poured concrete.

When they invited people over to dance, they would park the cars outside and throw sawdust on the floor so their shoes or boots would slide. With their electric lights, they could dance all night long if they wanted.

Another improvement was setting up a family telephone company. There was no commercial phone service that far from town but they managed to run a wire along the fences and under the highway from the old ranch to Hal's place. The system used two old hand-crank phones and batteries. The setup made it possible for them to talk to each other just like in town.

Alyce Lee said it wasn't used for anything urgent – much like today's smart phones. The two families would call each other and check up on rainfall or ask if they'd seen one of their cows.

One of Hal's great friends was General Hugh Milton. They used to hunt deer in the mountains north of Hal's ranch. In his 1976 interview with Hal, Milton told the following story and Hal endorsed the tale as being true:

Halff and I had been hunting up in the San Andres and I had shot a buck on the

According to Rob Cox, this photo of his grandfather, W.W. Cox, was taken in 1906 with the family patriarch on his "pet" horse called Lightfoot. Photo courtesy of Rob Cox.

other side of the canyon. Halff suggested, rather than going down the steep side of the canyon, that we go up to the head of the canyon and cross over. It'd be easier riding.

After awhile we came to an adobe hut which was occupied by an old goat herder who came out to greet us. He had only one leg. The wooden leg was made out of a broomstick. I'm certain that everyone has seen that type of wooden leg.

Halff and I engaged him in conversation and while we were talking, around the side of the house there came a three-legged sheep and after awhile we looked down and there was a three-legged cat. For I do not know why, Halff looked at me and I looked at him and we were impressed with the fact that here were three animals, one a man of course, who had one leg missing.

Next, I presumed that both of us, with one accord, but without any spoken word, decided that were going to get into the house. At any rate, we went in and this man was evidently a very devout individual. Around the walls of that little one-room house there were any number of niches and in each one of them there was a santos and everyone one of them had one leg cut off...Halff and I often refer to it (this tale) as the one legged Jesus story. I don't consider that as a sacrilege, but nevertheless, around the walls of this room were more one-legged Jesuses than any of us had ever see before.

Milton explained in the interview that his wife tried to analyze the herder's behavior thinking it was probably some sort of psychological complex. On the other hand, Milton and Cox lived at a time when a good story was a thing to be valued, nursed and improved with each telling....

The other brother, A.B., eventually moved over to the west side of the Organ Mountains where he developed the Dripping Springs ranch in the 1950s. In the late 1980s, a complex deal was struck involving the descendants of A.B., the Nature Conservancy and the BLM to set aside the ranch. It became a recreational area now maintained by the BLM. Today the house serves as a visitor center, and hiking trails take visitors to the mouth of Ice Canyon where the

remains of Van Patten's mountain hotel still stand.

Jim and his wife Fannie raised three boys at the San Augustine ranch. The oldest, William, was serving in the U.S. Army when he was killed in an airplane crash in the Philippines in 1945. Jay served in the U.S. Navy during World War II while Robert, the youngest, served in the Army's Armored Corp. Rob commanded tanks at the Battle of the Bulge and won the Silver Star.

Jim not only gave up a son to World War II, he also was forced to sell 90 percent of the San Augustine ranch to the U.S. Army. For Hal it was even worse as he lost his entire ranch to what became White Sands Proving Ground after the war.

At the beginning of the war, military officials swarmed into the Southwest to survey and establish a large number of training ranges. Planners were drawn by the good weather, very low population densities, and the remoteness of their potential sites. Bases popped up all over Texas, New Mexico and Arizona.

In fact, before the war began, officials were already snooping around the Tularosa Basin. Supposedly the basin was being looked at as a possible training area for British aircrews. After Pearl Harbor, those plans went by the wayside as the United States needed to train its own crews.

At the beginning of World War II, Fort Bliss moved north onto the Cox ranch's basin lands to develop training ranges. Today, debris from an anti-aircraft gunnery range can be found east of the missile range's main post near Launch Complex 33.

The training range was used to fire .50-caliber machine guns mounted on jeeps at small radio-controlled aircraft flying overhead. In addition, to simulate the extreme speed of Japanese dive bombers, small rockets made of pipe with wooden fins were also used as targets. These could be equipped with flares for night exercises.

More land was taken to the north to form the Alamogordo Bombing Range. This huge chunk of land extended north all the way to U.S. Highway 380 and was used to train B-17 bombing crews. Later in the war, B-29 crews used it.

The headquarters for the bombing range was where Holloman Air Force Base is now located west of Alamogordo.

This use of the ranch lands was meant to be temporary, but at the end of the war the Army established

White Sands Proving Ground using the same lands. Through force of will and a persuasive argument, Jim Cox was able to keep the main house and the lands immediately to the south, north and west of it.

Someone in the Army must have had his eye on the old ranch because early on an official visited Jim Cox. According to his son Rob, the Army wanted to move the family out and take over the rest of the ranch. The Army representatives explained that it was unsafe for the Cox family to live so close to the missile testing going on out in the basin.

Jim Cox didn't take any guff from anyone and calmly explained the facts. He pointed out the Army had its offices, barracks, homes and mess halls between his ranch and the missile test areas. There was no way it could be safe for them and not him.

The Army didn't try again.

This last anecdote might make it sound as if there was a great deal of friction between the Coxes and White Sands. Initially there was. But eventually a working relationship developed and the two parties were reconciled to each other.

In one famous incident, one of Jim's bulls managed to get himself stuck in a large water tank just west of the house. Jim and his cowboys couldn't get the bull out.

The engineers at White Sands came to the rescue. They used a wrecker and some straps to lift the bull to safety.

Eventually, personnel at White Sands learned to respect Jim's integrity and honesty. He saw things simply and with clarity. When he told them something, they knew he was being honest.

Rob once related a story about his father's reputation that spoke volumes. When Rob was a young man, Jim gave him a personal check to deliver to an automobile dealer in town. When Rob tried to make the payment, it was discovered Jim had failed to sign it. They went in to see the manager who simply said the check was good as gold and that Rob should just ask his father to stop by the dealership and sign it the next time he was in town.

When Jim died in 1982, there was a huge turnout for the funeral. General

Hugh Milton attended and, out of respect for his friend, stood by the grave until everyone had said good-bye and left. He then made his farewells and walked away.

When the missile range built its new range control center, someone suggested the range name it something other than "Building 336." After casting about and looking at the typical military names, someone suggested Jim W. Cox. I don't think it took more than a few minutes to convince all the movers and shakers that it was perfect.

In 2000, the new building was dedicated as the "J.W. Cox Range Control Building." The building has a large entry area called a "customer service area." To go along with the naming of the building, there is a display of Cox family photos and murals inside the front door. After Rob's death, a display of his World War II medals and decorations was added.

Most people would say that Jim's son Rob was a chip off the old block. When it came time to decorate the display areas in the new building, Rob insist-

Murnie and Rob Cox are framed by an old metal gate outside their home in 1983. WSMR photo.

ed there were many other ranchers who also gave up their way of life to form White Sands Missile Range. At his suggestion, much of the customer service area and some hallways are dedicated to those cattle and goat ranchers who once made a living in the harsh environment of the Tularosa Basin. Ranching photos and murals cover many of the walls.

Rob and Murnie Cox took over the San Augustine ranch in 1976 when his parents moved into Las Cruces. The relationship between White Sands and the Coxes grew into a warm friendship largely due to the gracious and affable manner of both Rob and Murnie.

In June 1984, when Major General Niles Fulwyler was commander, the range hosted the "Joint Logistics Conference" for the chiefs of logistics from all

the services. It meant a weeklong visit by a briefcase full of four-star generals with their staffs and wives.

Fulwyler became a great friend of the Coxes and felt comfortable enough to ask them if he could host a BBQ for the generals and their wives at their old 19th-century home. Rob and Murnie said yes and the visitors, dressed as dudes, got to hear a little about the real old West.

In turn, Rob and Murnie became White Sands VIPs. They were invited to most of the missile range's important ceremonies as guests of each succeeding commander. Toward the end of his life, Rob was often introduced to the crowd as the "patriarch" of White Sands Missile Range.

Rob died in October 2008. Murnie still lives in the old house.

Old friends Gerald Thomas and Rob Cox take a break during their visit to the W.W. Cox dugout. Thomas was a former president of New Mexico State University. He and Cox both served gallantly in World War II. Cox was a tank commander at the Battle of the Bulge. Thomas was a dive-bomber pilot who fought against both the Germans and Japanese. Photo by the author.

4

The Wild West

Murder And Mayhem Punctuate Early Settlement

The Cox family was certainly part of the old "Wild West" we've come to know and love from television and the movies. After all, the legendary Pat Garrett pursued a wanted man into the Cox home and the result was a dead man on the kitchen floor.

The problem with those old TV shows and movies was that most individuals were one dimensional heroes or villains. Most situations were presented as black and white problems with simple solutions.

Of course, the real world is rarely ever that easy. Those folks who inhabited the New Mexico Territory were complex, multifaceted individuals. And, just like today, it was sometimes difficult to determine who should be wearing the white hat and who should be under the black hat. Maybe there should have been more gray hats.

Some of the people who make up the Wild West stories around White Sands Missile Range include Garrett, Albert Jennings Fountain, Oliver Lee, Albert Fall, Jim Gililland, Bill McNew, and Eugene Manlove Rhodes.

Not one of these people was ever involved in a shootout at high noon on a dusty main street with heroic music playing in the background. However, they played roles in the most interesting murder mystery in New Mexico's history, the deaths of Albert and Henry Fountain. It is a mystery that has remained unsolved for more than a century.

During my time working at White Sands, I was involved in several quasi-investigations into the murders. I often found myself coordinating and escorting visits to chase clues on where the bodies might be buried. Being a skeptic I always approached these visits with real doubt since there was no evidence

and we were acting on what amounted to as hearsay. On the other hand, this is a real mystery and it would have been exciting to be there when it was solved.

Civil War

My version of the Wild West story begins with the Civil War. With the huge battles in the South and East, most people have no idea there was Civil War action right here in New Mexico. As a territory, New Mexico was part of the Union, while neighboring Texas was part of the Confederacy.

In July 1861, Confederacy troops moved out of El Paso, up the Rio Grande, toward Fort Filmore south of Las Cruces. Union troops skirmished with the rebels near Mesilla but it was an insignificant event with nothing decided.

As the Confederates moved toward the fort, Union Commander Major Isaac Lynde abandoned the fortress to the Southerners. He led his troops and their families northeast trying to get to Fort Stanton, about a hundred miles away.

One popular story says discipline was lax and many of the men chose to fill their canteens with liquor instead of water. As the formation fled east over San Augustin Pass, the scorching heat took its toll on the soldiers, women and children. The line stretched for miles as more and more dropped out for lack of water. They desperately needed to get to San Augustine Springs.

Richard Wadsworth, in his book *Incident at San Augustine Springs*, thinks the story of soldiers marching off with the rum instead of water is complete prattle. The problem was they couldn't carry much as individuals and what water stores they took in wagons wasn't much good with the column stretched out for miles.

According to another popular myth, Confederate Commander Lieutenant Colonel John Baylor chased after the fleeing soldiers but took a shortcut over the Organ Mountains. They went over a gap to the south, now called Baylor Pass, and were able to get to the springs before the Union soldiers. This supposedly gave Baylor the edge he needed to capture the Union soldiers.

Again, Wadsworth thinks this account of Baylor taking the shortcut is just local legend. He points out that Baylor repeatedly wrote about coming upon the abandoned and hurting Union troops on the road to the pass. He couldn't have been an eyewitness to what was happening on the road if he was taking the shortcut at the same time.

Baylor's after-action report is available on the internet and Baylor mentions being at San Augustin Pass and seeing Union soldiers ahead on the route down to the springs.

Baylor met with the Union commanders and demanded their surrender. Major Lynde, with everyone suffering from lack of water and burdened with women and children, chose to surrender without firing a shot. Many of his officers protested his decision and would later testify against him when the Army investigated Lynde's behavior.

The surrender contributed cattle, horses, and other supplies to the Confederate force.

Word of the Confederate invasion spread quickly. Various volunteer units were formed in places like Colorado and California to move out and meet the threat. The California force was composed of over a thousand men and headed east in April 1862. They didn't arrive in New Mexico until August. One of the volunteers was Albert Jennings Fountain.

Meanwhile, after their easy victory at San Augustine Springs, the rebels eventually moved north under General Henry Hopkins Sibley. This led to more typical Civil War battles where fatalities were high and injuries on both sides were horrific. At the February 1862 battle of Valverde near Fort Craig, south of present-day Socorro, thousands of soldiers clashed. Many were mangled by artillery. One Confederate company, armed with only lances, charged a Union line only to be mowed down like moving targets in a shooting gallery.

In March 1862, the two sides met again at Glori-etta Pass, near Santa Fe. By most accounts, the battle was being won by the Confederates when Union forces stumbled upon the Southerners supply train. They proceeded to burn the wagons and kill or drive off all the horses and mules.

Without any source of supplies, the Confederate commanders had no choice but to retreat. It was the end of large-scale Civil War activities in the Southwest as the Confederacy never attempted to come back.

When the California Column arrived, there wasn't anything for them to do. They hung around for a while just in case the rebels tried to retake New Mexico. As their enlistments ended, most headed home.

Some decided to stay. Albert Fountain was one of those who chose to take his chances in New Mexico. He eventually settled in Mesilla, marrying a local girl.

Over the years after the war, Fountain grew to be a prominent lawyer, newspaper publisher, leader of his political party, and an elected lawmaker.

Billy the Kid & Pat Garrett

In late 1880, Lincoln County Sheriff Pat Garrett captured Billy the Kid, also called Henry McCarty, William Bonney and William Antrim, in northeast New Mexico. The Kid was charged with killing the previous sheriff of Lincoln County, William Brady, and was taken to Santa Fe where he was held for trial.

Instead, Garrett ended up transporting the Kid to Mesilla in March 1881 for trial on two murder charges. The first charge of murder ended up being thrown out of court on a technicality. The court-appointed lawyer to defend Billy on the second case was none other than Albert Fountain.

On Wednesday, April 13, the jury for the Kid's murder case retired to deliberate. Fountain had nothing to work with in defending Billy. In mid afternoon the jury returned a verdict of murder in the first degree. Judge Bristol, later in the afternoon, sentenced Billy the Kid to be "hanged by the neck until his body be dead." The hanging was set for Friday, May 13, 1881.

The buildings where this took place are still standing in Mesilla around the square.

Soon after the verdict, a heavily guarded Billy the Kid was hauled by wagon back to Lincoln, New Mexico. To do this, the party traveled along the old wagon road over San Augustin Pass and down the east side near the San Augustine Ranch. It was close to the same route followed by Major Lynde and his Union soldiers.

The rest of the Billy the Kid story is well documented. Maybe it was the execution day of Friday the 13th, but things didn't turn out as ordered by the judge. On April 28, the Kid escaped from the Lincoln County jail, killing two guards in the process.

Sheriff Pat Garrett eventually tracked down the Kid at Fort Sumner and killed him on July 14. It was probably the high point in Garrett's life as he was instantly famous for killing such a notorious outlaw.

Garrett tried to capitalize on the deed by collecting a reward and writing a book about the kid. He never received the reward. The book, *The Authentic Life of Billy the Kid*, was published in 1882. It was ghostwritten by Garrett's friend Ash Upton and is reputedly full of inaccuracies. It did not make him rich.

His life continued a slow spiral downward as he ran for several public offices without success and tried other enterprises without much luck. Also, he was hounded by the rise of Billy the Kid's celebrity as he saw his own popularity sink.

It seems to be just another typical American story where a dashing criminal, given the right public relations treatment, flips the story on its head. Billy the Kid quickly became the hero of this tale while readers looked down their noses at the taciturn and plodding Garrett.

Pat Garrett & the Albert Fountain Case

In 1896, Garrett received a chance at redemption when he was called back to the area to investigate the disappearance of Albert Fountain and his eight-year-old son Henry. He was initially appointed Dona Ana County sheriff and then was elected to the job in January 1897.

The disappearance and presumed killing of the two Fountain men remains the great murder mystery of New Mexico. In January 1896, Fountain drove his

> *Pop-Up: Note the difference in spelling Augustin and Augustine. It is, of course, the same name but spelled and pronounced differently. Augustin is the Spanish version and sounds like "a gust tin." The English version sounds like the month "August" with "teen" tacked on. It makes sense that place names like the pass kept their Spanish origins but the springs and ranch name became Anglicized by their various English-speaking owners.*

buckboard to Lincoln, New Mexico to conduct business with the courts. He was getting indictments against a number of individuals for cattle rustling.

The family insisted young Henry go along because, in those days, it was almost unthinkable for anyone to hurt a child. To deliberately hurt a child was against the code of the West and they thought, by being there, Henry would protect his father.

On his return trip on February 1, Fountain and his son disappeared at Chalk Hill in the heart of what is now White Sands Missile Range. The hill is just a low ridge, about 15 feet high, running basically northwest to southeast. U.S. Highway 70 now cuts through it just east of the Dona Ana/Otero County line. In Fountain's time, the old wagon road went up and over the ridge. The crossing point is just a few hundred feet south of the current highway; the ruts from the old road are still visible.

As Fountain approached the ridge and crossed it, he never would have seen an ambush if men were waiting on the west side.

When Fountain didn't show up at home, a posse was dispatched from Las Cruces. They found the buckboard near Chalk Hill, empty cartridges and blood-soaked sand. The posse followed tracks to the east toward the Oliver Lee place and then lost them.

Despite days of searching no bodies were found. Everyone assumed they were looking for bodies because of the blood on the ground. To this day, no bodies have been found.

Most people assume Fountain was killed because of the indictments he obtained in Lincoln. The implication is that by killing Fountain somehow the indictments would go away. Apparently it worked because it doesn't appear anyone went back to the court to find a record of the indictments and follow up on them. Maybe no one else wanted to disappear like Fountain.

After interviewing people such as W.W. Cox, listening to accusations and reading Pinkerton reports, Garrett focused on Oliver Lee, Jim Gililland and Bill McNew as suspects. He faced an uphill battle as Lee was popular, powerful and politically connected.

In fact, some of Lee's allies, to include Las Cruces lawyer Albert Fall, introduced a bill in the territory's legislature to have a new county carved out of Dona Ana County. The belief was that the place of a crime dictated who prosecuted it and where the trial would be held. Fall and his friends wanted a new county so the murder site and all subsequent legal action would be out of Dona Ana County, a Fountain stronghold.

At that time, there were few counties in New Mexico so they were huge, some covering thousands of square miles. The current 33 counties come from the original nine. Over the decades they were split into smaller, more manageable chunks of territory.

To help their chances, the new county proponents cleverly suggested the new county be named "Otero" after Miguel A. Otero, who was New Mexico's Territorial Representative to Congress 1856-1861. It was clever because the New Mexico governor at the time, the one who made the decision, was Miguel Otero, the son of the Otero being honored with the new county name.

Because the father and son shared the same name, some folks today assume the new county advocates were suggesting the county be named after the governor himself. The proponents weren't that dumb. They knew the junior Otero could safely name something after his father without tremendous political repercussions.

The new county deal went through and when the boundaries were drawn up, the Fountain murder site and Chalk Hill resided inside Otero County with Alamogordo as the county seat. In fact, the boundary makes it easy today to find Chalk Hill when driving down U.S. Highway 70 because the ridge is less than a mile east of the county line. At the county line, the missile range has a roadblock point.

Governor Otero had quite a colorful career which included writing a few books. In 1936 he published *The Real Billy the Kid; With New Light on the Lincoln County War*. The book is based on Otero's many conversations with the Kid and portrays Billy as a sympathetic character.

As Garrett chased his three murder suspects around southern New Mexico, a soon-to-be popular writer stepped into the picture. In 1899, Gililland and Lee sought refuge at the Rhodes Canyon ranch of Eugene Manlove Rhodes. The canyon was later named after Gene when he achieved some national fame in the early 20th century.

According to Leon Metz in his biography of Pat Garrett, Rhodes eventually accompanied the two men when they turned themselves in to authorities in Las Cruces to stand trial. Rhodes went along to make sure Lee and Gililland were not shot as they were arrested.

A Trial Without Much Evidence

After Gene Rhodes left Lee and Gililland in Las Cruces, Albert Fall stepped in as their lawyer. The other defendant, Bill McNew, was already in jail having been arrested months before.

Fall immediately requested the men be sent to Alamogordo for trial. All that maneuvering by Lee supporters to establish Otero County and move the trial venue turned out to be fruitless. The judge ruled Las Cruces had primary jurisdiction. However, Fall did successfully argue that the men would not get a fair trial in Las Cruces.

The judge set the trial for Hillsboro. At the time Hillsboro was the county seat of Sierra County and a booming little mining community. The exact population then is unknown, but by 1907, the town had some 1,200 residents.

Interestingly, Albert Fall and Albert Fountain (the "two Alberts" in the Gordon Owen's biography of the two men) were in some ways polar opposites. Fountain was the local leader of the Republican party while Fall was the leader of the Democrats. They sometimes opposed each other for public office. They often opposed each other in court. Also, they backed different business and cattlemen's groups. This is why some suspect Fall may have had a hand in Fountain's disappearance although there is no evidence of such involvement.

In my job at White Sands, I escorted researchers to Fall's old Sunol mining development north of U.S. Highway 70 on the missile range. It is very near Alamo Spring and the dugout W.W. Cox lived in earlier. The idea is that Fall could have ordered the killing and then kept track of it safely up at his place of business with plenty of witnesses around.

The researchers wanted to see if a person equipped with powerful binoculars could see Chalk Hill from the home site. We determined you couldn't see it from Fall's boarding house because of an intervening ridge. Moving south of Sunol, back toward Highway 70, it was possible to see Chalk Hill.

Only Lee and Gililland were brought to trial at

Hillsboro for the death of the Fountains. It was the event of the decade. Hundreds of people flooded little Hillsboro to watch.

It took the lawyers three days just to select a jury. The trial itself started on Monday, May 29, 1899.

Then testimony dragged on day after day. Garrett and the prosecution did not have much in the way of hard evidence so they presented a circumstantial case. Meanwhile, Fall painted Lee and Gililland as young Robin Hoods being slandered for political reasons.

After 18 days, the case was given to the jury. Maybe because it was late at night and everyone was tired, Fall called for the jury to vote immediately. In just eight minutes the jury rendered a "not guilty" verdict. All three of the suspects were quickly freed.

The families and friends of the people involved in both sides of this case are still around. Since no one was ever convicted of the crime, suspicion still abounds. During a recent reenactment of the trial, attendees in Hillsboro took to shouting at each other. At least that is all it was – no guns were drawn.

The McNews

In early 1982, I got to spend a lot of time with George Lee McNew, the youngest son of the same Bill McNew who was arrested by Garrett. George was intent on proving his father had nothing to do with the Fountain disappearance and wanted to visit some of the sites on the missile range associated with the case.

Yes, George's middle name comes from Oliver Lee. He explained that his dad and Lee were great friends.

That friendship started soon after Bill McNew moved to the Sacramento Mountains with his parents who homesteaded near Cloudcroft. By chance one day, Bill rode down into the Tularosa Basin from the mountains and heard shots fired from down below. When he went to investigate he discovered three men shooting at one. He could have ridden away but, as George McNew described him, Bill was proud, haughty, honest and fair. He didn't like the odds so he started shooting over their heads. The three must have thought reinforcements had arrived for their intended victim because they hightailed it away.

After the men left, Bill went down to see if the single man was hurt. He was fine and he turned out

to be Oliver Lee. He thanked McNew and invited him home for dinner. It was the beginning of a long relationship, one that benefited McNew in his endeavors to build a ranch.

Eventually, McNew married and set out to establish his own ranch by putting together smaller properties. He bought the Pellman, Wait, Dewey, Antelope Lake, and White Water Ranches. Some of these are now on the missile range along the east side from U.S. Highway 70 south to Orogrande.

The Pellman place is just north of the highway at one of the White Sands roadblocks. Like many wells in the basin, the well at Pellman was contaminated with lots of minerals. Pellman water was particularly rich in sulphur and took some getting used to. According to Jimmy Baird whose grandfather and uncle once owned the place, the original owner would take a barrel of the water with him when he went into town.

It wasn't that he liked the water. He took it to drink so he wouldn't have to reacclimatize himself to the nasty stuff when he went back home. Apparently it required many days before a person's bowels would accept the water and not reject it within minutes.

Between 1915 and 1917, McNew sold most of those properties to concentrate on his Orogrande spread. This ranch's headquarters was located just west of present-day U.S. Highway 54 and at the north end of the Jicarilla Mountains. From there it stretched west across the basin until it touched W.W. Cox's spread. It covered over 300 sections of some of the harshest desert in southern New Mexico. Together McNew and Cox once controlled most of the land across the south end of the missile range.

What made the ranch work was a deal McNew struck with Oliver Lee in 1909. The agreement allowed McNew to take 15,000 gallons of water a day from Lee's allotment from the Sacramento River Pipeline. He paid $4,000 for the rights. Again, water in a form other than rain made these ranches possible.

McNew then pumped the water west out to eight different holding tanks in the desert. Suddenly, like Cox, he had plenty of water no matter how dry it got.

However, again like Cox and others, he still needed the the weather to get cheap grazing provided by Nature. The rains dictated how much grass would grow which dictated how many cattle he could run.

George said his mother, Hattie, wanted the kids

to receive some schooling even with all the work to be done at the ranch. George said he remembered one summer when two of his older brothers, aged 11 and 8, handled one of their father's properties all by themselves.

This was a common strategy in the early part of the 20th century. Both cattle and goat ranchers usually couldn't afford to hire hands so the whole family pitched in. Young boys were often expected to fend for themselves, run machinery and protect livestock for weeks on end. Imagine youngsters in today's America doing anything like this.

George turned out to be the exception to the rule. His siblings all went into ranching although one brother attended what is now New Mexico State University for a while. He was invited to leave when he was part of a prank that put three hogs in the girl's dorm. George was a success in school and took the academic route for his path through life.

While attending school in Alamogordo, George helped his mother with her flowers and garden – she lived in town with the children while they were in school. He thinks some of his interest in plants may have come from this early experience.

George went on to college at NMSU and graduated in 1930 with a degree in biology. He did his graduate studies at Iowa State University and earned his doctorate in plant pathology.

He then went on to organize and manage a laboratory on agricultural chemicals for the U.S. Rubber Co.; he served as head of the Botany and Plant Pathology Dept. at Iowa State; and from 1949 to 1974 he served as the Managing Director of the Boyce Thompson Institute for Plant Research in New York.

In 1978, he returned to Las Cruces to serve as Distinguished Scientist and Consultant to the Dean of Agriculture at NMSU.

So when George contacted Public Affairs, we found ourselves dealing with a well educated, articulate family member who wanted to do some investigating. Range Rider Tom Dayberry and I took him to Pellman Well, Parker Lakes, Luna Well, Chalk Hill, and two old Baird ranches that were once owned by Bill McNew. Also we drove into Albert Fall's old Sunol development.

George grew up with his father around and he refused to believe the old man could have had anything to do with the Fountain case. Also, he believed his mother who always said she served dinner to Bill

and Oliver Lee the night Fountain disappeared. The distances were too great for the two of them to have killed Fountain and then gotten home in time for the evening meal.

At the time, George liked Ed Brown from San Marcial as the actual killer. Also, he was suspicious of Albert Fall who could have paid for the deed.

Another Point of View

Just as George was sure his family was not involved in the murders, Martha Raley DeArman was sure the three men arrested were involved. Martha was the daughter of Lucy Gililland which made Jim Gililland her uncle.

I escorted Martha onto the missile range on June 27, 1998 to visit some old ranches up north. One of the places we visited was the Jim Gililland place east of Sheep Mountain.

Martha said she had no use for her uncle - that he was an "SOB." She said her mother knew Jim was one of the Fountain killers and that he knew she knew. That made for an awkward relationship, one that led to Lucy fleeing her ranch life up north to start over in El Paso.

On her way to the train station she ran into Robert Raley and fell in love. They were married and started a family. However, Robert was shot and killed when Lucy was pregnant with her eighth child. She ended up raising the kids by working a goat ranch all by herself.

Martha blamed Bill McNew, an associate of Jim Gililland, for the murder of her father.

I never got to ask George McNew about Martha's claim, but it points out the difficulty of trying to find the truth years after an event when the prime players are gone. Since Martha Raley and George McNew have contradictory stories, it is likely one or both are wrong.

Of course, George McNew never solved the Fountain mystery. He said he knew most of the evidence was long gone and all the adults alive in 1896 were now dead, so there was little hope. However, he was quite happy because all the digging reconnected him with many members of his family. They also discovered the grave of one of his grandmothers and got the family together to clean it up and plant flowers.

Since the mystery of Fountain's disappearance has not been solved, it has remained a topic of interest for decades. In my 30 years at the range, I dealt with many people who wanted access to Chalk Hill, Sunol and other sites associated with Fountain's journey on the day he was killed. In some cases, like George Mc-New, we actually went out and looked around.

Also, I took calls from several people who knew, or knew someone who knew, where the Fountains were buried. Some sites were off White Sands, but most were somewhere on the missile range. I escorted several searches or should I say "wild goose chases" over the years.

Some old-timers theorized the bodies where buried in the mud of Parker Lakes. These playas are west of Chalk Hill and would have been convenient. In those days the flats were often dotted with ponds large enough to attract ducks and duck hunters.

For one search we drove all the way north to Sheep Mountain in the San Andres Mountains, looked around for a few hours, and came home empty handed.

At this writing, local archaeologist Karl Laumbach is following leads to another site just north of the old Pat Garrett Ranch which is north of Mineral Hill. That puts the site miles west of Chalk Hill.

This recent search is based on information passed down from Hal Cox to Tom Dayberry, the former White Sands range rider. Of course, neither man had first-hand knowledge but both are considered reliable folks. In other words, if they believed the story, it is probably worth investigating.

On the other hand, we have seen in other areas how unreliable information can be as it gets passed along from one person to the next. It doesn't seem to matter how "reliable" folks are thought to be, mistakes quickly creep in.

Finally, a group with some television backing asked in 2012 about searching on the missile range at Jim Gililland's old ranch. There is an old story that the bones of the two Fountains were moved to Gililland's ranch so he could guard them. This group had no idea where the ranch was located and seemed to be homing in on Dick Gililland's ranch on the west boundary of the missile range. Dick was Jim's brother but a respected rancher with a sizeable family.

The problem with all these searches is that there are never any markers for the graves and no nearby permanent landmarks to refer to. Obviously, the murderers didn't seem to want the bodies found, so it is a bit like looking for a needle in a haystack.

Add to these searches authors now fictionalizing the events. In 2005, W. Michael Farmer published *Hombrecito's War*. The book's plot revolves around the idea that young Henry Fountain didn't die but escaped. He was raised by an old Indian and seeks his revenge as he matures.

The End of Pat Garrett

Before the killing of Billy Reed at the Cox Ranch in 1899, Garrett had purchased a ranch east of San Augustin Pass and north of Mineral Hill. It butted up against W.W.'s ranch. A few months later Garrett added a property north of there in Bear Canyon.

Also, Garrett decided not to seek re-election as sheriff of Dona Ana County. In 1901, Garrett had his family living at the ranch near Mineral Hill when he got lucky. President William McKinley was shot on Sept. 6 and died on the 14th. Vice President Teddy Roosevelt was quickly sworn in as the 26th president.

Although Roosevelt had never met Garrett, he was an admirer of the tough old lawman's image painted by Garrett supporters. When it came time to appoint a new El Paso customs collector, Roosevelt nominated Garrett. Garrett was confirmed on Dec. 20, 1901.

Unfortunately for Garrett, he couldn't take advantage of this break either. His personality and poor decisions alienated a lot of El Paso residents and federal officials. By the end of 1905, Roosevelt relieved him of his job.

Some historians say Garrett was fired because he and some of his gambling and drinking buddies posed with Roosevelt for a photo. When Roosevelt, who was a teetotaler, found out who the men were he canned Garrett.

Leon Metz, in his Garrett biography, downplays the photo angle. Apparently, Garrett was often absent from work and Roosevelt cited him for not doing his duty and for being inefficient.

So, in 1906 Garrett returned to New Mexico and his ranch on the missile range. According to Cal Traylor and David Thomas, who have been doing research on Garrett for a new book, Garrett was often in financial difficulty during these times. They found that he rarely paid his debts or bills. Supporting the Traylor and Thomas contention is the fact that Metz found a letter Garrett sent to the New Mexico governor saying he was in dire straits and to please send fifty dollars.

This wonderful photo by L.B. Bentley shows the two-room rock house in Bear Canyon that supposedly belonged to Pat Garrett. Some historians claim it was part of the ranch Poe Garrett leased to Wayne Brazel. According to Dave Kirkpatrick, Human Systems Research, when he searched local land records for a missile range report, he found no proof this house belonged to Garrett. Kirkpatrick surmises the land Garrett controlled in Bear Canyon was simply pasture land less than a mile from the house. This structure still stands today but is mostly a ruin. Note the sharp edge on the arroyo wall behind the horses. It probably means there was a major rainstorm just months before the photo was taken. Human Systems did some stabilization work on the house in 1999. Photo used with permission of New Mexico State University Library, Archives and Special Collections.

In 1908, Garrett was looking to make a little money off his northern property in Bear Canyon. Because of some confusion with his son Poe, the place ended up being leased to Wayne Brazel.

When Brazel showed up with goats instead of cattle, Garrett was furious. He and Brazel argued and in typical Garrett fashion he threatened Brazel.

In late February, it looked like a solution was at hand when another party came forth and was willing to buy Brazel's goats, take over the lease, and run cattle on the property. On the morning of Feb. 29, 1908, Garrett left his home near Mineral Hill heading for Las Cruces via buckboard. Riding along was Carl Adamson who was one of those looking to take over the Bear Canyon Ranch.

When they got near Las Cruces, in the Alameda Arroyo, they ran into Wayne Brazel. Garrett and Brazel argued again. As a result, Garrett ended up shot in the back of the head and stomach. He died on the spot.

There are a couple of versions of what happened.

The version I always heard from Rob Cox was that Garrett was so mad at Brazel, he bent down to retrieve his shotgun under the seat. As he did so, he yelled at Brazel that he would get him off the property one way or the other. Brazel drew his pistol and shot Garrett to defend himself. Since Garrett was bending over to get the shotgun, this explained why he was shot in the back of the head.

This is the version the jury believed when the trial of Brazel was held a year later. The jury quickly ruled it was self-defense and Brazel was found not guilty

The other version is that Garrett got out of the buckboard to urinate and had his trousers unbuttoned when he was shot from behind by someone hiding on the ridge. This is the story many historians and writers believe.

In June 2012, I was at a luncheon where Jerry Lobdill talked about his recent article in the *Wild West History Association's Journal* (4th quarter, 2011) called "Rethinking the Murder of Pat Garrett." Lobdill told us he thinks "Killin' Jim" Miller was hired to take out Garrett.

Miller was a known hit man or assassin in Texas, New Mexico and Oklahoma. Lobdill said investigators now think he may have killed 50 people during his career. He said Miller was a psychopath who would kill anyone.

On the other hand, it appears Miller was a good Christian as he regularly went to church and did not smoke or drink.

Miller was very open about the killings but had powerful friends and excellent lawyers to free him if he was arrested. Also, he and his associates threatened witnesses and sometimes made them disappear. People and lawmen generally feared him.

According to Lobdill, Miller got off a train from El Paso to Alamogordo out in the desert where he picked up a waiting horse. He then rode the 35 miles through Soledad Canyon in the Organ Mountains to the road Adamson and Garrett were to take. Oh, by the way, Adamson was Miller's cousin.

Lobdill thinks Adamson had Garrett stop the buggy at just the right spot so Miller could shoot him with a rifle. Miller then got back on his horse and rode back the way he came to catch a train back into El Paso that evening.

Supposedly Brazel was hired as the fall guy because they knew no one would convict him.

If Miller did the killing, he didn't get to enjoy his freedom from prosecution or even suspicion for very long. In February 1909, he killed a former deputy U.S. marshal near Ada, Oklahoma. For this killing he was captured and charged. When the case against him didn't look too strong, as often happened, a group of townspeople took the law into their own hands. They charged the jail on April 19, 1909, took Miller and lynched him.

There is no transcript from Brazel's trial to recount the testimony of the witnesses, so these various versions of the Garrett killing freely float around for people to pick the one they like.

On Feb. 23, 1985, I went with Major General Niles Fulwyler, then White Sands commander, to escort Jarvis Garrett to see the old Garrett / Mineral Hill Ranch. At the time Jarvis was the last living child of Pat and Apolinaria Garrett.

Jarvis was almost three when his father died so he didn't remember the man. Soon after the killing, he said his mother moved the family to Las Cruces where Jarvis grew up and went to high school. As a child he picnicked once with the family at the old ranch. Other than that boyhood trip, he had not seen the ranch until 1985.

During his visit, Jarvis told us some of his thoughts on his father's death. He was obviously interested in what happened and had done some inves-

Jarvis Garrett and Jim Eckles during Garrett's visit to White Sands in 1985.

tigating over the years.

In many ways Jarvis told a story similar to Jerry Lobdill. Jarvis thought the killing was a planned assassination and Brazel, who was easygoing and generally thought of as incapable of committing murder, took the blame and the murder charge to draw the law away from the instigators.

Jarvis believed that the men who came to his father with an offer to lease the Bear Canyon place for cattle grazing used the story to lure Garrett onto the open road so they could ambush him.

During our visit to the old ranch, we also took Jarvis to the Brazel graves beside the road to the Hazardous Test Area further north of Mineral Hill. Many have wondered if one of the graves belongs to Wayne Brazel. Lee Myers, who was a Brazel relative, wrote a letter to me in 1980 explaining the grave belongs to Wayne's uncle. The marker reads "Captain W.W. Brazel."

There is an unmarked grave beside the four Brazel ones. According to Rob Cox, it belongs to an unknown cowboy. The Coxes found the man's body along with his dead horse and dog down near the old road. All three had been killed by a lightning strike.

There was no identification on the body, so the Coxes hauled the bodies of the cowboy and his dog up to the little Brazel cemetery and buried them there.

Pat Garrett is buried in the Masonic Cemetery in Las Cruces. Wild West enthusiasts often visit to pay homage and have their photos taken by his headstone.

Almost nothing is left of the old Garrett Ranch but it is still one of the most requested tour spots for missile range visitors. The house is gone but visitors can still see a flat area and a few stacked rocks where it once stood. Also, the ground is littered with pieces of glass and crockery as well as a few cast iron pieces from an old wood-burning stove.

To the west of the house is a small enclosure made of stacked rock with the walls about four feet tall.

Most artifacts probably walked off long ago. We know some disappeared with an Air Force officer named James Braddock in the late 1960s because he wrote about it in *Relics* magazine.

In the spring 1969 issue of *Relics*, there is a two-page article he wrote about finding the ranch and extracting a number of artifacts. He said the first intact thing he found was a bottle bearing the words, "Mexican Mustang Liniment." Using a metal detector, he moved to the arroyo below the house and found a silver spoon and fork. Digging further, he found a number of bottles and pieces of toys.

Since the items were removed from their setting, it is impossible to know if they were actually used by the Garrett family or were left later by cowhands working for the Coxes.

Paso Por Aqui – Gene Passed By Here

One of the most interesting characters to touch the Albert Fountain murder mystery has to be Eugene Manlove Rhodes. Unfortunately, knowledge of him and his writings is fading fast.

Born in Tecumseh, Nebraska, Rhodes came to New Mexico as a young boy when his father received a job as an administrator for the Mescalero Indian Reservation.

Rhodes didn't spend too much time in school because he loved the cowboy life. He worked for many ranches in and around the San Andres Mountains and reportedly could rope and ride with the best. After becoming a famous writer, he would complain no one took note of the fact he once could ride just about anything with four legs.

He also thought of himself as a great wrestler. Once he heard that a student at the New Mexico College of Agriculture and Mechanic Arts in Las Cruces, now New Mexico State University, was a champion wrestler. Supposedly Rhodes rode to Las Cruces just to find and challenge the young man on campus.

Rhodes confronted him and said, "I hear you are a good fighter." The man simply said, "That's what they say."

Rhodes threw off his coat and challenged the student saying, "Let's have at it." After finding himself repeatedly thrown to the ground with the student standing over him, Rhodes got up, shook the man's hand, and retrieved his coat. As he walked away, he said, "They're right."

Although Rhodes didn't have much formal education, he was a vociferous reader. While out herding or babysitting cows there often wasn't much to do. Rhodes always had a book going.

He even read while he rode. In one incident, he was riding along the side of a steep canyon in the San Andres Mountains. As usual he had a book in hand with one leg hooked over the saddle horn, letting the horse follow his comrades. At one point his horse lost its footing and tumbled down the canyon side.

The two cowboys with Rhodes hollered down to him when everything stopped moving, asking if he was alright. Rhodes shouted back up that he was fine but that he had lost his place.

Eventually Rhodes acquired his own ranch in what is now called Rhodes Canyon in the San Andres Mountains on the missile range. The cabin is long gone but a concrete pool or "spring box" still collects water at "Rhodes Spring."

In 1899, Rhodes married May Louise Davison Purple, a widow from New York. They tried living on his ranch but eventually gave it up and moved to New York.

In June 1939, *New Mexico* magazine ran a piece by May Rhodes about those days in the San Andres Mountains and the Tularosa Basin. She wrote she was a real tenderfoot and the cowboys she came in contact with were always pulling her leg.

She was once told vinegaroons were deadly poisonous and smelled like vinegar when crushed. She fearfully kept an eye out for these harmless giants and one day finally saw one of the jet-black bugs. She chased it around the cabin, finally cornered it and crushed it.

There was no vinegar odor. Later she discovered she had killed an ordinary cricket.

She was very afraid of rattlesnakes and especially shaken when her husband's foreman told her "he saw forty rattlers when he was riding fence out at the ranch one day." When she told this to another cowboy, he just spit and said that the foreman must have been drinking something that makes you see snakes.

In New York, Rhodes greatly missed New Mexico and his former way of life. With a talent for remembering the places and people of New Mexico, Rhodes turned to writing short stories and a few small novels about the place. Many of the people he knew were thinly disguised in his stories with fake names but were obviously friends or enemies from his days in the Southwest. Some even got to keep their names.

More than 60 short stories were published in such periodicals as *The Saturday Evening Post, McClure's* and *Redbook* during the early 20th century. He is also credited with creating the New Mexico state motto – Land of Enchantment.

His most famous novel is *Paso Por Aqui* which translates to "He Passed By Here." The book was turned into a movie in 1948 starring Joel McCrea as cowboy Ross McEwen. Charles Bickford played Pat Garrett. Called *Four Faces West,* the film was shot in California. Instead of yucca plants in the desert, the landscape is populated with Joshua trees.

In the book, however, the landscape the hero rides through is very correct. With some knowledge of the peaks and canyons of the San Andres Mountains, a reader can follow along and anticipate where McEwen will go next.

Part of that landscape included a choza or hut where McEwen encounters an ill family near the Point of Sands in the Tularosa Basin. This site is north of U.S. Highway 70 on the missile range at the old Baird Ranch.

According to an article written by Mrs. Tom Charles in the February 1953 issue of *New Mexico* magazine, before World War II the Alamogordo Rotary club restored the hut and put up a sign for visitors. For decades Mrs. Charles was the driving force in Alamogordo for keeping the memory of Gene Rhodes alive and well.

In the end of *Paso Por Aqui*, Rhodes paints a very sympathetic picture of Sheriff Pat Garrett as a man who lived by the code of the West. McEwen saves the sick family at the remote ranch while risking his own life and liberty. Garrett catches up to McEwen but sees what the cowboy did to save the family. In return, he lets McEwen go.

So, even though Rhodes hid Lee and Gililland from Garrett, he must have had a healthy respect for the sheriff.

Although Rhodes never achieved great wealth from his writings, he became a somewhat famous and popular writer. It never went to his head. In the 1920s, he wrote some things for the Atchison, Topeka and Santa Fe Railroad. They asked him for an autobiographical sketch they could use with his articles. Not able to take himself seriously, he wrote the following:

Eugene Manlove Rhodes came to New Mexico in 1881, as a boy of twelve. From 1881 to 1886 he worked for several cattle outfits, known respectively as the KY, KIM, John Cross, Bar Cross on the Jornada del Muerto. In earlier days he did a little mining and freighting; later set up a ranch of his own in the San Andres. Held four aces in El Paso, 1893; in Organ, New Mexico, 1896; in New York, 1908. Held a straight flush in New York, 1913.

Rhodes died in 1934. He had requested to be buried in his beloved New Mexico. Land alongside the old highway that ran through the San Andres Mountains from Tularosa to Hot Springs (now Truth or Consequences) was donated and Rhodes was laid to rest in what is now Rhodes Pass. It is at the top of Rhodes Canyon and just inside the western boundary of the missile range. In 1952, the New Mexico Legislature charged New Mexico State University with taking care of the grave.

At one time the site was fenced with a gate and turnstile for visitors. It was designed to keep cattle out but that is no longer a problem. One year, boy scouts from White Sands did some cleanup at the site but received a scolding from the range's environmental office for not getting the proper permission first.

The marker for Gene's grave is a large red sandstone boulder with a bronze plaque on it. The plaque says, "Paso Por Aqui," "Eugene Manlove Rhodes, Jan. 19, 1869 – June 27, 1934."

As of this writing, the missile range was still allowing an annual visit to the gravesite in October. The visits are sponsored by New Mexico State University in Alamogordo and the Geronimo Springs Museum in Truth or Consequences. Pregistration is required for all attendees.

Unfortunately, it can be difficult finding Rhodes' literary works. His stories aren't filled with the exciting but imaginary gunfights of writers like Louis L'Amour. Therefore, they don't get much attention in today's world where it is mandatory that books and movies be fast-paced and punctuated regularly with violence and a sex scene or two.

In 2013, I found *The Best Novels and Stories of Eugene Manlove Rhodes* still available at *Amazon. com*. This is a large paperback collection published way back in 1987 by the University of Nebraska Press. The tome includes *Paso Por Aqui*.

Gene Rhodes had an impact over many areas of southern New Mexico's history but I think he would have appreciated being put in the "Wild West" chapter here.

From left to right are Pete Eidenbach, NMSU at Alamogordo; Dave Townsend, NMSU at Alamogordo; and Parry Larsen, Geronimo Springs Museum, lecturing and reading from the works of Eugene Manlove Rhodes during one of the annual visits to the Rhodes grave site on White Sands. Traditionally visitors gather round with their picnic lunches and these local historians inform and entertain them. Photo by the author.

The Ranching Business

When the military moved into the Tularosa Basin in 1942, the landscape was a patchwork of cattle and goat ranches. By 1950, more than 80 ranches like the Coxes were affected by the military takeover of the area.

Successful ranching in this section of the Chihuahuan desert, unless you have money to burn, requires the use of federal and state lands. It all comes down to the "carrying capacity" of the land - how many cows or goats a square mile of real estate will support.

The typical ranch on what is now White Sands Missile Range was composed of small pieces of privately owned land supplemented by large parcels of federal and state lands leased for grazing purposes. While under lease, the public lands remained open to the public for such activities as hunting, fishing, and mineral exploration. (I know it takes water to have fishing but it is a traditional activity on other public lands – besides there are fish on White Sands.)

Since I'll be referring to Dave McDonald later, I will use his ranch as a typical example.

McDonald was part owner of a ranch on the north end of the missile range, just southwest of Trinity Site. The ranch headquarters was used as base camp by Manhattan Project officials when they came to test the first atomic bomb in 1945. Today it is called Pond Site.

McDonald and his two partners, other family members, owned 640 acres of land. That is one section or one square mile. This entitled them to lease surrounding lands from the government for grazing. The McDonalds leased over 22,000 acres – about 35 square miles of land.

It is quite a bit of land by Eastern or Midwestern standards, but in the desert Southwest that much land was necessary simply to get by.

The various government agencies leasing land for grazing calculate the carrying capacity for each chunk of land based on water and food. In some places around the missile range, the average carrying capacity is only five or six cows per 640 acres. The McDonald allowance was for a little over 12 cows per square mile.

The Homestead Act of 1862 never foresaw ranching in the Southwest. The act allowed individuals to claim 160 acres of federal land if they farmed it and made improvements for five years. In the McDonald's case, such a small amount of land would have supported three or four cows and farming was impossible. No one could have survived on such a small parcel of land on what is now White Sands.

The leased lands meant the McDonald partnership could raise over 400 cows on their ranch, enough to buy, sell and make a living at it. Of course, if it didn't rain, the carrying capacity could be significantly lower because of the lack of grazing for the cattle.

Most people who settled in and around the Tularosa Basin couldn't afford to buy that much land. The reality is most couldn't even afford to pay the taxes on that much land. Also, most families couldn't find the extra dollars to hire help, so women and children usually pitched in to make the operation sometimes profitable.

Cattle and Goats

In simple terms, most of the ranch families out

on the missile range raised either cattle or goats. At the beginning of the 20th century, sheep numbers were high but most owners switched to goats by 1940.

Obviously, individual goats and sheep consume less native material than cows do. To account for this difference, federal grazing agencies traditionally have set a ratio of five to one to even the equation. This means five goats or five sheep are equal to one cow when calculating carrying capacity and leasing fees.

Generally, the cattle outfits were located on the flats or foothills of the mountains while the goat operations were in the heart of the mountains. There were exceptions to this. The Joe Pete Wood Ranch at the top of Bear Den Canyon started out with sheep and goats and then switched to cattle.

The Wood Ranch headquarters is located in a broad grassy valley that extends north for miles. With its higher elevation up between mountain ridges, the valley received more rain than the desert floor and had a great deal of grass.

Joe Pete's brother John lived just a few miles north of the Wood headquarters and raised goats. According to his daughter Dorothy Wood Miller, "We always had between 900 and a thousand head goats. They were probably half nannies and half muttons." (Nannies or "does" are females and muttons are castrated males. The more accepted term for muttons is "wethers.")

Angora goats found a regular grocery store in the steep, brush-covered slopes of the San Andres Mountains. In return, the goats provided their owners with a variety of goods.

The goats were raised for their hair which is called "mohair." It is one of the oldest textile fibers used by man and is noted for its luster and sheen. Typically, the goats were shorn in the spring and fall. In the 1930s, the fiber was used in all kinds of clothing, including all those military uniforms for countries building their armies. Also, it was used for blankets and upholstery in cars and furniture.

As World War II loomed, goat ranching took a hit from international political maneuvering. To as-

sist our European allies against Germany, the United States purchased all the wool coming out of Turkey. This was to keep it out of German hands.

The wool was put up for sale in the United States at a low price that undercut American producers and flooded the market as well. Some families said they chose to store their mohair for a year or more hoping for a rebound in prices.

The families milked the does and children drank it straight up or put it on their cereal if they didn't have a milk cow.

Also, goats were slaughtered for meat, especially if an animal had a broken leg or some other issue making it impossible for the animal to function normally.

Unlike cattle, Angora goats were fairly labor intensive. There was always a herder with them when they were out on a mountain browsing. A dog might be included to help protect them from predators.

The goats were susceptible to lice and other parasites, so they had to be dipped regularly. Many old WSMR ranches have concrete troughs with pens on either side to accomplish this regular task. Goats would be forced into the trough to be submerged in the bug-killing solution and then climb out on the far side.

Just after shearing they were at risk from cold, wet weather, so most families built low-level covered shelters to get them out of the wind and rain. The shelters also provided shade during the hottest summer days.

In Dorothy Wood Miller's letter to me about raising goats, she went into great detail about the kidding or birthing process. She wrote:

> *The first of May, we were ready to start kidding goats. Everybody worked in the goat pen.*
>
> *The men folks cut out the nannies that would have their kid that day and left them in the corral until they could get them staked on a wire where toggles were already placed. (Author - A toggle was a bit of rope with an*

> **Pop-Up:** *Grazing is consuming grasses and forbs. Browsing is the consumption of leaves, soft shoots and bark from woody plants like shrubs and trees. Browsing can be a drawback because some of the material may be very low in nutritional value. On the other hand, many browsers can stand on their rear legs to reach high and capture low hanging tree leaves and limbs. Some, like giraffes, have evolved even better strategies for getting higher into trees.*
>
> *Cattle and sheep graze while goats and deer browse.*

---

adjustable loop at one end that fastened to the new kid's leg. The other end of the rope fastened to a length of wire.)

When the little kid was born, a Roman numeral was placed on both the kid and the nanny. If twins arrived, all three had the same number. Red paint was used to paint the number.

Each kid had a little tent-shaped shed made of tin or wood. We used tin." (Author - Most of the tin shelters were metal tent liners or sleeves used to support a large Army tent where a pole was placed. By cutting a door into one side, the little shelters were perfect for kids.)

In the afternoon, if the nanny had suckled her baby, she was let out to go for a drink and graze around. Come evening, the nannies would come back to their babies and bed down beside them for the night. Once in a while a mother wouldn't come to her baby, so she was hunted up and staked back over night.

Shearing the goats was a big job. In the early days it was done by hand clippers. Shearing a thousand goats was not for today's couch potatoes. It was hard work that required skill to ensure the goats were not gouged and the mohair was kept as long as possible.

Later, engine-driven clippers were used. Dorothy Wood remembered the families doing the work

The two kinds of shelters used to protect new-born kid goats. The one on the left is from an old military tent and has a door cut into the sheet metal. The other one is made of wooden boards held together with nails. Photo by the author.

themselves at first but later hiring it out to professionals. She said before the pros started doing the work, the men always had contests to see who could shear the most goats in a day.

She also said, "We children picked up the mohair, put it in the wool sack, and tromped it down."

At the Potter Ranch in Bosque Canyon, the family had a shed along with other goat-related improvements. In their operation, the hair was simply pushed across the floor to an opening where a big sack hung down below. Here as well children were used to hop into the sack to compact the hair.

During a ranch family visit, we talked about the children doing this job. I said it sounded like fun. A young women in the group said she had done this on her parent's ranch, and it was definitely not fun. She said the hair is dirty and oily, so it smells bad. Plus it is filled with briars, stickers and other hazards that scratch and prick.

Cows, on the other hand, didn't need day-to-day attention like goats and often roamed great distances if not confined by fences. Ranchers like Jose Lucero divided up their land into large pastures, each with a source of water. This allowed them to move cattle from one area to the next when the cattle had grazed most of grass. While the cattle were feeding elsewhere, the used pasture was given a chance to recover before being grazed again.

Often cattle from adjoining ranches ended up mixed together. Since most of the animals were branded, a joint roundup would be conducted. Then the various owners would cut their cattle out. It was a convenient way for ranchers with limited people resources to help each other.

Cool, Clear Water

Without potable (drinking) water for both humans and livestock, there couldn't be any ranching in and around the Tularosa Basin.

Most people don't realize there is literally a sea of water under the surface of the Tularosa Basin. Unfortunately, it so mineral-laden it usually measures out to be saltier than ocean water.

There is so much water underground in the Tularosa that in many places it is almost at the surface. Near White Sands

National Monument, digging a hole a couple of feet deep will result in a puddle of water in no time. Early missile range recovery teams discovered, when they went to pick up V-2 rocket debris, that the impact craters were slowly filling with water.

Some of this water near the surface is not as salty as the rest because it exists in isolated pockets separated by layers of clay. Livestock can build up a tolerance for this water, but humans have trouble drinking it.

While underground water from the basin bottom was mostly unusable, water in the foothills and mountains was excellent. It turns out that fresh water percolating down through the limestone mountains often formed large pools or aquifers at the edges of the basin like the one under the main post at White Sands.

Drilling wells into these pockets provided potable water for man and beast. In some places the water simply flows out onto the surface at springs or seeps.

One rancher, Felipe Lucero, tapped into San Nicolas Spring on the slopes west of his home to provide a constant flow of good water. This is a major spring known to area inhabitants for centuries. It was a reliable water stop on the old salt road running out of Mexico up to the playas east of Salinas Peak where workers would collect salt.

Felipe and his brother Jose had adjoining ranches just east of the San Andres Mountains and north of U.S. Highway 70. Jose's place was north of Felipe's and bordered the playa now called Lake Lucero.

They also used to trade off working in the Dona Ana county sheriff's office in Las Cruces. After Wayne Brazel killed Pat Garrett, he turned himself in to Deputy Felipe Lucero. According to the family, when Jose was in charge of the county's jail he would use inmates to work his ranch.

Using a two-inch pipe, Felipe brought the fresh water from San Nicolas Spring down almost two miles to his ranch headquarters. In addition to watering livestock and using it for the family's needs, he used to irrigate a garden and orchard.

Price Sanders, one of Felipe's grandsons, remembered it from his childhood and said the place was lush and green because of the water. He said the pipeline had a number of checkboxes that relieved the pressure in the line and allowed the family to divert water to different locations.

With such a glut of water, Felipe stored water in a large dirt tank to the west and stocked it with goldfish. Price said the boys learned to swim in the tank but the girls used the "nicer" concrete cistern closer to the house.

According to Price, their cattle were mostly watered from around the headquarters so the landscape for a mile or so in any direction was generally stripped of vegetation. He also remembered being left alone for several weeks at the age of 14 to water the cattle, check them for screw worms (the parasitic larvae hatched from eggs left in wounds by screwworm flies) and generally make sure they were getting along.

Some other ranchers were lucky to have access to good flowing springs for their water. The Smith family at Sweetwater Ranch on the south side of Salinas Peak tapped a spring and stored the fresh water in several tanks. As the name of the ranch implies, they always had a source of pure fresh water.

Alice Smith was one of Dick Gililland's daughters. She and husband Clay ran goats around two sides of Salinas.

The two-seat outhouse at the Sweetwater Ranch is one of the wooden buildings still standing although it is leaning precariously left. Photo by the author.

The ranchers running animals in or near the mountains made the effort to develop all of the springs and seeps. Usually they would dig a pool at the spring to collect as much water as possible. Sometimes the rancher would build a concrete box to hold the water or line the pool with stone. Animals could then come and drink.

Inevitably weeds and brush would grow up in and around the water. The vegetation had to be cleared out periodically so it didn't consume all the water and to allow the animals to get to the box.

If the spring had a good rate of flow, the box could be fairly large and create a nice reserve of water. It meant many animals could drink before draining it.

On the other hand, some seeps were so slight that the rancher might create just a small bowl or depression out of concrete to hold water. I've seen some of these that would probably only hold a few quarts of water. They wouldn't water very many animals before it was gone. It was, however, convenient for some of the wildlife like the mule deer and bighorn sheep found in the mountains.

Most ranchers did not have the surplus of water that Felipe Lucero or the Smiths owned. They relied on a number of strategies to acquire water and store it.

The most common tactic was to hand dig or drill wells and use windmills to pump the water out of the ground. Of course, the hand-dug wells were fairly sizable which allowed debris to settle to the bottom over time. Tom Dayberry, being a small person, remembers being lowered to the bottom of a well at the San Augustine Ranch and repeatedly filling a bucket with muck. Someone up top would haul the bucket up, hopefully without spilling too much of it down on Tom, dump it, and pass it back to Tom to refill.

Usually, wells were conveniently placed so the animals could be easily watered and, at the same time, the families could get water for their own use. Since most families wanted some distance between themselves and their animals, the well typically wasn't at the back door.

Price Sanders remembers that at the Lucero home, with all that water from the spring, they still hauled water into the house a pail at a time.

The Bennetts in Bosque Canyon were uptown when it came to getting water into the house. In March 1989, I took a number of family members to see the old ranch. The group included Nolene Bennett Nowell and Ann Bennett Kameese. The women were daughters of Arthur and Bernice Bennett who owned the goat ranch.

They were amazed at how small the one-room adobe house seemed to them after all the intervening years. The house was built in 1928. The one room acted as the kitchen, dining room, living room, den, ballroom, and bedroom – the bathroom was an outhouse. Only two beds were in the house as the kids slept in a log cabin next to the corral.

For water Arthur Bennett used a windmill to pump ground water into a large dirt tank up the hill and west of the house. It was used to water the goats, but Arthur also ran a pipe from the tank down to the house. The pipe went through one of the adobe walls where he hung a sink under it.

Gravity was enough to keep water flowing from the tank down into that sink. They used a simple cork to stop the flow when they didn't need water.

During the visit the two daughters laughed at how proud their mother was to have running water in the house.

Others went quite a distance to get water. Lealon and Agnes Hardin Miller moved from Arizona with 1,200 goats in 1933. Their son J.D., an eighth grader, did as much work as an adult hand. In 1994, J.D. told me his parents never told him what the initials stood for. He jokingly said he always assumed it was for "John Doe."

They settled in what is now called Rhodes Pass in the San Andres Mountains. They were just south of a place owned by Agnes' brother Charlie Hardin and his wife Lois.

For some reason the Millers never developed a well near the house. There is a well and windmill down Rhodes Canyon about two miles to the east that they used. It meant they hauled barrels down to the well in a wagon, filled them, and then brought them back to the house.

The well also provided enough water for a garden that had to be fenced to keep wildlife and livestock from eating the plants. The windmill and fencing are still there.

Charlie Hardin had a different strategy. He drilled wells for his ranch and had water developed in a couple of different spots. The well at the Hardin ranch was used to fill a large metal tank. According to Elma Hardin, Charlie and Lois' daughter, the water was used for livestock and the house. Like the Luceros, the tank was also used to teach kids how to swim or at least tread water.

Sometimes the wind just didn't blow and your windmill wouldn't produce much. This was a big problem when you were trying to sell water.

According to Paul and Anna Lee (Bruton) Gaume, the family living in Fleck Draw used mule power to pump water when the windmill was still. A mule would walk around in a circle and turn a geared mechanical pump. In 1990, when I escorted the Gaumes onto the missile range, they thought the family used to charge five cents a head for cattle to drink from the troughs.

Out on the flats where cattle needed lots of land to roam, a well or two wasn't enough. The cattle needed to drink each day. If they had to walk out very far to find grass, the equation didn't work. They couldn't walk far enough to find new grass and still get back to the well that day for a drink.

These ranchers built dams across drainages on their property to capture any kind of runoff during spotty rains. A well-designed dirt tank with a good rainstorm could hold water for weeks if it was big enough. This allowed the ranchers to move their cows to different pastures and have good water for them to drink.

Some ranchers, like Frank Martin on the Jornada del Muerto at the north end of the missile range, cleverly built dirt tanks to take advantage of the slight slope. When the tanks overflowed with rainwater, the water spread out over the desert and irrigated it. A good rain provided drinking water and, at the same time, grew more grass for the cattle.

During the 1930s, some of these catchment tanks were built by the Civilian Conservation Corps (CCC) to improve grazing in the desert. According to Howard McDonald, whose grandfather lived in the drainage southeast of Mockingbird Gap, the CCC established a small "side camp" just north of his grandfather's place to work local projects.

Workers from this camp built the huge Red Tank south of Range Road 12. McDonald said the tank always had water in it. He explained how they rigged a can on a long stiff wire so they could dip down deep into the water to get a good cool drink.

In 2012, amateur historian David Soules was researching historical places in Dona Ana County for the proposed Organ Mountains/Desert Peaks

National Monument. He was looking for the CCC records for the county and stumbled across a letter about the Mockingbird camp. The letter was addressed to the Dept. of Interior's Division of Grazing, attention Mr. Isom Newby in Albuquerque and was dated July 28, 1938. The letter was a plea for a larger generator so the men could watch educational films at night.

From the document we learn the camp had 25 men, Lieutenant King was the camp commander, and it was called a "side camp" from the main Carrizozo camp.

Basically, their current generator only put out 350 watts, enough for a few light bulbs. The movie projector they wanted required 750 watts all by itself. So they needed a larger unit. We also learn the 350-watt generator was so puny they were relying on gas lanterns for light in many areas at night.

The letter, signed by Cecil Butler, points out that a bigger generator would eliminate the lanterns and light the camp with electricity. He then listed what he thought would be required in light bulbs: two 40-watt bulbs for the recreation hall; two 40-watt bulbs for the mess hall; one 40-watt bulb for the kitchen; six 25-watt bulbs for the barracks; one 25-watt bulb for the showers; one 25-watt bulb for the latrine; one 25-watt bulb for the Foreman's quarters; two 25-watt bulbs for the street; and one 40-watt bulb for the tool room.

Such penny pinching seems remarkable to us today but this was during the Great Depression. Many people in the West were living a lifestyle that would have looked familiar to folks in the late 19th century.

One catchment tank on the north side of the Poison Hills, northwest of Salinas Peak, was a little different because it was built by farmers, not ranchers. A major arroyo drains the east side of the Poison Hills. It cuts through a low ridge before pouring down a gradual slope to the north.

Someone built a fairly sizeable dam across this arroyo, complete with a spillway chiseled into the rock at one end. Also on the site are a couple of stone huts and a scattering of tools.

When I started asking around for information, no one at White Sands knew anything about the site. It was not listed in the property inventories done in the 1940s when the Army first leased the lands, so it was probably constructed much earlier.

At a Ranchers Day event on the missile range

one year, one of the visiting families said they were aware of the ruins and had been told it was some sort of cult that had tried to develop the site. Apparently, this religious group came to the desert hoping to farm. They dammed the drainage to store water for irrigation.

Unfortunately for them, the only time the arroyo ever has water in it is after a good rain. If it was a particularly dry year, their dam probably collected nothing more than a puddle.

Our source said the settlers didn't last long and moved on.

Many ranchers, like Franz Schmidt, used their houses to collect rainwater for household use. No ground water could compete with the purity and clarity of Nature's water from the sky.

Most houses had tin roofs so it was simply a matter of putting gutters around the roofline to collect all the rain running off it. Normally this untainted water was piped to a concrete cistern where it would be protected from contamination and evaporation. In many places, the cistern was buried to help keep the water cool.

Homes

Ranch houses came in all shapes and sizes and were made from a wide variety of materials. As one might expect, since this is southern New Mexico, many houses were built of adobe bricks. It was a building material you could make yourself on site and then build what you needed.

Many were quite small like the Bennett house in Bosque Canyon. Franz Schmidt had the money and time to build the well-constructed and sizeable "McDonald" Ranch house near Trinity Site. Dave McDonald's Ranch house, about nine miles away, is also adobe.

The two Lucero brothers, Jose and Felipe, had adobe houses. Since they lived in a transition area between the bottom of the Tularosa Basin and the mountains, they were near the same areas used by Native Americans. Their adobe bricks were made on site, so Indian rock flakes and other artifacts accidentally made their way into the bricks. Archaeologists look closely at the exposed brinks to see what might have been caught in the process.

Normally the bricks were covered with stucco to protect them from the erosion of the occasional rains and spring's blistering winds.

One of the great advantages to adobe construction was the material's ability to moderate temperatures in the house in both summer and winter. Since the bricks are just dried mud, walls tended to be thick which provided a large mass to insulate the interior of the house. Couple that with the desert's tendency for a big difference between daytime highs and nighttime lows and you have natural heating and cooling.

The strategy was simple. In the summer, the daytime highs might be in the 90s or low 100s, but at night it usually cooled down into the 60s. At night, owners opened their houses up and let the cool air flow through bringing everything down in temperature. The next morning, the house would be shut up with the adobe protecting the cool interior. If done correctly, the inside would be very slow to heat up.

Conversely, in the winter, nights might drop into the 20s or 30s with the daytime high in the 50s or higher. In this scenario, the owners would open their houses up during the afternoons and let the sun and warm air naturally raise the inside temps. In the evening, they would close everything up and the interior would stay cozy for hours.

Of course, this system would have worked much better if the ranchers had modern insulation for their attics, double-paned windows and tight-sealing doors.

Also, the adobe was a very flexible building material. When the Bennetts put their water pipe through the wall to the sink, it was easy to bore the hole and then seal around the pipe with mud. On interior walls, it was possible to simply carve shelving in walls to provide some storage or niches for lamps.

One of the nicest houses on the missile range is an adobe structure that last belonged to the Woolf family. It is very isolated being located at the east base of the Chalk Hills and at the top of Hackberry Canyon.

According to members of the Woolf family, who visited the old place on April 25, 1998, the house was built in the late 1920s by an Alamogordo banker for his daughter as a wedding gift. The banker hired a construction company that hauled all materials to the site by mule except for the adobe bricks which were made on site.

For an early 20th century ranch house, this was a nice place. There were fireplaces in several rooms and French doors with glass doorknobs separating the living room from the rest of the house.

Unfortunately for the banker, his daughter couldn't tolerate the isolation and left after just six months. In 1934, the Woolf family acquired the house. They brought thousands of goats onto the ranch that browsed the surrounding canyons and hillsides.

At the opposite end of the spectrum, some people built houses made of logs they cut themselves. Probably because of our cultural penchant for labeling log structures, these houses were usually called "cabins" instead of houses.

They are scarce because there are only a handful of sizeable trees on the missile range. The small stand of Ponderosa pines on Salinas Peak would work, but hauling them down the peak and then to the ranch would have been a Herculean task.

The Greer family built a log house in Lee Canyon just below Silver Top Mountain. They also built a true two-room log cabin on the top of nearby Sheep Mountain.

The cabin is very isolated on the north edge of the relatively flat-topped peak. The walls of Sheep Mountain are mostly cliffs which makes getting to the top a tough hike up one of two trails built by the Greers. They used the cabin to house herders when they ran goats on top. According to the family, it was also used as a hunters shack during deer season.

The trail up the north side is well developed and was used to drive the livestock up and down. In some spots this trail is narrow with a dangerous drop off the side. In these places, the Greers erected what can be described as a low railing to keep goats from accidentally pushing those on the edge over the precipice.

The trail up the southwest corner of the mountain only has two developed switchbacks. The rest is simply a matter of trying to pick the best route through the loose rock on the slope and the brush on top. This trail is closest to the Greer homes and might have been used by the family herders to get back and forth from the mountaintop without their livestock.

Pop-Up: These efforts to stabilize some of the old ranch structures were done before funding dried up at the beginning of the war on terrorism. In the 1990s, archaeologists Bob Burton and Mike Mallouf used to request and receive money from the Department of Army to take a few select structures and try to keep them off the ground. Since many were in bad shape to begin with and there was only enough money for a few, they tried to preserve selected examples of the various styles of construction.

The Sheep Mountain cabin is so isolated it has been protected from looters and vandals by its inaccessibility. In May 1997, the missile range's environmental office gathered some of its volunteers and several handy folks from the White Sands fire department to go up and stabilize the cabin. They reshingled the roof and sealed up the door and windows to keep the rain and wildlife out.

Inside they found two bed frames, a table with two chairs, a wood-burning stove, and various tools still hanging on one wall. In one corner of the bedroom, the Greers had built a small stone fireplace.

Another log home sits northwest of Salinas Peak near the north end of Grapevine Canyon. It belonged to Lum Wood. According to the family, his real name was Columbus but he preferred Lum.

Here too, work was done by the environmental office to preserve the structure. The roof was collapsing so officials erected a roof over the house to keep the rain out. The roof is just sitting on poles and the structure is open on the sides.

Another abundant building material, especially in the mountains, was stone. The Joe Pete Wood house at the top of Bear Den Canyon is probably the best of the lot. The stone is a mixture of yellows and browns and is very attractive.

The house has a large cellar under it that is very unusual. It is almost like a regular basement. Also, there is a large fireplace in the living room and a nice covered porch on the west. For many of the ranch families, their porches served as bedrooms for children, especially during hot weather. The porches were screened in to keep bugs out and allowed the space to cool down quickly in the evening. Some families rigged tarps that rolled up in good weather but could be lowered to cover the screens to seal out rain and wind.

Another very nice house that appears to be stone is the Hardin house just north of Rhodes Pass. According to Elma Hardin, her father made the walls of the house from poured concrete and faced the outside with stone. She said he hand mixed all the concrete and then poured it into the forms a bit at a time.

This may account for the walls tipping out away from each other. Decades ago, the missile range ran steel cables through the house to the walls on the north and south. These cables keep the walls from spreading any further.

Elma said she had the northeast bedroom when she was home from school in Las Cruces. Her parents slept in a smaller bedroom on the southeast that is all windows on two walls. Worked into one wall of this wonderful, light room is an Indian metate and a large chunk of limestone bearing ancient plant fossils. Also, the house has a large kitchen, living room and a bathroom.

Because of the house's qualities, size and location, it is the one ranch house that has been maintained by White Sands for use by security personnel, environmentalists and researchers. During my career, I used it when escorting reporters and writers on multi-day trips on the range.

to get the U.S. mail into newly formed Lincoln County and such towns as White Oaks, a booming mining burg, and Lincoln, the county seat. At first the mail was supplied by stage from the end of the railroad in Las Vegas, New Mexico.

As the railroad moved south to Socorro and San Antonio, it was shorter and easier to run a stage line from there, across the Jornada del Muerto, to White Oaks. Urbain Ozanne won the contract in 1886 to carry the mail to White Oaks and beyond using this route.

Fairly soon after Ozanne started, the railroad extended east to a little coal mining community called Carthage. There is nothing left of the town but tailings piles and a historic marker along U.S. Highway 380.

According to an Ozanne Stage Line schedule, stages heading east from Carthage traveled 30 miles to the ranch station and arrived at 5 p.m. Passen-

Hardin Ranch after missile range personnel quit using it on a regular basis. When there were numerous range riders, they kept the house ship-shape. Now, with the ever-present rodents, the scare of hantavirus keeps many away. Photo by the author.

A stone house in the Oscura Mountains with a rich history predating the 20th century was last owned by the Bursum family. The house was built in the 1880s by the Ozanne family who used it as a stagecoach stop called the "ranch station" on the route from San Antonio, New Mexico to White Oaks, New Mexico.

At the beginning of the 1880s, there was a need

gers could eat (the place was sometimes called the "supper station") and rest. In fact, if they were really tired, they could spend the night in one of the guest rooms.

After a short break in the Oscura Mountains, about three miles south of the current U.S. Highway 380, the stage continued on and arrived in White Oaks at 6 a.m. after travelling 60 miles. The stage then made stops at Nogal, Fort Stanton and Lincoln.

Passengers were charged about 12 cents per mile to make the 135-mile trip to Lincoln.

Urbain Ozanne's son Alfred and his wife Olive managed the mountain station for 2 1/2 years beginning in 1888. When she became pregnant they moved into White Oaks and built a fine house.

Olive later wrote about her time at the station and said she didn't know much at first. She was lucky enough to hire a "smart woman" who taught her "that my little white hands could do lots of things besides crochet and play the piano."

She went on to say, "After she left I took over. Breakfast and supper for the drivers, and if there were passengers, they had to be fed. Often they did not want to ride all night and I had to keep a couple of rooms to take care of that situation. Sheets and tablecloths to be washed added to my other duties made up a full time job."

The work also opened up opportunities to meet interesting people. She wrote that she met a millionaire and his wife, the mayor of St. Louis, and the governor of New Mexico.

After the first mail contract ended in 1890, Ozanne was renewed for another four years.

Unfortunately for the family, events conspired against their stage business. The silver market crashed in the early 90s and mining communities like White Oaks went into decline. With the drop in population, the stage line had fewer customers and less mail to deliver.

In addition, the railroads started creeping into the area. If residents had their choice of getting their mail a day earlier via the railroad, they didn't care if the stage businesses went belly up.

When the Bursums acquired the property as part of their 200,000-acre ranch, they eventually used the large stone structure as a headquarters. Holm Bursum said every room had a fireplace and water came from two wells up the canyon.

Currently the house is a ruin with nothing but rock walls standing. Holm said that once the Army took it over, it was used as a hunting lodge and was accidentally burned. Charred wooden supports can still be seen amongst the rocks.

Scattered through both mountain ranges are numerous miner's cabins that are simply one-room rock structures. There was plenty of rock around, so it was fairly easy to dry stack four walls. To say the least, they are very crude and needed mud chinking to keep the wind from coming through.

The other building material for houses was a wood frame usually covered with boards and batten. Boards-and-batten siding means covering the house with wide boards, say a foot across, and then covering the seams or gaps between these boards with narrow strips of wood called batten.

Even with the batten to cover the gaps, this siding wasn't very weather-tight. Also, the wood had little or no insulation rating so it could be cold or hot. To stop the wind from creating too much of an airflow in the house, families often covered the interior walls with another layer of something. It could be anything from another layer of board and batten to linoleum to cardboard to newspaper and magazine pages. There is a great interior wall in the Greer frame house in Lee Canyon that is still covered with newspaper pages.

This kind of inventiveness was necessary for these people. They were living during the Great Depression so they had very little spending money. If they did have some money, the nearest hardware store was hours away by roads that started out rocky and rough and went to sandy and soft.

When the Millers decided to expand their house, they took up the outdoor dance floor used for holiday events and created a new room with the wood. In some frame homes, instead of buying new lumber for battens that fell apart, owners used all kinds of other materials. It is not uncommon to see the board gaps covered with strips from tin cans that were neatly cut from the trash. Others cut strips from old metal signs to cover the gaps.

The frame houses have not fared very well on the missile range. Once the roof starts leaking and the empty windows allow the water in, the base starts to rot. Eventually, they simply blow down during a windstorm. They kind of fold over and fall as if they just couldn't take it anymore. The Smith house at Sweetwater and the Potter place in Bosque Canyon are perfect examples.

In this dry climate, the frame homes may have been a little more susceptible to fire. We know of a few structures that burned down. Franz Schmidt built his nice adobe house just south of Trinity Site in 1913 because his original house burned.

In Hembrillo Canyon, the Ritch family had a line shack or cabin at Rock Art Spring. It may have been small but it sat on a concrete slab that is still there. Anna Lee (Bruton) Guame told me on a visit to the missile range on August 25, 1990, that one of the Ritch boys using the shack threw a log into the little stove. While he napped, the burning wood fell back out and started the place on fire.

I later checked the site and found several globs of glass that must have been formed when bottles or jars melted in an intense fire.

Most of these houses and shacks were heated by burning wood in fireplaces or stoves. In the early 1940s, the Love Ranch, northeast of the NASA facility, was very modern and had a butane tank. They heated the living space by burning wood or coal and saved the valuable butane for heating water, cooking, and running a gas-driven refrigerator.

According to the family, the drawback to butane was the gas wouldn't flow in freezing temperatures. They used to build fires under the storage tank to keep the butane moving.

The best fire story I heard thankfully didn't involve a house. Elma Hardin said her father was wiping down the wood surfaces of the chicken coop with gasoline to kill blue bugs. Blue bugs are a kind of tick found on poultry that suck blood just like a tick on a dog or cat.

Elma's father forgot what he was doing and lit a match for a cigarette. Luckily, he was not hurt but the coop burned down.

Common to all the houses, regardless of their type of construction, was a lack of door locks. All the families I took to visit their old homes said they never feared for their safety or their stuff.

Like the old urban neighborhoods, these families were true neighbors. They looked out for each other, helped each other accomplish big chores, and celebrated together. Of course, the big difference was they were many miles apart and only saw each other occasionally.

Like most neighborly people, these folks welcomed visitors. A cowboy, a herder or a family could stop by someone else's home and count on a meal and place to rest before going on. When no one was home, it was accepted practice for the visitors to go inside, if they really needed something, and help themselves to food, coffee and water. They were expected to clean up after themselves and leave everything like they found it. The visitor was expected to reciprocate in kind.

It was a system founded on trust and the need for survival in a rather harsh environment. During certain times of the year, a sudden snowstorm or scorching hot temperatures could drive a traveler to seek temporary shelter.

Even though these old relics have stood empty for many decades, they are still not safe from vandalism. Many of the buildings, sealed in an attempt to preserve them from the elements, have been attacked by range employees, project personnel and hunters – they are the only people with access to the uprange areas. For instance, the plywood cover over the door into the Jose Lucero house has been ripped off. The Potsy Potter house in Rhodes canyon is a frame house, so it was easy for someone to tear off some of the wooden siding to gain access to the interior. The front door on the Woolf house was still intact until someone pried the padlock hasp out of the doorframe.

When Mike Mallouf was the missile range archaeologist, he tried to stop the vandals. He knew there was no way to patrol the areas. We surmised people broke into the houses because they wanted to see what was inside. Of course, 99 percent of the interiors were in ruin. That didn't matter to some people. They seem to have a nuclear-powered curiosity that won't be satisfied by anything but an "I was there" experience.

On some of the stabilization projects, Mallouf cut screen-covered viewing ports in the plywood sheets to let in a little light and allow visitors to look in. As far as I know, no one has surveyed the stabilized structures to see if the viewing ports were successful in reducing vandalism or not.

What's For Dinner?

Food for ranchers was a challenge for two reasons. The first problem was the distance to the nearest grocery store. For many of these folks the nearest store was many hours away. It could take all day to go to the store and return home. If the roads were bad, it might take a couple of days.

The second challenge in the desert and elsewhere across America at this time was the lack of refrigeration. Fresh foods from the store and leftovers from meals weren't going to last long with no way to keep them cool.

Ranchers had no easy solution for the distance problem. Mostly they purchased dry and canned goods from the store to take home – things that would keep for weeks without a cooler. When they had perishables, they tried various strategies for storing food in a cool environment.

Many used the tried-and-true cellar to isolate food from the hot air above ground. Others used their water cisterns.

When you peer into the cisterns on the old ranches, you usually see heavy steel wire hanging down from the ceiling or cover. This wire is bent into hooks or tied into loops and was used to hang food items over the water. The shady inside of the cistern was somewhat cooled by evaporation of the water inside.

Many families said they used to hang chunks of beef or goat to preserve them until the family could consume the leftovers. Milk could be stored in the cool cistern to preserve it and make it more drinkable.

Some families didn't have cisterns and had to be more inventive during the summer. A couple of families said they would wrap up uneaten meat in waxed paper and burlap before wrapping it in a quilt after a cool night. They would then store it in the coolest spot in their house. For some it was under the bed in the middle of the house.

A few families also rigged window evaporative cooling. They would build a frame that would slide into an open window. One end would jut outside. A couple boards placed across the frame would provide some shelving.

On the outside of this box they would drape fabric like canvas and then wet it down. Air passing through the canvas to the inside of the box would be cooled by evaporation and would cool the items on the shelves. If the air was really dry, the air entering might be cooled as much as 20 degrees or more.

By the end of the 30s, some ranchers were buying the new gas-powered refrigerators. These devices burned propane to drive the system instead of an electric compressor. Many a cowboy who knew nothing about physics was intrigued by a box that had a fire down below and produced ice cubes up top. These refrigerators opened up all kinds of new food possibilities for the ranch families.

However, the bottom line for most families was the need to eat all the fresh foods very quickly and rely on dry and canned goods the rest of the time.

I often asked visiting ranchers what they ate during the 20s and 30s. It didn't seem to matter too much to the men as they gave mostly vague responses mentioning beans, bacon and biscuits. Not much variety. The women were more responsive. In fact, Dorothy Wood Miller wrote me a letter in June 1992 outlining how her parents handled food. I'll let her tell it in her own words:

In the early years of my life, Grandpa and Grandma lived on the place, and Grandpa raised turkeys, hogs, chickens and a big garden. He divided with us and Uncle Dick Gililland. When one would kill a beef, it was divided. That way, we had fresh meat most of the time. We hung the meat out at night and put it under the mattress after the day began warming up. We ate goat meat regularly. When Daddy marked the goats, there was usually some reginals which were billy kids that had one testicle missing. These were marked for eating.

We had three or four cows to milk. When the feed was short, I burned cacti every evening for them to eat (Author - she burned the thorns off them). We had plenty of milk to drink and to make butter and cottage cheese. When we didn't have a cow milking, we kept canned milk and made sourdough biscuits instead of milk biscuits.

In the early days, we ordered supplies from Wards or Sears catalogs. The orders would come to Engle and someone went for them. The best I remember, the items were 100 lbs. flour, 100 lbs. pinto beans, 48 oz. baking powder, 24 oz. baking soda, 25 lbs. salt, 1 horn cheddar cheese, 10 lbs. elbow macaroni, 1 case tomatoes, and a case of peaches, pears and apples.

We got a side of salt pork, one gallon black strap molasses, one gallon Blue Hill peanut butter, 100 lbs. sugar and 100 lbs. of potatoes.

The McNess truck came out in our area for years. He supplied us with pudding mixes, extracts and laundry detergent. He had a Rex Strawberry Jelly that I'd like to find again.

On the weekend, we baked a four-layer cake. If we had milk and eggs we made a cake, yellow vanilla with powdered sugar icing or cooked white icing and sprinkled it with coconut. My Dad especially liked coconut cake with cooked pinto beans over it.

When we didn't have milk or eggs, we made what was called a poorman's cake. We boiled 1 cup raisins in 1 cup water until tender, added 1 cup sugar, 1/2 cup shortening, 1 teaspoon soda, 1 teaspoon cinnamon, 1 teaspoon nutmeg and allspice, mixed well with flour, and baked in a hot oven.

We had dogs and chickens that had to be fed, so we never tried to keep left-over food unless we had leftover cookies or cakes for lunches. Lunches were a problem. We carried our lunch (to school) in a paper sack then tied it in another cloth sack and on our saddle. Several times our biscuits, salt pork, eggs and peanut butter and jelly were mixed together.

If families were going to have a lot of meat, they often "jerked" it. This meant it was cut into thin strips and dried in the sun. Sometimes it was rubbed with salt to speed the drying process. In the dry New Mexico climate, such meat could last for weeks before rotting.

The Lucero family often jerked beef for long-term storage. During a family visit in February 1994, some members remembered beating the jerked beef with a hammer so it could be used to make gravy for biscuits.

One thing the families seemed to miss while living in the boonies was fruit. Many tried to grow their own fruit with different degrees of success.

The best-documented fruit producer had to be Felipe Lucero with his orchard irrigated by water from San Nicolas Spring. The government inventory of the orchard in the 1940s listed the following trees: eight apple, six peach, four pecan, three plum, two fig, one cherry, one apricot and one quince. Also there were 36 grapevines, 11 cottonwood trees and 8 Chinese elms that provided shade. Family members on a visit in 1994 remembered there was always canned fruit in the cellar.

The Joe Pete Wood Ranch at the head of Bear Den Canyon had an apricot tree that was still alive and blooming into the 21st century. The lack of water and care plus age may have caught up with it as it appeared dead during a 2010 visit.

On June 5, 1994, I met Bill Threadgill and his twin sister, Pat Brown. Their parents bought what is now known as the Hardin Ranch in 1928 and then sold it in 1935. They said the house had all kinds of fruit trees around it. When I first saw the place shortly after arriving at White Sands in 1977, many of the trees on the east side of the house were still alive. Today, there are only one or two left.

Down Rhodes Canyon, the Potters also grew fruit trees on the west side of the house. According to family members, they had an irrigation system fed by a water tank up the hill. Those trees are now dead as well.

One reason these folks tried so hard to raise their own fruit was the almost total lack of it in the wild. The one fairly common fruit that was found in the mountains was the algerita bush. This evergreen bush can grow well over six feet in height and is covered with holly-like leaves. It produces small, bright red berries about the size of baby peas. These berries are very tart but can be made into jelly if you use enough sugar.

Dorothy Wood Miller, in her letter about food on the goat ranches, said that one year they couldn't order any canned fruit. The algerita berries were plentiful so they set about gathering them. She wrote, "We picked and canned, I think two dozen quarts. Mama really made good cobblers from them. Mama and we kids left early each morning on horseback to go to Good Fortune where the berries were thick. My younger sister, Lorena, and I were expected to fill a half-gallon bucket full of berries before we could go home. My, those buckets were big!"

Elma Hardin remembered algerita berries as a young girl as well. During her visit in 2006, she recalled her initial exposure to algerita berries in her aunt Agnes Miller's kitchen. She said her aunt had a big pot of berries cooking on the stove in preparation for making jelly.

She watched in horror as her aunt went to the stove periodically to scoop off little white worms that floated to the top. Apparently, the berries were infested and the boiling water killed the little critters. After that, she said she refused to have anything to do with algerita berries.

Health Care

Because of the great distances to the nearest town and a possible doctor, ranch families had to be remarkably self reliant when it came to illness and injury. On the other hand, being so far away from town and each other, families were rarely exposed to contagious diseases.

Coal tar and coal oil were used by many families to treat minor problems. Coal tar is a thick tar-like paste produced from distilling coal. It is a witches' brew of chemicals, some of which have been used in skin applications. Today, it is still used in dandruff shampoos.

In the early 20th century, it was used in many veterinary treatments. Many ranchers felt that if it was good for their horses, cattle and goats, it probably would work on themselves. One family told me that one of the men accidentally struck his foot with an axe while chopping wood. It made a gash to the bone with blood practically gushing out.

They stopped the bleeding by applying kerosene. Then they held the edges of the cut together while applying a layer of coal tar over the cut and then tightly wrapping it to keep the gash closed. After a week or so, they removed the poultice of tar and the wound was almost healed.

They said the coal tar sealed the wound and kept it clean. Also, the sticky stuff kept the edges of the cut together so it would heal without stitches.

By the middle of the 20th century, coal oil meant kerosene. Everyone had it because it was the fuel in their lamps.

One family said that when the kids caught cold or had sore throats, the parents made them gargle with kerosene. After going through the cure once, kids said they were reluctant to admit they were sick the next time around.

Another family said they poured a little coal oil on piles of sugar and lit each pile with a match. The oil would burn and caramelize the sugar. They then used the little lumps of sugar residue as cough drops.

Elma Hardin Cain talked about using the kerosene and sugar trick all her life, even when modern medicines were readily available. She related she had a friend undergoing chemotherapy who was hit hard with nausea from the treatments. When nothing seemed to work on the nausea, Elma suggested the treated sugar trick. She claimed it worked great.

To hear these old-timers talk about their folk cures, one would think they were using miracle drugs like penicillin or some new antibiotic. In many cases, especially with colds and other ailments, the treatment more-than-likely coincided with their

body's immune system kicking in to get rid of the infection.

One story revolving around a folk remedy involved the bite from a rattlesnake. A quick-thinking family member cut the flesh between the two fang holes and filled the cut with snuff. They claimed the snuff drew out the venom and the victim suffered no consequences. Of course, the more likely scenario is that is was a typical dry bite where no venom was injected under the skin.

More serious injury or illness required a trip to town, although some families remembered getting a doctor to travel to their homes for a house call.

Pregnancy and where to deliver the baby were serious matters. Most of the families I visited with usually opted to have the mother move to town and stay with friends or relatives during the final months of the pregnancy. Others would have a midwife or experienced relative stay with the expectant mother and help deliver the baby.

Every once in a while plans would go awry and mothers had to make do. On one of our ranch visits, Alice Gililland Smith vividly remembered her mother, Ginevra Wood Gililland, delivering her baby sister Lola all by herself.

Ginevra was scheduled to go to Albuquerque the next day to stay and have the baby there. Instead, Ginevra went into labor the day before with no one around but Alice, 13, and Dixie who was 8.

Ginevra, in bed, told Alice to go to the top of a hill and light a signal fire for their father, Dick Gililland. Alice and Dixie had no idea what was going on so they stayed out most of the day after the fire was built.

Dick Gililland didn't respond to the fire because he never saw it.

When Alice went back to the house, Dixie reported she heard a baby crying. Alice didn't believe her and went inside to investigate. When she looked in her parents' bedroom, Ginevra was holding baby Lola who was still attached to the umbilical cord and was a quite a mess.

Alice said she wanted to run – she was used to seeing baby goats and cows, not children. Her mother ordered Alice to get the scissors and hot water to clean up the baby. Alice then assisted her mother and learned a little more about life.

Mother and baby were fine.

Dick Gililland was one of two men who ranched

The Joe Pete Wood Ranch headquarters at the top of Bear Den Canyon during a tour of WSMR ranches. Over the years many groups requested ranch tours. At one time, ranch tours were co-sponsored by the New Mexico Farm and Ranch Museum and the WSMR Public Affairs Office. Photo by the author.

on White Sands and proved genetics and a common family background do not dictate the character of siblings. Lester Greer was the other. Both were respected, honest, hard-working ranchers who lived not too far from each other near Salinas Peak. Both had relatives who were something of the opposite.

Dick's brother was Jim Gililland, the man tried for the murder of Albert and Henry Fountain. Gililland was arrested by sheriff Pat Garrett and stood trial in one of the most famous murder cases in the history of New Mexico. Gililland and his co-defendant, Oliver Lee, were quickly found innocent because there was no hard evidence and no eyewitnesses testified against them.

Although Jim Gililland was exonerated by the law, many historians and even some of his own relatives think he was involved in the killing.

According to Charles Barnum, who married into

the Greer clan, Lester Greer had two brothers, John Franklin and William Randall, who were known outlaws.

The main culprit was John who tired of mining and ranching and turned to a life of crime as a young man. Barnum wrote that Greer committed many crimes that were never attributed to him. However, by 1910 he was the leader of a gang that openly robbed and killed for a living.

On Dec. 22, 1910, he singled-handedly robbed a train out of El Paso and in February 1911, Greer and a partner murdered and robbed a bar owner in El Paso.

He often fled to Mexico to hide or to the mountains in New Mexico where family members hid him. In an age where automobiles were quickly replacing horses, Greer still found it advantageous to escape his crimes on horseback. It allowed him into rugged, road-less country where the machines still couldn't manage.

Barnum wrote that Greer tried to unburden the superintendent of the Chino Copper Company of the mine's payroll in August 1911 but only netted $80 and some nice watches. A posse sent after Greer was ambushed and sent packing without their horses or rifles.

Finally in November 1911, a posse caught up with Greer and his accomplices. John Greer and one man charged the posse while another comrade hid in the rocks to cover the two with a rifle. Greer managed to kill two of the posse members before receiving a fatal neck wound.

According to Barnum, the accomplice in the rocks was John's brother, William Randall, who managed to escape. Family members concealed him and he eventually fled to California, changing his name to Fred Lindsay. Years later he volunteered for the Army during World War I, but died from influenza in 1917 before being sent overseas. On his deathbed he confessed to being William Randall Greer of the famous Greer Gang in New Mexico – the last gang of outlaws in the U.S. to operate on horseback.

In 1921, Lester Greer named his newborn son, "William Randall."

Learning the Three "R"s

Again distance made a big difference in how much schooling ranch children received. Kids went to small schools in such places as Cutter and Engle on the west side, Bingham on the north, and Oscura and Brice on the east. To get there, they walked, rode horses, were delivered by car, or rode in some sort of bus.

Another common strategy, especially when there were several children, was a second home in a larger town like Hot Springs, Tularosa, Las Cruces or Socorro. Usually the mother would live in town with the children and care for them while they went to school.

Some children were sent away to a boarding school. Elma Hardin Cain attended the Loretto Academy in Las Cruces. She only went home on a few holidays and for the summers.

Also, a few families home-schooled their children.

Finally, families living in and around the north end of the San Andres Mountains had their own school. In the early part of the 20th century, it was located in Bear Den Canyon, a couple of miles north of the Henderson Ranch and a couple of miles south of the Wood Ranch.

Eventually, this spot was abandoned and a school house was built just east of the Dick Gililland Ranch. It was called the Ritch School.

Children nearby walked and some went by horse. The rest were picked up by a little community bus that was driven by J.D. Miller for several years. He was under contract to Socorro County to provide the service.

It wasn't a real bus but a car. J.D. said he hauled nine kids in the car, so small kids had to sit on the laps of the bigger kids.

In the morning, he would start at the south end of his route picking up Potter kids in Bosque and Rhodes Canyon and work his way to the north.

To try and make ends meet, J.D. and his wife Dorothy also got the contract to maintain the little school. Years later, J.D. said it was a losing proposition with the cost of gas, tire replacements and the bank loan on the car. He thought he was lucky to break even.

Dancing

Ranchers often got together for dances. Many remembered dances at both the Bear Den and Ritch schools. Lealon Miller, J.D.'s father, was known as a promoter and would hold dances and rodeos on his ranch.

Miller had a now famous portable dance floor he would erect for these events. The boards were all numbered and could be taken apart and then reassembled whenever he wanted. Sawdust was a common lubricant on the floor so boots would slide smoothly when dancing.

Music for the dances was provided by other ranchers who brought their instruments. When the WSMR Public Affairs Office arranged for family reunions at the old homes, it wasn't unusual for some, like the Wood family, to bring their fiddles and guitars. After a potluck lunch, everyone would gather around for some down home music. Every once in a while someone would sing along.

The dancing often went on through the night until sunrise. During the day, there would be roping and other rodeo contests on the flats just east of the ranch house.

Attendees camped in the juniper forest around the Miller house.

The Wild Man

The Wild Man of the San Andres was a common discussion topic when talking to these old ranch families. During the 1930s, a solitary man roamed the mountains on foot.

No one knew when he showed up in the San Andres or what eventually happened to him. No one knew his name or why he was out there. He tried to avoid people but to survive he needed the generosity of the ranch families who often fed him. He seemed harmless enough, but women and children were often alone at these ranches and they didn't entirely trust him when he'd show up.

Most of the time he would mooch off the families when no one was around. Without locks on doors, it was easy for him to watch a place and go help himself in the kitchen when everyone was out.

Sometimes he'd make a mistake and enter a house when someone was still home. Most of these storytellers laughed at how they were so surprised by the Wild Man and at how surprised he seemed to be as well. When this happened he usually ran.

At times, he seemed to be a bit more comfortable around men and would provide news about what was happening on other ranches or what he had heard about events in the bigger world.

Dixie Gililland Tucker related that she ran into him a couple times at her Grapevine Canyon home. She was there and he asked for food. So she cooked him a meal and he went on his way.

Dixie and others noticed his shabby and dirty clothing and his long matted hair. One rancher said the Wild Man would build fires against large rocks before going to bed during the winter. After the fire died down, he would scrape the coals off and sleep on the warm ground against a warm rock. That supposedly explained why his clothes were always black with soot.

More Civilian Conservation Corps

I mentioned the Civilian Conservation Corps (CCC) in regard to building dirt water tanks on the missile range. They did other work in the 1930s on what is now White Sands.

In Rhodes Canyon they upgraded the old road from Tularosa to Hot Springs. It became New Mexico State Route 52.

The Tucker Ranch in Grapevine Canyon during a visit by relatives and friends. G.L. Tucker spent his youth on the ranch and during such visits told stories about what it was like living on a goat ranch in the shadow of Salinas Peak. G.L.'s mother was Dixie Gililland Tucker. She was the daughter of Dick and Ginevra Wood Gililland who lived just a few miles to the west. Dixie's sister, Alice, married Clay Smith and together they ran the Sweetwater Ranch on the south slopes of Salinas Peak. Photo by the author.

Evidence of their work can be found where the roadway is carved out of the canyon wall and rock cribs were built to hold the wall in place. Also, there are places where cribbing was used around culverts under the roadway. The nice rockwork looks like a lot of effort was put into the construction.

The Army abandoned this old roadway in places so they wouldn't have to maintain the cribs. With modern dirt-moving machines available, they found it easier to simply regrade the road in the bottom whenever big rains caused damage.

In Bosque Canyon, rock cribbing around culverts is still visible to travelers who pay attention to the roadway.

For this work the CCC employees were housed in a tent camp in Rhodes Canyon. Hazel Potter Johnson supplied the missile range with a nice photo of the camp. It was just above a spring box to the west of the Potsy Potter home. Two stone pillars that were once a gate into the camp are still standing near the current road.

The CCC also had a recreation area on the west edge of the missile range at a place called Ropes Spring. It is north of the NASA site and at the west base of San Andres Peak. Ranchers say it was a place for CCC employees to go to relax when they took some time off.

According to Robert Julyan in his *The Place Names of New Mexico*, the spring is named after Horace Ropes who bought the Goldenburg Ranch in 1885. Ropes was the brother-in-law of Albert Fall and became a professor of engineering at New Mexico A&M in Las Cruces.

Ropes Spring usually has a nice flow of water down through an area with brush and large trees. In fact, it is like a little stream running through a small riparian area. At least that is the way it was before the very dry 1990s.

To take advantage of this oasis, the CCC built a number of facilities. Down along the stream, scattered through the trees and tall brush, are a number of concrete picnic tables. Each has a fire grate and its own water spigot. The water feeds down a pipeline from a storage tank above the facilities.

Below the picnic area is a swimming pool that must have been filled using the same pipeline.

Above the picnic area is a fairly large stone building that has a center entry area with rooms of equal size to the north and south. I could never find any records on the camp, so we don't know if this was a dining hall or maybe a dormitory.

To the south is a large collapsed wooden privy with seating for four. Nearby is a small stone privy. It is square with the corners at the roofline built up to look a bit like a castle parapet. In essence it is a little stone castle tower.

This stone privy is probably the only building on the entire missile range built a bit beyond the utilitarian need. It isn't just a toilet. Someone had a sense of humor or a touch of whimsy. Whoever erected this castle-like tower to create a throne room for the toilets deserves a knighthood.

Ranchers Lose

The Situation Defies A Simple Explanation

World War II changed life on the planet for most of its inhabitants. Out of the war came advances in science and technology that must have looked like science fiction to Americans who lived through the 1930s. Atomic bombs, radar, plastics, jet aircraft and rockets are just a few examples.

The war changed the traditional world power structure. The United States and the Soviet Union emerged as "super powers" while Europe declined.

Societies changed. In the United States, before the war, less than half of Americans graduated from high school. After the war, the GI Bill paid veterans to go to college. Returning veterans married, started families and needed places to live. Low-interest government loans led to a housing boom and the "suburbs."

During the war, minorities were thrust into responsible positions as everyone worked for the common cause. After you've been shot at and bombed by the Nazis and the Japanese, you don't scare easily anymore. It didn't take long for minority leaders to emerge who bravely championed equal rights.

Finally, the war effectively ended the Great Depression.

For the White Sands ranchers, the war completely changed their lives as well.

In 1941, federal officials began looking at the Tularosa Basin as a possible training site for British Royal Air Force bombing crews. The United States was trying to remain neutral in the European conflict but President Roosevelt and others knew it was just a matter of time before America would be forced into the great war. Until then, they quietly assisted our British allies in many indirect ways.

Information about this land survey may have gotten out to the ranching community, as many seemed to be expecting some action by the federal government. Years ago I asked Fred Hollis, former chief of engineering at Stallion Range Center, to look at property records for the George McDonald Ranch near Trinity Site to see who owned it between the Schmidt family and McDonalds. With the assistance of the Socorro County Clerk, they looked through the old records. They were surprised to find no records or transactions for the property until 1941. In that year George McDonald filed a homestead claim for his ranch.

We surmise, like much pre-war business, dealings on the ranch were conducted verbally and with a handshake. When word got out that the government was thinking of establishing a training range, McDonald probably realized he needed a deed to prove ownership of his ranch. He filed his paperwork and got the documents needed to prove to the government his ranch was indeed his.

The bombing of Pearl Harbor changed the government's plans to provide the British with a training range. Instead, it was necessary to look for locations to train U.S. military forces that were going to be sent to fight on many fronts.

The Southwest was an obvious location for these training facilities. West Texas, New Mexico and Arizona were sparsely populated, blessed with wide-open spaces, and had weather that is rarely cloudy all day.

On January 20, 1942, an executive order established a training range in the Tularosa Basin. It turned out to be simple to turn the idea of a British bombing range into an American one. In fact, the runways were built using the plans for the British strips. In late May 1942, the first units arrived at the Alamogordo Army Airfield to begin training. After the war, the facility morphed into Holloman Air Force Base.

Of course, before the B-17s could fly, Army officials had to remove all the humans and livestock from the newly created bombing range. The military carved out an area from White Sands National Monument north to near U.S. Highway 380, taking up the middle and west portions of the Tularosa Basin, Mockingbird Gap, and the plains west of the Oscura Mountains. Included was the eastern portion of the San Andres Mountains.

Representatives of the Army Corps of Engineers spread out through the area to visit ranches and mines and tell the owners they had to move out. They carried lease agreements stating the lands would be needed until the end of the war and the owners would receive annual payments based on the size of their ranch units.

In addition, the ranchers were told to get their livestock off the land because they were not going to be allowed back to take care of them before the end of the war, whenever that was.

Of course, most of the ranch families complied right away. The war was on and it was going to take a national effort to win it. They performed their patriotic duty.

Culture Clash

When simplified this story sounds pretty typical. However, when you examine the details you see a clash of cultures, one that eventually led to great animosity toward White Sands, the Army and the federal government.

On the one hand, you had a rural lifestyle characterized by hard work, independence, a sense of trust, and a love for the land. On the other hand, there was a layered bureaucracy with no one person in charge, where decisions were often driven by budget considerations, and the cogs in the machine expected instantaneous compliance. Also, there was always a squad of lawyers making sure it would all stand up in court. Some people illustrate it as a conflict with human beings on one side and a heartless governmental machine on the other.

When the families were told to move themselves and their livestock off the land, they weren't given much time. Some were told they only had two weeks. Those who balked at the short timeline were told to move themselves or the Army would move all their possessions to the boundary and dump them there.

Since the Army gave them no money for moving expenses, most had to use their savings to pay for the move and to pay for someplace else to live. This was the Depression; probably no one had a fat savings account to draw on. They couldn't afford the cost of moving the livestock to someone else's land and then leasing it for grazing. Instead, many tried to sell their livestock.

This, of course, created a glut of animals on the local and Southwest markets. If they could even sell the animals, the ranchers received very low prices.

Not only did they not receive any moving expenses, most ranchers have testified they didn't receive their first year's lease payment until well after the year was over. For many it meant no income for at least a year while they had to spend and spend again to survive.

Imagine growing up on a ranch, going to a one-room school house for an eighth-grade education, taking over your parents' ranch, and then suddenly finding out you had to find a job, probably doing something else, to support your family. Many tried getting jobs in town because they fully expected to get their ranches back after the war. They figured they just had to last a couple of years.

Alyce Lee Cox, Hal Cox's wife, said, "With the war and all its anguish, there was no reason for the ranchers to be treated in the rude and dictatorial manner by these employees of the government."

Other Plans

Fate double-crossed the Alamogordo Bombing Range ranchers when Germany began launching V-2 rockets against England. Suddenly, here was a weapon most U.S. military leaders did not see coming. They were vaguely aware of some rocket research in the United States, but few had the imagination to see a rocket's real possibilities. When Robert Goddard showed his stuff, he was buried in a minor program. Then the Germans came along in the war and put on a full-blown demonstration for everyone to see.

In the fall of 1944, it became evident to military officials that America needed a land-based range for testing this newfangled rocket technology. This was especially true as teams prepared to rush into Germany, even before the war was over, and scour the countryside for the Nazis' superior rocket paraphernalia. They were ordered to bring back as much of it as they could.

Pentagon personnel used the following criteria in looking for this test site:

*The range should be within the continental United States, with large expanses of uninhabited terrain where firings could be conducted without jeopardy to civilian populations.

*It should have extensive level regions, surrounded by hills for observation stations.

*It should have predominantly clear skies to afford year-round operation.

*It should be accessible to water, rail and power facilities but should not be crossed by railroads, major highways or airline corridors.

*It should also be near a permanent Army post and, if possible, be near communities that could meet the off-duty needs of the personnel employed.

Through the study of topographic maps, highway and commercial air routes, weather charts, and other records, the officials found no single spot to meet all the requirements. These officers and civilians from the War Department and the Corps of Engineers then visited all the possible sites.

They found that the area occupied by the Alamogordo Bombing Range was closest to meeting the requirements. It was not as large as they desired, being about 100 miles long and 40 miles wide, but it was chosen as the best possibility.

Suddenly, ranchers weren't going to get their lands back when the war ended.

After selection was made, the Corps of Engineers issued a real estate directive in February 1945, declaring the use of the area to be of military necessity. In addition to the Alamogordo Bombing Range, they included the Fort Bliss antiaircraft firing range and a few small target ranges associated with Fort Bliss.

Original site plans for the installation were prepared in Washington during April and May of 1945. On June 12, 1945, Major Richard Crook of the Corps of Engineers submitted a memorandum to the District Engineer at Albuquerque outlining the buildings, roads and other developments needed for the new proving ground. Construction began on June 25.

Since it was felt the activity would be short lived, temporary buildings such as old Civilian Conservation Corps structures were moved from Sandia Base in Albuquerque. Nevertheless, consideration was given to possible future growth and the main post was divided into four areas or quadrants. This arrangement allowed each area to grow separately.

Since the war was still on, all this work was done without the ranchers' knowledge. However, in June 1945, with the construction of the main post for White Sands it was obvious something was up.

As the war ended, the leases for the ranch land simply continued. Originally it was thought White Sands might be temporary, so the leases were renewed on an annual basis. This arrangement ended in 1950 as it became evident there was much more to rockets and missiles than first thought. At this point the ranchers were forced into 20-year agreements for the use of their land.

Co-Use Operations Unworkable

During the late 40s, many of the ranchers on White Sands were allowed back on their property in a co-use arrangement. The idea was that the ranchers could go about their normal activities but would have to evacuate the range when V-2 rockets and other vehicles were tested.

In a report called "The Story of White Sands Proving Ground," dated April 30, 1946, the ranch leases stipulated, "No firing period under a given notification will exceed 20 days and that during that period the ranchers are authorized to return every third day for the purpose of watering and feeding their cattle."

This might have worked if it was just V-2s. Only twice were there more than two V-2s fired during a single month. However, because more vehicles like the Nike were brought onto the range, the number of firings and the need for evacuations escalated.

But maybe a bigger factor was the problem of getting word to the ranchers and making sure they evacuated. When a launch was scheduled, the Army, being the Army, sent out teams to notify the ranchers. The system was a typical government arrangement, being rigid and self-centered. Officials expected someone to be home so they could leave word. Well, sometimes the ranchers weren't home and claimed they never got the message.

Sometimes the test was delayed and the ranchers were evacuated on the wrong day. In those early days of developing the technology this might have happened a lot.

Many ranchers say that through carelessness or oversight by the Army, they were never notified and didn't leave. The Lucero family always retells the story about how they were home when a V-2 crashed near their house. It created a big explosion, shook the ground and scared them to death.

When the Army recovery team came out in their caravan of jeeps and trucks, they were very upset that the Luceros were home instead of being evacuated. To top it off, the crews simply drove through fences instead of using gates and generally acted like they owned the place.

The miscommunication is easy to understand. In those early days, there were problems internally as well. Austin Vick, a WSMR pioneer from the technical side of operations, once told a story of a little problem he had.

Vick, as a young man, was assigned to operate cameras for recording missile tests. For a series of Nike Ajax tests he went to Oboe Site to run an Askania cinetheodolite. He noticed the missiles hitting all around him during the tests. It was a little scary.

When he got back to the post, he mentioned the closeness of the missile impacts to Nat Wagner, chief of missile flight safety. Wagner asked, "Where were you?" Vick explained he was at Oboe. Wagner shook his head and said, "You weren't supposed to be at Oboe. That was our target."

Although none of the records survive, it is very easy to imagine the top officials at White Sands throwing up their hands and saying the co-use program was not worth all the rancher complaints, worry about their safety, and possible delays to test programs. The easy solution was to end co-use.

During the 50s and 60s, most ranchers realized they were not getting their land back and moved on to other endeavors. Some continued to look for ways back onto the missile range. They forwarded arguments directly to White Sands or through congressmen and senators for allowing, at least, co-use.

One pointed out that the lack of grazing on the missile range for years had allowed the grass to grow back and cover the rangeland. They said this was a fire hazard and the solution was grazing.

Oddly, another complained that the government's lack of care for the land was allowing a great deal of erosion. The large amount of new plant life and extraordinary erosion seem contradictory, so such arguments rarely received much attention.

Another rancher sent in news clippings about the lack of food. He said the United States was being forced to import beef from Australia. He argued this dependence on foreign sources could be solved by allowing ranchers to run cattle on White Sands again.

Someone pointed out that co-use worked on McGregor Range at Fort Bliss so it should work at WSMR. Finally, someone argued that allowing oryx on the missile range to forage was unfair to ranchers.

At the same time these co-use requests were coming in from former ranchers, others wanted to use the missile range as well. A Pennsylvania congressman requested permission for one of his constituents to explore two locations on the range. He didn't say it was for a treasure hunt, but that was a common query in those days. Also, there were requests to open mines and quarries for various business enterprises.

Other people wanted the old state highway through Rhodes Canyon opened on weekends so they could haul their boats to Elephant Butte Reservoir. Someone else wanted to introduce a buffalo herd on the range.

To say the least, the decision to exclude co-use activities on the missile range was never seriously questioned once these kinds of requests started coming in. Shooting missiles daily and trying to accommodate secondary users would have been a costly nightmare.

In 1970, new lease agreements were put into play for the ranches. In the new contracts, the 84 ranchers involved lost the right to be compensated for the public domain lands within their ranch units. For many, where the ranches were composed mostly of public land, there was a dramatic reduction in the annual fees paid by White Sands.

By 1970, the missile range was about 2.2 million acres or 3,200 square miles – about the size of Puerto Rico with its 3.5 million people. Of that area, only 72,000 acres (less than four percent) were privately owned. So the vast majority of the ranchlands were leased from the New Mexico and federal governments for grazing.

Until 1970, part of the lease payments included money for ranchers to continue their leases. The courts ruled that the ranchers had received rental payments in excess of 25 years and this was adequate compensation for the loss of the public lands which were withdrawn for military purposes.

Ranchers cried foul. They argued that such a situation was akin to renting one's house to someone for 25 years and then having the court rule that the rent paid for the house. They said the renter (the Army) was unfairly granted ownership.

Ranchers fought this decision but their appeals reached the end of the line in 1973 when the U.S. Supreme Court, in U.S. versus Chester Fuller, 409 U.S. 408, ruled the taking of a ranch unit which has an enhanced value as a result of actual or potential use in combination with adjacent federal grazing permit lands, requires no compensation for any value added to fee lands by the revocable federal permits.

The problem with the rancher's rental house analogy or argument was that they didn't own the house to begin with.

The Army had attempted to buy the private lands on White Sands since the 1950s. To do this Congress had to authorize the purchases and provide the funds. The request was always dropped off the budget in Washington.

Finally, in 1974, Congress authorized the purchase of the private ranch lands and about 200 mining claims on White Sands. Because of rising land values, the money ran out after 62,500 acres or 86% of the land was purchased. White Sands continued to lease the remaining 9,500 acres until 1980 when more money was appropriated.

In 1980, there were 34 owners left. Most sold voluntarily except for a few like Dave McDonald. In cases where the owners refused to sell or agree to a particular settlement price, the Corps of Engineers filed in federal court, under the law of eminent domain, to have the land "condemned for purchase."

Under this procedure, the Corps had the land appraised independently and then made a deposit for the value of the appraisal with the court. The money was available to the owners for their use until the court decided on the value of the land in question. If the court decided on an amount higher than the deposit, which was frequently the case, the government paid the difference.

The Dave McDonald Story

The Dave McDonald Ranch is a good example of how this history played out for many ranchers. I feel comfortable using Dave McDonald as an example (with the actual payment figures involved) because he made himself a public figure when he, his niece Mary McDonald and reps from the *Albuquerque Journal* stole onto the missile range in 1982 to reclaim his ranch. The numbers were published soon after in response to queries from the news media and congress.

Dan Duggan was an Army colonel and deputy commander of White Sands Missile Range when Dave made his move. In 2009, Duggan wrote this about the event for the White Sands Historical Foundation newsletter:

It was Wednesday, October 13, 1982 and a typical, beautiful fall day at White Sands Missile Range. The commanding general, Major General Fulwyler, was on a speaking engagement in Idaho and the acting commander, Colonel Dan Duggan, was looking forward to a typically quiet day with the boss out of town. Maybe there would be an opportunity later for some quail scouting time.

Jump forward to the Oct. 14 headlines in the local newspapers and you would discover that my Wednesday didn't turn out to be a 'typical quiet day.' The headlines read: 'RANCHER RETAKES HOME ON THE RANGE: Armed Rancher Retakes, Fortifies Home On The Range.'

The Albuquerque Journal went on to say, 'Armed with two rifles and an old pistol, an 81-year old rancher and his niece slipped across the boundary into White Sands Missile Range at dawn Wednesday, setting up occupancy in the isolated house from which he was evicted 40 years ago.'

This was the basic situation that was reported by Dale Green, Up-Range Coordinator, to the command group at about 1145 hours - just in time to ruin the lunch hour.

White Sands range rider Tom Dayberry, who was on location, reported that initial contact indicated that Mr. Dave McDonald (81), his niece Ms. Mary McDonald (32), and two Albuquerque Journal reporters were at the ranch site. Mary McDonald, armed with a .30-30 rifle, appeared to be the initial spokesperson for the group.

In addition they had posted the area with

homemade signs stating 'Road Closed to the U.S. Army – Deeded Land, No Trespassing.

As noted at the beginning of the Ranching Chapter, Dave was part owner, along with his brother Ross, of a ranch composed of 640 acres of private land and over 22,000 acres of leased government land. In 1942, he and other family members with ranches in the area were all forced off the north end of White Sands.

The idea for Dave's armed resistance in 1982 may have been seeded in 1942. The family story is that when the Army showed up at Tom McDonald's door, just southeast of Mockingbird Gap, he stood on the porch armed and ready to resist being moved out. Tom was Dave's father.

Laura McKinley, married to B.O. Burris, lived nearby in 1942 and witnessed the confrontation. In 1983, she wrote:

A day or two before we started moving our cattle, a man came by our house and told us our neighbor Tom McDonald, an elderly man, was expecting trouble with the military people because Tom told them he was not leaving his home. The man who talked with us said he didn't know if he could get word to Tom's sons in time or not. The military sent word to Tom that an escort would be there that day to take him out. We hurriedly drove to Tom's ranch and saw the military jeep with a gun mounted on it, two military police and a United States Marshal. The Marshal was standing by the jeep while Ross McDonald, Tom's son, was standing by his Dad talking to him. As we walked up, Ross put his hand down Tom's arm and took a pistol from him. Tom was talking and crying, and the whole scene was heart breaking as Ross helped his Dad into his pickup. It was hard to believe what we were all going through.

Beginning in 1942, the Dave McDonald Ranch partnership received $1,385 per year from the federal government. This fee was paid through June 1948. The owners were also paid $1,000 for restoration of their improvements.

In 1948, the agreements were extended and fee payments rose. The McDonald payment went to $7,055 per year from 1948 to 1950 and to $7,635 per year from 1950 to 1970.

In 1970, Dave McDonald lost the compensation for federal grazing lands. Since most of his land was federal, the annual payment dropped to $2,048 per year. However, in 1980 the courts ruled the annual payment was too low and the McDonalds were given an additional one-time payment of $13,057 for the ten-year period 1970-1980.

When additional money became available in 1980 to purchase the rest of the private lands, the Dave McDonald partnership refused to sell. The ranch was appraised and the government put $35,000 in the bank for the McDonalds until the case was settled.

In October 1983, the court rendered a judgment valuing the land at $160,000, less the deposit, and $60,000 in interest payment.

On October 26, 1983, the government was awarded the deed to Dave McDonald's 640 acres.

So when Dave and his niece snuck onto the missile range, Dave was in the middle of his court battle with the government. He told Colonel Duggan he wanted $960,000 for the ranch.

Because of the *Albuquerque Journal* reporters,

Dave McDonald with his Public Affairs escort, Debbie Bingham. Dave showed up at a Trinity Site open house and asked to take relatives to his old ranch. Debbie accommodated them. WSMR photo.

word spread like wildfire about Dave being back home on his ranch. It was immediately billed as the 80-year old rancher in a stand-off with the big, bad U.S. Army. In 24 hours, we in Public Affairs were taking calls from all over the United States and Europe.

Instead of confronting McDonald, the missile range stood back and let Congressman Joe Skeen, Senator Pete Domenici, the New Mexico Cattle Growers Association, and others talk with him. Major General Niles Fulwyler agreed to forward all details of the land purchases to the appropriate Washington offices.

In the end, Dave and Mary McDonald peacefully left the ranch four days later.

One result of the incident was Congressional hearings on the matter. Many ranchers testified in person or by letter about how they were treated and how meager and unfair the payments were.

Evelyn Claunch Greer said:

I will always remember the day the first Government man arrived at the ranch. I was there alone as Fred and Les were out checking the camps. I heard the car long before it came and this man got out, came up to the house and said he was from the Government and showed an identification badge and wanted to know if this was the Greer Ranch. I said yes it was. He wanted to talk to the owners and I told him that Les and Fred were out checking camps. He said, 'Well tell me how to get there.' I asked him if he could ride a horse (knowing he couldn't) and that I would saddle two and we would go look for them. He informed me he wasn't riding any horse so I said we can walk then over the mountain to the west and the other one to the east. He asked me then when they would be back and I said not until late in the afternoon but if he would like he could come in the house and wait and I would fix him something to eat. He looked at me and said, 'I don't have time to stay around here and anyone that would live in this godforsaken place is crazy. I will be back in two days with some other officials. See that someone is here.' With that he left.

In about two days they were back and informed us – this was in February – they were from the military and they was going to use

our ranch and it was for the defense of the country. We had two weeks to move all our possessions, all of our livestock. Les tried to explain to them you didn't move ewes that were going to have kids in a month or cows that were going to have calves in the Spring. They told us, quote 'YOU HAVE TWO WEEKS AND IF YOU AREN'T GONE WE WILL BRING ARMY TRUCKS AND SOLDIERS AND MOVE YOU TO THE BOUNDARY LINE BELOW HERE. YOUR STUFF WILL BE TAKEN OUT OF THE TRUCKS AND YOU CAN GET IT FROM THERE THE BEST WAY YOU CAN AND IF YOU DON'T HAVE YOUR STOCK MOVED THEY WILL BE LEFT HERE.'

This attitude by Army officials in the 40s and early 50s doesn't appear to be uncommon. In a historical monograph on the Nike Ajax for the U.S. Army Ordnance Missile Command, author Mary Cagle wrote about public relations problems the Army had in developing missile sites around the country. One complaint voiced by many city leaders and landowners was the "high handed attitude" of those charged with land acquisition.

Florence Martin was more succinct in her graphic description of dealing with the government over all those years. She said, "We had been dealing with Uncle Sam since 1941, and had experienced the tactics of the Corps of Engineers. Each had horns, a tail, and carried a pitchfork, none had the attributes of the Gods living above."

Like most, the Martins were forced to move out quickly in awful winter weather. After selling most of their cattle at fire-sale prices, Florence described the day their business essentially disappeared when the cattle were collected and shipped: "Chaos, heartbreak, cattle and men knee-deep in mud, snow and ice in the corrals, cattle milling and bawling, Army standing by with guns, frozen water. Have you ever had an experience like that? Do you wonder why I sat and cried when those cattle trucks passed through town? Tears rolled down my cheeks and sobs could be heard as trucks faded from view. Our dreams, many years of sacrifice to build a good herd of quality cattle had vanished."

One of the most galling things about the whole process for these ranchers was how they were treated.

One day they went about their business on land they called home for generations. Then, lightning struck and the next day as they walked their land they were guarded by armed soldiers like they were common criminals planning to steal the landscape.

Those who testified went to great length to point out that other government agencies like the IRS viewed their ranch units as a whole commodity. In other words, if a rancher died and passed on the ranch to his kids, they would have to pay an inheritance tax to the IRS on the total package of private and government land, not just the private lands.

On the other hand, federal lawyers argued that public lands obviously belonged to the people of the United States and were merely being used temporarily by the ranchers. They were granted use for grazing only on a year-to-year basis and no "ownership" was implied. When purchasing the ranches, they said there was no reason for the American taxpayers to pay for something that already belonged to them.

In the end, Dave never got that pot of gold. Congressman Skeen introduced a bill in the House to further compensate White Sands ranchers for the loss of their lands. The bill called for a seven-member commission to distribute $17.5 million to individuals who lost their land because of White Sands Missile Range.

The bill was debated in committee and died there.

My Two Cents Worth

As in most complex situations, the more you know, the more you see grey areas instead of black and white.

I would say it is obvious the Army Corps of Engineers acted legally in their dealings with ranchers from 1942 to the recent past. To my knowledge they won all the major cases that went to court. They occasionally lost when it came to the exact amount of payment – they were often low – but when it came to interpretation of the laws themselves, they prevailed.

On the other hand, I think the government behaved badly throughout the process. This is not how any of us want to be treated by our government when there are hard decisions being made. It was wobbly ethics or morality at best.

When the Army expanded Fort Bliss by acquiring McGregor Range, they did it right. They moved the process along and purchased the private lands

right up front. Those ranchers received that large lump sum you get when you sell a house or piece of land and it allows you to invest it elsewhere. You get a running chance to try something new.

At White Sands, the ranchers were kept on the annual rental payments for decades. They didn't get the lump sum needed to reinvest until they were getting old and grey or already dead.

Unfortunately, current leaders and personnel at White Sands still carry the burden of those decisions made decades ago. Some descendants of the original ranchers are very bitter about what happened to their ancestors. It colors their dealings with the missile range and its current personnel. In other words, the Army lost the hearts and minds of many who live around WSMR.

Also, because of the publicity around the Dave McDonald incident, a myth was let loose saying ranchers like McDonald were never paid for their ranches. This myth is so old now it is almost impossible to convince people otherwise.

The reality is that Dave and his partner were actually paid almost $450,000 over the years for the leases and the final purchase of their 640 acres of patented land.

At one of our Trinity Site open houses, a docent from the National Atomic Museum spread the myth by telling two busloads of people at the George McDonald Ranch house that "the government never paid them for the ranch." Once a myth is born, it rarely dies.

Ranchers in the call-up areas and beyond keep a watchful eye on White Sands. They are wary of the government. Any hint of a change in land status at the missile range will rouse these folks to query their congressional reps and notify the news media. They are fearful that the Army is looking to make another land grab.

It means that White Sands will never be able to expand by purchasing more real estate. For the foreseeable future it is politically impossible. The call-up areas on the west and north have worked only because the ranchers still have full control of their land and they are given generous financial compensation. There are some that make out quite handsomely but that is another story covered in Chapter 16.

Like any complex situation the rancher issue is looked at from many points of view and, to me, they all hint at some truth. Many citizens support the cause of the expelled ranchers. In its purest idealistic terms it is summarized by Lloyd Crockett, a former rancher from the Sulfur Canyon area, who said, "The Government certainly took our legacy to our family. Our general way of life was destroyed leaving our children robbed of their heritage."

On the other hand, some people point out that many ranchers made good money out of the deal – money they never would have made struggling to get by in the livestock business. The records show three families received well over a million dollars each in payments.

Others say, in the long run, most of the ranchers were better off. One rancher's wife said, "God used the Army to move them off the land before they all starved."

This south wall of the Jose Lucero house shows the original adobe structure. Normally it is covered with stucco to protect the mud from weathering. Here, a wooden structure was attached to the house at this point. It has collapsed (see the straight edge of the stucco on the right) and left the adobe open to the elements. As a rule, the bricks were made on site. On close examination of the eroding bricks you see the different materials scooped up to put in the mix. Sometimes there are sherds of Indian pottery mixed in by accident. Photo by the author.

Birth Of The Bomb

When The World Changed In An Instant

There is probably no other place or activity on White Sands Missile Range that stirs people's emotions more than Trinity Site. It is where the first atomic bomb was tested on July 16, 1945. The landmark is currently open to the public twice a year and attracts several thousand curious visitors each open house.

Most don't know the plutonium-based bomb tested at Trinity was identical to the one dropped on Nagasaki, Japan on Aug. 9, 1945 or that WWII ended just six days later when Japan's Emperor Hirohito broadcast his surrender message on Aug. 15 to the people of Japan.

What they do bring to the site is a vast variety of backgrounds, everything from World War II vets to young families to motorcycle gang members to school science groups, with a smorgasbord of opinions reflecting their upbringing, education and generation.

When they get there some are disappointed there is so little to see. At ground zero (GZ) there is an obelisk marking the exact spot where the bomb was exploded. A bit of rebar sticks out of the ground marking one of the tower legs that

supported the bomb. In the parking lot is what remains of Jumbo, and after a short bus ride visitors can see the Schmidt/McDonald ranch house.

Trinity Site is so obviously important the National Park Service proposed making it a national monument in 1946 and many times thereafter. Since it was on the newly established White Sands Proving Ground, the Department of Army declined the offer and continues to reject any attempts that might change who would control the area.

I worked my first Trinity Site open house in October 1977 when the missile range only opened the site to the public once a year – on the first Saturday in October.

Between the open houses we also took special groups and individuals to Trinity. This included news media types like Walter Cronkite when he was doing the CBS nightly news and lots and lots of Japanese reporters. We also took in military leaders, scientists, Boy Scouts, school groups, and historical societies. Basically, any group that seemed to have a legitimate interest in the site or someone important enough could catch a special tour if a public affairs specialist was available and test missions didn't interfere.

The most famous person I escorted to the site was Cronkite on Oct. 21, 1978. It was a chilly and windy day. If you remember him, he had that thin wispy hair on top. At Trinity Site his crew had a terrible time keeping those strands of hair in place. I swear they used most of a can of hairspray to get it stuck down for his stand up at the obelisk.

For almost 30 years I escorted the majority of these "other" tours. I've run a Geiger counter for Japanese TV, unlocked and locked gates for many photographers (to include Japan's version of *Playboy Magazine*) and spent long days waiting for sunset photo opportunities or for complete darkness so star tracks around the obelisk could be captured on one negative.

One television crew I escorted just before I retired was shooting for a British "sciencey" program and went to some length to try to explain how a nuclear chain reaction works. As an on-camera spokesman, they used a movie actor who had a recurring role in the Harry Potter movies.

Toward the end of the day, the writer/producer asked the actor to do a little 30-second standup out in the desert to plug one of their future shows. The actor blanched, got visibly upset saying he was not prepared for such a task and it wasn't fair of the boss to ask him. The actor then stalked off and hid in their van. Either he was acting like an eight-year-old or was practicing some future dramatic role as a prima donna.

Eventually, the producer prevailed and he did the standup, quite well I might add.

One special request we had for a Trinity Site visit I'm sorry we weren't able to do. One day in 2004, I received a call from a producer at VH1, the cable music network. Out of the blue, he asked if it might be possible for the network to film a free U2 (the Irish rock band fronted by Bono) concert at Trinity Site in conjunction with the group's new album release. He didn't offer why they wanted to use Trinity.

I was taken by surprise but gathered my wits and pointed out it was in the middle of nowhere with no hard power for miles. Having been to a few rock concerts, I knew they would need lots and lots of electricity for big sound and big lighting. It didn't seem to discourage him. He said they would bring everything.

I said there was no way we could handle any kind

of a big crowd (I was imagining 25,000 attendees for a "free" event, maybe more). That didn't bother him either. He said we could tell them how many people would be allowed in.

I then said we would have to do some thinking about it and would call him back. I immediately did a search on the web and learned U-2 was preparing to release their new album in November. It was going to be called *How to Dismantle an Atomic Bomb*. The proverbial light bulbs went on when I saw the title.

When I told the rest of the office, we had a good laugh. Then, I called him back to tell him it wasn't going to work. I said such a request would end up in the Pentagon itself, and we didn't see the current administration approving such a venture. It would have been a fun event to work.

I once escorted a photojournalist from Japan to the site. A photo of me opening the Trinity gates ended up in *Playboy* (what a great conversation piece that is).

However, my favorite tour was on April 24, 1997, when I escorted two buses of astronomers to the site. They belonged to the International Astronomers Union that was holding a conference in Socorro on radio emissions from galactic and extragalactic compact sources. I always liked this kind of group because I never had to explain the science behind nuclear fission. They understood the science. All they needed was the history.

This group was special because weeks before we found out a website was predicting that an alien spacecraft would land at Trinity Site that day to make first official contact with the human race.

It was great. I was going to be at GZ literally and figuratively for a cosmic convergence. There would be dozens of astronomers from all over the world at Trinity ready to meet the aliens in their first-ever ceremonial landing.

Or was there more to it? Might the astronomers have already known about the event? When I called Dave Finley, my contact at the Very Large Array radio telescope west of Socorro, he said he knew nothing about aliens and denied "extragalactic compact sources" might be alien space ships.

To say the least, the aliens didn't show. Maybe they were held up in traffic. Anyway, the astronomers and I were greatly disappointed. Looking back on it, it seems likely the landing announcement was secretly posted by one of the conference organizers to boost attendance for the bus tour to Trinity Site.

Trinity Site Origins

The Trinity Site story begins in the turmoil of the 1930s. It was a time of great political chaos and violence as the authoritarian governments of Germany, Japan, Russia and Italy used military force and bloodthirsty tactics to further their nationalistic and ideological goals. The world learned later that these governments marked whole populations for slavery and some for extinction.

At the same time, the Great Depression was stifling the world economy and people worldwide scrambled to find their next meal. The weather even contributed as drought triggered huge dust storms in America's Southwest after decades of poor farming practices left nothing to anchor the soil. The wind blew away valuable topsoil and turned it into choking blizzards of dust blotting out the sun. It was dubbed the "Dust Bowl" or "Dirty Thirties."

At the same time, physics was making headlines as scientists around the world made huge strides in doing the laboratory experiments necessary to prove various theories about the nature of the subatomic world.

In 1932, Englishman James Chadwick discovered neutrons inside atoms. Physicists around the world quickly realized the neutron, without a positive or negative charge, could penetrate all the way to an atom's nucleus without being repelled. It made splitting an atom into smaller pieces possible.

In an Italian lab in 1934, Enrico Fermi successfully split uranium atoms using neutrons - he just didn't realize it at the time.

In December 1938, Otto Hahn and Fritz Strassmann, working in Germany, bombarded uranium atoms with neutrons and came up with evidence of a lighter element, barium, as a result of their activity. With the help of Lise Meitner and Otto Frisch, they realized they had broken apart uranium atoms with the resulting pieces being less complex elements with lower atomic numbers. They used the term "fission" to describe the process.

When fission occurs some of the energy holding the nucleus together is released. At the level of a single atom this is hard to detect but multiply it by millions and billions of times and in the blink of an eye you have an atomic bomb explosion.

In 1939, physicists around the world looked at the structure of uranium and started crunching numbers. In January 1939, Fermi met with legendary physicist Neils Bohr to discuss the possibility of a nuclear chain reaction. They quickly came to the conclusion that chain reactions might be slow moving and could continuously produce almost endless energy, or they might be sudden uncontrolled reactions that release energy in a quick burst like no one had ever seen before.

What's Fission Got To Do With It?

Although there can be chain reactions running at different speeds, the principles are the same. The idea is that a neutron can strike the nucleus of an element, like uranium-235, and cause the core or nucleus to split.

When the nucleus splits, in addition to the enormous release of energy, two or more neutrons are ejected. These two neutrons then split two atoms and, in the next step, we have four neutrons flying out to split four atoms. In the next step there are eight neutrons in play, then 16, then 32 and so on. This doubling quickly grows into the millions and billions.

If each of these neutrons strike and split neighboring atoms and so on through a continuous series of divisions, there is exponential growth – it grows faster and faster. In an atomic bomb, this reaction is uncontrolled and happens in a fraction of a second. In a nuclear reactor, the chain reaction is controlled or maintained at a certain level, so the output of energy is steady instead of an instantaneous spike and drop off.

Maintaining a steady chain reaction is accomplished by absorbing some of the neutrons, so they cannot split atoms and expand the reaction.

Only a few elements will sustain the uncontrolled chain reaction required for an atomic bomb. Uranium-235, an isotope of uranium, is the only naturally occurring element that is fissionable.

An isotope like U-235 is a form of the element that behaves the same chemically but differs in a radioactivity sense. For instance, uranium-238 (the number refers to its atomic weight or mass and also is its number of protons and neutrons added together) is the most common form of the element found in nature. In fact more than 99.2 percent of all uranium is the 238 form. Uranium-235 accounts for only .7 of one percent, but it is the form necessary for a bomb.

Both forms have 92 protons in their nuclei and 92 electrons in the outer shells to balance the core's positive charge. This means that in a chemical reaction such as exposure to the air (oxidation), the different isotopes will behave the same.

Uranium-238 has 146 neutrons in the nucleus while the 235 version only has 143 neutrons. This makes uranium-235 less stable, easier to split and, as a result, more radioactive.

The term "enrichment" is used to describe the process of increasing the percentage of U-235 present. The term "depleted uranium" (DU) refers to uranium with the U-235 removed leaving a dense, hard metal that has been used in some conventional weapons.

Until recently, the element uranium was considered very rare. It turns out it is more abundant than tin, silver or mercury. It is about as common as arsenic. It is much more dense than lead but not as dense as gold.

European Physicists Make The Difference

By the late 1930s, many of the brightest and best scientists from Europe had fled German and Italian tyranny. Men like Albert Einstein, Edward Teller and Hans Bethe went to the United States while others took positions in Britain.

Enrico Fermi was awarded the Nobel Prize in 1938 and used it to escape Mussolini's Italy. His wife was Jewish and he feared for her safety as well as the rest of the family.

He took his family with him to Stockholm where he was awarded the prize in physics on Dec. 10, 1938. At the end of the month he sailed, with his family, to the United States not to return to Italy except to visit after the war. When he got to the United States in early 1939, he reportedly said he was establishing the American branch of the Fermi family.

Leo Szilard was a Hungarian physicist who initially fled to Britain but then moved on to the United States in 1938. While officials in America didn't take much notice of the nuclear possibilities budding in the world's physics laboratories, refugees like Szilard put two and two together and saw a dim future.

These men had the imagination to see the theoretical possibility for atomic bombs. Also, they knew what Hitler and his followers were like. To them it was a doomsday situation that probably meant hellfire and Nazi domination for the entire planet.

Working with Hungarian physicists Edward Teller and Eugene Wigner, Szilard drafted a letter to President Roosevelt warning him of the possibility of atomic bombs and that Germany had the scientific capability to do the research and build them. He said a single one of these bombs placed in a ship might destroy a whole port and much of the city around it.

Szilard realized the U.S. government probably wouldn't pay much attention to him, so he convinced his old friend Albert Einstein, the most famous scientist alive, to sign the letter.

The letter was signed on Aug. 2, 1939, but didn't get to the president until Oct. 11. It did not create an immediate sensation. One can imagine the staff of advisors and military commanders scratching their heads wondering what Szilard was hinting at in the letter. It was well beyond their everyday experiences and required someone with some science knowledge and the imagination to see through to the possibilities.

An advisory committee was formed with almost no budget to look into the matter. Since nothing much happened, many of the European physicists voluntarily censored their work. They were afraid that publishing any additional experimental work would only be advantageous to the Germans.

In 1940, the government's committee slogged through past research and conducted some original research to see if Szilard was right. After all, this was a government project that didn't have a high priority yet. They wanted to make sure good money wasn't going to be wasted based on some theoretical scientific mumbo jumbo.

Bomb Ingredients

By the end of the year, one report to the committee stated gaseous diffusion could successfully separate the U-235 from its more common brother, U-238. This method would use uranium in its gaseous form and force the gas through a series of very fine filters. The larger U-238 atoms would eventually be filtered out by the barriers while the smaller U-235-atoms passed through to be collected after thousands of passes – an atom at a time.

To put into perspective how tedious this process would be, the ratio of U-238 to U-235 is about 138 to one. To get one atom of U-235, the process has to discard 138 atoms of waste.

In May 1941, a positive report was prepared concluding that an atomic bomb was possible and it could be done in a reasonable amount of time.

In October 1941, President Roosevelt gave the approval to build a bomb. On December 6, the day before the Japanese Pearl Harbor attack, he signed the document to establish the Manhattan Project.

In December, scientists and engineers started looking into using another method, an electromagnetic process, to separate the U-235 from U-238. In this process, a cluster of raw uranium ions would be accelerated around the curves of a racetrack in a magnetic field. The heavier U-238 atoms, since they have more mass, would fly a little further out in making the turn. The lighter U-235 atoms would make a tighter turn and could be picked off – an atom at a time.

Much the same thing happens on a NASCAR track. At the same speed, a lightweight stock car would carve a path much tighter in the turns compared to a stock SUV.

Once the United States was officially in the war in December 1941, things started to move with more urgency and more money. In September 1942, Leslie Groves was appointed head of the Manhattan Project and was promoted to brigadier general to give him the clout necessary for such a job. In October, Groves appointed Robert Oppenheimer to head the scientific research needed to build the bomb.

Together Groves and Oppenheimer picked the old Los Alamos Boys Ranch in northern New Mexico as the headquarters for bomb research. In the spring of 1943 work started at Los Alamos.

The Real Start Of The Atomic Age?

Meanwhile, on December 2, 1942, Enrico Fermi provided large-scale dramatic proof that fission was the real deal by creating the first controlled atomic chain reaction. It was a clear demonstration of why he earned a Nobel Prize. For his experiment, Fermi and his team built the first nuclear reactor in a squash court under the football stadium at the University of Chicago.

They built the reactor, or "pile" as some called it, out of graphite blocks - over 350 tons of the slick stuff. Graphite has the ability to slow down and diffuse neutrons. This was done to prevent a sudden, unexpected spike in the reaction that might happen so quickly they would not have time to respond.

With the graphite slowing everything down to a human scale, Fermi could monitor the slow ramp-up of the chain reaction and restrain it to a safe continuous level.

Spaces were hollowed out of the blocks to accept lumps of uranium oxide and metal placed inside the structure to fuel the reaction. Over 90,000 pounds of uranium was used. This was the natural mixture of U-235 and U-238.

Holes were also drilled so cadmium control rods could be inserted into the pile to act as emergency brakes. Cadmium can absorb huge numbers of slow neutrons, so with the rods inside the pile, it was just that - a pile of components not doing much. Many neutrons were absorbed by the rods while other neutrons were not splitting atoms fast enough to sustain a chain reaction.

As the men built the pile, they created a critical mass of uranium because of the amount and its density. As they stacked the blocks and placed the uranium, the cadmium prevented the radioactive mass from taking off in an uncontrolled chain reaction.

Later, after the reactor was completed, by removing the cadmium rods the neutrons were not absorbed but were free to smash into uranium atoms and split them, releasing more neutrons to split other atoms.

Enrico Fermi. Department of Energy photo.

Fermi had made such meticulous calculations, all but one cadmium rod was easily removed to get to the point where the chain reaction was notable. Then, as Fermi monitored his instruments, the last rod was removed a few inches at a time until he was satisfied he had the reactor running at a very low and safe level. He had precise control and there was never any danger of a runaway reaction.

Even though Fermi ran the reactor for less than 30 minutes, it was a clear demonstration that validated many of the theoretical ideas postulated at the time. In fact, many experts say the Atomic Age really began in that squash court in 1942, a couple of years before the first atomic bomb test at Trinity Site. It could be said the bomb was simply the next technological step and was a forgone conclusion after Fermi's test.

In 1943, construction was underway at Oak Ridge, Tennessee to build the various separation plants needed to gather U-235. Later in the year construction started at Hanford, Washington for the first nuclear reactor designed to run continuously. Hanford also saw the construction of a reactor in early 1945 for the sole purpose of producing plutonium, another element capable of fission like U-235.

Plutonium was discovered in 1940 when samples of uranium were bombarded with neutrons as if they were in a reactor. Scientists discovered some of the uranium (U-238) was "transmuted" into another element, neptunium, which then decayed or broke down into another man-made element, plutonium.

The first sizeable batches of plutonium were created in an early reactor built at Oak Ridge. Enough was made to do tests and characterize its radioactive profile. Scientists quickly discovered plutonium would work in an atomic bomb.

There was a catch to using plutonium in making a bomb. In April 1944, Emilio Segre, already working at Los Alamos, analyzed some of the plutonium from the Oak Ridge reactor. He discovered plutonium would not work in the bomb they were building for U-235. Calculations showed such a bomb design using plutonium would be a low-yield fizzle. Another design would be needed to use plutonium.

At the same time, it became obvious that turning uranium into plutonium was easier, cheaper and quicker than the industrial-sized efforts needed to separate U-235 from U-238. Unlike separating alloys, which requires a physical process to collect one

atom at a time, plutonium can be separated from other elements using chemical reactions.

The Hanford "B" Reactor, the first reactor built to do nothing but make plutonium, came on line in early 1945. The process soon was known as "breeding" the new element which led to the term "breeder reactors." By the summer it had made enough plutonium for the bomb tested at Trinity Site on July 16, 1945 and the one dropped over Nagasaki, Japan on August 9, 1945.

Two Bomb Designs

Early on, scientists and engineers under Oppenheimer's leadership at Los Alamos were planning a gun-type design for their U-235 bomb. The design was utter simplicity and called for using high explosives to propel one piece of non-critical U-235 down a tube to strike another piece. When they met, the pieces would compress together to form a single critical mass that would fission immediately. By smashing the pieces together, the atoms would get closer together and were more likely to be split by neutrons flying about in the event.

Because of this mechanism, the bomb assembly and casing around it were long and slender. The bomb's "Little Boy" name was derived from its shape.

This fairly failsafe design wouldn't work for plutonium because of its higher levels of neutron activity. If plutonium were used in the gun-barrel bomb, the pieces would start to fission before they came solidly together. In other words, the early energy released would tend to blow the pieces apart before they became a super critical mass. The result would be, by comparison, a tiny blast.

Because of the relative ease of generating plutonium as a bomb fuel, it was obvious the Manhattan Project needed a different bomb design that could use it. It was Seth Neddermeyer who pushed the idea for an "implosion" design for a plutonium bomb.

The idea of smashing a ball of fissionable material with high explosives was originally proposed by Richard Tolman, but most people considered it too difficult to accomplish. The idea resonated with Neddermeyer as he realized using high explosives to crush a noncritical ball of plutonium into a critical mass would be fast enough to work for plutonium. It was a "sweet" design.

The famous mathematician John von Neumann added to the process by suggesting the high explosive material not be a single mass but individually shaped charges – 32 in the final unit. The explosives could be formed into "lenses" that focused each individual shockwave downward to form a single wave to completely envelop the sphere from all sides. If that could be accomplished, the sphere could be uniformly compressed from something the size of a grapefruit down to a blob the size of a golf ball. In addition, von Neumann predicted such a mechanism would be so efficient they could reduce the size of the bomb's core.

Eventually the design called for a sphere of plutonium weighing about 14 pounds to be surrounded by high explosives. To help trigger the chain reaction that would occur at detonation, a smaller sphere composed of beryllium and polonium, a natural neutron generator, was placed in the center of the plutonium ball.

To make this work flawlessly, the individually shaped charges had to be perfect. If one or two were flawed, the shockwave wouldn't be evenly distributed over the surface of the core. Such an imbalance might simply blow the core apart making a "dirty" bomb – lots of radioactive fallout but not much bang.

Also, each charge had to be detonated at the same instant or, again, the shockwave would be distorted. When you look at a photo of the plutonium bomb on top of the tower for the Trinity Site test, you can see all the wiring required to connect the charges to a single firing source.

Trinity Site Is Needed

Because of doubts about getting the compression event just right, the decision was made to test the plutonium design before trying to use it against Germany or Japan. The test gave the project the opportunity to see if they got it right. At the same time, if there was a problem, they would collect enough data during the test to fix it for the next attempt.

During the spring and summer of 1944, teams led by Ken Bainbridge went out looking for the ideal place to test that first bomb. They looked at San Nicolas Island off of the coast of California and an Army desert training base near Rice, California. Sandbars off the coast of southern Texas were also studied. All three of these sites suffered from being too far from Los Alamos.

Sites near the Great Sand Dunes National Monument in Colorado and in northwest New Mexico

near the lava fields around Grants had difficulty with rough terrain and land ownership issues.

Finally, the search narrowed to two sites on the Alamogordo Bombing Range. The site in the middle of the facility was further away from Los Alamos and, maybe, too close to Alamogordo and Tularosa. Also, using that site would have cut the bombing range in half, thus negating most of its use.

On the other hand, the northern site was closer to Los Alamos, major highways and a rail line. It was on the north end of the bombing range making the rest of the facility still useable. Downwind there were no sizeable communities.

The area is bounded on the east by the Oscura Mountains. The land generally slopes down to the Rio Grande some 25 miles to the west. Between the mountains and the Rio Grande, all the way south to Las Cruces, is a desolate stretch of desert called the "Jornada del Muerto."

The name originated from when the Spanish owned this part of North America. They established a route from Mexico City to their northern capital, Santa Fe. Called the "Camino Real" or royal road, it threaded its way through the scrub desert many miles east of the river. Most travelers on the road walked, rode horses and hauled things in two-wheeled carts.

The stretch of road from present-day Las Cruces to San Antonio was bone dry with the river too far away to use. Also, the Apache would raid the parties traveling on the road.

Because of these difficulties many people died on the route. Usually Jornada del Muerto is translated as "road of death" or "journey of death." However, authors are always trying to come up with new angles, so there are many other translations out there.

This tidbit of local history has been used by many writers to create a spot of easy symbolism for their articles and books about the test. Many could not resist forcing a connection between the birthplace of the atomic bomb and the name Jornada del Muerto.

Seeing it so frequently got to be annoying. Eventually, as I escorted reporters to the site and explained the history, I started to make fun of what was becoming an old cliché. It worked. The number of allusions to atomic death and the Jornada del Muerto decreased.

What's With The Name?

The most asked question at Trinity Site open

houses is "Why is it called Trinity Site?" After the war Groves wondered the same thing. He sent Oppenheimer a letter asking him to recall why he named it Trinity.

Oppenheimer was a bit vague in his reply saying he didn't remember exactly but he knows he was asked to name the site. He told Groves he remembers reading John Donne poetry at the time and was struck by lines that referred to the idea of resurrection coming through death. For the name, he pulled another Donne line out of the air that seemed to fit his mood, "Batter my heart, three person'd God." From that he moved to "trinity."

Since then a lot of books and news articles have been written about Trinity Site. Most of the authors of short pieces simply retell this story.

Book authors have a problem with doing that. They are writing a whole volume on the atomic bomb that has been pretty well covered in the many books already published. Nobody wants to buy a book with information already contained in other books freely available at the library. The pressure is on for new writers to come up with something new and this name business is so vague, it invites speculation. For many, that means coming up with new explanations.

These writers devote pages to nebulous stories and creating links to Hinduism, Native American customs, and other Christian stories. It gets rather mystical.

After a while, we in the White Sands Public Affairs Office even got into the act. We reasoned that the bomb test was the culmination of the work done at three sites – Oak Ridge which provided the uranium, Hanford which provided the plutonium, and Los Alamos which designed and built the bomb. It was a triad or trinity working together to accomplish the task at hand.

Of course, we knew we were blowing smoke, and never seriously advocated the story as the truth either.

By Extension, The Glass Is Trinitite

Another question frequently asked by those delving into the history of the test is, "When did everyone start calling the glass Trinitite?" The most complete answer I have comes from William Kolb who has done very detailed work on the Trinity story. He is co-author of a book called *Trinitite, 1999, The Atomic Age Mineral,* and has analyzed hundreds of

pieces of Trinitite. He has even published a detailed radiation map of GZ.

Also, he is co-author of the very comprehensive *Living With Radiation: The First Hundred Years.* If you want to see all the ways radioactive sources are used in our everyday lives, get a copy of this book.

Kolb put his summary of the name in an email quoted here with his permission:

Time Magazine from September 17, 1945 calls it 'glass.' The September 24, 1945 issue of Life refers to the material as both 'fused earth' and 'glass.' The February 18, 1946 issue of Time calls it 'glass' and 'atomsite.' The title of a front page article in the May 17, 1946 Los Alamos Times reads, 'Trinitite' Data Sought By Director.' The November 1946 piece in Holiday calls it 'atomsite.' In the July 25, 1949 issue of Time, it is called 'trinitite.' The earliest use of the term 'Trinitite' I've come across was in an October 22, 1945 letter from Louis Hempelmann, who I believe was in charge of the Los Alamos Health Physics group by then. Before that the material was variously referred to in official correspondence as Trinity Dirt, Crust and Slag, Glass, Fused Glass and TR Glass. Hempelmann doesn't explain the term in his letter, which suggests 'Trinitite' was then a familiar word at the Lab.

Jumbo

In August 1944, Groves approved the northern bombing range site as the location for the test. Also, because of the uncertainty of the bomb actually working, Manhattan Project scientists ordered "Jumbo" from Babcock and Wilcox that same month.

The idea was to place the bomb inside Jumbo for the test. If the bomb worked, Jumbo would either be blown to a million pieces or vaporized, i.e. turned instantly into a white hot gas. If the bomb was a fizzle, Jumbo was designed to contain the high explosive detonation and prevent the plutonium from being blown all over the countryside. It might even be recoverable after such an event and reused if Jumbo survived.

Jumbo needed to be 25 feet long, have a 10-foot inside diameter and have rounded or "hemispherical" heads or ends. Initially the Army asked for the walls to be 12 inches thick but soon changed that to 15 inches, just to be safe.

Babcock and Wilcox is an old company founded in 1867 when Stephen Wilcox and George Babcock set about building water tube boilers. By World War I, their boilers were powering a large number of U.S. Navy ships.

At a meeting with company officials, the general requirements for Jumbo, a large cylinder closed at both ends, were laid down. Many people in the past have described its general shape to be like a thermos bottle insert.

Babcock and Wilcox had no idea why they were building such a monstrous container. They looked at the specifications and realized it was bigger and heavier than anything ever constructed before.

According to the company's history of special projects during World War II, they planned to assemble the container in sections and build it up as they went. They first built an inner cylinder or shell using 6.5-inch-thick plate steel. The 15-foot length was "made up of two courses, two plates each, and represented the thickest plates ever rolled up to that time." The heads were composed of several pieces as well to get the appropriate curve.

The shell was then turned on a lathe so the wall thickness was cut down to six inches, which gave them a perfectly smooth surface for the banding process. The next step was to add steel bands around the shell to bring it up to specifications. This was done layer by layer. Each band of steel was a quarter of an inch thick so 36 layers were added to bring the wall thickness up to the required 15 inches. For added strength each layer of banding was laid so the joints would alternate like the joints in a brick wall.

Because it was many pieces, Jumbo required significant welding to hold it together. Visitors at Trinity Site often look for those welds in the cylinder section of Jumbo that is now on display. Some visitors speculate that Jumbo later failed in 1946 because of the welds. The Babcock and Wilcox analysis of pieces afterwards showed that the welds remained stronger than the plate steel used in construction.

Company officials said in their history that as Jumbo got heavier and heavier, the supporting equipment started to sink into the floor. The final product weighed in at 214 tons.

Once it was complete, they knew of no way to move it out and had no idea where it was going. The Army showed up with a railcar from U.S. Steel that was specially designed for huge weights. U.S. Steel used it to haul gigantic pots of molten steel around their mill.

Jumbo was loaded onto the railcar and a single switching engine was hooked up to move it out of the plant. One account said the engineer wasn't im-

The contractors who moved Jumbo from the rail siding at Pope to Trinity Site pose below it. It is tied down on the 64-wheeled trailer used to carry it cross country. Many visitors mistake Jumbo for the bomb. WSMR photo.

pressed by pulling a single railcar until he hooked up and only managed to spin the engine's wheels. Using lots of sand for traction, he eventually was able to move Jumbo.

Since the railcar was unique, the Army train reportedly traveled at only 20 miles per hour to insure the bearings lasted all the way to New Mexico.

Babcock and Wilcox's efforts ended when Jumbo left. It wasn't until after the war they found out what it was used for.

According to Babcock and Wilcox's records, photos were taken periodically of the construction process. An FBI agent was on hand and when the negatives dried he always took them away.

The company was proud of the role it played in the war effort. According to the company's history, they tried several times after the war to retrieve the photos but were unsuccessful.

Buried away somewhere in government archives, like in an *Indiana Jones* movie, there may be some nice photos of very old equipment being used to assemble a steel pipe with caps at both ends. It is hard to imagine any kind of sensitive military information being contained in the photos. Perhaps the simple explanation is that the FBI misplaced the photos.

Building The Trinity Site Test Bed

Once the test area, an 18- by 24-mile rectangle, had been selected on the north end of the bombing range for the plutonium bomb test, Bainbridge went to work planning and building. The first order of business was to select the general area for detonating the bomb. The placement of all instrumentation sites, observation points and base camp would be dictated by that single point or "ground zero."

One of the persistent questions visitors ask at Trinity Site open houses is why GZ is where it is. Why not a few miles west, north or south? It is a question we never found an official answer to, as there are no records on the topic at White Sands Missile Range.

However, there is one assumption that can be made about positioning GZ. Because of the known radioactive fallout hazard, all the observation points and base camp would be built upwind based on normal wind conditions. That means these points would be toward the west side of the box with GZ on the east side.

We think that is why GZ sits fairly close to the face of the Oscura Mountains with everything else scattered out to the west on the Jornada del Muerto.

Bainbridge established base camp at the Dave McDonald ranch, about 10 miles southwest of GZ. It is directly upwind of GZ since typical winds are out of the southwest.

The ranch was actually a partnership with Dave's brother Ross owning part of it. They owned a section or one square mile of land and leased over 20,000 acres (640 acres in a square mile) from New Mexico and the Bureau of Land Management for cattle grazing.

The ranch buildings had been empty since 1942 when the Alamogordo Bombing Range was established. Ranchers and miners were forced to lease their lands to the military for the World War II training range. The Manhattan Project declared the ranch facilities as necessary for the war effort and moved in.

Visitors and reporters are often confused about locations because of the other "McDonald" ranch where the plutonium core to the bomb was assembled. It is just two miles southeast of GZ. This ranch belonged to George McDonald who was the third McDonald brother.

They were the sons of Tom McDonald who owned a place in Mockingbird Gap, a small pass south of Trinity Site. Tom's ranch was headquartered in a drainage at the foot of a cliff and was blessed with good water. The missile range calls the place "Ben Site" now.

According to the family, Tom McDonald was ready to resist losing his land to the government during WWII. When the Army's Corps of Engineers personnel visited the ranchers to inform them they had to leave, McDonald met them with a gun in hand. Family members were present and able to coax the gun from him and get his cooperation.

There is no proof that bombing range personnel held this against McDonald, but during the war they loaded his house onto a flatbed trailer and hauled it to what is now Holloman Air Force Base. The bombing range needed buildings and someone decided to take this one.

According to Howard McDonald, Ross' son and Tom's grandson, the house stood on stone footings to keep it level on the slope where it was placed. That made it easy for the military engineers to slide the house off the piers and onto a trailer.

Ross said the family found out about it weeks

later from friends who said they saw the house going down the highway through Tularosa, New Mexico. The family finally found the house on the bombing range but couldn't get any compensation until they hired a lawyer to confront the bombing range officials.

Who Were The Schmidts?

Until 1986, the house used for the bomb core assembly was always called the George McDonald place. That was modified when the missile range Public Affairs Office heard from Frances Schmidt. She had seen some of the national publicity generated by the restoration of the house in 1984 and contacted our office.

Through a series of letters written for Frances by her daughter Rosemary Hall, we learned the house next to GZ was built by Franz Schmidt in 1913.

Franz Schmidt immigrated to the United States through Ellis Island at the age of 17. The young German moved west where he eventually met Ester Holmes of Pearsall, Texas. They were married in 1906.

They moved to New Mexico, still a territory, and established a huge ranch below the Oscura Mountains. Frances, the oldest child, was born in 1908. In 1912, their house burned down while Ester was in town giving birth to their second child, Thomas.

Franz set about building a new four-room adobe house about a mile to the east. The family lived in their barn until the house was complete in 1913. Frances thought they moved in during September.

In one letter Frances remembered many details about the house where she spent her childhood. She said the exterior was "pebble dash" and the interior walls were smooth plaster. The kitchen was painted gray, lit by two kerosene lamps and had a Magic Chef range for cooking. The master bedroom was painted pale green and Frances' room was painted blue.

A highlight in the house was the painted border around the top of the living room. Frances said the walls in the living room were a tan or peach color. The scroll work at the top was painted by Mike Walsh, a ranch hand who had come from Chicago seeking relief from tuberculosis.

Since the well water was salty, rain flowing off the house's metal roof was diverted through a box with a charcoal filter into an underground cistern on the west. Also on the west side of the house was a cellar and icehouse. Ice was cut from the water tanks

The Franz Schmidt/George McDonald house as it appears today. The frame in the foreground is a reproduction of the original. It was to be used in July 1945 to hang a hoist to assist in unloading heavy items from vehicles. Pit assembly personnel I've spoken with said it was never used. Photo by the author.

in winter to keep the icehouse cool. The thick, but hollow, door was filled with insulating sawdust.

To the east of the house they built a bunkhouse. Frank Holmes, Esther's brother, lived there. Also, part of the bunkhouse was used to store groceries and supplies. They only went to town twice a year for supplies so they needed plenty of space for storage.

A barn with attached garage sits just south of the bunkhouse. A large set of corrals is east of the water tanks and barn.

When Frances visited the house when she was in her 90s, she explained that the gates were double-duty gates. You could swing them open to allow horses and cattle in. Also, along the bottom edge, was a short, flap-like area that allowed the sheep to come and go when the main gate was closed. It worked much the way a dog door does.

According to Frances, the family ran about 12,000 sheep and 1,000 cattle. The sheep were divided into six smaller herds, each with a herder and dog. She said the bales of wool were great fun to play on.

Because of health problems, the family sold the ranch and moved to Florida in 1920.

Subsequent owners, maybe the McDonalds, built a stone addition on the north side of the house. It held another bedroom and a bathroom. Before the addition, residents used an outhouse on the west side of the home.

Working At The Test Site

Construction at Base Camp began in the fall of 1944. Contractors were used to assemble Civilian Conservation Corps (CCC) buildings on site. The buildings included barracks, a mess hall, various shops, warehouse, a PX, a dayroom, and a latrine containing showers. Equipment was brought in to generate electricity, pump water and maintain a motor pool.

The first people to occupy Base Camp were military police who arrived on Dec. 30, 1944. In that group was Marvin Davis, a corporal who eventually reached the rank of sergeant.

Davis was born in 1922 in Illinois and was inducted into the Army in 1942. He was trained as a military policeman to include time at the cavalry school learning to ride and care for a horse. He was sent to Los Alamos in April 1943 as part of the mounted police unit providing security at the laboratory.

When he arrived on the hill they had no equipment, no horses and no weapons. He said they rode patrol on horses from the old boy's school and carried flashlights and nightsticks. Soon stock was purchased from Las Vegas, New Mexico that gave the young soldiers a taste of "cowboying" as they had to catch these horses and try to saddle them. Eventually, better horses were brought in and were part of the group that went to Base Camp.

In 1945, Davis was soon promoted and put in charge of one of the security shifts at Trinity Site. They worked 12-hour shifts – one week of days, one week of nights and one week off. The week off wasn't actually time off but a time when the soldiers pulled other details around the camp.

Mostly the MPs manned a number of checkpoints and towers. Given a little elevation, they could monitor miles and miles of the flat treeless desert with binoculars. One of Davis' jobs was to get his soldiers back and forth from these various checkpoints.

Davis said one day he was changing shifts near Mockingbird Gap. He asked the soldier who had been there for several hours if he had seen anything. The soldier replied he had not, but he was surprised by the number of crawdads in such a dry environment.

Davis asked if he had touched any of them. When the soldier replied in the negative, Davis proceeded to explain what a scorpion was and advised him to be careful.

Apparently scorpions and black widow spiders

Marvin Davis with two of the military police horses used at Trinity Site. Photo courtesy of Marvin Davis.

were a problem in the latrine, especially around the toilet seats. Newcomers had to be advised to be careful when using the facility – check under the seat before sitting.

The 16 horses they brought down to Base Camp were quickly abandoned for work. The distances between sites were too great for the horses to be practical. Instead, the horses ended up being used for recreational purposes.

Captain Howard Bush, who was in charge of security and was also the camp commander, worked hard to provide recreational opportunities for his soldiers. They worked in a hot, dry and dirty environment without knowing anything about what was going on. After their work shifts there was very little

Personnel play polo just west of base camp using the military police horses. Photo courtesy of Marvin Davis.

for personnel to do, so Bush did what he could to boost morale.

Through connections back East he acquired enough real polo gear to equip two teams. The uneven terrain proved unworkable for the official wooden balls and small mallets at both Los Alamos and Base Camp. Instead, the men improvised by using a volleyball that easily rolled across the soft sand and brooms that any beginner could use to swat the ball.

In 2000, I received a query from *Polo: Players' Edition Magazine* asking about what they thought was a rumor – soldiers playing polo in the desert during WWII. I gave them the background information and sent some photos. The March 2001 issue carried a nice one-page article about the Trinity Site polo exploits. The only problem was the opening sentence said, "About 40 miles outside San Antonio, Texas, the U.S. Army had a top-secret site . . . ." Some editor must have thought there was only one San Antonio in the United States.

Other recreation included volleyball matches in the evening. In one of Davis' letters to Public Affairs he said, "In the evenings we played a lot of volleyball, we had the net stretched between the latrine and our barracks. I wonder what people would think of volleyball teams with names like Enrico Fermi, George Kistiakowsky and Norris Bradbury on them?"

In another letter, Davis explained that Bush would let trusted soldiers use the Army carbines to hunt deer and antelope. The meat usually ended up in the kitchen as something fresh to supplement whatever the Army was shipping in. He said the antelope was very good but the venison steaks were excellent.

In addition to hunting, work often brought the soldiers into contact with other desert wildlife. Davis said he retrieved a young hawk from a nest and proceeded to raise it. On patrols they were always finding jackrabbits and he periodically would bring one back for his hawk. He said, "he (the hawk) could really make the fur fly."

As the bird matured Davis set it free, but it hung around the camp for some time. For a while it would land on the telephone pole that acted as the camp's flagpole. Davis would put a piece of meat out from the mess hall and watch the hawk would swoop down to eat it.

Felix DePaula, an engineer working at the camp, made more of a pet out of a raven and tamed it enough it would rest on his arm.

DePaula was only 18 when he entered the Army after growing up in New York City. I met him years ago when he visited Trinity Site with a Smithsonian film crew doing oral histories about the Manhattan Project.

He said he was assigned to the Base Camp engineering detail. Since he had no skills, he raised his hand to volunteer when they asked for someone to collect the trash. During his visit, he was able to point out the approximate location of the camp dump to the White Sands archaeologist.

DePaula said he was deathly afraid of snakes and carried a long stick whenever he walked in the desert around camp. He would beat the ground in front of him to scare snakes away.

One day, he and a friend came out of the barracks and saw a snake slither behind some boards stacked against the next building. It was only a bull snake so DePaula took his stick and tried to pry the snake out. He got the end under the snake and tried to lift it out but the stick caught in the boards.

He worked the stick a bit and finally just gave it an energetic heave. The stick suddenly released upwards and the snake was catapulted right over the building.

He said he gave his friend a look of "oops" and started around the building. Before they got to the end to look out, DePaula said he swore his friend to secrecy to not breathe a word.

When they looked out from the corner of the building, they saw a large group of men all looking up in the sky. It turned out the snake flew into the middle of a line of men waiting to get into the mess hall. All they knew was that a snake had dropped on them. Luckily for DePaula, they all thought a hawk had dropped the snake. When he came out, they were looking to see if they could spot the bird flying away.

When DePaula told this story during his visit, he said it was the first time since 1945 he had ever told anyone what had actually happened that day.

Like most of the soldiers stationed at Trinity, DePaula put in a good word for Captain Bush. He said one time General Groves visited on a Sunday and saw men just sitting around relaxing. Groves immediately ordered everyone to work seven days a week. Bush saluted and said "yes sir." Later he told his men he would continue to arrange their schedules so they still received a day off each week.

This is a good example of the difference between a leader and a manager. Groves displayed that typical upper management attitude that hitting the workers with a sledgehammer would get them going. He viewed the men at Trinity Site as mere cogs in the big machine. He wanted all the parts moving to make it look like the work was getting done.

Of course, whether or not the military police, cooks, engineers and others got a day off here and there made absolutely no difference to when the bomb would be completed and ready for testing. Bush understood this and knew he would have harder working, more loyal troops by treating them like human beings instead of machines. He was the real leader that day, as those soldiers would have gladly followed him into whatever hellhole he led them. For Groves, maybe, maybe not.

Another man sent to Trinity Site was just the opposite of DePaula in that he had a real skill set. In 1945, Carl Rudder of Chattanooga, Tennessee was an experienced power lineman for the Tennessee Valley Authority.

In a letter to the White Sands Public Affairs Office in 1984, Rudder said, "I volunteered for a special assignment under the impression that I was going to Oak Ridge which was near my home. I was inducted on Jan. 26, 1945, passed through four camps, took two days of basic and arrived at Trinity on or about Feb. 17 where I immediately became supervisor of what I named the 'East Jesus and Socorro Light and Water Co.'"

He went on to say it was a one-man operation and he maintained five generators, three wells and five pumps. He also did all the line work.

You would think that with three wells, the camp and personnel had plenty of water. Not so. Most of the men said the water coming out of the wells was very hard. It was impossible to rinse the soap off your body, and the plumbing at base camp succumbed to calcium buildup in the pipes in just a few weeks.

According to Marvin Davis and others, they eventually resorted to driving into Socorro and hauling potable water in a tanker truck to Trinity for their cooking and personal use.

In addition, Rudder was obviously a trusted man as Bush made him second in command at the camp for most of his stay.

After a short correspondence with Public Affairs, Rudder mailed his photo scrapbook to us and allowed White Sands to copy his pictures. Some have now been published in various histories of the test.

Rudder also provided us with a copy of a letter sent to his wife in December 1945 by a friend of his, Sergeant Loren R. Bourg. Bourg's situation at Base Camp was similar to Rudder's as he turned out to be a one-man operation as well.

In his letter, the Houma, Louisiana native explained how he received the title of "chief" at Base Camp. He said he was in the fire department in his hometown but was inducted into the Army in November 1942 as a military policeman. Initially he worked a German prisoner of war camp in Oklahoma. In September 1943, he was reassigned to a fire-fighting unit at Fort Bliss, Texas.

They were supposed to go overseas but instead

were shipped to Los Alamos where he was assigned as the "station sergeant." He wrote, "In April of this year (1945) I was sent down here (Base Camp) to take over the fire prevention and fire department. Upon arrival I found I was the fire department period. I was assigned as fire chief and safety officer."

He included a bit of current news when he said, "Carl and I just came in from a fire call. Upon arrival at the scene, we found that it was an overheated coal heater. The soot burnt out of the pipe causing the pipe to turn white hot."

Bourg finished his letter with, "This is my fourth Christmas to be celebrated in an Army post. Every Christmas day so far, I had to work. This Christmas Eve night I will be in charge of quarters. That means no sleep. So Christmas Day I will be asleep, I hope." He added a postscript saying, "This is the first time I was ever real homesick on Christmas."

What happened to Rudder and Bourg was fairly common for soldiers serving at Trinity Site. Brand new personnel like Rudder, more experienced folks like Bourg, and a few veterans who had actually experienced combat ended up in the middle of the desert without a clue as to why they were really there. Some of them had signed on expecting to go out and contribute to the war effort.

Working in the desert in secret conditions didn't seem like much of a contribution. Many were frustrated by their initial time at Trinity. That, of course, changed on July 16, 1945 when they saw the test – they joined a very select fraternity of men and women who made a unique contribution.

To Collect Test Data

You test something new to see if it works as advertised and collect as much information during the test as possible. If it doesn't work, that data can help fix it afterward.

Since the test at Trinity was a cutting-edge, first-ever item, they needed to not only find out if it worked, but how it matched their theories and calculations, and what its effects were.

Mostly there were very few off-the-shelf instruments that could be used to collect this data. The scientists and engineers had to be ingenious in developing new instruments or modifying common devices to get the data they wanted. Also, they had to invent ways to protect instruments so they would survive the radiation and blast effects.

In many ways the collection of data became a series of "experiments" in itself, since this had never been done before. This reality is reflected in the title of the brochure written by Thomas Merlin of Human Systems Research for White Sands Missile Range concerning the instrumentation. It is called *The Trinity Experiments*.

The size of the workforce at Trinity Site in the months leading up to the test is a testament to this fact. Soldiers, scientists and engineers spent weeks laying out communication lines to shelters, bunkers and mounts for the hundreds of instruments scattered around the test bed.

During this buildup of test equipment and experiments, a committee was established to review and approve or reject proposals. This was necessary because Bainbridge was quickly flooded with requests by scientists wanting to collect all sorts of data. As the test date approached, they simply shut off all requests because they couldn't deal with them all.

One scientist told me that some of them conducted a few experiments on their own. One group was interested in biological effects of the blast. There was no time to put together any kind of complex task, so the experimenter simply acquired some lab rats and tied them by their tails to wiring cross arms at various distances from GZ. Because of safety restrictions, he had to place the rats too early in the day and was not allowed back into the area. One of the security people noted that night that the rats all died before the explosion. They figured it was just too much time in the heat without water or shade.

Contractors like Brown Construction out of Albuquerque did much of the heavy work. Ted Brown, founder of Brown Construction, said in an Associated Press story in August 2000, that his company built 45 miles of roads, shelters and several towers to include the one on which the bomb was placed. He said the operation was so secret he signed a blank contract with the dollar amounts to be filled in later.

At 10,000 yards from GZ at points south, west and north of the tower, Brown constructed shelters with concrete roofs. These shelters housed a few men with instruments and cameras. These observers were the closest people to GZ at the time of the explosion.

The shelter at the south point was the control center. Robert Oppenheimer watched from here, the countdown originated from here, and the signals sent to trigger the instrumentation and the gadget started here.

Although these shelters are given direction names, they do not sit on points directly south, west or north from GZ.

Also, a number of small instrumentation bunkers were constructed closer to GZ. For instance, one bunker visitors see as they drive into the site during open houses is only 800 yards from GZ. That bunker was originally built to protect Fastax cameras.

According to Berlyn Brixner, Los Alamos photographer, he had to change plans for some of these cameras. Tests determined that cameras close to GZ, like the ones at the west 800-yard bunker, would be exposed to high levels of radiation and the film would never survive.

Before the test, the cameras were moved to a sled outside the bunker. Brixner and his team fabricated lead boxes to protect the cameras. The boxes were mounted on the sled that was placed next to the 800-yard bunker. The cameras were pointed straight up through windows made of leaded glass. Mirrors were positioned over the cameras and angled so each camera was focused on the tower.

After the test, the crews used the thousand-foot cable attached to the sled to pull it back to their position where radiation levels were fairly low. This eliminated any unnecessary exposure to the high levels in the immediate GZ area.

When you stand in the west 800-yard bunker, you can look out through pipes that acted as viewing ports in the east wall and see GZ. There is also a pipe on the south wall that is angled to the southeast. I have no record of what the angled pipe was for, but it seemed to provide a view of the 100-ton TNT test site south of GZ. I assume initial plans called for a camera to be mounted in the bunker as part of the May 7 100-ton test. No one seems to know if it was used or not.

Cameras alone varied from simple pinhole boxes to measure gamma radiation to 37 motion picture cameras. Fastax cameras running at 1,000 frames per second captured those images of the initial stages of the explosion. Mitchell 35-mm cameras were used to track the rise of the mushroom cloud and track it as it moved northeast.

Some of the instruments like cameras and seismographs required power to operate. Others like blast gauges and crusher boxes were simply set up beforehand and retrieved when convenient.

Miles of communication and power cable were strung or buried all over the test bed. Some of the poles and cross arms for these lines are still standing today.

Moisture was an issue for the wiring laid on the ground or buried. To protect their work, the crews went into town and purchased as much garden hose as they could get. They then ran the wire through the hose to keep the water out.

As in any complex undertaking, not everything went right. For instance, Robert Walker worked to protect cables going to dozens of gauges he had in the field, but still ended up with no data from the blast. Given that fact, he said he made a big mistake during the test because he paid so much attention to his equipment; he missed seeing the first part of the explosion.

On the night of the test, personnel stationed at various bunkers didn't receive much information about the delay from 4 to 5:30 a.m. for the detonation. On one of his visits to Trinity Site, Brixner told me he knew there was a delay at 4 a.m. but had no idea what the new test time was.

Brixner was on top of the North 10,000-yard bunker and was one of the few people allowed to watch the test from outside a bunker. He was manning a motion picture camera mounted in a machine gun turret that required him to track the fireball and cloud.

He said he never heard when the new detonation time was, but some seconds before the blast his camera was powered up and he knew it was time to go to work. The camera was switched on by the automatic-sequencing system located in the South 10,000-yard bunker. When the switch was thrown to start the process, cameras and other instruments sprang to life, flares were ignited, and the bomb was triggered at a precise moment in the sequence.

With those dozens of cameras scattered around the test site, have you ever wondered why you never see color movies of the Trinity test? If you do see some, you know they are fake or from some other test.

Public Affairs was often asked to look at nice color photographs of a mushroom cloud and verify they were from the Trinity test. Most of the time it was a no-brainer response because they were color, plus it was obvious they were taken in broad daylight – not before sunrise.

Brixner said there were numerous cameras at the site loaded with color film. However, none of it turned out. In a 1985 letter to Brigadier General Niles Fulwyler, then commander of White Sands, Brixner said two cameras at his location "didn't run, my other cameras recorded all phases of the explosion." He added that the stop-action photos of the early moments of the test everyone uses are "enlargements from my 35-mm movie films."

However, there is a single color still image that was taken rather unofficially by Jack Aeby. He wasn't a photographer and described himself as a jack-of-all-trades for the Health Physics Group. He had nothing to do on test morning so his boss, Emilio Segre, gave him a camera and sent him out into the dark near base camp to take pictures.

He said he sat on a straight-backed chair with the back in front of him so he could prop his arms and the camera on the back. Thinking the test might be a dud, he started with the camera's shutter wide open to catch whatever spark or puff might be seen from 10 miles away.

In a visit to Trinity Site decades after the test, Aeby said, "When it became apparent that it was a successful detonation, I released the shutter and cranked the aperture down and shot three in rapid succession. The middle one was about the right exposure. I'd have taken more, except I ran out of film."

That iconic color mushroom cloud has been used worldwide for decades. It is the only color image from the test. When he was interviewed at White Sands, Aeby said he has seen the photo so many times, he sometimes wished he could get a nickel for every T-shirt, cap, mug, newspaper or magazine story using it. He laughed and said the only payment he ever received was $200 from *Life* magazine after his wife got after them.

The 100-Ton Calibration Test

On May 7, 1945, Los Alamos conducted a calibration test and dry run at Trinity Site. A 20-foot wooden platform was constructed southeast of the GZ tow-er. Wooden crates filled with 100 tons of TNT were stacked on the platform.

PLaced in the stack of TNT boxes was plastic tubing filled with a radioactive slurry from Hanford.

The test was used to calibrate many of the instruments with a known quantity of explosives. Since then, we have seen the yield of nuclear explosions equated to the explosive force of so many tons of TNT.

The test also acted as a dress rehearsal for the real deal with a countdown and automatic switching to activate some of the instruments.

Finally, measuring radiation levels from the slurry in and around the crater afterwards gave scientists some hint at what to expect during the real test. They even drove one of the lead-lined tanks into the small crater – about five feet deep and 30 feet across – to retrieve soil samples.

Jumbo's Final Role

Jumbo arrived by train from Ohio in early June.

What 100 tons of TNT looks like stacked in boxes on top of a 20-foot wooden platform. The wooden structure disappeared in the test on May 7, 1945 but personnel found bent bolts and other parts that survived. WSMR photo.

It was unloaded from the special railroad car at Pope siding about 25 miles west of the test site. It was rolled onto a special trailer equipped with 64 axles to evenly distribute the weight.

Bulldozers were used to pull and push the trailer across the soft sand to GZ. By the time it arrived, the scientists had already decided not to use Jumbo. One reason was they were confident the test would work and Jumbo was irrelevant. Also, if they decided to use it and the bomb was successful, the 214 tons of steel would interfere with collecting data on those first few milliseconds of the explosion. Thirdly, by not using Jumbo, they eliminated spraying 214 tons of activated steel (made radioactive by neutron bombardment) into the atmosphere to become fallout.

Instead, they hauled Jumbo to a tower about 800 yards west of GZ. There it was unloaded and hung in the tower just a few feet off the ground.

A photo of it in this position has led many to assume it was hanging during the test. For the test, Jumbo was lowered onto a concrete pad with a dimple in it to accommodate the curved end of Jumbo. Thus it was standing upright for the test.

The explosion did not damage Jumbo. However, the blast crumpled the steel tower standing around Jumbo and scoured the earth away from some of the tower's foundations.

On April 16, 1946 at 11:30 a.m. with Jumbo still standing on end, eight 500-pound bombs were exploded inside it. According to First Lieutenant Richard Blackburn who filed a report afterwards with Sandia Base, "The foundation was pulverized and scattered over a large area. Both ends were torn off 'Jumbo' and fragments were thrown as far as three-quarters of one mile. A piece, estimated to weigh over fifteen tons, landed 750 feet from the site."

The report was sent to Lieutenant Colonel A.J. Frolich, the commander of Sandia. Frolich, in turn, sent a memo up the chain of command saying he approved Blackburn's request to dispose of the eight bombs in Jumbo because "the charge was less than the total supposed to be set off in 'Jumbo,' I approved..." He then added, "I regret Jumbo was destroyed, but wish to state that all responsibility for the decision is the undersigned."

Frolich also added that since Jumbo was destroyed it could be salvaged to alleviate "the present shortage of steel." However, nothing was done with Jumbo for years. It rested partially buried on its side until someone salvaged the steel bands off of it. The question is, when did that happen?

Military personnel from the missile range often hunted pronghorn on the plains on the north end of White Sands. One of those old soldiers let Public Affairs copy a photo he had of Jumbo taken in the early 1950s. In the photo the nine inches of banding are still there.

As best as I can determine the bands disappeared before 1960. My suspicion is they were removed as

Today, what is left of Jumbo sits in the Trinity Site parking lot for all to see when they walk (or ride) down to Ground Zero. This photo was taken during one of the mountain bike rides to the site as part of the Socorro Fat Bike Fiesta. Photo by the author.

scrap. The Jumbo tower also disappeared at some point in the 50s. I assume the bands and steel from the tower made a sizable and valuable scrap pile.

Of course, this has implications for the current weight of Jumbo. Since the banding and ends probably accounted for almost 70-75 percent of Jumbo's mass, I estimate there is approximately only 60 tons of steel left. I suspect after the bands were removed most people who saw Jumbo for the next few decades didn't realize much of it was missing and thought it still weighed close to 180 tons.

It may have been that false perception of Jumbo's extreme weight that saved it from being given away. Preston Pond, president of the Socorro County Chamber of Commerce, wrote a letter on June 27, 1960 to Captain Norman Banda, Commander of Stallion Site on White Sands, requesting Jumbo be donated to Socorro to create a historical monument to that first test. He said, "If the cylinder were donated for that purpose, we plan to place it in a tourist park on both U.S. Highways 85 and 60, with a large sign on the highway to inform travelers of its historic significance."

He also said, "Inasmuch as Trinity Site is open to the public only one day a year." Missile range records are spotty but this proves there seemed to be regular public visits to the site before 1960.

On July 1, 1960, Captain Banda sent a memo to the missile range's troop commander saying, "Request the cylinder be released to be used in the monument, and that the Post Engineers assist in its movement to the site in Socorro." Later in July, Lieutenant Colonel Donald Jones, Chief of Logistics at White Sands, sent a letter to the Atomic Energy Commission. He told the commission Jumbo was not on the missile range's property book. He assumed it was part of the Trinity test and asked the commission to check their records and donate it to Socorro if possible.

Eventually, according to press reports, Jumbo could be donated to Socorro if the city could get it moved. Dale Green, who worked for the Post Engineers at Stallion in 1960, said he always heard Jumbo was too heavy to be hauled over the Rio Grande bridge at San Antonio. That is why it is still on White Sands.

If the planners were thinking Jumbo still weighed close to 180 tons, they didn't have a trailer that could handle or distribute the load enough to make it legal on the highway or meet the bridge's load capacity.

Jumbo rested peacefully in the sand until 1979 when Public Affairs convinced the White Sands command group to move it up to the Trinity Site parking area, so visitors could see it. Instead of trying to lift and carry it to a new location, the engineers at Stallion Range Center used a little ancient Egyptian technology. They bulldozed a ramp down below Jumbo. This allowed them to back a flatbed trailer down the ramp so the bed was level with Jumbo. Then they rolled Jumbo onto the trailer using a bulldozer.

At the designated resting site in the parking lot, another ramp was dug. With the help of the dozer, the truck hauled Jumbo to the main gate and backed down the ramp. The engineers then rolled Jumbo off to its final resting spot.

Visitors now walk right past it as they make the walk down to GZ. Kids love trying to run up the inside curve of Jumbo. There is a large amount of gouging and damage on the inside at one end of the tube. This is the end that was on the ground in 1946 when the 500-pound bombs were placed inside it.

Bomb Preparation

At first Los Alamos officials were looking for a test on July 4 – the ultimate firecracker. However, more testing at Los Alamos was required, so they pushed the test to the middle of July. Once the scientists and engineers deemed it ready, the whole process fell into the hands of the weather forecasters.

July and August in New Mexico are known as the monsoon months as the southern half of the state gets most of its moisture in those two months. Thunderstorms build as the summer heat pushes moist air up the slopes of the many mountain ranges. The storms drift off over valleys and plains bringing violent winds, heavy rains and hail.

Long-range forecasts predicted a break in this pattern around July 16. It became a target for the men to get everything done.

On Thursday, July 12, the two pieces of the plutonium core were transported to the Schmidt/McDonald ranch house in an ordinary Army sedan. The main part of the bomb with its thousands of pounds of high explosives followed on Friday, July 13.

The ranch house was perfect because it was a good solid structure and only two miles from GZ. The men turned the master bedroom into a primitive clean room. They nailed plastic over the windows to try and seal them. They taped the edges of the plastic and the various joints in the room to keep dust out. They even chalked a warning on the front door telling all who entered to wipe their feet outside.

The plutonium arrived at the ranch house about 6 p.m. and was delivered to the clean room by Sergeant Herbert Lehr. There is a famous photo of Lehr carrying a box with rubber bumpers through the door of the ranch house.

In the photo there is a hat hanging on the wall. According to an interview in 1983 with the Department of Energy, Dr. Robert Bacher said that was his hat. He went on to say he didn't remember being there for the plutonium delivery, but recognizing his hat made him believe he was there. Bacher was head of the Gadget Division at Los Alamos.

Also, Bacher said the idea in the ranch house was to use one of their special kits to assemble the core. Some of these kits with tools and parts were already on their way to the tiny Pacific island of Tinian where scientists would assemble the bombs for delivery to Japan. Testing the tool kits was essential to ensure their adequacy for the job a few weeks later.

Dr. Phil Morrison accompanied the plutonium and carried two initiators in his pocket. Lehr referred to the initiators as "urchins." Both he and Dr. Boyce McDaniel later related how Morrison played a game with the two urchins, asking people to guess which one was the real one and which one was the dummy.

People were flabbergasted as he freely mixed the two up, making it impossible to visually tell them apart. They were worried because the initiator was made to naturally eject neutrons at detonation to help start the chain reaction in the plutonium.

The initiator was made of polonium and beryllium. At the bomb's very center, when the two were crushed together, alpha particles released by the polonium would trigger an in-kind release of neutrons from the beryllium into the plutonium that surrounded it. This was designed to happen just as the plutonium was being crushed into a critical mass and was all that was needed to jump-start the reaction.

What many people didn't realize was that the radioactivity of the initiator made it warm to the touch. Morrison had no trouble telling which was which.

The plutonium hemispheres and the initiator spent the night in the ranch house. The next morning the pit assembly crew gathered to put it together.

McDaniel said Dr. Marshall Holloway and Dr.

Raemer Schreiber did most of the work. Lehr said in an interview that McDaniel and Schreiber put it together. They had to smooth some of the surfaces of the metals, but basically they simply placed the initiator into the hollowed out area in the plutonium hemispheres and put the plutonium pieces together.

Lehr described this core as being the size of a baseball. Others describe it as the size of a grapefruit. Most authors say it weighed about 14 pounds. For plutonium that means it had the volume of something like a 12-ounce can of root beer. It was a remarkably small package to be able to destroy a city.

This ball was then placed in a circular column of uranium. If we continue the can analogy, the ball of plutonium was placed into the center of a slug of uranium shaped like a large can. This is a step often missed by reporters.

Already inside the bomb apparatus at GZ was a larger sphere of uranium with a hole drilled in it to accept the plutonium/uranium package. This larger sphere surrounded the plutonium to keep the chain reaction going for a few billionths of a second longer before the core blew itself apart. The longer the chain reaction ran, the bigger the blast.

So the plutonium core, enclosed inside the heavier column of uranium, was taken down to GZ in the afternoon. In his interview at Trinity Site in 2005, Lehr estimated the package weighed about 40 pounds.

One of the photos taken at the ranch house shows two men carrying a box between them on a litter with a car nearby. This photo is often wrongly interpreted as showing the plutonium being taken from the car to the house.

As can be seen in the Lehr photo in the ranch house doorway, it only took one person to carry the 14 pounds of plutonium into the house. According to Lehr and others, the second photo was taken as Lehr and Harry Daghlian were moving the assembled 40-pound core to the car for its trip to GZ.

I should point out that I fell victim to this misinformation. Years ago when I put together the permanent, and I stress "permanent," signs at Trinity, I wrote an incorrect caption for the assembled core photo on the sign in front of the Schmidt/McDonald house.

The sign is metal with the text and photos etched into the surface of a solid piece of aluminum. Because the signs are supposed to last for decades, the error will be there longer than I am going to be around. I am sometimes tempted to try and scratch out the offending words during a visit to Trinity Site.

Under the tower at GZ, a tent had been erected to protect the bomb mechanism that rested between the tower's four legs. At this stage "Friday the 13th" bad luck almost struck the scientists. As they went to lower the plutonium / uranium cylinder into the recesses of the bomb, it balked. It wouldn't fit.

As they scratched their heads and each took a turn at peering into the opening to see what was the matter, the temperatures of the cylinder and the bomb's inner core equalized. Finally, much to their relief, the cylinder slid home into the center of the bomb.

After they buttoned up the bomb they assembled everything to the point of installing the detonators. They took the rest of the day off.

On Saturday, July 14, the crew removed the tent at 8 a.m. and hoisted the bomb to the corrugated steel shelter at the top of the tower. This was a slow process. The Department of Energy timeline from 1983 states the bomb traveled about one foot per minute.

The slow ascent gave nervous personnel a chance to stack mattresses under it as it went up. They were anxious about being blown to smithereens if the bomb somehow dropped from the cable.

The bomb made it to the top safely and by 5 p.m. was completely assembled and ready to go. At that point the test site was evacuated and only essential personnel were allowed in.

One of the essential people was Boyce McDaniel. He climbed the tower every four hours until early in the morning on July 16, in order to pull a long manganese wire out of the bomb and replace it with a new one. A tiny gap had been left so this could be accomplished.

The wire was a clever way to measure neutron activity in the core of the bomb. Neutrons activated the manganese and made some of the atoms radioactive. The more neutrons, the more radioactive the wire would be. The measurements proved steady throughout the night.

People gathered at various points throughout the night and early morning of July 16 to watch the test, perform assigned duties, and be ready if needed. The closest personnel were at the shelters 10,000 yards south, west and north of GZ.

When visitors ask why there was no east bunker,

the answer is simple: prevailing winds would have carried the radioactive fallout that direction.

That hasn't stopped writers from playing with the idea. In 1981, science fiction writer David Houston published *Tales of Tomorrow – Invaders at Ground Zero*. The novel was written as a public disclosure and claims there really was an east shelter manned by scientists. What happened there was supposedly buried in secrecy by the government.

The story line was that an alien spacecraft crashed near the site just a day or so before the test. The scientists responded and found a dying creature. Unknown to them was the fact the alien was dying because he was infected with a virus-like entity that could jump from one species to another and control the individual's actions. These microbes possessed a "group intelligence" and communicated with each other.

Just as the alien died, the virus jumped to one of the humans. As the virus tried to take control, it killed its human host and jumped to another and then another, gaining more control each time. In the end, the humans figured it out, but were dropping like flies. Finally, a man and woman were infected, they knew it, and they isolated themselves from everyone else.

In a heroic act, they walked to GZ and sat under the tower. They heard the countdown knowing the explosion would not only kill them but kill the virus as well and prevent it from taking over the earth.

The Explosion

Most personnel watched the test from base camp safe from the explosion and any aliens who might come by. In fact, there were probably a couple of hundred people there to include the support soldiers like Feliz DePaula and Carl Rudder and other much more famous people like General Groves and Enrico Fermi.

A number of VIPs including Edward Teller, Hans Bethe and Ernest Lawrence were taken in buses to a small hill south of U.S. Highway 380 and about 20 miles northwest of GZ. *New York Times* reporter Bill Laurence also watched from there. The hill is variously called Campania, Compana, and Compagna Hill by reporters and Manhattan personnel.

On current maps, Cerro de la Compana is a hill at the north end of a cluster of hills just northwest of the missile range's Stallion Range Center. According to former missile range archeologist Bob Burton, the named hill does not provide an unobstructed view of GZ. Other ridges get in the way. Red Butte, however, which is just southeast of Cerro de la Campana, gives a great open view out toward Trinity Site. In surveying Red Butte, Burton identified some old disturbed ground that might date to the viewing site in 1945.

The witnesses had no facilities and tended to not know much about where they were in the local landscape. One told me he arrived on a bus in the middle of the night and the bus left before the sun rose. He never saw anything too clearly.

Others, such as military police, medical personnel and soldiers, were on the perimeter of the test area providing security and monitoring radiation levels after the blast. For instance, Sergeant Marvin Davis escorted a technician with a Geiger counter as they traveled north along the west boundary.

Other soldiers and technicians with radiation monitors were stationed north along U.S. Highway 380 and northeast, near Carrizozo, waiting to see if it was necessary to evacuate the towns or ranches downwind from the test.

Some people didn't get invited but took it upon themselves to find a viewing spot. Harold Argo described himself as a junior guy "who punched a calculator." He wanted to see the test so he studied topographic maps of the area and selected Chupadera Peak, just south of Socorro and west of the highway. He said he could see the site with binoculars but was obviously way too far away to hear the loudspeaker announcements. He didn't realize the shot was delayed because of weather.

At 5:25 he decided to leave. He threw his blanket over his shoulder, took 10 steps down the hill, and suddenly everything lit up.

He tried to photograph it using Kodachrome film. Afterward, without thinking of the security consequences, he sent the film to Kodak for developing. Security intercepted the film and kept it. He said he got it back years later. Not exactly overnight service.

Personnel out in the open such as Brixner at the 10,000 yard shelters, at base camp and on Compania Hill, were all issued a piece of welder's glass mounted in a piece of cardboard. They were told to look away from the tower at detonation; after the first few seconds, they could hold their piece of dark glass up to their eyes and look at the explosion through it.

As the night progressed, thunderstorms rolled through the area. The test was scheduled for 4 a.m. but was delayed because of the storm. After discussions with the weather forecaster, Oppenheimer and Groves decided to delay until 5:30 instead of waiting for another day.

There were two reasons for not waiting a whole day. One, the meteorologist thought the storms might clear out by 5:30. (He proved right.) Two, with the rain, winds and electrical strikes, every delay increased the chances of serious problems with the bomb and all the associated equipment.

Given all the histories written since 1945, one would think it rained buckets that night. I've asked many people who watched from base camp if it was muddy when they laid down on the ground at 5:25. They have all said "no."

For his family, Stanley Hall wrote about his experiences at Los Alamos during the war and his time at Trinity Site. At GZ he worked on a device to measure neutrons and transmit that data to a remote underground bunker. The information was to be used for analysis if the bomb failed.

About the rain at base camp he wrote: "Hollywood movies portraying the event usually show a heavy downpour the night of the test, but all I remember is an occasional drizzle. Base Camp was really on the old McDonald Ranch where there was a ranch "tank" (that's what it is called) made by a bulldozer. We spent all night on the slope or side of the tank and certainly would not have done that in a heavy rain."

So apparently it didn't rain at base camp. Richard Watts, in his recollection of the night, said Oppenheimer and Groves would go out into the rain at the South 10,000-yard shelter and dodge puddles on the asphalt as they discussed their weather decision. They must have had at least a light shower there.

Based on these folks' experiences, it appears there were typical New Mexico thunderstorms that night. By that time of night, many of the storms may have lost their ferocity and only managed to produce light rains to drizzles.

At 5:30 the bomb was triggered. It was immediately obvious that it worked, maybe beyond their wildest expectations.

There were hundreds of eyewitnesses and they generally agree on the sequence of events. However, like most events reported by human eyewitnesses, they disagree on some of the details. Edwin McMillian watched from Compania Hill and said in his memo on July 19, "None of my estimates of times or magnitudes can be considered very accurate, as I have found by comparison with others a wide variation, illustrating the difficulty of personal judgment without instruments."

The first thing they all experienced was an incredible flash of white light. Most describe it as many times brighter than the noonday sun. At the same time they felt heat on their skin.

McMillian reported, "I was watching the shot through a piece of dark glass such as is used in welders' helmets. An exceedingly bright light appeared and expanded very rapidly. I was aware of a sensation of heat on my face and hands, which lasted about a second. After about two seconds, I took the glass away. The sky and surrounding landscape were brightly illuminated, but not as strongly as in full

sunlight. The 'ball of fire' was still too bright for direct observation…"

So how bright was that flash? O.R. Frisch, a member of the coordinating committee, watched from Compania Hill. He filed a report a few days later saying, "Suddenly and without any sound, the hills were bathed in brilliant light, as if somebody had turned the sun on with a switch. It is hard to say whether the light was less or more brilliant than full sunlight, since my eyes were pretty well dark adapted."

Philip Morrison was at base camp and tried to take into account the vagaries of personal observation. He said, "I observed through the welding glass, centered at the direction of the tower, an enormous and brilliant disk of white light." He later qualified that with, "On subsequently looking at the noon sun through these glasses I have been led to estimate this initial stage of the gadget corresponding to a color

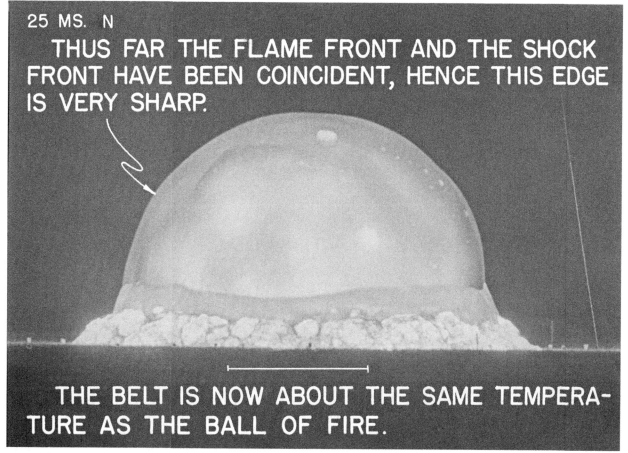

Normally these photos of the first milliseconds of the explosion only have the timing information imposed on them. This version must have been a briefing slide as it explains a bit about what is happening. The timing info is at the top and shows the photo was taken just .025 of a second after detonation. The fireball has enveloped the tower, hit the ground, and is pushing dirt and debris along the surface. Los Alamos photo.

much whiter or bluer and a brightness several times greater than that of the noon sun."

Robert Serber watched from Compania Hill and said, "I was looking directly at it with no eye protection of any kind. I saw first a yellow glow, which grew instantly into an overwhelming white flash, so intense that I was completely blinded." Within a minute Serber started to regain his normal vision.

Another perspective was provided by Luis Alvarez who was seated in a B-29 flying at 24,000 feet about 25 miles from GZ. He said, "My first impression was one of intense light covering my whole field of vision. This seemed to last for about 1/2 second."

Alvarez did not have a direct view of the event because of the clouds that filtered and dispersed the light.

McMillian reported feeling heat during the flash. Marvin Davis, the military policeman, reported it was like opening an oven door to look at what you were baking. Nobel Prize winner Enrico Fermi watched from base camp. He said, "My first impression of the explosion was the very intense flash of light and a sensation of heat on parts of my body that were exposed."

In anticipation of this intense infrared radiation, both Richard Rhodes and Lansing Lamont report in their books that Edward Teller and others at Compania Hill applied sunburn oil to their exposed skin.

After the initial bright flash, most agree that a huge fireball glowing in shades of red and orange expanded and started to rise. Smoke and dirt were mixed in the flux. It was a boiling, roiling, self-lit phenomenon. John Milton certainly would have used it to illustrate one of his levels of Hell in *Paradise Lost*.

Philip Morrison described it well. He said the white disk stopped growing horizontally and began "to extend in a vertical direction while its appearance had transformed into that of a bright glowing distinctly red column of flame mixed with swirling obscuring matter. The column looked rather like smoke and flame from an oil fire. This turbulent red column rose straight up several thousands of feet in a few seconds growing a mushroom-like head of the same kind. This mushroom was fully developed and the whole glowing structure complete at about 15,000 feet altitude."

The next step in the fireball's progress was the radioactive glow. Edwin McMillan reported, "When the red glow faded out a most remarkable effect made its appearance. The whole surface of the ball was covered with a purple luminescence, like that pro-

8.0 SEC.
N

⊢—⊣ 100 METERS

At eight seconds after detonation, the fireball is just beginning to push up from the ground. Los Alamos photo.

duced by the electrical excitation of air, and caused undoubtedly by the radioactivity of the material in the ball. This was visible for about five seconds."

Cyril Smith, looking from base camp, called the glow a "bluish ionization zone." Victor Weisskopf reported on July 24, "At that moment the cloud had about 1,000 billions of curies of radioactivity whose radiation must have produced the blue glow."

Next came the shock wave from the explosion as it spread in every direction. Most seemed disappointed by its strength. However, Brigadier General Thomas Farrell, Groves' deputy, reported "several of the observers standing back of the shelter (South 10,000) to watch the lighting effects were knocked flat by the blast." They were not injured.

O.R. Frisch witnessed the test from Compania Hill with his fingers in his ears. He said, "The report was quite respectable and was followed by a long rumbling, not quite like thunder but more regular, like huge noisy wagons running around the hills." Also at Compania, Edwin McMillan agreed: "It was remarkably sharp, being more of a 'crack' than a 'boom.'

At base camp, Kenneth Greisen said, "I noticed no sharp crack, but a rumbling sound as of thunder." Philip Morrison, also at base camp, agreed with Greisen as he reported, "The arrival of the air shock at T +45 on my stop-watch came as an anti-climax. I noticed two deep thuds which sounded rather like a kettle drum rhythm being played some distance away."

Enrico Fermi also watched from base camp but had a different take as he tried to use the shock wave to estimate the yield of the explosion. In his report he said, "I tried to estimate its strength by dropping from about six feet small pieces of paper before, during, and after the passage of the blast wave. Since at the time, there was no wind, I could observe very distinctly and actually measure the displacement of the pieces of paper that were in the process of falling while the blast was passing. The shift was about 2 1/2 meters, which, at the time, I estimated to correspond to the blast that would be produced by ten thousand tons of T.N.T."

A friend who is into doing these kinds of calculations finds Fermi's statement problematic, since he never states what formula he used. As it turns out, it wasn't much of a calculation because he was way too low.

By far the most grandiose observations made about the test were provided by Brigadier General Thomas Farrell and included in the Groves report of July 18.

At one point he wrote, "No matter what might happen now all knew that the impossible scientific job had been done. Atomic fission would no longer be hidden in the cloisters of the theoretical physicists' dreams. It was almost full grown at birth. It was a great new force to be used for good or for evil. There was feeling in that shelter that those concerned with its nativity should dedicate their lives to the mission that it would always be used for good and never for evil."

Probably because of this kind of sanctimonious verbiage, very few people quote Farrell today. However, I liked his description of the explosion and decided to use part of it on the cover of the missile range's Trinity Site brochure.

As he saw it:

The effects could well be called unprecedented, magnificent, beautiful, stupendous and terrifying. No man-made phenomenon of such tremendous power had ever occurred before. The lighting effects beggared description. The whole country was lighted by a searing light with the intensity many times that of the midday sun. It was golden, purple, violet, gray and blue. It lighted every peak, crevasse and ridge of the nearby mountain range with a clarity and beauty that cannot be described but must be seen to be imagined. It was that beauty the great poets dream about but describe most poorly and inadequately.

There is more. He said the shock wave was an "awesome roar which warned of doomsday and made us feel that we puny things were blasphemous to dare tamper with the forces heretofore reserved to The Almighty."

I can imagine his fellow generals in the Pentagon, dealing with the realities of invading Japan, reading this and shaking their heads wondering, "Who is this guy?"

Observers' accounts of the shock wave vary based on their location. Not everyone heard the "awesome roar." This is understandable since shock waves behave rather erratically. They can roll across relatively flat ground but seem to bounce over some things on the surface. They can be reflected and amplified by the terrain and even by clouds.

For instance, the shock wave did not significantly damage the Schmidt/McDonald ranch house only two miles from GZ. It only smashed windows and doors and broke a few rafters in the roof. The shock wave probably bounced right over the house. If someone had been inside, away from the windows, they might have survived.

Groves, in his July 18 report to the Secretary of War, stated, "The light from the explosion was seen clearly at Albuquerque, Santa Fe, Silver City, El Paso and other points generally to about 180 miles away. The sound was heard to the same distance in a few instances but generally to about 100 miles."

Somehow the terrain and atmosphere seemed to channel the shock wave to the northwest because it rocked Gallup, New Mexico about 170 miles away. During World War II, Fort Wingate, just east of Gallup, was used for munitions storage. The fort has rows and rows of large earthen-covered igloos used for the storage of explosives.

Shortly after 5:30 a.m. on July 16, Gallup residents were awakened by a loud boom coming from the direction of Fort Wingate. Officials called each other and the fire department, gathered together, and headed for the fort. They assumed one of the igloos had exploded.

At the fort they carefully drove every road looking for the damaged igloo. The igloos were all intact. The officials were mystified until the news of the Trinity test was released after the first bombing of Japan.

But on July 16 Gallup officials, as well as everyone else in New Mexico, heard a different story from an official news release issued by the Alamogordo Army Air Base. It was one of many prepared by the Manhattan Project to cover a number of possible outcomes.

This release said: "Several inquiries have been received concerning a heavy explosion which occurred on the Alamogordo Air Base reservation this morning.

"A remotely located ammunition magazine containing a considerable amount of high explosives and pyrotechnics exploded.

"There was no loss of life or injury to anyone, and the property damage outside of the explosive magazine itself was negligible.

"Weather conditions affecting the content of gas shells exploded by the blast may make it desirable for the Army to evacuate temporarily a few civilians from their homes."

A Los Alamos scientist who visited Trinity told me the news release didn't fool some of his colleagues from across the country. Instead, it gave those working on the periphery of the project a clue that something big was afoot. He said he received one telegram from a friend in the Midwest congratulating him and the others on a job well done.

One bomb test witness most people are unfamiliar with was Navy Captain Deke Parsons. Although born near Chicago, Parsons' biographer Al Christman pointed out in a *New Mexico Magazine* article in 2001 that Parsons spent some of his boyhood in Fort Sumner, New Mexico. He jumped ahead in high school and entered the Naval Academy at the age of 16.

Parsons was an ordnance expert and spent the early part of World War II as the military lead to develop the proximity fuse. The fuse made it possible for projectiles shot at airplanes to explode just before impact. This allowed for a shotgun effect of shrapnel that had a much better chance of bringing the enemy airplane down.

Because of his New Mexico ties, Parsons convinced the project to have the shells tested by E.J. Workman, head of physics at the University of New Mexico at what would become Sandia National Laboratory in Albuquerque. Parsons then introduced the shells to the Navy in the Pacific.

After such a successful project, Parsons expected some sort of combat command. Instead, he found himself back in New Mexico as the head of Ordnance at Los Alamos. He watched the test at Trinity Site and then headed for Tinian.

Parsons was onboard the Enola Gay to complete the final assembly of the atomic bomb in the bomb bay while in route to Hiroshima.

After the war he was promoted to rear admiral and became the Navy's spokesman on nuclear issues.

General Groves' Assessment

In his message to the Secretary of War, Groves also tried to summarize for leaders in Washington just how strong the blast was around GZ. Two days after the test, he already had a calculated yield for the bomb and told the secretary, "I estimate the energy generated to be in excess of the equivalent of 15,000 to 20,000 tons of TNT."

Groves went on with concrete examples of damage. He wrote, "A crater from which all vegetation had vanished, with a diameter of 1,200 feet and slight slope toward the center, was formed. In the center was a shallow bowl 130 feet in diameter and six feet in depth. The material within the crater was deeply pulverized dirt. The material within the outer circle is greenish and can be distinctly seen from as much as five miles away. The steel from the tower was evaporated. 1,500 feet away there was a four-inch iron pipe 16 feet high set in concrete and strongly guyed. It disappeared completely."

> ***Pop-Up:*** *The general's estimate on the bomb's yield was pretty good. Most sources now say anywhere from 18 to 21 kilotons of TNT. One question frequently asked at Trinity Site open houses is how much plutonium was actually consumed or turned to energy in the explosion. Given the estimate that the core was about 14 pounds of plutonium, it figures that about two pounds was transformed from matter to energy – only about 15 percent of the total.*

Groves also described what happened to the tower standing over Jumbo. He said, "This tower is comparable to a steel building bay that would be found in typical 15 or 20 story skyscraper or in warehouse construction. Forty tons of steel were used to fabricate the tower which was 70 feet high, the height of a six story building. The cross bracing was much stronger than that normally used in ordinary steel construction. The absence of the solid walls of a building gave the blast much less effective surface to push against."

After this setup, he said, "The blast tore the tower from its foundation, twisted it, ripped it apart and left it flat on the ground." He added, "I no longer consider the Pentagon a safe shelter from such a bomb." Of course Groves should've known, since he built the Pentagon just before coming on board to head the Manhattan Project.

Within minutes of the explosion, two of the three dangers from a nuclear bomb detonation were past. The first two, radiation burst and shockwave, were easily overcome using simple shelters and keeping a calculated distance away from GZ. The third, radioactive fallout, was an entirely different story.

The Fallout And Radiation Levels

The fallout of radioactive particles from the mushroom cloud was much more difficult to control especially as the cloud rose higher than expected.

Luis Alvarez, flying nearby in a B-29, reported, "In about eight minutes the top of the cloud was at approximately 40,000 feet . . . and this seemed to be the maximum altitude attained by the cloud."

It was high enough that upper level winds tore the cloud apart and carried it in various directions. The teams of soldiers and technicians went to work monitoring the cloud and measuring fallout as it rained down to the north and northeast.

Later, as all the data was put together, the fallout "corridor" proved to be on a northeasterly line from GZ heading toward Claunch, Vaughn and Santa Rosa – New Mexico villages and towns. The center of that line had the highest radiation readings. As you traveled perpendicular to that line (i.e. to the northwest or southeast) the radiation levels dropped and dropped. Also, the farther you went away from GZ, the lower the readings.

In his July 18 report Groves said, "It (the fallout cloud) deposited its dust and radioactive materials over a wide area. It was followed and monitored by medical doctors and scientists with instruments to check its radioactive effects. While here and there the activity on the ground was fairly high, at no place did it reach a concentration that required evacuation of the population. Radioactive material in small quantities was located as much as 120 miles away. The measurements are being continued in order to have adequate data with which to protect the Government's interests in case of future claims. For a few hours I was none too comfortable about the situation."

Groves felt relief because the vast majority of the fallout missed any large concentrations of population. The most radioactive areas proved to be in the middle of nowhere except for a few cases where ranch homes received large doses.

Groves and others were assured the radiation levels in these areas would drop quickly and there was no reason for concern. But, as can be seen in his report, he was obviously anxious about those levels and wanted to make sure he had real numbers if any lawsuits were filed.

In *Project Trinity 1945-1946*, a report prepared by Carl Maag and Steve Rohrer for the U.S. Defense Nuclear Agency, actual readings have been published. According to the DNA report, on shot day a team monitoring radiation levels in a canyon of the Oscuras east of Bingham found a gamma intensity of about 15 Roentgens per hour. Five hours later the intensity had dropped to 3.8 Roentgens per hour. One month after the test, the area was measured again and showed .032 Roentgens per hour. (The abbreviation for Roentgens per hour is R/h)

The Maag and Rohrer report states, "Significant fallout from the TRINITY cloud did not reach the ground within about 20 kilometers (12.5 miles) northeast of GZ. From this point, the fallout pattern extended out 160 kilometers (100 miles) and was 48 kilometers (30 miles) wide. Gamma intensities up to 15 R/h were measured in this region several hours after detonation. One month later, intensities had declined to .032 R/h or less."

These numbers offer a dramatic demonstration of how quickly radiation levels drop after a nuclear blast before they level out for the long haul. The canyon levels dropped 75 percent in just five hours. Of course, some of that fallout is still in the canyon, probably buried under several inches of dirt, and is still slightly radioactive. Like GZ today, there is no hazard left unless you eat the contaminated soil.

Other than a few reports, public exposure to radiation in the hours and few days after the 1945 test has largely been glossed over by officials and historians. That may have changed when Thomas Widner and Susan Flack published a paper in the March 2010 issue of *Health Physics* entitled "Characterization Of The World's First Nuclear Explosion, The Trinity Test, As A Source Of Public Radiation Exposure."

They spent years looking through tens of thousands of records relating to the Manhattan Project and came to some striking conclusions. Basically, in the rush to accomplish the test and then using inadequate equipment and procedures to measure radiation levels, some people were obviously overlooked. It turns out a small number of ranchers probably received excessive doses of radiation even by 1945 standards.

Dose levels for the public were not very well defined in 1945 because before nuclear weapons there was little chance for a John Doe to come into contact with much non-natural radiation.

Widner and Flack found that before the test, when the Army surveyed the area for residents outside the test area, they missed several families in isolated areas. Some of these people were then discovered the day of the explosion when radiation survey teams scoured the area following the path of the radioactive fallout.

One of these sites was the Ratliff ranch in Hoot Owl Canyon, subsequently dubbed "Hot Canyon" by Los Alamos personnel. The ranch was on the Chupadera Mesa about 20 miles northeast of GZ. It was occupied by an elderly couple and their grandson.

Near the house, monitors at 8:30 a.m. on the morning of the test were registering 20 R/hr. By 1:30 p.m. the rate was down to 6 R/hr. Perplexed by the high numbers, Dr. Hempelmann visited the site the day after the test and decided the numbers were then not high enough to warrant evacuation. Later calculations estimated the family members probably received radiation doses that exceeded the standards of the day.

But this is only part of the picture. It is a calculated guess at an exposure to the exterior of the body. The much more complex calculation, because of the myriad variables, concerns the consumption of fallout materials. The fallout was everywhere. Residents, like the Ratliffs, talked about seeing a fine white ash covering everything outside. If they worked outdoors and stirred it up, they breathed it in. No one from Los Alamos did nasal swabs to measure how much may have entered their lungs and lodged there.

Another way to consume the fallout was by eating or drinking it. For instance, the Ratliffs collected rainwater off their roof for drinking. The night after the test there were rain showers in the area. That means the fallout was probably washed into their cistern and mixed into their drinking water. It probably quickly settled to the bottom, but who knows how the family withdrew their water – from the top or the bottom.

Finally, no one did real medical and scientific follow-up with these ranchers. For a couple of years after the test, Los Alamos personnel discreetly inquired about the health of these folks without cluing them in on their concerns.

Scientists are currently trying to calculate the range of conditions and possibilities for this consumption of fallout and will eventually make their report public.

Of course, readings at GZ were much higher than elsewhere because of the activated soil that was emitting radiation in addition to fallout in the crater area. According to Maag and Rohrer, gamma intensity at GZ was estimated to be between 600 and 700 R/h. One week later the readings at GZ were down to 45 R/h and at 30 days they were 15 R/h.

These and many other survey readings were collected from all over the test site by scientists and doctors. It allowed the Medical Group to set up barricades around GZ at safe distances and to limit exposure times for those needing to go inside the perimeter. As levels decreased, the barriers and signs were moved in closer to GZ. Before the test they had set an exposure limit of five Roentgens during a two-month period.

To measure how much radiation each individual received, they were required to wear film badges at chest level outside their clothing. These badges measured gamma exposure and were turned in regularly for analysis.

Records were kept on everyone getting anywhere near GZ from July 16 to the end of 1946. Maag and Rohrer found that approximately 1,000 people, to include family members, visited the site in that time. Most did not go inside the fence that was built around the GZ area. In fact, no one in 1946 entered the fenced area and therefore no one received an exposure greater than one Roentgen.

The same could not be said of those days and weeks immediately after the test. According to Maag and Rohrer, "On the day of the shot, five parties entered the Ground Zero area. One party consisted of eight members of the earth-sampling group. They obtained samples by driving to within 460 meters (500 yards) of Ground Zero in a tank specially fitted with rockets to which retrievable collectors were fastened in order to gather soil samples from a distance. The group made several sampling excursions on 16 and 17 July. The tank carried two personnel (a driver and a passenger) each trip. No member of this party received a radiation exposure of more than one Roentgen."

Another tank was lined with lead and was equipped with a trapdoor in the bottom. This tank made five trips to within 90 meters (98 yards) of GZ to gather soil samples. The passenger would open the trapdoor and scoop up the soil. On two trips this tank drove across actual GZ.

One driver took the lead-lined tank to the GZ area three times and received one of the highest cumulative doses of radiation at 15 Roentgens.

Also on shot day, a photographer and radiation monitor went in to examine Jumbo and photograph damage. They were about 800 yards from GZ from noon to 1 p.m. Their estimated exposure was between one half and one Roentgen.

Again, Maag and Rohrer looked at the safety and monitoring reports and found that by the end of 1945, over 94 percent of visitors and workers had received radiation exposures of less than two Roentgens. There were 23 individuals who "received cumulative gamma exposures greater than two but less than four Roentgens." A total of 22 individuals received gamma exposures between four and 15 Roentgens.

Scientists quickly gathered what information they could from Trinity Site as the emphasis immediately shifted to the war against Japan. Within a few days or weeks, only military police and few others were left at Trinity. They secured the site and monitored visitors entering and leaving.

News Media At The Site

In September, Groves and Oppenheimer took the news media to Trinity Site. A famous photo taken by the Associated Press shows the two of them and others examining one of the footings to the tower. The buried rebar and concrete stand about two feet above the crater floor.

In the photo, all of the visitors are wearing booties over their shoes. This was not to protect them from the gamma radiation at the site as gamma rays are as penetrating as X-rays. No clothing could stop that form of radiation.

The booties prevented the visitors from carrying any radioactive dust away on their footwear. In other words, when they left the site, they completely ended their exposure because they weren't carrying any fallout with them.

In this age of instant and universal communication brought on by the Internet, a variety of people have posted articles about Trinity Site. In one the author claims that when Groves took the media to Trinity Site, the reporters were afraid to enter because of the news stories coming from Japan. Supposedly, to allay their fears, Groves ordered his driver to enter GZ. The website reports the driver ended up spending 30 minutes there and supposedly received an exposure of "100 rads." The author claims he died a few years later of some cancer due to his exposure at Trinity Site.

First of all, we see a different unit of measurement used by the web author. He uses rads instead of Roentgens. Roentgens are the units used in the forties but have now been replaced with rads and rems. However, for gamma exposure, one Roentgen equals one rad so they can be used interchangeably here.

We know from the records that by the middle of August the radiation levels at GZ were down to 15 Roentgens or rads per hour. When the press visited almost four weeks later, the level would have been even lower. A good estimate might be five rads if they spent the whole 30 minutes at GZ.

There is no way the driver or anyone else visiting GZ with Groves received an exposure of 100 Roentgens in 30 minutes. The only way would be if black magic were employed.

A few days after the visit hosted by Groves, there was another press visit but it was very low-key in comparison. On Sept. 15-17, 1945, George Cremeens, a young radio reporter from KRNT in Des Moines, Iowa, visited with soundman Frank Lagouri. They were flown to New Mexico by Captain C.L. Rutherford of the Iowa Civil Air Patrol.

During his visit, Cremeens flew over the crater and recorded his comments. Also, he interviewed Dr. K.T. Bainbridge, the Trinity test director, and Captain Howard Bush. In addition, he interviewed some of the soldiers still at Trinity Site and some of the eyewitnesses in the surrounding communities.

Cremeens then traveled back to Iowa and produced a four-part series of 15-minute reports on the first atomic explosion. They aired on Sept. 24, 26, 27 and 29.

A 15-minute segment was compiled from the material and broadcast nationwide by the ABC Radio Network. For his work Cremeens received a local Peabody Award for "Outstanding Reporting and Interpretation of the News."

I first wrote about Cremeens in 1986 after he returned to New Mexico to visit Trinity Site. After we escorted him to the site, he provided Public Affairs with copies of his letters, scripts, photos and a tape of the ABC broadcast.

From that material I made a display, with photos, to explain the tape we once played in the McDonald ranch house. It was his 15-minute network piece. When you do a search on the Internet for Cremeens and Trinity Site, it is amazing how many websites now quote the original display information.

For a couple of years after 1945, Cremeens was a fairly famous man in the Midwest. After the shows aired, he traveled through Iowa, Nebraska and other areas giving talks about the bomb and his experiences, and playing the ABC telecast. We received a copy of the script he used for those talks, and they provide some insight into Trinity Site.

For instance, during his visit he entered the McDonald ranch house and commented that as the shock wave went by blowing out the windows, "the suction created pulled all the ceilings down into the rooms." Also, he said Captain Bush experienced the bomb explosion from the South 10,000 shelter where he sat outside with his back to the bomb. Bush told Cremeens that the instant of detonation was so bright he had to physically touch his eyes to make sure they were closed.

Finally, for his show on Socorro, Cremeens said

George Cremeens, left, with radio station KRNT in Des Moines, interviews Ken Bainbridge, the Trinity test director, at Ground Zero just two months after the test. Photo courtesy of George Cremeens.

they set up their portable transcribing equipment at the town post office. They asked everyone that came by what they experienced on July 16. Cremeens summarized by saying, "Everyone I talked to was awakened by the sound of the explosion."

This is also where he recorded an interview with Mr. Greene, whose daughter was completely blind. Somehow she sensed the light from the blast as she was being driven to Albuquerque.

As an aside, Cremeens, being a radioman, would tell audiences he was impressed that at GZ the communications shack containing $4,500 worth of "intricate radio equipment" was vaporized in the explosion.

Writer George Fitzpatrick visited the site later in 1945. His article about the visit appeared in the January 1946 issue of *New Mexico Magazine*.

Fitzpatrick accompanied a party of National Park Service officials interested in the site as a national monument. Captain Bush was their escort and he took them to GZ, the Schmidt/McDonald ranch, South 10,000, West 10,000 and base camp.

Fitzpatrick said a chalkboard was still in place at West 10,000 showing the location of recording instruments. At South 10,000 Bush showed the group the wiring in the bunker and the switch that was thrown to trigger the bomb. Also, he pointed out where he sat on the ground outside the bunker during the blast.

At GZ, Fitzpatrick explained how they drove to

An unknown soldier examines one of the 100-foot tower stubs long after the explosion. From the Carl Rudder scrapebook.

a fence around the crater with an armed guard at the gate. The guard had them sign in and put their entry time beside each name. When they exited, he recorded the time so their exposure was recorded.

In talking to the men at Trinity, he learned that the mess hall was an equal opportunity facility. Every diner carried his dirty tray to the kitchen after eating and cleaned it himself. This included the VIPs who visited.

In a related incident, when Brigadier General Farrell visited base camp once he immediately got out of his normal uniform and donned a pair of work coveralls. The next morning he appeared in the mess hall queue with everyone else for breakfast. He was accosted by an attendant who said, "Hey, soldier, don't you know the Captain don't allow no breakfast unless you shave!" Supposedly the general skedaddled back to the lavatory to shave.

Fitzpatrick related one incident that spoke volumes about Captain Bush. He wrote, "The day we were there Captain Bush received notification of the award of the Legion of Merit for his part in the atomic bomb project. 'I'm not kidding myself,' he said. 'My men got this for me.'"

The Crater – A Pond of Green Glass

From the very beginning, starting with the scientists, then the news media and then the general public, visitors were all impressed by the glass covering most of the crater. Cremeens aptly described it as a green, brittle, low-grade glass.

Its thickness varied from a half inch to just small slivers. Its color could be gray to grayish green to a deep emerald green. There were other colors like red Trinitite but it was relatively rare. The pieces were usually very porous with many gas bubbles inside. The bottoms were rough and the tops were usually smooth.

At the time the accepted explanation was that the intense heat of the fireball – after all, it was supposedly many millions of degrees – melted the sand on the floor of the crater to create the coating. More on this later.

Over the years most people have described the crater at Trinity Site as a saucer-like depression as opposed to a gigantic hole in the ground. Discovering old documents, we now know that is only partially true.

In a Los Alamos report dated Oct. 3, 1945, F. Reines summarized a study of the crater area in terms of "permanent earth displacement." By the way, the men doing the work were at GZ on Aug. 12 and 13. Reines reported they were at GZ about three hours and the highest radiation dose received was four Roentgens.

In his results section, Reines said, "The most marked feature of the crater was its great width, approximately 1,100 feet, and its small depth, about 9-1/2 feet at the center." Most of that depth was confined to a small area, about a 150-foot radius out from the tower base. From the outer edge of the big crater to that inner edge there was simply a slight incline down to the center.

Reines concluded all the sandy soil, out to 1,100 feet, was compressed by the pressure of the explosion above. Then, in the inner area at zero to 150 feet, soil was actually gouged out and hurled into the air.

Proof that the inner crater area was greatly compressed came in the form of the bases or piers for the four legs of the tower. The top two feet of these bases were burnt off, and they were also pushed down five to seven feet below where they originally stood.

The report suggested digging up one of these bases to see how much damage there was to the concrete and rebar. Reines said this would be important information in trying to build protective shelters in the future.

The recommendation was taken and from Oct. 8 through Oct. 10, four individuals excavated two of the buried piers – the ones on the northwest and southwest corners. They were on the site for three days and their gamma exposures totaled between 3.4 and 4.7 Roentgens.

Such earth displacement and uptake of soil to create radioactive fallout did not happen in the bombings of Hiroshima and Nagasaki because the bombs were exploded about 1,800 feet above the ground. Most people don't realize the Trinity test created a much larger radioactive fallout cloud than either explosion over Japan.

Although part of the new White Sands Proving Ground, Trinity Site remained under the control of Los Alamos until 1948. Fences and warning signs probably did not keep out curiosity seekers. Many of the artifacts left on site certainly began disappearing right away.

Public Affairs once received a letter from an individual possessing a Trinity Site warning sign. He asked if the office would verify its origin so he could sell it as a rare artifact. We declined.

Shortly after the Trinity Site test, the uranium bomb was used over Hiroshima on Aug. 6 and a plutonium bomb just like the Trinity bomb was dropped on Nagasaki on Aug. 9. Japan announced its surrender less than a week later.

After The War

The war was over but a number of soldiers were left at Trinity Site to provide security, maintain facilities, and give support to personnel coming down to conduct studies. According to Felix DePaula, everyone received a bump up one rank at the end of the war plus a 20-day furlough.

Captain Bush wanted to give the men a longer break after their protracted stint in the desert. There wasn't much for them to do anymore and little hurry to do it. They were bored.

So Bush told them as they went on their vacations to send back a request for a 10-day extension. He told them to just come up with some sort of feasible excuse, and he would grant it. DePaula said he spent a month at home in New York before heading back to New Mexico.

According to Marvin Davis, Bush invited some women from the Women's Army Corps (WAC) stationed at Los Alamos to help the men celebrate Christmas 1945 at Trinity Site. In a letter to Public Affairs, Davis said about 20-25 women showed up on a bus. He added there was plenty of beer and "most of the women were wilder than the antelope."

Also, Bush took company funds and had special rings made for the military police and the engineers who served at the site. Davis said the ring had the words "First Atomic Bomb" on top along with the military insignias for the police and engineers. The numeral one is there under a spur signifying the MP unit was "Detachment One." At the bottom were the words, "silencio servicio" which translates to "silent service."

At a higher level, all military personnel who served in the Manhattan Project were issued special patches for their uniforms. The 3,500 patches had a blue background that represented the universe. In the middle a white cloud and lightning bolt formed a question mark that symbolized the unknown results and secrecy surrounding the project. The lightning bolt extended down to split a yellow atom that represented atomic fission. A red and blue star in the center of the question mark was the insignia for the Army Service Forces to which the Manhattan Project military were assigned.

When Davis left the site in February 1946, there were still a few dozen people there to support any operations that came their way.

In 1946, Los Alamos returned to Trinity with new projects. At the same time, the National Park Service proposed turning Trinity Site into a National Monument.

The park service recognized the importance of the site, but the idea was rejected by the military. Los Alamos was still using the site, plus it sat in the northern half of the new rocket proving ground. By turning it into a monument open to the public like Yellowstone, White Sands would have lost the use of the top 20-25 miles of its basic real estate.

The Los Alamos projects in 1946 revolved around using explosives to crush initiators and measure the output of subatomic fragments like alpha particles and neutrons. To accomplish this they built three underground cells about 1,600 feet from GZ; a distance far enough out, radiation levels were very low.

Sleeping Beauty

In the bunker southeast of GZ, they placed an experiment containing polonium 210 and a light element. The setup used an explosive device to close the switch to turn on equipment and trigger the explosives to crush the two elements.

It was triggered on Sept. 8, 1946. Nothing happened.

Officials decided to leave the experiment instead of running the risk of digging it up. After all, it was buried under 40 feet of sand and the initiator was not a fissionable material. Neither the polonium nor the explosives posed a hazard up on the surface. The test soon acquired the name "Sleeping Beauty."

A second experiment in another bunker was successfully conducted. The third bunker was never used.

In March 1967, as the agencies argued over the status of Trinity Site, Los Alamos returned to the site to clean up Sleeping Beauty. With the number of visitors growing, someone decided it was time to

According to Marvin Davis, these were some of the support personnel who worked at Trinity Site after the test. The group included military police, cooks, and engineers to maintain the facilities. His listing of who they are is just last names and each row is from left to right. Back row - Smith, Snodgrass, Jeffery, Agnew, Glode, Stockton, Lerner, Spry, Kymer, Leby, Gibson, and Capt. Bush. Middle row - Sisson, Davis, Coleman, Ferguson, Dirksen, Bourg, Fisher, Maher and Wendelin. Front row - Ballard, Kadow, Loyd, Grashock, Wheeler, Bresnahaw, Rudder, Harrison and Wilhite. Photo courtesy of Marvin Davis.

destroy the high explosives still down in the bunker. Although the explosives were buried deep, it was considered better to be safe than sorry.

This and other decisions about "safety" at Trinity were actually made for legal reasons. The lawyers didn't want the government held liable in the unlikely case of some sort of accident or claim of injury. They wanted the risk to be as close to zero as possible. Of course, the obvious answer to limiting risk is to close it to the public. They lost on that alternative.

Using heavy equipment, crews dug down to the Sleeping Beauty chamber door and carefully pried it open. Inside they found the explosive switch had fired, but it failed to close and start the rest of the experiment.

The team then placed a 100-pound charge in the bunker and destroyed the high explosives and equipment inside. Afterwards they filled the hole and eliminated the mound over both bunkers.

Because of growing public concerns about radiation, they uncovered a small storage bunker about two miles from GZ that contained ten galvanized 30-gallon garbage cans filled with Trinitite. The glass contains a great deal of radioactive material and is the source of most of the radiation at the site. Because of that, much of it was scraped off the crater floor and buried. The idea was to reduce the radiation at GZ.

These ten garbage cans were each placed in their own 50-gallon drum and taken to Los Alamos where they are currently buried in one of the lab's disposal areas.

Also in 1946, William Laurence's book *Dawn Over Zero* was published. Laurence was a Pulitzer Prize-winning science writer and *New York Times* reporter who was the only journalist allowed inside the Manhattan Project. He witnessed the Trinity explosion from Compania Hill.

Laurence may have been given such a unique inside view of the project because of his various articles before the war highlighting the possibilities of atomic energy through fission. One article was classified secret by the government at the start of the war and libraries were asked to note down anyone asking for a copy of the magazine. Somebody within the project must have felt he had the vision to document the bomb's development.

On the other hand, Nicholas Metropolis reported Laurence had to ask what the noise was when the shock wave hit Compania Hill about a minute after detonation on July 16.

Trinity Site Transitions To Local Control

By 1948, research activity at Trinity Site was at a minimum. The Atomic Energy Commission was losing interest in the site, especially since it was smack dab in the middle of the White Sands test ranges. On Aug. 10, 1948, a memorandum of understanding was signed between the Atomic Energy Commission and the Air Force concerning the disposition of Trinity.

The agreement was with the Air Force and not the Army because, at that time, control of the White Sands real estate was still divided between the two services. Holloman Air Force Base was home to the Air Force's missile test command and they were using the east side of White Sands up through the north end where Trinity Site was located.

Before the Air Force was to take over the area, the AEC was required to erect a chain link fence to encircle GZ at a radius of 1,500 feet. That fence is still there and is what is now called the "outer fence." They were to "erect appropriate signs in and about said Trinity Site, warning trespassers to stay off the property."

Also the commission was to remove "all personal property." We haven't seen any records on when base camp buildings were removed, but this may have been the point in time.

The agreement called for the Air Force to assume responsibility for maintaining fencing and signage, and for protecting personnel from safety hazards.

All of that changed in 1952 when the military "integrated" the proving ground, putting all the real estate and the testing mission under the control of the U.S. Army. At that point all the lands controlled by the Air Force, to include Trinity Site, were transferred to the Army.

Following through on a plan that was devised the year before, in March 1952 the AEC announced it was letting a contract to have the Trinitite at GZ cleaned up. The AEC's announcement created a flurry of public and government interest in Trinity Site. Many people in New Mexico didn't want the site "cleaned up." They felt it had more value as a historical site if the original crater was left alone.

Los Alamos fought against cleaning up the crater, saying there was no scientific reason to clean it. The risks were not great enough to warrant the effort.

Visitors and historians have wondered for decades what the crater was like in 1952 when the AEC made their announcement. Based on all the accounts of people sneaking into the site to steal the glass, we thought there might not have been all that much left. Nobody knew for sure. Then, in early 2013, I received a couple of scanned slides from Robert Alley.

Alley was a "broomstick scientist" stationed at White Sands in 1951 and 52. He worked on the V-2 project and as a draftee corporal was in charge of the last flights. He and a couple of friends visited Trinity Site in April 1952. They were able to get to the crater through a hole in the fence and Alley snapped his two shots.

Not only do they show the ground still almost covered with large chunks of glass, they are in color. The substantial area of vibrant green is remarkable. Unfortunately, the original slides are significantly damaged by age, but they energized the small community of Trinity geeks trying to pin down every possible detail of the 1945 test. One or both of the photos will probably show up soon in publications.

In the end, it was an all-too-common legal factor that motivated the AEC to deconstruct the site. In a July 1951 letter to Los Alamos, Dr. John Bugher, the Deputy Director of the Division of Biology and Medicine for the AEC, said they didn't care about the science – it was a "medico-legal" decision. He said their main concern was about being sued. Basically, he said a jury could find in favor of someone claiming their lung disease was caused by Trinity Site no matter how much science was brought to bear. Cautious lawyers and upper-level managers went for the "safe" solution.

On March 10, 1952, U.S. Representative Antonio Fernandez of New Mexico introduced H.R. 6953 to establish a Trinity Atomic National Monument.

On April 3, 1952, a conference was held in Washington, D.C. concerning Trinity Site. It was attended by members of Congress from New Mexico and representatives from the Department of Defense, the AEC, and the National Park Service.

One thing they eventually agreed upon was protection for a portion of the original Trinitite on the crater floor for a future exhibit. The AEC was going to have its way. Everyone agreed the Trinitite outside the planned protected area was to be removed in "the interest of public health and safety."

Key players then met at a field conference on May 20, 1952 at Trinity Site. Attendees included several reps from the National Park Service, the AEC, and the commanders of Holloman and White Sands.

Out of this meeting came an agreement to protect the sample plot of Trinitite already under shelter about 250 feet west of GZ. The plot was estimated at 20 x 50 feet. At the time the shelter was basically just a roof on poles. The agreement between the parties was to better protect the green glass by adding sides to the shelter down to the ground, thus creating a wooden box over the area.

They also agreed to protect the "wrecked tower" by fencing it to keep out unauthorized persons. This is a reference to the Jumbo tower. Obviously, officials at White Sands didn't pay much attention to the agreement as the tower disappeared in the 50s, Jumbo lost its outer bands of steel, and they tried fearlessly to give Jumbo away in 1960.

The National Park Service efforts in 1952 to protect Trinity were as unsuccessful as those in 1945, 1946 and later years. Each National Park Service probe was countered by the Department of Defense with, "the area around Trinity Site is essential to the defense of the country."

There was no way Trinity was going to become a national monument open to the public every day. Such a move would have crippled the missile range. The biggest asset White Sands has is its large empty space – no tourists in Bermuda shorts driving hither and yon. The emptiness allows violent things to happen in the sky with big chunks of jagged, deadly debris raining down indiscriminately. No one is in danger and no property is damaged.

Protecting the Site

For those who have never served in the military or worked for it, you should know that commanding generals are very similar to kings in their local domains. In many areas they have unquestioned authority with a court of senior knights ready to defend the ruler. That single leader can affect most things happening in his realm, even the attitudes of the people working for him. Everything trickles down from the top.

What I'm driving at is what shapes the attitude of lower-level employees concerning a place like Trinity Site. If the commander doesn't care, why should they?

In that light, many generals commanding White

Sands have viewed Trinity Site as nothing but a sore on their backsides. It is not part of their mission, so they get no credit from higher headquarters for doing anything there. Because they receive no funding or manpower to do anything at Trinity Site, they run the risk of criticism or censure if they divert funds or workers for improvements.

It is not surprising that many White Sands commanders let the Jumbo tower disappear and almost let Jumbo follow suit. In the 60s several of the Trinity bunkers, including the main control bunker (South 10,000), were bulldozed and burned. The reason given was they were unsafe. In any large organization, be it military or civilian, it is always hard to argue against safety claims – you look like a barbarian if you do.

The South 10,000-yard bunkers (there were actually two structures left) were sprayed with diesel fuel in July 1965 and lit up. The WSMR photo archives contain some nice color footage of the event. Those dry timbers survived an atomic bomb but couldn't escape a few gallons of fuel. They burned fiercely on a windy day.

The National Park Service called the destruction an "irreparable catastrophe."

That happened while Major General J. Frederick Thorlin was commander. He happens to be the same general who ordered the lava obelisk constructed to mark the precise spot of GZ at Trinity Site. Some say the general put up the obelisk to improve the site for visitors. Others say it was a clever way to immortalize himself.

The obelisk sits between what would have been the four legs of the tower. The lava rock came from the lava flow on the east side of the Oscura Mountains where the missile range's Oscura gate is located.

According to Dan Duggan who was an officer on Thorlin's staff, the bronze plaque for the obelisk came back from the foundry with a misspelling in it. It had to be sent back and remade. Since time was of the essence, they had to fly it back and forth.

Duggan said the delay was almost disastrous. Thorlin left WSMR at the end of July 1965 and had scheduled a little ceremony at Trinity to dedicate the obelisk and plaque. Duggan said they had to work the night before to finish the obelisk and get the corrected plaque mounted.

We know the obelisk was complete and had the plaque on it by mid-July because the *Wind and Sand*

newspaper ran a photo of it on July 16, 1965. However, it is a poor picture and half the plaque is cut off. It looks like the date may be wrong, but it is hard to tell from the newspaper. They must have sent it back after this photo was taken.

The plaque says, "TRINITY SITE--BIRTH-PLACE--OF--THE ATOMIC AGE--WHERE--THE WORLD'S FIRST NUCLEAR--DEVICE WAS EXPLODED ON--JULY 16, 1945."

Given the fact that one of the most important artifacts at Trinity Site, the control bunker, was torched on Thorlin's watch, it seems possible he might not have ordered the obelisk as an altruistic act.

Here's another clue. At the bottom of the plaque, in admittedly smaller letters but taking up almost 25% of the plaque, it is written, "ERECTED 1965--WHITE SANDS MISSILE RANGE--J. FREDERICK THORLIN--MAJOR GENERAL US ARMY--COMMANDING." Basically it was his official signature block. See the photo on page 132.

Over the years I took a lot of Trinity Site scientists and support personnel on visits to GZ. A common question was, "Who in the hell is General Thorlin and what did he have to do with the Manhattan Project?"

Also in the July 16, 1965 issue of the *Wind and Sand* was a short science fiction allegory concerning Trinity Site. It was written by Hi Anderson with a headline or title of, "Did 1st Nuclear Blast Signal World's End."

The scenario is a space ship exploring earth. They say earth is a "lifeless planet" that no ship has landed on in a thousand years. The crew detects a rectangular metal object below and they descend to check it out.

At the end the commander files this report in his log, "Space time 6-1-1500 Atomic War Year, on the planet called earth, in a northern latitude was located a metal plate bearing the following legend, "Trinity Site where the world's first nuclear device was exploded on July 16, 1945. Erected 1965 White Sands Missile Range . . . and the rest of the writing was destroyed by weathering."

It is interesting that Thorlin's signature block is what disappeared in the story.

National Park Service Tries Different Tactic

The next White Sands commander fought another perceived Trinity Site battle in the ongoing war with the National Park Service. On December 21, 1965, the Park Service lowered its expectation of getting Trinity as a national monument and placed the site on the National Historic Landmark list. A letter notified the Secretary of the Army that Trinity Site was on the list.

The historic landmark program began in 1960 and recognizes buildings, sites like Trinity, other structures, objects, and whole districts for their historical importance. For instance, in New Mexico, it includes Kit Carson's house, the Santa Fe Plaza, and the V-2 launch facility at White Sands. Nationwide there are about 2,500 properties.

Under the program, recognition is provided by the National Park Service, but it has no control over the properties. In fact about half are private property. For instance, if an owner decides to tear down the historical property, the Park Service can't interfere. The owner simply loses the designation.

It is a little more complicated for landmarks on federal lands because most agencies (the Army in the case of Trinity Site) have regulations in place to support the landmark status by preserving and protecting it.

When the letter from the Park Service about Trinity got to White Sands, Major General John Cone was commander. Paranoia struck the staff at White Sands.

One memo stated making the site a landmark was just the first step in the Park Service's plot to make the site a national monument with unlimited public access.

In my 30 years at White Sands, I noticed this was a very common perception. Staff and command were always fearful of encroachment of any kind. Cooperation with non-military agencies and, in some cases, other military organizations was usually seen as surrendering control. These historical programs, endangered species programs, and others always had WSMR officials wringing their hands saying, "they are going to shut the place down."

I suspect some of that paranoia comes from working at an installation at the bottom of the food chain. There are lots of bosses stacked above White Sands all the way to Washington. Not a single one will ever be blamed for anything negative that happens at the missile range – even if they order it. Scapegoats don't come from the top levels of huge organizations.

In his February 1966 response, Cone said, "We are protecting the site. Hence we are carrying out the spirit of the Landmarks program as well as the letter and spirit of the Historic Sites Act." This, of course, was just seven months after WSMR burned the control bunkers.

But, mainly, Cone relied on the safety and welfare argument. He appealed to the growing American fear of radiation. A long paragraph in Cone's letter talked about radiation levels at the site and quoted federal regulations about exposure. He said, "Understandably, the need for limiting access to any radiation source is obvious."

Eventually, both sides recognized Trinity Site as a "historic landmark." In 1975, 10 years later, a bronze plaque was added to the obelisk acknowledging that fact. During my time at White Sands, the National Park Service did not make any maneuvers to have the site declared a national monument.

The probable reason for the Park Service's low profile is found in a 1973 letter from Major General Arthur Sweeney, Jr., White Sands commander, to the New Mexico Environmental Improvement Agency. In the letter Sweeney said, "United States Senate Bill, S-288, January 12, 1967, authorizes the transfer of Trinity Site to the National Park Service, Department of Interior, upon the termination of the Army military use of the area and when such a transfer is consistent with National security." The Park Service simply was never going to get any commitment firmer than that.

As time passed after the test at Trinity, scientists and medical researchers learned more and more about radiation and exposure effects. The standards imposed in 1945 were replaced with stricter and stricter standards as the decades unfolded. Awareness was also growing and the general population became more fearful as some research showed long-term exposure at low doses could make you sick. General Cone's use of radiation hazards in his letter may have been a result of this.

On March 30, 1966, Cone was returning to White Sands from a speaking engagement in El Paso when he and his driver came across an accident along an empty stretch of War Highway. Cone found a soldier seriously injured and trapped under the wrecked vehicle. The general and his driver tried to lift the car off the victim but Cone, who had a heart condition, suffered a heart attack and died. The accident victim was eventually rescued.

During the 1975 Trinity Site open house, the new Park Service plaque that was added to the obelisk earlier in the year was unveiled. The plaque notes that Trinity Site is a National Historic Landmark. WSMR photo.

In October 1966, Major General Horace Davisson took command of White Sands. Davisson picked up on Cone's concerns about Trinity Site and he asked the Atomic Energy Commission to look into the safety of the site.

Radiation Risks at Ground Zero

This triggered the 1967 efforts by Los Alamos to clean up Sleeping Beauty, remove the cans filled with Trinitite, and survey the area again for radiation safety. The survey was quite extensive, involving

systematic measurements for most of the area inside the Trinity Site fence and outside as well.

In his April 17, 1967 report, Charles Blackwell stated areas outside the fence were the same as background radiation for that area of New Mexico. Inside the fence, levels were highest near the very center of the crater with diminishing levels as you walked outwards.

He said, "Briefly, the levels vary with distances from Ground Zero with a level of 2.5 mR/hr (milliroentgen per hour) out to the fence where the level is reduced to .03 mR/hr. There are a few spots within this area that will read up to 3.5 mR/hr where the concentration of Trinitite is fairly heavy."

He pointed out that all personnel wore film badges to measure their exposure while working around Trinity Site. He said, "The two personnel that were exposed within the area for the greatest length of time were Jack Richard and Gerald Eagan of H-1 as they spent about 85% of the 10 days within the fenced area making the survey."

Earlier, when talking about radiation levels in 1945 and immediately after, the scientists were using Roentgens. A milliroengten is one one-thousandth of a Roentgen. In other words, an exposure of 3 milliroengtens is .003 Roentgens.

So how much radiation did Richard and Eagan receive? The threshold of the badges they wore was 20 milliroentgens - they had to receive a cumulative dose greater than 20 mR to even be detected by the badges. The threshold was not reached for either man.

To put that in perspective, various organizations now estimate the average American receives about 300 mR per year in exposure from natural and medical sources.

Blackwell concluded his report with a reference to one of those natural sources. He said, "I feel that the area was left in a safe condition from an industrial safety viewpoint and considering the amount of radioactivity found within the area that personnel could be exposed to by just visiting the area would be very small. We have checked many pieces of ore brought into this office from weekend hikes in the back country that showed much higher levels of radioactivity than would be found at Trinity Site."

On April 26, health physicist Fred Fey at Los Alamos filed a report using the same data. Given a visitor's proclivity to wander around the site instead of sitting in one spot for eight hours, he concluded "The whole body exposure rate received by a person visiting Trinity Site would probably average no more than 1 mR/h."

Since much of the radiation at Trinity is in the form of alpha particles, it is not particularly dangerous. Alpha particles are stopped by the dead outer layers of skin. A person would have to ingest a large quantity (about 400 grams or almost one pound of Trinitite according to Fey) to have enough remain in the body to become a hazardous source. Experts

and most reasonable people I've talked to consider it unlikely for a human to consume a pound of sandy glass.

Fey concluded, "After a thorough evaluation of the data gathered during a survey of Trinity Site, it does not appear that anyone could receive any radiation injury through a visit to Trinity Site."

In a June 23, 1967 letter, the Atomic Energy Commission reported back to White Sands. Author L.P. Gise talked about the federal regulations and pointed out that the few spots at Trinity Site measuring 3 mR/h exceeded the national standard for the general public. Things were certainly different from 1945 where such a reading would have been background noise.

Gise wrote, "In view of this regulation, and especially the part listing a maximum radiation level of 2 mR/h, I do not believe that the entire area should be opened up for unrestricted access." He added, "I agree with the LASL that visitors to the proposed national monument would not, under any credible circumstances, receive a significant exposure of ionizing radiation."

Gise suggested that another fence be used at Trinity Site to encircle the area with radiation of 2 mR/h or greater. He proposed this as a restricted zone where visitors would only visit for short periods of time.

The missile range responded to this suggestion with an inner chain link fence imposed on the crater area that is 700 feet long and 400 feet across. Its intent is to better control visitors to the site and limit their time at GZ to about 90 minutes. With all the visitors inside the fence, military police and others could prevent visitors from digging up Trinitite or stealing anything else they might find.

By the end of July, the approval for the fence came from Davisson. His staff suggested using chain link fencing from the old Nike Zeus program.

The fencing could have been brought up from the Nike facilities on the south end of the range or from a nearby site called ZURF. The ZURF Site is just a few miles northwest of Trinity. The acronym stands for "Zeus Up Range Facility." The facility was used to launch Nike Hercules missiles as targets back to the south. It would have been a very convenient site to scavenge.

In September 2009, Austin Vick, once chief of data collection in National Range Operations, confirmed the fence was simply moved from ZURF to Trinity Site. It was just another demonstration at the missile range's talent for reusing old things.

Another question about safety

In October and November 1972, Charles Hyder made a rather big splash in New Mexico by publicly criticizing the Atomic Energy Commission for being lax on the dangers of radiation. In particular, he said visitors to Trinity Site were at risk from being there and from the Trinitite they took away with them. He demanded the state of New Mexico investigate.

Hyder made a name for himself in the decades after this by criticizing government and industry for polluting the planet and endangering all life on the planet. In 1986, he began a long fast in Washington, D.C. to protest war. In 1999, he started what was supposed to be a "terminal fast" in Carlsbad, New Mexico to protest the Waste Isolation Pilot Plant where radioactive waste was stored.

The news media ran with his Trinity Site accusations; suddenly everyone was trying to explain radiation and how it is measured. In June 1973, the New Mexico Environmental Improvement Board responded by voting to investigate "health hazards associated with public visits to Trinity Site."

In his criticism of the government, Hyder seemed most intent on the pieces of Trinitite visitors stole during each visit to Trinity Site. He claimed visitors were not warned about it.

In response, the missile range published the news release and a handout used for the Oct. 1, 1972 Trinity Site open house. Under Rules and Restrictions, number three stated, "No digging is permitted in the area," number four stated, "Visitors may not pick up objects in the area," and number seven stated, "Visit is restricted to one and one-half hours after time of arrival at Trinity Site."

Finally, in August 1973, a staffer from the Environmental Improvement Agency visited Trinity Site to make his own survey.

Soon the agency concluded, "Public visitors to the site who obey the rules established for their control will receive insignificant radiation exposures."

The uproar moved officials at the missile range to make more improvements to the site. At the end of November 1972, WSMR erected a barbed wire fence corridor from the outer fence to the gate at the inner fence. This helped to better control the visitors by further confining where they could go. There was to be no more wandering about inside the large outer fence. On the surface, it was a move to protect visitors from themselves, but it also protected the government from accusations of not doing enough to protect folks.

Of course, the basic problem here is rooted in human nature. Tourists love souvenirs. When not buying them, they are picking them up – rocks, plants, furniture, pieces of buildings, almost anything not nailed down, can disappear with a tourist.

Years ago, when I was the coordinator for Trinity Site open houses, I got tired of so many people stealing the Trinitite. The obvious pieces on the surface were getting harder and harder to find.

I had a sign fabricated that now stands right at the gate to the inner fenced area. Everyone entering has to pass by it. The sign states that removal of Trinitite is theft of government property punishable by fine and/or prison time. Did that, what I consider a fairly clear warning, stop visitors from collecting Trinitite? Nope.

We also stationed Department of Defense police inside the inner fenced area to discourage the theft of Trinitite. Does that work? Nope. Some visitors actually bend down to pick up pieces of the green glass right under the watchful gaze of an officer.

The only foolproof way to stop the collection of Trinitite or souvenirs at any other site is to close the places permanently.

A few people must feel some guilt after taking Trinitite because periodically we'd receive some back in the mail. In one box there was a letter from a young man in Gaithersburg, Maryland. He said, "While within the circular fenced in area where the bomb was detonated, I picked up from the path the enclosed rocks which probably are Trinitite. This was despite the posted warning..."

Interestingly, he wasn't even sure it was Trinitite. This is quite common. There are usually a few visitors who come up to us and ask, "Is this Trinitite?" Sometimes it is, sometimes it is just a chunk of limestone and sometimes it is a pile of rabbit droppings. They usually drop the rabbit poop very quickly when informed what they are holding.

Some people visiting Trinity Site collect the strangest things. I know of two instances where we had visitors stealing the toilet paper out of the porta-toilets on site.

The kind of safety controversy stirred up by Hyder put Trinity Site in the headlines and made more people aware of the site. During the 1970s, the number of visitors rose and soon missile range personnel were dealing with a thousand people at each visit. During the 30th anniversary year, the October event drew an estimated 2,500 visitors.

The Numbers

Radiation levels in the fenced, GZ area at Trinity Site are very low. The maximum levels are only 10 times greater than the region's natural background radiation. Many places on earth are naturally more radioactive than Trinity Site.

The radiation comes from the nuclei of individual atoms of several different elements. Not only are different elements involved, but there are several kinds of radiation – some harmful and some less so. These different radiations are called "ionizing" and they are harmful when they strike and alter atoms in our DNA and cell structure. The resulting damage can cause physical injury and can lead to cancer development.

Health physicists are concerned with four emissions from the nuclei of these atoms. One of these radiations is the alpha particle that is relatively large and travels fairly slowly compared to other atomic particles. Alpha particles are composed of two protons and two neutrons. They travel about one to three inches in the air and are easily stopped by a sheet of paper.

Another radiation is the beta particle, basically a very light electron that moves at less than the speed of light. These particles are more energetic than alpha particles, but can be stopped by a thin sheet of metal or heavy clothing.

The third form of nuclear radiation is the gamma ray. This is a type of electromagnetic radiation like visible light and radio waves, but is on the energetic end of the spectrum next to X-rays. They travel at the speed of light. It takes at least an inch of lead or eight inches of concrete to stop them.

Finally, neutrons are emitted by some radioactive substances. Neutrons are very penetrating but are not as common in nature. Neutrons have the capability of striking the nucleus of another atom and changing a stable atom into an unstable and, therefore, radioactive one. Neutrons emitted in nuclear reactors are contained in the reactor vessel or shield-ing and cause the vessel walls to become radioactive.

Americans, even military officials, aren't very good at dealing with these different terms. In 2013, Fort Bliss officials had a contamination issue in a bunker once used to store nuclear weapons in the 1950s. One of them told the public "no gamma particles" were detected. That is the same thing as saying, no "sunlight particles" were detected.

Radioactive elements emit various levels of these radiations until they have reached a stable state. For some man-made radioactive materials, this occurs in a few seconds. For other elements a small amount can emit radiation for thousands of years. As they break down they turn into other elements.

At GZ, the elements emitting gamma rays and alpha and beta particles are europium, cesium, cobalt, strontium and plutonium.

Here are some typical radiation exposures **per year** for Americans according to the American Nuclear Society:

*One hour at Trinity Site GZ = one half mrem

*Cosmic rays from space = 47 mrem at Denver, 28 mrem at St. Louis

*Radioactive minerals in rocks and soil = 63 mrem on Colorado Plateau

*Radioactivity from air, water and food = about 240 mrem (mostly from radon)

*Getting A chest X-ray = six mrem and a CAT Scan = 110 mrem

*Watching television = less than one mrem

*A plutonium-powered pacemaker = 100 mrem

Even with this kind of factual information, many Trinity Site visitors allow their emotions and fears to trump any kind of logic or reason. In 2009, after an open house, we found three pairs of good athletic shoes, with socks, laying together in the big parking lot. We didn't feel it likely that all three people would forget their shoes. Instead, we concluded the visitors were afraid to take the shoes and socks home because they might have tiny quantities of radioactive dust on them.

This is a perfect example of how little Americans know about radiation or science in general. For years we have tried to educate visitors by having a radiological display at each open house. The display is manned by missile range technicians who use different instruments to detect the radiation emitted by many common, everyday items. A typical setup has a pack of cigarettes, a banana, a home smoke detector, an old Fiestaware plate, pieces of colored , and a piece of Trinitite. The technicians lecture on the different types of radiation and how common they are. Also, they run a Geiger counter over the items to show how radioactive each is.

Years ago, technician Robert Huffmeyer had his thyroid gland destroyed with radioactive iodine for medical reasons. The procedure was done just days before an open house.

All day Lisa Blevins, another rad-health technician, would run the instrument over the items on the table. Each object would cause a weak audible clicking from the device. Then she put the monitor up to Huffmeyer's throat and the clicking went to a loud and constant buzz. Huffmeyer's thyroid was the hottest thing at Trinity Site that day. That is why patients having the treatment done can't hug their kids for a few days.

In 2010, I escorted astronaut Leroy Chiao to Trinity Site for a visit. When Chiao was with NASA, he flew three space shuttle missions and then spent six months at the International Space Station in 2004-2005 for his fourth mission into space.

We talked about the fact that astronauts receive much higher doses of radiation than the rest of us on the earth's surface. He said that while in the space station there was a solar flare that set off the alarms in the orbiting laboratory. On the second day, as the flare was dying down, they were still receiving 10 times their normal radiation exposure.

The earth's atmosphere absorbs much of the cosmic radiation coming at us from space. There is a direct correlation between altitude and the amount of radiation we receive. That is why Denver residents receive twice as much cosmic radiation as folks in New York City.

Given this fact, it stands to reason that people in commercial airliners flying at altitudes over 35,000 feet receive significantly more radiation than people on the surface. For the average passenger, these levels are not significant. However, for crews that fly several times a week for long periods, the accumulated dose can be higher than that received by many nuclear energy workers.

Most people are surprised to learn that some airline employees and organizations have advocated for radiation standards for the crews just like those standards for the nuclear industry. It turns out that really busy air crews receive radiation, doses just as high as

some workers in common nuclear jobs. Of course, the airline industry has always opposed such a move, and the government has supported them, saying it is unnecessary.

Open Houses

Most documents and old-timers agree the first real public tour of Trinity Site took place in the fall of 1953. Another one was held on the July anniversary date in 1955 and is usually referred to as a religious service with prayers for peace. By 1960, the tours were annual but they were being staged in October because July was just too hot. Attendance was usually in the hundreds.

Early on, these October open houses were scheduled for the first Sunday in the month. By setting the open house on the same Sunday every year, it was the simplest of tasks to look at a calendar and set about planning for the event. All anyone needed was a calendar for the year they were interested in.

Originally, the open house was held on a Sunday because it was basically a religious pilgrimage requested by local churches. Eventually it shifted to Saturday as the religious aspect dwindled and Trinity Site emerged as a true historical place. Chambers of commerce replaced churches as the cosponsors.

My first Trinity Site open house was in October 1977 on a sweltering day with a high close to 100 degrees. The rigid structure of the event made it a bit uncomfortable for the visitors.

Visitors met in Alamogordo or at the Stallion Gate to be escorted by military police to Trinity Site.

The two caravans of cars were timed to arrive about the same time at the site. Everyone parked in the large parking lot on the south side of the outer fence. People were then herded down to GZ. There wasn't much to see except the lava obelisk.

When the hundreds of people were crowded into the inner fenced area, someone from Public Affairs stood and gave a briefing about the history of the test. After that, a ceremony was held with remarks by the WSMR commander, comments from a representative from the Alamogordo Chamber of Commerce, prayers for peace offered by a local minister, and a talk by a featured speaker who saw the test and shared his memories.

It was a long time for people to stand out in the sun. In 1977, it was sweltering and I saw why people fainted every year.

The very next year I was assigned as the Public Affairs coordinator to organize the open house. One thing that caught my eye was that the open house was billed as an event "sponsored by the Alamogordo Chamber of Commerce in cooperation with White Sands Missile Range."

To coordinate the event, I dutifully copied the paperwork from the previous open house, assigning 13 different missile range organizations with their tasks. Requirements ran the gamut from the engineers cleaning up the site and roads; logistics providing water buffalos, buses and other support vehicles with drivers; security manning the gates and escorting the caravans; soldiers providing shade netting and chairs; and finally, we needed those vitally important portable toilets. The document was almost five pages long and ended up requiring dozens and dozens of people to work on a Saturday while putting in hundreds of hours of overtime.

What did the sponsor (Alamogordo C of C) do? They put out a news release, organized the caravan in Alamogordo and got it to the Tularosa gate so our police could take over.

Public Affairs even provided them with the handouts they distributed to each vehicle.

The open houses kept this form until the mid 1980s. I didn't coordinate every one of those early open houses, but I remember my biggest problem each year was finding one of the elderly Trinity Site veterans willing and healthy enough to make the trip and give a talk. That sometimes took weeks to accomplish.

Ranch House Restoration

Then Major General Niles Fulwyler assumed command of White Sands in September 1982. As an Army officer involved with nuclear weapons earlier in his career, he took a great interest in Trinity Site. When he visited the site, he was appalled at the condition of the Schmidt/McDonald ranch house.

Since 1945, the house had simply been abandoned and left to the elements. When I first saw it in 1977, the doors and windows were missing, some adobe walls inside were collapsing because of the leaky roof, the front porch had collapsed, stucco from the outer house walls was laying in piles, the rock wall around the house was knocked down, and all manner of animals lived in and around it.

If we took visitors over to the house for a spe-

cial visit, we always had to warn them to use caution. In the early 1980s, for a visit by Japanese officers to Trinity, I drove one car. When we got to the house, we warned them about rattlesnakes and walked up to the back door. Right in the middle of the step was a big bull snake all curled up.

Those officers took one look at him and practically ran back to the cars. They didn't care if it was a harmless snake. They did not go back to the house.

Fulwyler took immediate steps for White Sands to stabilize what was left at the ranch house so it wouldn't fall into further ruin. Then he convinced the Department of Energy and Department of Army to share the cost of restoring the ranch house to its July 1945 condition. He was able to get the National Park Service, with their decades of interest in the site, to do the restoration planning and work.

The Department of Energy was involved because the United States established the Atomic Energy Commission in 1947 to oversee all things nuclear. That included the development and production of nuclear weapons.

In 1974, the AEC was split up and the resulting agencies given new names. In 1977, the nuclear weapons research and production function ended up in the new cabinet-level Department of Energy. The Manhattan Project legacy passed on to this new organization.

The cost was something less than $250,000 and the project was completed in 1984. There was a bit of controversy about the venture in the form of criticism from the ranchers who lost their property during World War II to form the missile range.

Former rancher Dave McDonald had snuck onto White Sands in 1982 and reaped worldwide publicity for the displaced ranchers. Many felt they were not fairly compensated for the government takeover.

So, when ranchers heard a quarter of a million dollars was being spent on a single ranch house to restore it as a historical exhibit, they cried foul. Many said the money should have been given to them instead.

In addition to restoring the ranch house, some of the money was used to build a new shelter over the preserved portion of the GZ crater floor. We asked for windows or an opening in the roof so visitors could look in at the Trinitite.

Unfortunately, the Trinitite was safely cushioned by several inches of sand and turned out to be completely invisible. In 1991, archaeologist Bob Burton and I removed the sand from a square foot of Trinitite to make sure it was really there. Later we had several feet uncovered so visitors could see it. Within a year, blowing dust had covered the glass deep enough to make it almost impossible to see through any of the openings.

At that point we decided to forgo trying it again. The Trinitite was so fragile, even using fine brushes to remove the dust did some damage. It wasn't worth risking any further harm when there are nice large pieces on display at the radiological exhibit near the inner gate.

The Schmidt/McDonald ranch house was open to the public for the first time during the October 1984 Trinity Site open house,. Interest in the house generated a big crowd that day, matching the record anniversary crowd of 2,500 in 1975. In addition, we still had a ceremony at 11 a.m. with guest speaker Bob Krohn.

There was no parking at the ranch house, so we supplied a number of buses to provide shuttle service back and forth from the parking area to the house.

We had an instant problem. Everyone wanted to be at GZ at 11 a.m. to hear Mr. Krohn, plus everyone wanted to catch a bus to the ranch house. And they were only going to be at the site a couple of hours.

The line to ride the buses quickly crossed the parking lot and created traffic congestion. At the ranch house, a very proud Fulwyler wanted to give small groups of people guided tours of the house, so he could relate its history and what had been done to restore it. People were standing in a line a hundred yards long waiting just to get in the house.

It was all taking too long. It was very obvious to us we needed to change our approach to the open houses if we were going to have such large crowds. We couldn't subject visitors to such long lines and long waits.

The solution was to deemphasize the personal touch. The main roadblock we encountered was our woeful lack of resources – lack of money, space and manpower. The best and cheapest method was to simply spread the crowd out so our limited infrastructure could work.

In 1986 we added a second open house in April, hoping to move some visitors from October to the spring.

Also, we eliminated the whole ceremony – no more speakers or prayers. After that there was no reason for all the visitors to want to be at the site at the same time. They could visit in the morning or early afternoon.

We had already eliminated the old caravans from the Stallion Gate to the site. Visitors were able to check in and drive themselves the 17 miles to Trinity Site. Eventually, we widened that window from 8 a.m. to 2 p.m. If a visitor showed up anytime between those hours, they would be allowed to drive down to the site. The ones showing up at the end of the day usually experienced a limited visit as everyone supporting the event was tired and either gone or packing up to leave.

Since we could no longer provide briefings for each visitor, we had to resort to signs and handouts to tell the history of Trinity Site. At first, we used temporary signs but eventually missile range archaeologist Mike Maloof got us the money to erect permanent signs at the ranch house, Jumbo and GZ.

In addition, I put together a brochure that is given to every vehicle entering the site. We printed them by the tens of thousands.

The new procedures worked. Then, for some reason, crowds began to grow even more. However, we found we were able to deal with them using our new system. In April 1989, we set a new record with 3,400 visitors. In April 1992, we saw 3,600 visitors. Outside of peaks like these, the crowds have been fairly consistent at 2,000 to 3,000 people per open house since 1990.

Most of the big crowds were in April. Since the weather is usually worse in April, the only explanation we had was the great amount of activity in October throughout New Mexico. For instance, the October open house is always the same weekend as the Albuquerque Balloon Fiesta and other celebrations throughout the area.

The timing of the April open house has created some problems in that it is sometimes on the day before Easter. When that happens, the office receives many calls from people wanting to know if the site is really going to be open.

Other questions are a bit harder to understand. Debbie Bingham, a co-worker in Public Affairs for almost 30 years, once took a call from someone asking about the day. The caller said they understood the open house was always on the first Saturday in April but this year the first of April was going to be on a Sunday. "Could it be," the caller asked, "that White Sands considers the Saturday before April 1 as the first Saturday of April." Debbie about fell out of her chair but calmly explained, "No, that would be the last Saturday in March. The first Saturday in April will be on the seventh."

In 1995, for the 50th anniversary of Trinity, we underestimated the public's interest in the site. First of all, we had to get command approval to open the site on the actual anniversary date which happened to be on a Sunday. Then CNN and some members of the public called about being on the site at exactly 5:30 a.m., when the bomb exploded. The news network planned to broadcast live via satellite at 5:30.

We basically set up the open houses like the regular ones but eliminated the Alamogordo caravan, using only the Stallion gate, and opened the gate from 5 a.m. to 11 a.m. With the early morning hours, we thought we could accommodate the few who wanted to be there at 5:30 and also get most people off the site before the heat of the day.

When the day arrived, we expected a hundred people might be waiting at the Stallion gate at 5 a.m. We were very wrong. The line of cars was backed up for miles. We took one look and thought "these people are nuts."

Eventually we counted over 5,300 visitors.

It was also our only real encounter with protestors. Very early on, someone rushed toward the obelisk and threw a red liquid on the monument, saying it was symbolic blood. The military police quickly grabbed the person and carted him off to the Stallion gate.

Still very early in the morning, we had a group of 50 to 60 people who looked, smelled and talked very much the way I remember college students in the late 60s. Eventually, they linked hands to form a circle around the obelisk and chanted as they danced around it. They called for others to join in but everyone just watched. They were really leftover hippies.

The military police wanted to wade in and arrest them. We asked for restraint since they weren't a threat to anyone - there were a lot of them. It was not very long before they tired of the song and dance and quietly went away.

By 7 a.m. we were running a quiet and typical open house. Visitors, for the most part, were appreciative of the opportunity to be there on the 16th.

Once in a while, a problem would arise at an open house that no one had foreseen. During the October 1991 open house, only the first 37 cars in the Alamogordo caravan made the turn in the town of Tularosa to go to the missile range gate. The other 120 cars just kept going straight north headed to Carrizozo on U.S. Highway 54.

Apparently, in making its way from Alamogordo to Tularosa through the many stoplights along the way, the 38th car totally lost contact with the car in front of it. Its driver just keep going straight through Tularosa. Many locals told us later they knew it was wrong to head to Carrizozo, but there wasn't much they could do.

Most of the lost visitors made it to Trinity Site anyway by going west from Carrizozo to the Stallion Gate. It was a long drive for them.

We learned our lesson there and hinted that the Alamogordo Chamber of Commerce might want to make sure they have someone at the turnoff making sure the whole caravan got to Trinity. A few years later that arrangement led to a different kind of problem.

Again, the caravan was stopped and pulled apart by stoplights on the way to Tularosa. This time there was an officer at the turn off with his vehicle's lights flashing. He stood by the side of the road and mindlessly signaled cars to turn to the west.

When the caravan arrived at Trinity Site, a young girl, not more than 16, got out of her car shaking and crying. She asked where she was and how was she ever going to get to the wedding rehearsal in Tularosa from out in the desert.

It turned out she got mixed in with all the cars heading north out of Alamogordo, saw the officer, with lights flashing, signaling to the left. She thought something was wrong so she followed the crowd.

Once we assured her it would be all right, we gave her some gasoline and one of the police officers escorted her back to Tularosa. I doubt she made the rehearsal, but she was back in plenty of time to attend the wedding.

Probably the best thing I ever did for the Trinity Site open houses was convince my boss and the Alamogordo Chamber of Commerce to change the caravan starting point to jettison the drive through the minefield of stoplights. I knew it was politically impossible to kill the caravan so I found a way to make it run smoother for everyone.

The suggestion was to organize and start the caravan at the football stadium parking lot on the west side of the village of Tularosa. From that lot it is almost a straight shot on a back road, without traffic lights or traffic, to the missile range's gate.

Because of this change, state police and sheriff's deputies are no longer required – no more lost caravans or hijacked drivers caught up in the rush.

A Powerful Symbol

For most open house visitors Trinity Site is a historical curiosity. They come to see what all the discussion is about.

For some, however, Trinity Site is a powerful emotional symbol for them personally. They feel or believe they can pray there, chant there, or engage in some ceremony that will make a difference. We have had people sit or kneel on the ground at GZ and say they are praying to heal the earth. At the very least it makes them feel good.

Those two bombs dropped on Japan killed a lot of people very, very quickly. For decades, people all around the world have feared such weapons might actually destroy mankind. In America, Christians have been the main proponents for symbolically praying for peace at Trinity Site. The U.S. military, like Congress and other government entities, has no problem with "Christian" prayer, so the original open houses started with prayers for peace.

When a similar request came in 2005 from individuals representing a group of Japanese Zen Buddhist monks, officials took a long hard look at the request. Some of use wondered if Buddhist prayer would be allowed. In the end, it was decided these monks were the real deal, and White Sands had no overwhelming reason to deny their request.

Their story was that when Hiroshima was bombed in 1945, they lit a fire from the smoldering ruins and kept it burning for 60 years. During much of that , they trekked all over the world carrying a portion of the flame to promote peace and the end of nuclear weapons.

In Buddhism, 60 years is a complete cycle, like the life of a man. Since the atomic bomb cycle was coming to an end in July 2005, they believed that by extinguishing their flame where it began (Trinity Site) they might end the "nuclear cycle."

So a small group of supporters and the monks were allowed to walk into Trinity Site on Aug. 9, 2005. It was 60 years to the day from when a nuclear weapon was last used on human beings. In a short ceremony at the obelisk, they extinguished the flame to close the circle.

The ceremony was filmed by the monks' support group. A summary video is now available on *YouTube*.

The Real Trinitite Story

Just when you think you really know some fact or truth – not believe it, but know it – something comes along to rock your boat. That is the great thing about science. It allows for better explanations that only require better proof. No holy books need to be rewritten.

That happened to us in 2003 when we got involved with Robb Hermes and Bill Strickfaden from Los Alamos. Hermes was a polymer chemist with the lab at that time and Strickfaden was a retired physicist and independent investigator. Their work has completely rewritten the story of how Trinitite was formed.

They contacted us and asked for samples of sand from both GZ and an area outside the outer fence. They said they could use the samples to recalculate the yield of the bomb.

And, by the way, they added, could they get some samples of anthill sand from GZ? We said sure, and on the next trip to Trinity Site we filled some quart plastic bags with the appropriate sand and mailed them to Hermes.

Not long after, Hermes contacted me excited about the ant sand. He said there were small balls or spheres of glass mixed in with the sand. In other words, there were tiny beads of Trinitite mixed in. Some weren't much bigger than a pinhead, but some were larger and clearly balls, not sherds. People have found larger spheres that are about the size of pearls which are appropriately called "Trinitite pearls."

Plus, they were easily identifiable as Trinitite because they were radioactive, just like the big chunks.

Hermes said that many of the sample chunks of Trinitite stored at the lab were shiny and smooth on top but rough and irregular on the bottom. On some of the pieces, spheres were clearly embedded in the mixture.

The old explanation that was accepted for 60 years about the formation of Trinitite was that the fireball simply melted the surface of the crater and turned it to glass. Kevin Casey, who was in Public

Affairs at the time, called it the "Trinitite crème brulee effect."

This old explanation did nothing to account for the spheres.

Strickfaden said he modeled the explosion knowing the height of the explosion, its basic yield, and the kind of sand found at GZ. Using different models, he could not generate enough heat on the surface to form Trinitite over a half-inch thick. The fireball just wasn't there long enough.

That set them on a course looking for another mechanism to form the glass. When they looked at old reports and photos of the crater, as in the Groves account, they realized quite a bit of material was actually gouged out of the crater. The crater wasn't simply smashed down and compressed forming a nice dinner plate surface.

The two quickly realized that if this material was thrown up into the fireball, the tremendous heat would have melted the sand and turned it to a mist of liquid rock.

At this point, it became something like raindrop physics. Droplets bumped into each other to form larger ones. Eventually, they fell back to the ground. In some cases, the tiny spheres were suspended long enough to solidify and remain beads after they hit. Other drops hit as a liquid and spread into puddles.

"Much of the layer was formed not on the ground but by a rain of material injected into the fireball that melted, fell back, and collected on the hot sand to form the observed puddles of Trinitite, especially within the radius of the hottest part of the event," they concluded in an article for the Fall 2005 issue of *Nuclear Weapons Journal.*

"After falling to the ground, the top surface of the Trinitite layer was still heated somewhat by the fireball and thus developed a smooth surface . . . We calculated an average fireball temperature of 8,430 Kelvin," they reported. That's about 14,710 degrees Fahrenheit.

Their theory nicely explains the spheres. It also explains why there was Trinitite found on asphalt and on top of fence posts and rocks afterward.

In this process of examining Trinitite, they were

Some of the Trinitite beads collected by Robb Hermes and Bill Strickfaden at Trinity Site. Many of these tiny spheres and dumbbells were unearthed by ants on the site. Stickfaden made many of his photographs of the Trinitite samples using an ordinary computer scanner. Photo by Bill Strickfaden.

able to confirm that the green color of the glass is simply caused by the amount of iron found in the sand. Since ancient times, craftsmen knew how to add iron oxide to liquid glass to tint it green.

In one trip to Trinity with them, we discovered a few chunks of the very rare red Trinitite. Los Alamos analyzed one piece and Hermes reported the red is from copper mixed in with the glass. There were large copper coaxial cables running up the north side of the tower; that wiring is probably the source of the copper. Supporting that idea is the fact that the red glass was found north of GZ.

During the October 2011 Trinity open house, I was answering questions at GZ when a young boy and his father approached me. The man told his son to show me what he had found pawing around in the dirt. The boy held out a glob of Trinitite, not quite a sphere, that was mostly white with just a tinge of turquoise.

In visiting Trinity Site for more than 30 years, I had never seen such a color. I thanked the boy and tucked the Trinitite away for safekeeping. I then sent it to Hermes at Los Alamos for analysis. He reported their quick-look showed the white was caused by calcium, probably from the calcite or caliche in the soil.

Having an imagination that sometimes wanders outside the confines of scientific analysis, I quickly theorized the calcium could have come from the bones of some poor slob chained to the 100-foot tower at the time of the test. We just might have a murder case on our hands. Wink.

Since the initial report, Hermes has pursued his quest to learn as much about Trinitite as possible. He has even acquired a piece of glass from the first Soviet test site where Joe-1 was exploded. That glass is a deeper greenish black but has the same texture and qualities of Trinitite including the spherical inclusions on the bottom. Since Joe-1 was a carbon copy of the Trinity event, including a 100-foot tower, it means their glass was probably formed the same way.

Then in early 2010, Hermes discovered a buried Los Alamos report from 1947 that postulated the same theory he and Strickfaden had come up with for the dispersion of Trinitite. This document was classified as "secret" when written, so very few people were privy to the information. If the document had been available earlier, maybe the crème brulee theory never would have grown into the myth it has become.

In addition to their reformulation of the Trinitite story, Hermes and Strickfaden waded into the issue of the size of the GZ crater. Previously I have quoted measurements presented by Groves and F. Reines.

Hermes and Strickfaden examined aerial photos taken of the crater the day after the test. The very dense negatives were perfect for enlarging – so much that they could clearly see the four tower footings protruding from the surface.

From this and other information in the Los Alamos archives, they calculated the crater had a diameter of about 250 feet and the spread of Trinitite covered a circle with a diameter of close to 2,000 feet. They concluded various people, over the years, have confused the crater with the covering of Trinitite at the site.

The bottom line here is that we have new numbers from very reliable sources.

Myths And Misinformation

Over the years we worked hard to present factual information about Trinity Site and its history. If we made mistakes, we corrected them. However, correcting other people's mistakes proved pretty much impossible.

The news media are always making mistakes. Because the Trinity Site story is a little history and a lot of science, many reporters are not equipped to retell the tale.

In 1989, *New Mexico Magazine* ran an article on Trinity Site, stating the bomb tested was uranium based and not plutonium. This seems like a pretty big oops when you are talking about the very first bomb.

The author also called Jumbo a "bomb casing." Actually this is a very common error. We often hear visitors at the site talking to family or friends explaining that Jumbo is the Fatman bomb casing.

This error seems a bit remarkable when these same people seem astounded that the Schmidt/McDonald ranch house survived the explosion. To them an atomic explosion is so big it destroys everything for miles and miles. Given that belief, I've always wanted to ask how would a bomb casing survive the test?

Also, the author botched the entrance procedures by telling visitors they had to drive in a caravan from Stallion gate. That was old information from years before. His error gave us fits because lots of people read the magazine and wanted to show up at the time the caravan left. So much for spreading out our crowd during the day.

Sometimes we wondered what a writer was thinking, especially when they have the correct information readily at hand. Years ago, a historian who visited Trinity Site several times wrote a short piece about Jumbo for one of the *Smithsonian* magazines. In it he told readers that if they wanted to see Jumbo, they would have to go to Alamogordo and enter with the caravan.

He didn't mention the Stallion gate or that 75% of the visitors enter there. I wrote the magazine that the author's directions were a bit like suggesting the best way to see the Washington Monument was to fly into Baltimore first. The distances are similar.

Sometimes writers get the day completely wrong and say it is the first Sunday or some such thing. This obviously causes the missile range some bother, but it has to be a major headache for those who act on the wrong information and show up for nothing. Sometimes they are quite irate to be turned away – they wasted a great deal of time and money.

When the Internet started to grow and Public Affairs established a webpage, I was able to develop a page devoted to Trinity Site misinformation and myths. Some of the postings seemed to make a difference.

For instance, there were a number of people regularly selling pieces of Trinitite on *eBay*. Most of them said the glass was from Trinity Site located in the Tularosa Basin, Otero County or near Alamogordo. None of that is true. So I posted quotes from their ads and web pages along with the correct info. After a while, they started to change their statements and eventually most were at least getting the location correct.

Other myths and misinformation include: the idea that radiation at the site will fog your film; that there were soldiers taken to the site on a train and forced to observe the blast from close-in trenches; that you have to pay to get into the site or reserve a spot with some outside organization or company to get in; that the gypsum sands at White Sands National Monument are white as a result of the bomb test; that roadblocks along U.S. Highway 70 during the 1950s were for atomic bomb tests on the missile range; and that you can see GZ while flying on a commercial flight between El Paso and Albuquerque.

Concerning the last myth, I was on a commercial flight where the crew pointed out what they thought was GZ to the east of the airplane – the missile range's airspace is off limits to commercial aircraft. What they pointed out was a warhead impact target area on the west edge of White Sands, called Stallion WIT. The target area is graded regularly so it is barren sand. It shows up very well against the surrounding grasslands. GZ is visible but it is covered with grass and much harder to detect, especially from the distance of a commercial airliner.

Trinity And Aliens From Inner Space

Finally, my favorite story about Trinity Site involves a package I received years ago from Mark Harp in Memphis, Tennessee. Basically he sent a thesis and supporting letters explaining how the earth was really hollow. At one time he even had a webpage devoted to this pet project.

He said the governments of the world know the earth is hollow and they are keeping it a secret from the rest of us. There is supposedly access to this inner world through large holes at the earth's poles. I'm not sure what keeps the water out of the hole at the North Pole since that pole is in the ocean.

Inside the earth is a sun-like energy source floating in the center of the void and a humanoid civilization living in this subterranean realm. I suspect Mr. Harp saw "Superman and the Mole Men" on television when he was a boy.

His story continues that on July 16, 1945, the atomic bomb explosion at Trinity Site so shook the planet that these humanoids were, hmmm, shaken by the experience. They wondered what it was. Maybe there was some danger approaching.

So they built a flying machine and sent a team out the hole at the North Pole to fly down to New Mexico and investigate. Unfortunately, their vehicle malfunctioned and crashed in the desert northeast of Trinity Site. You guessed it – near Roswell.

What the rancher and military personnel found when they investigated was not an alien ship from "outer space" but an alien ship from "inner space."

Right Or Wrong Or Is It More Complicated?

Frequently visitors to Trinity Site want to discuss or argue about the use of the atomic bomb on Japan. Sometimes they try to engage the government officials and sometimes they connect with each other.

Most are very civil but sometimes tempers flare. During the 50th anniversary open house, the military police had to step in and physically separate three individuals who seemed ready to let fists fly.

Here are the main arguments for and against presented in no particular order:

*It was inhumane to target civilian population.

*The military should have done a demo for the Japanese government.

*They were ready to surrender anyway.

*Fighting month after month, island to island, demonstrated that the Japanese, military and civilians alike were ready to fight to the death. Huge numbers seemed to be ready to commit suicide for the emperor.

*An invasion would have cost America and its allies, tens of thousands of lives and probably over a million Japanese lives.

*The bombs provided a quick and surprising end to the war. It was so sudden that most Japanese POW camp commanders never had a chance to carry out their "kill them all" order, thus saving thousands of POWs from extermination.

*The Soviets declared war on Japan in August and prepared to invade. If the war had continued, Japan would have ended up as a divided country like Germany. Over the decades, millions of Japanese probably would have disappeared to work camps in Siberia and elsewhere in support of the Soviet empire.

*The horrors of Hiroshima and Nagasaki left indelible images for decades following World War II. Because of those graphic photos and stories, so far, no world leader has been willing to "pull the trigger" on the use of nuclear weapons. President Truman fired the very popular General McArthur for proposing and publicly advocating their use against the Chinese in Korea. Without that Japanese example, McArthur might have gotten his way, and the result could have been a major exchange of nuclear weapons killing tens of millions of people.

*Finally, I heard one story about a British philanthropist who was invited to the annual Hiroshima memorial service. He was invited because of his humanitarian work around the world and in Japan after the war. I guess the assumption was that he would be very sympathetic to the organizer's cause. When he arrived, he was questioned by the Japanese news media. They asked what he thought about what the Americans had done to them at Hiroshima. The man took a second to consider the Japanese atrocities in China, Korea, the Philippines and Indochina. He then said, "I think you probably got what you asked for." He was immediately uninvited to the event and left standing on the airport tarmac.

Trinity's Contribution To Extinction Theory

Supporters of big budget military research projects often say you never know what non-military information or advancement you might get from the research and development of weapons. For instance, the German V-2 rocket quickened the civilian effort to put a man on the moon, and the Department of Defense's Global Positioning System (GPS) has made an easy and revolutionary move into the civilian world.

In 2012, information gleaned from the Trinity Site test was being used to defend a controversial theory about an asteroid impact that may have almost overnight cooled and dried the planet. The cooling lasted for over a thousand years before the heat was turned up once again.

The asteroid impact theory is a bit controversial now with a great deal of opposition. However there are supporters, just like in the early days of the plate tectonics theory, who are rushing to find supporting evidence. At this point, no one can tell if this new idea will have a positive result like plate tectonics.

Toward the end of the last ice age 20,000 years ago, the earth began a steady warming program that was running smoothly. Ice sheets were retreating and the average temperature was on the rise. From a modern human's point of view, things were definitely looking good.

Then, 12,900 years ago, there was a sudden hiccup in the big thaw. It is called the Younger Dryas period. Temperatures dropped and much of the planet was plunged into a drought.

Of course, this wasn't the effect everywhere. Weather patterns were altered and local results were as varied as the different continents. For instance, in some areas there was increased snowfall in mountain ranges, forests disappeared in places like Scandinavia to be replaced with tundra, and in North America human beings may have had some difficulty finding enough to eat as many animals went extinct. Some say the people responsible for the Clovis culture may have declined because of this occurrence.

Explanations for what happened are varied. In 2012, a look at *Wikipedia* revealed the prevailing theory was linked to a flood of fresh water into the Atlantic Ocean from melting glaciers that, in turn, interfered with the warming effects of tropical waters flowing north. Another explanation was increased volcanic activity may have created a "nuclear" winter scenario. Finally, some propose a solar flare may have altered the atmosphere.

The *Wikipedia* authors also mention an asteroid impact theory but generally spurn it as highly unlikely with little physical evidence. That may be changing rapidly.

So what is the impact theory? Basically, it is the nuclear winter idea with an asteroid or comet instead of a hydrogen bomb exchange being responsible for the tremendous gush of dust and smoke into the atmosphere. One problem with this idea is that the event was not long ago, and there is no big impact crater anywhere to be found.

However, two impact events – one here on earth and one in the far reaches of the solar system – triggered the imaginations of a few scientists. The first event was the asteroid/comet explosion over Tunguska, Russia on June 30, 1908.

When scientists went to Tunguska, they found 80 million trees covering 830 square miles flattened. They also found no gigantic crater.

It took several years, but scientists eventually figured out that something, an asteroid or comet, exploded about three to six miles up with the force of one thousand Hiroshima atomic bombs. And it never touched the ground to leave a crater like the huge Meteor Crater in Arizona.

Since then we have learned that both comets and heavy items, like asteroids, can explode in the atmosphere and create the equivalent of a high altitude nuclear burst.

The second event was the breakup and collision of Comet Shoemaker-Levy 9 with Jupiter in July 1994. This event ignited the imaginations of scientists around the world who watched the event unfold. People started to see the possibilities of such an event.

It was electrifying because it was man's first eyewitness experience of seeing a big object strike a planet. Of even more interest was the fact the comet broke up into many large pieces on approach over a period of about a week.

Because of the timing and the rotation of Jupiter, each comet chunk hit a different spot on the planet. Suddenly, applying the scenario to earth, questions started to bubble up. What if a busted up asteroid hit the earth 12,900 years ago in a series of impacts spread around the world creating a series of huge explosions? And secondly, what if the chunks hit at the right angle and exploded in the atmosphere leaving few craters, if any?

So, the proposal is that the pieces of asteroid were big enough to blast large sections of the planet and send lots of smoke and dust into the atmosphere to create an "asteroid winter." So far researchers have found only one crater and that doesn't seem like enough smoke. Now the question is, how do you prove there were other explosions?

Robb Hermes, our Los Alamos Trinitite guru, has been pulled into the effort to prove the impact theory because of his research and knowledge concerning the glass formed in the Trinity test in 1945. It turns out that nuclear explosions are similar to high-speed asteroid explosions in that they are hot enough to liquefy minerals and turn them into glassy substances.

This is important because scientists have recovered glassy spheres and other blobs from sites in Asia, Europe and North America. Mostly these glassy items are made from minerals common to asteroids, not earth-bound rocks, and they have been consistently recovered from a layer of soil easily dated to 12,900 years ago.

According to Hermes, there were no Fatman atomic bombs 12,900 years ago to make these glass spheroids, and other human activities like firing pottery and making glass couldn't generate the heat needed until well into the industrial age.

Scientists looked at natural possibilities like wildfires, volcanoes, lightning and collisions from space. It turns out the first two are not hot enough.

Lightning is hot enough but its ground impacts are pretty much confined to making fulgurites in very small areas – like a few feet. Materials found in association with the Younger Dryas research are spread over miles. In comparing the lightning-generated glass to the samples found in association with Younger Dryas sites and Trinity Site, they are nothing alike.

That leaves the asteroid collision/explosion explanation. It turns out the glasses created in the Trinity Site test match very well with the material found so far on several continents dating back 12,900 years.

As with any new theory or explanation, it takes a lot of evidence and reasoning before the majority of scientists accept it. Sometimes it can go one way or the other very quickly, if the science is good. It will be interesting to see in the next few years if there is enough evidence to feed and nurture this new theory.... or will it be overrun by something else?

Captain Bush on his horse Honesty. Bush was much appreciated by his men. Everyone on record spoke highly of him and of his civil treatment of the men stuck at Trinity Site. Photo courtesy of Marvin Davis.

How A Test Range Works

For decades White Sands Missile Range has been referred to as a huge outdoor laboratory, a place where weapons and civilian products can be tested to see if they worked as advertised. At one time the range's welcome brochure stated the labs and personnel "shake, rattle and roll the product, roast it, freeze it, subject it to radiation, dip it in salt water, and roll it in the mud. We test its paint, bend its frame and find out what effect its propulsion material has on flora and fauna." In the end, if the item was a missile, it might actually be fired at a target.

White Sands is a unique combination of geography, laboratories, weather, personnel and support activities making it almost ideal for modern testing. Most people only see the range on their radar if there is a missile firing requiring a roadblock on the highway and they are stuck in it. Sometimes they see the contrail in the sky left by a rocket after it has been launched. But as a rule, folks in the communities surrounding the missile range have very little real knowledge of what goes on.

First of all, who can use the services provided by White Sands has grown to include almost anyone. It could be the U.S. Army, another U.S. military service, another U.S. government agency, a university, a foreign ally or an organization, company, or individual with the where-with-all to pay for the service. There is one caveat. If the testing service is readily available from a commercial source, non-government users will have to go there first for testing services.

The users at White Sands are often called customers since they pay for the missile range's support. The fees for the services are scaled depending on the customer. Since White Sands is a taxpayer-support-

ed institution, it doesn't make much sense for other taxpayer organizations like the Navy to pay full price. They get the cheapest rates. A commercial enterprise, on the other hand, is at the highest cost levels, since it wouldn't be appropriate for the taxpayer to support their endeavors.

This brings up one of the great problems White Sands has in trying to be self-supporting, as in trying to model itself as a business.

When President Reagan and others pushed hard to "make government more like business" they put places like White Sands at a huge disadvantage. For decades now, men and women running for the House and Senate proclaim their business backgrounds and promise they will fix the government by making it run like a business.

On the surface, it looks great. The idea is that by making WSMR live by a strict budget and compete for work like a business that rents cars or cleans carpets, White Sands will supposedly become more efficient.

The big problem, and it is BIG, with this idea is the larger, overriding principle that government cannot compete with private enterprise for work. If a company wants to test its umbrellas at White Sands, the missile range probably won't be able to accept the work because, more than likely, the testing can be done by a private outfit. The rule shrinks the customer pool to a handful of possibilities when you can't compete against your competition.

The rule is very understandable since White Sands was built and is maintained with taxpayer dollars. It would be unfair for such an organization to compete against private companies. The bottom line here is that all those Congressmen and Senators who say they are businessmen and know how to fix the government will have to perform magic because White Sands is not really like any company.

It leaves folks at White Sands in an interesting position. Their work is absolutely necessary for usable, modern military equipment. Without such testing, the country would be sending out its men and women with equipment that just might let them down and send them home in a casket. But it is an esoteric task.

In the end, the folks who manage WSMR facilities and the range itself use many of the best business skills so valued by those in private enterprise. Just because an organization like White Sands has a bad quarter or year doesn't mean it should fail, as you might expect in private industry. The test function is going to be needed again. So, WSMR's bureaucrats and upper-level managers carefully and deftly balance budgets, workloads and personnel strength, getting the most from their meager resources.

They can bend but they cannot be allowed to break. As long as there are military personnel in harm's way, White Sands needs to continue to function. There may be times when the business version of WSMR can't pay cash dividends but the payoff in lives, our own sons and daughters, is more valuable.

Testing Capabilities

In the beginning, the testing was pretty simple with WAC Corporals and V-2s being fired. However, the V-2 is an excellent example of how White Sands testing includes much more than simply launching missiles.

For example, the V-2's propulsion pumping system was pretested by performing a dry run on a small test stand located just to the west of the main V-2 assembly building. For safety and convenience, the pumps circulated just water as they were measured to see if they would push the prescribed volume of liquid oxygen and alcohol to the engine.

After this calibration test, the propulsion unit or the rocket with the unit in place was strapped in a static test stand and actually fired using live fuel to see if it was working correctly.

In the end, the V-2 was buttoned up and launched with its payload.

Over the years the testing needs have grown tremendously. In response, White Sands developed a profusion of test capabilities and organizations to run them. To try and trace that development would require a very long and esoteric chapter, maybe a whole book actually. Suffice it to say, the organizations running the test mission have been split up, rearranged, reunited and renamed many times as the demands have changed.

Sometimes the reorganizations were done because some influential individual or higher-level organization thought they had a better idea on how things should be run. It has not been unusual for a series of changes to occur over a 20-year period only to end up back where they started. Only those who are there for a career get to see such "reinvention of the wheel."

Regardless of the organization and what the offices are called, the kinds of testing are still very recognizable. Subjecting a missile's launcher to freezing rain hasn't changed much over the decades no matter what jargon is used.

In addition, the methods of collecting information haven't basically changed but they sure have improved. These changes/improvements have been driven by each generation of whiz-bang weapon system tested at White Sands.

Labs

One kind of testing which is easy to understand is climate simulation. Everybody knows the weather can affect the machines we use.

So it is July in the New Mexico desert and the customer really wants to see how his missile will perform in Alaska in January. The solution is easy. White Sands can provide a large portable freezing unit to take the missile down to the desired temperature – say 20 below zero. When it comes time to fire, the missile can quickly be removed, placed in its launcher, and at "zero" there is fire and smoke.

It isn't unusual to see testers wearing heavy gloves and parkas in the summer as they tend a cold chamber. On the other hand, when they are testing at temperatures way over 100 degrees, the same kind of clothing protects the technicians from the blistering heat.

Want rain? The range can generate a nice steady drizzle or a monsoon downpour of 27 inches per hour. Want wind with that? Giant fans can be used to blow the rain sideways at speeds up to 40 miles per hour.

Even though WSMR is in the middle of an arid desert subject to huge spring dust storms, they can't be summoned on demand. So, dust storms have to be artificially created in a dust chamber. High altitudes can be duplicated in special vacuum chambers.

Sometimes these things come in handy for other uses. After the big flood of 1978, valuable documents in basements were soaked. Some of them found their way into a vacuum chamber to be dried in a very gentle way – by literally sucking the water out of them.

Another area that is easily understood is dynamics. This is where items are subjected to the shock and vibration they might encounter in the real world. For instance, an entire missile can be placed on a special table that can vibrate so fast you can't see it move. However, the missile experiences the kinds of stress it might experience during flight. Afterward, the missile can be taken apart and checked for damage.

Large shaker tables can accommodate whole vehicles and can move several inches in any direction. These can be programmed to simulate the potholes and washboard conditions of road transportation and, in just a matter of hours, simulate a journey of many days.

Part of this testing is the simple drop test. End users want to know if the missile is still usable after they accidently drop the shipping crate off the truck. Drop tests will provide some parameters in deciding to use it or send it back.

The range used to have a microbiology lab. One of its most important functions was to perform standard fungus tests. For instance, back in the 60s, the lab found that those first electronic circuit boards, if left untreated, could be made useless in a matter of days. Fungus was able to live off nutrients found in the mounting material and, as it grew, it bridged the wiring and shorted everything out. The testing became standard after some unpleasant experiences in Vietnam when new electronic gear quit working simply because of the environment.

Scientists at the lab also showed that fungus could live off a little water trapped in a vehicle's diesel fuel tank. As the fungus multiplied it would eventually clog the fuel filter and bring everything to a halt.

One area of testing not related to your normal, everyday environment is for equipment on the battlefield where nuclear weapons have been used. In such a hostile situation, the radios, tanks, helicopters and missiles must continue to work.

The organization responsible for this kind of testing used to be called the Nuclear Effects Laboratory. Years ago the organization dropped the taboo term "nuclear" from the title and went to something a bit more generic which doesn't give away what kind of work they do. The new title is the "Survivability, Vulnerability and Assessment Directorate" or SVAD for short. Outsiders might guess they test anything from helicopters to umbrellas to chocolate chip cookies.

Actually, the organization's managers could say they like the vagueness of their title because they just might snare a new customer who calls asking for details.

In nuclear effects, electromagnetic pulses can be generated over specific pieces of equipment; whole vehicles can be exposed to huge static electricity discharges or gamma radiation; and a solar furnace can produce the surface heating found in a nuclear blast.

The solar furnace is one of the most obvious objects on White Sands. Its large arrangement of mirrors and sits right beside the road coming in from the El Paso gate.

It was built in the late 1960s at Natick, Massachusetts but was moved to White Sands and put into operation in 1972. When the mirrors are nice and clean and the sky perfectly cloudless, the furnace can focus the sun's rays to generate about 5,000 degrees F. over a four-inch circle. It can melt a hole through a quarter-inch-thick piece of stainless steel in well under a minute.

For tours of the facility the guides used to pull out some common objects that the employees burned holes through. One of the favorites was an old cast iron frying pan with a nice hole burned through the bottom. The melted material was still stuck to the edges.

The furnace is pretty simple. The "heliostat," a flat panel of mirrors measuring 40 feet by 36 feet, can move and track the sun. Most all of the light from the mirrors is directed to the "concentrator," a cluster of spherical mirrors. Each concentrator mirror is pointed and focused back into the test chamber that sits between the two sets of mirrors.

Also, between the heliostat and the concentrator is the "attenuator." This is basically a huge Venetian blind that can be left wide open to let all the sunlight through or closed to any desired degree to reduce the

The missile range's solar furnace just west of the El Paso gate. The concentrator is in the vertical gray box on the left while the heliostat is the flat reflecting panel on the right. The attenuator is just to the right of the concentrator with the test chamber elevated to the right of it. WSMR photo.

amount of light hitting the concentrator and thus the test cell.

Inside the test cell, the testers can mount a shutter system to provide very short bursts of light – like one might find in a nuclear blast.

So, what kind of testing do you do with sunlight? A test done decades ago was for the Air Force to see if some fancy new aircrew goggles would darken instantaneously when exposed to a blinding flash – like if an atomic bomb went off nearby. It was easy to do at the furnace.

They put a life-size mannequin in the test cell dressed in his flight suit, helmet and a set of the goggles. Behind the goggles, where the eyes would be, sensors were placed to measure the strength of the light coming through the goggles for the duration of the flash.

Apparently the goggles worked very well, but the site's test crew reported the pilot's clothing caught fire because of the intense heat from the flash.

Another example was a totally non-military application. A research group wanted to see if the sun's heat could be used to "gasify" coal. The coal was ground up into a fine powder and exposed to the sun's rays. The coal flashed to gas with useful end products being natural gas and methane.

Radiological sources at Nuclear Effects can be used to expose components and whole missiles or vehicles to gamma radiation like that found during a nuclear explosion. On a smaller scale, there is a semiconductor lab to test computer chips in a nuclear environment.

The nuclear effects group runs a couple of electromagnetic pulse (EMP) facilities. There is a great deal of EMP test capability because the potential impact from an EMP during an overhead nuclear explosion could be devastating to modern military equipment.

The entertainment business has grabbed this idea. In the movie *Red Dawn 2*, puny North Korea is able to invade the United States because they are able to create an EMP that puts the country and military out of business.

An electromagnetic pulse moving from its source wouldn't affect humans but would induce an electrical charge in any conductor it encountered. Theoretically, the charge imparted could be big enough to fry electrical components. That could render tanks, jeeps, helicopters, airplanes, communications – all kinds of equipment – useless until fixed.

What most people don't realize is that transmissions from radio stations, CB radios, and cell phones are electromagnetic pulses as well, just much weaker.

Back in the early 1980s, as airbags were being developed and installed in automobiles, someone asked what would happen if the airbag's controlling microchips encountered the electromagnetic radiation from a nearby radio station transmitter or the radiation from the CB radio in the car next to you. The issue was about the very low voltage in the little processors and whether enough current could be induced in the system to accidentally fire the airbags. This would not be a good thing to experience doing 75 miles per hour on the freeway.

Many car manufacturers came to White Sands to test their air bag assemblies and, in some cases, whole automobiles in the EMP facilities. At the time it was a service long offered within the military, but not readily available in the private sector. Missile range engineers could dial up just about any electromagnetic environment specified by the automakers.

In Public Affairs, we thought this was a great story for White Sands. It was an excellent example of non-military testing at the range. However, when we asked the car companies if we could do an article about the testing, they refused.

Basically, we assumed it came down to consumer confidence. It looks like the companies didn't want to admit to buyers that EMP was a possible problem.

Obviously, if there were problems, they were fixed. Over the years we haven't heard any news stories of air bags mysteriously exploding in people's faces because a passing trucker was talking on his CB.

Also, the nuclear effects operation has a fast-burst reactor to provide the neutron environment found during a nuclear explosion. The "reactor" creates a great deal of confusion both locally and at the national level. People see the word "reactor" and start thinking Three Mile Island.

After the 9/11 attacks, leaders in Washington must have been quite addled on learning they had a reactor at White Sands. I can hear the conversation:

General – "You say the Army has a nuclear reactor at White Sands. Where is White Sands?"

Colonel – "Sir, it is in New Mexico."

General – "Why in the hell is it in Mexico?"

Colonel – "No sir, its "New" Mexico which borders Mexico but has been a state since 1912. It is between Texas and Arizona.

General – "Well, who gets the electricity from it?"

Colonel – "Sir, it is a small device with very little nuclear material. It is used to provide a neutron and gamma radiation environment for individual pieces of equipment."

General – "Dammit, we've got to protect this thing. Get some soldiers with real guns out there right now!"

For several years after 9/11, a succession of National Guard units were ordered to White Sands to add security for the facility. By then the reactor, with its storage system, was decades old and had been inspected by every conceivable concerned organization in the federal system. The operation had been tweaked and adjusted many times to prevent or contain any imaginable incident, internal or external.

So, it was a total waste of time to rip these citizen soldiers from their homes to guard a reactor in one of the most secure facilities anywhere in America. Thick concrete walls and a dedicated guard force have always protected it. The members of those National Guard units experienced a year of incredible boredom instead of being at home or deployed some place where they could have been useful.

The missile range also has chemical and metallurgical labs to test things like propellants for proper combustion and metals for corrosion.

Targets

In addition to these labs, there is much more. For example, an air defense system must have a radar system and some powerful computers to find targets and calculate where they are going and how to get the interceptor missile there. Behind every missile shown on the news flying to kill its target are systems of complex components that are all necessary for success.

Before ever firing the missile, testers might fly real airplanes over the range at various altitudes, azimuths and speeds to see how well the missile system does in acquiring the target and preparing to fire at it. Missile range equipment provides the baseline for the new air defense system to compare to.

White Sands has always been a proving ground for all the military's tactical missiles. Their broad categories are: ground-to-ground, ground-to-air, air-to-ground and air-to-air. In the case of the Navy missiles, just substitute "shipboard" for ground.

All of these systems require realistic targets eventually. In the early days when something like a ballistic missile (ground-to-ground) wasn't all that accurate, a stake or X on the ground would mark the target and then they would measure out to the actual impact point.

For antitank tests, they would stretch red "target" cloth over an appropriately sized frame and shoot at that. Need a moving target? They mounted the frame on wheels and towed it through the impact zone.

As these weapon systems matured, so did their capability to detect a target, discriminate one from another, and precisely home in on it. A cloth target wasn't good enough anymore. For a while, contractors built plywood replicas of real foreign tanks that were mounted on a truck chassis to be presented as targets.

After Israeli victories over various Arab states that used Soviet equipment and after the end of the Cold War, real tanks and other armored vehicles became available to be used as the ultimate "realistic" target. One of the difficulties the contractor has in keeping these vehicles running is finding spare parts.

Instead of stakes in the ground, the range can provide mockups of real buildings or bunkers. In some cases, actual bunkers are built.

For aerial targets, there have always been subscale drones and remote-controlled obsolete aircraft. Immediately after World War II, old B-17 bombers (the Flying Fortress) were used extensively as targets at White Sands. The "Post Diary for 1959" states that on Aug. 6, the droned B-17 flown by the Air Force for the Navy's test was the last of the big planes flown as a target at WSMR. The entry stated "more than 600 Flying Fort target missions" had been flown over WSMR.

For anti-aircraft tests, subscale, propeller driven mini-planes were flown for testing the Nike Ajax, our first air-defense missile system. Jet-powered, subscale drones were soon brought in to provide the realistic speeds and altitudes needed for a full test.

To provide the full-scale jet fighters, the Air Force has made available, at a bargain price, obsolete planes. Many an old fighter has been turned into useful trash at White Sands instead of going to some boring storage yard. In 2007, the range was using old F-4 jets. I say "old" hesitantly because, although the F-4 is a Vietnam-era plane now out of the U.S. inventory, they were still being used by many air forces around the world.

This killing of any kind of a drone can get expensive. Remember, White Sands is trying to run a business and the customer pays for such things. But when a developmental program lasts for years, it is important to show the people controlling the purse strings that progress is being made. There is no better way than to have the system destroy a real honest-to-god jet fighter.

At other times, to make the testing more reasonably priced, the missile range can ask the program to plant a little offset in the weapon's computing system, so they shoot at a box near the target, thus saving the target to fly again some other day.

So, how do you tell if they hit that designated spot representing an imaginary plane? The flight of both the missile and the target have to be measured very precisely, since there won't be any obvious visual evidence as when the plane blows up. Being off 10 feet would mean a miss for a hit-to-kill missile, but perceiving that can be difficult when human observers are safely miles away.

The instruments used by the range detect the fly-by and record the distance. Analysts can look at the data and film to see if the missile hit the target "box" next to the drone.

Data Collection

Collecting the data during a rain test or in some other laboratory setting can be very straight forward. However, when a missile is flying at supersonic speeds and the target itself is going 600 mph, collecting the information can be tricky.

One tool for checking the missile's accuracy is to put equipment in the target drone that can measure the distance between the two objects as they pass. The other tools are the ones usually called upon for a missile test – optical, radar and telemetry systems. No one instrument or family of instruments provides a complete picture, but when you combine data from these many sources, evaluators have a pretty good idea of what went down.

Optics

Optical instruments involve cameras used in a variety of ways. Everyone has seen the super slow-motion moving pictures of bullets exiting gun barrels. The same thing is done at White Sands to check how a missile exits its launch tube.

Cameras can safely film the missile flight from a great distance and capture problems. For instance, if a fin falls off during flight and the missile goes haywire, it is something observers might not catch in real-time. Instead, it will probably show on the film and send investigators in the right direction.

Optical instruments really get sexy, in a nerdy way, in devices like cinetheodolites. The first ones showed up at White Sands with the German V-2 materials. These Askania cinetheodolites were used to film missiles in flight and to calculate their positions in three-dimensional space afterward.

In addition to being a motion picture camera equipped with a telephoto lens, the cine employs the surveyor's tool, a theodolite, for measuring angles. As the instrument records the missile in flight, it is also recording the azimuth angle of the lens, it's elevation angle, and the time the frame of film was exposed. This takes us to those geometry classes we had in high school.

Azimuth refers to the direction the lens is pointed. North is zero degrees, east is 90 degrees, south is 180 degrees and so on until you fill the 360 degrees of a circle.

The elevation angle is how many degrees the lens is above the horizon. Zero would be dead level with the earth's surface and 90 degrees would be straight up. Again, this is based on being able to rotate the full 360-degrees of a circle. Of course, here the camera would not be pointed down.

For decades it took two people to operate a cinetheodolite. One would turn a crank to raise and lower the lens while the other turned a crank to rotate the whole device. Working together, after much practice, they could smoothly track a missile moving across the sky in front of them.

Later, with computers and sophisticated controllers, a single person could control a cine using a joystick to follow the missile. The next step was to automate the whole process. By the time I retired, it was possible to do but complicated sky conditions made for a bumpy track. The optics and computer would get fooled by certain sky conditions and might even track something other than the missile. A human's motor skills and training made for a nice, smooth movie with the missile or target clearly in the center of each frame of film.

This wasn't true for a camera close to a launch where the subject crossed the field of view in a fraction of a second. Here a machine reacted and moved quicker than a human could.

Since the missile range puts these cinetheodolites on very precisely surveyed markers on carefully constructed concrete pads, everyone knows exactly where the instrument is during the test. Using the azimuth and elevation angles from a single frame of film, analysts can draw a nice line into space from a camera's position that intersects the item being tracked.

At that point, they still don't have much except a record of the event because it's not possible to discern how far away the missile was on that line. It could be a mile or six miles away.

Some complex calculations could be made based on the known size of the vehicle in the image in relation to the size of the film and lens being used to determine distance - but it is difficult.

Instead, the data collectors position a second cinetheodolite miles away from the first one and film the same event, running on the same clock. This provides a sweet solution for finding position. By taking the angles from the second cine, the analysts can draw a second line into space to the missile. Bingo, the two lines intersect. Those two lines from the missile to the two cines are also two legs of a triangle.

Going back to our two cines, they can draw a line between them making the third line or leg of the triangle. Plus, the two sites have been previously surveyed as part of the missile range's hundreds of precisely located points for placing instruments. They know exactly how far apart the sites are which means they know the length of the triangle's third leg.

Using the data from the film, they know two angles of the triangle so they can easily figure the third. Put that information with the length of the one leg and using the Law of Sines, the other two sides of the triangle – the distance from each recording site to the missile – can be calculated.

From this the technicians can calculate the missile's position in three-dimensional space at a particular time. However, using just two cines provides a rather rough measurement. To get to the precision test programs really want, three or more cines are needed – more triangles means accurate information. The data from all the units is massaged by computers and refined into a very exacting location.

But that is just the beginning. In the analysis, by moving forward in time, other positions in space can be calculated. Since the time and distance between point A, B and C is easy to figure, the speed of the missile can be calculated quickly. Run with that idea and a bunch of data points and acceleration can be calculated – the change in speed as the missile flies.

For decades this was done using film. White

Sands had a large laboratory for developing lots of motion picture and still film. That has been phased out in the 21st century and it can all be done digitally now.

Although the optics measurements are very precise, in the days of film, they didn't provide feedback in real-time. They weren't much good for managing a test while it was happening and deciding if the missile was going astray and needed to be destroyed. Radars were the workhorses for that mission. Now that the optical instruments are shooting moving pictures in digital formats, the images can be fed to range controllers in real-time, to help keep track of the test items. It has evolved into another tool for making testing safer.

Radars

Not all radars are created the same. Most people know radar is a device that sends out radio waves and that if the waves strike an airplane, missile or UFO, some will bounce back. The item flying about then shows up as a bright light on some sort of screen indicating a "bogie" is present. If it is a more sophisticated system, an icon might show up on some sort of map indicating its position relative to things in the local area.

We see this kind of surveillance radar in movies, television shows, and on the news when they show us airplane traffic around an airport. In addition to that positional information displayed on a nice map, over time a line can be imposed on the map to show the aircraft's past – where it came from. A more sophisticated display can also show the airplane's speed and altitude.

This is all derived from radar. Such radars are well and good for simply keeping track of airplanes in an airspace and White Sands has used them for decades to do just that. Currently, because of the various mountain ranges, it takes three to give complete coverage of the WSMR airspace. One is by the Orogrande Gate, one is near the Oscura Gate, and the third is on a hill above Stallion Range Center.

Data from these radars is fed to the Air Force airspace controllers. They monitor air traffic, guide aircraft during tests, and make sure no airplane strays into a test area, be it a trespasser or legit but lost military aircraft. These radars sweep around in complete circles to provide 360 degrees of coverage.

For missile testing, more precise information is required so "instrumentation" radars are used. These radars have a very narrow field of view – I've heard them referred to as "pencil-beam" radars. They have a tiny view of the sky, kind of like looking through a wrapping-paper tube. They don't see the rest of the sky.

To put that in perspective, humans have a wide field of view of around 180 degrees. Because most of that is peripheral vision it is fuzzy and vague, but we do see contrasts in light and dark, and we can detect motion. As the field of view narrows, we get to the point where we have three-dimensional vision and can differentiate color.

The area of sharpest vision is in the center and is not all that wide. If you take a page of magazine text set in three columns and focus on the middle column, the text is nice and sharp. You can easily read it. Now, while keeping your eyes pointed at the center column (no movement of the eyes allowed) you will be aware of the other two columns, but they will be blurred and you probably can't read them. At least that is the way it is for my old eyes.

When we read, we shift our eyes side to side to move the focus point across the page, so the letters and words properly resolve themselves. This smallish spot of resolution and focus is the main reason speed-reading doesn't really work - if you want to glean any of the information contained on a page.

Instrumentation radars have an even narrower focal point. Beginning in 1946, the first radar used to track the V-2 rockets and provide position information was the SCR-584. This was a radar developed in World War II with only a 4-degree view of the sky. That might sound fairly narrow but is wide compared to more precise radars developed later specifically for the test ranges. The SCR-584 needed a narrow point of view because it was originally used to focus on enemy airplanes and point anti-aircraft guns to shoot them down.

Because of the specialized nature of these instrumentation radars, they aren't turned on to lazily scan the sky between tests. With such a narrow beam, such scanning would be a waste of time. In other words, depending on the test load, they sit idle for days at a time.

For decades UFO researchers queried White Sands about the state of range radars in 1947 when the alien spacecraft supposedly came down northwest of Roswell. Some have a very exaggerated view of early radar capabilities, and have no idea how different kinds of radar are used at WSMR. Some claim these early SCR-584s were used by the Army to track the aliens and direct recovery teams to the crash site. The reality was these things were certainly good at tracking a single object once it was acquired, but lousy for finding that item in a big empty sky. When the Roswell event supposedly happened, the WSMR radars probably weren't even turned on.

So, you ask, how does one of these fancy, narrow-beam radars pick up the target to track? There were/are a number of ways to get the radar pointed in the right direction. According to Austin Vick, who worked decades at White Sands for National Range Operations and is now a WSMR Hall of Fame member, one way was to have a human operator on the radar who would be given coordinates for the missile's location and he would manually turn the radar so it pointed at the right spot to acquire the vehicle.

Vick said another way was to place a "beacon" in the target vehicle that emitted a signal that was readable by the range radars. The radars could be pointed at the strongest signal, its source, and track it. This was more accurate than a skin track of the target vehicle because it never changed. For a skin track, the surface of a missile might shrink and expand depending on how the missile tipped and turned.

The third way for the radar and other instruments to acquire the target was through what developers called a "chain radar system." The 1952 brochure "An Introduction to White Sands Proving Ground" has a nice two-page spread explaining the proving ground's chain radar system. In a way, it was like the manned idea where coordinates were provided to the instruments, except here we are talking about instruments being slaved to the system so they are automatically pointed at the target.

The brochure's explanation comes with a diagram showing that the radar located at C Station could easily lock onto a V-2 as it lifted off for its flight. Position data could then be computed and relayed to other radar sites and camera sites uprange. That information could drive each of the instruments scattered around the range and point them in the right direction, so they too could acquire and track the missile.

Such an arrangement is still being used at White Sands. It is easy to imagine how valuable such slaving is for a launch where the missile comes over the horizon from a place such as Fort Wingate in northwest New Mexico or Green River, Utah. The missiles would be invisible at launch and would suddenly pop above the horizon as they climbed toward apogee.

In the 1950s, an instrumentation radar was designed and built specifically for test ranges like White Sands. It was so good it is still out on the range today. Of course, it has been digitized and greatly improved, but it is still the AN/MPS-16. Again, because of this radar's narrow beam, it was only capable to tracking one target at a time. With several of them deployed, a test involving a few vehicles could be completed.

Data collection changed when programs wanted White Sands to track a bunch of targets, all at the same time. For instance, programs wanted more complex scenarios with many airplanes and missiles in the air at the same time. Also, new smart weapons were being developed that could be dispensed from a delivery missile and then attack targets on their own. An excellent example of this was the BAT submunition.

In a typical BAT scenario, a single Army TACMS missile could be launched to attack an enemy column of vehicles 100 miles away. When the TACMS missile got over the target area, it would break open and dispense 13 BATs, each capable of finding and destroying a tank or truck.

The project's test requirements included wanting to know what happened to the mother-ship missile and each BAT. That was 14 items at one time. It was an impossible task with the few MPS-16 radars available.

The need for a new way to track weapons fell to the range's old Instrumentation Directorate (ID). It was their job to keep the optical, radar and telemetry systems on White Sands up-to-date and capable of handling any test scenario.

To tackle the future that BAT and complex tests represented, ID worked with RCA to develop and build the Multiple Object Tracking Radar (MOTR). This is a phased array radar which means it has a very wide field of view and uses a multiple individual antenna to scan the sky. It is very versatile because it can track up to 40 items simultaneously. Just what the customers needed.

Today MOTR is called the AN/MPS-39.

One thing notable about these instrumentation radars is they are very, very accurate. They are often used as the baseline for weapon system radars that

The Multiple Object Tracking Radar is capable of tracking dozens of aerial targets simultaneously. WSMR photo.

are under test at White Sands. Evaluators compare the position solutions derived by the weapon system with the solutions from missile range radar. In the past, some projects have had to go back and make adjustments to their systems.

Because radars use electromagnetic waves, everything is traveling at the speed of light. The only holdup is in the computing devices that take the data and display it so the human controllers can understand and respond to it. By human standards, the processing and displaying of radar data is very quick – many times a second. So, although it does take some time, White Sands has always talked about "real-time" displays of data.

For missile flight safety this is obviously important. Any delay in responding to a malfunctioning missile traveling at supersonic speeds increases the possibility the errant weapon might make it out of the White Sands safety box.

Originally, radar data was displayed for safety personnel on paper maps on plotting boards. The radar's position data was translated into commands to the ink pens in the plotter and it would draw a line on the map showing where the missile was at any given instant.

As the computing power increased for this process, the range was able to add the "instantaneous impact predictor" or IIP. With this capability, not only did the display boards graphically show where the missile had been and where it was at that moment, it could project a point on the map showing where the missile or its debris would land if the safety officer destroyed it at that instant.

This additional capability was necessary because a missile moving across the sky at a thousand miles an hour doesn't just drop straight to the ground if a destruct action is taken. The missile or its debris would continue to coast forward for some distance.

So a safety officer has to keep an eye on the IIP if there is a problem. He or she will have to take action as the IIP approaches the safety boundary on the display, not when the missile body itself approaches the defined limit.

In the 1980s, there was a gradual transition to displaying this information digitally. It was a great boon as more data could be displayed in a variety of ways instead of just lines on paper.

Telemetry

Telemetry data is the other major source of data about a missile, usually its health and status. The term means data is telemetered or transmitted to ground stations for recording. The information collected is whatever the project wants but usually includes information like skin temperature, internal pressures, battery levels, fin inclinations, and timing info.

In 1977, the missile range installed and then spent three years perfecting a position-calculating instrument using telemetry signals from the missile or target. It was called the Three Object Angle Measuring Equipment (TOAME) and worked passively without any moving parts.

TOAME worked using two sites, each with an array of small antennas to capture the telemetry signals. The computing system would look at the ever-so-slight timing difference of the signal hitting one antenna versus another. From this, the computer could calculate the same elevation and azimuth angles as those from a cinetheodolite or a radar – without any of the moving machinery. Using two sites the lines drawn into space would meet at the missile.

According to Forrest Dozier, an early engineer on the TOAME project, the system worked in all weather, had instant acquisition of the missile, was unaffected by countermeasures, and could provide data for the instantaneous impact predictor. However, it was a labor-intensive system and was costly to use.

With Global Positioning Systems now found in some missiles, the GPS information can be transmitted to telemetry sites and used for tracking as well. Of course, a White Sands GPS device can also be installed in the missile if there is room and the position data can be passed along or recorded for later analysis.

Range customers order up this data collection effort depending on what they need to know about their system. White Sands collects the information during the tests and presents it to the customer in a report form.

In addition, White Sands needs to collect the real time data necessary to safely conduct the test. Keeping missiles and targets out of surrounding communities is the range's obligation.

For a shoulder-fired missile or an artillery round that doesn't generate enough energy to leave the missile range or hit a populated White Sands asset, the range's data collection for safety will be minimal. On the other hand, when a system like Patriot is firing at a supersonic drone, both vehicles are capable of leaving White Sands. Safety becomes a big driver in those kinds of tests. I was told once that for the big tests, about half of the data collection equipment was there for missile flight safety. Knowing exactly where a missile is, where it is going, and how it is performing, all figure into a safe test.

Missile Flight Safety

As I have pointed out, many data sources feed the displays used for missile flight safety. Safety is a subject that runs through many of these chapters

because out-of-control missiles are a real danger to personnel on the missile range, neighbors living next to White Sands, and to those living under the flight corridor from Fort Wingate and southern Utah.

Outsiders tend to think of missile "flight termination" as simply blowing it up. Usually this is not done – for several reasons. If you blow the missile to smithereens, there won't be much left to analyze, to determine what went wrong. That won't help prevent a repeat.

If it is blown to pieces, instead of one or two big chunks of metal coming down, dozens of potentially lethal pieces will come raining down. More pieces actually increase the chance of damage or injury.

The smarter thing to do is to shut off the missile's rocket motor. Tricky. Since missiles today use solid propellants, there is no shut-off switch. When they are burning, they are on full blast and can't be extinguished. But, by popping holes in the top of the motor, high-pressure gases are vented in the opposite direction. These counteract the gases coming out the nozzle and the net effect is zero thrust.

In most cases, the missile will break up into a few pieces and will not behave like an arrow anymore. It may tumble and spin which slows it down. Ultimately it should fall to the ground in an unpopulated area, if the destruct action is taken in the preplanned safety footprint.

There is a section of engineers in National Range whose job it is to look at the missiles and decide how best to terminate their flights, if needed. Some missiles are too small to load extra explosives on board to knock holes into rocket motors. One solution is to allow the missile flight safety personnel to explode the missile's warhead and bring it down.

White Sands Missile Range has safely fired over 40,000 rockets and missiles. Never has anyone in the public been injured from any of the many stray missiles that have left the established safety box and its invisible lines. It may be because of this excellent record that many people assume the missile flight safety people can actually guide an errant missile to a safe impact. That is not quite true.

I ran into this assumption when we were having public meetings concerning the reopening of the missile corridor from Fort Wingate and southern Utah. For those proposed flights, as well as the ones in the past, the missiles flew down a defined corridor of airspace over the heads of people in towns, on ranches and driving down highways. No one was evacuated in the past nor was anyone being asked to leave their homes for the new launches.

In planning for the meetings, I ran into Army officials and contract personnel who wanted to say that in case of a faulty missile, White Sands safety personnel could guide the missile to safe impact. I had to object to the use of the word "guide" as it implied more control than we actually could muster.

The reality has always been that these big missiles are not like radio-controlled drones. They are equipped with a termination package, one for each booster, that can punch holes in the rocket motor while that motor is burning. That would effectively terminate thrust and drop the vehicle to the ground.

This only works when the rocket motor is firing. Punching holes in the motor after it has burned out accomplishes nothing. It is still a big piece of metal coasting through the air on a ballistic trajectory just like a baseball thrown in from the outfield. It is going to carry on in a straight line based on how much energy went into accelerating it.

What control White Sands has over these vehicles boils down to knowing when to push the red destruct button while the rocket motor is still burning. Timing is everything and it works because of probabilities.

For example, the flight corridor from Fort Wingate to WSMR is generally not densely populated. In fact, the range surveys the area to find any concentrations of people. Outside the few dense clusters, there are miles and miles of empty land. That means dropping something out of the sky in most areas has a very, very small chance of actually striking someone. Driving into town to buy groceries is probably a more dangerous activity for those folks.

During a test, the missile flight safety officer sees the flight of the test item or target imposed over a map displayed on a color monitor. Imposed on the map are the safety boundaries for the corridor as well as population clusters, roads, and other significant items.

It should all look familiar to them because they practice before the actual firings. Using data about the vehicle and its capabilities, computer simulations are run using different scenarios. The safety officers working with that particular program basically rehearse for the tests so there are no surprises, and they feel comfortable with the speed of events. They

know from the start what a second or two means in the end result.

During a test, if the missile begins to misbehave and the safety officer is ready to terminate its flight, he or she might wait a second to push the button so the projected debris passes over a ranch to safely crash a few miles away. Or, the safety officer might destroy it immediately, before it can reach a small population cluster.

The data coming in from many sources and the lightning-fast computers crunching it into meaningful displays makes this all possible. The bottom line is that White Sands can't take over a missile and fly it to an impact point but it can precisely control the risk to make sure no one is hurt. So far they are perfect.

Overland Advantage

One of the great advantages White Sands has over test ranges that use the ocean as their test bed is the ease with which test vehicles can be recovered. Recovery teams can usually find missiles or rocket payloads in a matter of minutes and proceed to retrieve them.

When things go wrong, this can be very valuable. The debris can be taken to experts for a "post mortem examination" to try and figure out what went wrong. It is kind of like doing an autopsy on a perfectly healthy young person who dies unexpectedly.

If the failure had taken place over the water, there might never be a recovery of the test item.

A concrete example of this happening was during Theater High Altitude Area Defense (THAAD) testing. In the early stages of testing, one missile appeared to be on an intercept course with its ballistic missile target. In the end, it didn't get there and missed.

The THAAD does not have a warhead. It has to physically strike its target to destroy it, so close doesn't count.

When the recovery team picked up the THAAD, they discovered the booster and the kill vehicle were still connected by some cabling that was supposed to disengage once the rocket motor burned out. This meant the kill vehicle was dragging the booster behind as it maneuvered to intercept its target. It simply ran out of gas because of the extra load and couldn't get to the kill point.

The contractor was able to make changes to the hardware to ensure this didn't happen again.

Normally, recovery of missile debris or a rocket payload is accomplished by sending ground crews to a site based on positional data from range instrumentation. In the early days, aircraft were used to search and find the item beforehand with the pilot then directing the recovery crew. This was useful when impact point predicting was primitive at best.

Also, helicopters are used to retrieve some rocket payloads to get the experimental packages back as quickly as possible.

In 1962 and 1963, White Sands tried using a new technique called the Mid-Air Recovery System (MARS). It was based on the Air Force's efforts to grab film capsules falling from Space over the Pacific Ocean.

On Aug. 19, 1960, a C-119J cargo plane out of Hickam Air Force Base was used successfully for the first time to snatch film out the air that had been dropped by an orbiting satellite. The program was part of Corona, a Cold War spy effort that sent up short-lived satellites to photograph the Soviet Union and China. The film was then jettisoned and plucked out of the sky as it descended on parachutes or picked up out of the sea after splash down.

According to the Dec. 5, 2008 *Hickam Kukini* newspaper, the Air Force's recovery unit retrieved over 200 film canisters before the end of the program. Because of its rather unusual mission, the unit took on the motto, "Catch a Falling Star."

At White Sands the idea was modified to use helicopters to snag parachute-borne packages like sounding rocket payloads out of the air and return to base.

According to Major Myron Wilson, who was chief of the Aviation Branch of the Range Services Division, the technique provided a soft landing for packages, made for a very quick recovery and guaranteed recovery over areas of rough, inaccessible terrain.

The benefits look sizable but there is the little problem of those rotor blades turning to keep the helicopter in the air. What might happen if one of those parachute cords or other material was caught up in the blades? It was a tricky procedure, something you might see at an airshow, that required excellent timing.

The White Sands *Wind and Sand* newspaper reported on Oct. 5, 1962, "In a maneuver more dramatic than found in science fiction, the helicopter swoops across the desert sky like a giant hawk and darts in to make the 'catch.' The chopper was equipped with 'talon-like hooks' that trailed below the craft and these would engage the parachute. A loop of cable anchored in a hoist onboard ended up encircling the parachute shroud and was used to reel in the payload for the flight back to base."

The system was used extensively in the Vietnam War to recover remotely piloted reconnaissance drones.

Just The Facts Please

In all the testing White Sands has done, you've never heard WSMR personnel commenting on the success or failure of a system or item being put through its paces. As a rule, White Sands prepares a test report containing all the data collected and leaves it at that. You might say the missile range is discrete and leaves interpretation to the customer paying the bills.

The May 12, 1998 failure of a THAAD missile is an illustration of this relationship in operation. It was a frustrating morning for those of us in the White Sands Public Affairs Office.

Any release of information about a program and its tests is usually strictly controlled by the customer, even if it is a fellow Army agency. For THAAD testing, WSMR Public Affairs personnel could talk about missile range activities to support the test, but we had to wait for the project to release results before we could pass along any other information.

For that May test, we went to work early to watch and answer phone calls afterward. This was a very high profile and expensive program closely followed by the various military journals and reporters covering the military beat. The money was big, but they were also intrigued by the state-of-the-art technology being perfected.

Many of them were cozy with sources inside the military-industrial complex, so they knew exactly when tests were scheduled. In fact, they knew more about the project than we did. They usually started calling within 30 minutes of launch time to get results.

That morning, well before daylight, we went outside the building to watch the usually spectacular THAAD launch from just a few miles away. As we looked on, the missile lit up the launch pad as it exited its tube and quickly shot into its spiral to bleed energy. As it came out of the curl, it headed north and then flew apart, crashing into the desert about two miles north of the launcher. It was much more spectacular than a normal launch, but was over in just a couple of seconds – except for the debris burning out in the desert.

We went back inside and waited for the project to give us some sort of release about the obvious failure. And we waited and we waited. Calls started coming in from numerous reporters on the East Coast asking how the test went. Of course, we knew how it went – it did a magnificent job of intercepting the ground in record time.

We couldn't say that, and since we had nothing from the project, we confirmed there was a launch and we were awaiting word from the project on how it went.

Well, we waited for what seemed like hours to get the blessed words. After all that delay, the project came out with this: "Preliminary investiga-

This spectacular time-lapse photo shows the entire flight of the May 12, 1998 THAAD missile. Army photo taken by WSMR photographer.

tion indicates that the THAAD missile lost control shortly after launch. The missile impacted on the White Sands Missile Range about 2 miles north of the launch site. The THAAD interceptor and target debris landed on the White Sands Missile Range as planned in the event of a failed intercept. Analysis of the flight data is underway to determine the cause of the malfunction."

The rest of the news release was boilerplate, stuff that is put in every release about the project history, its purpose, etc. In fact, the quoted material above is mostly boilerplate. It is hard to imagine why such a release would take more than 10 minutes to devise, but times have changed and programs are deathly afraid to use the word "failure." They were probably feverously looking through a thesaurus for a good synonym.

In concert with putting the best light on a subject is the ever tightening of the control of information. The release probably had to be shuffled for review from one layer of approval to the next and then the next, until it reached some officials at the very top in the Pentagon. That takes time.

Sometimes reporters or television producers feel they are getting the runaround when they call White Sands because Public Affairs usually has to send them elsewhere looking for the proper point of contact in someplace like Huntsville, Alabama or Washington, D.C. Sometimes I would try to talk them into doing a story on the missile range's support of the program, but very few wanted to report on optical instrumentation, radar, telemetry, or missile flight safety.

Invisible White Sands

Behind the scenes at White Sands is a whole world of other support organizations that play their part in making the fire, smoke, and explosions possible. For instance, even though southern New Mexico usually has clear skies, weather plays a major role in missions at WSMR. The team of forecasters can make or break a test.

When bad weather does postpone a test, some outside the test community scoff and say the equipment should be able to perform in any kind of weather. The truth is that the delay is not for the project under test but for the range's ability to collect the required data – the information the project is spending big bucks to gather.

Visibility is a big one because many tests require

good photographic coverage. If there is blowing sand or fog or clouds, the cameras might not catch all the action.

Sometimes the weather unit saves the day. If a missile test calls for the missile to intercept a high-flying jet at 30,000 feet, but there are clouds at 5,000 feet, the weather people will check the satellite images to see if there might be a break coming. If there is, the test might be delayed a few hours and still get done. Having to cancel and reschedule another day means getting all geared up again which can get expensive.

Winds have a major impact on a number of tests. Low-level winds must be monitored during sounding rocket shots because they can push a rocket to the point it might land off the missile range. At the same time, upper-level winds might be strong enough to push the rocket's payload off the missile range as it descends hanging from a parachute.

Upper-level winds are important in high altitude intercepts. Some of these tests involve debris way up in the jet stream which can carry pieces a long way. The jet stream can howl along around a hundred miles an hour but sometimes exceeds two hundred miles an hour. Light materials can travel a great distance in that kind of a wind, and the weather team is constantly modeling the winds and projected debris to make sure it is all safely contained.

It may not seem like much, but White Sands has to have a master clock that all test equipment and all missions follow. In the after-action report, data presentations are tied to the time the information was gathered. If there was an explosion at a particular time, evaluators can quickly find the photos, radar information, and telemetry data by going to that instant in the record and look for clues.

To get the timing and all kinds of other information around the range, there is a huge communications network. It includes telephone, radio, computer networking, fiber optic cable, and secure transmission for sensitive data.

An independent organization monitors frequency use in the radio world on White Sands. They have fixed and mobile stations for making sure radio signals used throughout WSMR are on their assigned frequency and at their proper strength.

This is important because errant frequencies might interfere with the transmission of valuable data or prevent a destruct signal from reaching a missile gone haywire. When television crews visit White Sands with their satellite trucks for live broadcasts, the transmitters have to be checked first. The frequency monitoring folks will compare the truck's output with the station's license to ensure it is functioning correctly.

Another organization flying below the radar at White Sands is the countermeasures group. They provide various kinds of jammers and decoys to fool weapon system radars, heat-seeking missiles, and other detectors. If they find an American-made missile can be easily misled, no one advertises it. Instead, they quietly get to fixing the problem and making the missile less vulnerable to countermeasures.

Electronic countermeasures can use complex technical devises while other measures may simply involve ejecting hot burning flares. Action movies have portrayed the classic flare drop for some time now. In a typical scenario, the bad guys fire a heat-seeking missile at the airplane with the good guys aboard. The missile detects the hot exhaust from the plane's jet engines and targets the warmest spot. The good guys, in turn, pop a dozen or so flares out of the rear of the plane in hopes the missile will be confused and home in on a white-hot flare.

There is much more to WSMR. For decades White Sands has published a capabilities handbook to provide users and potential customers with information on what is available at the range. If you are interested, the last time I looked (early 2013) it was available as a PDF online and titled *WSMR, Range Customer Handbook*.

With all this testing capability and the variety of its users, White Sands is a very unusual place. At the same time, it has the typical infrastructure of most military installations. It is much like a small town with a rather specialized workforce. It has homes and apartments, a school for the kids, library, grocery store, department store, health and dental clinics, service station, golf course, post office, banks, restaurants, bars, weekly newspaper, swimming pool, police force, baseball and soccer fields, fire department, museum, fitness center, bowling alley, cable TV, tennis courts, car wash, and a chapel for religious services.

All of these things are relatively small-scale. At its height in the 1950s and 60s, the population was well over 10,000 military personnel and their families, civilians and contractors. Since the end of the

Cold War it has shrunk significantly. Instead of three swimming pools there is only one. There is no separate "officers club" anymore – it is a community club open to everyone on post. The large mess hall for enlisted men was torn down years ago. The commissary and post exchange have very limited offerings; many post residents go into town for their essentials. The golf course is only 11 holes and is usually available to just walk on unless there are leagues. This is an excellent example of the quirkiness of WSMR – who else has something other than a 9- or 18-hole golf course?

Many WSMR facilities have very limited hours now because demand is low. Some are open only a few days a week and are only one-deep when it comes to personnel. It is a far cry from huge Fort Bliss just down the road with its thousands of troops, shopping malls and all the rest.

In the end, White Sands has been successful for more than 65 years by being flexible. The missile range has had to respond to the needs of its customers and sometimes try things that haven't been done before. White Sands has had to grow and shrink in response to the flood or decline of customers. The institution has had to find creative ways to keep the doors open when funding tends to shrivel year after year.

Of course, this flexibility is rooted in the decades of dedicated personnel who have passed through WSMR. People are flexible, government organizations – not so much.

Halloween 1953 in Jane Moore's first grade class at the White Sands school. They each have a cupcake and one of those frozen paper cups of ice cream. In the proving ground's first few years, children were bused over to Las Cruces for school. For the 1948-49 school year, Dona Ana County established a school at White Sands with Laura Sandiford as the sole teacher. It was a one-room affair with her teaching several grades. The school quickly expanded and by 1953 there were large numbers of students in every grade. WSMR photo.

9

German Vengeance Weapons

How The Space Age Started

The first rockets fired at White Sands were not German V-2s. In fact, the very first rockets seen in southern New Mexico were U.S. developments, trying to catch up with the Germans.

It is hard to overstate the rocket's impact on American life in the 1940s and 50s. The news media followed the rocket research at White Sands with rapt attention. They published long feature articles and gushed over the amazing technology. In fact, most authors wrote about rockets as if they were delving into Einstein's theory of relativity – it was just too much for the average American to understand.

The look of a V-2 or a rocket in general became a symbol in America for something state-of-the-art, cutting-edge, sleek, fast and powerful. A variety of companies used actual photographs from White Sands or rendered images of rockets in their advertisements. They wanted to show the buying public they offered the latest and greatest products.

For example, in 1949 General Motors introduced the Oldsmobile 88 with a "Rocket V8 Engine." It was hugely popular. One advertising slogan for the car was "Make a Date with a Rocket 88." In 1951, Ike Turner recorded a rhythm and blues tune called "Rocket 88" that praised the vehicle and became a number one song that year. Ike's fame was eventually surpassed by his wife Tina.

The first hood ornaments for the Rocket 88 were stylized chrome rockets with wings. The center section looked pretty much like a V-2 with its large fins on the tail. The GM artists then added wings and

A typical magazine ad for the rocket-inspired Olds 88. Author's collection.

elongated rocket engines on the ends of the wings.

The designers weren't done there. On the trunk of the car they added a chrome badge with the number 88 and a rocket flying through it.

Other companies tapped into the rocket rage as well. Anaconda Copper ran an ad showing a missile launch and bragged how its copper made the electrical connections work inside the rocket.

Chesterfield cigarettes used a series of photos from a missile launch at White Sands with soldiers doing the work. After the launch, an Army captain is congratulated on the test and the ad declares he deserves his Chesterfield.

Havoline Motor Oil compared its engine oil to a guided missile. The company's advertisement pointed out that a missile "thinks" for itself when it guides itself to a target. Havoline claimed its new multi-grade oil also thought for itself to provide engine protection in various conditions.

Of course, any company that actually built the missiles or any of their subsystems played up its role in this advanced technology and defense of the country. General Electric (GE), which held the V-2 Hermes contract, ran some wonderful color ads based on photos of their V-2 work at White Sands.

The 3.25" Rocket-Propelled Target

This vehicle was not a research rocket or a sophisticated guided missile but was probably the first "rocket" fired in the Tularosa Basin. It was basically a long pipe with plywood fins powered by gunpowder.

In February 1985, Public Affairs received a call from Clarence Tacquard, a missile mechanic with the Raytheon Company. He told us he had found an old rocket stuck in a sand dune east of the White Sands main post.

On investigation the rusting rocket turned out to be a target rocket used during World War II to train antiaircraft gunnery crews. Tacquard's rocket was probably fired sometime between November 1943 and the end of the war; it had been sticking nose down in the sand dune since then.

Tacquard said he actually found the rocket back in 1975 but couldn't interest anyone in it. He left it and forgot about it until the Christmas break in 1984. He said he went back out to the dune area to see if it was still there. When he found it again he called us.

The rocket was used at the south end of what is now White Sands by the Antiaircraft Artillery Training Center at Fort Bliss. In November 1943, the center established a mobile combat course at Condron Field. Condron was then a dirt runway and is now the missile range's main airfield just southeast of the main post. The course was designed to train crews to be able to engage and destroy a variety of ground and air targets.

According to Army Technical Manual 4-236 dated March 7, 1942, the "rocket target had been developed in order to introduce into automatic weapons training the degree of alertness required under combat conditions." In other words, the towed targets and drone aircraft couldn't simulate the high speeds of strafing planes and dive-bombers. This simple rocket with its plywood fins was supposed to safely provide the needed speeding target.

The rocket isn't much. It is a steel pipe or tube about five feet long and 3.25 inches in diameter. Each of the three plywood fins are set in what looks like a hand-fashioned metal frame. The frames simply slide under flanges on the sides of the rocket and lock in place. Because the fins are so flimsy, they were not put on the rockets until just before they were fired. In addition, a yellow flare was attached to the nose to provide a night target.

The rocket was fueled with a solid mixture of nitroglycerin and nitrocellulose. Just before firing, a black powder igniter and an electric squib were placed in the combustion chamber.

When fired, the propellant was completely burned up in the first 30 feet of flight. By the time the rocket reached the top of its arcing trajectory, it was traveling between 250 and 300 miles per hour. It was supposed to have a maximum range of 2,000 yards.

Tacquard's rocket was retrieved by the missile range's Explosive Ordnance Disposal Team and then turned over to the White Sands Museum after a safety inspection.

Private F

A series of Private F missiles was fired from Hueco Range on Fort Bliss during the first two weeks of April 1945. These winged missiles were launched from a ramp and used a solid propellant booster to quickly get the Private up to speed so it would fly.

According to an Ordnance Corps report, "A total of 17 rounds were fired including two dummies to test operation of the launcher and boosters. Tests were conducted for the purpose of investigating some of the problems of winged missiles, particularly aerodynamic problems of stability and drag at high speeds and to check on the feasibility of extending the range of a missile by the use of wings. When the missiles were fired, in no case was satisfactory steady flight produced."

As the tests were conducted near the New Mexico / Texas border, the researchers tweaked the missile between flights trying for stability. They tried bending and shaping the fins to see if it would make any difference. Nothing helped.

Afterwards they concluded some sort of autopilot would be necessary to keep such a vehicle stable in flight.

Overall the Private F weighed 506 lbs. with 175 lbs. being the propellant. It was 92 inches long, 9.6 inches in diameter and had a diameter around the fins of 33 inches.

Private F launches followed Private A launches that took place at Camp Irwin, California back in December 1944. Essentially the F was a version of the A with larger wings.

The Privates were developed by the Guggenheim Aeronautical Laboratory at the California Institute of Technology (GALCIT). The group started out life with a small government grant for developing the "Jet Assisted Take Off" (JATO) for aircraft. In 1941, they demonstrated to the Army how these rockets could accelerate conventional airplanes to take-off speeds in very short distances.

In 1943, Theodore von Kármán, Frank Malina, and others from the project established the Aerojet Corporation to manufacture JATO motors for the military.

In November 1943, the rocket group at GALCIT was broken out and named the Jet Propulsion Laboratory (JPL). The organization was basically under contract to the Army to develop more rocket technology with the contract administered by Cal Tech.

WAC Corporal

In addition to the Privates, which were basically test vehicles to investigate flight characteristics, JPL received orders from the Army to build a usable rocket capable of carrying a 25-pound package of meteorological instruments to an altitude of 100,000 feet, basically 20 miles. In the first months of 1945, the WAC Corporal was hastily conceived to satisfy

the requirement. A few months later, JPL was flying their WACs at White Sands.

A few years later, after the launches, legendary comedian Jack Benny was photographed sitting on a saddle that was strapped to a display WAC Corporal. In the photo, actress and singer Ann Blyth looks on admiringly as Benny waves and prepared to ride the rocket. The same rocket is on display in the White Sands Museum - along with the famous photograph.

The name of the rocket causes some confusion today. The Corporal part is simply in line with JPL's penchant for using Army ranks to name their vehicles. They started with the Private, moved up to the Corporal, and finished their Army work with the Sergeant.

Some assume the "WAC" stands for Women's Army Corps, but most White Sands old-timers support the story that WAC stands for "without attitude control." Since the rocket needed to simply go straight up, it didn't need any complicated control devices that would have required additional space and added uneccesary weight.

The JPL engineers came up with a rocket 12 inches in diameter and 16 feet long. The rocket's smallish motor burned acid and aniline as propellants while generating about 1,500 pounds of thrust. The motor could burn for about 47 seconds.

To make the WAC as light as possible, the JPL designers did a number of clever things. For instance, conventional wisdom in Army circles was that, like bombs, the rocket would need four fins to give it stability. JPL engineers had to go to some lengths to convince their Army overseers that three fins would work just as well and save weight.

The fins were designed to be like the feathers on an arrow. They would drag through the air and keep the backend steady behind the front end.

Also, the outside skin of the rocket was welded to the oxidizer, fuel tanks, and other internal components. This meant that the tanks provided the structural strength to support the skin and weighty internal bracing wasn't needed.

A side effect of this design was that the tubing to carry the fuel and oxidizer to the motor was routed outside the vehicle. JPL covered the lines with lightweight cowlings to protect them. This distinctive feature was carried through to the much bigger Corporal ballistic missile.

Since the launch weight of a WAC was around

Frank Malina, aeronautical engineer from the Guggenheim Aeronautical Laboratory and the newly formed Jet Propulsion Laboratory, stands beside one of his WAC Corporal rockets before loading it into the launch tower at White Sands in 1945. WSMR photo.

660 pounds, it was woefully underpowered. To get it off the ground as quickly as possible and up to a speed where the three large fins would stabilize it in flight, JPL used a Tiny Tim motor as a booster. The Tiny Tim was a Navy aircraft rocket that blasted out 50,000 pounds of thrust for just six-tenths of a second.

To keep the whole thing secure and pointed straight up during that second of liftoff, the whole package was launched from a 100-foot steel tower. Using the Tiny Tim, the WAC Corporal vehicle was

traveling several hundred miles an hour when it hit the top of the tower and transitioned to free flight with its own motor powering it.

Like many of the later V-2s, the weather instruments in the WAC Corporal were supposed to be ejected at the top of the flight and gently descend under a parachute. Just like the V-2 experience, the idea didn't work very well.

In late September 1945, a series of Tiny Tim boosters were fired from the 100-foot tower at the launch complex at White Sands. We assume the blockhouse was complete and usable for protecting the JPL engineers.

On Sept. 27 and 28, 1945, Tiny Tim boosters were fired with simulated WAC Corporals stacked on top. On Oct. 1 and 2, partially fueled WAC Corporals were placed on Tiny Tim boosters and launched. Finally, from Oct. 11 to Oct. 25, six full-up WAC Corporals were fired.

The rockets greatly exceeded their requirements. Instead of 20 miles, the best rocket reached an altitude of 43 miles.

Such success must have pleased Dr. Frank Malina, the WAC Corporal designer, and his JPL comrades. If it wasn't for the German V-2s arriving at White Sands at the same time, the WAC Corporal probably would have been used by American researchers to conduct upper atmospheric research.

Instead, the V-2 suddenly provided scientists the capability to carry thousands of pounds to altitudes double what the WAC Corporal could provide. However, mated together in the Bumper rocket, the two vehicles would grab the world's attention with the WAC Corporal being the first man-made object in space.

Birth Of A German Vengeance Weapon

The story of the V-2 rocket is a bit of a "Jekyll and Hyde" tale in reverse. In Robert Louis Stevenson's novella, Dr. Jekyll eventually makes a permanent transformation into the evil Mr. Hyde. In contrast, the V-2 started out life as a German terror weapon during World War II, but then the United States transformed it into a peaceful research tool.

America's use of the V-2 rocket at White Sands Missile Range (then a proving ground) propelled the United States into the Space Age. Launch Complex 33 at White Sands, where most of the V-2s were launched, is now a National Historic Landmark because of that early work.

The V-2 rocket and its predecessor, the V-1 "buzz bomb," owe their existence to World War I. At the end of the war the winners imposed restrictions on Germany's military that were spelled out in the Versailles Treaty. The limitations were meant to prevent Germany from rearming and threatening her neighbors again.

To get around the treaty, Germany looked for weapon developments not covered in the agreement. Rockets were not mentioned. Eventually, as Hitler grew stronger and more brazen, he was able to simply ignore the whole treaty.

But how did simple gunpowder rockets used in celebrations turn into vehicles capable of carrying large cargoes into space?

Two men, an American and a German, kickstarted the idea of developing rockets that were real machines capable of traveling into space and possibly to other planets. Although the principles are the same, they weren't talking about the Chinese rockets that flew a short distance in the direction they were pointed. Both men wrote about self-contained vehicles that would use multiple stages to propel the rocket up and out.

In December 1919, the American professor Robert Goddard published a small paper entitled *A Method For Reaching Extreme Altitudes*. In it he proposed using a multi-stage rocket to send a charge of flash powder to the moon and have it explode on impact so it could be seen from earth using large telescopes.

It was not well received. Goddard never forgot the ridicule he had to endure from ignorant editors at newspapers like the *New York Times*. They called him foolish and said everyone knew a rocket couldn't go to the moon because there was no air for the rocket to push against in outer space.

Americans have never been very good at distinguishing real science and technology from hokum, myth, fakes and outright lies. After all, we live in a country where most kids want to be athletes and

singers – not scientists and engineers. The *Times* reaction was typical.

In Goddard's case, reporters in 1919 had very little if any science background, and things haven't changed much today. Ask a room full of reporters to explain the basic electrical principle behind the toaster and incandescent light bulb and see how many correct answers you get.

Of course, Goddard was absolutely right. He understood the implications of Newton's third law of motion, published way back in 1687. The centuries-old idea seemed to escape the editors at the *Times*.

In simple terms, Newton's law states that for every action there is an equal reaction. That means when the super-hot gases blast out the rear opening of a rocket engine, there is an equal reaction or push in the opposite direction. It works in the complete vacuum of outer space better than in earth's atmosphere because there is no air resistance and very little gravity to slow the vehicle down.

A more down-to-earth example of the law in action is when a hunter fires his rifle. When he pulls the trigger there is a small explosion of gunpowder in the cartridge. The rapidly expanding hot gases push the bullet out the barrel towards the target. At the same time there is an equal push or reaction in the other direction that the hunter experiences as recoil – the butt of the rifle slams against his shoulder as it is pushed backwards.

If the hunter was on roller skates and rapidly pulled the trigger over and over, the recoil would push him backwards. Given enough bullets and a big enough rifle, the hunter could become a rocket.

In 1923, German professor Hermann Oberth published *By Rocket To Interplanetary Space*. Using math he showed how a man could ride a rocket beyond earth's gravity field.

Three years later, Willy Ley, a well-known German science writer, took the idea and popularized it in Germany.

So, the idea of using rockets to travel into space came to light at almost the same time in the two countries. The results were completely different, however.

In America, Robert Goddard was ignored but for a few backers. Supporters included Charles Lindbergh and the Guggenheim Foundation. They put their heads together and liberated the money Goddard needed to move to a ranch near Roswell, New

Mexico where he could build real working rockets and carry out experiments.

During the 1930s, Goddard worked with a small team in the desert slowly perfecting the various mechanisms to make a liquid-fueled rocket a reality. He lived an isolated life of scientific obscurity.

Probably because of that, very few Americans know about Robert Goddard. It is a shame because he independently developed the guts to the working space rocket. Many call him the father of the modern rocket.

To make matters worse, he did this work near Roswell - where businesses now seem more interested in promoting space alien visitations than science. The city museum has a mockup of his workshop with many of his actual rockets on display. It is very informative. Regrettably, most visitors to Roswell mob the space-alien museums with their boring collections of newspaper clippings. They never learn about Goddard and the gigantic footprint he left in the world of space exploration.

In Germany, thanks to Oberth and Ley, rocketry literally and figuratively took off. Hundreds of people joined rocketry clubs or "societies." They tinkered and competed with each other to build vehicles to go faster and further. Opel put rockets on a car to make it go faster. Someone mounted rockets on the back of an ice skater to try and make him faster. There didn't seem to be any limits.

Some people laughed at these ideas but large groups seriously debated what the effects would be on the human body when riding a rocket into space.

Wernher von Braun was part of the rocket culture emerging in Germany. He joined Oberth, Goddard and many others who were energized by rockets. They saw the rocket as an exciting new tool to explore well beyond the earth's surface, maybe even to send a human being to other planets. Von Braun was the only one of these early luminaries who got to see his dream become a reality when he watched Americans walk on the moon in 1969.

Early on in Germany, von Braun was recognized by the military as an up-and-coming leader in the field and was quickly hired by the Army. To survive, von Braun had to twist his dreams to meet the requirements of the country's maniacal dictator.

Soon after Hitler took power in 1933, the military basically seized hold of rocket research in Germany by banning the rocketry societies from doing any work. Unlike Goddard on his lonely quest, in the subsequent military buildup, German rocket scientists and engineers were blessed with teams of experts and workers, funding and up-to-date facilities for their work.

The Germans quickly moved ahead at a very smart pace. By late 1934, they were already sending experimental rockets to altitudes in excess of two miles, something Goddard never achieved.

As the army work expanded, the young von Braun was chosen to be the technical director of the development group that ended up at the Peenemunde Experimental Center. There they developed many rockets and missiles, including the Aggregate 4 rocket or A-4. Later it became known as Vengeance Weapon 2 or simply the V-2.

The first successful V-2 flight was on Oct. 3, 1942 when the rocket reached an altitude of 60 miles and impacted about 120 miles from the launch point. It was by far the largest and most capable rocket ever built and would be for years.

The V-2s were 46 feet tall and five and a half feet in diameter. At launch they weighed about 27,000 pounds with 19,000 pounds being propellant and 2,000 pounds being the warhead.

Fred Simmons, in a letter to the missile range, said he worked with the Germans in 1946 at White Sands. One of the German engineers told Simmons they originally were looking to build their rocket out of aluminum to save weight. However, in an early accident, the aluminum caught fire and the whole vehicle was incinerated. They switched to steel after that.

Konrad Dannenberg, one of von Braun's paperclip engineers, wrote in *From Peenemunde To The Moon* that they designed the V-2 to use liquid propellants to make the rocket more transportable. He said, "The use of turbo pumps for the pressurization of the propellants was a major advance . . . This permitted light-weight tanks so that the missile could be erected at almost any launch location. The German rocket troops were trained to erect three missiles at a time, and to fuel, to align and to launch them in a matter of two hours."

V-2s had a range of about 200 miles and fell on their targets at 3,500 miles per hour, just five minutes after launch.

At that speed, the vehicles were coming in much faster than a bullet from any standard pistol or rifle.

A German "Vergeltungswaffe 2" or V-2 being prepared for launch in Germany during World War II. It was also called the "Aggregat-4" or A4. WSMR photo.

Forget the warhead, the V-2 fuselage with residual fuel amounted to a four to five-ton kinetic-kill vehicle. The energy released on impact alone would have been equal to just over 2,000 pounds of TNT. In other words, the impact effectively doubled the explosion of the warhead.

So, even if the warhead malfunctioned and didn't explode, a V-2 still had the capability to destroy buildings and kill many people simply by hitting a target area.

What made it so intimidating was that it struck without warning. The German V-1 or "buzz bomb" was propelled by a pulsed jet engine. With its "putt-putt" sound, victims knew the engine was still running and it was flying by. When the sound stopped, they knew the bomb would soon be hitting the ground somewhere in the vicinity.

The V-1 had a 25-foot fuselage and an 18-foot wingspan. It was effectively the world's first cruise missile and carried a warhead weighing about 1,800 lbs.

It flew along at 360 miles per hour, so it was susceptible to some countermeasures. According to the May 1954 issue of *Army Information Digest*, fighter pilots shot down 1,800 V-1s, while 232 were brought down by barrage balloons, and 1,878 were knocked out of the sky by antiaircraft guns and rockets.

Toward the end of WWII, the allies, especially the United States, took wrecked V-1s, examined them, and made plans to make their own. By the summer of 1945, the United States was beginning to build the "Loon," based on the V-1, for the impending invasion of Japan. One sits in the missile park at White Sands.

Since the V-2 fell from a great altitude at velocities way beyond the speed of sound, the impact explosion and the sonic boom were pretty much simultaneous. In addition, there were no countermeasures. British fighters had many chances to machine-gun V-1s as they slowly flew toward their targets. With the V-2 they were helpless.

German attacks using the V-2 began in September 1944. An estimated 1,115 V-2s fell on England with half hitting London and its suburbs. Targets on the continent included several Belgium cities and Paris. About 1,780 of the V-2s targeting the mainland were fired at Antwerp. This went on for seven months and resulted in the deaths of about 8,100 people and wounding some 28,000 people.

The worst V-2 incident in England occurred on Nov. 25, 1944 when one struck a Woolworth's store in New Cross High Street during the noon hour. Reportedly 168 people were killed.

The biggest loss of life on the continent from V-2s was during an attack against Antwerp where a rocket struck a theater filled with civilians and soldiers. This Dec. 16, 1944 attack resulted in 567 deaths.

Hitler had hoped the V-2 would terrorize Britain and its allies into surrender. It obviously didn't. In fact, the V-2 did not significantly affect the war and was considered a failure as a weapon.

In hindsight, from a German point of view, the V-2 did not justify its great expense in resources and manpower. In fact, more people died manufacturing V-2s in the slave labor facilities than were killed by its use as a weapon.

If Hitler had focused his scientific efforts on the atomic bomb instead, things might have been different.

V-2 Mechanics

The heart of the V-2 was the propulsion system. The two propellant tanks took up most of the space inside the rocket. The alcohol tank (fuel) was stacked on top of the liquid oxygen tank (oxidizer). Each tank had a volume of just over 1,200 gallons.

Why alcohol instead of some more energetic fuel? Konrad Dannenberg, a propulsion expert for von Braun at Peenemunde, said at a 1997 Fort Bliss History Forum that it was what was available. "Since Germany had no oil wells, the fuel for the V-2s was ethyl alcohol," he explained. He went on to say that the alcohol could be made in any moonshine still, and stills were not illegal in Germany then. The government simply went to the booze makers and had them distill as much ethyl alcohol as possible from potatoes.

Dannenberg also pointed out another war factor that played a role in the design of the V-2. The rocket had to be moved all across Europe, which meant it had to be small enough to fit through tunnels and across railroad bridges. Those dimensions prevented them from building a bigger rocket.

Using gravity to feed the combustion chamber or engine could not deliver enough propellant to provide the necessary thrust to get the hulking V-2 off the ground. Also, in the reduced gravity of a space environment, little or no propellant would even reach the engine if it was left to gravity.

To supply large amounts of both fuel and oxidizer to the engine, the V-2 was equipped with a pumping system positioned just below the tanks. There was a pump for each of the propellants.

Goddard was also working on liquid propellants on his ranch outside Roswell. He too quickly realized he needed pumps to provide a continuous supply of fuel and oxidizer to the engine.

Much of Goddard's work was inventing the different systems to bring rockets to life. For decades historians and others have been arguing about how much Goddard's work influenced the Germans. Some suggest the Germans used many of his ideas and had the personnel and resources to rapidly perfect the technology.

This area of who did what first gets a little complicated. Some say the Germans didn't really need Goddard's work to move ahead. Others say the Germans simply stole everything and wouldn't have gotten anywhere without Goddard's patents.

It turns out there is evidence for both arguments. In 1970, the U.S. Congress published a booklet called "Congressional Recognition of Goddard Rocket and Space Museum" with "Tributes to Dr. Robert H. Goddard." The booklet points out Goddard had 214 patents. Many of the early ones were not restricted and would have been available to anyone who asked.

The booklet then described how captured German military leaders, at the end of the war, were closely questioned about the German rocket program. One lieutenant general asked the questioners why they didn't ask Dr. Goddard. The Congressional report said, "Goddard had always felt that the Germans knew more about his work than did his countrymen."

Werhner von Braun wrote a tribute for this booklet, saying, "In the history of rocketry, Dr. Robert Goddard has no peers. He was first. He was ahead of everyone in the design, construction and launching of liquid-fuel rockets which eventually paved the way into space. When Dr. Goddard did his greatest work, all of us who were to come later in the rocket and space business were still in kneepants."

Wow! That is pretty strong stuff. However, von Braun later states, "In 1950, when I had the opportunity to examine Dr. Goddard's many patents, I was virtually overwhelmed by the thoroughness of his early work and found many design solutions in the V-2 rocket were already covered."

This last statement would indicate von Braun and his team had not seen much, if any, of Goddard's work in the 1930s and that they arrived at their designs independently. It is very possible because, contrary to the popular saying about things being easy compared to "rocket science," a lot of this work was simply solving new engineering problems.

German engineers designed propellant pumps driven by pressurized steam generated in a chemical reaction. The chemical reaction was created when sodium permanganate and hydrogen peroxide were sprayed into a pressure tank. The chemicals reacted instantly to create, among other things, steam. This pumping system was fueled from small tanks holding 34 gallons of peroxide and three gallons of permanganate.

The steam blew into turbines that in turn ran the pumps.

The alcohol and oxygen were fed into the top of the engine through 18 injectors. Each injector had rows of nozzles that turned the fuel and oxidizer into a fine spray. There were over 3,000 nozzles atop the engine to thoroughly mix the two propellants for combustion.

The engine was double walled with a small space between the two walls. To help cool the inner wall and prevent burn through during the combustion process, cooling alcohol was pumped into the space. In addition, small holes on the inside wall allowed alcohol to seep into the engine and help cool the wall.

When a V-2 was ignited, it took several seconds for the propellant pumping system to come up to speed and provide enough fuel to reach full thrust for lift off.

To provide guidance from the instant of lift-off, small maneuverable vanes made of heat-resistant graphite were mounted in the engine's exhaust plume. The rocket's guidance system could rotate these four vanes to deflect the exhaust in different directions and alter the V-2's course.

It was similar to riding in a car with the window down and your hand stuck out into the wind stream. If you keep you hand parallel to the ground, your hand slices through the air. If you tip the leading edge up or down, your whole arm is immediately deflected one way or the other. The carbon vanes would do the same thing in the engine exhaust.

Large fins on the tail section of the rocket provided stability as the V-2 rose through the atmosphere. As the air got thinner, these became less effective. In fact, early film of V-2 flights showed the rocket tumbling end over end in the upper atmosphere as it headed down range. When the rockets headed back to earth and encountered denser air, the V-2 would return to a nose-first trajectory and hit the ground like a dart.

At the top of the V-2 was the nose cone where the warhead was normally located with the control section immediately below that. The warhead weighed just over a ton and was composed of TNT and ammonium nitrate. At White Sands, this area was used to house the various experiments lifted to the edge of space.

The control compartment contained gyroscopes, accelerometers and other devices used to guide the rocket to its target. In addition, there were timing devices to do things like shut off the flow of fuel to the engine to control the length of the flight.

V-2 guidance was primitive by today's standards. On March 17, 1945, the Germans fired 11 V-2s at the Ludendorf Bridge in Remagen, Germany – the last bridge standing over the Rhine River. They were trying to slow the advance of allied troops.

One rocket was an obvious failure as it fell 40 miles short. The other 10 all fell within a few miles of the bridge from a launch point 130 miles away. It was impressive for such a new weapon but not accurate enough to actually destroy or even damage the bridge. In other words, the few incidents during the war of great loss of life in a single impact was sheer luck for the Germans.

Headed To Texas and New Mexico

Toward the end of World War II, von Braun and most of his scientists and engineers made a decision to surrender to the United States as opposed to any of the other allies. They felt their best treatment would come from the Americans and their worst option was with the Russians.

At the same time, special U.S. forces were looking for V-2s and related material. At Mittelwerk, soldiers found almost 250 V-2s in various stages of completion. Since this was an area that was eventually going to be turned over to Russia, the Army hurriedly removed the best material and shipped it west. While this was playing out in Europe, plans

were underway for the establishment of White Sands Proving Ground (name changed to White Sands Missile Range in 1958). The post was initially meant to be a temporary facility for testing the newfangled rocket technology emerging from WWII.

Von Braun and crew surrendered to the United States on May 2, 1945. Eventually, several hundred German scientists and ships filled with V-2 parts and associated equipment made their way to the United States. By the time these specialists reached the United States, the war was over in Europe. However, the Germans were still held captive. Von Braun referred to his group as POPs or "Prisoners of Peace."

In August 1945, almost 300 rail freight cars filled with V-2 components arrived in New Mexico. Every train siding from El Paso, Texas to Belen, New Mexico was used to hold the freight cars. Then, ten cars per day were delivered to Las Cruces where they were unloaded and their contents trucked to White Sands.

Colonel Harold Turner, the first White Sands commander, boasted about the rather large task of moving all the material from Las Cruces out to the new installation. In an interview back at White Sands in 1964, long after he had retired, he said they had no transportation support yet at White Sands, so under the terms of the General Electric contract, "we hired every trucker in this county."

Turner also recalled the German material as "the most horrible bunch of junk." When these V-2s were finally put together, they were not sleek and shiny like the ones in science fiction films. David DeVorkin, in an *Air and Space* magazine article in 1986, said the rockets looked like they were made from junkyard scrap. The skins of the V-2s were rippled and pockmarked like an automobile body that had been in many accidents and the dents had been hammered out.

DeVorkin went on to write *Science With A Vengeance* in 1992. The book is a very detailed history of the rockets and science of the V-2 era.

The railcars full of components included over 200 engines, 180 sets of propellant tanks, 90 tail units and 200 turbopumps. Contrary to popular belief, there were no rockets intact and ready to fly.

General Electric was awarded a contract to assemble, test and fly V-2s at White Sands so they had to learn how to put them together. The onsite manager was Leo "Pappy" White.

The contract was dubbed "Project Hermes." There is often confusion about what exactly is "Hermes" because there were also several rockets named "Hermes."

In January 1946, many of the German scientists and engineers were sent to Fort Bliss, Texas where they had two missions.

One mission was for some of the Germans to go to White Sands and assist General Electric in assembling and launching V-2s. It's estimated that the number of Germans working at White Sands peaked at 39 in March 1946. The number quickly diminished as the GE personnel became familiar with all aspects of the V-2. A GE report stated, "By the spring of 1947 all German specialists had been replaced."

The second mission that engaged the larger number of Germans was work on new rocket and missile designs. The White Sands Museum has a copy of the Fort Bliss Christmas Menu from 1946 for the "Research And Development Service / Sub-Office (Rocket)." The menu lists traditional American foods, basically turkey with all the trimmings. In a sign of the times, the menu also includes "cigars and cigarettes" at the end.

What makes the menu interesting is an alphabetical list or "roster of scientists." The list has 152 names on it beginning with Wilhelm Angele and ending with Helmut Zoike. Both of the von Braun brothers, Wernher and Magnus, are listed.

Assembling and testing the V-2s was tedious. Each rocket required weeks of preparation. All of the individual components were inspected and tested. When they were assembled into a subsystem, it had to be inspected and tested. Because of the crude nature of many of the original parts, repair or making things from scratch was often necessary.

According to GE, the early goal for the program was to fire 25 V-2s and do it in a fairly short time. Eventually the number was increased and, with the difficulty in testing components and the experiment-

GE employees on the V-2 contract ham it up by posing on the missile range's display rocket. In the back, Pappy White, the GE manager, holds a torch as if he is going to light the rocket's engine. I've always liked this photo, so I submitted it as one of the images to be turned into a mural in the new range control building's customer area. It is now larger than life and was "colorized" for the painting. WSMR photo.

ers needing time in preparing their payloads, GE could not maintain the one per week schedule originally planned. After it was all done, GE stated they kept a workforce of 34 to provide a V-2 every two weeks.

As useable German components ran out, GE started building their own parts. In an article by GE's Charles Green, he noted when they used German steering systems there was a large number of rocket failures attributable to the steering. After they started using GE's replacement parts, steering failures dropped dramatically. Also, the performance of the rockets was increased. Having parts made from good materials and put together by a well-fed, highly-trained workforce seems preferable to items made from subgrade materials by starving slave labor.

There is some indication that GE was a bit miserly about expenses on this contract. One of the German scientists wrote how frustrated he was watching GE personnel share their single wrench to assemble parts of the rocket. He suggested they buy a couple more so several people could work at one time. The idea was rejected.

The scientist then went to the White Sands machine shop with the wrench specifications and had one made. Suddenly, the GE personnel were working twice as fast.

Tom Starkweather, former head of the Data Reduction Division in National Range Operations at White Sands, used to collect historical information about White Sands for a book he planned to write. Before he retired he was in great demand to give talks about the range's history. One of his anecdotes about GE concerned their creative solution to dust on small parts.

The blowing sand and dust were impossible to keep out of buildings so it often migrated to small mechanical and electronic parts – items that needed to be kept clean. One GE engineer came up with the idea of placing cleaned parts in condoms and tying off the open end to keep them spotless until used.

It worked perfectly. Locally, GE management purchased a gross of condoms and submitted the bill to their headquarters. Headquarters was not amused; they wrote back that they would not pay for employee trips to questionable places in Juarez.

Of course, anyone who deals with a large bureaucracy quickly learns how to game the system. The next month, the local GE purchasing agent submitted the bill as "144 elastic storage tubes, sealed at one end." They were routinely reimbursed.

Test Stands

Subsystems were often tested in specially built facilities at White Sands. For instance, the 100K Static Test Stand, just south of the main post, was needed to test the rocket's propulsion system. The whole rocket or just the propulsion system itself could be mounted in a steel frame and then fired. A small blockhouse protected men and equipment during tests. Contracts for the facility's construction were let on Oct. 26, 1945.

The frame is gone but the blockhouse is still standing.

The concrete throat of the test stand is still there as well. The throat was designed to channel the flames and super-hot gasses down and away from the rocket motor. Some called it a "flame bucket." There was one obvious issue with the flame bucket right away.

The White Sands Museum has a manuscript written by Robert Bolles, a former GE engineer who went to work for White Sands, recounting the problem. In it he said,

One of the major problems with the small static test stand was the fact that the blast from the missile exhaust would melt the concrete lining of the flame bucket during each firing and it would flow out the bottom of the deflector like green lava or molten green glass.

Our first approach to saving the deflector concrete was a brute force attempt. We lined the deflector with 1/2 inch thick iron plates about 3-foot by 3-foot square. They were secured at the top of each plate with lag bolts into the concrete, and each row of plates overlapped the plates below so there was no way the exhaust gas could get under the plates (we thought).

Then a water manifold was placed at the top of the deflector under the missile support structure so that the manifold was protected from the blast. A high velocity stream of water was then directed along the surface of the plates to keep them cool during a firing. This, we thought, would protect the concrete on the sides and bottom of the blast deflector from eroding during each static firing.

The first static firing after lining the deflector was a sight to behold. The heavy iron plates blew off and were hurled out across the desert like dried leaves in a fall breeze. The difference from leaves was that the hot iron plates set fire to every sagebrush plant they touched as they were hurled across the desert by the force of the exhaust plume.

I thought I could fix the problem since I knew all the Germans south of us at Fort Bliss. I'd just call them up and find out how they protected the blast deflectors at Peenemunde. Whomever I talked to, I don't remember who it was now, said they just lined the deflector with tank tracks bolted to and protected by a header up under the thrust mount.

This was more of the brute force or brawny approach which we understood, so we got hold of some tank tracks and bolted them in place, checked out the water system to keep them cool and got ready for the next static firing of an engine. The tracks were only secured at the top and lay against the blast deflector. Their own weight was supposed to hold them down against the deflector surface during static firing, but to our consternation, it was a catastrophe. The tracks flapped in the exhaust like clothes on a clothesline in a windstorm, and eventually snapped off and rolled out of the deflector and into the desert.

Bolles went on to write they eventually came up with a more elegant system using water to cool the throat that worked very well.

Colonel Turner was at the small test stand on March 15, 1946 when the sheets of steel were launched in the test of a V-2 engine. Turner recounted the event in his January 1964 conference with then WSMR commander, Major General Frederick Thorlin.

Turner said VIPs from El Paso and Las Cruces were invited to be there. He said a battalion of the 69th AA from Fort Bliss under General Barnes was there as well. As they watched, Turner said, "Great sheets of incandescent steel were hurled across the desert. It was the most fantastic show of power I have ever seen."

Another test facility was a calibration stand built on the west side of the tech area. This stand held the steam generation and propellant pumping system in place and was used to calibrate the amount of fuel and oxidizer the system delivered to the engine.

V-2 mounted in the 100K Static Test Stand. The photo has no caption but most believe it is from March 1946 as there are several other photos from that first V-2 engine firing. WSMR photo.

Each rocket's system would be tweaked while the pumps moved water instead of propellants.

Beginning in 1947, GE used the stand to perfect the ratio of alcohol to oxygen. At the end of the program, they said the pumps needed to provide 123 pounds of alcohol per second and 152 pounds of oxygen per second or 275 pounds of total propellant per second.

As a result of these calibration efforts, GE said they got more consistent results and were able to increase the carrying capacity of each rocket. In fact, later payloads weighed as much as 700 pounds more than those flown early in the program and the rockets went just as high.

Only the small blockhouse from this facility remains.

Another facility developed at this time but little known or used was a "static test pit" at what is now Launch Complex 33. The pit consisted of a large concrete pad with a hole or opening in the center. The sand was excavated under the hole in the pad to create a large deep pit opening to the east. The pit was lined with concrete and became another flame bucket for static tests.

The idea was to bolt or tie-down a fully assembled rocket on the test pad just over the hole. When fired, the engine's flames and exhaust gases would go through the pad, down into the pit and blow out the east side into the desert.

By deflecting all the debris to the east, viewers in the blockhouse and cameras mounted in the area had an unobstructed view of the rocket.

After all the testing on the main post and with the rocket fully assembled, it was placed on a German-made trailer called the "Meilerwagon" and towed to the "Army Launch Complex." An integral lift frame on the Meilerwagon elevated the rocket to a vertical position onto a low portable steel launch "table" or "stool."

Once the rocket was erect, engineers and technicians loaded the propulsion system with alcohol, liquid oxygen, sodium permanganate, and hydrogen peroxide. Often the payload would be placed in the rocket at this time as well.

To assist in this process at the launch complex, a gantry was constructed from August through November 1946. The gantry was made of two open steel towers, each 60 feet tall and tied together at the top. It was almost 30 feet wide and rode on railroad car wheels on tracks. There was a hoist at the top to assist in erecting rockets and missiles. Also, there were three pairs of adjustable platforms that allowed easy access to the rocket at all levels. Scientists and engineers could walk right up to an erect rocket and work on it from a solid platform instead of a ladder.

The gantry stood on crane track, and with electric motors at each corner, could be rolled one way or the other. After erecting and preparing a V-2 or Corporal for launch, the tower was slowly moved out of the way.

According to Arnie Crouch, who worked on the V-2 program as a Broomstick Scientist, the electric motors "were not controlled by rheostats and had only on/off controls causing the top of the gantry to sway significantly when starting and stopping."

Others who worked on rockets using the gantry have told stories about other scary moments. One very real hazard was someone at the top accidentally dropping tools or heavy objects and having the item bound off one support to another, so it was possible to be struck even if you weren't under the offending worker.

Another hazard was getting off the gantry quickly when an alarm was sounded for an evacuation. With the liquid-fueled rockets standing there like ticking bombs, technicians were motivated to get to cover. They moved fast. Unfortunately, they usually descended using the steel ladders built into the gantry. As the first man went down, the next would hop on as soon as the first guy's head disappeared.

This is all well and good except we tend to leave our hands on the rungs above us as we climb down a ladder. That means the guy above, who is hurrying, is likely to step on your fingers. There were more mashed and bloodied fingers at the launch complex than injuries from explosions.

Another way off the gantry was to use the cable slide. This was something like today's zip-line attractions we see everywhere. In this case a cable was stretched from the gantry, according to GE's final report, 200 feet toward the blockhouse. In an emergency, a worker could grab a small device with a pulley on the cable and a handle hanging from it, step off and slide to safety. Homer Newell in his book *Beyond the Atmosphere: Early Years of Space Science* said "if things went wrong, one could slide and then run like hell to safety."

According to Gil Moore, who worked for the

Physical Science Lab during the V-2 days, this method of escape was used when a V-2 payload started spraying acid on workers. One worker didn't get to the zip line though.

At the time, there was a program to photograph V-2s as they climbed in order to capture the vapor trails on film over a period of time. As the smoke trails were pushed one way or another by upper level winds, it was possible to figure the direction and speed of those winds.

The work was done by the Signal Corps in cooperation with the University of Michigan and Edgewood Arsenal. The only problem was the rocket's engine nominally only burned for about a minute. The V-2 kept coasting much, much higher but it left no further contrail to observe. Somebody came up with the bright idea of creating a second smoke trail, starting after a minute, so they could collect data on winds in the 100,000 to 200,000-foot altitudes.

Various methods were proposed for doing this in the 1948-49 timeframe. One was to spray a fine powdery dust of talc out from the V-2. Another used the smoke puffs of grenades to be ejected at regular intervals. Still another involved loading a tank of sulfuric acid and a tank of water in the payload of a V-2 to create a smoke trail.

The plan was to rupture a diaphragm between the two liquids and vent the resulting boiling, steaming vapor to the outside. On the launch day, the tanks were loaded in the V-2 when they sprang a leak or the diaphragm ruptured. The reaction sent boiling acid/water out onto the gantry platforms.

Most of the men got off on the cable slide except for one man who got his ankle hung up in one of the ladders. Acid was raining down on him, and he was hollering for help when a fireman down below responded. The fire department was often on hand when hazardous materials were being handled.

According to Moore, the alert fireman opened the nozzle on his water hose and was able to direct a spray of water on the man. He kept washing the man down, diluting the acid, until the tanks ran dry and they could safely mount the gantry to retrieve him.

Moore said the victim received some significant burns, especially to his scalp, that he would show off at parties. He obviously was not terribly injured thanks to the quick-witted firefighter.

The gantry is now a relic standing at Launch Complex 33.

The Blockhouse

The blockhouse at Launch Complex 33 is one of the original buildings constructed at White Sands. It and the old V-2 assembly building on the main post are the only two buildings left from 1945.

Unlike the advanced rockets and missiles launched at LC-33, the old blockhouse is a primitive, brute-force solution to protecting men and equip-

---

Pop-up: *When you step back and listen to people discuss historical events, it is easy to see how our past gets forgotten or rewritten. When I got to White Sands, there was a keen debate ongoing about whether or not there was a German railroad V-2 launch car ever located at LC-33, just east of the blockhouse.*

Many old-timers pooh-poohed the idea, saying there were no tracks from Orogrande (the nearest railhead) to LC-33, while most simply didn't know. Finally someone came up with a couple of photos of LC-33 taken in 1946 that clearly show the railroad car sitting near the blockhouse on a very short stretch of track. Apparently it was not there long as it doesn't show up in any other photos. I also discovered a video on YouTube clearly showing the railroad launch vehicle. There is no local record that it was used for anything.

Then I found more information in a report called "The Story of White Sands Proving Ground" dated April 30, 1946. I have a photocopy of the report with no other information except on the edge of each page it says, "Reproduced at the National Archives." The report states, "some auxiliary equipment – huge railway type launchers – had to be shifted by rail to Alamogordo, dismantled there to sections transportable by Ordnance trailers over Highway 70, and reassembled on a 1000 foot stretch of track constructed for them in the launching area."

The speculation is that the railroad car was shipped to White Sands with all the other equipment with some thought they might need it to better understand how the Germans used the V-2.

---

ment during firings. The walls are reinforced concrete, about ten feet thick. The pyramid-shaped roof or cap is about 24 feet thick – no one has measured it lately and claims vary from 20 to 27 feet thick.

It was designed by Dr. Del Sasso from CalTech with some push by the first range commander, Lieutenant Colonel Harold Turner. As Turner remembered it, they had no standards for building the structure. He said there was lots of discussion and uncertainty. In his typical take-charge fashion, he stepped in and declared the roof would be 24 feet thick.

We have no idea if the engineers and Turner got it right. It has never been tested. However, it successfully protected the men inside when V-2 number 55 exploded out on the launch pad on June 14, 1951.

T. Dungan was in the blockhouse and wrote about it in *The Broomstick Scientist* newsletter for September 2001. As the V-2 exploded, men hit the floor looking for cover even though 10 feet of concrete stood between them and the rocket. He said, "My most vivid memory was of wondering if the burning liquid fuel and LOX were going to come roaring thru the tunnel that allowed the missile wiring to enter the blockhouse."

No one was injured. Dungan concluded, "I swear the blockhouse was bouncing up and down! I don't think I had been that scared since World War II."

Both Arnie Crouch and John Schoneman were young enlisted soldiers working on the V-2 program in 1951 and spent some time in the old blockhouse. Crouch, in an article in the Fall 1998 issue of *The Friends Journal*, wrote about the "launch control panels that illuminated from behind when certain functions in the launch procedure were achieved." There were quite a few of these panels.

According to Crouch, someone must have had a sense of humor because on one panel, if a malfunction occurred, the panel lit up with "TILT" to indicate the countdown was stopped.

Schoneman, in another article for *The Broomstick Scientist* newsletter, revealed he was in the blockhouse for the V-2 explosion. He wrote that after the explosion, "We all smiled when we got back on our feet and saw that the control panels were dark except for one panel that proclaimed, 'Aw Shit.'"

Blockhouse construction began in July 1945 and was completed in September. The cost was $36,000.

At first the control room, on the north side of the box, had two small slit windows for viewing what was happening out on the launch pads. Later, a third window was jack-hammered into the eastern wall to provide a view of launches on that side.

Since the walls are so thick, peering through the windows is like looking through a tunnel or tube with a very narrow field of view. The openings are protected by a series of very thick slabs of glass. They are sufficient to keep debris and a shock wave out of the building.

In addition to these few windows, personnel inside the control room had access to two periscopes mounted on the north wall. These could be used to scan the launch complex to make sure it was clear of people and track the vehicle once it left the ground.

Besides protecting people on the site, the blockhouse housed a collection of equipment for launch

This early photo of the first launch complex (now LC-33) at White Sands shows the blockhouse on the left, the WAC Corporal tower in the center and the V-2 gantry on the right. You are looking north, into the heart of the proving ground. WSMR photo.

control, communication, and recording the flight and data from the rocket. It didn't leave much space for people inside.

Artist Don Alfredo was allowed to make some drawings of White Sands in 1947. In describing the blockhouse he wrote, "It contains more doodads, jimcracks, doohickeys and gadgets than you can shake a stick at."

It turns out the blockhouse was very safe but absolutely the worst place to be if you wanted to watch the rocket fly. During the first V-2 launch on April 16, 1946, the control room was packed with people – maybe not all were essential for the mission. It was a big deal as it was the first attempt to fly a V-2 in the United States.

As soon as the V-2 left the ground, it was basically out of sight for everyone in the blockhouse. They scrambled out the blast door on the west side of the building to watch the rocket climb.

Unfortunately for the spectators, that V-2 behaved erratically and the engineers sent a message to kill the engine. So the V-2 only reached an altitude of 3.4 miles and started falling back to the ground.

It is a well-known phenomenon that when you look up into the clear blue sky and lose sight of the horizon, things will soon appear as if they are right overhead, even when they are far away from vertical. The people who had made it outside the blockhouse to watch suddenly thought they saw a huge missile headed back at them.

As these people turned and fled to find safety in the blockhouse, other folks were still trying to get out. To say the least there was much confusion and many people didn't make it back inside. Luckily the V-2 crashed to the ground well east of the blockhouse and no one was injured.

The incident did provoke a safety response from the command. On later launches, an armed guard was stationed at the door and he would not allow anyone to leave the building until the safety officer said it was OK.

This story about personnel leaving the blockhouse early and having the rocket missile head back at them is not unique. Joe Gold, in *As I Remember*, recounts being in a blockhouse for an Aerobee firing. The booster successfully pushed the rocket for a couple of seconds but the sustainer did not ignite. That meant, as Joe and others got out of the Navy blockhouse, they looked up and saw the rocket headed back down. Like the V-2, this rocket crashed harmlessly some distance from the blockhouse.

The Army blockhouse was expanded in 1947 with the addition of a communications room on the south side and a small shed on the west side to house a large 3,000 P.S.I. compressor and storage tanks. The air was fed to the launch pads via pipes.

Compressed air had innumerable uses. For example, it was very useful in cleaning things, but it was also used in many missiles to provide force. In the V-2, compressed air was used to push the sodium permanganate and hydrogen peroxide into their combustion chamber to generate the steam for the turbines. The compressed air tanks had to be charged while it was on the launch pad. An easy way was to tap in to the lines running around the launch complex.

The blockhouse is no longer used by the WSMR test community. It was turned over to the missile range's museum years ago. The museum and Public Affairs personnel used to take tours to the building but there has been no money to clean out the rodents and their droppings. The rats and mice have made the building a health hazard to visit.

On Nov. 18, 2004, Konrad Dannenberg related stories of being in a similar blockhouse at Peenemunde, Germany for the first-ever V-2 launches in 1942.

Dannenberg was a young propulsion engineer working on Wernher von Braun's team during World War II. In 2004, he was visiting White Sands to participate in the dedication of the new V-2 rocket display, with its own building, at the missile range's museum. After the ceremony, attendees were bused down to the old blockhouse at LC-33.

Dannenberg said he sat in a blockhouse about half the size of the one at White Sands for the first two V-2 flights. He couldn't see a thing. Unlike the White Sands blockhouse, there were no windows at all in the German version, and only the bosses got to look out through the periscopes.

Those first two flights were failures; Dannenberg was disappointed to not see any of the fireworks. He said, for the third launch in October 1942, he stayed outside and watched from the roof of a nearby building. He was lucky. He got to see the first successful flight of the world's largest and most complex rocket.

At the end of WWII, he followed von Braun to the United States as part of the "Paperclip" group of

German scientists who worked on rocket technology for America. He lived at Fort Bliss with the group and visited White Sands many times before moving onto Huntsville, Alabama where he worked for both the Army and NASA.

Just southeast of the blockhouse is a lone structure many people assume dates back to the V-2 firings. It is a tall concrete box with large steel doors on one side – looks like it might be a square silo.

In fact, that is what it is. The structure was built in the late 1950s and is known as the "Reduced Scale Test Facility." It was part of a series of tests for the Nike Zeus system to see how designers should build the "tactical cellular launchers" for the big missile. In this case everything was scaled down in size and Nike Ajax missiles stood in for their larger brothers.

Accomplishments

The V-2 program at White Sands had three goals: 1) gain experience in handling and firing large rockets; 2) obtain technical information on rocket ballistics, and 3) make measurements of the upper atmosphere.

A great deal of credit has to be given to the military for incorporating universities and other researchers in pursuing the third goal. The famous American space scientist James Van Allen gave the credit to Colonel Holger Toftoy.

Van Allen gave a speech on March 26, 1986 at New Mexico State University in which he said, "The Army's principal purpose in assembling and firing the V-2 rockets was for military assessment and experience. But a far-sighted ordnance officer, Colonel Holger Toftoy, had the view that they might be used for scientific purposes as well, if equipment could be mounted in the warhead in place of the sand that had been planned as ballast…"

At the end of WWII, Toftoy was in Europe and commanded a group that was charged with investigating reports of unusual or interesting German weapons. Major James Hamill worked for Toftoy and was in charge of the unit that entered the tunnels at Mittelwerk where V-2s were assembled by the Nazi slave workforce. Although the leaders of the Allied nations had agreed to split up German weapons when they were found, it was Toftoy and Hamill who rushed to remove as much V-2 material as possible before the Soviets got there.

Toftoy went on to oversee the movement of the German V-2 scientists to the United States and would later command Redstone Arsenal. Hamill eventually landed at White Sands as the chief of the ordnance unit there.

Van Allen was a young physicist out of Iowa State after the war. He provided some of the payloads in those V-2s at White Sands. Later, his instruments discovered the radiation belts surrounding the earth that are now called the "Van Allen belts." Also, he is credited along with Wernher von Braun and William Pickering for the success of America's first satellite, Explorer I.

Toftoy's V-2 Upper Atmosphere Panel was formed with both military and civilian scientists on board to review payload proposals for V-2 rockets. This led to an eclectic array of experiments that flew on the V-2s and paved the way for manned space exploration. Some of the players were Johns Hopkins University, Harvard, Princeton, the University of Michigan and the California Institute of Technology.

Like Toftoy and Hamill, many of the military officers engaged in these early days of missile development were bright and pretty good at looking into the future. In Douglas Larsen's 1946 article for Newspaper Enterprise Association (NEA) about push-button warfare and the first successful V-2 launch, he talked to some of the officers on hand about the implications of the V-2.

Vice Admiral W.H.P. Blandy said one possibility was to fire a V-2 from a ship with an A bomb on board.

One insightful officer commented about using a V-2 for going into space. Larsen wrote, "Another ordnance colonel said that it would take once again as much power to get the V-2 completely away from the earth into space. But he added: 'We don't want to do that, because we would just be cluttering up space with ersatz meteors which would get in our way later when we fly to the moon.'"

During the early decades of space exploration, you didn't hear much about the little problems scientists would encounter, like dealing with potential collisions with deadly space junk. Yet in 1946 one Army officer saw that possibility.

This examination of the upper atmosphere was needed because we simply didn't know much about its composition and how it affected us on earth's surface. Writer Daniel Lang of the *New Yorker* magazine interviewed Dr. Charles Green of GE who said our knowledge of the upper atmosphere in 1946 was similar to what a fish knows about land.

In the article Green pointed out one gee-whiz fact scientists discovered - the distance between air molecules in the upper atmosphere was 370 inches while on earth the distance was one millionth of an inch between molecules.

Later in the V-2 program, *National Geographic* magazine flew cameras on board a V-2 and took "look-down" photos of the earth. The magazine published pages of the photos. The curvature of the earth was clearly visible, thus proving that our planet is round and not flat.

Also, these photos showed the distribution of clouds over a huge area. A few meteorologists must have recognized the advantages of getting such a bird's eye view of the weather. Instead of getting barometer and temperature readings, the forecasters could actually see the clouds and fronts. The logical conclusion was to put cameras and other devices on satellites to give the weathermen their 24/7 looks at the entire planet's surface.

Pop-up: When looking down a list of V-2 launches, they are numbered 1,2,3 etc. and are in nice chronological order. However, when you get to #25, it jumps from #24 to #26. There were problems with #25. Three attempts were made to launch it, but each time some problem with the rocket or the payload sent it back to the shop. It was finally launched on April 2, 1948 and successfully reached an altitude of 89.5 miles. On board were air-sampling bottles, Geiger counters and a solar spectrograph.

Because of this rocket's apparent reluctance to leave the launch pad, it was jokingly referred to as the "Hanger Queen."

The *National Geographic's* efforts were not the first photos to show a round earth. On March 7, 1947, the Naval Research Lab put two K-25 aircraft cameras on a V-2. The cameras were mounted in the body of the rocket pointing straight out. Each had a right-angle prism so that the angle of view was down toward the tail of the rocket.

The team's cameras managed to take photos from 100 miles above the earth. The flight is often credited with taking the first space photos of earth. At the rocket's apogee it was tilted several degrees to the northeast. That means the cameras were looking to the southwest. Visible in the collage of photos are the Colorado River, the Gulf of California, the Pacific Ocean and Baja California.

The news media loved the photos, but probably more important to scientists was the new data from a spectrograph on board that captured some of the sun's ultraviolet light. The earth's atmosphere absorbs a lot of the ultraviolet light coming from the sun which means scientists had never seen some of the sun's spectrum lines. By putting instruments at the outer edges of the atmosphere, scientists were able to capture that data. The spectrum lines provided insight into what elements are found in the sun's inferno.

Devices were sent aloft to gulp samples of the air at all levels to determine what gases were present and their concentrations. Other instruments measured the level of cosmic radiation at various heights. Eventually, seeds were sent up, exposed to cosmic radiation, and then planted after their return to see if the radiation had damaged them.

One experiment involved firing rifle grenades from the side of the V-2 during a Dec. 17, 1946 launch to see if such a method could be used to make artificial meteorites. The V-2 was launched at 10:12 p.m. and reached an altitude of 116 miles. The grenades were not visible during the test and did not show up on any of the film shot of the event.

The rifle grenade experiment still gets some play in the Blogesphere. No one knows if the rifle grenades even fired since there was no evidence seen from below. However, some speculate one of the grenades may have fired and, if it was pointed in the right direction, it or pieces of it could have become the first man-made, earth-orbiting object.

Often lost in the fanciful discussion about artificial meteors are the facts about this launch. It was the first night firing of a V-2, it attained a very high altitude for such an early firing, and the glow of the carbon vanes was clearly seen by everyone on the ground.

According to Lieutenant Colonel Turner, the carbon vanes mounted in the exhaust stream from the rocket engine were heated to a red incandescence. Fritz Zwicky, of the California Institute of Technology, stated afterwards he thought the vanes could have been seen at the Mount Palomar Observatory in California, if a telescope had been pointed east.

Several experiments were conducted using mammals as test subjects in flights sponsored by the Air Force and Cambridge Research Labs. There was a series of Albert shots where Rhesus monkeys were sent aloft. The first shot (Albert I) on June 11, 1948 was a total failure because the monkey died before the rocket even took off.

On the next flight (Albert II) on June 14, 1949, the V-2 reached an altitude of 83 miles, and good heart and respiration data for the monkey was collected. Unfortunately for the monkey, the recovery system (separating the payload from the rocket and then deploying a parachute) failed miserably. The monkey died on impact with the ground.

For the third flight the rocket failed. However, on Dec. 8, 1949 (Albert IV) scientists collected good data from their little astronaut.

Although scientists failed to bring back a monkey alive, something that eluded them for several more years, they had valuable respiration and heart data from the flights. In a nutshell, the animals' respiration and heart rates were within normal ranges during the stressful parts of the flights.

The results showed that a mammal could survive the extreme G forces at liftoff and the zero gravity experienced at the top or apogee of the flight. This must have given scientists confidence that a large mammal like a man would some day safely ride a rocket into space.

Another biological experiment involved placing a mouse in a clear plastic cylinder and filming his reactions during a flight. After the Aug. 31, 1950 test, Dr. James Henry stated, "The pictures showed the mouse floated around, with no apparent air of confusion." This flight disproved a theory of the time that mammals might "go crazy" when exposed to the weightless environment of outer space.

Other tests were conducted to improve rocket technology and the methods employed during a test. Engineers experimented with various explosives and eventually found that a few pounds of TNT placed in a V-2 could be used to separate the nose cone. They also looked at using compressed air to eject the payloads from the rocket once the data was collected. This, coupled with parachutes that would automatically deploy, was to allow for a softer landing for payloads – when they worked.

These developments were vital to recovering any data from the flights. Many early photos of V-2 impact craters show soldiers and scientists in the craters with picks and shovels hoping to find their instruments still intact. Remember, a V-2 could hit the ground with such velocity it was like a 2,000-lb. warhead exploding – easily enough force to destroy the experiments.

They were lucky to find anything but small pieces until they figured out how to soften landings. Here is a GE description of the V-2 impact after the first successful flight on May 10, 1946:

The appearance of the crater indicated a very high velocity impact with no chemical explosion or fire following. It was estimated to be at least thirty feet in diameter at the top and thirty feet deep. The earth at this point consisted of a mixture of wet sand and gypsum, dry on top, overlaying hard gypsum rock. Many large boulders had been blasted out of the rock, a few being tossed as far as fifty or sixty feet from the crater, others falling back into the crater and sliding to the bottom. Some loose masses of wet sand and gypsum were thrown to great distances, perhaps as much as five hundred feet.

No parts of the rocket were to be found in the crater, although it is possible that some were buried under the boulders at the bottom. Most of the parts were found at distances up to a thousand feet, the distribution being most dense at one to three hundred feet and to the lee side of the hole…..All together a two-hour search netted only about 50 pounds of scrap parts.

Also, the writer reported that although there was no fire, the effects of great heat were evident on pieces of the metal. The leading edges of the V-2 may have been glowing red hot as it smacked into the ground.

One interesting aspect of this smashup is the total destruction of the vehicle and the huge hole created simply from the kinetic energy released on impact. There was no secondary explosion of propellants because they had been spent.

Contrast that to the impact from the first flight in April 1946 that only climbed to an altitude of 3.5 miles. In "First American Showing of the V-2," R.W. Porter from GE said the V-2 propellant tanks were two-thirds full and the "resulting explosion raised a plume of dust hundreds of feet into the air." Porter's article appeared in a publication called *The Guided Missile* in July 1946. It was published by the Joint Committee on New Weapons and Equipment under the Joint Chiefs of Staff.

From descriptions such as this, many people have drawn the conclusion the V-2's alcohol load exploded on impact like TNT. In reality, the alcohol is like gasoline. It has to be turned into an aerosol (mixed with air) so it can burn explosively. Such an explosion is called a "deflagration" as opposed to a "detonation" like you might have with TNT. It is an explosion, but the over pressure is much lower and there is much less blast energy.

The impact of a V-2 then is really a two-step explosion. The kinetic energy of the impact is like a TNT detonation and creates the crater. That explosion instantly destroys the tanks holding the alcohol and oxygen, mixes the two, and they ignite to burn fiercely in another explosion that is dangerous but one that doesn't dig craters. The alcohol explosion is the same as the military's fuel-air bombs.

Porter reported, "many of the sturdier parts of the rocket were found reasonably intact in or near the crater and instruments packed in the warhead for tests were found with records in useable condition." So the speed of the V-2 when hitting the ground was the main cause of damage to the vehicle and the size of crater created in the desert floor.

The GE engineers quickly found a solution for this problem. It was absolutely necessary if they were going to get any data from the experiments being sent aloft in the V-2s. One of the final GE reports stated, "Unless experimental requirements dictated otherwise, it became standard practice to effect warhead separation at 40 miles, or higher, on the downward leg of the trajectory. With proper separation, the impact of the after end of the missile was surprisingly gentle."

Sometimes this atmospheric effect is forgotten even today. On March 8, 2012, I was lucky enough to meet Gene Kranz, a former NASA flight director. He is probably best known as the director who led the effort to bring home the astronauts on the ill-fated Apollo 13 mission.

I showed him around the missile range museum and Launch Complex 33. In our conversations about V-2s, he mentioned they were surprised at how much of the space shuttle Columbia survived the fall to earth from orbit when it disintegrated. He said pieces must have tumbled or spiraled, instead of crashing through the air like arrows, and were slowed enough to make it to the ground.

GE engineers also tried ejecting the experiment using compressed air and have it tumble to the ground separate from the dart-like V-2. This was successfully done for the first time on Oct. 10, 1946.

With other adjustments GE made to the rockets over the years, V-2s were able to carry heavier loads to higher altitudes. The first V-2s only reached altitudes of 60-70 miles. In 1951, an altitude of 128 miles was attained.

In one GE report, the company stated they developed many changes and improvements that were never used on the rocket. It would have been too time-consuming and expensive to make the changes with very little gain for the program.

The Navy In The Desert

The Navy was invited to participate in the V-2 program from the very beginning and set up shop at White Sands in 1946. The service became a major player in the V-2 program.

Lieutenant Colonel Turner liked to take some credit for the Navy being at White Sands although the idea originated elsewhere. According to Turner's 1964 interview at White Sands, he invited General Campbell (Army Ordnance) and Admiral Parsons (Navy Ordnance) to his office after the first successful V-2 firing. This is the same Parsons who worked on the proximity fuse and atomic bomb during World War II. In fact, he armed the Little Boy bomb on the flight to Hiroshima.

At the meeting, Parsons asked Campbell if the Navy could put some people at White Sands to work on the V-2. Campbell said, "What do you think Turner?" Turner said he responded with, "Sure, we can get along with anybody." They initially sent about 50 people.

The German nosecones for the V-2 were designed to provide a dart-like, aerodynamic body for cutting through the atmosphere. It wasn't very good for packing with instruments. The Navy ended up fabricating most of the nosecones for the V-2 flights, some being specially built to house very specific items.

For instance, there was a University of Michigan

experiment that flew three different times needing a nose cone with four small openings in its sloped sides. The openings were for small tubes that would push out and retract repeatedly during the flight. They were used to measure pressures so scientists could eventually calculate the temperature for the different layers of the atmosphere.

Also, the Navy was obviously interested in missiles aboard ships, so it could reach out to defend the fleet. As Larsen pointed out in his article about the May 1946 V-2 launch at White Sands, some in the Navy already glimpsed a future of shipboard missiles armed with atomic bombs.

On September 6, 1947, GE and the Navy launched a V-2 from the deck of the aircraft carrier Midway several hundred miles out in the Atlantic Ocean. The test was called "Operation Sandy."

It didn't go too well. The V-2 tipped immediately on liftoff and oscillated side to side. Luckily, the rocket didn't hit any superstructure on the aircraft carrier and successfully propelled itself away. Not long after the rocket broke up over open water.

This did not give Navy officials a warm and fuzzy feeling about launching liquid-fueled missiles from their ships. They headed back to White Sands and eventually did some "what if" testing.

During a program dubbed "Operation Pushover" in 1949, the Navy deliberately tipped over two V-2s, with rocket motors burning, on mock ship decks to see how much damage would be caused by such an accident. Most historians say the Navy abandoned the idea of using liquid-fueled missiles afterward.

The tests were conducted at the Navy's Launch Complex 35. One of the mock-up decks is still sitting out in the desert. There is a gaping hole in the deck from the test.

Bumper

One very successful V-2 program at White Sands was the Bumper series. It captured the world's attention as the White Sands team put the first manmade item into Space.

The program's name comes from the idea of using a V-2 rocket to "bump" another rocket, or stage, up to higher altitudes and higher speeds. The idea of putting the V-2 and WAC Corporal together apparently came from Toftoy who, with his many suggestions, really put his stamp on the early days of American rocket research.

The program gave engineers a chance to look at techniques for putting a two-stage vehicle together and then have them separate at high speed. Also, it gave scientists a chance to look at what happens to vehicles at even higher altitudes and speeds than ever seen before. At the same time, new records could be established which were proof to the public that these folks were profitably spending taxpayer dollars.

General Electric basically used a regular V-2 rocket with the nose modified to accept and hold the rear of the WAC Corporal. The WAC Corporal was modified by JPL to use four fins instead of the normal three. Also, small spin motors were added. These modifications to the WAC provided stability as it flew through the much thinner atmosphere at very high altitudes.

On Feb. 24, 1949, the WAC Corporal or "second stage" on a fully fueled Bumper reached an altitude of 250 miles and a speed of 5,150 miles per hour. It

Bumper - a V-2 coupled with a WAC Corporal on top - shortly after launch at the Army Launch Area. WSMR photo.

was the first manmade item in space and the fastest any manmade object had traveled. There is no bullet or projectile leaving a rifle muzzle that comes anywhere close to that speed.

According to Dr. Frank Malina, director of JPL at the time, "Thus the WAC became the first recorded man-made object to enter extra-terrestrial space, and the "space age" could be said to have been opened in the U.S.A. in 1949."

One myth about that flight is that the WAC Corporal was never found, that it simply disappeared. Army records show it was found a year later.

For the fifth launch in the Bumper series, Frank Hemingway did something he wasn't sure he would have done later in life. At the time he was a young engineer who came to White Sands with the Ballistics Research Lab at the very birth of the range.

It was 1949 and Hemingway's team put together a refined instrumentation package for the vehicles. It was equipped so the ground crew could send signals to the rocket and the rocket would answer.

After the rockets were fueled and pressurized, Hemingway's team couldn't get a signal from their instruments on board. "I asked if anyone wanted to climb up the gantry and fix it. Nobody would go. I can't blame them because those rockets were just

like big bombs. So I took a screwdriver and climbed up the gantry. I had to take out 28 screws to get the panel off and get to the instruments. I didn't even know if I could fix it, but luckily it was just a loose cable connection. I fixed it and the bird successfully flew," he said.

As the program continued, scientists wanted to collect aerodynamic data on the Bumper while in the thicker, lower atmosphere. They needed to launch the rocket at a lower angle, so that it didn't fly very high but would go a great distance - more parallel to the ground.

There wasn't enough room at White Sands, so the team shifted their efforts to the newly established Cape Canaveral center in Florida. On July 24, 1950, a Bumper package was the first vehicle launched from the cape. In this flight the WAC Corporal reached a speed of Mach 9.

Oh, by the way, the first commander of the "Joint Long Range Proving Ground" at Cape Canaveral was Colonel Harold Turner, the first commander at White Sands. Turner arrived at the cape in 1949 and went out with his personnel helping to survey and place the various facilities that would be constructed. In other words, he did much the same thing he did at White Sands when he arrived in July 1945.

The White Sands Missile Range's Museum V-2 is now housed indoors and is displayed horizontally so visitors can peer into the various openings to see the internal machinery. Photo by the author.

For a summary of two V-2 rockets that went astray, see the later chapter on missile mishaps, called Oops!

Display V-2

The V-2 on display at the White Sands Museum once stood in the old missile park when it was across the street from the headquarters building. Before it was mounted for permanent display in the 1950s, this may have been the V-2 that White Sands regularly towed to surrounding communities for display. Historians guess this because all the internal components were clearly marked with painted labels that would have been visible when the various compartment doors were open.

The towed version was dubbed "Betsy." According to an article and photo in the *Wind and Sand* newspaper from December 1950, Betsy had been taken for display in El Paso, Las Cruces, Alamogordo, Albuquerque, Phoenix, and Florida.

When the V-2 was mounted in the old missile park, a steel pole was welded into the engine and mounted into a huge block of buried concrete. In addition, more than 10,000 pounds of concrete were poured into the tail section to insure the spring winds didn't topple the display.

By 2001, it was evident the V-2 was losing its battle against the winds, sand and rust. There were places where you could actually poke your finger through the crumbling skin.

In 2002, the museum staff asked the Cosmosphere and Space Center at Hutchison, Kansas to look at the V-2. The space center was asked because they had previously restored several V-2s. Their inspection revealed that the rocket was in dire straits.

At the same time, they found that the White Sands V-2 might be the most complete rocket of the 19 existing V-2s in the world.

A decision was quickly made to fund a complete restoration of the rocket by the Cosmosphere and Space Center before it was too late to save the vehicle. In September 2002, the V-2 was moved to Kansas where it was completely taken apart, treated, and reassembled with a new skin.

To protect the V-2 from the desert's harsh environment and to provide better access to it, the museum staff decided to put the V-2 in a protective building and display it horizontally so visitors can see inside it.

Along one side, the skin and even some of the components have windows cut in them so visitors can see what is inside. It is a rare peek at some vintage technology.

The V-2 is painted with a yellow and black paint scheme just like the first successful V-2 launched at White Sands on May 10, 1946. The paint scheme was designed to be highly visible but turned out to be just the opposite as the rocket climbed into the dark sky of near outer space. Later paint schemes used a white background with black lines and blocks.

When the Cosmosphere personnel took the V-2 apart, they found serial numbers on some of the parts. This allowed them to do some research on the rocket's provenance.

Through their contacts with rocket enthusiasts in Europe, they discovered the museum's V-2 is "German rocket #FZ04/20919." According to European records, it came off the Mittelwerk assembly line in December 1944. Rockets with serial numbers prior to and after #20919 were launched at the end of 1944 by Battalion 836 of Gruppe Süd. Rocket #20919 was sent to firing sites in Westerwald, but was sent back to Kleinbodungen for repair.

In April 1945, American tanks and infantry rolled into Kleinbodungen and found a number of complete V-2s. One of those liberated and packed off to the U.S. was #20919. It became a public display at White Sands.

Whatever Happened To All That German Loot?

Many of us who have worked at White Sands have wondered what happened to all the V-2 stuff once the program ended. We know large numbers of components and pieces arrived at WSMR in 1945-46. At the end there should have been dozens of rocket engines, propellant tanks, fuselages, small parts (you name it) left behind.

When I arrived at White Sands in 1977, no one seemed to know what happened to the relics. For sure, there were a few odds and ends around. For instance, a set of propellant tanks was donated to a museum, and a few components ended up in the WSMR Museum.

Although no one could say for sure what happened to the material, one story was repeated by many folks. It was that a trench was bulldozed in the desert, and all the V-2 parts and pieces were dumped in and buried.

A similar story goes along with the old German films taken of their V-2 tests back when they were developing the rocket as a weapon. Supposedly, dozens of cans of this film were sent to White Sands along with the V-2 components to assist in studying this new technology.

The account goes that the film was nitrate-based which means it is very volatile and a fire hazard. Supposedly, in the 1950s, the White Sands fire marshal discovered the old film in the vault at the pictorial building. He stated it was a hazard and ordered it removed. Since the V-2 program was long gone, no one saw any use for the film, so it was taken to an open area and burned.

Whether these stories are myths or real, I cannot say. Having worked at White Sands for 30 years, I will say the actions taken by Army officials in these stories are perfectly believable. A short-sighted bureaucrat, be it an officer, enlisted man or a civilian, really has a lot of power to make the most blindingly ill-advised decisions when no one else cares.

Unfortunately, we are now deprived of seeing this material and deprived of the potential information it may have yielded. In a matter of just a few decades we are left wondering "How did that work? How did they do that?"

This is V-2 Number 55 exploding on the pad on June 14, 1951. It was carrying a package of equipment from the Naval Research Lab to measure solar and cosmic radiation. The photo is very revealing. The air around the rocket's nose is filled with debris for dozens of feet. Obviously some sort of explosion has done this. Yet the lower rocket body, housing the motor, pumps and propellant tanks is intact yet - not a propulsion system failure. In fact, it looks like the alcohol tank was probably ruptured in the initial explosion and the fuel is starting to vaporize and burn. The fireball is just beginning at the nose. Speculation based on the photo is that the explosive charges to be used later to separate the payload from the rocket triggered prematurely. WSMR photo.

10

The San Andres Tram

A Ski Lift To Clyde Tombaugh's Optics Site

The problem with most mountaintop viewpoints is getting there. The top of San Andres Peak offers one of the grandest views on White Sands Missile Range but is miles from and thousands of feet above the nearest road. However, for a few years starting in 1947, an aerial tram carried range employees to the top with relative ease.

San Andres Peak is 8,235 feet high and is in the middle of the San Andres Mountains to the west of Lake Lucero. From the top the view is easily 50 to 100 miles in almost every direction. It includes an unobstructed view of many of the range's launch complexes and most of the range itself. In the late 1940s, that meant a view of V-2 missions from just after liftoff to impact without the interference of ground haze.

Initially, range officials used the top of San Andres Peak as an observation point for plotting V-2 rocket impacts. By combining information from several sites on the range, it was possible to pinpoint the location of an impact through triangulation.

According to old-timers, it was astronomer Clyde Tombaugh who proposed using the mountaintop for photographing V-2 flights. See the photo of him on site at the top of the mountain.

Years after discovering the planet Pluto, Tombaugh joined White Sands in 1946 to run the optics branch. He basically taught White Sands personnel how to photograph objects like missiles in the big, empty New Mexico sky.

To get equipment and personnel to the top of the mountain, planners decided to put in a tram instead of a road. The site is in the middle of the San Andres National Wildlife Refuge, a non-military piece of land, so a road was probably frowned on.

According to Charlie Brink, who was chief of the range's survey unit, the construction of the tram was contracted out. He surveyed the mountain for the project, but a Colorado firm installed it in 1947. It is 7,200 feet long and ascends 2,200 vertical feet from its terminal on the west side of San Andres Peak to a point just below the top.

The tram is anchored at the bottom and top to small but beefy steel frames which are pinned to solid rock. There were 11 pairs of towers in between to hold up the cables.

The towers were put together like the scaffolding used in building construction. Each tower was apparently carried up the mountain in pieces and then bolted together on site – much the way a child would put together a Tinker Toy tower. The bottoms or feet on the towers were not anchored to the ground. Instead guy wires held each tower erect the same way they hold a radio station antenna in place.

When I first visited the tram the towers were still standing. Not anymore. In the 1980s, there was an incident where a helicopter clipped one of the cables during a bighorn sheep survey. The helicopter was OK, but officials decided to knock down the towers to prevent a more serious accident. A team went up and cut the cables on each tower and allowed them to fall in place. They are still where they fell.

At each tower site, there were two towers standing side by side. A stationary cable hung from each tower and was anchored at both the top and bottom. This stationary cable acted as a rail for the cable cars to hang from.

The term "cable car" is a bit of a misnomer as

they weren't much more than metal baskets. They were very small with room for only one person to ride in comfortably. Those who actually rode it said two people could go together, but they would have to sit side by side with their legs dangling out the side.

The second cable attached to the cable cars and was a continuous loop going up through one side of the towers and down the other side. One car was fastened to this loop at the base of the mountain while the other one was on the opposite side of the loop and fastened at the top.

To get people to the top, an operator would run an engine that pulled the cable loop on one side while the visitor rode the opposite car to the top. If a second person wanted to go up, he would get into the car on the opposite side that had come down to the bottom as his buddy was pulled to the top on the other side. The operator would reverse the engine to pull the other side and raise the occupied cart.

This meant that if the photographers approached the tram base and got into the south basket for the ride up, the north basket was already at the top of the mountain. As they ascended, the north basket came down the peak and ended up at the base as they hit the top. This simple system insured there was always a basket at both the top and bottom.

The cable was driven back and forth by a small gasoline engine at the bottom. Whenever the tram was used, two soldiers stayed at the bottom and operated it. They communicated with the instrumentation techs at the top over a telephone line strung below the tram. The engine was equipped with a transmission so it could run at various speeds. Typically a ride took 15 to 20 minutes one-way.

The mountaintop quickly grew into a real instrumentation site, equipped with an Askania cinetheodolite to film missile tests. A cement-block building was built on the east edge of the peak. Beside it a small shelter was constructed for the instrument. Electricity was provided by a portable generator and heat came from an oil heater. A radio provided launch information and timing data for the crews.

All the building materials and equipment were carried up the mountain on the tram. The construction crews rode it back and forth. They even carried pipe and a portable welder to build a railing along the east edge, so no one would fall off the cliff on that side.

Lester Christiansen was in charge of the cine site on San Andres Peak and says he probably rode the tram more than anyone. It took two men to operate the old Askania cine; Christiansen said he never had

Clyde Tombaugh, Virginia Farquhar and Major LLoyd Smith visit Clyde's new optics site atop San Andres Peak at 8,235 feet, circa 1949. They rode the tram from Ropes Spring to get there. The roof to the shelter has blown off but the walls are still there. WSMR photo.

Harry McCaffrey on one of the tram towers to provide perspective. The photo was taken in the early 1980s before the towers were knocked down. McCaffrey eventually retired from White Sands as the head of the Contracting Directorate. Photo by the author.

to look far for a fellow operator. Many people were interested in the adventure of riding above a steep mountainside covered with piñon, scrub oak, sotol, cholla, ocotillo, century plants, and mountain mahogany to get to one of the best viewpoints in southern New Mexico. It was certainly an unusual journey.

Christiansen said he once saw a mountain lion down below on a ride. John Phillips, the chief of the Askania units for White Sands at the time and Christiansen's boss, also rode the tram frequently. He said he once surprised a desert bighorn sheep on top. The startled animal leaped down the ledges on the east face of the mountain. Phillips and Brink both talked about the rattlesnakes they saw at the top.

But the most unanticipated inhabitants on the mountaintop were the ladybugs. Phillips said it was common to have them crawl up your pant legs. I noticed this same phenomenon when I visited the peak. There were hundreds and hundreds of the orange and black bugs on the rocks.

In early 1950, *National Geographic* magazine photographer J. Baylor Roberts made the tram ride. He was looking for a photo of an instrumentation site being used in support of a V-2 firing involving the *National Geographic*. The magazine had cameras in the payload of the V-2 to take still photos of the earth as the rocket slowed to apogee.

Roberts took a photo of Christiansen and Phillips manning the Askania at the site. The color photo appeared in the October 1950 issue of *National Geographic* magazine in an article called "Seeing the Earth from 80 Miles Up."

The article was written by Clyde T. Holliday and talks a lot about the future use of high altitude photography of the earth. All the photos in the articles were shot at White Sands.

Working on the mountain did not always go smoothly. Christiansen said during summer the top cable would warm, expand and droop. Then, when he and his partner rode over areas close to the ground, the basket sometimes dragged on the rocks and cactus. On the other hand, winter temperatures seemed to be especially cold on top. The oil stove didn't help much.

In addition, Christiansen said there were several days when he was forced to walk down from the summit because of high winds. The tram also stalled occasionally, leaving men dangling between towers until the soldiers could get it going. Phillips remembered a time when it quit as the basket he was riding in was less than 100 feet from a tower. After waiting 30 minutes, he decided it wasn't going to be fixed anytime soon so he went hand over hand on the top cable to the tower and walked down.

According to Christiansen, the scariest part of working on the peak and riding the tram was the lightning. He said the peak was a great lightning rod and sitting on top during a thunderstorm was an experience in helplessness. Once a lightning strike blew out some of their equipment.

Safety seems to be the main reason for closing the site in 1952. In addition, the inaccessibility of the place and number of man-hours required in getting the data made the site unattractive.

The cinetheodolite and other equipment were removed. The building was left behind and has since lost its roof to the high winds that race across the top.

The towers, cables and baskets are still on the side of the mountain. An equipment shed and the bottom frame, with its counterweight and gasoline engine, are also still there.

The base of the tram sits just east of the old Civilian Conservation Corps (CCC) recreation site at Ropes Spring.

11

Hand-Me-Downs To Start

Wobbly Buildings, HAWKS, And Polar Bears

Maybe it was working the first half of my 30-year career at White Sands Missile Range in one of the original 1945 buildings that colored my impressions of the installation's physical plant. That crummy old rundown building and many more were polar opposites to the cutting-edge weapons technology tested at White Sands, the advanced optics, radar and telemetry systems used to gather data, the computers and other paraphernalia used to turn raw data into reports, and the collection of highly paid scientists and engineers to put it all together.

When I arrived in the fall of 1977, I reported to Bldg. 122, one of the earliest structures, which had just been turned over to Public Affairs a few months earlier. This wobbly structure was a warren of small and large rooms that defied explanation to someone coming from work in a tall office building in downtown St. Louis. Everything about it was warped, drafty, old and worn out.

For heat there were a few radiant gas heaters located around the walls. There wasn't an ounce of insulation in the building – not in the walls or the attic. We were required to basically turn off the heaters at night, so each morning, depending on the low the night before, we'd enter a cold or a really cold building. The first order of business was to crank up the heaters and then stand around them until the place started to warm up.

In the summer, the rooms were cooled by huge swamp coolers mounted on the roof. Or in the language of the day, it was a "washed-air cooling system." That makes it sound sort of appealing.

These things blew so much air, the exterior doors would not close by themselves. If you didn't strategically deploy paperweights around the top of your desk, your correspondence would often launch and drift toward someone else's desk.

At the end of the day we would shut them down. Luckily temperatures at night usually cooled enough that the building wasn't scalding in the morning. Besides, the "hurricane coolers" could refresh the building's air in just a couple of minutes.

The floors were covered with 1950's asphalt tiles that were buckled and uneven. You could try to roll a marble down the center of almost any room and there was no way it would travel in a straight line. It would bend and curl as it bounced around and eventually end up against one of the walls.

The dreary paint, ancient all-metal grey furniture, antique fixtures, leaky roof and, in general, its decrepit, neglected nature were only relieved by getting out on the range to watch a missile shot or explore an old ranch. When we were forced to move out because of asbestos and lead paint found inside, we were a little reluctant because the building had so much "character." It was, after all, one of two original buildings still standing on the main post. We got over it in a few minutes.

Starting From Scratch

To support the rocket and missile projects arriving at White Sands, the Army needed a typical military post but with an emphasis on engineering and testing. So, in addition to erecting standard installation facilities for things like housing, food services, a post exchange, a chapel, and administrative support, White Sands was home to some interesting early test capabilities. For instance, the first two static test stands were seen as state-of-the-art in their day but quickly became "white elephants."

Interestingly, Bldg. 122 was already well used when it arrived at White Sands. At the very beginning of White Sands Proving Ground, the plans were for a temporary facility to support a few tests of rockets and missiles. There was no reason to build anything new for such a task. That changed in the fall of 1945 with plans to ship tons of V-2 parts and equipment to White Sands for in-depth analysis.

In order to house troops and engineers, provide offices for administrative support, supply space for shops and maintenance, and feed and entertain everyone involved, the Army simply collected excess buildings. Most came from the New Mexico Civilian Conservation Corps (CCC) camps and regional military installations like Sandia Air Base in Albuquerque. The buildings were systematically disassembled with many of the parts numbered so they could be properly reassembled at White Sands – just like a kit home house from Sears.

When it became evident White Sands was going to be a permanent facility, the Army continued to move old buildings onto the post because there

wasn't enough money or time to magically create a whole new post from scratch. New structures gradually went up while some of the old buildings, like Bldg. 122, lived on for decades.

One range history entitled *Origin and Construction of White Sands Proving Ground* put it this way: "By taking advantage of buildings at de-activated stations, it was possible to acquire certain storehouse facilities, maintenance shops for maintenance of special technical vehicles used at the post, and a chapel at very favorable out-of-pocket cost." That emphasis on cost has always been a factor in building the range's infrastructure. Cinder block boxes with occasional brick boxes seemed to be the building strategy for decades. As an employee, you might get lucky and work in a box with a window.

That chapel was rebuilt at White Sands in 1947. According to research done by Dave Ussery many years ago, the chapel was originally constructed during World War II at Camp Luna near Las Vegas, New Mexico. Camp Luna served as a basic training and advanced aerial gunnery training facility for the U.S. Army Air Force.

The chapel was dismantled after the war and

This photo of the first post chapel was taken on Aug. 26, 1947. When it was taken apart at Camp Luna, the siding was stripped off but the tar paper under it was left. If you look closely, you can see the vertical lines in the tar paper between each window where the wall panels were joined. Under each seam is a small concrete pier to support the structure and get it off the ground. Some of the old buildings imported in 1945 weren't placed on nice, sturdy concrete blocks like these. Instead, they were placed on rocks found at the base of the Organ Mountains. This chapel is still used today. WSMR photo.

moved here to serve the religious needs of the proving ground. Originally it was used for all faiths. When the new chapel was built, Sierra Chapel became the focus for Catholic services.

The chapel is not unique. It was built as part of the Army's Series 700 Mobilization series of buildings. It is a rectangular, two-story wood-frame building with a simple gable roof. The building rests on a concrete foundation.

It may not be unique but it may be the only surviving, primarily unaltered 700 series military chapel in New Mexico. There probably aren't very many in other places either.

White Sands was established to test the new-fangled rocket technology in World War II. The Army's Ordnance Corps recognized the need to investigate rockets in 1944. Major General G.M. Barnes, then chief of Research and Development Service within the corps, put together a team to find a place within the United States to conduct such testing. The team of officers, scientists and engineers included Lieutenant Colonel Harold Turner who ended up as the first commander of White Sands.

According to a short history of White Sands published Sept. 30, 1947, the team was looking for these features: "extraordinarily clear weather throughout most of the year; large amounts of open, uninhabited terrain, over which firings could be conducted without jeopardy to civilian population; accessibility to rail and power facilities; and to whatever degree possible, proximity to communities to provide for the cultural needs of personnel to be employed at such an installation."

They hit on the land already occupied by the Alamogordo Bombing Range and the Fort Bliss Anti-Aircraft Artillery ranges. By adding lands to the sides of the bombing range, the Army jury-rigged a testing range 100 miles long and 40 miles wide.

Even at this very early stage, the planners knew the range wasn't large enough. The 1947 history states, "While it was recognized that both in length and width the range was not as large as might be desired, it could be utilized efficiently for the early types of missiles to be developed and for reduced scale prototypes of later and larger types."

Plans for the post or cantonment area were drawn up in Washington. Turner arrived around the 4th of July ready to take command. He was picked for the job because he had a background in rocketry. In a transcript of a recording made by Turner, he stated he was overseas at the close of World War II where "I had the privilege of conducting a very highly classified mission involving the installation of Army rockets on airplanes with the hope of greatly improving the accuracy of these rockets."

When he visited the area selected for the main post, the Corps of Engineers personnel were already at work and needed more information. The plans devised in Washington didn't exactly specify where to place headquarters and the buildings around it. It was generally in the southwest corner of the new proving ground.

Planners obviously knew what they were doing. Even with several thousand square miles to work with, they knew to place people and the support facilities at the very edges of the range. Big, heavy chunks of metal and various explosive devices were going to be falling from the sky; so to maximize safety, everyone needed to be miles from the action.

Engineering preparations began in June 1945 with actual work starting on the 25th. On the 27th, a contractor was on site to begin drilling water wells and making preparations for a sanitary sewer system. By the 29th, the engineers were ready to start erecting buildings. The question was where to start.

According to Turner's transcript, this kind of fine detail had not been part of the planning. He knew he didn't want to get into a long discussion with others about what would be best because he figured it could drag on and on. He said, "I looked around, made a cross on the ground with my foot." That became the spot for headquarters. After that it was simply a matter of following the plan.

Looking back on his choice, Turner jokingly said, "It can be seen immediately, this was a very scientific decision, and actually, as years went by, it was clear it was not precisely the optimum but nevertheless very adequate."

The engineers worked quickly to make the place operational. On July 7, they started work on the access roads so personnel didn't have to drive down a sandy desert road from San Augustin pass through the Cox ranch to the headquarters.

On July 10, work began on the launch complex 6.2 miles east of headquarters to include the concrete blockhouse and WAC Corporal launch tower.

On July 13, the order activating White Sands Proving Ground as a Class II activity was published.

The order was effective July 9 so that is the anniversary date for White Sands (not the 13th).

At the same time, the authorization for personnel at White Sands was set at 163 officers and enlisted men. Also, the 9393rd Technical Service Unit was activated to provide support.

There are two superb aerial photos of the post at its birth. We know the photos were taken several months after July 1945 because the initial buildings are in place. They include headquarters, the V-2 assembly building, mess halls, quarters for officers and hutments for enlisted personnel, the diesel power plant, and roads. It looks like an image documenting the end of the initial construction.

At the same time, we know they must have been taken before February 1946 because that is when a contract was let for construction of a new missile assembly building just west of the V-2 assembly building. Construction probably didn't start until March or April but we have no start date on file.

This building is a large open-bay structure with clerestory windows to light the bay and a large overhead crane that could be moved the length of the workspace. It was known as the Mill Bldg. In these photos, there is no evidence of construction on that piece of desert. Once completed the Mill Bldg. was used for V-2 buildup.

The largest building in these images is the V-2 assembly building. It is a large Quonset hut.

Quonset huts were used in many places during World War II so they were easy to acquire. One estimate is that the military used over 150,000 of the prefabricated steel buildings during the war.

A Quonset hut is semicircular in design. It is one continuous arc from one side, over the roof, to the other side – looking a bit like a French loaf of bread sitting there. They can be made in almost any size and, because there is no support structure inside, imagination is the only limit on what can be placed inside.

Other smaller Quonset huts were added later for storage and office space. In my time at White Sands, an old Quonset, probably erected by the Navy, was turned into a roller skating rink for residents.

The other buildings in the photos are mostly wooden CCC buildings. The foundations for these structures were very short stonewalls or pilings meant to get them off the ground. Whereas the

This aerial photo of the main post, looking north, was probably taken in late 1945 and shows the facility based on the Army's earliest plans. The only building in the photo still standing is the large Quonset hut just left of center. It was the first V-2 assembly building - in fact, enlarging this photo shows a V-2 on a trailer to the left of the building. The first headquarters is the white building immediately north of the Quonset. The next building to the north is the old mess hall that evolved into the Officers Club and the Public Affairs Office. WSMR photo.

Quonset hut was placed on the ground or a concrete slab, these CCC buildings had crawl spaces under them, perfect for bugs, rodents, and the snakes hunting them.

Also visible, because of their white tops, are the hutments for enlisted men. There are 25 on the south and 22 on the north.

These little buildings are 16x16-foot squares with a plywood floor, walls and roof. Apparently the hutments didn't stand up too well to the spring winds, and pieces often headed toward Texas.

Construction of 76 sets of permanent structures for quarters that wouldn't blow away began in May 1947.

The hutments were used all over America during the war. In the South, where temperature and humidity were high, there was a tented version where the plywood sides only went up so far and the rest of the walls and roof were made of canvas and screen mesh. This provided better ventilation. In colder climates, the sides and roof were plywood and an oil or coal-burning stove could be used to provide some comfort.

How many people could fit into a hutment depended on status. They were used in prisoner of war camps, military camps, and places like Los Alamos and Oak Ridge where work on the first atomic bomb took place. The higher an occupant's status, the fewer the number of people assigned to the 250-square-foot box. Generally, however, they were used for prisoners, enlisted military personnel, and African Americans. If available, officers and prominent civilians were placed in more permanent facilities.

The first headquarters building was placed, facing south, across the street to the north of the V-2 assembly building. The Mountain View cafe sits on the spot now.

Electricity was provided by a diesel-powered generating system on the northeast corner of the post. Eventually lines tapped into power from the Elephant Butte Dam and then from El Paso Electric's system to provide uninterrupted power.

Surprisingly, electricity generated on post continued until the mid-1950s as a way to augment the imported power. In a June 11, 1953 *Wind and Sand* newspaper article, the author said the range was buying 12,000 kilowatts of "electric power" from Elephant Butte and generating an additional 3,000 kilowatts on post.

The initial small-scale generating plant from 1945 was moved south and placed behind the post engineers headquarters. In 1951, this was upgraded to eight generators of varying capacity. According to the article, the generators were never all run at the same time.

Each generator was powered by a 340-horsepower diesel engine. These big engines consumed 18 gallons of fuel per hour to generate the electricity. They were run every day during the peak hours of 8:15 a.m. to 4 p.m.

Luckily, this generating station was located east of most buildings, so the westerly breezes would carry much of the roar out into the empty desert. The *Wind and Sand* article said that even with a seven-foot muffler it was almost impossible to talk to another person anywhere near the system.

The Original Officer's Mess Hall

Building 122 didn't start out as the Public Affairs Office at White Sands. It began life in 1945 as the officer's mess hall. Since my building's demise, the only one of the original 1945 structures left is the old V-2 assembly building. It has been modified inside but the exterior looks much the way it did when built. Because of its use in putting together the first V-2 rockets, it is considered a historic structure and is still standing.

My old building was the first real eatery for officers on White Sands. In the early 1980s, I interviewed Charles Brink, a surveyor who came to work at White Sands in August 1945. He was needed to survey the new roads, power lines, water and sewage pipes, and the placement of buildings.

He said before the mess halls were finished and operational, food was served out of a tent with Italian prisoners of war doing the cooking. During the war, prisoner of war camps were scattered across New Mexico, to include Las Cruces where Germans and Italians picked crops. Eventually, there was a very short overlap period where you could hear Italian, German, Spanish and English spoken in the mess hall at White Sands.

During the war, Brink worked for the Army Corps of Engineers doing site work for new installations all across the Southwest. He even did some work at Trinity Site for Los Alamos.

It was a tough job because there was very little community support available to Brink and his wife as they moved around. Housing was almost impossible to find. With food rationing, he said meals often consisted of "peanuts or bacon and a plate of eggs."

He knew it was getting time to settle down when he actually went to inspect a chicken coop to use as an apartment. The chicken house had cardboard on the walls for wallpaper. There was no bathroom -- the outhouse was nearby -- and the only water in the coop was from a faucet in the middle of the floor. His wife was not amused when the owner suggested she get a washtub for bathing.

Brink grabbed the surveying job offered by Lieutenant Colonel Turner and worked for White Sands until he retired in 1972.

He told me one of his first jobs was to establish the route for Range Road 7, the main north/south artery through the range. The initial instructions were to head north from the original launch complex. The thinking was that a road from Launch Complex 33 would allow recovery teams a quick start as soon as a missile was fired.

That line took them across the usually dry playa known as Lake Lucero on the west side of White Sands National Monument. Brink said that after they lost two bulldozers in the muck of the lakebed, they shifted to the west. In the interview, he said the bulldozers sank completely out of sight and, as far as he knew, were never recovered.

Not every facility or road was preciseley surveyed for location. One old-timer told me they simply used "Jeep PS" in those days in a takeoff of today's GPS capabilities. He said they had a requirement to locate a telemetry site at Parker Station at exactly five miles north of the launcher. Using a jeep, someone drove north until the vehicle's odometer read five miles.

The tent mess hall quickly gave way to the building that was my initial work place. It was originally a short T-shaped structure with the top of the T used as the dining hall and the bottom of the T housing the kitchen.

When a larger and more modern mess hall was constructed to handle the growing population, the decision was made in 1947 to transform the old mess hall into the officers club. On the west side of the building, the top of the T, an open porch was added. The new wall for the porch was half native stone from the Organ Mountains. After a few years, the open windows were filled with real windows. Using

the same stone, a nice fireplace was built in the large room in the south part of the top of the T.

The whole east side of the building was enlarged by basically putting a box over the bottom of the T. This had the effect of turning the whole T into something resembling a square with some irregularities. This new area on the east was home to a ballroom with a larger fireplace made from the same Organ Mountains granite. The ballroom was called the "Rocket Room" and the fireplace andirons were decorated with stylized rockets. Also the new kitchen area was put in the southeast corner of the box.

The club was a place to go and relax after a long day at work. One old-timer told me the road to El Paso wasn't improved for quite some time. Initially it was basically a two-track ranch road winding through the dunes and yucca. With people driving off the road one way or the other, creating new two-track routes, it was difficult to follow the correct path at night.

From the club, men unwinding with a beer outside could look out to the southeast after dark and see the headlights of cars trying to follow the track to the post. He said they would bet on the different cars and whether or not they would successfully get to the post in one try.

There was also entertainment inside. Frank Hemingway, a White Sands pioneer and eventual Hall of Fame member, related that the club had slot machines for the officers and civilians to use. One night Hemingway went to the club and saw a large sign over the door. On it were pasted a number of Mexican coins personnel apparently found would work in the quarter slots. The only problem was the coins were worth pennies at best.

The sign said, "Officers and Gentlemen Don't Cheat." Hemingway said when he left, all the coins had been pulled off the sign and, presumably, pumped back into the machines.

The 1952 post guide, called "An Introduction to White Sands Proving Ground," said, "Officers of all services are welcome to join the Officer Mess. Recreational facilities of the mess include reading room, bar, pool tables, card tables, ping pong, chess and checkers." No official mention of one-armed bandits.

Hemingway was one of the pioneers to work at White Sands. In fact, he was supporting rocket testing in the basin before there ever was a White Sands.

In early 1945, Hemingway was employed by the

Ballistics Research Laboratory (BRL) at Aberdeen, Maryland. In March 1945, he was asked to be part of a team to work with Cal Tech on some rocket launches at White Sands. Cal Tech was testing their Private F missile; BRL was to provide instrumentation to collect data.

Since the land to make up White Sands wasn't completely locked down yet, the testing was done on the north end of Fort Bliss on their Hueco Range. The tests took place during the first two weeks of April.

When WAC Corporal and V-2 testing began at White Sands, Hemingway was frequently on post supporting BRL missions. Eventually he moved to White Sands as the assistant chief technical supervisor for BRL. He lived on post until he was married and then moved into Las Cruces.

With all the construction at White Sands, the ground was constantly being disturbed. Bushes, weeds and grasses were bladed off to make roads and flat spots for new structures. That meant the spring winds had plenty of fine dust and sand to whip up into huge clouds of flying sandpaper.

When I interviewed Hemingway in 1978, he talked about one dust storm so bad he said you couldn't see more than a few inches in front of you. He said he and others knocked off early to walk back to their rooms on the other side of the post. On the walk there were times he couldn't see his coworker beside him.

He said, "At one point I turned toward the person I was walking with and he wasn't there. He had disappeared."

It turns out they had crossed one of the primitive graded streets and didn't even know it. Someone was driving a jeep in the storm along the street and hit Hemingway's companion. When the wind let up momentarily, he saw the front tire of the jeep resting on his coworker's chest.

"He wasn't hurt. The jeep had been going very slowly and just nudged him over. The front end of the jeep was light so nothing was broken. I was lucky I guess. The jeep had passed right by me and I didn't know it," Hemingway said.

He pointed out that most windstorms weren't that bad. Normally, walking back to his quarters was not a problem. However, "Every night you could count on half an inch of dust on everything in your room," he said.

Hemingway went on to serve as the technical

director for the National Range Operations Directorate before retiring in 1977.

In 1947, artist Don Alfredo was allowed to sketch the "smoking room" in the Officer's Club in addition to the blockhouse at the launch complex. The drawing showed the knotty pine paneling covering the walls and ceiling. The heads of several wild animals hung on the walls. On the floor were rows of big comfy chairs and couches with a number of reading lamps.

The large fireplace is portrayed as very dark, almost like lava, although it was made from the same buff-colored granite found elsewhere in the building. When we were in the building, we always thought of the room as the ballroom but we called it the "pine box" because of the abundance of pine paneling.

Although we were never allowed to use the fireplaces in Bldg. 122, they turned out to be a little hot – all the time. In 1984, we discovered the fireplaces and the porch's stonewall were slightly radioactive.

The granite used for these things contains measurable amounts of radioactive elements like uranium and thorium. The "hot" rocks containing these elements were discovered in the summer of 1984 when personnel from the range's Radiological Health Office were testing new and very sensitive radiation detection equipment.

The specialists were out using the instruments to measure radiation in the blacktop on some of the parking lots. Some of the parking areas had the same rock used in the aggregate, so they were also radioactive.

The level of radiation found in the granite is pretty much undetectable with standard equipment, but using the new, super-duper instruments the specialists were able to pick up a reading.

When Rodney Patterson, a radiological health technician, walked into Public Affairs to use the phone, his detector registered the radiation from the fireplace right in front of my desk. He knew the levels were incredibly low, but his office prudently ran a study of the fireplaces to make sure there was nothing unexpected in the level of radiation.

It turned out that working 40 hours a week just 12 feet away from one of the fireplaces, a person would receive a fraction of one millirem of radiation per year. In other words, a year at my desk was about the same as spending a day or two in Denver.

In 1960, Bldg. 122 was jointly occupied by the

Army recruiters, Girl Scouts and Post Chaplain. The Resource Management Directorate also used the building before Public Affairs moved in during August 1977.

When the missile range established its Hall of Fame in 1980, the initial display of inductees was exhibited in Bldg. 122. The Rocket Room and dining area on the east became display areas to tell the story of White Sands. So in addition to housing Public Affairs, the building became the range's Visitor's Center until a museum was established. The Visitor's Center was just another mission placed on the Public Affairs plate.

Change In Plans

Toward the end of 1945, with the post built according to Washington's plans for a temporary establishment, things changed dramatically. After receiving word German V-2s and equipment would be shipped to White Sands, planning shifted to a whole new level. More people were going to be coming and more facilities of all kinds would be needed.

In fact German material started arriving in November and December 1945. In "WSPG In Retrospect On Eighth Anniversary," by Eve Simmons, she notes four men from the 1st Guided Missile Battalion were put on temporary duty (TDY) in Las Cruces to "guard captured railway equipment." This could be the German railroad launch car that showed up in a few very early photos of the Army launch complex.

Also, she stated "enlisted men were assigned to guard a German V-2 on the railway siding at Las Cruces." The reference could be an early-arriving V-2 or it could be a reference to the train cars filled with V-2 parts.

From then on, the order of the day was "build." By the mid 1950s, White Sands had blossomed into a small town in what was once Cox pastureland.

In 1959, White Sands published a historical report covering the base's first 10 years – 1945 to 1955. In it, authors Brown, Robertson, Kroehnke, Poisall and Cross wrote, "Apart from the barracks buildings, there were 430 housing units and 93 trailer spaces, with gas, water, sewer and electrical facilities. Food could be obtained at the Post Commissary and the Cafeteria, and clothing and other essentials at the Post Exchange Store. A branch U.S. Post Office and a branch bank (Otero County State Bank) were in operation. A Post newspaper (*Wind and Sand*) was

issued. Telephone and telegraph facilities, as well as a service station were available. To fill the educational and religious needs there were an elementary school, a Post Chapel and Sunday School. Recreational facilities established included a swimming pool, bowling alley, theater, library, athletic fields, hobby shops and officer's and enlisted men's clubs. Also, there was a nursery, laundry and dry cleaners, a barber shop, dispensary and dental clinic."

By 1950, things were booming at White Sands. At the end of the year, the bank had 165 accounts and over four million dollars in assets. The post headquarters building was being completed while plans were being finalized for a 500-seat theater – the same one in which Jack Benny appeared in Christmas 1951. The post newspaper *Wind and Sand* started publication and the fire department moved into their new station on main post.

The post elementary school was started in the fall of 1948 with Laura Sandiford employed as the single teacher. It was a one-room school with all of 15 students, grades one through four, sharing the space. It was sponsored by Dona Ana County. In the fall of 1950, the elementary school had 80 students enrolled.

It was steady growth as the school enrollment was 250 in September of 1953. For the start of the 1958 school year, the school was expanded to cover all grades up to high school and had an enrollment of over 600 children. For the school year beginning in September 1961, enrollment was up to a peak of 791 students.

Soldiers arriving after the first couple of years would not have been surprised by the physical plant they found at White Sands. The facilities described in the historical summary are pretty typical of any Army post.

One nicety available at White Sands because of the large civilian workforce was a government-sponsored bus service running back and forth into the main civilian communities. This bus service developed into quite an enterprise. Service was offered from the three main communities surrounding White Sands – Las Cruces, El Paso and Alamogordo – but also included places like the tiny village of Dona Ana. My wife and I took advantage of it for a few years, riding from Dona Ana. I found myself snoozing on the ride into work and reading on the return home.

Bus service to and from White Sands was going great when this photo was taken in August 1953. People are streaming to the motor pool from their workplaces to catch a ride home. There are 28 buses lined up in the photo ready to move out in three directions from the post - Las Cruces to the west, Alamogordo to the east, and El Paso to the south. WSMR photo.

Early on the bus service was quite convenient as drivers actually drove through parts of town to pick up passengers at numerous stops. Eventually the buses left from single points in each city where passengers could park for the day and buses could be securely stored overnight. Then as fares were raised at the insistence of higher headquarters and attitudes changed about bus transportation, ridership dwindled until the system died in the 1990s.

As the main post was expanded, new streets were established. To keep them straight and provide addresses for the facilities, the streets were given names. The street naming system, much like the rest of the early-day post, was not very imaginative. Also it was a bit confusing.

Basically, the streets used letters and numbers like any city laid out on a grid. However, the post was not a nice, neat set of streets looking like a piece of graph paper. Instead, streets started and stopped, continued on beyond some obstacle, some made 90 degree bends one way or the other, and the naming system wasn't totally consistent.

For example the main east/west street, now Aberdeen, was simply 3rd St. The streets running perpendicular across 3rd were avenues with letter designations and an indicator of whether they were north or south of 3rd. For instance, Avenue A was what is now Dyer. Things north of 3rd were on Avenue A North.

Having said that, on old maps there is a street east of Avenue A (presently Crozier), running north and south called "Z" street. It looks like the letters

progress to the west and then at some point jump back to the east and continue back to their starting point so after "Z" there is "A."

The main north/south street running through the post was called "Main Access Road" and the original road from the pass through the Cox property was called "Ranch Road."

Effective Jan. 1, 1957, the streets were all renamed. Officials came up with a system for naming the streets that is typical military. It is a bit arcane which explains why nobody living or working at White Sands today can tell you anything about the names – names like Hof and Crozier.

The idea was to name north/south streets in the Army admin area after former Army chiefs of ordnance. Major General Samuel Hof was chief in the 1930s. Major General William Crozier was chief from 1901 to 1918. Ripley St. is named after Brigadier General James Ripley who served as the chief at the beginning of the Civil War. The Main Access Road was named Wadworth Boulevard in 1957, after Colonel Decius Wadsworth, the very first chief of ordnance.

Although these streets bear names of people pretty much no one has heard of, no effort has been made to change the names to something more meaningful like the missile range's Hall of Fame members or past commanders. The Navy, on the other hand, chose to name the short streets in their administrative area after Navy heroes. Thus there are streets named after Dewey, Parsons and Halsey.

The primary streets running east/west were

named after Army Ordnance Corps installations such as arsenals, depots and proving grounds. In 1957, the old ranch road became Picatinny Ave. and 16th St. became Rock Island Ave. Some of these streets can still be associated with recent installations but many have disappeared from existence and current consciousness.

The planners did a decent job when it came to the housing area streets. Here they used the names of Army and Navy missile systems, many of which were actually tested at White Sands.

In the old Navy area there are Aerobee and Viking Streets while the Army has LaCrosse, Hawk, Dart, Honest John, Zeus and many more. Some missiles used as names, like Thor and Atlas, were never fired at White Sands but meet the basic requirement. For many of the street names, personnel can visit the White Sands Museum's Missile Park to see real examples of the missiles.

Eventually, using Wadsworth for the main street must have bothered some commander enough to have the name changed to Headquarters Ave. in February 1964. Also, Raritan Ave., named after Raritan Arsenal near Edison, New Jersey, was changed to Martin Luther King Ave. in the mid 1980s, at the time President Reagan signed the bill to create a federal holiday to honor King.

> *Pop-Up: Raritan Arsenal was created in 1917 as a storage depot for shipments overseas. It sat on 3,200 acres on the banks of the Raritan River, just 20 miles from Manhattan, New York. Because of its strategic location, its existence continued after World War I. Vehicles were stored there as well as all kinds of munitions and explosives.*
>
> *After World War II, activity declined through the 1950s, and the facility finally closed in 1964. It was then cleaned up and sold by the General Services Administration.*
>
> *The site is now divided into a highly developed industrial park and county college with the other half being mostly wetlands.*

The Navy

For decades White Sands has boasted it is a true tri-service facility where the Army, Navy and Air Force cooperate to make the complex testing mission possible. It seems to be a rare arrangement given the many inter-service squabbles that exist, but each service brings important capabilities to bear at White Sands and its test mission.

The relationships between the three services were a bit rough at the beginning. Disagreements, especially as the Army gained more control, were serious in the first decade.

In the fall of 1945, the Army Chief of Ordnance invited the Navy's Bureau of Ordnance to join the party at White Sands.

When Army Lieutenant Colonel Harold Turner recalled how this started, he said he had Admiral Parsons from the Navy and General Campbell from the Army in his office after the first successful V-2 flight. Turner said Parsons asked Campbell if the Navy could put personnel at White Sands to work on the V-2. Campbell then asked Turner what he thought. Turner responded with, "Sure, we can get along with anybody."

Navy journalist James Glynn, in his history of the Navy facility, wrote, "As he stood, shielding his eyes from the glaring sun, he (Admiral Parsons) turned to Lt. Col. Turner. Wiping his brow, the admiral – visibly impressed with the Army's technique – thundered his approval and asked, 'Colonel, could you use some Navy help on this project of yours?' The colonel viewed the admiral through dark sunglasses. 'I sure could,' he replied."

Both of these stories are apparently myth. The first successful V-2 firing was in May 1946, placing this exchange well after the important matters were already decided. According to Glynn's history, "a high-level Secret conference was held on April 23, 1946 in Washington where representatives of the Navy and War Departments finalized operating agreements." So, these officers may have talked about the possibilities at the local level, but the wheels were already rolling in Washington to put a Navy unit at White Sands.

On June 14, 1946, the Naval Ordnance Missile Test Unit (NOMTU) was formally established at White Sands. Even before that date, marines were on White Sands with Commander J.A. Coddington laying out the Navy's allotted spot west of the missile assembly buildings. They got off to a speedy start by bringing in dozens of Quonset huts and using them for everything from administrative support to a dining hall to sleeping quarters. They even turned one into a small bowling alley.

The first officer in charge of the new Navy unit was Commander Robert McLaughlin who served from June 1946 to February 1948. He was succeeded by Captain William Gorry.

McLaughlin created quite a stir in 1950 when *TRUE* magazine published in its March issue his article about UFO sightings on White Sands by his men (April 1949) and himself (May 1949). The article was quite lengthy as he went into a great deal of detail about what was seen. He even proposed that the alien spacecraft were powered by nuclear "radiation pressure motors." The detail, speculation and positive tone probably didn't help his career.

The article must of have been quite a sensation. Hell, it still is. Here was a Navy commander, still on active duty, who worked at America's primary rocket and missile testing facility pontificating about UFOs. In 2013, a simple *Google* search revealed people still commenting and arguing about the sightings. As in most UFO cases, supporters point to McLaughlin's rank and position to imply he couldn't have made a mistake.

In the *True* magazine article McLaughlin is terribly sure of himself. In fact, a bit too sure. For instance, he states the UFO seen by his balloon observers was 105 feet in diameter, was flying at 56 miles in altitude, and moving at five miles per second (that's about18,000 miles an hour). The object was visible for about 60 seconds.

In reality, if you don't know what the object is, you can't know how large it is. If you don't know how large it is, you can't tell how far away it is. Is it a 25-cent piece in front of your face or Venus millions of miles away? These two examples can appear to be exactly the same size to an observer if he doesn't know what they are to begin with. Also, you can't deduce speed if you don't know the other variables.

Given McLaughlin's dimensions, the object would be about the same length as a Boeing 737. Its fairly easy to see a 737 overhead at their cruising altitude of seven miles, especially when they leave a contrail or the sun is glinting off their skin. Now imagine that plane at an altitude of 56 miles, eight times higher, with no contrail. It would probably be pretty invisible.

Also, given the UFO's speed, in 60 seconds it would have traveled 300 miles. That would have put it way east out over the Texas panhandle. Again, it would have been quite a trick to track such an object

that far from the Rio Grande valley near Arrey, New Mexico where the team was stationed.

According to newspaper reports at the time, the Department of Defense issued a denial there were alien spacecraft flying over America. No mention was made of what might have happened to McLaughlin.

In addition to its Quonset huts and other structures, the Navy built a "training" pool in 1948. Since there was no large body of water at White Sands, the local unit justified a swimming pool as something necessary for all sailors stationed in the desert.

This pool turned out to be a great boon to White Sands as all personnel were able to use it. The thing was 50 yards long and 20 yards wide and held 480,000 gallons of water. It was huge for such a small post.

In 1953, Gunner's Mate First Class George Holland, a volunteer lifeguard and instructor at the pool, was killed in a motorcycle accident. On Sept. 12, 1953, the Navy and the Post renamed the pool in honor of Holland. In 1958, the pool was turned over to the Army – it was too much for the Navy to run and maintain.

When I arrived in 1977, the pool was still operational. In fact, my wife and I swam there a few times. It was located just south of the bowling alley and Bell Gym.

Eventually, as water usage became an issue and maintenance of the pool became burdensome, the pool was closed and demolished. Removing the Navy pool was not the problem it might seem. At that time, the post had two other swimming pools – one at the Officers Club and one at the NCO Club.

After the Navy built their permanent headquarters building, Captain James Parham, Navy Commander, had a ship's bell installed outside the building. It was installed in October 1956, according to noted science fiction writer G. Harry Stine who worked for the Navy at the time as a missile flight safety officer.

In an article in the March 1986 *Whispering Sands Pioneer Gazette,* Stine wrote, "Capt. Parham felt that the Navy's presence should be more audibly heard at WSPG, and the bell was sounded by the watch officer's orderly every thirty minutes in accordance with naval 8-bell tradition." Stine added, "There were rumors (unfounded) that it was the ship's bell from the battleship U.S.S. New Mexico but this was untrue; it was a surplus bell from a battleship that was never built during World War II."

Initially, when the Navy had a large number of sailors, the bell was rung seven days a week at half-hour intervals from 6 a.m. to 10 p.m. Now the bell is only used for ceremonies in front of the Navy headquarters building.

Stine made a great point at the end of his article when he pointed out, "What few people realize is that WSPG was primarily a proving ground for people who went on to do other things in guided missilery and space flight."

Many old-timers who served at White Sands in the 1950s remember the Navy's dog mascot. Army Staff Sergeant Gilbert Smith was stationed at White Sands from 1948 to 1956. In the August 2008 issue of the *Hands Across History*, the WSMR Historical Foundation's newsletter, Smith wrote this about Guns, the mascot, "The Navy, which then had well over 200 personnel and was one of our contenders in softball, had a mascot – a dog named 'Guns.' Guns was quite a dog. He rode in a jeep just like the sailors, to and from the Desert Ship. Old Guns liked everyone, but if you were not in Navy dungarees, you could receive a wet pants leg. For some reason or other he didn't like people in khakis. For the protection of the officers and chiefs, poor old Guns had to be tied up during inspections."

In addition to building their own pool and other facilities, the Navy chiefs started their own chief petty officer's club in 1950. According to Smith, "Since there were only a few chiefs, they invited the Army master sergeants from all the White Sands units to join and assist. Those of us who were interested worked at nights and weekends with the chiefs in the construction of the first CPO club. Later it expanded and took over the entire building. We all donated $10 to establish a starting fund and took turns tending bar and cleaning – for free. It turned out to be an excellent club for many years."

According to employees at White Sands during the 50s, this club created some friction between the Navy and the Army landlords at White Sands. The club was too successful. It took Army personnel away from the post's club system. The scuttlebutt is that White Sands pressured the Navy to close its club forcing sailors, civilians and AWOL soldiers to frequent the officially funded facilities.

In addition to the main post facilities, the Navy immediately went out beyond the Army's launch complex, about 10 miles east of the main post, and built their own launch complex at what is now LC-35. Not seeing any need to reinvent the wheel, they built a smaller version of the Army's blockhouse in 1946. The first Viking sounding rocket launch from the site was No. 9, on December 15, 1952.

In the summer of 1947 they started construction of a tower for Aerobee sounding rocket launches. The Aerobee was very much like its precursor, the WAC Coporal. It was unguided and needed a booster to accelerate it to a speed where stable flight was possible and the sustainer motor could be used. It was just a lot more capable than the WAC.

According to Gregory Kennedy in his book, *The Rockets and Missiles of White Sands Proving Ground 1945 – 1958*, Lieutenant Colonel Turner stopped construction. In May, White Sands had lost V-2s in Mexico and near Alamogordo. Turner wasn't convinced that unguided rockets were such a good idea at the time.

James Van Allen, the Navy's chief proponent for the Aerobee, went to work and came up with solutions to satisfy Turner's concerns. The tower was modified so it could be tilted up to seven degrees to account for low-level winds. This would be used to compensate for the winds blowing the rocket off course at its most vulnerable time – at liftoff.

Also, he proposed a fuel cutoff system so thrust from the motor could be terminated if the rocket was veering off course.

These two techniques are still used today for sounding rocket launches and are key to keeping vehicles in the box of air over WSMR. The Army approved the precautions and the tower was completed. Demonstration flights started in the fall of 1947.

In 1965, the Air Force's Aerobee tower from Holloman was deconstructed and moved to the Navy launch complex. It was placed near the first tower. For some reason the Air Force tower was four feet taller than the Navy's and stood 152 feet high.

Navy officials said the second tower would give them the ability to launch two rockets, one right after the other, to basically double the size of a payload being sent up.

The first dual launch was on April 14, 1966 at 8 a.m. One lifted off at 8 while the other followed eight minutes later. The two payloads were built by University of Colorado students. The first rocket reached an altitude of 114 miles while the second one topped out at 120 miles.

In 1951, at the same launch complex, the Navy built the famous Desert Ship. According to George Helfrich in an article in the August 2007 issue of the *Hands Across History* newsletter, the building is often referred to as a commissioned ship stuck out in the desert. He wrote it never was, but "The contractor crew, upon completion of the building, did conduct a mock christening. Congressional approval was, however, required to name it the USS Desert Ship. It is also know as the LLS-1 or Land Locked Ship Number One."

In reality, the Desert Ship has always functioned as a blockhouse for Navy guided missile launches right outside the door. The interior of the building was initially equipped with standard shipboard fire-control equipment to simulate at-sea conditions.

It also looked like a ship inside. In fact, I remember visiting and having to pass through bulkhead doors instead of office doors. When conducting tours at the site, getting through the bulkheads was tricky for some of our elderly visitors.

Outside the ship, Navy missile launchers were

The famous Navy Desert Ship at LC-35. WSMR photo.

placed for firing the first generation of ship-defense missiles – Terrier, Talos and Tartar. To complete that arrangement, in 1954 a replica deckhouse was added to the east. According to Helfrich, the deckhouse would have been part of a CG-10 class cruiser. Out in the desert, the White Sands Navy used it to test and fire production missiles while simulating shipboard conditions – there just weren't any rolling waves.

Of those early guided missiles, the Talos was the

most complex. It used a solid-fuel booster for liftoff and to get the missile up to supersonic speed where the ramjet-equipped second stage would sustain its flight to the target. The missile was 22 feet long and could reach targets 75 miles out.

The first full prototype was fired from the Desert Ship in October 1952. The system was under development for a long time as it wasn't declared operational until 1959. According to Gilbert Moore who supported Talos testing as a Physical Sciences Lab employee, because of the system's complexity there were often delays. For one mission, he says the Navy tried more than 30 times to launch.

In those days, Moore used to draw cartoons about the activities at White Sands. In one he put in a little sign showing that Talos stood for "Try And Launch On Schedule." He said he received an official reprimand for the cartoon. The Navy told him they were in competition with the Army Hercules air-defense system and didn't need discouraging gibes out in the public.

To provide cheap, high-flying targets with the correct radar cross-section, the Navy contracted with the Physical Sciences Lab at New Mexico A & M in Las Cruces. According to Moore, the lab came up with Pogo and Pogo Hi. This was a series of rockets with different-sized rocket motors. The rockets carried parachutes with metal thread woven into the fabric to be ejected at altitudes starting at 60,000 feet and eventually going to 100,000 feet.

The parachutes would float down and provide the right-sized target for the test system to see with its radar. They were used later in tests for the Army's Nike Hercules system at White Sands.

Moore says that during the first test in 1954, the rocket's body became tangled in the parachute and brought the whole thing crashing to earth. After that it worked great. They even dangled heat sources under the parachute for testers who wanted an infrared signature instead of a radar one.

An Integrated Range

The Navy club is a tiny example of the kind of friction between the three services as they vied with each other over land use, responsibilities, pecking order, future missions and, of course, dollars. At the very beginning, juggling everyone's needs wasn't too complicated, but within just a few years each service's presence and requirements grew tremendously.

In 1950, a proposal was made at higher levels to consolidate the Holloman range into the White Sands Proving Ground. The Holloman range ran up what is now the east side of White Sands from Holloman Air Force Base to Highway 380. In other words, the large 40-mile by 100-mile rectangle that is now White Sands was divided into two narrow corridors with separate controllers.

In this process, the Navy objected to how it was going to be treated in such a consolidation. Department of Defense planners ended up working with all three services to devise a plan to placate them all.

In 1952, the Secretary of Defense issued a memorandum to the secretaries of the Army, Navy and Air Force. First of all, the new "integrated range" was placed under the command, management, and operational responsibility of the Army. At the same time, the document stated, "In the interest of economy and efficiency, all facilities at White Sands Proving Ground are available for the accomplishment of the mission of each service on an equitable basis."

While the Army commanding general was to have overall range responsibility and operational control, the Navy commander at White Sands and the Air Force commander at Holloman were designated as deputies to the Army commander. The order states the deputies, "will be responsible for the exercise of command and management control of the property, equipment, personnel, and projects of their respective services and for operational control thereof except insofar as operational control for overall integration purposes may be vested in the Commanding General, White Sands Proving Ground."

This is why White Sands Missile Range today has three deputy commanders, one for each of the services. Of course, this didn't end disagreements, but over the decades the established structure gave the parties a way to negotiate their differences and move on.

A concrete example of the various sides getting together to work out their differences took place several years before I retired and shows how the missile range operates.

Funds to operate White Sands come down through various channels depending on the money's use. These are often called "stove pipes." Another reference to how money is used is by its "color."

The reason for this jargon is because there is no single pot of money that organizations and managers dip into to pay the bills. If new radars are needed, money will be assigned to that project from on high and it will come down specifically for that use. The same thing is true for maintenance of the facility or to pay personnel in support positions. It is very difficult, if not impossible, to move money from one account to another.

At the same time, White Sands offers a testing service to the Army, Navy, Air Force, other government agencies like NASA, private industry, and our allies. Anytime testing is done, the project or "customer" pays for the service. Big missions are very expensive.

For instance, if you want to fire an air defense missile at a droned supersonic fighter jet and have all kinds of data, like nice slow-motion film of the test, it is going to cost a lot. The droned jet alone could cost a million dollars.

Over the years, the system has evolved so the people who actually run and conduct the test missions at White Sands are paid from the monies collected from the programs under test. The more testing being done means there is more money of the right color to pay salaries. If testing dips, funding for employees begins to dry up.

Because of this, White Sands has been anxious in the last few decades to attract new customers. The missile systems developed in the Cold War supported a booming White Sands, but when the wall came down in Europe that large scale testing dwindled.

One customer White Sands found was Japan. As an ally, Japan has visited White Sands many times, usually to fire missile systems they have purchased from the United States.

It this instance, however, the Japanese built their own sophisticated air defense missile system but had no place to realistically test it in their homeland. Management at White Sands was glad to capture this business.

Of course, White Sands is a secure facility because of all the advanced technologies being tested, especially our own developments. So having Japanese military personnel and their civilian engineers on White Sands to test this missile became a hot topic.

Basically, White Sands had to build a method to deal with the foreign nationals so no one else's stuff was vulnerable and, at the same time, not offend the Japanese. The money was important enough to go the extra mile to make it so.

By escorting the visitors, controlling their movements, and hiding sensitive items, most organizations were ready to go.

Initially the Air Force had a different reaction. In the 1950s, Holloman existed as the Air Force's Missile Development Center. Although Air Force missile test missions often flew through Holloman out onto White Sands, missile testing is no longer the base's main mission.

Instead, Holloman is home to some of the latest and greatest fighter jets, aircraft that have just been introduced to the Air Force inventory. Pilots train in those planes in the airspace over and around White Sands.

When the Japanese proposal came up, the Air Force balked for fear the air defense system's radar might be used by the Japanese to light up these brand new planes and acquire rather sensitive information about them.

The Army countered saying the Japanese would only be allowed to fire up their radar during scheduled test missions. No Air Force jets should be around.

The Air Force came back and basically said, how will you know they are following the prohibition? The Army then demonstrated equipment they have to detect very weak electromagnetic fields at some distance. They showed they could park their equipment in the parking lot and detect someone inside a trailer turning on something as simple as a computer monitor.

It was a clear demonstration the Army would be able to easily keep the radar turned off. The Air Force objection was overcome. Even though the services still sometimes disagree, they usually settle their differences and march forward.

Movie Featured 500K Test Stand

To publicize the White Sands Co-op program and its use of university students, the U.S. Army released a short film in 1959 called *They Major in Missiles*. The 15-minute film explained how the program worked by focusing on one student who attended New Mexico State and then went on to become a

missile range employee. Filming at White Sands started in December 1958.

At one point the film points out other technical specialties occupied by a variety of students. The single woman in the film isn't portrayed at a missile launch but is shown at a big old mechanical calculator crunching numbers. There wasn't much out in the field yet for a woman.

Also, the film embraces the smoking cliché of the time. The university personnel are portrayed as pipe smokers. The student and his supervisor are filmed peacefully smoking their cigarettes.

In the film, the student worked at the 500K Static Test Stand during his junior year. By the time the film was made the test stand was just about out of business and certainly not something a young engineer would tie his future to.

In a way it was too bad the 500K facility became a white elephant in just a decade. When it was built, it was supposed to be able to test any future rocket motor. Circumstances and capabilities changed quickly in the 1950s. It was swiftly left behind.

The number in the facility's name means engineers could tie down rocket motors with lift-off capabilities up to 500,000 pounds of thrust, light them up, and not have the framework and engine fly away. To put that in perspective, here are some sample vehicles and what their rocket engines produced in pounds of thrust: V-2 = 56,000; Corporal = 20,000; Redstone (first stage) = 78,000; Pershing I (first stage) = 26,000; Saturn V moon rocket = 7,600,000.

According to a special report called the "500,000-Pound Rocket Static Test Facility" dated February 1957 and signed by Lieutenant Colonel James P. Hamill, the facility was designed in 1947, with the help of the German Paperclip scientists, and then constructed from 1948 to 1950. At the time, Hamill was chief of the ordnance mission at White Sands. Also, this was the same James Hamill who was in charge of the unit that entered the tunnels at Mittelwerk where V-2s were assembled by the Nazi slave workforce during World War II.

The report was a promotional device intended to publicize the test stand's capabilities and attract customers. By 1957, customers were getting scarce as alternatives were developed elsewhere.

The abandoned facility sits about four miles south of the White Sands main post at the base of Granite Peak, the eastern-most spur of the Organ

Mountains. Employees and visitors clearly see the 500K as they travel onto post via the El Paso road. Visitors and many range personnel assume it is some kind of mining structure. In fact, there is a black, shadowy area at the base of the huge concrete superstructure that looks like the dark opening of a mine tunnel. Others have equated it to some medieval castle you might see in Europe.

It is a massive complex with tons and tons of concrete, miles of plumbing and wiring, tunnels bored through solid granite, and was equipped with a huge array of measuring equipment for tests. In a *Wind and Sand* newspaper article on May 2, 1958, Jean Fredericks wrote, "Literally hundreds of electronic recording machines are installed for component testing of various valves, regulators, tanks, diaphrams, and other plumbing of a rocket's propulsion system." On top of that, there were instruments measuring pressures, temperatures, vibration, thrust, acceleration, and the sequencing of events in the systems.

If you burn off all the jargon, the idea behind the site was pretty straightforward. The facility was mounted against the very steep mountainside to make a vertical environment instead of a horizontal one – close to the actual orientation for most missiles. This had the great advantage of using gravity to bring propellants down to the test stand and water down from a 100,000-gallon storage tank.

At the top of the facility designers placed the water tank and two bunkers for the fuel and oxidizer tanks. The propellant tanks were stored inside big boxes made from lightweight, friable concrete. If there was an explosion, the concrete was to disintegrate into small fragments instead of huge, crushing pieces that might wreck the rest of the facility.

The propellants were fed by pipe into pumping stations – one for the oxidizer and one for fuel. The pumps would then feed the rocket engine mounted in the stand with the correct amount of fluid. These stations were later turned into machine shops.

To provide a safe location for a control room and data collection area, builders bored a space out of the solid granite only 50 feet from the test stand. The space is 936 square feet and all the granite debris from the excavation is still visible on the side of the mountain below the four control-room windows.

The eastern wall of the control room, where the viewing windows are located, is five feet of reinforced concrete. The windows are two feet by two feet and are made of two three-inch-thick panes.

Looking out the windows, controllers could not see the test stand or the item under test. Mounted on small rail cars outside the windows were four six-foot by six-foot mirrors. The mirrors could be moved and tilted to provide those in the control room a complete view of the test. Although the win-

The north side of the 500K Static Test Stand during construction on Feb. 20, 1948. WSMR photo

dows are still intact, the mirrors are long gone, shattered into thousands of pieces by vandals.

Access to the control room was via a tunnel cut through the granite from the north side of the facility. The tunnel entrance was equipped with a heavy steel door to effectively make the control room a bomb shelter in case of an explosion.

The tunnel is four feet wide and 11 feet tall. It runs 154 feet to a 90-degree bend to the east and then 85 more feet to the control room. At the bend there is a vertical shaft rising 60 feet to an emergency escape bunker. A metal ladder was to be used in case of an evacuation.

The escape bunker is located above the storage

The 500K test stand after it was out of business but is still intact. At the top are the bunkers for the fuels and oxidizers. Below that are the two pump houses - one for each propellant. In front, in the middle, is the frame for holding the missile or just its engine. To the left of the stand are windows in the side of the mountain that look out from the control room. Note the large cavity carved out below the facility where the rocket engine exhaust met the rock and was cooled with water. WSMR photo.

tanks and the testing area. If personnel needed to use this route they would have taken portable oxygen breathing devices to use in the bunker because of the possibility of toxic or suffocating gases.

Above the escape bunker was a 20-foot tall chimney used to blow fresh air through ducts down into the control room.

Electricity to the site was shut down decades ago, so walking through the tunnel to the control room requires a good light to avoid stumbling along in the dark. It is also handy to detect snakes and other critters that might have sought shelter in the dark.

I've been in several times, once escorting the commanding general. To say the least, I carried a Coleman lantern and a flashlight, in reserve, when I took him into the old relic.

It is a historical relic now. The designers saw a bright future for the facility, a future filled with customers wanting to test larger and larger rocket motors. After all, when completed it was the world's largest static test stand.

According to Hamill's history, in 1950 and 1951, a series of V-2 power plant tests were conducted followed by extensive modifications of the facility. To better test Redstone motors, the test stand was changed to a vertical orientation.

In its initial configuration, motors were mounted at 60 degrees so the exhaust shot out over the desert. In the vertical mode, the capability was reduced to 125,000 pounds of thrust which was fine for Redstone and the other military missiles at the time.

The change moved the exhaust plume from the rockets so it struck the granite mountainside below the frame. To quench that hot exhaust, a water system was constructed to flood 3,000 gallons of water per minute into the exhaust plume.

For thousands of years, humans have broken rock by heating it and then throwing water on it. The drastic temperature change causes the rock to fracture. It can literally explode, if conditions are right.

This happened to the granite where the exhaust plume hit the mountain. The solid rock was quickly eaten away by nothing but quick temperature changes. Eventually a large cavity was opened up under the test stand – the black, shadowy hole people see from the road.

In 1959, the *Wind and Sand* newspaper reported the cavity was 60 feet deep and 30 feet across. Later in the year the range installed a steel, water-cooled

deflector below the engine mount to push the super-hot exhaust out away from the rock. To feed water to the deflector, a new 20-foot-diameter water tank was installed high above on the ridge.

From 1953 through 1955, a long series of development and acceptance test firings for the Redstone power plant were conducted at 500K. In 1956, Nike Ajax and Nike Hercules liquid sustainer tests were done there.

In 1957 into 1958, the Corporal missile system's propulsion system was tested at 500K.

In 1958, according to the *El Paso Times*, 500K was further modified with the addition of the Redstone test stand moved in from Alabama. The article said, "A Redstone power plant test package weighing more than 30 tons has been cut away from its stand at Redstone Arsenal . . . shipped to White Sands Missile Range and welded onto the 500,000 pound static test stand."

The article lauded the effort, pointing out it only took 42 days to cut out the package, move it, place it, and start testing. The equipment was to continue Redstone motor testing for "program plant acceptance" and "product improvement testing."

In other words, after Redstone propulsion units were built by the manufacturer in California, they were shipped to White Sands for testing. If they passed, they were forwarded on for incorporation into the finished missile. Also, if changes were made to the fuel and engine system, those changes were tested at White Sands.

By 1959, the 500K was used only occasionally. There is a photo of two folks from Roswell, along with their White Sands escort, watching a test at 500K on May 24, 1960. It may have been the last test as the site was mothballed in 1961.

In an interview with Carlos Bustamante in 2013, I learned the site's original 15,000-gallon, pure aluminum, alcohol storage tank was no longer used by the mid-50s.

Bustamante was working on a requirement for a large water storage tank out on the range. When he learned about the empty alcohol tank at 500K, he convinced his boss it would be perfect for the task.

They pulled the tank out of the bunker and transported it to a flat area where they could fill it with water. Bustamante remembered how proud he was to realize the water would be much denser and, therefore, much heavier than the alcohol originally stored in the tank. He said he had the foresight to reinforce the tank before filling it with a test load of water.

After they filled it and the boss blessed it, Busta-mante left the site telling the worker to go ahead and drain the water. Much to Bustamante's chagrin, when he went back to the tank the next day, he found it almost completely flat. It had been squashed like a bug.

The worker had opened the drain plug on the bottom without venting the tank. Eventually, because of the vacuum created inside the tank as water trickled out, the atmosphere crushed it.

It was an excellent demonstration of the weight of the air all around us, but for Bustamante and his people that was of little consolation. He said there wasn't much that could be done so they buried the tank as just so much junk.

Not mentioned in the movie *They Major in Missiles* was the 300K static test facility built in the 1950s to fire solid-fuel rocket motors. Like the 500K, it is located at the base of Granite Peak but is three miles south of the main post. Because it was designed to test solid-fuel engines that come ready to fire, all the plumbing and other infrastructure of the 500K facility was unnecessary.

The 300K was built with four concrete bays and a blockhouse. Two of the bays were designed to handle thrusts up to 300,000 lbs. These were 43 feet deep, 25 feet wide and lined with concrete walls 11 feet high. They were open at the top and at one end.

The missile's rocket motor or the whole missile was mounted in the bay horizontally and fired. The exhaust harmlessly shot out the open end.

Two of the bays were smaller and set up to handle thrusts up to 5,000 lbs.

In the *Wind and Sand* article, Fredericks mentioned plans for White Sands to modify one of the 300K cells so it could handle thrusts up to one million pounds. This didn't happen. The idea was probably overcome by the sheer amount of testing to be done and its movement to other facilities springing up across the country. As the 1950s ended, White Sands was beginning to lose its position as the center of the missile-testing universe.

On Sept. 30, 1955, Clyde F. Wofford, age 27, was killed in a Nike rocket motor explosion at one of the proving ground's static test stands. Unfortunately, no official information about the accident is read-

ily available. The White Sands Safety Office, said the records were long gone. They checked with Army Safety in Washington and found their records don't go back that far. To top it off, there are no copies of the White Sands newspaper from that year in the missile range's Public Affairs Office.

I found stories about the accident in the *Las Cruces Sun-News*, *El Paso Times* and the *Albuquerque Journal*. They agree that Wofford was a mechanical engineer who grew up in Las Cruces. He attended Las Cruces High School and then earned his college degree from New Mexico A&M in Las Cruces. After serving in the Air Force for three years he returned home to a job at White Sands.

In addition to Wofford, eight other men were involved in the accident but received minor injuries. They were: Lyle McCain, John Bornachien, William Schumacher, Donald Nyre, William Orr, William Stipp, Fred Renfro and Jess Clark. All were from Las Cruces except Nyre who was from El Paso.

The explosion occurred around noon. All the injured were taken to the White Sands dispensary for treatment. There, Wofford died about 3 p.m.

Wofford was a White Sands federal employee while the others all worked for Douglas Aircraft which built the Nike missiles.

What is not clear from the reports is what exploded and where. The *El Paso Times* reported on Oct. 1, "Witnesses said the men were testing a Nike engine at the time of the explosion." In talking to old-timers it appears the motor was the sustainer engine or second stage to the new Nike Hercules.

Hercules started life using liquid propellants for the second stage. Eventually, it was equipped with solid fuel. The liquid oxidizer and fuel used early on were Inhibited Red Fuming Nitric Acid and Unsymmetrical Dimethylhydrazine. An explosion would have blown these hazardous materials on everyone and would account for some reports of acid burns on the victims.

Also, the location is not clear. The newspapers just say it was in a facility "near the 500K test stand."

The reason I've included so much detail about Wofford's death is that there has never been a death at White Sands from an actual missile launch. This wasn't a launch but was awfully close.

Lots of people have died at White Sands but most deaths have been the result of auto accidents. Also, there have been a number of industrial-type accidents resulting in death. Technically Wofford's death would probably be classified as an industrial accident as well.

HAWK Missile

The film *They Major in Missiles* ends with a dramatic HAWK firing against a drone jet aircraft. The missile blows the jet to smithereens as the narrator explains how these students are helping protect America from future aggressors.

The HAWK (Homing All-the-Way Killer) has to be one of the most successful air defense missile systems ever built. The original specifications were proposed in the early 1950s for a missile capable of hitting low-flying targets and being portable enough to travel with the Army. It was deployed in 1959.

The original HAWK missiles could hit targets up to 16 miles out at altitudes from 200 feet to 36,000 feet. The improved HAWK missiles had an extended range of 22 miles and could fly as high as 59,000 feet.

At just 16 feet long, the HAWK missiles were much smaller than their Nike predecessors. HAWK used a solid-fuel, single-stage propulsion system that cleverly acted like a two-stage system. The rocket motor burned two different propellants, one after the other. The first was very energetic and burned

for the five seconds needed to launch the missile and accelerate it away. The second section of propellant then burned for about 20 seconds and sustained the missile to the target.

At White Sands, HAWK meant lots and lots of testing during development and then follow-on testing for improvements. It was the kind of system that insured work and income for years.

Also, HAWK was used several times to successfully shoot down small ballistic missiles at White Sands.

Raytheon built the missile so their people were on hand at White Sands putting together missiles and firing them. Vern Haverstick, a Raytheon employee, wrote about those early days in the May 1986 issue of the *Whispering Sands Pioneer Gazette*.

Haverstick said when they first arrived they shared spaces with other missile systems. Down at the Army Blockhouse, they were allocated half of an old Nike assembly building. Before their first flight, they left the HAWK components in the building overnight, planning to start final missile assembly the next day. When they returned to the building the next morning, they found black widow spiders had worked all night spinning webs throughout the missile parts. Haverstick said, "Here was a case where

Soldiers prepare a trio of HAWK missiles on the M192 launcher/trailer for a public display. WSMR photo.

debugging the electronics had a literal meaning."

The first HAWK firing at White Sands was scheduled for Aug. 16, 1955. Prior to this, company crews had fired HAWKs out to sea at the Navy's Point Mugu, California facility. For those ocean tests, firings were delayed many times as fishing boats evaded patrol boats and often sailed right through the test area while they were returning to port with their catches.

According to Haverstick, the team was much relieved to be at White Sands, out in the desert, where such delays just weren't possible. He went on, "It was approximately minus twenty seconds in the countdown when Nat Wagner flashed a hold fire command. On investigation, it was learned that a truck had run the Highway 70 roadblock. The truck was carrying a fishing boat."

In 1956, HAWK was actually shooting at aircraft at White Sands. On one mission, the radio-controlled target was an old B-17 bomber from World War II. After a direct hit by the missile, the bomber crashed near Highway 70 and members of the public saw it come down. One of those folks called the military police to report a plane crash.

When the Raytheon people finally got to the impact site, they found an ambulance crew from the base going through the wreckage. When they tried to approach the old plane so they could evaluate what damage their missile had done, the base crews wouldn't let them in. The rescuers said they were still looking for survivors in the debris. It took some explaining to call off the rescue effort.

One of my favorite Haverstick stories concerns a test using a QF-80 as the target. The QF-80 was a radio-controlled F-80 which was America's first operational jet fighter. The thing was developed at the end of World War II but did not see action during the war.

The test involved flying the jet at only 50 feet above the ground into the intercept area. This was to test the HAWK's radar system, its capability of distinguishing targets from ground clutter, and its ability to actually kill a real target. The flight path for the test took the fighter jet over Lake Lucero on the west end of White Sands National Monument.

> **Pop-Up**: *The name of the missile did not start out as an acronym for "Homing All-the-Way Killer." Initially it was simply called Hawk after the birds of prey. The acronym was added later.*

According to Haverstick, "As the drone neared the firing point, the HAWK search radar detected an unidentified object behind the drone, and Ellis Beymer, the test conductor, held fire. But Range Control reported that the range was clear; the Range's radar's had not detected the bogey."

As the drone was routed around to repeat the approach, the UFO disappeared. Then, as the drone passed over Lake Lucero again, the item appeared a second time and a hold fire was called.

Haverstick continued the story, "Range Control, obviously annoyed, had no sign of a bogey, and notified Ellis Beymer there was only enough fuel for one more pass of the target. This time Ellis was in contact by phone with a cameraman near the intercept point, who was asked to see what kind of plane was flying over Lake Lucero. The cameraman told him, "There's no airplane. Every time the F-80 flies low over the lake, a flock of ducks flies up, circles around for awhile, and goes back down."

On the next pass, the HAWK successfully killed the drone.

After its first decade of service, the basic HAWK was upgraded to the Improved HAWK or I-HAWK. After that the system was continuously tweaked to make further improvements.

These improvements and upgrades were not minor changes. New radars, a new guidance package, better resistance to countermeasures, solid state circuits as opposed to tube technology, quicker reaction time, a missile that went further and higher, were just some of the improvements. Of course, any change needed to be tested before it could be passed along to the troops – steady business for White Sands.

In the years between 1955 and 1970, there were 562 HAWK firings at White Sands.

This incredibly long-lived missile system lasted for four decades in the U.S. inventory. It was phased out in the 1990s and replaced by Patriot.

I remember attending HAWK launches at White Sands in the early 1980s as they were demonstrated for potential customers. So who bought the HAWK system? When looking at the *Wikipedia* entry for HAWK, it appears most of our allies (about 20 nations are on the list) bought it and at least one country that is no longer friendly. Iran shows up on the chart as an operator. Many of these countries still use HAWK as an air-defense system.

Polar Bears

In the Nov. 30, 1956 issue of the *Wind and Sand* newspaper, there was a report about personnel from White Sands being "heckled" by polar bears.

No, it wasn't some exotic introduction of wildlife on White Sands. It was the beginning of a period where the proving ground was a major player in launching sounding rockets from the frozen wastelands of northern Canada. The launches were part of a joint United States/Canada research effort during the International Geophysical Year (IGY). IGY was actually 18 months running from the second half of 1957 and all through 1958.

With White Sands personnel having a great deal of expertise in sounding rocket preparation and launches, it was logical the range would be called on to work at the Fort Churchill site. Fort Churchill and the nearby town of Churchill are on the shore of Hudson Bay in Manitoba, about 700 miles north of the U.S. border with Canada. It has a subarctic climate with long, cold winters and very short, cool summers.

Because it is on Hudson Bay, it does provide Manitoba with a seaport. Unfortunately for the province, it is usually only ice-free about three months of the year.

The site was selected because it was a convenient northern location that allowed scientists to study the aurora, cosmic radiation, geomagnetism and other phenomenon found near the earth's poles. During IGY, the Van Allen radiation belts around the earth were discovered.

According to the *Wind and Sand* article, about 30 men from the White Sands Signal Corps Agency were at the site installing radar and communications for the upcoming rocket launches. When the bay froze over, the ice allowed polar bears to wander into the compound looking for food. In response the soldiers were issued rifles but told they could only use them in self defense.

According to an Air Force history of the rocket range, close to 200 rockets were launched at Fort Churchill during IGY. Those were mostly Aerobees and Nike Cajuns.

At the end of 1958, the site was closed down. Scientific groups from Canada and the United States

pressed to have it opened for further research. In August 1959, it was reopened under the control of White Sands Missile Range. Periodic launches of sounding rockets took place at Fort Churchill until the disastrous fire on Feb. 28, 1961.

A fire broke out in the facility's diesel generator plant in the middle of the night. When an attendant tried to call for help he couldn't get through because the lines were already burned through. He was forced to drive to another facility to call for fire fighters. By the time they got there the place was pretty much gone.

"The Churchill Research Range" published in 1964 by the Air Force noted, "The generator building, helium storage, diesel storage, helium compressor building, Aerobee assembly and preparation building, mess hall, launch control building, and a portion of the tunnel connecting the launch control building and the Aerobee tower were all destroyed." The destruction of most of the site left the Army frosty, as officials didn't want to pay for reconstruction. The Air Force eventually moved in and restored the facility.

By 1990, use of the Churchill facilities had ended and the community could no longer rely on jobs and income from visiting scientists. The town rebranded itself as the polar bear capital of the world and now plays host to thousands of eco-tourists. They visit to get up close and personal with one of the big white bears. Others visit in the summer to watch Beluga whales in the Churchill River.

Choral Competitions

Normally you wouldn't expect that the Army would encourage singing groups and hold competitions for them. Yet, in the 1950s and 1960s such things did happen. At White Sands, Army personnel put together a small choral group of about a dozen men to sing for fun and to compete. They called themselves the Missile Rangers.

The group was led by Private First Class John Puchinsky and included both officers and enlisted men. In November 1962, these singers won the small chorus competition at the 4th Army's Choral Contest.

There was also individual competition. Private First Class Steve Brainard took home first prize in the Popular Vocal Soloist category. Private First Class Glenn Gray finished second in the Classical Vocal Soloist competition.

In May 1965, White Sands sent a number of acts to the same contest. While no one took a first place, Specialist 4 Melvin Hueston and Private First Class Stanley Stenner, performing as the "Shakers," took second place in the vocal group competition.

Unfortunately, when I worked at White Sands singing had descended to karaoke at the clubs on Friday nights.

Looking west at the White Sands main post in March 1947. What is obvious in this photo is the new Mill Building just west of the original V-2 Assembly Building. The V-2 Bldg. is the large Quonset hut on the left. Also, west of the Mill Bldg. are the new Navy Quonset huts. WSMR photo.

12

Broomsticks And Co-ops

How To Man A Missile Range

In addition to the typical military and civilian workforce at White Sands, management had to search for the technically qualified people needed to do the work. There was even a need for a few cowboys, not your usual military fare, out on the range.

This was just after World War II and prior to 1940 most Americans didn't go to college. In fact, before then, less than 50% of Americans even graduated from high school. To say the least, there was no big pool of potential employees with the math, science and engineering backgrounds for the work.

Then, if you throw in the fact that the workplace was in thinly populated southern New Mexico, a place many thought was a foreign country, there was difficulty filling positions.

For instance, in the data reduction area, it was tough finding a group of people who could run the trigonometric functions necessary to calculate missile data. One early solution was to contract for the help. Where did the range get people with the necessary backgrounds? A university was one place to start.

In the spring of 1946, the Ballistics Research Lab at White Sands entered into a contract with New Mexico College of Agriculture and Mechanic Arts in Las Cruces to support Army testing by reducing data. This meant taking film and tediously turning the information in each frame into meaningful numbers or measurements. Before long they were reducing data from telemetry instruments as well.

Thus the Physical Science Lab was born. Dr. George Gardiner was the first director. At the time he was head of the school's Physics Department.

Because of the need to do complicated math functions in reducing the data, the first students hired were promising kids in engineering, math and physics. Anna Gardiner, a math instructor at the school and Dr. Gardiner's wife, supervised the group. Their first work was looking at film from V-2 launches.

The lab quickly grew, taking on more tasks at White Sands to include work for the Navy. The permanent staff expanded and the lab got its own annex on campus.

Because of his work in establishing PSL and the lab's great value in getting meaningful information from those early missile flights, Dr. George Gardiner was elected to the White Sands Hall of Fame in 1986.

Joe Gold and Benjamin Billups were students in that first group working under Anna Gardiner. They went on to full careers at White Sands. Billups was elected to the range's Hall of Fame in 1980, in the original group. Gold was inducted into the Hall of Fame in 2006.

Sometimes folks flipped the arrangement. Jed Durrenberger, a photo-optical engineer at White Sands from 1951 to 1981, retired from his federal job and went to work for PSL. In 2004 he was inducted into the Hall of Fame.

Joe Gold, in his autobiography *As I Remember*, wrote about the uncertainty of the early days of White Sands because of budgets and personnel limits. After his graduation from New Mexico A&M and armed with a degree in engineering and work experience at PSL, he sought work at White Sands. He was told there was nothing full-time available and was offered temporary work.

He was glad for the job and jumped on it. Unfortunately, it was only a 60-day appointment. In his book he wrote, "At the end of 60 days, Art Ditmar came to me and said my 60 days were up and handed me a personnel action form, signed by the Chief of Civilian Personnel, terminating my temporary employment. What a panic that caused me! When he had allowed sufficient time for the implication of that shocker to sink in, he produced a similar piece of paper, also signed by the Chief of Civilian Personnel, which informed me that as of the same date, I had been temporarily hired again for a period not to exceed 30 days."

After 30 days, Ditmar did the same thing to Gold. This time the new temporary period was to be 15 days. After 15 days, Ditmar struck for the third time with a termination notice. This time, however, he followed it with a probationary appointment that was good for a year. Upon satisfactory completion of the year, Gold became a regular, full-time employee.

Austin Vick's hiring was a little more straight forward but was certainly a bolt of lightning out of the blue. After he graduated from New Mexico A&M in 1950, Vick was headed north for a job. He loaded his few belongings into his pickup and headed out of Las Cruces.

On the way out of town, he stopped to get gas. The station attendant struck up a conversation with Vick, asking where he was going. After Vick explained, the attendant told him he ought to drive over to so and so's house and apply for a job at White Sands. He understood White Sands was hiring.

Vick followed the suggestion and drove over to the indicated house. The range official turned out to be the head of personnel and was out mowing his lawn on a Saturday morning when Vick drove up. Vick interrupted him and asked about possible work at the range. When Vick indicated he had taught others in school how to use theodolites, he was hired on the spot and told to report for work at White Sands the next week.

Broomsticks

As G. Harry Stine said, White Sands was a proving ground for many professionals who wandered in and then moved on. The young soldiers stationed at WSPG in the early 1950s as part of the Army's "Enlisted Scientific and Professional Personnel Program" are an excellent example.

This was another way to get workers with technical backgrounds for White Sands. In 1950, the draft

was started up again at the beginning of the Korean War. Using the draft, the Army was able to bring into the service young men with partial or actual degrees in the sciences and engineering, and put them in a variety of technological jobs. Many reservists were also activated and inserted into the program.

For instance, a young man with an aeronautical engineering background might be drafted and sent to work on helicopters. Someone with a chemistry degree might be sent to the Army's Chemical Corps. And someone with mathematics, physics or engineering training might end up at White Sands to work on missiles.

Chuck Mullis was one of these draftees. In the April 1988 issue of the *Whispering Sands Pioneer Gazette*, he wrote how he completed basic training at Fort Leonard Wood and then went to Fort Meyer, Virginia for processing.

Many of the men in this program have written about the processing process. They were often given a number of possibilities to select from, but it all boiled down to some faceless clerk making the final assignments. Men with degrees in mathematics were very versatile and could count on being sent almost anywhere.

Mullis was sent to White Sands and arrived at 2 a.m. on March 3, 1951 aboard a Union Pacific train. The train dropped Mullis and a few others off at the Orogrande station where there was no life and a single light bulb burning in the distance. Mullis asked the conductor where the station was and he pointed toward the light bulb.

The men walked up the tracks to the light, went inside the small station, and found a sign reading, "To call White Sands Proving Ground for transportation, turn crank." The phone beside the sign was an old Army field phone with a hand crank to ring the phone at the other end.

Mullis was assigned to the 9393rd Technical Service Unit. He said there were over 250 men in the unit; 220 had some university credits and 180 of the total had at least one degree. Most were assigned to the 1st Ordnance Guided Missile Support Battalion for duty assignments. Because of the composition and circumstances, Mullis said they "had a spirit more akin to a university." And that was a problem.

These young men didn't appreciate the strict discipline of the Army, didn't like doing things simply to be doing them, and openly questioned the seemingly meaningless regulations. In April 1951, Mullis sent a letter to Gale, his fiancée, in which he enclosed a cartoon from the *American Legion Magazine*. The cartoon has a young private saying to a sergeant, "Is there some accepted form of salute that shows respect for an officer's rank, but at the same time expresses a low opinion of him personally?" Mullis' comment to Gale is, "Thought you would get a kick out of this. The tragedy is a lot of us feel this way."

For instance, Broomsticker Carl Haskett remembered being lectured on the limitations of toilet paper and being told they were to use only four sheets. These guys were not your normal draftees and they didn't believe it for an instant.

The fact they were commanded by many officers and non-commissioned officers who were "old school" certainly didn't help. Also, their quick promotions didn't sit well with old-timers who spent years working through the ranks. In one example, a soldier went from private to staff sergeant in just four months.

One officer was berating the unit one day for some typical error when he told them he was not impressed, and they were about as useful as a bunch of broomsticks. The men loved it. They jumped on the insult and quickly turned it into their own moniker, calling themselves the "Broomstick Scientists." It became a badge of honor.

One NCO commented how surprised he was to enter the Broomstick barracks because, instead of men reading comic books and listening to honky-tonk records, these guys were reading textbooks and listening to classical music.

Many of these supervisors didn't understand the technology being investigated. One lieutenant later said, "I just told them what we needed and then disappeared while they produced it."

These men were also handy and built things for their needs – like tables in the barracks to provide work surfaces, places to put records and books, etc. One of their officers was a hardcore regulation man. At a formation, he ordered the men to remove all non-regulation tables from the barracks. One of the men raised his hand and asked if that included "integral tables." The officer didn't get the dig and told them all tables must be removed. They all had a good chuckle about that.

Of course the officer shouldn't be blamed; most Americans today wouldn't know that integral tables are used in calculus. The tables were reference material essential to solving the problems the men faced in their jobs on the missile projects.

In another example, an officer was castigating the unit at morning reveille for being late. According to Dom Toscani they were always late.

The officer was fed up and told the men that if they didn't straighten up, he was going to order reveille 30 minutes earlier for every minute they were late. Immediately, one scientist drew a graph showing what time they would hold reveille for each minute they were late. The conclusion was that being late by 40 minutes make make reveille the next day at a very comfortable 10 a.m. The graph was duly posted on a bulletin board, but the old school cadre didn't seem to understand the joke.

Eventually, one Broomsticker mouthed off to the wrong non-commissioned officer. Dom Toscani ended up being court-martialed for his "insubordination" and was sentenced to 30 days in the brig.

Bill Ezell remembered the event in the April 2000 issue of *The Broomstick Scientist* newsletter. He wrote, "As I recall, Dom also forfeited 1/3 pay for the month (which we restored at the party) and had to serve an extra month to make up for the 'bad' time. I also remember that Dom was marched to the mess hall for each meal and received a standing cheer each time he entered – as a thanks for taking the medicine for all of us who didn't talk back....I do remember that Captain McGaffick asked me (I was in an office just down the hall from him at the time) what happened to cause Toscani to be court-martialed. When I told him, he surprised me by expressing, in colorful terms, that 'an injustice had occurred!'"

On the other hand, these young men knew their stuff. They were assigned to missile systems such as the V-2, Corporal, Loki, Nike, Terrier, and Hermes. They occupied technical positions in propulsion, guidance, tracking, and launching. Some were sent on temporary duty to contractor facilities such at the Jet Propulsion Lab, North American Aviation, and General Electric.

They were featured in the April 5, 1952 issue of *Collier's* magazine as the Army's "Whiz Kids." Bill Davidson, the author, quoted General J. Lawton Collins, the Army Chief of Staff, after he visited White Sands, "I never have come across such soldiers. There were recently inducted Pfcs who were electrical engineers in civilian life, sergeants who have their master's degrees in engineering and officers with PhDs in physics. Why, when they pulled out their best lecturer to brief me in basic electronics, it was a corporal!"

The article pointed out another corporal who was given great responsibility. When the General Electric contract expired, a group of these young soldiers was called on to assemble and fire a V-2, dubbed "Test Flight 1" or TF-1. To head this group, Lieutenant Colonel Matthew Collins (the men called him Curly) selected Corporal Robert Alley. Alley had an electrical engineering degree from the University of Michigan.

The team worked for weeks with the informal goal of beating the old altitude record of 114 miles set by GE for a V-2. The Broomstick V-2 was launched on Aug. 22, 1951 and reached an altitude of 132 miles.

A very dapper Staff Sergeant Robert Alley before leaving White Sands - taken after his effort to lead the team firing the V-2 known as TF-1 when he was still a corporal. Photo courtesy of Robert Alley.

There were several more launches after this for the soldiers, but none were as successful as the first.

As quickly as it began, this special program began to disappear as the Korean War wound down. Men served out their two-year commitments and were released. Some of these men turned to the air and space industry for their careers while some received technical jobs with the government. They were definitely influenced by their stay at White Sands.

Arnie Crouch, who started and edited *The Broomstick Scientist* newsletter (1999 – 2005), collected as many White Sands soldier/scientists that he could find. In the end he had found about 100 of them and was mailing them copies of the newsletter. I had the honor of helping him put together a reunion of many of the Broomstickers back at White Sands in 2001.

In one of Crouch's newsletters, he quoted a few of the men on their experience at White Sands. George Gianopulos said, "I agree that this experience was unforgettable and valuable. For me, it changed my life entirely, for which I am forever grateful – despite the fact I hated the Army!"

John Schoneman said, "It was a unique experience for us at White Sands. I think I learned more about my abilities and myself there than in any previous experience."

Mr. Stine was right about White Sands; it was a "proving ground."

Co-op Students

Around the time the Broomstick soldiers were leaving White Sands, the proving ground and New Mexico A & M came to an agreement to further help fill the need for engineering and science talent. The program, called The Cooperative Student-Trainee Program, was quickly extended to Texas Western College in El Paso in 1954. Of course, those organizations today are known as New Mexico State University and University of Texas at El Paso.

The first class to participate in the program started in the fall of 1952. Students made $1.20 per hour that first year while working at White Sands.

Although there was a great deal of detail and bureaucratic structure to the program, the idea was pretty simple. White Sands made part-time positions available in various organizations for engineers, physicists, mathematicians and other technical fields. Students in these fields could apply for the positions.

It was arranged so students would attend school for six months and fill one of these White Sands positions the other six months. For their efforts at White Sands, the students would be paid on the government's General Schedule pay scale. As freshmen they were paid at the GS-2 level. As sophomores, they moved up to GS-3 and so on until, as seniors, they were at the GS-5 level. While working at White Sands, the students were allowed to live in student housing back on their campuses.

When the students graduated, there was usually a job waiting for them at White Sands.

The program quickly took off. In January 1959, the post newspaper reported 102 co-op students were returning to school and 75 were coming to White Sands to start their work cycle. On Dec. 1, 1961, the *Wind and Sand* reported that after nine years, 70 percent of those in the co-op program who earned their college degree went to work at White Sands.

For decades this program was described as a win-win situation for everyone involved. White Sands gained access to future highly qualified professionals who might be inclined to spend a career at the installation. Also, while the students were still in school, they provided valuable labor in support positions at White Sands.

For the universities, it gave them the opportunity to expose students to real-world jobs and to see if they really wanted to pursue a particular course of study. Also, it allowed them to keep bright hardship students who might not have been able to complete their degrees because of financial burdens.

The only downside for the students was the additional time it took to earn their degrees. Going to school only halftime usually extended their stint at school.

On the positive side for the students was the experience gained in real jobs in their chosen fields of expertise. It looked a whole lot better on the resume than flipping burgers over the summer. They also received a decent wage for their time at White Sands. In the early decades of the program it was plenty to pay for school, books and housing.

While working at White Sands, the students were technically government employees, covered by health insurance and sick leave. Also, they earned retirement credit and other benefits.

John Sweem, a member of the second co-op class at the Range, went to work as a mathematician in 1957. In a July 6, 1958 *Las Cruces Sun-News* interview, Sweem said, "The co-op program gave me a really firm foundation for the work I'm doing now. I feel that without the co-op experience behind me, and as a graduate just out of a regular college cur-

This is the first co-op class for 1957. The 18 students are from both Texas Western (UTEP) and New Mexico A and M (NMSU). Seated, left to right, are: Clyde Imagna, Robert Witholder, Jr., Lawrence Crouse, Glenn Ramsdale, Robert Elliott, and Charles Sullivan. Standing, left to right, are: Chester Claghorn, Donald Kassner, Harry Gilbert, Robert Stanfield, William Dial, Jr., Luigi Perini, Lance Presnall, Donald Bickel, Ralph Flowers, Richard Beliun, Hubert Plumlee, and Jerome Chaffee. WSMR photo.

riculum, I could never step into this job I have now." Sweem also said the program gave him a great boost financially and ability-wise when compared to other college graduates with similar degrees.

One of the White Sands people credited with making this program a reality was Ben Billups, a technical guy in the data reduction world at White Sands. His pioneering work in the early days of White Sands earned him induction into the missile range's Hall of Fame in 1980's initial group.

The co-op program quickly spread across the country and was used throughout the military, NASA and other government agencies.

Many of the White Sands leaders emerged from this program. Jim Scott was a co-op student at New Mexico State when he studied electrical engineering. He received his degree in 1958 and went to work at White Sands right away as an electronics engineer.

Known as "Scotty," he moved through the Instrumentation Directorate and then to the National Range Directorate in 1975. He worked there until he retired from federal service in 1990. During his last year he was the senior civilian for the organization and responsible for providing technical leadership.

Because of Scotty's influential work in data collection and its processing, missile flight safety, resource management, and running day-to-day operations, he was elected to the missile range's Hall of Fame in 2004.

Officials quickly realized the co-op program could be expanded to other fields – it was too good to be restricted to just the sciences and engineering. An example of someone taking advantage of the expanded opportunity was Monte Marlin. Marlin entered New Mexico State in 1977, studying journalism with an emphasis on public relations and marketing.

Marlin entered the co-op program late, in 1980, so she only participated in two work cycles at White Sands in the Public Affairs Office. Those two six-month work cycles delayed her graduation from NMSU to 1982.

Immediately after her graduation and passing the civil service exam of the day, she hired on at White Sands as a permanent employee in the Public Affairs Office. When Larry Furrow, Chief of Public Affairs, retired in 2008, Marlin was selected to replace him.

Cowboys

Known variously as Range Inspectors and Range Riders, for decades White Sands had a need for employees who possessed the skills to ride horseback in rough country, handle livestock, track both animals and humans, repair equipment, and be the spear point for public relations with the missile range's ranch neighbors. Many reporters and members of the public called them "government cowboys." Those who loved the outdoors often said it was probably the best job on White Sands.

With several hundred miles of unfenced boundary, White Sands has always had a problem with cattle seeking greener pastures on the military side of the dividing line. In a few cases, neighboring ranchers might even have encouraged their animals across the line to pick up a little free grass. The solution was a small group of employees hired in the early 1950s to patrol the boundary.

Initially they were part of security and were used as an arm of law enforcement. Floyd Adams, the first chief inspector, and his assistant, Tom Dayberry, attended security training at the Army's Military Police School in the 1950s.

Toward the end of the 50s, John Snow and Bill Bates joined the crew. When I first met the range riders in the late 70s, Dayberry, Bates and Tom Emanuel were the three full-time cowboys.

Using their government horses, the range riders used to patrol the boundary lines looking for trespass livestock. When detected, the riders would contact the owner and arrange to escort the rancher onto the range. The range riders would then help round up the strays and move them off the missile range. This meant they had to be aware of all the local brands so they could contact the appropriate ranch.

While patrolling the boundary, they were also looking for two-legged trespassers. This was important because looters used to sneak onto the range to pilfer items from the old ranches. Also, in the Hembrillo area, treasure hunters were numerous and persistent for decades. In fact, during the early 1970s, a house trailer was placed at Hembrillo Pass so the range riders would have a more permanent presence in the Victorio Peak area.

These skills of getting into rough country on horseback and being able to track people were very useful when performing rescue work – say for an injured or lost deer hunter or someone lost in the national monument dune fields.

After 1960, range riders picked up the task of

delivering evacuation notices to the ranch families in the call-up areas on the north and west side of White Sands. To make sure ranchers evacuated and that there were no excuses, the missile range hand-delivered the notices to each family.

Knowing every nook and cranny of the missile range made the range riders valuable for other efforts as well. When I first got to White Sands and needed to take reporters to Victorio Peak or an old ranch, I depended on the range riders. Also, they helped the environmental folks and the New Mexico Department of Game and Fish when they were doing wildlife studies on White Sands.

Since most of their work was done in the middle to northern end of White Sands, it made no sense for them to work out of the main post. Hours would have been wasted each day just driving back and forth. Instead, they used the Hardin Ranch house on the western boundary at the head of Rhodes Canyon.

That is the reason the two-bedroom house has been maintained for years. It had a nice set of corrals for their horses and a good windmill to provide potable water. Inside, the house was comfortable with a small kitchen, living room and bathroom. A large government propane tank supplied gas needed for the stove, light and refrigerator. There was even a telephone so they could communicate with the main post.

Over time an urban legend has grown up that this house was turned into some sort of lodge for the commanding general and his hunting buddies.

Range Rider Les Gililland is interviewed by a television crew about his role in the horse roundups at WSMR. Photo by author.

During their workweek, the range riders would spend the night at Hardin so they were always close to their next day's work. I had lunch with Bill and the two Toms a couple of times at Hardin; they always had beans on the stove and whipped out fresh-baked biscuits very quickly. The entertainment was good too - it wasn't hard to convince Bill to pull out his fiddle and play a few tunes.

These men and their unusual job on a high-tech weapons testing facility attracted attention from the news media. The November 1965 issue of *Western Horseman* has a nice article about the "inspectors" supported by lots of photos. The same year Major Vincent D'Angelo, an Army radio correspondent, interviewed the men for an audio story. For the piece they put D'Angelo and his recorder on the back of a horse so he could ride along on a patrol.

All good things come to pass, however, and the range riders have dwindled to one. As trespass cattle and humans diminished and budgets shrank, the range riders were bumped from security to the environmental organization.

This didn't go over too well with the men. Within a year or so, they all retired.

Eventually the range rider function ended up under National Range Operations because it was the organization needing people to deliver evacuation notices in the call-up areas. The government horses were sold, and the Hardin ranch house was pretty much abandoned.

When I retired in 2007, there was still one range rider. It was Les Gililland. He came from the same kind of rancher stock as the first ranger riders. Those skills made him invaluable when the wild horse die-off happened at WSMR. His abilities made it possible for White Sands to successfully conduct the roundups and adoptions.

The Numbers

Obtaining personnel strength numbers for White Sands is an Easter egg hunt for the necessary records and never knowing what exactly you'll find in each egg. However, even with the lack of early records and the vagaries of later ones, it is pretty easy to see the overall trends.

As might be expected, the population rapidly grew through the first two decades as rocket and missile technologies were explored. There was a lot to look into. Teams of scientists and engineers studied everything from the chemistry of different fuels to how to guide a missile to a tank or a supersonic jet – two very different situations.

In response to the Cold War, military leaders dreamed up a huge variety of missile systems to deal with the land, air and sea threats posed by the Soviet Union. There was everything from small, shoulder-fired, anti-aircraft missiles to hulking ballistic missiles which could carry atomic bombs.

All of these technologies, all of these systems needed to be tested, and White Sands was the go-to facility in those early days. In turn, the missile range population shot forward like the rockets being tested.

Much of the early work was labor intensive. It took many people to do everything from billing to maintaining radars to recovering debris to supporting the workforce with food, drink and places to sleep.

Eventually the workforce numbers reached a plateau and then started to fall. There were ups and downs but if you rough out the spikes and dips, a graph might look like a very steep climb to a flat-ish period and then a gentle slope down the other side.

The decline had many causes – White Sands equipment got better and more automated, meaning fewer people were needed; there were fewer and fewer tests as the missile technology matured – you didn't have to reinvent the wheel with each system; missile systems got more expensive which meant the program couldn't fire hundreds of missiles like Nike did – instead more had to be packed into a single test; and finally, as the Cold War wound down, the reduced Soviet super-power threat meant fewer missile systems to test.

The Public Affairs Office has a single typed page that some unknown person put together years ago to summarize personnel strength for the first 15 years of White Sands. After that there are numerous summaries and factsheets outlining the numbers.

In 1945, the very first number was 163 officers and enlisted men allocated for White Sands. The initial group was soon increased with another 25 officers and 200 enlisted men.

In 1946, the total strength was estimated at 600 people. We know there were civilians on site working on projects and providing support but we don't know for sure if they were included in the 600.

A 1947 summary is more specific and states that on July 28 there were 32 officers, 600 enlisted men and 200 civilians. However, we don't know if this includes the Navy personnel who began arriving in 1947.

For 1951 there is a single entry showing 1,862 people at White Sands. Again, there is no breakout, but clearly the workforce is ramping up fast.

After this there is a big gap until 1957 where the range reportedly had 9,000 people. The summary states the total is military and government civilians. At the same time, Holloman reportedly had 8,000 personnel. There is no indication of whether or not these totals include contractor personnel.

In 1961, we finally have a report breaking out the numbers to segregate the workforce. The total was 11,400 with 4,100 military, 5,100 civilians and 2,200 contractors. Also, Holloman was folded in for a joint WSMR-Holloman workforce of 17,000 folks. Whoever compiled the numbers estimated the payroll at $100 million.

In an October issue of the *Wind and Sand* that year, an article pointed out that out of the 5,000 civilians on WSMR, 370 were considered "handicapped."

During the 1960s there was an effort to report a WSMR-Holloman number which White Sands briefers called the "WSMR Complex" data. In 1967, management could boast that the WSMR complex included 20,124 people. Pulling the Army, Navy and NASA numbers out of the total, the White Sands portion was 11,200 workers.

In 1969, White Sands compiled and published a nice fact sheet about the range, something that would continue almost every year until the end of the century. The total workforce that year was 9,355. On the surface that looks remarkably low compared to 1967 until you read the little note on the factsheet indicating the number does not include NASA or any of its contractors. Still it is a decline.

This statistics factsheet does provide a little more insight into the makeup of the workforce. It states that out of the Army civilians, 886 were women and 3,722 were men. By age they were: 18-30 = 820, 31-50 = 2,804, 51-60 = 829, and over 61 = 155.

Finally, it tells us where they lived. About 35 percent lived in Las Cruces and another 35 percent in El Paso. Only 10 percent lived in Alamogordo while 20 percent were scattered in places like the WSMR main post, Socorro and Carrizozo.

In 1971, without NASA contractors included, the total WSMR population was reportedly 8,600 people. In 1976, the number had declined to 6,900 but was up to 7,600 in 1977 when NASA numbers were included.

During the 1980s, there was quite a bit of fluctuation with 7,800 in 1980, 8,600 in 1983, and 9,500 in 1989. The military numbers were shrinking while civil service employee and contractor numbers were going up.

In 1992, the total dropped down to 8,000 as the end of the Cold War started to impact the testing business at White Sands. In 1996, the total was 7,000 and in 1999 it was only 6,000. According to the 1999 statistics factsheet, there were only 370 military (Army, Navy and Air Force) personnel working on White Sands.

The last published statistics factsheet in 2004 indicates the workforce was stabilizing with 6,200 people at the range, a number very similar to 1999.

So, you might ask how good are these numbers? Well, they aren't too bad but there is no way they are exact in any way, shape or form. They should be viewed as "ballpark figures."

For a couple of decades before she retired from Public Affairs in 2006, Debbie Bingham compiled the statistics factsheet for White Sands each year. It took her weeks and sometimes months to collect the data. I think she likened preparing the factsheet to beating her head against a brick wall.

It included much more than workforce numbers so it was more complicated. In addition to collecting manpower numbers, she went looking for the range's total payroll and how much money was spent locally through contracts. Those numbers were incredibly hard to nail down.

Doing this factsheet is a perfect example of why people who work inside bureaucracies don't have much sympathy for outsiders who complain about some incident in dealing with a government office. When you work at a place like White Sands, pretty much everyone and every office you deal with is part of the bureaucracy. That means working with all those rules and, sometimes, mule-headed personnel

for eight hours a day, five days a week, year after year. It does require patience.

For Debbie, getting the personnel numbers was a mixed ordeal. Many organizations quickly added up their numbers and sent them over. For others, she often wondered if they received the original request.

Some people might have let it go at that point, but Debbie always wanted to make sure the factsheet was as accurate as possible. Every year she would have to shift into babysitting mode and remind the late organizations they were late. For some entities this became a weekly ritual until they broke down and sent the numbers over.

In other cases there were tenant organizations on White Sands that simply didn't want to be bothered. Debbie would have to go to work persuading those in charge that their report was needed to complete the snapshot of White Sands for that year.

In a few cases Debbie ran into organizations that didn't want it known they were even on White Sands, let alone how many people they had. In those instances Debbie would have to work her way up their chain of command, explaining there was no threat, no danger, as their organizational numbers would simply be folded into a single big number. No one would be able to differentiate one tenant from another.

Finally, there would be an organization or two that simply didn't send any number in, ever. If she could back into a guesstimate, she would. Sometimes they simply weren't counted in the total.

Because Debbie was the sole author of this factsheet for years, we have confidence the numbers from year to year were consistently collected and tabulated. Before Debbie took on the task, we have no idea how the numbers were compiled. In some sense, comparing Debbie's numbers to previous ones might really be like trying to compare apples and oranges. Actually, if Debbie's numbers are oranges, previous ones might be apricots or watermelons for all we know.

Again, in the end, the best advice is to round off the numbers and always preface a workforce number with the wonderfully imprecise word "about."

13

Red Devils Lead The Way

Miscellaneous Sports Stories

Since World War II, sports have been a major part of life on military installations. Lots of money has been poured into facilities and equipment for soldiers and their families. Most of it, of course, goes into support for ordinary soldiers and their everyday use. Intramural competition and fitness usage are the norm on ball fields and in gyms all across America. But there is also an emphasis on properly equipping teams of the best athletes that would represent the installation against outside teams.

White Sand Proving Ground tried to keep up with the larger Army posts by fielding installation teams, but was hampered by its small military population and odd mission. There just wasn't a very big pool to draw from compared to the forts found in the Southwest.

Also, military personnel at White Sands were from a great variety of backgrounds with many having some technical expertise – not exactly where you find great athletes.

Finally, the range's missions, with tests scheduled day and night, often prevented athletes from attending practice sessions or the games themselves.

Given all that, the post managed to field a football team for a couple of years. They were never competitive but were winners off the field – see their story below. In basketball and baseball, White Sands easily fielded teams for decades as those sports never required a lot of personnel to compete.

Additionally, White Sands put together a track and field team for a while and had a swim team in 1956. This was pretty remarkable given the chances of having enough young men from these minor sports to make a go of it.

The swim team did it by having a few people compete in a lot of events. According to the *Wind and Sand* in 1956, there were only 12 men on the team when they went up against big Fort Bliss. That included diver Louis Braddi who competed on both one-meter and three-meter boards.

There is no caption but the photo is from the right time frame to be Braddi practicing his swan dive at the Navy pool. WSMR photo.

Braddi grew up in California where he learned to dive in junior high and high school. He said he received some great coaching and he thought he had a future in big-time competitive diving if life hadn't gotten in the way.

He ended up in the Army and in Korea. On his return to the States he was assigned to the motor pool at White Sands where he drove just about everything available.

With his junior swimming background, it was an easy leap to join the White Sands swim team. He said he doesn't remember what other installations they swam against but he thought there were quite a number of competitions.

The *Wind and Sand*, in reporting the Fort Bliss meet, said the swimmers only had four pairs of racing trunks between them. The paper reported the men would run to the locker room and trade out trunks after a race so the next guy could go. Braddi said this didn't affect him as he had a different style of shorts for diving.

Despite the shortage of men for the team and shortage of trunks for the swimmers, they beat Fort Bliss.

Braddi got out of the Army at the end of the year but signed on with the Air Force in 1957. In addition to his regular job, he volunteered as a swimming and diving coach for the Air Force. In addition, he competed for the Air Force in both swimming and diving. He swam the individual medley plus the freestyle and butterfly in individual races.

After getting out of the Air Force, Braddi returned to White Sands as a civilian working in Logistics. He worked there from 1974 to 2005. While at WSMR, he acted as a flight instructor for the range's flying club which had been organized in 1953.

So there are no stories of great White Sands teams conquering all the neighboring competition and going on to win All-Army accolades. However, there are some interesting stories where the range brushed up against greatness in one way or another.

Football

At one time, when V-2 rockets were still being tested, real football was played at White Sands. This wasn't the flag or touch football now played by the post team. These were full-grown men in real pads and uniforms going up against other teams.

In 1949, the team was winless. In 1950, the team played other military and school teams. They even played in a game billed as the "Silver Bowl."

It is hard to grasp how good or bad the team was because there are no White Sands records and only one post newspaper still around to reference. By searching through newspapers from Las Cruces and other military bases, I found the results of three games in 1950. According to Don Lloyd, who was a guard on the offensive line, there were only three games - so I may have found them all.

Unfortunately, the evidence doesn't point to a "rocket-powered" team. Instead, the clippings indicate it was not a very competitive team and the "bowl game" was a local attraction that promoters tagged as a bowl game. The White Sands team lost all three games and scored only 22 points while the opponents scored a total of 113 points.

The team may not have been a powerhouse, but it did enjoy some novelty as one of the few and maybe only true all-service football organization. The starting offensive lineup included an Army backfield with the linemen coming from the Army, Navy, Air Force and Marine Corps. Included on the roster were some of the Broomstick Scientists, enlisted men with technical educations in science and engineering who were drafted and assigned to White Sands to assist on several missile projects. For instance, the starting quarterback, Dom Toscani, was a broomsticker.

One game, probably the season opener, was on Sept. 28 against the freshman team at New Mexico A and M, now New Mexico State in Las Cruces. Although the final score was A&M 13, White Sands 7, the game wasn't all that close. According to the university's newspaper, the school scored all of its points in the first half while the White Sands offense didn't cross the 50-yard line until the second half.

In the second half, White Sands crossed the 50 twice and only managed a score in the closing seconds when Bill Poteat caught a pass and got himself into the end zone. The paper said Poteat had been an All-4th Army performer in 1949 and was an obvious bright spot for the proving ground team.

On Nov. 4, the team traveled to El Paso to play the Fort Bliss Rockets. In its lead sentence the following day, the *El Paso Times* reported, "After a scoreless first quarter Fort Bliss poured on the coals and trampled White Sands, 47-7, on Armstrong Field at Fort Bliss Saturday afternoon."

White Sands scored its only touchdown thanks

to Bill Poteat again. In the first half he burst through the Rockets line for a 12-yard run to pay dirt. Basically, the White Sands team was again outmanned – except for Bill Poteat.

According to team captain Walter Patton, it was a difficult situation because of the lack of players and command support. He said there were about 2,000 troops on post, which is not a large number to draw from. In addition, the commanding general didn't really like football and didn't back the team. Without that support, the team members had to participate strictly on their own time. With all the players working in so many jobs and programs, getting them together at one time and place for practice was just about impossible without some command emphasis.

Walter Patton played tackle for the White Sands Red Devils. He was a double captain. By day he was a Marine Corps captain working as a missile project officer. In the evenings and on weekends, he was the captain of the post's football team. Photo courtesy of Walter Patton.

Then, to top it off, they had to practice on a dirt field littered with large stones and goat heads, a nasty ground-cover plant with seed pods covered in thorns.

Patton came to White Sands in the summer of 1950 as a young Marine Corps captain working as a missile project officer. He played high school football and had worked for the athletic department at Auburn University when going to college. He volunteered to be the line coach for the team.

According to Patton they only had 27 players on the team, so the coaches decided to check out uniforms as well, just in case they were needed. In the first game, two of the tackles were injured and Patton had to step in and play. "I played about 56 minutes in the first game and couldn't get out of bed the next day," he said.

At the time, Patton weighed about 200 pounds and stood six feet tall. He ended up as the starting tackle for the rest of the season.

So the question is, how did this team make it to a "bowl game?" Details are sketchy, but Nellis Air Force Base, outside of Las Vegas, Nevada, did invite White Sands to play in the Silver Bowl on Dec. 3. Nellis always hosted this bowl game and played in it.

Patton said, "somebody got our record fouled up and thought we were better than we were." Patton's point is certainly true because the *Las Vegas Review Journal*, in an article printed before the game, said, "The White Sands aggregation has yet to taste defeat this season but has two deadlocks." Well, we know that's not true.

We'll probably never know if the error was an honest mistake or a deliberate attempt to make the game look more attractive to fans. The Las Vegas paper did hype the game, saying the White Sands team was a bevy of "behemoths who will crash heads with the Nellis Air Force Base Mustangs" and "A pair of huge, rugged pigskin organizations...run full tilt up against one another this afternoon at 1:30 in the annual Silver Bowl football game before an estimated 3,500 fans in the Last Frontier Sportsdome." The Nellis coach also was quoted as saying his team would need at least four touchdowns to win.

What may have added to the confusion about the proving ground's record was the team name. On the program for the Fort Bliss game, the White Sands team was called the "Buzz Bombs," presumably because of V-1 testing at the range. The local paper referred to the team as the "Tigers" before they traveled to Nevada and the Las Vegas papers called them the "Red Devils." It's no wonder there were errors concerning the team's wins and losses.

Whatever the name, the team received permission to go to the game, but with a general who did not support them, the question was how to get there and back. Nellis solved that problem by flying one of their planes to White Sands and picking up the team and coaches on Dec. 2. The Air Force then flew them home on Dec. 4.

Besides being a bowl game, the battle was a fundraiser with proceeds going to the Nellis chaplain's fund for their annual children's Christmas program. To defray costs, Las Vegas businesses stepped in to help. For instance, a local casino paid for printing the game programs.

So this may have been the force behind the game and the phony hype. The base and the community were working together to raise money for a very good cause. It really didn't matter who Nellis played as long as spectators showed up and paid their admission fee.

The White Sands team probably should have gone to the casino instead of the stadium because the Nellis team scored more than the four touchdowns their coach predicted they would need. The *Las Vegas Review Journal* said, "In what turned out to be a game of one-sided keep-away, the Nellis Air Force

Base Mustangs obliterated the White Sands, New Mexico, Red Devils ... by an astronomical 53-6 count before 1,000 subdued fans."

White Sands scored in the second quarter after a drive that started on its own 30-yard line. The touchdown came on a 15-yard pass from quarterback Bob Plenert to end Art Guglielama. They missed the extra point.

The Las Vegas paper described the game in terms of "carnage." Patton said they were completely "outclassed." He said Nellis carried a huge roster of around 55 players with 18 of them being former college players. It was an understandable loss but still a disappointing day for White Sands.

The *Wind and Sand* newspaper, was a bit more positive with a headline, "Hard-pressed Tigers lose to rampaging Nellis." In the story's first sentence the writer said, "White Sands football team finally went down under the overwhelming power of a slamming Nellis Air Force eleven to the tune of 53-8."

Note that score. The Las Vegas reporter must have left early because the *Wind and Sand* reported the Tigers scored a safety in the closing seconds to get to eight.

Instead of "carnage" the post paper favored a more favorable description. Their reporter said, "It was a contest of a determined, hard-fighting group bucking up against the granite-walled drives of a highly trained team."

In this rare photo from the Silver Bowl, number 50 is White Sands running back Army Corporal Robert Pienert who has broken through the defensive line. It was too little, too late, as the scoreboard in the background shows a score of 47 to 6 in favor of Nellis. Photo courtesy of Walter Patton.

The article singled out a few players for their outstanding play: Corporal Bob Pienert, Sergeant Poteat, Torpedoman's Mate 3 Johnston, Gunners Mate 1 Lafata, and Sergeant Parker.

What happened next wasn't reported in any of the newspapers but was more important than a football game. It showed the true nature of this White Sands team.

After the game, Patton took the team into town to buy them a drink. He said they played hard and they deserved to relax and have a beer. Getting that simple glass of beer turned into a small battle for the multi-service unit.

Patton said he had trouble getting a drink because the first half dozen bars they entered would not serve the black soldiers on the team. Apparently, Jim Crow laws and barefaced segregation were alive and well in Las Vegas in 1950.

Patton said he led the men into a bar, was told the black players wouldn't be served, and led the team right back out. Finally, they found a place that would serve all of the team members and they had their drink.

The team may have been outclassed on the field, but that was a minor detail when facing the realities of everyday life. Confronting adversity both on and off the field turned these diverse human beings into a cohesive unit. They had reason to return to White Sands with their heads held high. No man left behind!

Basketball

The greatest basketball player to ever lead a New Mexico team did not attend any of the state's high schools or universities. He played on the White Sands Proving Ground team in 1955 and 1956. His name is Sam Jones and in 1996 he was named one of the 50 greatest players in the history of the National Basketball Association (NBA).

Jones was born in 1933 in Laurinburg, North Carolina. He played high school ball in Durham, North Carolina where he was selected to the All-American high school team in 1951.

He then attended all-black North Carolina Central College. He was relatively unknown on the national scene but did captain the college's basketball team for two years and was voted its "most valuable player."

In September 1954, Jones entered the Army and took basic training at Fort Jackson, South Carolina. He then attended the Pole Lineman's school at Camp Gordon, Georgia.

At White Sands, in addition to his commo job, he played basketball. His talent was obvious to everyone. He led the post team to second place in the Fourth Army Basketball Championships. He averaged more than 26 points per game even though he only played the first half in a couple of games. When awards were given afterward the *Wind and Sand* reported, "Sam was given a standing ovation, longer and louder than for any other player in the tournament."

His talent was soon in demand by other Army teams. In basketball, when it came time for the big "All-Army" and "All-Service" tournaments, installations would put together all-star teams to be as competitive as possible. Sam Jones was asked to join the

Boston Celtic great Sam Jones in action in the NBA. Imagine what Fort Bliss and Holloman personnel thought when they had to guard him. Photo courtesy of the Boston Celtics.

Camp Chaffee, Arkansas team as it entered the All-Army Tournament.

According to the *Wind and Sand* newspaper, "Jones led Camp Chaffee to the All-Army championship . . . after being with the team only two weeks. His work on the back boards, plus his better than 18-point game average, gave Chaffee the shot in the arm they needed as they came back from the loser's bracket to defeat the Fort Lewis All-Stars in two straight games to cop the crown for the Fourth Army quintet, their second All-Army championship in three years."

For his efforts Jones was picked for the All-Army team and the All-Service team. He was also given a chance, with other military stars, to try out for the U.S. Olympic Team. Although he didn't make the Olympic squad, he would soon join gold medalists K.C. Jones and Bill Russell with the Boston Celtics.

After Jones left the Army, Red Auerbach of the Boston Celtics selected him in the first round of the 1957 NBA draft. Jones, at 6'4", was paired in the backcourt with K.C. Jones. Add the likes of Bill Russell and John Havlicek and a dynasty was born.

Sam Jones played in the NBA for 12 years. The Celtics won the NBA championship 10 of those years and at one point ran off eight in a row. Jones averaged 17.7 points per game for his career and almost 19 points a game in the playoffs. His best year was 1965 when he averaged 25.9 points per game and was fourth in scoring behind Wilt Chamberlain, Jerry West and Oscar Robertson.

Jones was in five All-Star games and was inducted into the Basketball Hall of Fame in 1983.

Having a world championship ring for all 10 fingers certainly qualifies for greatness.

Golf

On Oct. 27, 1964, the ninth best golfer to ever play the game professionally, man or woman, visited White Sands. Her name was Mickey Wright and she was in Las Cruces to play in the Las Cruces Ladies LPGA Open.

Wright is considered by most experts to be the greatest woman golfer ever. A golf magazine once ranked her the ninth greatest golfer ever – man or woman. In the list she is only behind the likes of Jack Nicklaus, Arnold Palmer, Bobby Jones and Gary Player.

Wright retired from regular play at the very young age of 34 because of physical ailments. By then she had already won 82 tournaments, 13 of which were majors.

The year she visited White Sands she won 11 times to include the U.S. Women's Open. She also led the tour in earnings. The year before she won 13 of the 28 events she entered. She was incredibly dominant, like Tiger Woods in his 20s.

On her visit to White Sands with other players, a staff photographer posed Wright standing on top of the display V-2 rocket in the missile park. At that time the rocket was displayed resting on its side. She is poised on the missile with driver in hand, ready to rocket a ball down range.

In that first Las Cruces Open, other notable players included Althea Gibson and Kathy Whitworth. Whitworth was from Jal, New Mexico and she came back to win the third and final Las Cruces Open in 1966. In fact, by 1966 Whitworth was surpassing Wright as she won nine times that year and was the tour's leading money winner.

Wright did not win the Las Cruces tournament that concluded on November 1. Sandra Haynie was the winner. Haynie received $1,300 for her victory. The second Las Cruces tournament, in 1965, was won by Clifford Ann Creed.

According to the *Wind and Sand* newspaper, the top 10 money winners on the LPGA participated in the 1964 tournament. By the way, the newspaper called the women golfers "proettes." That must have made some of them cringe.

Rich Beem is another professional golfer who played on the White Sands golf course many times and holds the course scoring record. Beem's father, Larry, was the White Sands pro and manager of the golf course from 1974 through the 80s. In 1998, Larry returned to New Mexico State University to coach their golf team.

Larry played golf at NMSU in the 60s and was the school's first All-American in 1964. Rich went to NMSU as well, played on the golf team, and graduated in 1994.

Rich turned pro after graduating from NMSU but initially was not very successful. In fact, he worked as a salesman until he won the Kemper Open on the PGA Tour in 1999. He has won two other tournaments to include a major, the PGA Championship.

Related to golf, I once received a phone call from the golf course at Fort Benning, Georgia. The caller said they were redoing their bunkers on the course and they thought using white sand would really look great. They knew the missile range had lots of white sand and wondered if they could have several dump trucks full of the stuff.

I confirmed that we had lots of white sand but that it was gypsum and not beach sand. I explained that lots of wear and tear would break the fragile crystals down into powder. Also, the stuff is soluble in water and wouldn't work very well where it gets soaked every day as they irrigate the course. It was an easy no.

Boxing

One of the more curious sporting connections for White Sands invovled Dallas Cowboys football great Ed "Too Tall" Jones and his boxing debut in Las Cruces back in 1979. Jones did some training for his first fight at the missile range's Bell Gym.

Jones grew up in Tennessee where he played high school baseball and basketball well enough to receive many offers to play at the next level. For baseball that meant turning pro and for basketball there were many offers to play at major colleges. He chose to go to Tennessee State and play basketball but eventually quit the team to focus on football.

He was drafted by the Cowboys in the first round of 1974 and went on to a stellar career with the cowboys. By the time he retired to box in 1979, he was an all-pro defense end and had a Super Bowl ring.

As a boxer Jones was imposing for his day. He stood 6'9", weighed around 250 lbs., and had a reach of 88 inches.

He was large and with the long reach he looked tough on paper. However, he had almost no experience, having boxed a little in Golden Gloves as a youngster. Las Cruces was his first step on the road to becoming a professional boxer.

His first fight was scheduled at the Pan Am Center at New Mexico State University in Las Cruces for Nov. 3, 1979. While training at a facility in Las Cruces, the boxing ring fell apart and his entourage looked around for an alternate site.

According to the Nov. 12, 1979 issue of *Sports Illustrated*, the manager "shifted the training site to a gym on the White Sands missile range, about 25 miles away and less than 100 miles from where the United States exploded the first atomic bomb. Too Tall posed for photographers among the display

rockets, folding his arms and looking like one of them himself."

It was a big day for boxing and Dallas Cowboy fans at White Sands. Word quickly spread and many workers and residents went to watch Jones train.

On fight day, Pan Am was crowded with 9,000 fans. Many were there to see Jones, but many were there to support his Mexican challenger, Jesus "Ya-qui" Meneses. The fight went six rounds with Jones winning on a decision.

Meneses fans booed the decision as their fighter stunned Jones in the last round by knocking him to the canvas. They felt Jones benefited from his celebrity status in his newly chosen sport. Jones reportedly received $72,000 for the fight.

Jones fought five more bouts, winning them all by knockout. For reasons not readily apparent, he then quit and went back to the Dallas Cowboys for the 1980 season. Most biographies say Jones was a better player when he returned to football because the training and concentration needed for boxing made him tougher.

He retired from football in 1989.

Beauty Pageants

I am putting beauty pageants in the sports section because there were very few competetive sporting programs for women at White Sands for decades. Eventually there were women's post softball, volleyball and basketball teams, but early on there was a different kind of competition for woman - the grueling appearance on stage in a swimsuit and high heels.

These competitions were held annually at White Sands for years. Women from different organizations on post participated voluntarily or were cajoled into the process. Eventually, the winner was named "Miss Nike." But that was just the beginning.

For instance, in 1956 Clara Melendres, who represented the Signal Corps at White Sands, won the Miss Nike title. She was a cheerleader in high school and college and was also chosen "queen" for a number of school-related events. She was experienced.

Immediately after winning the White Sands title she went to Truth or Consequences as the range's entrant in that town's seventh annual fiesta. The fiesta was the result of Ralph Edwards, the creator and host of the popular radio and TV show "Truth or Consequences," offering to appear in any town that changed its name to his show's title. Warm Springs,

New Mexico jumped at the chance and is now called "TorC" for short.

Until he was quite elderly, Edwards went to TorC which, in turn, built a fiesta out of his appearances. There was a parade in which White Sands sent a float. In 1956, the White Sands parade entry, appropriately enough, was a Nike missile on a trailer.

Edwards brought acts with him from Hollywood and they entertained folks. In 1956, he brought quasi-star Tab Hunter along. Hunter was just about at the height of his career and was very popular. He starred in many films, was considered a hearth-throb by women, and even had a hit record in 1957 called "Young Love."

Because of his appeal, Hunter was an obvious choice to be one of the fiesta's beauty pageant judges. According to the *Wind and Sand* newspaper, Melendres was "the center of attention" wherever the beauty contestants appeared. She also caught Hunter's eye.

When Beverly Sikes from Crane, Texas was announced as the winner, the paper reported that Hunter rushed the stage, gave Melendres a hug and

kiss and said, "This is my choice for queen." Apparently Hunter also publicly begged for a delay to allow the other judges to reconsider their decision.

I bet Miss Sikes felt good about the hotshot Hollywood star causing such a brouhaha in protesting her win. She and everyone in her family probably never bought another of his records.

Hunter lost his loud appeal and the rest of the places were announced. Melendres finished second.

Just like a sporting event, one could have said that Melendres was overcome by someone with more experience. It turns out that Sikes was previously chosen Sun Carnival princess in El Paso and held the title of "Miss Southwest" in 1955.

As society and the Army changed their views of women, the flimsy threads that supported missile range beauty pagents unraveled and the things mercifully disappeared. Unfortunately, competitive sports have pretty much disappeared at White Sands as well because military personnel only number a few hundred and the civilian workforce has an average age of 50 or so.

Intramural football in 1953. The only equipment needed for touch and flag football is a ball - much easier than trying to field an equipped team to play tackle against other installations. WSMR photo.

Instant Death On Sugarloaf

14

It is a very steep climb up to the ridge running south of Sugarloaf Peak just to the west of the housing area on White Sands. I've done the hike twice to visit the deadly crash site of an Air Force C-45 where six men died around 12:30 a.m. on April 5, 1951.

They must have died instantly. Their twin-engine plane looks like it was put in a blender and thrown onto the ridge. Parts and pieces still litter the mountainside above Rock Springs Canyon on the east side of the Sugarloaf ridge.

The crash site is not on the missile range proper but is in the Organ Mountains on Bureau of Land Management property. However, it is right in the missile range's backyard. In fact, personnel on the main post of White Sands saw the subsequent fires and reported the accident. A rescue party was immediately organized to leave White Sands just before dawn.

It turns out the most direct route to the crash site is through the Cox ranch which sits right at the base of Sugarloaf. One of the original rescuers was Tom Dayberry. At the time he was living at the Cox ranch and attending school at what was then New Mexico A&M in Las Cruces. Ranch owner Jim Cox woke Dayberry at 4 a.m., so he could help lead the search party to the crash site.

Because the fires had burned out, the searchers weren't sure of the exact location on the ridge. Dayberry, later a White Sands range rider, said it was a tough climb to the area where they thought the plane had crashed with its potential survivors.

They circled around to the west side of Sugarloaf and climbed the west slope. At the top of the ridge they found a spot where the plane first hit the ridge

on it way down the east side of the mountain. Air Force records show the search team found a propeller blade there.

The rescue party did not know how many people were on board, but it quickly became apparent there would be no survivors. As they worked their way down the steep, rocky slopes they started finding twisted pieces of metal in all shapes and sizes. There were other pieces that weren't aircraft parts either.

Dayberry said the one thing that sticks out in his memory is a remark made by one of the searchers: "There must have been at least three of them because here are three left feet." From that point the rescue party turned into a body recovery operation.

The search did not progress very far. The weather was windy with gusts up to 50 mph reported at the White Sands weather station. The slopes are steep and covered with thick brush, including cactus and yucca.

When I climbed up there in April 2005 with Kevin Cobble, manager of the San Andres Wildlife Refuge, we encountered bushes that had to be circumnavigated only to find ourselves blocked by cactus, yucca or boulders. It was tough going to just get from one point to another.

Searching for bodies must have been exhausting and gruesome. Dayberry reported human entrails hanging from one bush. Chuck Mullis was an enlisted man at White Sands at the time and wrote to his future wife about the incident, "Rescue operation complete; a very messy task. I'll always remember John McKenzie's comment: It's amazing how heavy a head is."

On the first search day, before returning because

of darkness, the search team did find the body of Navy Reserve Lieutenant James Giddings of Albuquerque. According to the April 6 *El Paso Times*, Giddings was just along for the ride at the invitation of the pilot. Giddings was the assistant manager at radio station KOAT in Albuquerque.

The plane was assigned to the Sandia Special Weapons Base in Albuquerque. The other five victims on board the plane were Air Force personnel from Sandia. The group was on a routine training flight when the accident occurred. They left Albuquerque on April 4 and flew to El Paso International Airport. For their return, they left El Paso at 12:10 a.m. on April 5.

The weather that night was not good. A strong storm front was just moving through, and winds were unusually gusty for that hour. Winds at the local weather stations were reported at over 30 mph from the west and northwest. There are no records of what it was like in the mountains, but past experience says it was probably very turbulent.

When the plane hit the mountain it was headed southeasterly. It may have been headed for Condron Field or back to El Paso. It lost enough altitude to just catch the top of the ridge.

The Air Force's Inspection and Safety Center reported after their investigation there was strong evidence the cause of the crash was due to the loss of one engine. The report indicated that the throttle, propeller and mixture levers for one engine were found "full forward" while the controls for the other engine were "full aft." This indicated one engine was at full power and the other was shut down for some reason.

These circumstances support the story I heard over the years from old-timers who were familiar with the accident. They said the plane "lost an engine" and the pilot was trying to get back to El Paso. With only one engine and the strong tailwind from the northwest, the pilot lost altitude too quickly to get over the ridge and was just a few feet from making it over. As the *Albuquerque Journal* reported, "the plane smashed into the mountain."

There was no search for the other bodies on April

Kevin Cobble, the manager of the San Andres Wildlife Refuge, accompanied me on my last climb to the Sugarloaf Peak crash site. He holds the frame to a window from the plane. Pieces of the plane were scattered over hundreds of square yards. Photo by author.

6. The Air Force reported clouds completely covered the mountains reducing visibility to zero. The report also said it rained and snowed all day.

On April 6, the *Albuquerque Journal* was quick to reassure readers by reporting, "authorities said there definitely was no atomic equipment aboard." The *Journal's* article had a peculiar ending. The last sentence said, "Before workers halted the search Thursday, five hats were recovered in the area strewn with the wreckage." I suppose the hats were proof there were five men aboard in addition to Giddings.

The *Journal* was right in its description of the area being "strewn" with debris. In my visits to the site I found pieces in many areas. Cobble and I found pieces of the fuselage on one ridge with wing parts on another. We found one of the engines in a ravine down below. I have never seen the second engine. It really looks like the plane was blown apart with a ton of TNT and scattered to the wind.

On April 7, a search party left to bring back the bodies. Listed as dead along with Giddings were: Captain Ralph Bowman, 29, pilot; Captain Amos Hines, 34, copilot; Major George Smith, 35, passenger; Corporal Kenneth Turner, 21, passenger; Private First Class David Washburn, 20, passenger.

The rescue effort was a combined Army and Air Force effort. Newspaper accounts said Captain R.N. Clark, the White Sands Provost Marshall, and Lieutenant E.P. Regrutto, from the proving grounds' rocket recovery team, were in on the hunt.

The bodies were brought down the mountain through Rock Springs Canyon and then out across the Cox ranch. Dayberry remembered bringing the body bags down the wet and icy canyon. He said he got in trouble with the Air Force major in charge because he didn't treat the bags gently enough on one icy slope. Dayberry said he thought getting himself down safely without a broken leg or neck might be more important than gently lowering body bags when there was ice underfoot.

The crash site has never been cleaned up because it is so tough to get at. It doesn't appear to be marked either. Apparently the Air Force considered the plane as "inaccessible wreckage." In such a case, Air Force regulations call for careful plotting and photography of the site. This information is then furnished to air search activities and the air rescue center, so it is not misidentified later as a new crash site.

One problem is that some of the crash site is slowly moving downhill. In my trips up the canyon I have seen airplane parts as far as two miles from the impact area. They have been washed down Rock Springs Canyon by runoff from thunderstorms.

By the way, the canyon seems to have gotten its name from wet areas where water usually flows. There are a couple of very pretty but small waterfalls over polished granite drops.

Also, going up the canyon we ran into huge Ponderosa pine trees and some fir trees as well. In places it was a hidden oasis – not at all like our start point.

15

Red Canyon Range Camp

Shootin' Missiles, Livin' In A Tent

I first heard from J.P. Moore in early October 1997 when he sent an email to the post newspaper looking for me. He told them he had read some of my articles on the Public Affairs webpage and wanted to contact me about a book he had just completed on Red Canyon Range Camp. He called it *The Malapais Missiles*.

It turns out that Jean-Paul Moore is a retired Air Force master sergeant who started out his military life as a missile man in the U.S. Army. He graduated from high school near Wichita Falls, Texas in the spring of 1954. He proudly got himself a job - but after moving thousands of 90-pound bales of hay in blistering heat that summer, he decided he needed a career change. He enlisted in the Army.

In early August he was sent to Fort Bliss in El Paso, Texas for basic training. He was excited by the experience because it was so different from farming in rural Texas. No hay bales to be thrown in his new life. This was all radars, computers, screaming jets and guided missiles.

Being a farm boy meant learning about the big world in general too. He says he still remembers the six words the Army chaplain provided for the recruits to sum up personal hygiene and health. He said, "Flies spread disease. Keep yours zipped."

There were some detours through guard duty and kitchen patrol, but eventually Moore got to play with the Nike Ajax air-defense missile system through on-the-job training, not the formal air-defense school. He then spent almost all of his Army years at Red Canyon Range Camp providing launch support, or working at Fort Bliss and White Sands on one of the review boards charged with testing changes to the Nike system. He left the Army in August 1957 but returned to the military in the Air Force.

Decades later, Moore harbored strong positive memories of his Army days, especially his time at Red Canyon. In his book he says, "Few appreciated the paradox of working on the most sophisticated anti-aircraft guided missile system in the free world, while living in a migrant camp straight from *The Grapes of Wrath* movie set."

Moore loved that contrast and, as it turns out, so did many other men stationed at Red Canyon. Where else could you go live in a tent, bathe in a 55-gallon drum, eat greenish powdered eggs reeking of gasoline fumes, and then spend the rest of the day operating a state-of-the-art radar to track missiles traveling over 1,500 miles per hour?

Like many good young boys in the service, Moore faithfully wrote his mother, telling her about his experiences. His mother saved them. Using the letters as a baseline, Moore was able to write about his experiences at Red Canyon. Then he used Internet postings and personal contacts to spin a web of Red Canyon connections. He became their focal point – the eye of the storm, so to speak.

By the time I got a copy of the book to read and review, he was incorporating the memories of other Red Canyon vets. They couldn't have asked for a better coordinator. He collected their input and gave them all a voice. This led to a website so others can now peek into that life.

Feelings in this group were amazingly positive, and Moore's gusto led to two reunions in Las Cruces and at White Sands. I was involved in both reunions and the enthusiasm of the men and their tales were infectious. It was great fun to sit around and listen to them correct each other and tell stories about Nike, the burro, and their own handmade rockets - things that could only have happened at a place like Red Canyon.

Moore did a great job on the book. He is one of those rare individuals able to tell a good tale and do it with humor.

In June 1998, I wrote in the missile range's post newspaper, "The final product is a fun read with humorous anecdotes, a factual history of the camp and some nice commentary about the sometimes preposterous nature of military life."

One of my favorite descriptions is his portrayal of payday. On payday the men would line up by rank. Everything was based on rank down to when you could take a shower. The lower your rank, the longer you waited in line.

For payday, Moore wrote:

When I finally get to the pay table, there sits the paymaster and an NCO, usually the first sergeant or the field first sergeant. Both are armed with 45-caliber automatic pistols, clips inserted. The guns are lying on the table in front of them, next to the large stack of cash.

I salute and report to the paymaster "Specialist third class Moore, Jean P., reporting for pay, Sir." The paymaster scans the pay roster looking for my name and the amount to be paid. If I'm lucky my name is there and does not have a red line through it. Then the paymaster picks up the big bundle of cash lying

in front of him, counts out the amount due me, and stuffs it in an envelope. He writes my name and the amount on the envelope, then seals it. You are probably thinking I get the envelope handed to me, right?

Wrong. The paymaster hands it to the NCO sitting beside him who waits until I report to him as I did before. Then the NCO opens the envelope, counts the money in front of me, has me sign beside my name on the pay roster, indicating that I was paid, then gives me the money.

Sounds like big bucks here, right? I think my pay was about $78.00 a month, or maybe a little more as a Spec-3, minus deductions for the quartermaster laundry and social security. That's right, you civilians reading this, we did pay social security.

When it came to the latrines, rank didn't seem to help much. They were awful. Moore wrote this about the latrines:

The base-camp latrines are fairly large wooden buildings with vents all around the edge of the roof. Inside there is nothing but a wooden box along the center with a dozen holes cut through it and a vent pipe leading through the roof. Wooden toilet seat covers are hinged over each hole, six holes per side. During rush hour six men can use one side and six more the other, back-to-back. Nice and cozy.

Modesty is out of the question and the stench is absolutely overpowering. Bags of quick lime are dumped through the holes into the pit that is dug below and that compounds the stench. Mounted on one wall are some galvanized metal urinals. In the winter it's freezing inside. In the summer the flies will drive you crazy. A favorite saying is, "Close the door, you're letting the flies out!"

Today, because of Moore's affection for Red Canyon Range Camp, there is an exhibit about the camp in the White Sands Museum. Various vets have donated artifacts to the museum. The children of Lieutenant Colonel John McCarthy, camp commander

The first headquarters at Red Canyon Range Camp was a tent. Photo courtesy of Mary McCarthy Elliot.

for most of its existence, donated a scale model of the famous built by the men who were assigned to RCRC.

Boom Town to Ghost Town

Red Canyon Range Camp is in the northeast corner of White Sands Missile Range. Once it was the booming center for Army public relations and troop training. Today, it is cracked concrete slabs, deteriorating roads, and a couple of crumbling fire control bunkers. Graffiti marks many of the remaining foundations. Deer and antelope are the most frequent visitors. It is a ghost town.

However, from 1953 through 1959 more than 10,000 visitors from 45 countries and 40 states passed through the camp to see some of the 3,000 Nike Ajax missiles fired by air defense troop units. About 300 troops were assigned to Red Canyon to run the facility. On some days the mess hall served as many as 1,500 meals to feed the cadre, troops shooting missiles, and visitors. It was a boomtown.

The camp was opened in October 1953 by Fort Bliss as a place to conduct Nike Ajax training and annual service firings. At the time, Fort Bliss did not have the necessary area for such a mission. White Sands allowed the use of the northeast corner of the range as a temporary facility. Eventually, Fort Bliss established McGregor Range closer to the fort and moved the air defense firings there in August 1959.

What is left of the camp is about four miles south of US Highway 380 with the turnoff 16 miles west of Carrizozo, New Mexico. That's 165 miles from Fort Bliss headquarters. At the turnoff, a gate made of red rock still stands where the camp had its outer entrance. At one time both sides of the gate were topped with Nike missiles.

Nike Ajax batteries received most of their training at Fort Bliss. When the units completed the basic required training, they moved to Red Canyon Range Camp. There they received further training that culminated in the firing of at least one successful missile. Once this was completed, the units would be considered fully prepared for around-the-clock operations at a Nike site somewhere in America.

Those visiting troops didn't use their own vans, radars and computers. All of the support equipment to fire the actual missiles was permanently stationed at Red Canyon and maintained by the cadre. The equipment was turned over to the shooters for their

tests while the cadre offered support when needed.

Red Canyon Range Camp was built from scratch in the eastern foothills of the Oscura Mountains. Initially, tents and then dozens of Quonset huts and other temporary buildings were erected in a flat area below Chupadera Mesa. Besides the usual barracks, mess hall, and motor pool, there was a small post exchange, dispensary, fire department, and a recreation and service club. The men also had softball diamonds and volleyball and basketball courts for their use.

Several miles southwest of the camp a missile assembly area was built on a low ridge. Nike Ajax missiles were repaired, assembled and fueled at this site and then moved to the launch area further to the southwest. The missiles were fired at drones as visitors watched from the ridges to the east. For decades an area west of the launch points was littered with Nike boosters that were stuck in the ground like arrows after being shot straight up in the air.

For targets the Army presented the Nike units with RCATs (radio controlled aerial targets). These small propeller-driven aircraft were about 10 feet long with a 12-foot wingspan. They were quite tiny compared to the Soviet bombers the Nike units were supposed to be protecting American cities from. They were equipped with radar reflectors that made them look much larger to the Nike radars.

The RCATs were launched from Oscura Range Camp south of Red Canyon on the eastern boundary of the missile range. Most of the targets were launched from a circular asphalt track just north of Oscura.

The RCATs were placed on a wheeled trolley on the paved circle. The trolley was connected to a center pole via a cable. Soldiers would fire up the RCATs engine, tweak its throttle and let go of it. The RCAT and trolley would roll forward, but the cable would keep it turning in a circle.

Eventually the target would get up enough speed to take off from the trolley. Once high enough, the RCAT could be tracked by radar and a controller could fly it up to Red Canyon to present as a target.

If these launches were not done with some precision, the RCATs sometimes went cart-wheeling into the desert creating interesting explosions – especially during night operations.

The men who manned Red Canyon (no women were stationed there) seemed to like the duty. Their tour was supposed to be a short five months because of the isolation of the camp but most stayed on for several tours. The last camp commander, McCarthy, liked it enough to stay four and a half years.

In fact, McCarthy was the spirit and guiding hand behind Red Canyon for most of its existence. He implemented dozens of projects to improve the camp and make it more fit for his soldiers and the many visitors.

Lieutenant Colonel John McCarthy, Red Canyon commander most of the camp's life. Photo courtesy of Mary McCarthy Elliot.

In addition, he didn't insist on busywork to keep the cadre moving all the time. He expected them to do their jobs, do them well, and then relax. The normal tour for cadre at Red Canyon was five months. According to McCarthy's daughter, over 90 percent of the men assigned to Red Canyon asked for at least one more tour at the camp. That is a testament to the leadership of McCarthy.

A Chapel From Trash

One of McCarthy's more interesting projects was the building of a chapel.

For several years the camp held church services in the small camp theater. McCarthy wanted something better but could get no funding for a chapel. So he and Master Sergeant William Sidell, the camp's senior NCO, drew up plans for a building and turned the project over to the troops. Over 100 men, representing 32 states, volunteered to work on the building. Work started in December 1957.

The men spent their spare time, weekends, and holidays scrounging materials for the chapel. They salvaged steel railroad track from the Southern Pacific Railroad for the frame. Bracing was cut from the steel doors of the old Lincoln County jail. The interior walls and roof came from the tops and sides of Nike booster crates. They quarried red rock from a nearby canyon for the walls and used plastered telephone poles as the pillars on the front entry. Using cellophane and shellac they were able to simulate stained glass windows.

For bells they hung three used Nike boosters in the steeple. The intense heat gave them a pleasant resonance. Since they were three different lengths, they produced three different pitches.

It might not sound like much of a building, but it was. The men referred to it as "90 percent junk, except in appearance." They worked hard and were able to give the chapel the appearance of one built by a regular contractor with large amounts of money.

McCarthy was proud of the chapel and of his men who worked on it. Years later he told the following story: "I recall on one very cold January Sunday when we started to work on it about 6 a.m. We were running cement for the floor and one soldier said to me during a brief pause, 'You know colonel, I don't go for this church stuff. The old lady likes it, but not me - I never go'. I replied, "What do you think you're doing now?" He said (sorta hesitantly) 'Well, this is different'. I countered by saying, 'For a guy who doesn't like it, I am glad you don't mind going the hard way'. He was a most conscientious worker, rolling one wheelbarrow full of cement after another and never complained. I guess there are all kinds of church goers."

Major General Patrick Ryan, then Army Chief of Chaplains, was impressed with the effort and made a special trip to Red Canyon from Fort Bliss in 1958 to dedicate the chapel. He told the men, "A building such as this means a great deal more than a large and more expensive chapel built by congressional appropriation. This has the heart and soul of you men in it."

According to McCarthy, having the Army's chief chaplain on hand upstaged a similar dedication at Fort Bliss the next day. All the news media loved the Red Canyon story and how the men built their own chapel. In most articles, the writers focused on the range camp effort and just added at the end that "Ryan also went to El Paso." Apparently, Army brass in Washington called Fort Bliss and wanted to know, according to McCarthy, "Why the hell that place in the desert got all the publicity?"

The chapel ended up being a cross-shaped building, 87 feet long and 36 feet wide in the main section. Officially, the only cash spent was $200 for shingles, which the men contributed. After he retired, McCarthy did admit to some creative administrative work to help the project. He said they transferred the building number from an unused temporary shed to the chapel. This allowed them to draw funds to maintain it once it was complete.

In 1965 McCarthy wrote, "General Snodgrass was enthusiastic about calling it Saint Barbara, after the patron saint of artillery. I felt, if anything, it should be called St. Dismas, after the good thief on the cross. After all a certain amount of conniving has to go into a project like that."

After the chapel was completed, McCarthy included it in the tours he gave visitors. Most of these visitors were part of "Operation Understanding," which was a special Army program to educate community leaders about the Nike Ajax. They were VIPs

Soldiers place the chapel's belfry using a telephone pole extension to the boom of their crane. Nike boosters were used as bells. Photo courtesy of Mary McCarthy Elliot.

from cities all over the world where Nike units were on site or where units were planned to be installed.

The visiting groups were made up of mayors and city officials, civil defense leaders, church, civic, educational and industrial leaders, and newspapermen. Occasionally, a governor or senator made the trip. They were all flown in military aircraft but paid their own expenses.

The program was dubbed "OU" and was credited with smoothing the way for many of the Nike installations. In 1957, the proposed location of a site at the Los Angeles International Airport drew adverse public demonstrations. After the mayor and other city officials went through OU and then told the citizens of Los Angeles about what they had seen, opposition evaporated.

When the groups went through the chapel, McCarthy always had someone there softly playing hymns on the organ. On one visit, the Norwegian Minister of Defense broke away from his group and asked the organist to play a particular hymn. He then sang along as the rest of the group listened. Eyewitnesses said they were all captivated by his beautiful voice.

The camp mascot, a burro the men caught and raised, also liked to sing in the chapel. They called him Nike and, according to McCarthy, he liked to try to attend the Catholic masses on Sunday. One Sunday, during a Protestant service, Nike managed to get into the chapel just as the congregation started a hymn.

Nike stuck his head into the chapel and started braying with the singers. There was hysterical laughter, even from the minister, and the service concluded right there. When the minister heard Nike seemed to prefer Catholic masses, he claimed he was proud to have converted the burro.

According to Joe Perry, one of Moore's Red Canyon vets, he and some other soldiers captured Nike as a baby. He said his wife made the blanket for Nike's back to use when there were special events. The blanket had the word "nike" and a cutout of a missile on both sides. When the camp was abandoned, Nike was turned out to go back to the wild.

When Fort Bliss left Red Canyon for McGregor Range, they removed the temporary buildings. The men who worked there remember leaving the chapel standing, since it was not an official building. Besides, they had put a lot of their own sweat and time into erecting it. Many soldiers and many local residents thought the chapel would remain as a tribute to Red Canyon and as a possible place of service in the future.

Then in 1961, someone who expected the structure to survive discovered it was gone. Only its concrete foundation and the stairs remained. What happened to the chapel was something of a mystery for a while.

Records from the Fort Bliss Real Estate Office showed that the building was sold for salvage for $219. Some people didn't believe this and during the 1960s there were hints that something else happened to it. "What" is unclear. There were even efforts to search for the structure on other parts of the missile range.

In the June 1972 issue of *Soldiers Magazine,* there was a full-page story on the "disappearance" and an appeal for information on the chapel.

In December 1972, *Soldiers Magazine* ran a follow-up. The magazine said the chapel was sold to Mr. R. F. Waterman of Los Alamos, New Mexico who wanted to move the building in one piece. It couldn't be done and they had to deconstruct the chapel and move it piece by piece.

What the buyer didn't understand was that the frame was made of railroad track set in a solid concrete pad, and the exterior walls were veneered with rock. Waterman reportedly lost $10,000 getting the building out of there.

Nike Ajax

The Nike Ajax, which was the reason for having the camp, now holds a special place in history as the world's first supersonic guided missile to become operational. Originally it was simply called "Nike" but the "Ajax" was added when the next generation, the Nike Hercules, was developed.

Nike Ajax was conceived in 1945 with most of the subsequent development testing done at White Sands Proving Ground. Early tests included static firings of motors, live firings of booster and sustainer motors, and tests of the guidance system and warhead.

In October 1951, for the first time, all Nike components were brought together in one missile and fired at White Sands. A month later a Nike successfully intercepted a droned B-17 bomber and sent it crashing to the desert floor north of Launch Complex 33.

This was exciting stuff for America. It was suddenly just one shot and the enemy airplane was probably going to fall to the ground in flames. No longer would defenders literally fill the sky with barrages of rockets and lead from "ack-ack" guns to kill airplanes.

On April 24, 1952, a White Sands camera-tracking crew photographed the intercept of another B-17 by a Nike. A still

Nike Ajax on its launcher. The black booster section is filled with solid propellant and the white, second stage is liquid fueled. WSMR photo.

image from the footage won an Ernie Pyle Award for "Outstanding Contribution to National Security by Still Photograph."

The Nike was almost 20 feet long, 12 inches in diameter, and burned nitric acid and aniline in the second stage. It was equipped with a solid propellant booster that was later used to boost NASA sounding rockets at White Sands for decades after the system was put out to pasture.

It could achieve a speed of about 1,600 miles per hour, reach an altitude of about 15 miles, and hit targets as far away as 25 miles.

Nike was designed to get close to its target; then a radio signal from the ground would fire the three warheads it carried. These warheads were made to fragment into a cloud of hardened shrapnel. Add to that the pieces of the missile body and it was very difficult for an airplane to survive any kind of close encounter.

The first Nike unit was put on site at Fort Meade, Maryland, and on May 30, 1954, became fully operational. During the mid-1950s, Nike systems were installed along the Eastern seaboard. Later, the system was deployed to Allied nations as air defense for industrial and metropolitan areas. Growing up in Lincoln, Nebraska, I remember one site southwest of the city guarding the old Lincoln Air Force Base.

In November 1964, after a decade of service, the last Nike Ajax was withdrawn from active duty. The system was replaced by the Nike Hercules and HAWK air defense systems.

Lieutenant Colonel McCarthy used to talk about the high morale of his men and how hard they worked. He said they were dedicated and enjoyed being at Red Canyon. It would be hard to argue with him. Years ago while in Public Affairs, I received a call from Ernest Littlejohn in Michigan who was once stationed at Red Canyon. He was a private first class and missile mechanic. He had helped build the chapel and wanted to know if he could get in to show it to his children.

I could sense his disappointment when I told him the chapel was gone, and only slabs of concrete were left. He was left with trying to describe the camp and its life to his kids. Hopefully, he got a copy of Moore's book to help out.

The completed chapel at Red Canyon as seen on a postcard from the time. Photo courtesy of Mary McCarthy Elliot.

Size Does Matter

Everybody Knows Bigger Is Better

When White Sands Proving Ground was established in 1945, the Army was making the best of what was available. With the German V-2 rocket already having a proven range of 200 miles, it was obvious flying it and as yet undeveloped U.S. vehicles would be greatly limited on the new proving ground. At 100 miles long, it simply wasn't big enough.

If I may use a sports cliché here, one of the greatest accomplishments at White Sands has been playing bigger than its actual size. In sports, commentators often speak of undersized football and basketball players having success against larger opponents using their speed or native ability or guile. They are usually said to be "playing big."

In the 1950s and 60s, White Sands developed a scheme for playing big. Since then, the strategy has allowed White Sands to do testing way beyond what can normally be accomplished in a box measuring 40 by 100 miles. To top it off, for decades the arrangement was financially a cheap alternative to simply buying more land.

According to Major Guy O. King in his 1963 thesis for the Air War College entitled "A Discussion of Overland Missile Flights in the United States," White Sands officials sought to expand the real estate footprint as early as 1947. The idea was to enlarge the proving ground by acquiring 36 more miles on the north end of White Sands and continue the east and west side boundaries on to the north. The new property would have extended the range almost to U.S. Highway 60, up near Mountainair, New Mexico.

Looking back on the idea, it is easy to see how impossible it was both economically and politically. Although most of the land was government property,

World War II had just ended and money was tight. It was going to be difficult to justify such an expenditure, especially when White Sands was originally billed as a temporary facility.

The bigger obstacle, however, was the vehement resistance from ranchers, their many support groups, and a large number of affiliated politicians. After the displacement and sometimes shabby treatment of dozens of families in WWII to form the Alamogordo Bombing Range, folks in rural New Mexico were determined not to let it happen again. To gobble up more land would have required a hard-fought and lengthy battle in congress and the courts, with public opinion possibly trumping any government action.

In 1950, the Department of Army announced it was giving up on the idea, at least publicly. In house at White Sands, groups continued to look at ways to accommodate longer-range tests.

Instead of simply adding more land to the original White Sands boundaries, these planners took a different route. What emerged in the early 1950s was the basic idea of creating a narrow passage or corridor of evacuated land heading out from White Sands to a series of missile impact points.

In 1954, White Sands conducted a paper study to find the best location for such a corridor. The researchers wanted to take advantage of the long, rectangular shape of White Sands and find the least populated areas to incorporate into the corridor. In addition, Mexico had to be nowhere near the corridor. We had already dropped a V-2 next to Juarez.

With that criteria, the most sensible direction to look was northerly. In the end, the study recommended a corridor from the launch areas at the

247

south end of White Sands to the northwest on a 337-degree azimuth. For those of you who don't remember your geometry, zero or 360 degrees would be straight north with east being 90 degrees, south at 180 degrees and so on around the circle. This makes a 337-degree line just left of straight north.

Map analysis showed they could have impact points at 250, 500, 750, 925 and 1,500 miles. The 1,500-mile mark would have been in British Columbia and they said 2,000 miles might even be possible which was southeastern Alaska. On maps produced at the time, the impact points were represented along the flight line as small squares on the ground.

Instead of trying to buy the necessary land, the idea was to step into agreements with landowners that would allow White Sands to occasionally use the land. Instead of buying, the government would be renting.

For safety, the plan was to evacuate the landowners in the particular impact area being used. In addition, planners were going to evacuate people living under the missile flight path.

Knowing what we now know about running evacuation programs in rural areas, it is not an easy task and this was a very ambitious proposal. The devil is in the details; such an arrangement could have been a bureaucratic nightmare to administer given the number of land agreements and evacuations required for the proposed long-range shots. It probably would have taken a small army of dedicated personnel to keep it running efficiently.

As the 1950s marched along, so did White Sands analysis of what it would take to make the off-range corridor a reality. Outside agencies like the University of Chicago were hired to run detailed risk analysis. Not only did they look at human safety, they looked at things like the possibly of starting a forest fire from falling debris or a missile smashing into Elephant Butte dam.

Teams from White Sands and various missile projects that wanted the longer ranges visited various decision makers back East. They briefed on the effort to form a generic flight corridor to be used by a variety of programs. In the meantime, specific, real requirements were arising for individual missile systems.

For example, the Army's Nike Zeus and Redstone, along with the Navy's Talos, needed more room than what was offered within the missile range's basic borders. The Air Force also wanted more room, but because they were flying vehicles that looked like something everyone was familiar with, they tried a little different approach.

In the 1950s, the Air Force was developing a series of missiles to attack ground targets. Some, like the Rascal, were air launched, while others, like the Matador and Mace, were ground launched. The Rascal was rocket powered so it had a relatively short range of only 100 miles while the Matador and Mace were America's first cruise missiles and could fly hundreds of miles using jet engines.

For one test of the Rascal at White Sands, the Air Force air-launched a missile on Nov. 27, 1956 from a spot southwest of Orogrande. According to Major King, it was the first intentional off-range over-flight at White Sands. Since it was basically a flight from Fort Bliss to White Sands, the test was not a complicated effort.

To better test the Mace and Matador, the Air Force wanted to use the same basic northwest azimuth or corridor proposed by White Sands. They proposed flying from Holloman, AFB to Wendover, Utah, a distance of almost 700 miles.

The Air Force had a great advantage in selling

A Mace on display at the National Museum of the Air Force. Mace had a cruising speed of about 650 miles per hour and could reach out to 1,400 miles. It is 44 feet long and has a wingspan of 22 feet. Air Force photo.

these tests. The missiles looked like small jet aircraft and they flew at the same speeds and altitudes as the Air Force's fighters. The Air Force ultimately convinced authorities they only needed an FAA flight plan to conduct the flights.

To overcome any safety objections about flying the unmanned missiles over the public, Air Force fighters accompanied each flight with the pilots prepared to shoot down any misbehaving missile.

On Sept. 25, 1957, a Matador missile successfully

flew through the corridor to Wendover and on Feb. 6, 1958, a Mace missile did the same.

The FIX

While the Air Force was up and running, White Sands couldn't gather all the necessary approvals for their corridor with its impact points. Time was getting short for upcoming tests involving Army and Navy missiles, so the northern extension idea was dusted off and reevaluated.

Learning from previous mistakes and borrowing some of the corridor ideas, the extension area was proposed again but this time as a co-use area. There would be no need to get Congressional action to purchase the property. The Army Corps of Engineers would put together contracts allowing the Department of Army to pay ranchers to evacuate for 12-hour periods – up to 20 times per year. It was a co-use arrangement where ranchers didn't have to worry about losing their land.

The Army approved the idea on Aug. 25, 1959, and everyone got busy coordinating with New Mexico officials, legislators, and landowners, and educating the public. A few days after the "official" approval, military officials held a public meeting in Socorro, New Mexico to explain the situation.

Attending were Assistant Secretary of the Army Dewey Short and Major General W.E. Laidlaw, the White Sands commander. Short was quoted in the Sept. 4, 1959 issue of the post newspaper saying to attendees, "In other words, it looks as though almost all of these Nike-Zeus test firings will be within the confines of the present missile range. However, the Nike-Zeus does have a longer range than its predecessors in the Nike family and its point of impact will be much nearer the northern boundary of the present range. Therefore, some spent projectiles, fragments of projectiles and other debris resulting from firings will fall in the area immediately to the north of the northern boundary of the present range. The Army's safety experts have estimated that such material possibly could fall as far as 40 miles to the north of the northern boundary. This safety area is needed for Zeus tests."

Laidlaw, being aware of past friction with the ranchers, said soothing things. He was quoted in the same article saying, "No seizure of the added land is contemplated by the missile range or by the federal government. Rather, we hope to temporarily lease these ranchlands for occasional flights and impacts for our newest most important missiles. All precautions will be taken to minimize any inconvenience on any rancher and his family living in the area involved."

In Dec. 1959, the New Mexico Highway Commission approved missile range roadblocks on U.S. Highway 380 lasting up to 1.5 hours. The highway divides the missile range proper from the extension area, and roadblocks would be needed to construct a continuous evacuated area for the intended tests.

On Jan. 1, 1960, the land-use agreements were in place and the 40-by-40 mile northern extension was born. It was called the "Firing In Extension" area or the FIX.

Ranchers were paid a fee each year that was based on the size of their ranch. The larger the property, the more valuable it was to White Sands and the larger the payment. So some small outfits received less than a thousand dollars a year while most were paid thousands of dollars; a few received tens of thousands of dollars.

Also, ranchers were paid per diem for each evacuation. This turned into a bit of a bookkeeping headache, as each rancher submitted claims for evacuating family members and workers.

Some skeptical officials claimed a few ranchers actively milked the system by having family gatherings during evacuations to bump up the number of claimants. A rancher could make several hundred

> *Pop-Up*: When I arrived at White Sands in 1977, the FIX and other call-up areas were called "extensions." Nobody gave the terminology a second thought. Then, at the end of the century as the political correctness movement grew, some sensitive soul objected to the term "extension." They said it implied the lands were actually part of the missile range. Ranchers supposedly felt that the use of such language was the next step in the government's bid to take their homes. In response, the missile range changed the language. They didn't change the formal names of the areas nor did any aspects of the relationship change, but the term "extension" was banished from any public conversation. In its place, we all were told to use "call-up" as our descriptor for the areas.

dollars extra per evacuation if he had enough people to move into town.

In addition to the regular costs to keep the FIX intact and the per diem payments, the missile range also was required to pay for any damages in the FIX caused by debris impacts or the activities of government employees. In my time at White Sands, there were claims from ranchers for fence damage and cattle killed by government vehicles.

The first evacuation of the ranchers in the FIX took place on Feb. 3, 1960. The *Wind and Sand* newspaper reported 130 residents were evacuated for the day. During the 12-hour period, White Sands fired a Nike Hercules that was destroyed over the FIX and a Nike Zeus.

As the decades passed, someone would occasionally question what government activities could be allowed in the FIX and other extensions. The original 1960 agreements stated the ranchers gave the government, "the right to fire projectiles over the general area of the premises described." Also, it granted the government, "the right to enter upon or pass through said premises after firings to investigate claims for damage or loss resulting from firings, to repair damage resulting from firings, and to search for, guard, and recover projectiles, fragments thereof, or other debris which may have fallen on said premises."

For 1963, the agreements were amended to clarify the contingencies. Officials learned if an event wasn't covered in the agreement, a rancher would want more compensation.

The new one read, "the Government also desires to amend such agreement, as written, to provide for additional uses, as follows: Fall-out areas for boosters; launching of missiles from within or over this extension area, and other missile research and development tests where no construction is required."

The agreement also discussed individual arrangements with landowners like paying additional fees for locating instrumentation on their property or launching vehicles from their property.

In the 1990s, using ranch lands was taken another step when White Sands needed a place to launch target ballistic missiles such as the Hera to be intercepted by the Theater High Altitude Area Defense (THAAD) missile or the Patriot Advanced Capability 3 (PAC-3) missile. The idea was to launch the targets from the middle of the FIX and intercept them over the southern end of the missile range.

White Sands entered into an agreement with a few ranchers in the FIX for the construction of a small launch complex and a few instrumentation sites. Dubbed "LC-94" because it was established in 1994, the actual launch facility was located on the Donaldson ranch. A large environmental shroud set on rails was constructed to be used in assembling the missile and prepping it for flight.

In the same decade, the missile range pushed the envelope some more by establishing a designed (not accidental impact) weapon impact target area on the Oliver Lee III ranch in the FIX. For this operation, a Lee pasture area was set aside as a target for the Army Tactical Missile System (ATACMS).

Some ranchers have viewed this evolution of the co-use agreements as a dangerous sign that the government will soon try to simply take their land. Again, the actions taken by the Army at the beginning of World War II continue to haunt the relationship between the two parties to this day. On the other hand, some ranchers have learned to hammer this point and maybe exaggerate their concerns about a hostile takeover in order to strengthen their position during payment negotiations. They view keeping the government on the defensive as a wise chess move.

The Corridor

Establishing the FIX was all well and good, but it didn't satisfy the long-range requirements for systems like Redstone. As a solution in 1960, White Sands looked to the proposed northwest corridor and picked out Fort Wingate for use in testing Redstone. The old fort had been used during World War II as an ammunition storage facility, but by 1960 had large areas of land standing idle.

In this timeframe, someone made the decision to turn the old off-range corridor proposal on its head. Instead of launching from White Sands to impact areas along the corridor, the new proposal was to launch from Wingate and use the whole missile range as the impact area.

I have asked many old-timers about this change and it seems impossible to attribute the new strategy to any one person. The idea might have been floating around for some time since it makes so much sense. Requirements finally drove the decision makers to switch their strategy.

It was the leap forward needed to make the whole corridor idea work. Target areas could be placed up and down the missile range to vary the distance and approach angles. Plus, a missile flying into a target area on White Sands could be 10, 20 or even 30 miles off and still impact on controlled government property – property already being used for missile tests and impacts. In retrospect it looks like a "no-brainer" decision.

In May 1960, missile range personnel visited Fort Wingate to select a launch site for Redstone. During the summer, White Sands officials coordinated with the FAA for the airspace over the proposed launch area, looked at places to put instrumentation sites, and worked with the local U.S. Forest Service office to establish a booster drop zone on public lands.

Redstone launch from the south end of White Sands. The Organ Mountains are visible in the distance. WSMR photo.

On July 29, 1960, personnel from White Sands and the Army Ordnance Missile Command briefed the Ordnance Corps staff. A few days later, on Aug. 2, the Army Ordnance Missile Command suddenly notified White Sands to shut down preparations at Fort Wingate.

According to Major King, this didn't keep the Army Ballistic Missiles Agency from having another go at it. They pounded out a feasibility plan and sent it forward, saying WSMR could support launches down the corridor. On Dec. 2, 1960, the proposal was staffed as a "request for work and resources" at White Sands.

Then, in February 1961, Headquarters at the Ordnance Corps, announced that there still would be no Redstone flights from Fort Wingate. Headquarters gave four reasons for the decision. The first was that they would not fly Redstone over populated areas. The next three were that it was cheaper to just fly at White Sands, it was easier to support at WSMR and, finally, the weather was better further south.

Carlos Bustamante, who worked for National Range at the time and was involved in Redstone planning, had an insider's view of what was going on. This is typical of test programs – what is seen by the public is not necessarily reality.

Bustamante says the Redstone was having technical difficulties with staging during launches. The project wanted to conduct some tests over a highly instrumented range like White Sands so they could get a handle on it. Before the off-range launch preparations could be completed, Bustamante says they fixed their problem. That, in turn, eliminated the need for costly, time-consuming tests shots from Fort Wingate.

I think another reason was probably the "why bother" factor. Although still a deterrent, by then Redstone was an old, doomed system that no one was ready to spend a lot of money on. There was no reason to go to all that trouble with Sergeant and Pershing in the pipeline.

Through the 1950s, the Army's ballistic missile arsenal was composed of the Corporal and Redstone. Both missiles were liquid fueled and required extensive support teams and a great deal of time to prep for launch. It was technology based on the old World War II German V-2 rocket.

Their replacements, the Sergeant and Pershing, used solid-propellant rocket motors and needed much less preparation before lighting the fuse. They were lighter, more mobile and more accurate. In other words, there was likely an emphasis on getting the new systems up and operational as fast as possible because they were so much better weapons than their predecessors.

Such pushes occur when the brass know they have a real winner and want to take a giant step forward. In my time at WSMR, the Pershing II (the missile following the original Pershing and then the Pershing IA) was rushed through testing with very few shots and then fielded in Europe. It was so good it helped change the strategic balance of power with the Soviets.

The Corporal missile was the first American missile to carry a nuclear warhead. It stood 46 feet tall and, being only 30 inches in diameter, it looked a bit like a pencil standing on the launcher. It was mobile but required a small army of men about nine hours to assemble and prepare the missile. In addition, it was difficult and dangerous to fuel because red fuming nitric acid was used as its oxidizer. Officials said it was sometimes accurate and sometimes horribly off the mark and you never knew what you would get when you launched it. It had a range of 75 miles.

In contrast, the Sergeant was 34 feet long, could carry a nuclear warhead and, with its solid propellant motor was ready to fire in only an hour. It had a range from 30 to 85 miles.

The Redstone was huge, about 70 feet tall on the launcher and almost six feet in diameter. It burned alcohol and liquid oxygen just like the V-2. That meant the support team included a portable liquid oxygen plant. Redstone weighed over 60,000 pounds at launch and had a range of over 200 miles. Obviously it was not very portable or easy to prepare for launch. This thing was so big part of it was the basis for the rocket used to launch the first American satellite.

The Pershing, on the other hand, was 35 feet long, weighed 10,000 pounds and had a range of 100 to 450 miles. Units could haul it cross-country and even transport it in C-130 airplanes. Everything about it was better than the Redstone.

By 1959, White Sands told headquarters that it could test the new Pershing missile. The missile range proposed using the Fort Wingate Redstone launch site for Pershing launches. In 1962, the missile range became more responsive to the Pershing Project's testing needs by proposing additional launch sites that included Black Mesa, just west of Blanding, Utah, and McGregor Range on Fort Bliss. The arrangement provided a variety of azimuths, ranges and terrains.

Eventually, the McGregor proposal was changed to the Hueco Range on Fort Bliss, so the launch point would be west of U.S. Highway 54 which runs from El Paso, Texas to Alamogordo, New Mexico. They were trying to lessen the impact on the highway in terms of safety roadblocks.

In July 1962, the Pershing Project and the Department of Army announced most Pershing testing would be done at White Sands Missile Range instead of out over the ocean. The advantages for the program were considerable. An overland range provides cheaper support since no boats and other exotic support are involved. The instrumentation used to collect data is more accurate since it is not on ships bobbing around and drifting on the water. Finally, it is a breeze to go out and collect the debris after a test – it doesn't sink to the ocean floor.

Before any Pershing missiles were launched, the smaller player, the Sergeant, snuck into the picture. In early 1963, White Sands made arrangements with state, federal and outside agencies to utilize a launch site on ranch land and fire Sergeants back into WSMR. From April 29 through May 8, the missile range prepared an off-range launch site for Sergeant near Horse Springs on the Plains of San Augustin in western New Mexico.

On May 13, 1963, the first Sergeant was fired from the primitive location and successfully impacted on White Sands. According to Major King, "This was the first Army missile fired off-range over a populated area."

Additional launches took place on May 15 and 16. King pointed out the launches "demonstrated to some degree, that the concept of firing over populated areas was valid."

According to Fred Walters who worked for the DOVAP tracking system for these launches, the test was needed to verify the Sergeant's inertial guidance system. The firings were from west to east to see if the missile's guidance system would be affected by the rotation of the earth on its axis.

In a newsletter article written by Walters, he said the missile range picked a launch site that just happened to belong to a rancher who had been previously displaced from a ranch on White Sands during World War II. According to Walters, "He was more than a little reticent to allow the Army to again inconvenience him as it had 20 years previously. After spirited discussions, negotiations, and many promises 'that this was a one time only situation,' he did relent and let us locate the launch area and several instrumentation sites on his property."

A Sergeant launch on Sept. 28, 1961. WSMR photo.

In the September 2013 issue of *Hands Across History*, Lawrence McFall wrote about the team sent out to prepare for the Sergeant launches. He said a caravan of 40 vehicles and 125 men left WSMR on March 5, 1963. They got to the launch area after dark and used the vehicle headlights to set up tents, latrines and a mess tent. They even hauled whitewashed rocks to the site to mark out "streets" and the HQ area. After erecting a headquarters tent and flagpole, the men moved out a ways to prepare the launch area.

The spring temperature swings in the desert caught McFall by surprise. He wrote, "Etched in my memory is the single greatest temperature change I have ever witnessed in one day. That final morning found the water that filled my aluminum washbasin the evening before, frozen solid. By two o'clock that afternoon, the late May sun was a scorching 96 degrees."

Even with the daytime heating, McFall said, "we learned that beer could be kept cool in a 2 to 3 foot hole dug in the floor of our squad tent with pasteboard covering the newly disturbed earth. An officer who liked beer as much as our small group went back to base and returned with six cases our second weekend out there. Except for the usual military discipline we experienced no harassment during our detail and I generally remember having a great time."

Walters, on the other hand, camped out high in the mountains. Many men in instrumentation support camped atop Mount Withington at just over 10,000 feet where some of their equipment was stationed. It provided a great view of the missile's flight and cool temperatures for the men's comfort.

In the evenings the men were often bored and played cards. Walters wasn't an enthusiastic player and often excused himself. He wrote, "One evening as I lay asleep in my tent, the card game got out of hand after one participant, who was in his cups, thought someone took his wallet. (It had fallen out of his pocket and was later located) He took umbrage, went back to his tent, got a gun and threatened the other players. When he didn't get his wallet back, he started shooting. He was restrained by the other players and those who awoke to the gunfire. The local sheriff was summoned and hauled off the miscreant. Quiet reigned again. Later I found one round had gone through my tent over my head. One of the joys of off-range operations."

In this same timeframe (1962-63), the Air Force introduced a new cruise missile to White Sands with launches of the supersonic Hound Dog from a B-52 flying near Del Rio, Texas. These missiles flew some 300 miles off-range before impacting in a target area on WSMR.

Then, on Sept. 24, 1963, the first off-range Pershing missile was launched from the Hueco Range at Fort Bliss to impact on WSMR. Four more missiles were fired in quick succession before the program moved to shots from Black Mesa, Utah and Fort Wingate, New Mexico.

Suddenly, the skies around and over White Sands were filled with incoming missiles from several different directions. Things started off so well the missile range and its customers just kept expanding the capability.

Green River

The most ambitious step was adding a major launch facility just south of Green River, Utah to accommodate the Air Force's Athena program. The reason for the program was to simulate, on a reduced scale, the reentry of warheads like those one might put on an intercontinental ballistic missile. The Air Force talked about "increased penetrability" for warheads and "hardening the vehicle and warhead against blast, X-Ray, neutrons, electromagnetic pulse." They also mentioned lowering the warhead's visibility both optically and from radar as well as using deception to get warheads successfully to their targets.

Of course, to test these strategies, radars and other sensors needed to be in place at WSMR to actually measure everything happening.

To propel their scaled-down warheads into space and then blister them down through the atmosphere onto White Sands at speeds over 15,000 miles per hour, the Air Force developed two versions of the Athena vehicle. The early version was a four-stage rocket and later the "H" version used only three stages.

The first firings were in 1964 and the last ones

were from Green River in 1973. The most famous Athena was number 122 launched on July 11, 1970. It went haywire and flew hundreds of miles into Mexico. See the Oops! chapter for the story of this international incident.

This was a big program that required lots of additional land. First of all, the launch site outside of Green River was "borrowed" from state and federal land managers. At 25 square miles, the facility included a number of pre-fabricated metal buildings, dozens of trailers, two FPS-16 radar buildings, a display building, a blockhouse, three launch pads with environmental conditioning chambers, a 500-foot meteorological tower, a meteorological rocket launch pad, and seven explosive storage buildings. Also on site was a complex of buildings used by the contractor (Atlantic Research Corporation) for missile assembly.

The empty land just southeast of each launcher served as a safety area in case there was a malfunction at lift-off. A WSMR missile-flight safety engineer once told me that if a solid fueled rocket motor was going to fail, it was most likely at liftoff during those first few seconds of acceleration. The launch area safety zone took care of that.

Next, White Sands and the program needed safety areas along the corridor to receive the boosters when they burned out. The first of these areas was just south of Moab, Utah and contained 424 square miles of land. The second area was 1,318 square miles of land near Datil, New Mexico.

The other common time for a missile failure is during staging, when one booster burns out, falls away and the next booster ignites. If the next stage fails to ignite, the Athena booster drop zones were large enough to receive the spent stage and the rest of the vehicle after it fell to earth. It is pretty simple physics. The spent booster and the rest of the rocket are traveling at the same speed and have the same momentum – they basically will fall very close to each other.

These two booster drop zones were called up as needed, and any residents inside the boundaries were paid to evacuate. Roadblocks and barricades were erected to keep visitors out during the missions.

The drop area near Moab would eventually cause heartburn with the National Park Service and the public. Canyonlands National Park, to the west of Moab, was established in 1964. The drop zone actually encroached onto thousands of acres in the Needles District of the national park.

In the 1990s, when White Sands and the Army's THAAD program proposed reopening Green River as a launch site for Hera target missiles, there was need to establish a booster drop zone along the eastern boundary of Canyonlands. This time there was a loud and powerful objection to the proposal. It came not only from the locals but from many of the visitors as well. Powerful lobbyists for parks, wilderness and open space flat out told the Army that if they tried to reestablish the drop zone, they would be in for a long battle in the courts. Eventually, the program decided on Fort Wingate as the target launch site.

> *Pop-Up:* In the 1960s, southeastern Utah populations and the number of park visitors were relatively small. Today, it is recognized as one of the more spectacular areas in the country. The number of visitors to Canyonlands today, a rather remote location, is around a half million per year. Tiny Arches National Park, right outside Moab, now receives over a million visitors a year.

Finally, the Athena program needed a couple of evacuation areas adjacent to the missile range's western boundary. These were to be called up individually depending on the trajectory of each mission. Dubbed the "Abres 4A" and "Abres 4A Extension," they essentially expanded the western boundary of White Sands almost to the Santa Fe Railroad tracks running through the Jornada del Muerto.

The term "Abres" was used because it was the acronym for the overall program that included Athena – the Advanced Ballistic Re-Entry System Program.

These new extension areas were set up just like the FIX with ranchers receiving annual payments and per diem for each evacuation. Later, a third area was added on the west boundary for Aerobee sounding rockets launched by the Navy. This area was called the Aerobee 350 Extension.

With three distinct areas on the west boundary, White Sands could surgically call up one, two or three of them as needed. Later, the missile range knitted the two Abres extensions into just one.

With just over 140 launches from Green River, the Athena was certainly a workhorse for White Sands. Even setbacks like the missile into Mexico didn't slow down the launches from off-range sites back into White Sands. The range was certainly playing bigger than its actual 3,200 square miles.

Compared to Pershing launches, the Athena was small potatoes when you look at the numbers. To add even more options for the Pershing program, White Sands established another launch point in a very remote area of Utah near the small town of Hanksville. Gilson Butte was a nearby landmark and gave its name to the launch area.

The original Pershing and its immediate successor, the Pershing IA, were key weapons in Europe. They were deployed to both American and German forces and their nuclear warheads were a major deterrent to the Soviet forces with their hundreds of tanks poised in Eastern Europe.

American and German troops were trained to maintain Pershing equipment and to prepare them for firing. They also needed to actually shoot one to see how it all came together. To make that happen, American and German soldiers were regularly shipped to launch facilities like Fort Bliss, Green River and Black Mesa and were allowed to fire a missile, sans warhead, at White Sands. Such training was done after support person-

A Pershing I launch from Black Mesa, Utah - west of the town of Blanding. WSMR photo.

nel graduated from Pershing school and then again for refresher training.

The first German Air Force firing was from the Hueco launch site on Fort Bliss in April 1964.

This training requirement added more support needs at these sites. Instead of a mostly government and contractor team launching a missile for a test, for these additional firings the sites were flooded with real-life soldiers who needed to be housed, fed and trained. Temporary and not-so temporary facilities had to be erected to accommodate them.

In the end, it was not unusual to see German troops in Utah as they went about their business of preparing and launching a Pershing missile. At the same time, White Sands tried to maintain friendly relations with local communities. At Green River, because the launch facility was so close to town, residents were notified about launches and they would come to the edges of the site to watch.

Missile range records for launches of Pershing and Pershing IA from off range show the following totals: Hueco – 18; McGregor – 95; Fort Wingate – 20; Black Mesa – 80; Green River – 60; and Gilson Butte – 29. That is a total of 302 launches, but it is not the end of the Pershing story.

In the late 1970s and early 80s, the Army began development of a completely new Pershing missile. It was not an engineering improvement on the previous models and their equipment. Everything about Pershing II was to be brand new. Key features would be much greater range and amazing pinpoint accuracy. With such incredible accuracy it was possible for the new missile to carry a much smaller warhead. If you hit the target right on the button instead of a hundred yards away, you didn't need as big an explosion.

While testing was ongoing, I was required to write up some notes for Major General Niles Fulwyler, WSMR commander, about current White Sands activities so he could brief the Las Cruces Chamber of Commerce. I knew a little about the accuracy of the Pershing so I thought it would be nice to provide a real-world example.

I called the Pershing project manager and asked him if I could have the general say that the Pershing II could be launched from 800 miles out, from Mountain Home, Idaho, and still hit the main parking lot next to the WSMR headquarters building. The colonel laughed and said, "You can tell the general and the chamber that the Pershing could hit the general's reserved parking spot in that lot."

To accommodate this missile that could reach targets more than 800 miles away, White Sands established a new launch site in southern Idaho. Called Shoofly, the site was on public land south of Boise. The nearest sizeable town was Mountain Home where an Air Force Base was located.

Pershing was on a fast track so White Sands moved quickly in coordinating with Idaho officials and building the launch site. Not much construction was needed as it was planned to be a bare bones tactical setup. The site was ready to go in just a few months.

For these flights, the Pershing's first stage was to drop into a safety evacuation area about 70 miles long fanning out from the launch point. Since this was just a two-stage missile, the second rocket motor was to just follow the warhead or reentry vehicle into the target area on White Sands.

However, when the first two-stage Pershing firing was conducted from McGregor Range on Fort Bliss in November 1982, after burnout the second stage did not behave as predicted by the computer simulations. That was not a problem for the real weapon but was an issue for testing at White Sands with friendly neighbors just outside the boundaries.

Based on the initial shot, if they fired from Shoofly, it was not certain that the second stage would actually land on White Sands Missile Range. It was a simple engineering problem that normally would have been fixed so the program could start testing as planned.

Because Pershing II was so good, military officials wanted to get it deployed to Europe as soon as possible. They decided against a delay. Instead, they reinvented the test series by dividing it into two parts.

The first part was to go ahead and fire full two-stage Pershing II missiles out over the ocean from Florida. This would give engineers the information they needed on general guidance, staging and other details up to the time where the warhead started directing itself to its target using its terrain comparison radar system.

For that reentry portion of the flight, tests were conducted at White Sands with the vehicles being launched at McGregor Range. For these tests, the missile was reduced to a single stage to propel the warhead to a very high altitude over White Sands. Then the guidance system would kick in and seek out the assigned target.

Testing was fast, furious and very successful. In June 1984, the first Pershing II battalion was completed and in place in Europe. In December 1985, the Pershing II system reached full operational capability in Europe.

It was during this time I learned something about the local news media. In anticipation of allowing reporters to watch the Pershing II launches from McGregor, we invited them to watch a Pershing IA launch from the same location. The idea was to give them a feel for the operation and also allow them to interview project and missile range personnel.

We had a decent turnout and were able to place the reporters back from the launcher in an area where non-essential personnel gathered. Any closer would have required being in a protective shelter at launch.

One of our reporters wanted to be closer. She worked for the *El Paso Times* but somehow finagled a deal to write about the event for *Time* magazine as well. She told us she was representing mighty *Time* magazine and demanded to be in the bunker with the soldiers who were launching the missile. We explained that was only for personnel essential to the launch because it was dangerous and she didn't qualify.

I don't think she received much sympathy from project personnel because she showed up dressed in Army surplus fatigues as if that would help her "fit in."

Later I noticed her talking to some of our missile range personnel who were there to run radars, optics and telemetry. After a while she came up to me and said, "I don't get it. I've been asking your guys what happens when the Pershing warhead hits the ground up north of here. They said it depends on the ground, that sometimes they bury themselves in the sand or mud or hit a rocky slope and bounce down the hill. Why doesn't that nuclear warhead make a huge crater when it explodes?"

I kept from laughing and resisted the urge to say a real *Time* magazine reporter would know about the international ban on above-ground nuclear testing set in 1963. Instead, I explained no weapons tested at White Sands ever carried actual nuclear weapons and the only above-ground nuclear explosion ever in New Mexico was at Trinity Site in July 1945. I don't

know if *Time* magazine ran anything from her or not.

Eventually, 25 PII missiles were fired from McGregor Range onto White Sands to test their guidance systems. The missile range would set up cameras in small, designated target areas and capture the warhead in slow motion as it crashed into the ground. It was very impressive video.

Since the Soviets had nothing to counter the Pershings, the new missile immediately influenced the negotiations on a treaty to reduce such weapons. For several years the two sides had been going back and forth with one proposal after another. The United States wanted total elimination of such weapons but the Soviets always balked. Finally, under the lead-

Pershing II launch on Feb. 26, 1983 from McGregor Range at Fort Bliss. This is after the decision was made to abandon the Idaho launches. This stubby version of the missile used just the first-stage booster and the re-entry vehicle to test the guidance capabilities of the warhead.. WSMR photo.

ership of Gorbachev, the two sides came to a zero game agreement. Just two years after becoming fully operational in Europe, the United States and the Soviet Union signed the Intermediate Range Nuclear Forces (INF) Treaty on Dec. 8, 1987. For America the treaty called for the elimination of all Pershing missiles while the Soviets had to give up the SS-20 and other weapons.

The treaty was remarkable in that it was the first agreement to actually reduce the number of nuclear weapons, not just put a cap on their numbers.

For the next couple of years, the two sides destroyed their missiles while inspectors watched. The treaty did allow a few of the missiles to be demilitarized and used for display. One of those spared missiles is standing erect in the WSMR Missile Park.

The kicker is that these display units have to be accounted for with detailed location information. For instance, when the missile range moved its Missile Park from the area in front of Headquarters Building to the area north of the Museum, the move, along with new location coordinates, had to be reported to the Russians.

All of the missile range's off-range launch sites were shut down in the 1970s except for the Pershing II firings out of McGregor Range at Fort Bliss. The unused Pershing II launch site in Idaho joined the others in mothballed status. White Sands preferred the terminology "caretaker status." Valuable equipment, trailers and other items were removed. Some places like Gilson Butte and Black Mesa were returned to the Bureau of Land Management and all improvements were removed. These sites then sat dormant until the early 1990s when new hit-to-kill ballistic missile interceptors needed to be tested.

The driving force behind reopening an off-range launch site in the mid-1990s was the new Theater Missile Defense program. This program sought to develop systems to protect military personnel and our allies from missiles launched within the theater. Attacks during the Gulf War of 1990 were cited as an example for their need.

Key systems in the program were the Theater High Altitude Area Defense (THAAD) system and the Patriot Advanced Capability-3 (PAC-3). These were the kinds of defensive systems to successfully emerge from the Star Wars programs started by President Reagan.

It wasn't lasers, magnetic rail guns or some other exotic technology that rose to the top after all the hype and testing. It turned out to be something we were all familiar with - thundering, fire-spitting, blazing-fast missiles. Unfortunately, no light sabers or tractor beams emerged.

But these new systems weren't your father's missiles. They were smaller, faster, and could hit tiny fast targets. In fact, they were so accurate, they didn't even need to carry a warhead. The interceptor's guidance system was so good it would simply seek out and crash into the target. This took place at such high speeds that the kinetic energy released on impact turned both vehicles to tiny pieces of junk and a cloud of smoke and dust.

This was a new approach to killing enemy ballistic missiles. Prior to this, military testers had been shooting down missiles with missiles for decades at White Sands. In 1960 alone, a HAWK missile intercepted an Honest John missile and a Nike Hercules was used against another Nike Hercules. In these tests the interceptors used explosive warheads that were supposed to blow up the target, destroying its capability. In its tactical mode, the Hercules could use a nuclear warhead that probably guaranteed a kill.

We know from Operation Desert Storm in 1991 that conventional warheads only work some of the time. During this conflict, Iraq launched numerous Scud ballistic missiles at U.S. and allied targets. The United States launched Patriot missiles at the Scuds and did manage to destroy some. However, the Patriot's explosive warheads often did not kill the incoming Scud's warhead, yet it still managed to explode on impact, wounding and killing many personnel.

At that time, Patriot had a warhead designed to explode when close to the enemy plane and spray it with a cloud of debris pieces. It was like a shotgun, hoping some of the pieces would kill or cripple the airplane. As evidenced in World War II, airplanes can take quite a beating with dozens of bullet holes in the wings and fuselage and yet keep flying. However, blanket them with a mass of shrapnel and the chances are good something vital will be destroyed.

This methodology doesn't work so well with incoming ballistic missiles like Scuds. The missile is simply falling out of the sky and a shotgun blast may or may not take out the actual explosives buried in the missile.

During the first Iraq war, the Patriot project and

contractor, in response to this problem, changed the software on the missiles so they would explode closer to the target and provide more punch. The changes were tested at White Sands and rushed to Iraq to make Patriot more effective against Scuds.

The Army's THAAD and PAC-3, along with a new version of the Navy's Standard Missile, were the new promise with their "hit to kill" technology. With the speed involved, it was often referred to as "hitting a bullet with another bullet." Briefers would ask the audience to imagine someone firing a hunting rifle at you and you raising your rifle to shoot the incoming bullet before it hits you.

Of course, the tests were much more involved than pushing the button to fire the missiles. To test the system's radar capabilities, targets needed to be presented from close by and from locations far away, over the horizon. At White Sands, targets from a hundred miles out could be launched from the new complex in the FIX. For farther targets, White Sands needed to return to the off-range corridor and one or more of its launch sites.

Unlike the 1960s and 70s, the rules for starting such a project were very different and very formalized by the 90s. Because of the National Environmental Policy Act, the Theater Missile Defense folks and White Sands had to write an Environmental Impact Statement (EIS) beforehand. The EIS was required to contain an analysis of federal actions that might "significantly affect the quality of the human environment."

An EIS describes the positive and negative effects of a proposed action and usually lists a few alternatives to it. The EIS is not the decision-making devise nor does it prohibit harm to the environment. The EIS is the tool to be used by the "decision maker" when making the final choices. Using the EIS, the decision maker will hopefully have a full understanding of the impacts, what might be done to mitigate them, and whether or not the need for the action outweighs the negatives.

Even though lots of missiles had once been fired from Green River, Utah and Fort Wingate, New Mexico, the new project needed to analyze what impacts there would be if target missiles were launched from there. It is a long and expensive process.

The process started in 1993 with public scoping meetings in Green River, Salt Lake City, and Moab, Utah. In New Mexico there were scoping meetings in Albuquerque and Gallup. These meetings were held to find out what concerns citizens and their communities had about the proposed actions.

After complaints from Native American groups, additional meetings were held at Window Rock, Arizona and Crownpoint, New Mexico.

Some of these meetings, especially those in Utah, were quite contentious. They were intended to gather information to be analyzed, but most people attended to protest.

When boiled down, most arguments against the proposal were about risk – risk to natural resources and risk to public safety. Also, some had very legitimate concerns about loss of business caused by closures or simple inconvenience to themselves caused by evacuations.

The risk issue was very educational and we in Public Affairs learned two things. The first was that Americans are terrible at assessing risk. The missile range and other experts had calculated the risk of injury from the proposed flights at well beyond one in a million. That is a very low level and is generally recognized as an acceptable risk in our everyday lives.

While protesting this slight risk, meeting attendees engaged in much higher risk activities like driving to the meeting or taking their smoke breaks or having a few beers afterward. There was an obvious disconnect there that was probably greatly influenced by the second thing we learned.

The second insight was that people don't like risk imposed on them. It doesn't seem to matter how low the risk really is, Americans seem to sense it as a form of being told what to do. That never plays well, especially in rural areas.

Everyday we find people who voluntarily jump out of airplanes, scale vertical cliffs on mountains, and sit around gorging on ice cream. They don't bat an eye at the risk they are incurring because they have made their own decision to do it. When the activity is imposed, we feel we are not in control.

That is why many people are afraid to fly. Their fate is totally out of their control. Give them the pickup truck steering wheel, however, and they feel they are in command of the vehicle and the risk. Of course, we know the reality is that driving your car to the grocery store is many times more dangerous than taking a flight to New York City.

After the scoping meetings were finished, a draft of the EIS was prepared, hopefully addressing the concerns, and made available to the public and concerned agencies. To see what people thought of that, we held meetings in 1994 in Moab and Salt Lake City, Utah; and in Crownpoint, Gallup, Ramah and Shiprock, New Mexico. Some of these were held in Navajo and Zuni facilities to make sure we gathered their input.

To address some concerns about the required booster drop zones for these flights, new areas were proposed and additional meetings were required to allow input. Those meetings were held in Monticello and Salt Lake City, Utah as well as Grants and Magdalena, New Mexico.

I attended most of these meetings and can say it is discouraging to sit for a couple of hours and have people rail against your organization. Luckily, no one really carried their anger to a personal level against any of us.

In early 1995, the executive decision was made based on a final EIS. For White Sands, the program announced it would launch target missiles from Fort Wingate only and intercept them over White Sands. After looking at all the impacts for resurrecting Green River, the decision maker dropped the Utah option.

Since Wingate is much closer than Green River, both one- and two-stage targets could be used as needed. The one-stage target was the Storm II assembled by Orbital Sciences Corp. Its motor was a surplus second stage from a Minuteman 2 missile. These have been used as targets for the PAC-3. No drop zone for a booster is needed as the motor follows the warhead into WSMR.

The two-stage missile was dubbed the Hera. It was put together by Coleman Research and consisted of surplus Minuteman 2 second and third stages. It was big, standing almost 40 feet tall, over four feet in diameter and weighed 25,000 lbs. A drop zone, located near Datil, New Mexico, was needed for the first stage of the Hera.

The testing of THAAD and PAC-3 started in 1995 with demonstrations of the Hera target. Once shown it could be flown successfully, launches moved off-range. There were no Hera launches from Fort Wingate until 1996. Before there could be any firings, WSMR had to build a Missile Assembly Building (MAB), a trailer shelter made of concrete and a launch pad with environmental shelter.

In addition, just like the launch areas at White Sands, personnel had to prepare sites for range control, radars, optics, telemetry and meteorological support. Some 25 vans were used on site, all linked by fiber optic and copper cable as well as microwave.

THAAD launches at White Sands started on April 21, 1995 with a simple launch to see if the propulsion system worked. No target was used.

Two more flights followed to test the various missile systems. On the third one a target was launched from White Sands but no attempt was made to intercept it. The test was to see if the targeting system saw the Hera and was correctly crunching the data.

Storm and Hera targets were eventually launched from LC-94 and Fort Wingate for THAAD tests. Unfortunately, THAAD failed to hit these targets in the first series of tests. In fact, it didn't score a kill until June 10, 1999.

Fireworks

During these early failures, while we certainly didn't have the excitement of an intercept, we in Public Affairs did have to deal with the light show visible in southern Colorado and Arizona. During that first successful launch of a Hera target from Fort Wingate in early 1998, in the 30 minutes or so before sunrise the second stage's contrail put on quite a show to the west.

The first time it happened the phones in Public Affairs lit up. News media and others called from Tucson, Phoenix, Flagstaff and Yuma, Arizona and Colorado Springs, Colorado because residents were seeing a contrail cloud lit by the rising sun. During one phase of the phenomenon, the cloud showed the various colors of a rainbow. A few people were worried but most were awestruck and just wanted to know what it was.

At first we had no idea what was happening but it didn't take long to figure it out. We started asking around and looking at the photos people sent in. It turns out the Hera's second stage left smoke and water vapor in the upper atmosphere as it blasted higher and higher. More than likely, the water vapor in the exhaust froze almost instantly at those high altitudes and created innumerable little ice crystals.

For the people in Arizona the sun was still well below the horizon, so it was quite dark as they went about their early-morning business. The vapor cloud from the Hera, however, was miles above the ground and more than a hundred miles to their east. The sun striking the cloud lit it up. Also, the ice crystals acted as tiny prisms and broke the light up into a rainbow of color.

After a couple of repeat performances, news agencies and photographers called White Sands asking us to notify them of the next test so they could shoot video or stills of the contrail. Toward the end I did send news releases to Arizona media outlets letting them know about the next test. One thing we learned was that if the launch of the Hera took place after the sun was up, there was no contrail phenomenon, at least none that was visible in Arizona.

I was in south Phoenix during one of these missions. Knowing the schedule, I went outside early in the morning to photograph the contrail. I stared to the northeast where I calculated Fort Wingate would be. I knew I would not be able to see the first stage burn because I was too far away. Hoping to see the second stage, I waited and was rewarded with a clear view of it burning for several seconds in the dark sky before it winked out and continued its invisible coast to WSMR. It took a while but eventually the sun's rays struck the contrail and lit it up in an unnatural display of cloud and color.

Finally on June 10, 1999, THAAD killed its Hera target. During planning meetings I went to for this project, one topic of discussion was the issue of detecting an intercept of a Hera target by THAAD. The engagement was higher than anything ever done before over WSMR, and with no warhead WSMR personnel wondered if it would be visible.

That June morning all doubt was erased as the cloud of debris created in the impact quickly ballooned into a large white cloud brightly lit by the rising sun. It was obvious and it was spectacular.

The program continued with several more successful flights at WSMR before shifting to Hawaii for tests over the Pacific Ocean using targets coming from much greater distances.

That shift also ended the light shows

for Arizona residents. Interestingly, the show came back on Sept. 13, 2012, when a Juno target missile was launched from Fort Wingate to be intercepted over WSMR by a PAC-3 missile.

Juno is a two-stage target using the same motor stack as the Hera, just a different company putting it together with other equipment. It was the same scenario as the Hera shots in the 1990s, so the second-stage contrail was very visible as it twisted and turned across the sky.

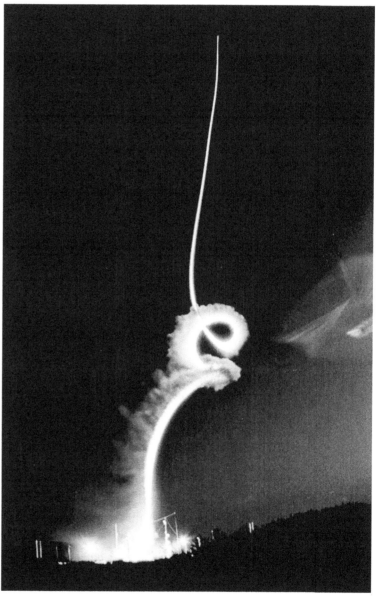

This dramatic, pre-dawn, time-lapse photo of a good THAAD launch captures the curling maneuver performed by the missile just after it left its launch container. The move was pre-planned to bleed energy during the boost phase so the missile didn't end up in Colorado if something went wrong. WSMR photo.

One curious aspect to this repeat performance was the reaction in Arizona. It was like all the news media from the 90s were gone (all the talent, writers, producers, directors, et al) and replaced by fresh faces who oohed and aahed about the cloud. They acted as if this had never happened before. You guessed it, the Public Affairs Office phones lit up again and it was deja vu.

Symbolically, the event put quite an exclamation point on the assumption of command at White Sands by Brigadier General Gwendolyn Bingham that day. She took command during a 9 a.m. ceremony after watching the test earlier in the morning. Bingham was not only the first woman to command WSMR, she also was the first black commander.

With the Green River launch facility being eliminated from possible use as a target missile launch site, it continued to molder and sink into the surrounding desert. Year after year weather and vandals took their toll on the few buildings and infrastructure.

In June 1997, *Popular Mechanics* magazine surprised us all with a large article featuring the Green River facility. The article basically said the Air Force planned to shut down Area 51 in Nevada and move the "top secret" testing activities to Green River, using the old missile range facility. Holy cow!

The article said the launch complex has this infrastructure already in place, that it is desolate and isolated, and that the Air Force will launch experimental vehicles to the northwest into Michael Army Air Field near Hill Air Force Base.

The truth was the complex was very small and very accessible from both the town of Green River and Interstate 70. Green River was only 1.2 miles from the site (not exactly remote) and the interstate ran right through the northern half of it. Not exactly a large hiding place for the kind of secret activity we associate with Area 51.

In fact one of WSMR's problems with proposing the complex as a launch site for target missiles was moving the launcher far enough south so we would not have to stop traffic on the interstate for a safety roadblock.

The article proposed flying experimental vehicles to the northwest from this launch complex. If that were true, the vehicles would have flown over the interstate very soon after liftoff. Such a scenario would have required roadblocks on Interstate 70 and maybe evacuation of the town of Green River. That

would be hard to keep secret.

The article also said there was an infrastructure already in place at the WSMR launch complex that the Air Force could walk in and use. The truth was anyone wanting to move a project into the site would have needed to bulldoze what was there and start over.

The bottom line was pretty much a completely fictional article. Not something one would expect from a prominent magazine like *Popular Mechanics*.

Since then White Sands has been going through all the requirements to return the land to its various owners. The biggest hurdle was cleaning up areas where hazardous materials were used or leaked into the ground. It has been a glacial process to remove the missile range from any responsibility for everything at Green River. Also, the site is now considered historic. Various state and federal officials are looking at the site's importance to assess possible requirements for preservation.

It seems unlikely White Sands will ever go back to Utah or Idaho for launches. The only thing keeping the off-range corridor alive in 2012 was the launch of targets from Fort Wingate. For a couple of decades, the corridor was very useful as it effectively made WSMR much larger during the height of the Cold War.

The northern and western call-up areas are still intact, although they don't get very frequent use. In fact, White Sands has spent a great deal of time trying to reduce the cost of the extensions. Of course, ranchers have actively resisted such moves.

The land in the extension areas totals 2,400 square miles, not quite as much as the missile range's own land mass of 3,200 square miles. There are some missions where all the extension areas are called up, and for almost 12 hours White Sands is about 5,600 square miles. That is a shade larger than the state of Connecticut with its 2010 population of 3.5 million.

In the case of the missile range, we are talking about an area almost devoid of population because of the evacuations for the test. It is quite a contrast to densely populated Connecticut.

Those extension areas have been useful for all kinds of missions. However, in 1993 the whole program received national attention when CNN did an attack story about the setup. The news network aired a feature story accusing White Sands and the Army of running a "cowboy welfare" operation. The narrator said the extension areas were mostly government land already, so why should the Army pay to use them?

In typical news media fashion they oversimplified the situation. Also, they distorted the numbers saying ranchers were only evacuated one time the year before, so they obviously were getting paid large amounts of money for doing nothing.

It turns out CNN received a complaint from a rancher on the west side who was just outside the extension area boundary. This person wanted into the extension program so she would be able to collect the annual fee but was denied by White Sands. The rancher hit out after that, accusing White Sands of all kinds of underhanded things.

After the piece aired nationally, we prepared for an onslaught of questions and complaints from the public. I prepared a two-page response for Army Public Affairs in Washington so they could answer queries there.

Our response pointed out that there was no way politically or financially White Sands could grab the 2,400 square miles as suggested by CNN. There would have been riots.

We also pointed out that most ranchers received small amounts of money for giving White Sands the right to evacuate them. At that time, 28 of the ranchers received less than $1,000 up front. Only four received over $30,000. Everybody else was in between with the majority, 53 ranchers, somewhere between $1,000 and $10,000.

In addition, we used real numbers for the actual number of evacuations. While 1992 was a down year, WSMR did evacuate ranchers between five and seven times, depending on which area they were in. Just a few years before, in 1988, most ranchers were asked to evacuate 22 times.

In the end there was no hue and cry as a result of the CNN attack program. The Department of Army received less than 10 queries and we only received a few. One gentleman received our response and forwarded it to CNN to see what they thought. CNN basically told him they stood by the story because their reporter won some awards once.

The man then sent a letter to the Department of Army saying, "I consider your response more complete and reasoned and their response defensive. Thank you for your explanation."

The interesting twist to this story is that Ted Turner, the billionaire who started CNN, bought the Armendaris Ranch in 1994, just a year after the negative story. A portion of the Armendaris place is in the missile range's western extension.

The ranch was established in 1819 as a Spanish land grant. It was then patented by the United States in 1881. That means the huge ranch, at 550 square miles, is privately owned. It does not include federal lands under lease like most ranches.

Some of the Armendaris Ranch bumps up against the missile range's boundary. Turner raises buffalo there as he does on most of his other ranches. One escaped through his fences once and found its way onto the missile range.

The big beast was spotted by range employees near Trinity Site and eventually up near the north boundary. Turner's people were contacted and, with White Sands cooperation, they were allowed access through a gate to corral and remove the bison.

When they had trouble controlling the animal, they shot and killed it to prevent it from escaping onto the ranches in the FIX.

This was apparently done to make sure no rancher could claim a Turner buffalo gave the rancher's cattle a bacterial disease called brucellosis. The disease may be found in buffalo and can be transmitted to cattle but not by casual contact. In fact, this looks like one of those risk issues where people get very excited about very low probability events.

Since the Armendaris Ranch takes up quite a bit of the western extension, Ted Turner receives annual government payments as part of the evacuation program. Because the ranch is much larger than any of the others, Turner receives the largest payment made by the missile range. It is tens of thousands of dollars. So it turns out Turner would be considered a "welfare cowboy" by his own network.

By the way, as far as I know, Turner has never refused the money.

17

Oops!

Things don't always go well with rocket and missile firings. This was especially true in the first few decades of their development when the technology was very young.

When you consider what is happening in a missile flight, it is not surprising. First of all, there is the rocket motor that is nothing more than a controlled explosion in a can. Then all the components are subjected to huge G forces and extreme vibration as most missiles quickly accelerate through the sound barrier. There is extreme heat from the burning motor and friction as it passes through the air coupled with extreme cold at high altitudes. To say the least, it is a severe environment that, even in the 21st century, challenges engineers.

To this day malfunctions still materialize in the most sophisticated vehicles. In my time at White Sands, I saw some spectacular mishaps. At a launch attended by hundreds of school kids, I sat with them for the firing of a round from the Army Tactical Missile System (ATACMS). The missile flew out a few seconds and simply exploded, erupting into flame as the pieces fell to the ground.

From the Public Affairs Office at White Sands, we used to go outside to watch the predawn launches of Tactical High Altitude Area Defense (THAAD) missiles. One morning the missile came corkscrewing out of its launch canister, did several flips, and crashed into the ground just seconds after launch. That was a spectacular light show in the dark predawn sky.

Most people viewing video of these incidents consider them humorous, although I'm sure someone responsible for the missile took the heat for the problem. There is great historical motion picture footage of an Honest John launch where the missile is still locked on the launch rail at ignition. The missile didn't break away but propelled itself and the launcher down range skipping along the ground every few feet. It was a very, very, very low-level flight.

Such mishaps used to be quite entertaining. After all, no one was hurt and it showed that all that state-of-the-art science and engineering was still fallible.

At one time, missile range officials showed a short film to the general public with nothing on it but missile bloopers. The movie made the important point that testing these vehicles performing at the edges of modern physical limits was vital before they were turned over to American sons and daughters in the military.

Testing goals haven't changed but attitudes have. Today, top officials and program managers do not want even a whiff of failure associated with their tests. When the THAAD missile essentially destroyed itself at launch and plowed into the ground, officials much higher than us delayed putting out any information for a couple of hours.

All the mainstream press and trade journals knew when the test was scheduled and called our office for a report on the test. Although the test took place at White Sands, our staff rarely had authority to speak for these programs. We usually read from prepared news releases when the media called.

In the end, the delay on the THAAD release was a waste of time. When reporters saw the footage later, they just laughed at the military's lame attempt to cover up a blooper.

Sometimes when things go wrong there is nothing funny about it. Out of the 45,000 rockets and missiles fired at White Sands, a few, very few, have left the missile range property and crashed out in the public domain where no one was evacuated or placed in a safe place like a bunker.

However, because of the foresight of those who picked the Tularosa Basin for a missile test facility, population densities around the missile range were really thin when most failures took place. The few vehicles that crashed off range have never injured or killed anyone in the public. There have been claims of cattle being scared to death but that is all.

Maybe it is lucky that White Sands still exists today. After the first successful V-2 launch in 1946 which was viewed by many reporters, Douglas Larsen with the National Editor's Association filed an interesting story about the event and White Sands.

The story's lead was, "Residents of New Mexico and neighboring states are getting worried about their back yards being used as a laboratory for push-button warfare." He claimed the local population was getting "a trifle peeved and a mite scared" about bigger rockets and rockets with A bombs.

Larsen then wrote, "Local politicians are telling the residents that they have the words of Senators Carl A. Hatch and Dennis Chavez and Secretary of Agriculture Clinton Anderson, all from New Mexico, that if so much as one civilian should be injured or killed by any of these tests, the Army would be moved out of the state, lock stock and barrel within 24 hours."

As any good reporter should, Larsen went to someone at White Sands for a comment. Larsen said, "This possibility isn't worrying White Sands Army officers, however. They are positive that no V-2 will ever get away from them far enough to hit a city or anyone who is not in the restricted area."

Given that context, read on.

V-2 Rockets Astray

After the first successful German V-2 launch at White Sands on May 10, 1946, the program took off with an average of almost two rocket firings each month. Things changed just a year later when, in May 1947, two V-2s crashed near population centers. Those accidents raised anxiety levels in the communities and pushed White Sands to come up with better safety procedures and technologies.

The first V-2 was launched on May 15, 1947 carrying instrumentation from the Naval Research Lab to measure cosmic radiation, atmospheric pressure, the solar spectrograph, and the makeup of the ionosphere.

According to both General Electric in their final report on the V-2 Missile Program and a report by the Army on Ordnance Department guided missiles, this V-2 flew almost perfectly except for one small detail. Instead of flying due north it "flew a remarkably straight course approximately 40 degrees east of north. That put its impact point about four miles northeast of Alamogordo. The Army report says the deviation from north was "undetected" during the first part of the flight.

Most old-timers say it crashed in the desert north of the current New Mexico Museum of Space History. In 1947, Alamogordo had less than 6,500 residents so there was no development yet in the area and no one was close by.

The General Electric report concluded that the guidance problem was probably caused by a faulty gyroscope.

The Army report states there was a premature explosion onboard the missile that was responsible for some parts and pieces being scattered at points west of the impact site. It says, "White Sands installed explosive charges to break up the missile to obtain lower impact velocities and thus aid instrument recovery. Premature explosion may have been caused by these explosive charges."

In 1995, Bob Callaway was interviewed by George House for an oral history with what is now the New Mexico Museum of Space History. Callaway was a high school student in 1947, just completing his freshman year. He and a friend, Bill Price, were in the street after school at Michigan and 15th Street, playing catch with a baseball.

He said, "About the time the ball was above the power lines, that we were throwing across back and forth to one another, the lines started shaking violently and we couldn't figure out what in the world was happening. About that time we got the sound wave from the explosion of the V-2." He said they didn't find out until later what had happened.

The next day was the final day of school and it was short. He said by 10 a.m. he and friends were in a truck headed to the crash site.

When they got to there, they were stopped by a

military perimeter and personnel working at the site. They sat nearby and watched as the soldiers winched the V-2 across an arroyo to a lowboy trailer. Once loaded, the military crew left.

However, one of the men went over to the boys and warned them to stay out of the hydrogen peroxide that was spilled on the ground and to beware of the spun glass insulation scattered about. According to Callaway, he added, "Outside of that, anything that's left you may have."

They didn't need any encouragement and began searching the crash site. He and his friends grabbed wiring panels and five steel tanks. Later they used the wiring to make model airplanes and the steel tanks were used to make portable welding units.

According to Callaway, some people went to the site before the military got there and relieved the V-2 of some valuable payload. He said that when the military arrived that evening, they discovered that five valuable cameras were missing. Security personnel from Alamogordo Air Base came in and started knocking on doors. They had the cameras back by midnight.

It really was a small town in those days.

Exactly two weeks later, on Thursday, May 29, a highly modified V-2 was launched from Launch Complex 33 as part of the secret Hermes II program. Like the Alamogordo rocket, this one flew fairly well but had that same kind of small guidance problem. Instead of traveling north, it went south and ended up crashing just outside of Juarez, Mexico within a half mile of Tepeyac Cemetery.

The site was about three and a half miles south of the Juarez business district.

Like the V-2 rockets that bombed London, this V-2 impacted at supersonic speed and created a whopper of an explosion. The next day the *El Paso Times* reported the crater was 50 feet across and 24 feet deep. That is pretty significant considering it hit on a rocky knoll.

The paper also reported the concussion shook buildings all through Juarez and El Paso. They reported an electric clock in the sheriff's El Paso office stopped at 7:32 p.m. and marked the time of the impact. The El Paso fire chief reported three windows broken in his office.

Alfonso Ariola Tejada and Jose Acosta Tejada, cousins, had just landed their small plane at Juarez's Buena Vista Airport when the V-2 struck just half a mile away. They reported to the *El Paso Times* that their plane shook and they could see the parked airplanes at the airport shake from the shock wave.

These two men rushed to the site. When they got there smoke was still rising from the crater, nearby shrubs were smoking, and the ground was still hot.

Apparently within minutes, nearby residents and those who hurried to the site started to gather the scattered small twisted pieces of metal as souvenirs. Mexican and U.S. military personnel eventually secured the site to prevent further theft of the debris.

There are many stories about what went wrong. Most focus on the gyroscope used for guidance and the belief it was wired backwards. So, instead of doing a slight pitch to the north after liftoff, the V-2 pitched slightly to the south and followed that path.

What is not clear is why the safety officer decided not to terminate the flight once it was determined the rocket was headed south. The *El Paso Times* reported that Lieutenant Colonel Harold Turner, the White Sands commander, said "there was an error in judgment on the part of the safety control department in not shutting off the rocket motor."

In the Army's report on Ordnance Department guided missiles, a summary states, "Observers at the emergency cut-off station realized the rocket was moving to the south slightly but judged the angle was so steep that the rocket would fall within the limits of the proving ground."

This is almost dead opposite of the legend that has grown up around this event. The word-of-mouth story is that the German safety officer realized the V-2 was headed south. He decided not to terminate the flight because he thought after shutting down the flow of fuel to the engine, the vehicle might coast far enough to crash in El Paso. To avoid such a catastrophe, he did nothing. If the story is true, he turned out to be right as the rocket flew over both El Paso and Juarez.

Could it be that a legend has grown to replace a mundane explanation with a more heroic one? Brilliant scientist quickly calculates the odds and makes the correct decision.

In addition to the news story the next day in the *Times*, the paper ran a commentary about the incident with the headline, "V-2 Rocket Too Close For Comfort." The first few lines were, "It could happen here! Standing on the rim of the gaping crater left by the wild V-2 rocket, I looked down upon the lights of

El Paso five miles away and shuddered. The 50-foot-wide cone could just as easily have been dug where the city lights seemed but a few steps away."

So, this accident was very obvious and very well documented by the news media. Since 1947, the relationship between the faceless government and its citizens has soured somewhat. Nowadays people don't believe government spokesmen and many assume embarrassing events were and are always covered up, that conspiracies abound behind the scenes.

For instance, while working at White Sands, I received an email asking when the government was going to come clean and admit that a V-2 had crashed outside Juarez. The writer pointed out that the May 29, 1947 V-2 flight is not on the official list of shots and he therefore assumed the U.S. was not admitting to the incident – a cover up was underway.

His suspicions are kind of funny when you see the articles, on the front-page no less, in the *El Paso Times*. Trying to cover that up certainly would have been like trying to put the toothpaste back in the tube.

But he was right about the launch not being in the later official lists of V-2 tests. That's because there is more to the story.

For starters it was not a standard V-2 rocket carrying a payload. It was part of a special program initially dubbed "Hermes II Project" that was launched to look into the idea of ramjet technology. It was classified stuff.

When Wernher von Braun and the other German paperclip scientists were sent off to Fort Bliss, they were not there just to assist in firing V-2 rockets at White Sands. In fact, according to most sources, within a year the General Electric personnel had a good handle on the V-2 and didn't need much in the way of help.

Instead, the Army and von Braun were interested in the German idea of a ramjet-powered vehicle. In theory, a ramjet-powered vehicle could go farther, faster and carry more payload than any other delivery system at the time. It is the

kind of technology that would give a country a big advantage in an arms race.

In a conventional jet engine, a large fan draws air into the engine and compresses it. Fuel is mixed with the air and ignited. The resulting hot gases exhaust out the rear of the engine providing a forward push or thrust.

This is the "V-2" that crashed outside Juarez on May 29, 1947. It was the first Hermes II rocket, number zero. It had much larger fins than a normal V-2 and the dummy wings on the nose were supposed to simulate the ramjet vehicle to be tested later. WSMR photo.

268

These engines are rather large, heavy, costly and fuel-hungry compared to a ramjet. A ramjet eliminates the mechanical fan by bringing air into a combustion chamber and compressing it simply by passing through the air at very high speed. Simply by going faster, it can bring in more air molecules and thus support even greater speed.

The Army's Hermes Project was looking for its ramjet vehicle to travel at 3,180 feet per second. That is 2,168 miles per hour. Their goal was for it to operate at an altitude of 65,000 feet.

Given the speed and fuel load goals, such a weapon could have delivered its payload to a target 225 miles away in less than seven minutes. This is very similar to missile capabilities but without the size and complexity.

The big problem with ramjet technology is that the jet has to be going very fast for it to work at all. In other words, it will not propel any kind of vehicle from a dead stop. It needs some kind of booster or other vehicle to get it up to speed, hundreds of miles per hour, before it can operate on it own.

The German idea was to use a modified V-2 rocket as that boost vehicle. They created a recess in the nose and top propellant tank to receive a mockup of their ramjet vehicle. Also, they modified and extended the fins to make it stable as it rose into the air.

The flight on May 29, 1947 was the first test and was designed to see how the package flew through the air and to check the V-2 performance.

Incidentally, the missile was numbered zero instead of number one. The legend behind this is that the project was told they could number their vehicles through five. Having worked with both German and U.S. bureaucracies, these creative people simply started with number zero so they could get an extra vehicle out of the program.

When this secret rocket crashed in Mexico and blew itself into a million pieces, the Army simply reinforced everyone's assumptions that it was just another V-2 flight. After all, it looked like a V-2, smelled like one and sounded like one. There was no evidence at the site to contradict the Army, so it was no effort at all to keep the Hermes project secret a little longer.

A Safety Tool Emerges

In response to these V-2s going awry in such a way that it was difficult for observers on the ground

to determine, early on, exactly which way the missile was going, Dr. George Gardner, with New Mexico State University's Physical Science Lab, developed "skyscreen" for Herb Karsch who was flight safety officer in those days.

As with many technologies where teams were involved, various other people are credited with developing the White Sands skyscreen. Colonel Turner, in a 1960s interview, said Carl Schooley "conjured up" the skyscreen. Tom Starkweather, in an article about PSL, wrote that PSL had a "cutoff" group under the leadership of Ivan Carbine. This group "designed, erected and operated the skyscreens." It is very possible all three gentlemen played a role in the development.

The original skyscreen was used until 1949 for the V-2s and Vikings launched at the Army launch area (LC-33) and Aerobees and Vikings from the Navy area (LC-35). It was the crude beginning of impact prediction as a safety tool.

According to retired Army Brigadier General Julius Braun who witnessed many launches at White Sands, the system was hard to use and not very accurate. The system was quickly outdated as the range was soon able to take tracking data from radars and present it on a plotting board with a nice map of the area.

Skyscreen was a simple viewing system that provided a reference for determining if the rocket was going too far left or right from the observer's perspective. The observer would look through a small telescope mounted on a pipe. Several feet away, on a straight line with the launch complex, was another pipe with a small open frame mounted on it – kind of like the opening in a picture frame. When correctly aligned, the observer could see the rocket on the pad by looking through the telescope.

A little further away from the observer was a second frame with two wires strung from the horizontal bar of this large pipe frame – another picture frame but much larger. The angle of these wires was calculated to correspond to the rocket's safe angle of attack when viewed by the observer.

The observer, by looking through the telescope, watched the rocket take off. As he continued to watch the vehicle, it would rise and be visible between the two wires.

As he watched, if the rocket stayed inside the space between the wires, they were assured it would

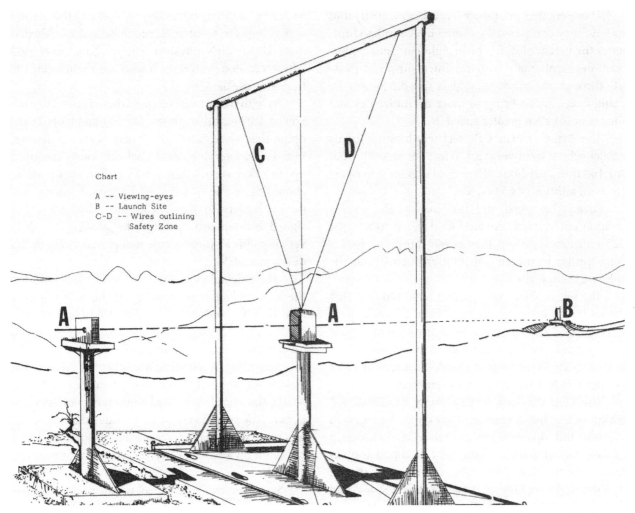

Chart

A -- Viewing-eyes
B -- Launch Site
C-D -- Wires outlining
      Safety Zone

From the old factsheet for the West Skyscreen. The other two skyscreens were placed behind the Army block-house and the Navy blockhouse for observers to look north and make sure the vehicles didn't stray east or west.

remain on White Sands. If it strayed beyond the left or right wire, the blockhouse was notified and the rocket was cut down.

Because one observer only saw one plane of the rocket's flight, a second observer was needed to see the other plane. So, there was a western skyscreen that told them if the rocket was going too far north and south. If this had existed for the Hermes II launch, the observer could have called for a flight termination very early and kept the vehicle on White Sands.

There were two skyscreens on the south to complete the coverage. These were located south of the launch complexes with the observers looking north through the launch pads. They could tell when the rocket was going too far to the west or east. If this had existed for the Alamogordo incident, the safety officials could have cut the missile long before it

got to the city – as long as the termination system worked. That's a different story.

Pershing Missiles Seek Their Own Destinations

The Pershing missile system was the Army's first really successful medium-range, ballistic missile system. For almost three decades, generations of Pershings were tested at White Sands and troops from the U.S. and Germany were given the chance to actually launch them.

All versions of the Pershing were two-stage vehicles with solid propellant motors. The total package of missiles and support equipment was very mobile and was designed to run along the roads of West Germany.

The Pershing I and IA were capable of flying 400 miles and the Pershing II had a range of 900 miles. The I and IA used the same missile but the support equipment was modernized and improved for the IA designation.

The Pershing II was a completely new missile with greater range and incredible pinpoint accuracy. The reentry vehicle or "warhead" could maneuver itself to the designated target. It was loaded with images of the target area, and the onboard computer compared them to the radar images provided by the onboard radar.

All versions could carry either a conventional explosive warhead or a nuclear one. Because the Pershing II was so accurate, planners were able to use much smaller nuclear warheads. If they had ever been used, the collateral damage would have been greatly reduced.

To say the least, with White Sands being only 100 miles long, it wasn't large enough to accommodate any full Pershing flight within its boundaries.

To make the tests possible, launches were moved off the missile range to a number of locations to give the Pershings both long- and short-range targets.

This led to launches from areas to the south on Fort Bliss at Hueco Range and McGregor Range. For longer shots, White Sands established launch points at Fort Wingate, just east of Gallup, New Mexico; Black Mesa, west of Blanding, Utah; Gilson Butte, south of Hanksville, Utah; and the Athena launch facility at Green River, Utah. The Idaho launch site for Pershing II was built but never used.

All totaled there were over 300 Pershing launches into White Sands from these sites.

On Nov. 19, 1964, a Pershing missile was launched around 3:30 p.m. from Hueco Range on Fort Bliss. It was supposed to fly north a relatively short distance, probably just over 100 miles, and hit a target area on the north end of White Sands.

It wasn't even close as the missile streaked 250 miles further north, crashing near the Continental Divide in the Rio Grande National Forest northwest of Creede, Colorado. Local residents heard the echoing sonic boom as it smashed into the mountains.

Missile range officials knew there was a problem right away. Radar information would have shown almost instantaneously that the Pershing was continuing north. Telemetry data also may have shown that the charges to end the flight did not detonate.

The Pershing predecessors, Corporal and Redstone, used liquid propellant systems. All that was necessary to stop the rocket motor from firing or thrusting was to cut off the flow of fuel. It could be done by a controller on the ground or by computer command.

Pershing, however, used a solid propellant. Once the motor was burning, there was no turning it off. It was a blowtorch with no switch.

Solid rocket propellant is self-contained with the fuel and oxidizer mixed together in a matrix that used to be rubber based. That is why you can launch them underwater or in the vacuum of space.

So, to get a Pershing to fly only 100 miles instead of its full range of 400, the program engineers had to find a way to cut off the thrust of the burning second stage. By today's standards, they came up with a rather primitive system but one that worked pretty well.

They devised a way to simply knock holes in the top portion of the rocket motor. This was accomplished with explosive charges that could be detonated on command. They were shaped charges that blew inward and punched the needed holes. With holes at the top and one at the bottom, the engine would have no thrust or push. At that point, the vehicle would simply coast on its current heading with gravity eventually pulling it down.

This method is still used today to terminate the flight of a rocket or missile that is judged to be going astray. With new guidance systems, such a technique is no longer used to stop a missile and have it drop on a target. In the case of the Pershing, the charges were part of the guidance system and simply used as part of the emergency destruct system.

Knowing everything there was to know about a Pershing and the laws of physics, the project people calculated exactly when to fire those charges on the rocket engine to bring it down on a particular point. On Nov. 19, 1964, however, the venting charges failed to fire - allowing the missile to just keep on flying.

The missile range responded immediately putting out notification to officials in New Mexico, Colorado and Washington, D.C. They told one little white lie when they talked to the news media. They said there were no explosives on board the missile.

They meant there was no warhead of any kind. However, since the venting charges obviously didn't work, there was a chance they were still with the vehicle. Luckily, no one was later injured by these explosives.

Radar coordinates and some computer analysis

put the Pershing up near Creede, and search parties were sent out. On the 21st, a helicopter was used to fly over the area, but nothing was found.

This continued to be the case for several days as helicopters flew search parties over the mountains. That late in the year there was already snow at the higher elevations, so trying to find a missile buried in fresh snow or in amongst the trees was almost impossible.

By the 26th, the Army gave it up as a lost cause because of winter conditions. In February 1965, they offered a $500 reward to anyone who found the thing.

In late June 1965, a small group of soldiers went into the area on the ground and spent over two weeks looking before giving it up. More soldiers returned at the first of August and rented horses and riding equipment from local ranchers to make better time searching in the rugged mountains. By late August, the military posses ended and everyone went home. However, they extended the deadline for the $500 reward to Sept. 30.

Then, near the end of September, Maurice Chaffee found an impact area with many pieces of debris. Chaffee was a geology student working on his doctorate.

Using the *Internet*, I found Chaffee in September 2009. He told me that for his project

someone took him up to the Continental Divide and dropped him off; he then walked down a different ridge each day surveying rock formations. The data was not only used for his thesis but also went to a mining company who paid him.

U.S. troops prepare a Pershing I missile for launch from Utah. WSMR photo.

One day he noticed, just by chance, a small indentation on the side of a ridge. He said he had heard about the Pershing so he looked closer and found twisted pieces of metal. He dug around until he found a piece with a serial number on it and turned it in at Creede.

He said he became a bit of a celebrity in tiny Creede for a while. The Army came back and flew him in "one of those banana shaped helicopters" so he could show them the spot. He said they showed him a rectangle on a map where they had calculated the missile had landed. He said the spot he found was right in the middle of it.

Since he found it before the reward expired, the government did send him a check for something less than $500. Taxes had been taken out. He said the money was a boon to a poor graduate student.

Others weren't so lucky. The reward offer attracted the attention of all kinds of people. The missile range received letters from folks in places like Montana and Idaho and as far away as Argentina claiming they heard or saw something that might be the Pershing missile.

Chaffee earned his doctorate and ended up working a 40-year career with the U.S. Geological Survey. He retired in 2000.

The Army didn't bother to tell him he only found part of the Pershing. He was surprised when I told him it wasn't until almost 18 years later that the second stage and other major components were found.

In the fall of 1982, a hunter showed the Army where the big pieces of the Pershing were located. Personnel from Fort Carson, Colorado and White Sands eventually responded. They found some pieces of missile weighing several hundred pounds each and those pesky explosive charges. They were still viable and an explosive ordnance disposal crew from Fort Carson destroyed them.

By the end of October 1982, White Sands was finally able to close the book on that Pershing. Only in the modern West did today's Army still put up reward posters and outfit soldiers like mounted cavalry from the century before.

A year later, on Oct. 6, 1965, a Pershing launched from Gilson Butte, Utah went astray and had to be destroyed. Calvin Wells reported finding pieces of the missile on Oct. 11, north of Blanding. An aerial search finally found the sensitive warhead section in Recapture Canyon near Blanding on the 13th.

Almost two years later on Tuesday, Sept. 12, 1967, two Pershing missiles were launched from the Blanding launch facility on Black Mesa. The second missile was launched at 1:48 a.m. and turned out to be a repeat of Creede but in the opposite direction. This missile crashed just across the Mexican border south of Van Horn, Texas more than 150 miles beyond the target area.

Troops from the U.S. Seventh Army, stationed in Europe, fired the two missiles as part of their annual service practice in Utah.

News coverage was immediate and widespread. That night Walter Cronkite mentioned it on CBS and The *Huntley-Brinkley Report* covered it for NBC. Since the impact area was very remote in our neighboring country, only a few Mexican newspapers reported on it.

Permission to search came fairly quickly from the Mexican government as long as civilian aircraft were used. In the meantime, Mexican rancher Felipe Chavez-Garcia showed up with a piece of debris from the missile.

On Sept. 22, the missile range announced they were still searching for the main missile components but they were seeing numerous scattered pieces. Officials concluded the second stage and reentry vehicle had broken up and scattered before striking the ground.

In a follow-up the next day, range officials were able to announce they had successfully concluded the search. They were able to find and return "critical parts" of the missile.

It wasn't so easy the next time.

Athena Missile Goes Deep

On July 11, 1970, Athena missile number 122 was launched from Green River, Utah, in the middle of the night. Like the previous firings, which the Air Force began in 1964, this Athena was programmed to impact on White Sands Missile Range. Instead project and range personnel watched helplessly as it rocketed south heading deep into Mexico.

In fact, the missile went so far south, radars lost the vehicle as it descended over the horizon and, at first, officials were not sure where it struck.

This international incident was made worse when it was soon revealed that the Athena nosecone or "reentry vehicle" carried two small containers of cobalt 57, a radioactive element. To top it off, the

Mexican government quickly reminded the United States about the Pershing missile fired from Blanding, Utah, in September 1967 that crashed just across the border in Mexico south of Van Horn.

One can only imagine the telephone lines glowing red hot as calls crisscrossed the country in the wee hours of Saturday (Where is it? Who calls the Mexican government? Do we call the president? Do we have to tell anyone there is a radiological source onboard?). While top officials dealt with notification, contractor and government managers called on key personnel and everyone scrambled for their emergency response plans. It was looking like it might be a long, hot summer.

At 50 feet tall and 16,000 pounds, the Athena was assembled as a subscale model or simulator for an intercontinental ballistic missile. The Air Force used it to study reentry characteristics of warheads and other space vehicles. Going this route saved the Air Force money and allowed them to collect high-quality data from the land-based instrumentation at White Sands. Full-scale testing was done at sea. The Navy was even involved as the flights provided information for their Polaris missile program.

The missile's four stages burned solid propellant. The first two stages were used to push the Athena to an altitude of about 200 miles. As the vehicle coasted, computers reoriented the final two stages so they were pointing down and toward White Sands. Once this was accomplished, stages three and four fired in sequence to shoot the reentry vehicle back through the atmosphere at speeds of 15,250 miles per hour – that's 4.25 miles per second.

They experimented with different shaped reentry vehicles and different materials to protect them. Their goal was to make the warhead survivable and invisible. Also, they brought the reentry vehicles in at different angles to see what difference that made.

The Green River launch complex was built to accommodate the Athena program with the first launch in 1964 and the last in 1973. A total of 141 Athena missiles were fired. Green River was also used for Pershing launches.

Other land acquired for the testing included booster drop areas south of Moab, Utah and near Datil, New Mexico. In addition, the two ABRES (Advanced Ballistic Re-Entry System) call-up areas on the west side of White Sands were established for the incoming missiles - in case they fell short.

To collect the data for these tests, a huge array of instruments, especially radars, was needed. Decades after these tests, the clutter fences shielding two of the radars still provoke questions like, "What is the elephant fence for?"

Clutter fences prevent signals from the edges of the radars from bouncing back from nearby objects like hills and buildings. Those stray returns can confuse and complicate the position calculations.

In the southeast corner of the missile range, just north of the Orogrande Range Camp, radars and associated clutter fences were put in place. The RAMPART (Radar Advanced Measurement Program) and RAM radars were erected and used by the Air Force to collect data on their Athena reentry vehicles coming through the atmosphere. The RAM, with its 84-foot diameter antenna, sits inside a clutter fence just over 100-feet high. The fence's circumference is 2,200 feet.

According to Colonel Len Sugerman, head of the Air Force's Inland Range Field Office at White Sands, the fence gave researchers almost 10 additional seconds of "clean" data from each test. Sugerman was on hand to insert the last bolt in place when the fence was completed in December 1969.

The RAMPART radar is outside the fence with the RAM slaved to it. It was needed to direct the RAM radar to acquire the vehicle to be tracked. RAM generated a very narrow pencil-like beam for precision tracking and was virtually useless in finding a small object in the big sky. Once it was locked on the object, the RAM provided excellent tracking out to a thousand miles.

The RAM radar was also used for Pershing and Navy sounding rocket shots.

At the same time, other organizations were interested in defending against incoming ICBMs so they piggybacked on the tests to see what kind of radar signatures they could collect during the different shots. Also they wanted to see if they could tell the difference between a real warhead and a decoy.

The Advanced Research Projects Agency (ARPA) built the AMRAD (ARPA Measurement Radar) just to the east of RAMPART. This radar had a 60-foot diameter antenna with a 104-foot-high clutter fence stretching around a 2,000-foot perimeter.

On a clear day, these clutter fences are visible from San Augustin Pass on U.S. Highway 70, almost 30 miles to the west. They look like large buildings.

It isn't until you get much closer that you recognize them as just very big fences.

Athena #122 was scheduled to launch at 2:40 a.m. according to news releases sent out by White Sands prior to the test. Area residents around Green River and Moab would often stay up late or get up early to watch the Athena and Pershing fireworks provided by White Sands.

There also were fireworks on the receiving end. According to Pat Quinlan, who was in Range Control at Bldg. 300 watching telemetry and radar data, the first part of the flight for #122 was textbook. Data from the telemetry and radar tracking systems clearly showed where the missile was during the first couple of minutes.

Quinlan explained that during reentry White Sands always lost contact with the Athenas. He said it was the same phenomena the space shuttle experiences when it reenters the atmosphere. There is a communications blackout caused by the plasma surrounding the vehicle that is generated by the intense heat from friction with the air.

Quinlan said he and others usually went out on the north fire escapes of Bldg. 300 to look for the telltale glow of the Athena coming into the atmosphere

Typical Athena launch at Green River. WSMR photo.

over White Sands. He said it always showed to the north about 45 degrees above the horizon.

On July 11, 1970, it was different. "Suddenly, the glow appeared almost straight overhead and the reentry streak trailed to the south," Quinlan said. He said it wasn't long before the phones started ringing.

According to a historical summary of this flight from the Air Force Systems Command, "An inflight malfunction, fourth stage motor ignition on V123D, caused both stage four and the payload to fly off course; for ignition of the fourth stage occurred prior to mid-course guidance maneuvers and provided a range extension of approximately 400 (nautical miles) and subsequent impact in Mexico."

Although the missile appeared in the wrong spot in the sky, Quinlan pointed out that the range systems did exactly what they were supposed to do. As the Athena emerged from the plasma cloud, telemetry signals started arriving. The data was processed and used to aim the narrow band radars so they could track the missile until it disappeared over the horizon. This information was used afterwards to forecast where the Athena should have impacted.

As officials wrestled with the unknowns the Athena dealt them, there was a more immediate problem up on the western boundary of the range. Dale Green, who was the Uprange Division Chief at Stallion, said he received a call early Saturday morning telling him to get a fire crew and equipment out to the Engel Gate. The gate is on the missile range's western boundary in the San Andres Mountains. The road out the gate leads to Truth or Consequences. Apparently, burning fuel falling from the Athena started a grass and brush fire near the gate.

Green said they couldn't accomplish much on Saturday because of the rough terrain. They went back on Sunday with a bulldozer to cut fire lines. However, the dozer's clutch went out on a steep incline and they ended up letting the fire burn itself out by Tuesday.

Then Green received orders to travel to the main post on Tuesday for a noon meeting with the commanding general. He was told he would be going to Mexico to retrieve the errant Athena when it was found. Planning started immediately to figure out what equipment and people would be needed.

Of course, the big question was, "Where is it?" There was some speculation that the nosecone could have burned up on reentry and never hit the ground.

For the first day or so, the newspaper stories reported officials saying it probably came down in a "remote mountainous area 150 miles south of Juarez."

Carlos Bustamante, who was working as the project engineer for SRAM (Short Range Attack Missile) in the National Range, got a call in the middle of the night from Austin Vick telling him to pack his bags, he was going to Mexico. Vick was with the Plans and Operations Office at the time and knew about Bustamante's background.

It turns out Bustamante was uniquely qualified to be on the team that went to search for the Athena. Earlier Bustamante worked as a project engineer for Athena and was involved in the selection of Green River as the launch site. So he knew the Athena program, he knew how White Sands worked, and he was fluent in Spanish.

Bustamante joined a small team led by Lieutenant Colonel Lowell (Buzz) Knight. The team's instructions were that they were on their own and Bustamante was the only one authorized to speak to the Mexican officials about the program and their efforts.

By the time the group left on July 16, the data reduction folks calculated that the Athena was 450 miles into Mexico in a south-southeast direction in the area of the boundary between Durango and Chihuahua. The team flew down in two small contracted airplanes while others drove two vehicles down for their use. They established a base in Torreon, the largest town in the area. They expected to be done in four days.

The team made contact with their Mexican counterparts who included some engineers and two army officers. After two days of answering questions posed by the officers nothing happened.

Back in the States, reporters were looking for answers. One news service correspondent asked Jim Lovelady in the White Sands Public Affairs Office when the Athena would be found. Lovelady told the correspondent it might take days, weeks or months. This was turned into a quote saying White Sands expected to find the Athena within 24 hours.

Of course, the folks in Washington were not amused; they put out the order that only they would answer questions about the incident.

In Mexico, Bustamante quickly realized the two army officers spoke English. After those first futile days, he invited them for drinks in the bar. He bought a few rounds, then told them he knew they spoke English and he was tired of translating.

It worked. They admitted they had trained in the United States at the War College and had done some liaison work with NASA. After that, the two sides got down to business. Another plus was that Knight could be directly involved since the talks would be in English.

In the meantime, the Athena impact point was further refined. Air Force specialists said the nosecone would be in an area 1.5 miles long and only half a mile wide. The only problem was no one could put that ellipse on a particular spot on the ground because there were no landmarks to go by. Bustamante said it was near a small town called Ceballos about 100 miles from Torreon.

The terrain is open desert and mountainous with very few people. The team flew aerial searches day after day. They took reports from anyone in the area who might have seen or heard something. They landed on back roads and pastures to interview ranchers.

According to Bustamante, the aircraft got quite a workout. The planes were flown by former Navy carrier pilots whose flying skills were perfect for searching empty desert. He said if anyone on board saw something in the desert below, the pilots had a knack for making quick tight turns and returning them to the exact spot for a second look. It was like searching over the ocean.

One day the second plane was coming in late, after dark. Normally this wouldn't be a problem but the one-man airport had closed down at sunset and turned off the runway lights. Landing in the dark on a primitive strip was not okay.

This is the one time Bustamante played his wildcard. The team wasn't quite on its own. Bustamante and Knight knew that the Mexican government had assigned one of their secret service agents to assist the Americans. All they had was a phone number and the guy's name.

On this evening Bustamante called the agent and explained the situation. The Mexican rep told them to just have the plane circle and the lights would be on in 10 minutes. They were.

Another time one of the team members became seriously ill. Bustamante called the special agent who sent a doctor. When the doctor said the man needed to get back to medical attention in the United

States immediately, the agent quickly made the arrangements for one of the search planes to fly unhampered to El Paso.

By the first of August, after days of searching, they still had not found the nosecone. On Aug. 2 the nosecone was finally found using a specially equipped aircraft from the Atomic Energy Commission operated by EG&G Inc. The plane was equipped with a scintillometer and a spectrum analyzer calibrated for cobalt 57. It was called ARMS, an acronym for Aerial Radiological Measuring System. It only took them three days to locate the package.

Since the cobalt sources were described as "two small pellets imbedded in tungsten" this was an impressive display of technology by EG&G.

Interestingly the Air Force Systems Command historical summary claimed "Except for the fourth stage, which was believed to have burned during reentry, V123D payload was successfully recovered on 18 July 1970." Given all the other reports and eyewitness accounts, one has to assume the Air Force's author made a significant error in fact.

Bustamante said his ground team then followed directions radioed from the plane to get to the general area. For the last dash cross-country, they followed a trail of flour sacks dropped from the plane to the impact site. Bustamante has a photograph of himself standing on a dune with a shovel overhead indicating to the aircraft crew that they were at the site.

What the WSMR team found was a small crater area with just a few pieces of metal and some contaminated sand.

The nosecone carried the two small pellets of cobalt 57 to measure the ablative material on the outside of the nosecone as it burned off and protected the vehicle during reentry.

Bustamante's team and the Mexican scientific team measured the radiation levels all around the site and found it to be about six tenths of a millirem per hour – just about what the levels are at Trinity Site today.

This is a very low level radiation. There are many places on earth naturally more radioactive. To put it in perspective, the American Nuclear Society estimates Americans receive between 26 and 96 millirems every year just from the sun -- depending on elevation. The top end of this spread is for people living above 8,500 feet.

The night they found the Athena the whole team, including the Mexican escorts, celebrated with a banquet in Torreon. Bustamante said White Sands reluctantly paid the $700 bill for the evening.

After conferring with the two Mexican colonels, Bustamante said he thought the whole thing was over. They found the debris from the nosecone and the radiological source (they never did find the third or fourth stages of the Athena). The radiation levels were very low and very isolated. Both parties thought they would fill in the hole and that would be it.

However, a few days later officials and radiological teams from higher levels of both governments showed up at the site and the situation changed. They confirmed the initial readings, but after lengthy negotiations the Mexican government requested the site be reduced to a radiation level of one half a millirem or less.

What followed were several more weeks of negotiations between the two governments on how to accomplish the recovery. The basic premise was that personnel from the U.S. would travel to Mexico to remove most of the contaminated dirt and bury the rest.

Every detail was talked about and planned. The folks in Washington prepared contingency news releases based on vehicle accidents and other vague possibilities.

There were many restrictions. For instance, according to Dale Green, the team had to travel by train and all military markings had to be removed from the railcars and the earthmoving equipment sent down.

The train consisted of three Pullman-type cars to house the personnel, one dining car, three boxcars, nine flat cars for heavy equipment, two water tankers and a fuel tanker. It left Orogrande late on Sept. 23 and was timed to clear customs in Juarez just after midnight on Sept. 24.

The recovery operation was dubbed "Operation Sand Patch" and was commanded by Colonel Thomas Kearns.

The train arrived at its destination on a siding at Carrillo, Mexico, about 4 p.m. on Sept. 24. From Carrillo the team would have to travel just over 20 miles cross country each day to get to the crash site. At the time Carrillo was a tiny community of about 100 souls with very few modern conveniences. The only electrical power came from a small generator used by a salt company outside of town.

The men ate breakfast and dinner in the train's dining car and had lunch delivered to the site. They slept on the train. Green said the food was good and sleeping quarters were air-conditioned.

On the 25th, team members unloaded equipment and started building a road to the crash site. Then the heavens opened up with rain falling for days.

The bad weather caused a huge delay. Team members spent a great deal of time just getting vehicles out of the mud each day. Green said on that first day every vehicle was stuck. The only vehicle not in the mud was a large bulldozer still on the train. He decided not to unload it yet because, "I figured we would just have one more vehicle to get unstuck."

Eventually, after several days, it quit raining and they were able to move back and forth to the site. The loading of barrels with contaminated soil was completed on Oct. 1, late in the afternoon. Sixty drums of soil were prepared for shipping plus three 19-gallon drums containing anti-contamination clothing, rubber boots and gloves.

The news reports of how much soil was being removed were greatly exaggerated. One newspaper stated that 200,000 tons of dirt would be shipped out.

Some very low-level radioactive soil was buried in two trenches, but basically the contamination was no deeper than a few inches across the site.

Once the barrels were back at the train it took a few days to clean and load everything. But there was a problem. They were too good at their jobs and finished early. The Mexican government wouldn't let them leave until the agreed upon date.

According to Green, that left the team with some time to do work for the Carrillo community. They bladed streets, reinforced the check dam above the town, and worked on the water system.

Also, they fixed the single television set in town and got it working with power from the salt company generator. Green said many of the residents had never seen a TV broadcast before. It probably explains why the locals were not disappointed when all they got on the set were ghostly images from a distant city.

The train left Carrillo just after midnight on Oct. 5. It hit the Juarez rail yard about 4 p.m. and was given almost immediate clearance. Green thinks the radiation warning stickers on the barrels probably hastened the inspection.

By the close of business on Oct. 7, Operation Sand Patch was complete when everything was unloaded from the train. The barrels of radioactive sand were stored near the missile range's El Paso gate inside the fences at the Nuclear Effects Laboratory.

According to George Wentz, former chief of WSMR's Radiological Health Office, the barrels of sand were eventually just dumped in the desert. He said the half-life of cobalt 57 is only 270 days. So, after 10 generations or just 7.4 years, the radiation in the drums was undetectable.

A report on Operation Sand Patch put the cost for the recovery effort at $104,000.

While this was going on, the Air Force halted Athena launches and investigated what went wrong. White Sands personnel I talked to mentioned the fourth stage igniting prematurely, causing it to tip up and head out on a trajectory to the south.

An Air Force history of the Athena project states that two failure modes were postulated, but without any of the third or fourth stage hardware to examine, the report concluded, "instrumentation data of Mission 122 did not provide conclusive evidence of the failure mode."

In the absence of factual information, myth and rumor often sprout. This incident is a perfect example.

Basically, the myth says there is an area in Mexico called the "Zone of Silence" that is like the Bermuda Triangle. The implication is that some physical anomaly in Mexico caused the Athena to head toward it.

Of course, such things usually require a conspiracy and cover-up because some government agency knows all about these things and keeps them secret. In this case the story is that the recovery team was actually a group of NASA scientists investigating the zone of silence. Bustamante, Green and the others should ask for supplemental pay from NASA.

Athena flights resumed on Jan. 9, 1971. The program ended in the summer of 1973.

In addition to an Athena missile in the White Sands Museum's Missile Park, the program donated one to the city of Green River, Utah in 1968. It stands in the city park.

To conclude, I have to throw in this Athena story simply because my wife and I live in Jim and Marion Carter's old house in Las Cruces. In 1968, Colonel Jim Carter was head of the Air Force's Athena Test

Field Office, coordinating operations with White Sands. On March 29, 1968 the 100th Athena was launched from Green River.

According to the Atlantic Research Corporation MSD News, the launch was extra special for Bruce Brawley, the project's guidance supervisor. In his time with the company he had participated in 98 of the previous 99 Athena launches.

As the first two stages of the missile fired normally, Brawley is quoted as very formally asking, "Project Control, the Guidance Supervisor requests permission to manually fire the 100th Athena." In response, Athena test conductor Colonel Carter coolly said, "Shoot the juice to her, Bruce."

Firefly Into Los Alamos

Another dramatic impact, for different reasons, occurred on Aug. 4, 1969. During the test of an Air Force vehicle called the Firefly, the little jet-propelled drone malfunctioned and parachuted itself right into the middle of Los Alamos, New Mexico. during the lunch hour. That's right, the same lab that developed the first atomic bomb.

The vehicle was the latest unmanned spy plane designed to fly thousands of miles and photograph targets inside China and elsewhere. The Air Force classified its very existence as "secret."

One slight problem - hundreds of people watched the thing softly and harmlessly land in town. In typical manner, the missile range's Public Affairs Office wrote a news release about the test and prepared to answer queries. In such a situation the program approves the release of all information.

Somehow some bright Air Force brass back in their headquarters missed the fact that this was seen and photographed by lots of people in a very public area. They really thought they could keep the lid on it. Maybe they thought Los Alamos was still a Manhattan Project facility with everything buttoned down like when General Groves ruled the day.

They dithered about for five hours tinkering with the news release trying to cover up what happened. Finally, they fell back on the story that the vehicle was a high altitude target.

During those five hours, the Air Force insisted on keeping the classification on the Firefly. The White Sands Public Affairs Office was requested to prevent publication of any photos. This earned White Sands a major headache as the media lambasted the range's lame attempts to hush it up. To no one's surprise, media outlets printed the photos anyway.

No One Noticed This One

Not every off-range impact drew as much attention as these well-known incidents. In fact, one didn't make the papers at all.

Vern Haverstick, a long-time Raytheon employee, wrote an article about the history of his company at the missile range for the White Sands Pioneer Group's newsletter in 1986. In the article he related many details of HAWK (an air defense missile manufactured by Raytheon) testing at White Sands. Over the years more than 800 test firings took place at WSMR.

He wrote, "One more unusual HAWK flight comes mind. This was an Improved HAWK fired from uprange. Probably no one in Alamogordo knows to this day that a HAWK overflew their city."

The self-destruct system failed as the missile headed for the White Sands boundary and, because of the missile's altitude and speed, it landed in the Sacramento Mountains. According to Haverstick, where the missile landed was "a freak of luck" because it crashed on "a ten acre piece of government property at a WSMR telemetry site in a remote area."

Haverstick was pleased there was no negative publicity about the HAWK gone astray. And it was probably a good thing nothing slowed down development of the missile system. By the 1980s, Haverstick wrote, "HAWK has proven itself to be the most effective and reliable surface-to-air missile in the free world."

18

Visitors

Jack Benny to JFK

When I decided to include a chapter on missile range visitors, it seemed like it would be an easy task. All I had to do was include a list of all the famous and important people who stuck their noses in the door. Turns out there are too many to list them all. To complicate it I had to figure out what constitutes being famous.

Some of the White Sands visitors are obviously very famous and everyone recognizes them. Examples are President Kennedy, Clint Eastwood and Walter Cronkite.

Others are a step back. Some readers will recognize Ben Burtt, the Oscar-winning sound producer for Lucas Films, but others won't have a clue he designed the sound effects for the Star Wars movies. Also, many young people probably won't be familiar with names like Jack Benny or Audie Murphy simply because they belong to a period now decades past.

Then there are visitors who are not necessarily famous but who are very important because of their position or stature. There are many behind-the-scenes people in all walks of life who are really movers and shakers – you just never hear about them. A lot of government and industry leaders fit into this category.

And now, in contemporary America, we have people who are famous for no apparent reason whatsoever. They are people without any real substance or character. They have accomplished nothing and hold no important positions. They are simply presented to us by the media and other outlets as a form of entertainment and for some reason Americans love to watch. I call them the "phantom famous."

I don't think any of the visitors I will discuss are

phantoms but I imagine that is open to debate.

The number of missile range visitors today is tiny compared to the early years when White Sands was the buzz for American cutting-edge weapons technology. In 1956, when the workforce totaled only 7,500 military and civilian personnel (contractors not counted), White Sands had close to 20,000 visitors. According to the White Sands newspaper, visitors ranged from individuals to several groups with as many as 400 persons.

In 1959, White Sands had a rare royal visit. The guest was Crown Prince Constantine of Greece who was only 18 at the time but in line to become king of Greece. On Feb. 3 he visited, received several briefings, and watched Honest John and Nike Hercules launches. Constantine must have been on a tour of the United States because on March 4 he met with President Eisenhower in Washington.

Like many royals he received quite a diverse education and training in many fields. For instance, he served short stints with all three Greek military services and attended NATO special weapons training. His background also included sports; he won a gold medal in sailing during the 1960 Olympics in Rome.

In 1964, the very-young Constantine was crowned king of Greece. The same year he married Princess Anne-Marie of Denmark.

The good times didn't last long, however. In 1973, he was essentially booted out when the country abolished the monarchy. He now lives in quasi-exile in England.

Many famous and important people tend to be a little different from the rest of us. Some of them are very demanding, in an unpleasant way, and it raises the proverbial chicken and egg question. Did fame and fortune turn them into difficult, demanding, egocentric characters or are those qualities inherent and responsible for pushing them ahead – making success possible?

Most of the famous people I ran into doing my job were agreeable enough, but my encounters were very limited. However, there were a few exceptions. In early 2006, I got to see Michael Bay, the Hollywood movie director and producer, in operation. I hesitate to say I met him because I was probably perceived as the "pain in the butt" bureaucrat sent to babysit his group.

He directed such movies as *Armageddon*, *Pearl Harbor* and the *Transformer* series. He has also been the producer for such gems as *The Texas Chainsaw Massacre: The Beginning* and *The Amityville Horror*.

I had no idea who he was as I worked with a Dream Works location scout, Richard Klotz, and location manager, Emre Sonmez, for the first Transformer movie. They were looking for some locations corresponding to planned scenes in the movie.

I spent a couple of days driving them around to look at empty desert landscape, sand dune areas, remote gates and roads. Also we took a look at the

missile range's "tank farm." The tank farm is located at the Small Missile Range just north of U.S. Highway 70. It is a place where dozens and dozens of tanks and other obsolete military vehicles are stored for later use as targets.

A contractor keeps a fleet of these vehicles running, so a whole column of tanks moving down a road can be presented as targets for any weapons program with such a need. It is not an easy task, since the spare parts supply-line for most of these vehicles dried up years ago. Also, much of the foreign equipment has no sources for parts except the Black Market.

One tactic the contractor employs is to scavenge parts from excess vehicles to keep some running. The donor vehicles can then be used as static targets.

When the tank farm was first established, many people driving by on the highway noticed it. Soon it was brought to our attention there were some paranoia-driven New Mexico militia who feared the old tanks were being positioned for the eventual takeover of the area by invading United Nations troops.

Over the years such a notion has been proven ludicrous for two reasons. The first is the unreliability of the equipment. There is no way such junk could

The missile range's tank farm at the Small Missile Range. These obsolete tanks become targets for weapon systems testing at WSMR. Dream Works used the facility in the first "Transformer" movie. Photo by the author.

be driven from the site to Las Cruces, Alamogordo and El Paso. Most of the vehicles would never make it.

The second reason is the idea that the U.N. could successfully invade the third most populous country in the world. It is so preposterous it is falling-down funny. When these rumors were going around, U.N. peacekeeping troops in 1995 were being captured by a few Bosnian Serbs and used as human shields by the Serbs to protect their assets. A large motorcycle gang might be a more realistic threat.

Michael Bay's scouts weren't interested in this history, however. They needed a weapons storage area that could be attacked by one of the gigantic alien robots starring in Transformers. When they saw the tank farm they were pretty sure it was perfect.

After we found a number of other likely sites to include several places in the white sand dunes on the eastern boundary of the missile range, it was time for Bay to fly in and look them over. First, Bay and his team inspected a number of places on Holloman Air Force Base and then came to White Sands.

I met them at Holloman and we drove to the prime sand dune site. As they trudged around in the sand I noticed the organization was very Army-like. At the center was Michael Bay, kind of like a high-ranking general, surrounded by a cloud of minions ready to respond to his every whim. Everywhere Bay moved, the cloud moved with him. "Yes sir, yes sir."

After looking over the site, Bay announced he liked it very much. In fact, he didn't even want to bother seeing the second site we had found. So it was on to the tank farm.

I led them in their cars and vans out through Holloman to U.S. Highway 70 for the 30-mile drive to the tank farm. I was in a government vehicle with Emre Sonmez, the location manager – a very nice person. Then again, Emre was not famous.

After a few minutes Sonmez's cell phone rang. He listened and then apologized to me before asking me if we could drive faster. Apparently Bay doesn't have a lot of patience and driving the speed limit is a waste of his valuable time. I had the cruise control set at the speed limit and he wanted to kick it up.

Here's the rub. I was driving a government vehicle with an obvious federal plate. There is nothing citizens like to do more than call in to report a speeding government employee. It happens all the time. Questions are asked, and if you are lucky, you

get a verbal warning telling you not to do it again.

There was no way I was going to risk the wrath of the U.S. Army simply to get him there a few minutes early. I told Sonmez we'd get there driving the speed limit, but Mr. Bay could go ahead to the gate and wait for us there if he wanted.

Once we got to the tank farm several people from Dream Works came up to me to apologize for Bay's behavior. Again, it was just like the Army where loyal officers cover for their star-studded bosses. They said he was often like that and they wanted to make sure he didn't alienate anyone from White Sands or the Army. They still had a movie to make.

I didn't make any big deal about it and just chalked it up as another interesting tale to tell about working at White Sands. After all, his movie had the backing of very high officials in the Pentagon. I'm sure any offense I might have taken wouldn't have gotten past the first person I talked to.

Once the company actually committed to filming on White Sands, the project was turned over to Patrick Romero and his project engineers in the Material Test Directorate. They took care of many of the paying military customers who came to White Sands to test. They were equipped to handle the required documentation, the flow of money and the many last minute requirements that always pop up in any project. Later they related similar encounters with Bay's needy nature.

Jack Benny and Ann Blyth

The Dec. 23, 1951 issue of the *Las Cruces Sun-News* reported, "Film and radio stars Jack Benny and Mary Livingston will brighten Christmas Day for servicemen 'marooned' at White Sands Proving Ground. Benny and his wife are scheduled to put on a personal appearance show in the post theater at 4 p.m. Christmas Day."

In 1951 there weren't many people more famous than Jack Benny. People all across America tuned into his radio show during the 1930s and 40s, and it was still going strong in the 1950s. He modified the radio program for television and during the 50s he was appearing in both mediums.

People loved the fact that every year he was still only 39 years old. They loved his stinginess and how spending a dollar for a Christmas gift for his announcer could drive him crazy. He originated the joke where he is held up by a thief who demands,

"Your money or your life." Benny hesitates and the thief repeats, "Look buddy, your money or your life." Benny then responds in an exasperated voice, "I'm thinking it over."

Audiences loved how he was a natural foil for his friends and guests like Fred Allen, George Burns, Bob Hope and all the other big names from that era. And they loved the whole set-up with his supposed inability to play the violin.

Jack Benny was born Benjamin Kubelsky but simplified it as he got deeper into vaudeville. At first he played serious violin with a piano accompanist on vaudeville stages. He soon realized he was getting more laughs, applause and attention by telling jokes. The violin was then relegated to a prop for his many humor routines.

It is hard to think of an entertainer in contemporary America who would be as well known and liked as Jack Benny was in 1951. By then kids had grown up listening to him and were raising families of their own. Others were growing old with Benny and would follow him through the early 60s to the end of his television days.

Mary Livingston was Benny's wife and often appeared on his shows. Her role was to make snide remarks at the expense of her husband.

Also visiting White Sands with Benny and his wife that Christmas was Ann Blyth, a young actress and singer.

The troupe appeared in the new post theater that was just opened the month before. There are photos in the White Sands archives of Benny and Blyth on stage together. In one photo he seems to be introducing her so she can sing. In another photo Benny is playing his violin, probably as part of some joke.

The best photo was taken outside and shows Benny sitting astride a WAC Corporal rocket waving to the crowd as smoke pours from the rocket's nozzle. The rocket is setting on a stand with the nose slightly raised and has "White Sands Proving Ground" painted on the side. Benny is sitting on a western saddle and holding a lariat in the photo.

Comedian Jack Benny seems to be telling actress/singer Ann Blyth, "Don't worry. I've ridden rockets much bigger than this." Soon after, range officials put a smoke grenade in the WAC Corporal's engine nozzle to make it look like the rocket was preparing to take off. WSMR photo.

On the ground, next to the rocket, Ann Blyth is laughing and looking up at him. The staging was probably a perfect time for some Benny adlibs.

Since this was part of a USO tour, the Benny entourage met with soldiers at Fort Bliss and White Sands. At the missile range they ate Christmas dinner with the enlisted men and at Bliss they visited soldiers stuck in William Beaumont Army Hospital.

Audie Murphy

On Jan. 26, 1945, a young second lieutenant named Audie Murphy found himself in France facing an attack of German tanks and infantry. Murphy's subsequent actions earned him the Medal of Honor.

Murphy ordered his men to withdraw into the woods while he stayed behind to call in enemy positions for artillery units. When the German tanks came crashing up to his position, he manned the .50-caliber machine gun from a nearby burning tank destroyer. Using this weapon he proceeded to clear the area of German infantry, killing at least 50 of the enemy.

The tanks retreated without infantry support and Murphy, even with a leg wound, organized his troops to counterattack. They forced the Germans to withdraw and were able to hold the woods the Germans were trying to capture.

Murphy's Medal of Honor citation states, "Murphy's indomitable courage and his refusal to give an inch of ground saved his company from possible encirclement and destruction, and enabled it to hold the woods which had been the enemy's objective."

Murphy went on to become the most decorated U.S. soldier from WWII (33 awards to include decorations from France and Belgium) and something of a movie star in Hollywood. He appeared in more than 25 films that were mostly westerns.

In 1949, Murphy's autobiography *To Hell and Back* became a best seller. He then starred in the film version, also called *To Hell and Back*, in 1955. The movie was Universal's highest grossing movie until it was surpassed by *Jaws* in 1975.

On Sept. 23 and 24, 1960 Murphy visited White Sands as part of an Army movie production. The Army was filming *Broken Bridge* which was described as a "full-length color documentary" by the Wind and Sand newspaper.

According to the paper, "The film takes Murphy back to Europe to revisit his wartime unit. The visit grows into a tour of today's Army defenses, the hardware undreamed of when Murphy and millions of other GIs were battling from the coast of Normandy to free Nazi-occupied Europe."

At White Sands, the crew filmed Murphy watching the firing of the Sergeant, HAWK and Honest John missiles. Also, mobility was demonstrated as a Little John missile was airlifted by helicopter, and two soldiers hand-carried a Redeye for the cameras.

Accompanying Murphy was Lieutenant General Arthur Trudeau who was the Chief of Army Research and Development. The film was produced by the Office of the Chief of Research and Development for worldwide release in theaters and on television.

Major General John Shinkle, the White Sands commander, also appeared in the film with Murphy and Trudeau.

Major General John Shinkle, WSMR commander, poses next to Audie Murphy with Honest John launchers in the background. WSMR photo.

For his role in the Army film, Murphy was awarded the Outstanding Civilian Service Medal.

Murphy was killed in a plane crash in Virginia on May 28, 1971. He was buried with full military honors on June 8 in Arlington National Cemetery.

Omar Bradley

Another World War II hero who visited the missile range was General of the Army Omar Bradley. He was the nation's last five-star general and was the guest speaker at the missile range's "Patriotism Day" on Feb. 18, 1981.

White Sands was lucky to get him as he died less than two months later while in New York to receive an award. In fact, in our decision paper to the commanding general we stated because of his questionable health we planned to have a backup speaker just in case Bradley couldn't come.

Bradley was born in Missouri and went to West Point. He was part of the 1915 graduating class that some have dubbed "the class the stars fell on." A total of 59 generals came out of that class including another General of the Army, Dwight Eisenhower.

Unlike Audie Murphy, Bradley was at the opposite end of the World War II power pyramid. As D-Day approached, Bradley was in command of a whole army of men like Murphy. His men took the brunt of the German counteroffensive at the Battle of the Bulge. Later his troops rushed into Germany to capture more than 300,000 German troops.

After the war Bradley served as the Army Chief of Staff and then President Truman appointed him the first Chairman of the Joint Chiefs of Staff. He was in that rarified atmosphere with Eisenhower, Patton and MacArthur.

In 1981, Bradley was one of the few living legends from the big war. Some White Sands staff member pointed out he was living in special quarters just down the road at Fort Bliss. Public Affairs was asked to contact the general's aide and see if he would agree to speak.

Although Bradley was in fragile health, he still enjoyed getting out and participating in special events. He said yes.

We arranged the luncheon so Bradley could speak first, while he was still strong, and then we would eat afterwards. We anticipated a huge turnout from the workforce so we allocated tickets to organizations based on their populations. It turned out to be unnecessary as only 300 people bought tickets.

The event was a success. Bradley talked for about 20 minutes on leadership and then took a few questions.

He was a meat and potatoes man so we had steak and mashed potatoes. The Officers Club even managed peach ice cream for everyone, one of the general's favorite desserts.

Bradley is remembered for his modesty and concern for his troops. He was also a reflective professional soldier who gave his profession some thought. He once said, "Ours is a world of nuclear giants and ethical infants. We know more about war than about peace, more about killing than we know about living."

Michael Todd and Friends

I was aware the opening scene of *Around the World in 80 Days* contained a missile shot from White Sands, but didn't think I'd include the story in this book. After all, missile footage from White Sands has appeared in lots of productions.

Then, the more I learned about the film's producer, Mike Todd, the more my curiosity grew. I'm pretty sure this guy would feel right at home in today's entertainment business. Todd was a handsome, confident, self-made man who lived in the fast lane. He was brash and yet charming, could get blood out of a turnip, and was fearless to the point of trying just about anything. He was a fast talker, wheeler-dealer who pushed and shoved to get what he wanted. Today, I'm betting he would have his own reality television show.

At White Sands he engineered a deal with the Dept. of Army to allow him to film the launch of a Corporal missile and use the footage in the prologue for his film version of Jules Verne's *Around the World in 80 Days*. The film was released in late 1956 and won five Academy Awards to include Best Picture. Being the film's producer made Todd a celebrity, someone to be taken seriously. Unfortunately for him it was the only movie he ever made. He died in a horrific plane crash near Grants, New Mexico on March 22, 1958.

His film opens in the tiny, square film format typical of the day with the famous newsman Edward R. Murrow in a library, sitting behind a huge desk nursing his ubiquitous cigarette. Murrow talks about the fantastic fiction of Jules Verne, who wrote the around the world tale in 1872, but focuses on Verne's

From the Earth to the Moon. That book inspired one of the first science fiction films every made, *A Trip to the Moon* by Frenchman George Melies.

Several minutes from the French black and white, herky-jerky film then appear. This is the famous movie where a group of men are blasted to the moon from an artillery piece and crash into the eye of the man in the moon. They are then captured by the inhabitants of the moon and have to escape. The movie was made in 1902.

Murrow then tells the audience that fiction now lags behind fact as the scene shifts to the present at White Sands Proving Ground. For this the curtains at the movie theater would open wider so the movie could be projected on a new, wide screen, wall to wall. In the middle of the screen a Corporal missile is poised in the sand dunes of White Sands as a countdown descends from 10 to zero and launch.

After following the missile's climb for several seconds, we eventually get a look-down view from the missile. At the time, reporters were told the footage was taken from a camera on the missile. I have my doubts about that. It could have been footage from any number of prior sounding rocket shots. It seems unlikely there would have been a camera onboard a Corporal.

Murrow then says something about our shrinking world and the movie kicks off in London circa 1872.

To film the launch, Todd used his specially designed wide-screen photography system called Todd-AO. He had been a partner in the early development of Cinerama, the wide-screen system that shot everything on three cameras and then required three projectors to show it. It was a very popular technology in the 1950s and 60s as it produced a bit of an IMAX sensation. For Cinerama, if you sat in the middle of the theater and close enough to the screen, you saw nothing but the images on the screen.

Todd contracted with the American Optical Company to devise a 70mm film system that used just one camera but gave the same wide-screen images. Being the modest person he was, he put his name on it.

Todd had very little to do with the nuts and bolts of these things. He dropped out of high school and, after a few jobs, became an entrepreneur. He moved from the construction business into producing Broadway shows to doing movies. In between

were many other ventures some left him bankrupt and some were great financial successes. It was up and down with the "downs" never bothering him. He picked himself up and quickly moved on.

His instincts for *Around the World in 80 Days* were good. He put together an almost three-hour long, quasi-documentary, partial travel film, with loads of famous actors. In fact, he is credited with coming up with the term "cameo role." The list of actors he cajoled into making very minor appearances reads like a who's who for the time and includes Charles Boyer, Noel Coward, John Gielgud, Trevor Howard, Jose Greco, Robert Morely, Cesar Romero, Peter Lorre, George Raft, Red Skelton, Frank Sinatra, Buster Keaton, Marlene Dietrich - and this is just a partial list.

David Niven played the lead role of Phineas Fogg and Mexican star Cantinflas played Fogg's servant Passepartout. A very young Shirley Maclaine played Princess Aouda.

The film was shot in many locations around the world and was billed as a spectacular show of the exotic. This was just at the beginning of television, so American audiences were still ready to be impressed by the colorful and mysterious cultures found elsewhere. The movie ran almost three hours so it required an intermission.

So Todd was an interesting guy, but it got better when he actually came to film that launch. He first showed up for the Corporal firing in early February 1956, but the launch was scrubbed because of "weather conditions and mechanical difficulties." He came back to White Sands on March 2 and brought two of his talented friends with him to watch. Those friends were Eddie Fisher and Debbie Reynolds, and they put on a show that night at 6 p.m. for the benefit of the White Sands Proving Ground Combined Charity Drive (now called the CFC).

This was a big deal. According to *Wikipedia*, Fisher was at the height of being a teen idol with 17 songs in the Top 10 music charts between 1950 and 1956. Meanwhile Reynolds was moving up in the world after playing a major role in Gene Kelly's *Singin' in the Rain*.

Considering what a negotiator Todd was, I would bet the benefit show was promised by him to help seal the deal allowing him to film the Corporal missile launch. Of course, these two stars were quite an attraction for White Sands. The *Wind and Sand* reported over 500 tickets were sold at a dollar each. The show was held in Building 1753, a large open bay building used for maintenance – it held more people than the theater.

According to the post newspaper, Fisher and Reynolds sang "Love and Marriage," one of the top songs from 1955 that was originally recorded by Frank Sinatra. Dinah Shore also recorded the song in 1955 and had success as well.

That Fisher and Reynolds came along with Todd makes some sense because Fisher was Todd's best friend and Reynolds was originally from El Paso. That particular song selection was spot on as Fisher and Reynolds had just been married the year before. The *Wind and Sand* reported Reynolds' grandmother, several aunts and uncles and a few cousins attended and sat up front with General Laidlaw and Todd at the performance.

The couple's daughter is the Carrie Fisher who portrayed Princess Leia in the original *Star Wars* movies. Of course, she is also a noted author who wrote *Postcards From the Edge*.

After *Around the World* hit it big, Todd enjoyed a short time at the very top of the entertainment business. It didn't last long.

His fame bought him into contact with newly-divorced Elizabeth Taylor. In February 1957, he became her third husband. He was so smitten with her, he named his personal jet the "Lucky Liz" in her honor.

According to Dr. Richard Melzer in an article in the Oct. 21, 2006 issue of the *Valencia County News-Bulletin*, on March 22, 1958 Todd was flying to New York City from Burbank, California to be honored by the Friar's Club as "Showman of the Year." Plans called for a stop in Albuquerque where Todd had just visited a few days before. With his own personal jet he easily zoomed around doing his business.

According to Melzer, Todd was then feted by the city as he hinted his next movie project would be Cervantes's Don Quixote with some filming in New Mexico. The press described Todd as "dapper and cocky."

On that March 22nd night, Todd's plane never made it to Albuquerque as it went down during stormy conditions over the Zuni Mountains near Grants, New Mexico. When rescuers got to the crash site, they found, according to Melzer, a 10-foot deep crater and just body parts.

Today, we think of celebrity fans as being aggressive, intrusive and just plain rude. The implication is that people weren't always that nasty. I'm afraid that is not true. When Todd was buried in Chicago, fans mobbed the cemetery and the police couldn't hold them back. They tore Elizabeth Taylor's veil off her head. They then stormed her limo and pounded on the windows. So much for allowing the grieving widow a little privacy.

Because these stars were perceived as being fabulously rich with their pockets full of money, myths about Todd immediately took hold. Treasure seekers swarmed the plane crash site for weeks looking for jewelry and money. Others actually dug up Todd's grave trying to find an expensive diamond ring Taylor supposedly gave him. Since the coffin just contained a bag of body parts, there wasn't much to that story.

Of course, as we now know after reading about sports and entertainment celebrities for decades, many of them don't pay for anything. They usually expect their handlers or the people who are drooling over them to pick up the tab. They just walk away.

Doug and Christine Preston

This is an excellent example of why I liked my job in Public Affairs so much and why others were envious of it.

In 1995, our office was contacted about writer Doug Preston visiting so he could write a piece for *New Mexico* magazine about the missile range. When I contacted Preston, he explained his article was to be about the flora and fauna, the environment of White Sands, and not the military mission of the place. His wife Christine, a professional photographer, would also be along to take pictures.

They wanted to see as much of the mountains and deserts as possible in a three-day period. To maximize their time, I arranged for us to "camp" for a few nights at Hardin Ranch in the San Andres Mountains. This eliminated the long drive back and forth from town each day and gave us time to experience sunsets and sunrises from spots in the boonies. We really had the "whole" day to ourselves.

Hardin Ranch is the one ranch house on the missile range that has been maintained for decades for use by range employees. Range riders, security personnel and environmental scientists have been frequent users. Occasionally I used it when a situation like the Preston visit arose. It eliminated hours of driving just getting to and from a site each day.

At the end of April when I met the Prestons, Doug was rapidly gaining national attention as the co-author, with Lincoln Child, of the techno-thriller-horror novel *Relic*. The book reached even more people when it was turned into a feature motion picture that was released in 1997. One website states there are now over a million copies of *Relic* in print worldwide.

Since then Preston has written many best-selling novels by himself and in partnership with Child. In fact, his visit to White Sands gave him some location details he needed for the 1996 novel *Mount Dragon* where a top-secret lab is located on the missile range.

This was in addition to his journalistic efforts for magazines such as the *New Yorker, National Geographic, Natural History, Smithsonian,* and *Harper's*. Also he has produced some non-fiction books. My favorite is *Cities of Gold: A Journey Across the American Southwest in Pursuit of Coronado*. The "pursuit" was accomplished on horseback and the book chronicles a thousand-mile ride across Arizona and New Mexico trying to follow Coronado's original route.

We spent a very pleasant three days hunting wildlife, flowers, historic spots and vistas. They got an earful about the missile range and I learned a little about the life of a best-selling author. The feature article appeared in the October 1995 issue of *New Mexico* magazine.

MLRS and the German Minister

So what happens when you endanger a high-ranking government official? Usually there is a general wringing of hands with some finger pointing, and then some action is promptly taken to remedy or appear to remedy the situation. This is what happened when the German equivalent of America's Secretary of the Treasury was hit by debris from a rocket firing at White Sands in the spring of 1989.

The Multiple Launch Rocket System (MLRS) is one of the most successful weapon systems ever developed and then tested at White Sands. It began life as the General Service Rocket System in the late 1970s with the firing of a rocket in December 1977. Since then it has been growing and evolving decade after decade and is now part of the defense forces of innumerable countries.

When it was introduced the system consisted of a self-propelled tracked vehicle carrying two pods of rockets. Most everyone around the project called the pods "six-packs" because there were six rockets in each pod. The pods were nice rectangular boxes that could be changed out in minutes once the six rockets were fired.

The rockets were about nine inches in diameter and 13 feet long. Each rocket was isolated in its own storage tube that doubled as its launch tube. The crew, up in the cab, could fire one rocket at a time, a few, one after another or a "ripple" of all 12 rockets in less than a minute.

Each rocket had a range of about 20 miles. When the rocket reached the target area, the skin would peel back and 644 small bomblets would be dispensed. Each bomblet was activated as it fell to earth so it would explode on contact.

These munitions were only about three inches long and 1.5 inches in diameter so they were good against personnel and light vehicles like jeeps and trucks. Each explosive was a smallish unit but the volume of them could be overwhelming. For example, if all 12 rockets were fired into an enemy's staging area, more than 7,700 explosions were going to take place in a span of less than 60 seconds. It was, and still is, the artillery's version of the BIG shotgun.

In the Middle East the system was used very effectively against the Iraqis who called it "steel rain."

Over the years, the system has become much more sophisticated and diverse. The range of the rockets has been extended, they can carry a variety of munitions, and there is a guided missile version now. Also a lighter, wheeled launcher vehicle is now available making it possible for smaller aircraft to deliver the vehicle close to the front lines. In typical military fashion the new vehicle's long title is "High Mobility Artillery Rocket System" which, of course, had to be shortened into an acronym – HIMARS.

Also, the heavier tracked launcher vehicle can carry two larger ATACMS (Army Tactical Missile System) missiles instead of the MLRS load. In the space of a pod or six-pack is a single ATACMS missile pod. However, the pod is disguised so it looks just like an MLRS six-pack. The lighter, wheeled vehicle can only carry one six-pack of rockets or one Army TACMS missile.

An Army TACMS missile is about two feet in diameter and 13 feet long. The extended range TACMS can hit targets about 200 miles out. On Oct. 17,

1996, a TACMS missile was successfully fired from Fort Wingate, New Mexico, near Gallup, to a target on the missile range.

Early on, the United States made the MLRS system available to our closest allies. Eventually, a license was drawn up that allowed the consortium of Great Britain, France, German and Italy to build their own units. If you sat at one of their fire control units, you could chose which language you wanted to use in communicating with the computer.

As part of this process, dignitaries from these countries and others interesting in purchasing the weapon would come to White Sands to watch an MLRS firing. The Germans were especially interested in MLRS at the height of the Cold War because

they were the first target, if the Soviets rolled their tanks and troops to the west. The Germans designed an anti-tank submunition to be dispensed by the MLRS rockets. Testing the submunition was done at White Sands.

At one of these MLRS demonstration firings for Germany, the audience was mostly civilian government officials. We bused them out to Launch Complex 33 for the firing. This was the project's regular firing point on the south end of the missile range and bleachers were permanently in place. They were positioned directly north of the old Army blockhouse with the MLRS launcher stationed a few hundred yards further north and straight ahead. From the bleachers, visitors could watch the rockets fly straight

A MLRS rocket emerges from the smoke left by the previous rocket fired in a series. The launcher vehicle carries two six-packs of rockets and personnel can fire rockets individually or any number up to 12. The rockets are fired one at a time and the timing between each launch is controlled from inside the cab. All 12 rockets can easily be fired in less than a minute. WSMR photo.

away from them and get the full concussive shock of the rockets igniting and roaring away. It was very loud and impressive.

When the rocket motors ignite, there is an explosive rise in the air pressure inside the storage/launch container. This pressure blows the metal covers off both ends of the launch tube.

Most of the time these metal disks, about 10 inches in diameter, fly off and tumble to the ground. But not always. Sometimes the covers develop a spin at launch and can either sail through the air like a Frisbee or roll along the ground like an upright bicycle wheel.

For the German demonstration I was standing beside the bleachers watching the show. Rockets were blasting off every three seconds or so. After a couple of shots, several of us noticed one of the rear tube covers rolling toward us at high speed.

There wasn't time to think about it much less shout a warning. In a second it rolled straight at the middle of the bleachers and hit the bottom row. It bounded up through the visitors and sailed over the bleachers and the blockhouse. We looked at each and said something more graphic than, "Holy cow."

The chief nurse, who was standing by, immediately walked out to where the cover entered the bleachers and looked up. I think we were imagining the disk hitting someone in the forehead and spilling his brains on the bleachers. The nurse tried to shout out to see if anyone was hurt, but rockets were still thundering away behind him. No one looked dead or excited so he got out of the way.

Later, as everyone was climbing down from the bleachers, one of the German ministers came down with one of his pant legs rolled up. It turns out the cover rolled up the bleachers and struck him a glancing blow just below the knee. He had a bit of a bruise but nothing serious.

Project officials retrieved the cover, autographed it and presented it to the minister. He seemed delighted with his souvenir.

The wringing of hands started immediately with people discussing "what if scenarios." Not long afterward, the viewing bleachers were moved to the east a quarter of a mile to get visitors out of the line of fire. There were no incidents after that.

A Demonstration for the Commander in Chief

On June 5, 1963 President John F. Kennedy vis-

ited White Sands to watch a series of missile firings. The event was called Project MEWS or "Missile Exercise White Sands."

The visit was just one of a long string of weapon demonstrations over the history of White Sands done for a bigger reason than the edification of a very important person. When you put them in their historical context, most seem to be sending a message. For instance, for Kennedy's visit you have to recognize that the Cuban Missile Crisis took place a few months earlier in October 1962.

There was a good deal of fear generated in the showdown between the Soviets and the United States over the placing of missiles in Cuba. Many Americans were panic stricken. Khrushchev said the Communists would bury the United States and many believed he could.

So, in 1963, the President went about bolstering American confidence in our ability to defend ourselves. In February he made a very public visit to Redstone Arsenal in Alabama to shine the spotlight on Army missiles. He followed that with the visit to White Sands in June to show off some of those missiles in action. After these demonstrations, it was evident the United States had the muscle to deal with the Soviets.

For Kennedy's visit, White Sands launched seven missiles against a variety of targets including another missile, a hillside and several remotely controlled jet aircraft. Also, there were briefings, a speech to be made, presentations of mementos, and some goodwill handshaking. Normally that is a lot of activity and would probably take the better part of day. Not so when it involves the President. All of this was scheduled for exactly 139 minutes.

The President, along with Vice-President Lyndon Johnson, Secretary of State Cyrus Vance and numerous generals, flew into Holloman Air Force Base. They were then flown by helicopter to the White Sands main post where the clock started ticking.

Dan Duggan was a young captain and project officer stationed at White Sands at the time and was assigned to give two the briefings. He said that the missile range went through 90 days of preparation for those 139 minutes. As well as his two briefings, Duggan helped coordinate some of the shots.

Duggan said the announcement of the visit, "immediately called for an ad-hoc group of some 15 principals headed by a major who was supervised daily by the deputy commander and the chief of staff and no telling how many others spreading like a web from the center."

He added, "I personally gave a total of 93 formal briefings, 'dry runs,' to everyone from the janitor to the chairman of the joint chiefs of staff. Every one of them had 'suggestions' on how to say it. I felt sorry for the Navy briefer who was told three weeks before the event that he could not use a script because the Army Zeus briefer didn't use a script. I don't think he liked me too much after that." Duggan was the Zeus briefer.

Kennedy and his party were scheduled to be seated at the parade field at 2:45 p.m. but ran a little late. The White Sands workforce attended this portion and Kennedy talked to them for about 10 minutes. The official party then went to Launch Complex

32 by car to begin the briefings and missile launches.

The first firing was an Honest John. According to the schedule, the briefer had two minutes to explain the system's capabilities and what the soldiers were doing to fire it. The missile was fired against a hillside target north of U.S. Highway 70.

Next, the Littlejohn and Sergeant ground-to-ground missiles were fired from the same place. Finally, a HAWK air defense missile shot down an F-80 jet fighter. By the way, the HAWK replaced the Nike air defense missiles and the name is often thought to be an acronym instead of a bird of prey. It is widely accepted that the acronym "Homing All the Way Killer" was dreamt up after the system was dubbed Hawk.

The group next moved to Launch Complex 37 where they witnessed a Nike Hercules launch against

President Kennedy takes time to shake hands with WSMRites during his visit. To the left is New Mexico Congressman Joseph Montoya. In 1964, Montoya moved into one of New Mexico senate seats. WSMR photo.

another Nike Hercules missile, a Navy Talos fired against another F-80 jet, and a Nike Zeus launch.

After the demonstrations, representative soldiers from the various missile crews presented JFK with a Sergeant missile model.

The last thing on the agenda was a 20-minute briefing for just the presidential party on the Nike Zeus system. The Nike Zeus was the new super-duper missile killer designed to knock out Soviet Intercontinental Ballistic Missiles (ICBMs) by exploding a large nuclear weapon near them. Its name was changed to Spartan as it morphed in the Sentinel System and then into the Safeguard System.

Duggan was the briefer for the Nike Zeus firing and then participated in the longer classified briefing. In his own words, this is how the classified briefing went:

> Not sure of just how smart this young captain was in discussing system capabilities and strategy with the president, the White House gave me plenty of support. My immediate backup was the Chairman of AT&T, followed by the president and CEO of Bell Telephone Lab, someone from Douglas Aircraft, a gaggle of more 'expert' contractors and, of course, our ever-present commander, Major General Thorlin.
>
> I pointed out to the President that we had some refreshments, even Heineken Beer (his favorite) should he like one. He declined, reminding me with that ever-present grin, that he and I were still working.
>
> I was ready to proceed with the classified briefing when he said, 'I know you have worked on this briefing for some time. How many dry runs did you make?'
>
> 'Ninety-three times,' I replied.
>
> General Thorlin turned a bit purple and then red.
>
> 'I am sure you are thoroughly prepared and have an outstanding briefing ready but we are running a bit late. Would you mind just sitting down and let's talk about a few things on my mind?' JFK asked.
>
> Wow. I still can't believe I was able to answer his questions and discuss the program intelligently without having to call on one of my many backups. Upon his departure he shook my hand and said 'My thanks to you

> and everyone for their hard work in making this an outstanding informative day. Now you can enjoy that after-action party.'

Pretty much back on schedule, the visitors flew to El Paso where the President spent the night.

Some people see Kennedy's visit in a different light. White Sands National Monument has an administrative history of the monument posted on their website. It is called "Dunes and Dreams" and was written by Michael Welsh in 1995. In it Welsh states Kennedy's "primary concern (for the visit) was the fitness of WSMR for the Apollo program."

In the early 60s, and many other decades for that matter, the Park Service was concerned about encroachment on the monument by the Army and Air Force. In fact, when you read the history there are many examples of the two services more or less bullying White Sands. After a while, the Park Service developed a deep mistrust of the military and exaggerated many threats or simply imagined some. Any rumor that came along became a call to action.

In this instance, the Park Service clearly feared NASA would end up on Alkali Flats and would loom over the north boundary of the monument. Nothing is mentioned in their history about the President watching missile launches in a huge display of firepower that took months to prepare and was openly covered by the national news media.

When the president didn't go flying out to the supposed Apollo launch site, Welsh concluded they ran out of time and had to move on. That conclusion seems unlikely if JFK's prime reason for visiting WSMR was to see the Apollo site. Instead, he took the time to shake hands with WSMR and Holloman personnel.

It is true politicians like New Mexico Senator Clinton Anderson, at the time, were politicking for Apollo-related work in their home states. Anderson and others proposed WSMR as a launch site for Gemini and Apollo vehicles. The main advantages sited for White Sands were the reasonably good weather and the fact the launch site would already be almost 4,000 feet above sea level.

Welsh's argument is also very questionable because presidents don't fly around to take a personal look at a potential facility site. It is a bit ludicrous to think Kennedy was weighing in on the selection process.

When you look back on it in the cold and harsh light of fiscal and political reality, there wasn't a snowball's chance in hell that NASA was moving its operations to New Mexico. Florida already was conducting Mercury launches and was equipped with a tremendous infrastructure for support. Plus the political support from a state like Florida and the needs of the administration to hold the Southern states outweighed any clout from tiny New Mexico.

Then there was this huge technical problem. The planned launch inclination to put the men into orbit required a basic west-to-east flight path. That meant for launches from White Sands, the Saturn rocket's first stage, weighing around 280,000 pounds after burnout and separation, would have hit the ground some 400 miles or so east of White Sands - somewhere in Texas. "Watch out Abilene!" Launches in Florida simply meant dropping boosters in the Atlantic.

Another clue here that the Park Service had nothing to worry about was the agency's own experience with the Army. From 1946 forward, the Army and WSMR always fought the Park Service's proposal to make Trinity Site a national monument or other

There is no caption for this photo but it shows a Nike Zeus on display at a viewing area, probably LC-37, with another Zeus being launched at LC-38. A lot of work and expense went into such an arrangement which leads me to believe this photo is from President Kennedy's visit in 1963. Everything about it fits what took place that day. WSMR photo.

kind of historic park. The Army's reasoning was that a monument would cut out the top portion of the missile range and effectively eliminate WSMR's capability to test many long-range missiles for the Army, Air Force and Navy.

Now imagine an Apollo launch complex in the very middle of the missile range with hundreds of people working there. It is a quantum leap worse than a national monument as far as encroachment on the missile range. Given such a scenario, WSMR would just about disappear as a test site for weapons.

Given these circumstances, the events provide an insight into how American politics work. Nobody in their right mind thinks Senator Anderson actually would have pushed to shut down WSMR to acquire the Apollo program. Also, he wasn't naïve enough to think New Mexico actually had a chance. So what was he up to?

By keeping the public and local supporters beating the drums for New Mexico for the space program, Anderson was able to dip his hand into the pork barrel and deliver a NASA Apollo spin-off.

It wasn't the whole program, but it was something useful, reasonable to New Mexico, and something that continues to this day. It came in the form of the White Sands Test Facility, established in 1963.

The facility is located on the very west edge of WSMR, out of the way so it does not encroach on the military mission at all, or the national monument either.

In 1964, the facility began testing the smaller rocket engines that were used in the Apollo program. Its mission has expanded over the years to include space shuttle support, hazardous materials testing, high-pressure oxygen systems and a number of laboratories.

Of course, there are some totally whacko claims about Kennedy's visit. Some say JFK used the visit as a smoke screen to go see Victorio Peak and decide what to do about all the gold bars and other treasure stored there. Cue the *Twilight Zone* music.

Other Demonstrations

In one of the most innovative shows in early television, NBC broadcast live the launch of nine missiles from White Sands on Sunday, March 3, 1957. The demo was part of *Wide, Wide World* with Dave Garroway as the host. It aired on Sunday afternoons from the fall of 1955 to the summer of 1958.

This program was very ambitious at a time when television support technology was very limited and primitive. The program ran 90 minutes each week and all the segments were live.

Some of the old shows are available on *YouTube* to watch. In one I watched, Garroway was introduced at the beginning to explain what was going to happen during the following 90 minutes. For this particular show he announced they had 74 cameras scattered about to provide the live coverage. The only thing similar today is the Olympics when a network may have to provide coverage from many, many locations.

For the March 3 program, the White Sands segment was only 20 minutes long. During the rest of the show, Garroway interviewed baseball legend Mickey Mantle, Karl and William Menninger of the Menninger psychiatric clinic in Kansas, actor and dancer Gene Kelley, Supreme Court Justice William O. Douglas, and two-time Pulitzer Prize-winning playwright Tennessee Williams. Current television has nothing like it.

Between the launches at White Sands, Garroway broke to interviews with Colonel James Hamill, Major General J.B. Medaris, Major General W.E. Laidlaw, and Dr. Wernher von Braun. Laidlaw was commander of White Sands and Medaris was commander of Army's Ballistic Missile Agency.

Hamill and von Braun knew each other from World War II. Colonel Hamill led American efforts to retrieve as much V-2 rocket material from Germany as possible before the Russians arrived. Not only did he capture huge amounts of stuff, most of which ended up at White Sands, but he also was in charge of the German scientists who surrendered to the United States. Those rocket scientists were led by von Braun.

In today's world of super-expensive weapons and tight budgets, it is hard to imagine the Army's largesse for *Wide, Wide World*. The White Sands segment wasn't until the end of the show, but the Army allowed two Nike Ajax missiles to be launched as "teasers" during the first part of the show.

The Army probably viewed the exposure of Nike Ajax as excellent publicity, since the system was already in place around many U.S. cities guarding against Russian bomber attacks.

The White Sands segment began with another Nike Ajax launch. This was followed by two Honest Johns, two Little Johns and then a Dart missile that destroyed a tank. The finale was the launch of a Corporal, the first American surface-to-surface missile. It was capable of carrying a conventional or nuclear warhead.

This effort was groundbreaking for White Sands, the Army and live television. In an oral history given by White Sands Commander Major General Laidlaw in 1978 he said, "I think I got some of my gray hair during that afternoon."

Afterwards, the White Sands newspaper said, "The presentation marked the first time in history that such an array of missiles was ever fired on a live television program – in full view of millions of TV viewers from coast to coast."

Rightfully so, the newspaper was also impressed by the effort needed by NBC to bring the program to the airways. The network had a crew of 40 technicians on base who were assisted by White Sands personnel.

To get the video signal to El Paso so it could be transmitted to New York, NBC hired the Mountain States Telephone and Telegraph Co. They put together a chain of 10 mobile microwave trucks to relay the signal to El Paso.

The audio was carried by special wire down to El Paso. The video, audio, background music and Garroway's narration were married together in New York and then sent out to the country.

The day after the show, Dorothy Knipe sent a letter to her parents in Indiana with news about the show. Her husband, Captain Willis Knipe, was the project officer at White Sands for the Corporal missile program.

She said the event was a huge success although her husband didn't appear on the show. She explained that the top ranking officers were on camera and the rest of the personnel shown were actors. Her husband stood in another room to direct the launch and pass along the count to the "actors" on camera.

Nothing was left to chance as the television crew and Army personnel rehearsed the event for three days. She said they ran through the whole thing with Dave Garroway twice via closed circuit television.

Unfortunately for residents at White Sands, the NBC affiliate out of El Paso was NOT the single channel they could receive at White Sands. In her letter, Dorothy Knipe said she drove down to Fort Bliss in El Paso with her two daughters to watch with friends.

Dorothy's comment about her husband passing along information to the actors was confirmed by Paul Arthur who worked missile flight safety in the blockhouse for the event. At one point, he said an actor on camera shouted into a microphone, "Get on that missile, get on that missile." It was a fiction created to liven up the action for folks at home.

In addition to the phony drama in the blockhouse, Arthur said much of the testing was faked for the show. The missiles were really launched, but they were simply and safely fired up into the heart of the range. He said the ground targets were all in one area so NBC could conveniently cover one explosion after another without needing dozens more cameras. Unbeknownst to the viewers, the missiles were never shot at the targets. The targets were pre-rigged with explosives and were triggered after each missile shot.

Arthur said one of the fake impacts failed to explode because a previous detonation severed the wire to the next explosive package and it couldn't be triggered. So, NBC never caught the conclusion of one of the "successful" flights. Arthur said afterward the men joked that White Sands must have accidentally put that missile into orbit since it failed to come back down.

Just a few weeks after the *Wide, Wide World* demo in 1957, top military officials from all 14 of the NATO nations visited White Sands. At that time NATO was composed of the United States, Belgium, Canada, Denmark, France, Germany, Greece, Italy, Luxemburg, the Netherlands, Norway, Portugal, Turkey and the United Kingdom.

It must have been some year because a few weeks after that tour, several hundred top Army officials and industry leaders, led by Army Secretary Wilber Brucker, visited on the afternoon of April 25, 1957. It was part of the "Association of the U.S. Army Guided Missile Symposium" that was held in El Paso.

Brucker was soon back at White Sands for what must have been a really big show. On June 30 and July 1, 1958 the Army filled the New Mexico skies with missiles and helicopters at Fort Bliss' northern ranges and White Sands in a demonstration of the newest weapon systems.

In all, nine different missiles were fired and crews of the Army's newfangled helicopters showed they could blast enemy ground forces with machine gun and rocket fire.

And the stars were out to watch. There were over

80 general officers from all the services and NATO allies on hand to be wowed. With them were more than 100 industrial leaders and 120 news reporters. It required 20 buses just to move the group around from site to site.

The demonstration was dubbed "Project AMMO" or the Army Mobile Missile Orientation. Invitations issued by the secretary and the chief of staff of the Army stated, "The purpose of this event is to acquaint key members of the executive branch, senior commanders, industrial representatives and informational media with the capabilities of the U.S. Army missiles." Unlike *Wide, Wide World*, this was an event that couldn't be faked.

In addition to Brucker and General Maxwell Taylor (he was the Army chief of staff), the military VIPs included Air Force General Nathan Twining, Chairman of the Joint Chiefs of Staff and Army Ordnance Missile Command Chief Major General John Medaris. Assistant Secretary of Army and New Mexican Hugh Milton also attended.

One newspaper estimated there were 150 stars present for the demo.

The industrial leaders who attended represented the many companies building the various missiles. For instance, U.S. Steel Corporation built Nike launchers and made materials used in many missiles. The company's president, Clifford Hood, and many subordinates were on hand. Donald Douglas Sr., the founder of Douglas Aircraft, attended because his company built the Honest John.

To cover the event, major newspapers such at the *New York Times*, *Chicago Tribune*, *Baltimore Sun*, *Washington Star* and *Los Angeles Times* sent reporters. Also, a few television stations sent film crews to capture the missile shots.

The actual demos started on June 30 at McGregor Range on Fort Bliss. Two Nike Ajax missiles were fired at a droned B-17 bomber and successfully brought it crashing to the ground. An Honest John, surface-to-surface missile, was fired at and successfully destroyed a target either five, six or 15 miles away depending on which newspaper account one reads. The Honest John launch was conducted after the various components were airlifted to the site using helicopters.

The group then moved to Orogrande Range Camp at the southeast corner of White Sands where they saw a Corporal firing.

Finally, the day ended at Bliss' Hueco Range where armed helicopters blasted the desert with rockets and machine guns. Then infantry soldiers were dropped off by helicopters into the cleared area.

The helicopter demonstrations captured the visitor's imagination as much as the missile flights. The news media started talking about helicopters being the "cavalry for the atomic age." Army officials, however, stressed that helicopters were still considered experimental and could be vulnerable on the battlefield.

On July 1, the throng moved to White Sands for six missile launches. In addition to the five Army systems (Nike Hercules, Hawk, Dart, Little John and Lacrosse) the Navy's Talos air-defense missile was part of the show.

All the missiles were successes. The only glitch was when the Talos warhead failed to detonate. It was the first flight for the warhead and the news media only mentioned it.

Targets varied for these missile shots. Some were very realistic. For example, the Dart was fired against a tank and the Hawk shot down a droned F-80 jet.

On the other hand, some were simulated. The Lacrosse was fired to a spot that was marked with a wooden stake. The Nike Hercules was successfully guided to an imaginary box in the sky. Since the Hercules could carry a nuclear warhead, it only needed to get in the vicinity to knock down whole squadrons of aircraft.

The news media were really impressed with the Hawk demo. Unlike the Nike Ajax demo, where a high-flying, slow-moving target was used, the Hawk engaged the F-80 at only 500 feet above the ground flying at 400 miles per hour. After launch, the Hawk climbed to an altitude well above the jet and then dove down hitting it directly and creating a huge fireball.

The Army's Redstone and Sergeant missiles were not fired but put on display with project personnel providing capability briefings.

The demonstration was used as a backdrop to assure the American public as well. In October and November 1957, the Soviets had put the first two manmade satellites into orbit around the earth. Many Americans were running around with their hair on fire because they believed the launches proved the Soviets had an intercontinental ballistic missile capability.

The Army told the news media that the Soviets still couldn't deliver a nuclear weapon to the U.S. because they had not solved the problem of getting the warhead back through the atmosphere on re-entry. The United States, on the other hand, had just finished testing materials that would solve the problem for American ICBM weapons.

Another topic that had the press abuzz was an Army "moon probe." In a press conference in El Paso, Army Secretary Brucker confirmed the Army was proceeding to work on a vehicle to send a payload to the moon.

In fact, an Air Force vehicle, Thor-Able, was selected to carry the first moon probe – the Pioneer series. The first launch on Aug. 17, 1958 failed. The next two failed as well.

The program then switched to the Army's Juno II rocket. The first launch had a premature shutdown of the rocket engine and it did not generate enough speed to break away from the earth's gravity. The second Juno II launch (Pioneer 4) was successful on March 3, 1959. The Pioneer vehicle sped by the moon at a distance of 37,000 miles.

It certainly was an electrifying time for the Army. At the demonstration, one three-star general was heard to remark, "Gad, I'm glad my retirement comes up next year. This stuff makes obsolete everything I've learned."

Demonstrations I Remember

On June 21, 1978, Secretary of Defense Harold Brown brought the national news media to White Sands to witness for the first time a flight of the Navy's Tomahawk cruise missile. By the demonstration standards set in the 1950s, this one was rather small but significant in that the cruise missiles, which had been in development for decades, were finally mature enough to be a real factor in conflicts.

In fact, during the press conference Brown told reporters the U.S. cruise missile would be able to penetrate any Soviet defense. This was in answer to criticism that the U.S. needed a new manned bomber to deliver bombs to targets.

The demonstration was very simple and not very exciting. Afterwards, it took a little imagination to see the weapon's future capability, something the reporters lacked. Most reporters who visit White Sands have no background in science, technology or the military. It is not surprising they couldn't imag-

ine that in just a few years, the United States would be launching cruise missiles that would fly hundreds of miles to a target area, find a particular building and then fly through a designated window.

Instead, the reporters asked about the cost of the system and its political impact.

The Tomahawk was mounted under a Navy A-6 Intruder Fighter-Bomber and flown to White Sands from the Pacific Missile Test Center in California. Most reporters missed the fact that the airplane was hooked into the missile guidance system and it was the missile that guided the jet to White Sands.

Once over the missile range, the pilot launched the missile and it flew preprogrammed maneuvers up and down the range for about two hours. Those of us in the media viewing area experienced long periods of nothing but burning heat, punctuated by periodic Tomahawk flybys.

Being a new employee in the office, I probably noticed the national reporters more than the flybys. I do remember it was very hot and dry. Really it was a typical June day in southern New Mexico.

The viewing area was no more than a spot in the middle of nowhere that was bulldozed flat to provide a gathering point and set up camera tripods for the photo opportunities. In that process of grading the desert, the dry, flour-like soil was stirred up. It was the finest of powders, and every step created a little cloud of dust that would rise to your knees.

Most of the local reporters were ready for the hot and dusty conditions. They wore jeans, short sleeve shirts and mostly cowboy boots. Even some of the national guys were prepared. I remember Ike Pappas from CBS News was dressed in some sort of sensible bush clothing.

One guy, however, stood out. He was the reporter from ABC News and he dressed in the traditional Washington, D.C. uniform – white long-sleeve shirt, navy blazer, gray flannel slacks and black loafers. It wasn't long before the jacket was off and the tie was hanging loose. But what got our attention were his nice gray pants. His shoes and his pants, to his knees, had turned a nice shade of light brown.

Secretary Brown was back in December 1978 with a bigger and more explosive demonstration. It had all the gee-whiz attributes needed to get some national attention. At least, if the high tech aspect of it didn't grab your attention, all the explosions and fireballs would.

It was billed as the "DOD Precision Guided Munitions Demonstration" and featured weapons from all three of the military services. Brown didn't bring many VIPs with him. He stressed the show was for the news media and by default the American public. He didn't want a bunch of straphangers to detract from the demonstration.

Five weapons were fired while many others were on static display and briefed during the morning. The significant thing about PGMs is their one-shot kill capability.

Instead of firing dozens of artillery rounds at a single tank target three miles away, with the Army's Copperhead it only took one round. Instead of dropping dozens of dumb bombs on a missile site to destroy the headquarters, why not drop one or two

laser-guided bombs or one TV-guided bomb and do the job in one pass.

This was and still is a major advantage. When the Cold War was raging and everyone worried about the thousands of Soviet tanks poised in eastern Europe, being able to knock out a tank with one missile or smart-bomb was a whole lot more practical than building a multi-million-dollar tank to match their tank, or resorting to nuclear weapons.

In preparation for the event, White Sands had to create an observation area at Cedar Site, which is a few miles north of U.S. Highway 70. The week before we had a spell of cold weather. December in southern New Mexico is usually sunny and warm with highs in the 60s. However, it can snow just as well.

Officials were worried about the comfort of the visitors, especially if we had a cold morning. When I saw their solution I realized I had come to work for a creative organization. The engineers tied tarps around the base of the bleachers. Then they fed large flexible ducts from portable furnaces under the tarps. The heated air was trapped under the bleachers and had no place to go except to rise up through the boards forming the seating and warm the VIPs and news media from their feet on up.

It was beautifully simple, effective and ultimately not needed. It turned out to be a beautiful day with the warm sun beaming down on us.

The first weapon demonstrated was the Army's Copperhead. This was an anti-tank round fired from a 155 mm howitzer. The round was fired in the general direction to the target and then, using fins that sprout after launch, the Copperhead's seeker found and then homed in on reflected laser energy.

This meant someone had to be lighting up the target by spotting it with a laser designator – think really sophisticated and powerful laser pointer. For the demo, the laser designator was used by a soldier on the ground, but the designator could just as easily have been mounted on any ground vehicle or aircraft.

Copperhead successfully killed both stationary and moving tanks.

Secretary of Defense Harold Brown (left) and New Mexico Senator Pete Domenici drink coffee and chat during the Precision Guided Munitions demonstration. WSMR photo.

Next, the Army fired a TOW missile from an attack helicopter at a tank. The TOW acronym stands for "Tube launched, Optically tracked, Wire guided."

The TOW was older technology that had already been fielded for quite some time. In fact, by then the U.S. had sold the weapon to some 20 other countries. The missile system could be mounted on a jeep or helicopter or carried onto the battlefield by infantry.

To fire it, the gunner had to find his target visually through the system's telescopic sight. Once fired, he was required to keep the sight's crosshairs focused on the target. This was so the system's computer could calculate the target's position and send guidance signals to the missile through wires connecting the computer and the missile. The wire would spool out behind the missile as it flew out.

The TOW successfully found its tank target with just one shot that morning.

The Air Force was up next with drops of a GBU-15 and four laser-guided bombs.

The GBU-15 was a TV-guided bomb. It had a camera mounted in the nose so the gunner could see the target area. The system was equipped with a targeting system visible in the video display. All the gunner had to do was place the video crosshairs on the target in the display before or after the bomb was dropped. The system's onboard computer then sent guidance commands to the bomb as it glided to the target.

For the demonstration, the 2,000-lb. GBU-15 destroyed a command vehicle protected behind a revetment. The bomb was delivered by an F-4.

Next a cluster of four 500-lb. laser-guided bombs destroyed a simulated fuel storage dump. Like the Copperhead, the laser-guided bombs homed in on a spot of reflected laser light. The laser designator could be mounted on the plane delivering the bombs or on another aircraft used as a spotter. In theory, the designator could be handled by troops on the ground. In this case, another F-4 was used for the attack.

The beauty of these bombs was that the "smart"

A Copperhead strikes the lased (marked) tank, not the one to the left, and is captured just as the warhead explodes against the turret. The smart projectile was fired from an artillery tube at the Small Missile Range several miles to the south. WSMR photo.

part of the bomb could simply be attached to the nose of an old general-purpose bomb. Suddenly it took fewer flights and fewer bombs to destroy specific targets.

The Navy came last with the drop of a 2,000 lb. Walleye from an A-7. Like the GBU-15, the Walleye was successfully guided to a hardened ground target via a TV link between the plane and the bomb's onboard camera.

Another category of weapons that was on static display and not demonstrated was the radiation seeker. No, not nuclear radiation. These weapons locked onto electromagnetic radiation coming from a target, like a radar or thermal source, and then guided themselves to the target.

For instance, the Army's shoulder-fired Stinger locked onto the heat signature (infrared radiation) of a jet or helicopter engine and flew to it. The Navy's HARM missile locked onto the radio transmissions of radars and other transmitters and, once launched, homed in on the source.

The program was completed around noon with most everyone headed home. Some reporters took the opportunity to visit the destroyed targets. When Ike Pappas, CBS-TV, saw one of the Copperhead targets with a neat hole punched in it, he said, "That sure would stop your Timex."

The demo was done at a time when Timex was running ads about how tough their watches were. Pappas was referring to the company's sales slogan, "It takes a licking and keeps on ticking."

In the end, the secretary of defense congratulated White Sands saying, "Clearly, White Sands provides a very good environment for such tests." He went on to suggest they now needed to figure out how to get a submarine to the missile range so the Navy could test the underwater launch of its cruise missile – the Tomahawk.

. . ."Here She Comes, Miss America"

On Oct. 31, 1965, Vonda Kay Van Dyke, Miss America for 1965, visited White Sands. During her visit, she gave an afternoon talk at the Post Chapel about her experiences leading up to winning the title and what happened to her afterward. That evening she gave an hour-long show in the Post Theater singing and performing her ventriloquist act.

Van Dyke grew up in Phoenix where, as a teenager, she was runner-up two years in a row for the title of Miss Phoenix. In an interview with the *Wind and Sand* newspaper, she said she was discouraged and thought she might quit entering pageants.

When she was asked to compete in the Miss Tempe, Arizona contest she was planning to say no. She said, "I went out anyway and won hands down. I was the only contestant."

That win triggered something and she went on to take the Miss Arizona title and then the Miss America pageant in September 1964. At the big event, not only did she win the crown, she was also named Miss Congeniality, the only person to ever take both honors in the Miss America contest.

Her sense of humor must have been a major factor in winning the congeniality prize. In addition to the story about winning the Miss Tempe title, she told the *Wind and Sand* that after being crowned Miss America she was very nervous. They arranged her first autograph session where she sat under a big banner and people lined up to get her to sign a photo.

She related there were a lot of teenaged boys in the queue. One came up and politely said, "Can I have your autograph Miss America?" She wrote out her whole name and gave the photo back to the young man. He stared at her signature and read it out loud to his friend. He then nudged his friend and said, "I told you her last name wasn't America."

She had a talent unique to these contests, having learned ventriloquism as a child. Her dummy was a red-haired youngster she called Kurley Q.

When she appeared in the WSMR theater, reportedly a standing-room-only crowd of 650 people was on hand to see her.

Nicolas Cage

Not all visitors come announced with a great deal of fanfare. When the missile range's Visitors Center was located in the Public Affairs Office, we received a call late one afternoon (in fact most people had already gone home) from the front gate inquiring if the center was still open. The guard said Nicolas Cage, the actor, wanted to come in and see it.

My reaction was split between, "Yes, I can stick around a little longer to meet a famous actor" and "It can't be the real Nicolas Cage. It must be someone with the same name." We told the guard to go ahead and send him to us.

Sure enough, a few minutes later, the famous Nicolas Cage walked through our door. I took him into the Visitors Center and talked to him a little. It turned out he was in the area to visit his friend Willem Dafoe who was over at the national monument filming the movie White Sands.

Clint Eastwood

Another actor to visit White Sands for just a few hours was Clint Eastwood.

One day I received a query from someone responsible for photography at the Malpaso Company, Clint Eastwood's movie production outfit. He explained they were planning a Clint Eastwood movie called *Firefox* where he would steal a super-secret Soviet fighter and fly it to the West. In that process he would need to land on an ice floe and have the jet refueled by a submarine.

The company had heard that Alkali Flat, in the middle of the missile range's old lakebed, was very white, maybe white enough to double as snow and ice. He wanted to know exactly how white the ground really was.

I explained the color was hard to describe, mainly because the color changes during different weather and lighting conditions. The flats are at their whitest when the lakebed is very dry while moisture can make them more of a camel color.

He asked for photos and I said we didn't have much in stock and, besides, a print can be altered and might not show the true colors. He asked if White Sands could shoot a few new photos. I said yes and volunteered to shoot a role of Kodachrome slides.

By using Kodachrome, we agreed he could see unaltered images of the lakebed.

So I went out and shot a series of photos around the space shuttle landing strips. I shot in all directions so they could see what the background would be like.

I mailed the roll of film to an address in California and got a call back in a week or two. They liked the look of the lakebed and Fritz Manes, the movie's producer, wanted to actually visit the place.

We arranged a day and I did the paperwork to get Manes and his crew onto the missile range. I drove them out to the flats and we looked around. In the process Manes explained they wanted to shoot the ice flow scene some place easy to get to and in comfortable weather. He said through their special effects magic they could mask out the mountains in the background and make the flat expanse look like

ice. This was before CGI in movies. Southern New Mexico was a far better location than the frozen North.

Before Manes left, he said Eastwood would need to visit to approve the site before they could go to the Dept. of Army with a formal request to use the lakebed for filming.

I said that would be fine and promptly lost control of the project. When the New Mexico Film Board, representing the company, called back to make arrangements for a spring 1981 visit, my office mate Debbie Bingham somehow intercepted the call.

She met Eastwood, his company reps and a couple of people from the New Mexico Film Board at the Small Missile Range and drove up to the flats. When they got out onto the lakebed, Debbie said she was surprised at how tall Eastwood wasn't. She always pictured him as a large person reflecting his roles as an action hero.

The film board personnel were quite excited about having Eastwood in New Mexico. When they made arrangements with Debbie, they explained that everything should be low-key with no one there to take Eastwood's photo. "Don't bother him," they said. Afterwards, Debbie said each board member seemed to have two cameras and showed no restraint in using them around the actor.

In addition to his physical appearance, Debbie wasn't much impressed by the star's demeanor. She said he seemed kind of "dull" about the lighting. When he got out of the car, he said it didn't look so white to him. She advised him to take off his sunglasses. Then the glare was blinding and he admitted it was bright.

The next problem was her request to get his autograph on one of the White Sands post guides to display in the WSMR visitors center. She asked him to sign it. He asked her to spell her name. She replied that it wasn't for her and he should just make it out to White Sands Missile Range. He then asked to her to spell that. Incredulously, she proceeded to spell each word in the name.

To be fair to Eastwood, Debbie did overhear them talking about all the margaritas in Santa Fe the night before. He may have been a bit sluggish from the late-night partying.

One real problem they discussed was time of year for the filming. The movie company's schedule called for them to shoot in June. When Debbie explained that temperatures on those flats usually exceed 100 degrees in June, it dawned on them that actors wearing winter parkas, heavy gloves and boots in such conditions might be difficult. It was something for them to address.

Eventually, the company decided the lakebed would meet their needs and went to the Department of Army to seek permission to film there.

There are offices, one for each military service, in Los Angeles that do nothing but deal with requests from film companies for military support in their projects with equipment, personnel, locations, etc. If the staffers are positive about a project, they start coordinating to see if it is possible. In this case, it meant questioning White Sands to see if the range could and was willing to support.

The answer from White Sands, as it has been for most movie requests, is that it is possible, but the filming has to be on a non-interference basis. That means the film company would have to work around the missile range's schedule and not the other way round. If there was a missile firing in that area or a planned impact or space shuttle pilot training, the company might have to evacuate for several hours or maybe even all day.

To say the least, such a restriction is almost impossible for a movie company to live with. They burn money so fast, a day or two of delay can probably cost them something into six figures. Plus, an unplanned delay might ripple out and mess up equipment and personnel schedules on down the line.

In the end, Malpaso withdrew their request to film at White Sands and went elsewhere. The movie was released in 1982, not long after the Space Shuttle Columbia landed on the nearby shuttle landing strip at White Sands.

Other feature-length movies that did film on the missile range were: *Convoy* starring Kris Kristofferson and Ali MacGraw (a convoy of trucks passed through the sand dunes on Range Road 10); *The Man Who Fell To Earth* starring David Bowie (Bowie came down the stairs from the test building at the Solar Furnace; *Transformers* starring a bunch of huge alien robots and, by the way, Shia LaBeouf, Megan Fox and Josh Duhamel (A Middle Eastern desert village was built in the sand dunes and the tank farm was used as a military base's weapons yard); and *Transformers: Revenge of the Fallen* starring the same characters as the first (sand dunes again filled in for Middle East-

ern desert - Egypt with pyramids inserted in post production).

The Sounds Behind The Death Star

A highly decorated Hollywood type who visited White Sands but is almost invisible to the public has to be Ben Burtt. He has won two Oscars for his sound and sound effects work (*Indiana Jones and the Last Crusade* and *E.T. The Extra-Terrestrial*) and two Special Achievement Awards (*Star Wars* and *Raiders of the Lost Ark*) from the Academy Awards.

To top it off, he is one of the nicest and most unassuming people you are likely to meet – at least he was back in 1978.

He visited White Sands twice that year to gather sounds for the Lucas Films sound library. Debbie Bingham and I each escorted him around for several days as he recorded everything from missile and rocket launches to elevators operating and vault doors being opened and closed.

He explained that for generations, movie studios had been recycling sound effects again and again. He had an ear for it, and when he went to movies as a kid he could close his eyes and tell you which studio made the film by the sounds of gunshots, car engines, sirens and other noises added after filming. They were always the same, over and over.

Eventually he went to college and majored in physics. Jobs in physics are hard to come by, so after college he took a job operating a special effects camera with Lucas Films. One day someone came through asking if anyone knew anything about sound. Burtt raised his hand and never looked back.

When the first *Star Wars* movie was in planning, he made a very deliberate decision to get away from the old sound effects. This was going to be a new and different space movie and the sounds needed to reflect the new viewing experience the movie was going to create.

Burtt and his team went out into the world outside the studio and started collecting all kinds of sounds. He told Debbie they went to zoos and aquariums to record all kinds of animals. On the other hand, he said the sound of water gurgling down a drain was one of the most intriguing they had run into. Many of these sounds were used in the movies and many effects were engineered by combining two or more sounds to create new and unique ones.

By the time we met Burtt, he was already pretty

important. He'd won his special award for the first *Star Wars* movie. The movie was a huge hit; once people found out who he was, organizations threw open their doors to welcome him. It was easy for us to coordinate the visits.

Capturing the noise from the missile launches was probably the hardest thing we did. He had a couple of very expensive tape recorders and some long cables to run the microphones out as close as possible to the missiles. Usually the recorders were near us in some relatively safe spot, so he could turn them on just before the shot and tweak the input as needed.

That became a challenge for one shot when I was escorting Burtt. We'd arranged with the Navy to record a middle-of-the-night NASA-sponsored Aries sounding rocket launch at Launch Complex 36. And I mean middle of the night as it was scheduled for 2:45 a.m.

The Aries utilized the rocket motor from the second stage of the old Minuteman ICBM system. At the time it was the largest thing fired on White Sands. The motor was 44 inches in diameter and close to 30 feet long. It weighed in at over six tons. For us it was BIG.

It was a very powerful rocket that enabled NASA to propel large payloads very high above the earth. On Dec. 16, 1976, an Aries launched at WSMR reached an altitude of 319 miles. The nosecone survived its freefell to earth and was put on display in the WSMR visitors center.

The night Burtt and I were there, the payload reached an altitude of 220 miles before coming down on a parachute up in the middle of the missile range.

The Aries was launched from a stool or stand and basically flew almost straight up in the air like the old moon rockets. That meant the safety footprint was essentially a circle radiating from the launch point.

Normally, the Safety Office would only allow project-necessary personnel outside the heavy concrete blockhouse for the launch. The problem for Burtt was the shelter was several hundred yards from the rocket to where he wanted to place his microphones. His cables weren't nearly long enough.

Lloyd "Gunner" Briggs was running the sounding rocket program at the time and he proposed a compromise. Briggs was an old Navy veteran who did things his way. He said he would let us get much closer if we would lie in a ditch and keep our heads down during the launch. Without thinking about it too much, we agreed.

So Burtt set up the microphones and ran cable over to a roadside ditch just about two hundred feet from this huge rocket. We sat beside each other in the sand and listened to the countdown blaring over a nearby loudspeaker.

At zero there was a loud explosion and a blinding flash of white light. A bit tense, we watched the rocket slowly lift off the stool with smoke and fire blowing out of the motor. The noise was overwhelming. As it got higher up, it appeared to be almost directly over us.

At that point I remember thinking, "Go baby, go. Just keep going."

If it had blown up or stopped thrusting, we would have been trying to dodge rather large chunks of burning debris. It would have ruined our night. Burtt was so intent on his recorders, I'm not sure he realized how exposed we really were in that ditch.

But it was a success and Burtt went on to more fame. I was convinced by others to contact him some weeks later and ask for a souvenir of his visit from *Star Wars*. He was such a nice guy he did not tell me to drop dead, but instead sent a replica Darth Vader mask that is now on display in the White Sands Museum with a note from him. It's just a Halloween costume mask but it was nice of him to go to the effort.

Walter Cronkite - The Dean of Newsmen

Walter Cronkite visited Trinity Site at White Sands Missile Range on Oct. 21, 1978. Because it was a Saturday, I suspect Jim Nieb and I got the job of escorting him because no one else wanted to give up their day off.

On Thursday, Oct. 19, we first met with John Ward, a CBS News associate producer, cameraman Pat O'Dell, and soundman Arnie Jensen. Ward was from New York while O'Dell and Jensen flew in from the CBS affiliate in Dallas.

We went over ground rules and found out what they wanted to accomplish. The next day Nieb and I drove to Alamogordo to pick them up. Ward took one of our warnings to heart and came out with a brand new pair of cowboy boots "to keep the scorpions off."

We spent Thursday and Friday shooting background material for the Cronkite standup.

When most news organizations contact White

Sands and want to visit Trinity Site, the crew arrives by car and is escorted to the site. Not when you are CBS and Walter Cronkite is your reporter. Nieb and I only drove to Holloman Air Force Base where we boarded an Army helicopter and flew the crew to Trinity Site.

On the flight up, we flew over some wild horses that O'Dell wanted to videotape. We said "yes" and he went to work filming the horses running below us. I remember as he leaned out, then a little more and a little more, I wondered how I would report a CBS cameraman falling out of an Army helicopter. About then Jensen reached out and grabbed O'Dell's belt. He hung on until we ran out of horses.

On Saturday morning Nieb and I split up. He met Jensen and O'Dell and escorted them to Trinity by car. I met Ward and we went to Holloman to meet Cronkite who arrived by charter jet. We then flew him to Trinity Site in an Army chopper.

The biggest problem the crew had at Trinity Site was the wind. It was a cloudy and breezy day with some gusts well over 20 miles per hour. No matter how much hairspray they put on his wispy hair, the wind blew it around.

They finally solved the problem by having him face into the wind so it blew the hair in the direction it was combed.

I wrote an article about the visit for the post newspaper and said this about Cronkite: "Incidentally, Cronkite's voice sounds as good live as it does on TV. He has a certain way of just turning it on and projecting this authoritative sounding voice. Some of those pauses he uses are not planned. At times he would forget the script and then ad-lib it. After one of these takes, the cameraman remarked that the ad-lib was better than the script."

The whole thing with Cronkite only took about 90 minutes. When they were done, Cronkite said, "As the saying goes, let's get the hell out of here."

As I recall, the piece aired on *CBS Evening News* on Jan. 1, 1979. It was the first of a series looking at the possibilities of "Doomsday."

And that's the way it was, October 21, 1978. A day like any other day except I was there.

Bataan Memorial Death March Marchers

At first glance, one would assume that an event featuring participants running or walking a marathon-length route through the desert should be in the Sports chapter. To complete the 26-mile course in a timely fashion certainly qualifies as an athletic endeavor. Couch potatoes and other unprepared individuals can suffer greatly trying to complete the course.

But completing this marathon is different from almost any other marathon in the country. This event has always been about honoring the thousands of American and Filipino soldiers who fought for the Philippines and then endured the horrible circumstances of the Bataan Death March at the hands of the conquering Japanese. A 26-mile run/walk with water stations every two miles pales in comparison to the real forced march where captives were pushed along at bayonet point without food or water, afraid to stop and rest for fear of being shot.

Nobody wants to see this event become just another marathon.

The event can get quite emotional as many of the Bataan survivors attend the opening ceremonies. They are quite elderly now. In fact, very few are left and the numbers shrink dramatically from year to year.

There are so few left now, reading the list of those who have died since the last march doesn't take much time.

Those that do come appreciate the marchers and what it means. Many of the survivors position themselves along the beginning of the route where they receive salutes and handshakes from thousands. For the marchers, meeting these men provides another jolt of adrenaline as they start the long day. Unfortunately, it is hard to maintain that energy high hour after hour on the trail.

Mingling with the crowd at the start is interesting and inspirational. I have seen several generations in one family walking to honor a father/grandfather/great-grandfather who endured Bataan. They wore matching t-shirts with his photo on the back.

I once saw a large group from a small rural community marching to honor their former minister who had survived Bataan and then served their needs for decades.

I have seen soldiers from the Wounded Warrior program marching with their prosthetic legs. During the first several years, I saw a Bataan survivor march part of the course.

I once saw a marcher covered with bandages to protect his burn-scared skin from the sun. He read about Bataan while recovering from an accident and said the Bataan soldiers' bravery and strength gave him the courage to fight his own way to recovery. His day on the route was a way to say thank you.

I have seen marchers whose feet look like raw hamburger after just six miles but they are determined to go on. At the same time, I have seen high school Junior ROTC cadets literally dancing through

Bataan marchers in the military light category await their turn to start. Photo by author.

the course, laughing and talking, looking like they could do it again in the late afternoon.

And I have seen, fairly frequently, two soldiers – one on each side of a third – supporting the weaker, exhausted soldier, working as a team to get all three of them home.

It can be a grueling march and an emotional experience. Having it on White Sands Missile Range will ensure it receives the proper balance between athletics and a memorial to many great American heroes.

The memorial march was started in 1989 by the Army ROTC unit at New Mexico State University to pay tribute to those World War II heroes. A high proportion of the Americans captured by the Japanese were New Mexicans, more than 1,800 men, because a whole New Mexico National Guard unit was there – the 200th/515th Coast Artillery. The rest of the men were scattered from all over the country.

As of 2012, about half of the few Bataan survivors left nationwide lived in New Mexico.

The first few marches were held in Las Cruces and on surrounding public lands. In 1992, with difficulties gathering around the event, White Sands Missile Range and the New Mexico National Guard stepped in to sponsor it. It was moved to the missile range.

At first the route left the main post on desert roads, crossed U.S. Highway 70, looped up around Mineral Hill, and came back to the main post on the west side of Owen Road. Eventually, range officials tinkered with the course to get it as close to the official marathon length of 26.2 miles as possible.

However, they do not plan to go to the effort necessary to make the course a certified marathon event. Again, having some sanctioned race is not the point of the event and many feel trying to make it into a "real race" would detract from the original intention. Besides, with all the soft sand to wade through and the 1,000-foot elevation gain, a time at this event would be meaningless when compared to another marathon.

For those who want to really challenge themselves, there is a heavy category. For military personnel in this category, they must carry a 35-lb. pack and wear combat clothing with the appropriate boots.

Years ago when Gary Johnson was governor of New Mexico, he visited White Sands to participate in Bataan. He entered in the heavy division as the New Mexico National Guard's civilian commander. To top it off, he didn't just walk the route, he ran it with one of the guard teams. We saw him out there well into the route with that dazed and determined look long-distance athletes get when they are lost in their world of keeping body and soul together.

Johnson received some flack from one of the Santa Fe pundits who objected to the news media calling Johnson an "athlete" when he did things like Bataan. The writer said Johnson never played football or basketball and didn't deserve to be placed alongside football players or other team sport members.

This was a very concrete example demonstrating how little these commentators really know but, for some reason, get to spout their opinions as if they were experts. I'm pretty sure Johnson finished Bataan faster than most any football player could have finished. Also, Johnson finished the Ironman Triathlon in Hawaii several times in very fast times for his age. He climbed Mount Everest, one of the most grueling endeavors man has dreamed up. It seems doubtful to me that most superstars in their respective sports could have done these things at the same age as Johnson.

Over the years, Bataan participation has steadily climbed to over 5,000 folks in 2013. There are several factors contributing to the increased numbers. One of the main things was the addition of a shorter optional course. Folks who are unable to complete the marathon distance can still take part by doing the 14-mile route.

Another factor is the amount of publicity. Every year people come from all over America and many foreign countries. Their stories get told locally and nationally and others notice – they decide to come the next year.

The Bataan Memorial March appears in a 2005 book called *From Fairbanks to Boston: 50 Great Marathons*. The editors collected details on interesting or unusual marathons from all over the country. I was asked to write the chapter on Bataan even though I have only walked the event a few times. They didn't care. I provided a different perspective, and for an event like Bataan it worked fine.

The future of the Bataan march will be interesting to watch. In the beginning, the event received all kinds of military support that was free or very cheap. Over the years that has dwindled. In response, White Sands has steadily raised the price. Some are wondering if many of the locals who have participated in it for years will soon decide it is too pricey.

The Neighbors

For decades, White Sands hosted open houses and invited the public to come and see what was going on at the range. Originally, these events were held in association with Armed Forces Day and later they were moved to be associated with the missile range's anniversary of July 9. As the testing mission shrank and missile systems only came occasionally

Looking west at the "missile midway" during the June 1965 open house at WSMR. Not only is there a huge Redstone missile in the front, its associated equipment is also on display to the right. WSMR photo.

to WSMR, there wasn't much to show off and the events died.

The best ones were in the 1950s and 60s. For instance, the Armed Forces Day event at White Sands on May 16, 1959 drew 10,000 visitors. The event included live firings of four different missiles and the static display of others in a "missile midway."

The launches were of the Nike Ajax, Nike Hercules, Lacrosse and Little John. The missiles in the missile midway included: Sergeant, HAWK, Nike Ajax, Nike Hercules, Honest John, Little John, Lacrosse, Talos, Aerobee, Corporal, Redstone, Pogo, Sidewinder, Falcon and Matador. If you know your missiles, you'll note that all three services were represented on the midway.

In addition, there were some target drones like the Q2 and Q5. For those not interested in missiles, there were displays all over post of more traditional Army gear like an ambulance manned by medics, an M-48 tank and a fire truck.

Paul Harvey

In November 1963, radio newsman and commentator Paul Harvey visited White Sands in the company of Las Cruces civic and chamber of commerce officials. He was given a briefing on the mission and operations at the missile range and given a tour of range operation and the missile park.

The post newspaper described Harvey as a "veteran broadcaster." That is a bit of an understatement.

Harvey started in radio in Tulsa at the age of 14. Initially he did custodial work but quickly began filling in for announcers by reading commercials and the news. For almost 60 years, he polished his unique and highly recognized delivery style.

In 1951, the ABC Radio Network started the *Paul Harvey News and Comment Program*. This show basically ran until his death in early 2009. His quirky delivery and salesmanship made him a legend for many in America. At one time an estimated 24 million people listened to him every week.

Harvey was noted for several catch phrases that were used over the decades. He would segment his broadcast by announcing "page two" and then "page three." He was famous for his, "You know what the news is, in a minute, you're going to hear....the rest of the story." And he always ended with "Paul Harvey....good day."

19

Two Roads Across The Range

One issue that seems to pop up like clockwork for White Sands is the question of opening old State Route 52 across the missile range for public use. The question comes from citizens, city leaders, county groups, and even the New Mexico state legislature.

The road is now designated as the missile range's Range Road 6. The state route used to connect Tularosa on the east side of White Sands to Engle and Truth or Consequences, then called "Hot Springs," on the west. East to west, the road crosses the flats of the Tularosa Basin, then winds its way through Rhodes Canyon in the San Andres Mountains, and finally drops down to Engle on the Jornada del Muerto. From Engle, State Road 51 finishes the route to Truth or Consequences. (See map on page 3)

Before World War II, this route was a gravel/desert road used mostly by local ranchers and a few hardy travelers going elsewhere. Former ranchers told me the road would be impassable in places of the Tularosa Basin after summer rains. The dirt road simply turned to a bog and they would have to wait a day or two to get through. Also, washouts occurred in Rhodes Canyon requiring road repair or small detours to get through.

Most of the time, the road was bone dry and produced huge clouds of dust every time a vehicle sped along it.

To support ranchers living along the route and those few traveling through, Uel (Pottsy) and Mellie Potter sold Phillips 66 gasoline at their ranch on the north side of the road in Rhodes Canyon. There was no electricity in the canyon,

so the gasoline was hand pumped from a 500-gallon underground storage tank into a glass cylinder mounted on top of the pump. There the gas could be visually inspected for impurities and measured before draining it with a hose into the vehicle.

During the 1930s, the Civilian Conservation Corps (CCC) improved the road in many spots. Some of their work, like taking the roadbed out of the canyon bottom and perching it along the canyon wall, is still visible today in the form of the cribbing or stone retaining walls holding the roadway up. Also, a number of stone-supported culverts can be found in Rhodes and Bosque Canyons.

At one time, the CCC had a small tent camp in Rhodes Canyon for the workers. It was off the south side of the old road just northwest of Rock House Spring which is west of the Potter gas station. The most notable remains of the camp are the two stone pillars marking the gate into the camp. Most drivers

According to Hazel Potter Johnson, who donated this photo, this is the CCC camp in Rhodes Canyon during the 30s. Barely visible are the two stone pillars for the gate at the top of the photo.

on the current road roll on by and never see these structures as they are pretty well hidden by brush.

In perusing a Public Affairs folder containing papers concerning the old road, I found a sampling of correspondence from a variety of folks asking WSMR to open the road on weekends. The documents ranged from responses to private individuals, to Senator Jeff Bingaman, to the Sierra County Economic Development Organization and others.

Over the decades it looks like most of the appeals have been generated by or at the request of Sierra County promoters. They look at a map of central New Mexico and see the missile range as a huge roadblock to travelers east of WSMR trying to get to Elephant Butte and Caballo Reservoirs. They figure opening the old state road would cut many miles from the trip that now forces drivers around the south or north ends of WSMR.

Since going through the missile range was obviously shorter, most supporters figured it was faster too. In fact, many merely suggested opening the road in its present condition and letting people through on Saturday and Sunday.

To counter this, in 1972, range personnel test drove the two routes and timed each trip. Driving from Tularosa to Truth or Consequences via State Route 52, a distance of 83 miles, took two hours and 35 minutes. In contrast, the trip from Tularosa to Truth or Consequences via U.S. Highway 70 and Interstate 25, a distance of 148 miles, took two hours and ten minutes. The time and distance difference clearly demonstrates how slow the road is when going through the mountains.

Of course, some people also suggested the road be improved. An early study in 1964 estimated it would cost $3.3 million to bring the road up to an acceptable standard for public use.

The most serious attempt to reopen the road took place in 1978 when the 33rd New Mexico legislature passed House Memorial 6. It tasked the state highway department to "perform and present to the first session of the thirty-fourth legislature a study that sets forth fully all arguments regarding the feasibility, in light of the continued operation by the federal government of the White Sands missile base and other military installation in the area, and the cost necessary for reopening of state route 52 . . ."

Some people miss the next part which states, "it

The old roadway for State Route 52 in Rhodes Canyon when it was perched on the side of the canyon wall to keep it out of the flash floods in the bottom. Note the dry stacked rock in the middle of the photo to keep the road from sliding into the canyon on the right. Photo by the author.

is the intention of the house of representatives that reopening state route 52 shall not be pursued if detrimental to the continued operation of White Sands missile base . . .”

The highway department's team visited WSMR to see the road and determine what would be needed to fix it. They also collected all kinds of economic data from the area, traffic patterns and public comment.

The resulting report nixes reopening the road on many fronts. From the White Sands side there are all the security and inconvenience issues. Range officials pointed out the road is through the very center of White Sands. All kinds of things fall out of the sky there and many sensitive facilities are near the road.

To protect the travelers' safety and the missile range's assets, security fencing and manned gates would be required along the route. Even with that, WSMR officials said there would be a risk of spies using the road to have access to the heart of the range.

Weekend missions at some facilities would have to be rescheduled and squeezed in elsewhere. Also, additional roadblocks might be required if missions were needed on weekends.

In the end, White Sands found such a move to be a huge inconvenience, costing lots of money and jeopardizing the security of range programs.

Next the highway department presented what would be required to bring the old road up to the standards of the day with a paved surface. They projected a construction cost of $31 million, an additional $5.4 million for engineering and contingencies, and $5 million just for the fencing. The math is pretty easy – over $40 million for a weekend road. Plus, this did not include reacquiring the right-of-way for the road.

They also made an estimate of how many vehicles would actually use the road each day it was open. They projected 388 cars per day for 1977 and by 1997 it would increase to 734 per day.

The report's conclusion was "the cost of constructing the road would exceed the benefits that would accrue to the road users."

Most of this information was shared with proponents at a public hearing on July 12, 1978 in Truth or Consequences. Many highway department personnel were there to explain their estimates and methodologies. Also present was Major General Tobiason, White Sands commander, and some of his staff.

Many people in the audience didn't like what they heard. They asked about making the road gravel instead of paving it to reduce costs. The state official said they didn't do a formal estimate for gravel but it wouldn't be a huge difference.

Of course, the proponents weren't taking into consideration the fact that many people with expensive RVs and boats probably weren't going to travel on miles of gravel to save a few miles. The spray of rocks would quickly remove valuable paint and dent expensive body features.

Some members of the audience took issue with Tobiason's claim there were missions in the center of the range all the time. They wondered if the general could provide them with an unspecified list of all the missions in that area.

When you look at all the petitions, proclamations, letters and other documents from citizens, there were a lot of people who favored opening the road. Even most members of the Truth or Consequences VFW signed a petition in favor of freeing the road.

One thing about this reaction that only some officials at WSMR understood was a popular view that the Department of Defense controlled way too much of the landscape in southern New Mexico. It was mostly military property from Fort Bliss in Texas to U.S. Highway 380 at the north end of WSMR. The military saw this as a great asset, but surrounding small communities that had residents displaced and pushed around by the Army weren't necessarily happy about the arrangement. Some saw it as more big government ruining their lives.

After the meeting, WSMR officials made the effort to reach out to local communities to tell them the range's story. Representatives visited towns and met with officials to brief them on current missions, to show them there really were multiple missions going on every day at WSMR. The one thing they really hit hard was the economic impact White Sands had on the local area.

With its thousands of highly paid employees living in surrounding towns and contracts for goods and services with local businesses totaling millions of dollars each year, the range was, and still is, a boon to these communities. Ultimately, by implying this gravy train would be endangered by propositions that might interfere with the mission, WSMR always won the day.

These efforts and arguments by White Sands in

the past haven't completely stopped the requests to reopen the road.

In 2001 many surrounding communities voted or decided to support a Road 52 reopening proposal originating from the Sierra County Commission. They tried a new angle. The proposal was billed as "opening a scenic corridor from Texas to Arizona to promote tourism and commerce."

The collection of groups endorsing the concept included the Village of Tularosa, Office of the Grant County Commissioners, Town of Silver City, Ruidoso Valley Chamber of Commerce, Village of Hatch, City of Truth or Consequences, City of Deming, and the City of Elephant Butte.

Of course the proposal eventually died. Interestingly, the effort did generate a call from a White Sands supporter that ended up being officially noted. The caller wanted White Sands to know about the effort being mounted to reopen the road. The caller warned that the undertaking might lead to lawsuits against WSMR or negative publicity for the range.

As range activity continues to shrink since the end of the Cold War, there will certainly be more efforts made to open the old road on weekends.

Surrounding communities have not been the only ones trying to use roads on White Sands. In the mid-1980s, WSMR came up on a list for possible placement of the Hard Mobile Launchers and their Small Intercontinental Ballistic Missiles. Playing off the name "Minuteman," critics dubbed this smaller missile "the midgetman."

This was an idea dreamed up just before the end of the Cold War to create a shell game for the ICBMs needed to counter a strike from the Soviet Union. Silos and their missiles were considered too vulnerable from attack and wouldn't be able to mount an effective retaliatory strike. The answer was to use smaller missiles and store them in mobile launchers that could randomly move around every day. The Soviets would never be able to find them all.

Of course, it was politically impossible to put these launchers and their nuclear-tipped missiles out on the public highways. Nobody wanted to be driving down I-25 behind a convoy of huge vehicles carrying nuclear missiles looking for a place to camp for the night. Then no one wanted them to camp nearby because that area automatically became a major target for a Soviet nuclear missile strike.

There was also the major issue of providing the required security detail for each convoy. It would have been a small army of personnel and vehicles moving like a cloud of ants across the landscape.

Instead, the shakers and movers for this shell game idea proposed putting the mobile missiles on large military bases like White Sands and Yuma Proving Ground. Although this would greatly restrict where the missiles could be positioned each day, it eliminated much of the public's concern – except for those folks living around White Sands.

Most folks at WSMR didn't see much future for the idea because of the range's mission. Whole airplanes and missiles, some with explosives still onboard, were falling out of the sky all the time. Heaven forbid, a test missile might come crashing down on a nuclear missile sitting in a supposedly hardened, blast-proof container.

Also, plans called for randomly moving the missiles daily. With the problem of coordinating daily with the range's shot schedule, the movements probably wouldn't have ended up being very random at all.

Finally, those roads on the missile range would have been destroyed. The launcher trailer and its tractor formed a unit close to 200,000 lbs. The roads at WSMR were never constructed for such weights. A train of these vehicles would have chewed up the fragile asphalt and left long stretches of cratered roadway.

The idea went away along with the Cold War.

The Ribbon of Death

It took more than three years to complete, but when the construction was finished in 1959 to make U.S. Highway 70 a four-lane road, many White Sands employees breathed a sigh of relief. According to those who drove daily from Las Cruces to the missile range, the highway was known as the "ribbon of death."

The main problem with the narrow highway from Las Cruces was San Augustin Pass, also known as Organ Pass in those days. In 1958, the missile range military police reported that 1,000 cars entered and left the post every day through the Las Cruces gate during the rush hours. Inevitably, most of those cars ended up stacked behind each other going over the pass.

Old-timers say semi-trucks used to crawl up the mountain at five to ten miles per hour and stymie normal traffic flow. They report it was a miserable drive. Some of those in a big hurry took to passing slow vehicles on the shoulder, thus running the risk of hitting rocks and other debris on the roadside.

The exact number of WSMRites injured or killed on the old road is unknown, but when looking through the post newspapers I was struck by the many headlines about personnel in auto crashes. In that first decade of White Sands, there were no seat belts and the roads themselves made for mayhem. A fix for the road part of the equation came about in the late 1950s.

In 1956, enough state and federal funds were rounded up to turn the narrow road into what would then be called a super highway. The construction was done in four steps or sections, so detours were not continuous or spread over the entire length of the road.

The first section constructed was a six-mile stretch from the northeast city limits of Las Cruces at Madrid and Main to a point about one mile east of the Jornada Range Station road. Brown Contracting Co. of Albuquerque started the work in May 1956 and finished in November the same year. The price tag was $684,223.

The second and shortest section of road was the 2.1 miles over San Augustin Pass from near Organ to just a quarter of a mile east of the pass. Work was started in July 1956 by Armstrong and Armstrong of Roswell. According to state and contractor officials at the time, the lowering of the roadbed by 34 feet was the biggest earthmoving project ever undertaken in this area. When completed it was also the most expensive stretch of four-lane in the state.

In lowering the roadbed the contractor used 80,000 pounds of explosives to break up the rock and earth. They drilled 20-foot-deep holes in the granite and filled them with explosives using about 4,000 pounds for each blast. In moving all this rock, the contractor foreman claimed his crews came across some very low-grade silver ore. He said it was there but not worth anyone's trouble to mine.

When the pass was completed in July 1957, the road was shorter and two curves were eliminated. It opened with the speed limit set at 60 miles per hour.

Also in July 1957, work started to finish the road down the mountain east from the pass to the range access road. Henry Thygesen and Co. of Albuquerque received the $966,698 contract. The 5.7-mile section followed the old right of way and was completed in April 1958.

Work on the last section, 8.75 miles, did not begin until February 1959. The million-dollar stretch was completed later in the year.

As traffic has increased on the highway, the section through San Augustin Pass was widened again. It now has a third lane for big trucks and other really slow traffic on the up-hill sections.

20

Caves And Tunnels

White Sands Missile Range is a land of holes. Some are natural but most are manmade.

Nature provided some beauties on the north end of the missile range with lava flows on the west and east boundaries. Deep cracks and lava tubes make for some intriguing holes.

The western flow is the older of the two and just touches the range's border. The flow is famous for its lava tubes that are home to huge colonies of bats. In fact, in the past, enterprising locals mined the thick layers of bat guano from the tube floors.

The eastern lava flow is much newer and originates off the missile range north of U.S. Highway 380. About 5,000 years ago, off and on over a period of about 30 years, lava spewed from Little Black Peak and flowed south into the Tularosa Basin. The flow reaches about 44 miles from its origin and is four to six miles wide. It is 160 feet thick in places.

The eruption was a slow ongoing process much like the eruptions in Hawaii. The lava is described as pahoehoe meaning it is rough and jagged. The surface is punctuated with fissures, pits, and openings into lava tubes. It is a difficult area to cross on foot and almost impossible on horseback. Wearing a new pair of boots into the lava field can leave them shredded after a day hike.

Geologists say the flow was able to reach so far south because it traveled most of the distance in lava tubes that insulated it from the cooling air above.

Most of the really obvious holes on the missile range predate military use of the land. They are from the legions of prospectors and miners who swarmed over the two mountain ranges found on White Sands. Mine dumps and their associated adits and shafts are still visible even though most haven't been worked in almost a hundred years.

When the government took over the lands that now form the missile range, not only did officials lease and then buy dozens of ranches, they also had to lease and then purchase the mining claims. At the beginning of the process there were several hundred claims, but only a few were still active at the end of World War II.

Frank Kottlowski, former director of the New Mexico Bureau of Mines and Mineral Resources, wrote that in the San Andres Mountains these miners found gold, silver, lead, vanadinite, copper, talc, bismuth, zinc and flourite. However, he concluded none of it was significant. The only place with large ore bodies that would support large-scale mining was in the Organ District around the small community of Organ and San Augustin Pass. Those mines included the Stephenson-Bennett, Torpedo and Modoc that produced millions of dollars in lead, copper and silver.

A few sizeable strikes certainly gave people a perceived chance at wealth and many went out seeking their fortune. Rob Cox, from the San Augustine Ranch, once said that during the Great Depression many a prospector came to the ranch looking for directions and a handout. Rob's father Jim Cox owned the ranch at that time and was always ready to provide them with a simple meal before seeing them off.

Add to that the stories and legends about the Spanish. They must have prospected the mountains on what is now White Sands Missile Range. The Organ and San Andres ridges and peaks were clearly visible from their main road, the Camino Real, which passed by on its way from Mesilla to Socorro and on up to Santa Fe.

The Spanish were the first generation of fortune hunters as they looked for the fabled seven cities of gold. They failed miserably, but it didn't stop subsequent generations of explorers and settlers from looking for something similar. Many follow-on stories, like the tale of Padre LaRue, told of Spanish mines and treasure lost because of one misfortune after another. Fake maps and documents sold to the gullible promised them the directions they needed to find it.

Bob Eveleth, the Senior Mining Engineer at the New Mexico Bureau of Mines & Mineral Resources in Socorro, has politely called them "eternal optimists." It is probably something akin to today's gamblers who play the lottery week after week, forever optimistic about their chances.

The names they gave their mines are a good indicator of this optimism. Some of the mine names on the missile range included Hidden Treasure, King Solomon, Quick Strike, Four Aces, Golden Lily Group, Crystal, Silver King, Silver Coinage and Copper King. In reality, most all of them lived up to the few realistic names such as Last Chance, Buzzard, and Hard Scrabble.

In a place with such legends as the seven cities of gold and a padre's 100 tons of gold, myths are still quoted and embellished. For instance, while working in Public Affairs, I was asked a couple of times about the story of a 14-mile tunnel from the San Andres Mountains toward the Rio Grande.

This is quite a fantastic story that was introduced to the world by David Chandler in his book *100 Tons of Gold*. In the story, Harvey Snow descends over a thousand steps inside Hard Scrabble Mtn. and finds a tunnel headed west with an underground stream

> *Pop-Up:* Years ago I was told by more than one person associated with mining that "adits" were the horizontal holes going into mines. They said "tunnels" was an incorrect term because a tunnel has to be open at both ends – like a highway going through a hill. For an opening to be a tunnel, it had to have an exit. Until my wife started editing this chapter, I just thought that was an interesting bit of trivia - some esoteric jargon from the mining world.
>
> In reading this, my wife questioned the usage. It sent me to the internet to do more research. It turns out the meanings and uses of words like adit and tunnel are just about anything you want. I checked in dictionaries, encyclopedias, glossaries of mining terms and professional word lists. Basically, I was able to find definitions from authoritative sources justifying using adit and tunnel interchangeably. Being a reasonable person and unable to find evidence that God has decided the matter, I have used adit and tunnel to mean much the same thing.

running down it – hot water instead of cold to distinguish it from Doc Noss and his Victorio Peak tale. He easily follows the water, finding a variety of artifacts along the way to include stacks of gold, silver and copper, and some things he refused to talk about. He then emerges out in the sands of the Jornada del Muerto using a hole covered with bushes. Supposedly it took him two days to make the pitch-black trip.

Another fanciful story is about a tunnel connecting the Gulf of Mexico to New Mexico so the Navy can bring submarines into the desert to test fire missiles at White Sands. I suspect this is one tale some sailors stationed at White Sands made up to tease locals when they were drinking in local bars. They probably told the story and asked, "Why else would the Navy have a unit in the middle of a desert missile range?"

Teagarden Cave

If you are fit and used to bushwhacking, it only requires a 45-minute hike and steep climb up to the mouth of Teagarden Cave on the east flank of Bear Peak. Also, it helps if you know where you are going because the opening is nothing more than a three-to four-foot diameter hole in a small outcropping of rock. It is very unremarkable and very difficult to find unless you step into it.

The hole drops about five feet before sloping back into the mountain and disappearing into complete darkness. The opening is small enough that crawling is the easiest way in or out.

I first saw the cave on July 20, 1987. It was an exciting trip because the cave has been described by some old-timers as a "mini-Carlsbad Caverns."

Jeff Osborne, formerly with the missile range's Explosive Ordnance Disposal team, had in a sense "rediscovered" the cave earlier that year and wanted to show it to me. When he asked around about it, he couldn't find anyone who had visited or knew anyone who had visited Teagarden in many decades.

Before entering, he gave me a set of kneepads, fingerless leather gloves, and a hard-hat equipped with a powerful electric light. The hat was to protect my hard head and provided a perfect place to mount the lamp so it would point wherever I looked.

We climbed down the little shaft after checking for rattlesnakes and then crawled through a ten-foot tunnel into the darkness. In those ten feet we moved into a completely alien world. The air was suddenly cool and damp. The walls sparkled under our lights and the formations caused fantastic shadows everywhere we looked. And when we turned off the lights, it was dark - very, very dark. It was the kind of dark where you can't see your hand in front of your face.

On a planet where most of the great geographical discoveries have been made, traveling just a few feet in a new cave offers the same sense of adventure and discovery explorers like Lewis and Clark and others must have felt.

Compared to Carlsbad Caverns everything about Teagarden Cave is tiny. But I felt a little bit like an explorer as we crawled and squeezed our way through the rooms, all decorated with formations. There were stalactites and stalagmites, columns, popcorn, soda straws, flowstone and draperies.

Most of it was white but some was stained brown; a few formations showed hints of green and orange. One room, which we dubbed the "pond room," had an eight-foot by three-foot pool of water in it. The water was only inches deep, but its dead calm surface reflected the ceiling making it appear several feet deep.

When you travel through Carlsbad Caverns you are basically going through a museum. The National Park Service provides the light and lots of rules, and you don't dare stray from the asphalt path. In Teagarden the only light was supplied by

our own headlamps and there were no rangers saying we couldn't explore a side tunnel if we so desired. It didn't matter that they were dead ends, our curiosity was satisfied.

This photo of four boys and a man is from the L.B. Bentley collection. It is not labeled but we know Bentley frequently visited Teagarden Cave because he left behind his name and a date many times on various cave formations. Based on the dates he left, I'd guess the photo was taken between 1900 and 1910. One of the boys is holding a candle, so they came prepared. Also, the man is wearing a tie indicating they may have been on some sort of Sunday picnic-outing. Photo from New Mexico State University Library, Archives and Special Collections.

On the other hand, Osborne briefed me beforehand about cave etiquette. We had to be very careful not to break any of the formations and not to leave any oily fingerprints on the limestone. Many caves have been damaged by the thoughtlessness of visitors.

Although there was a sense of adventure for a rookie like me, exploring Teagarden certainly was not like going into a newly discovered cave. Everywhere I looked there was evidence of previous visitors. Many of the cave formations had been broken off and many visitors had signed or carved their names on the formations.

Some of the ranchers drew their brands beside their names. It appears a lot of couples and small groups visited the cave after 1900. It may have been the hot spot to take a girl on a picnic. We even found an empty whiskey bottle hidden behind a rock.

The oldest signature we found was dated 1896.

One name that caught my attention was L.B. Bentley. His signature appears several times in the cave from different years - mostly between 1903 and 1917.

Bentley used to own the general store in Organ, New Mexico, run ore assays, act as postmaster, and mine the surrounding mountains in the early 20th century. Also, he reportedly refused to give Pat Garrett credit when Garrett was living on a small ranch just north of U.S. Highway 70 and Mineral Hill. The Garrett place is on the missile range in an area called the Hazardous Test Area.

According to Leon Metz in his biography of Pat Garrett, many authors have written Garrett stopped at the Bentley store on Feb. 29, 1908 and argued with Wayne Brazel. Later in the day, Brazel surrendered to the Las Cruces sheriff saying he had killed Garrett in self-defense. Garrett's body was discovered east of Las Cruces with a bullet hole in the back of the head.

Metz doubts the meeting in Bentley's store ever

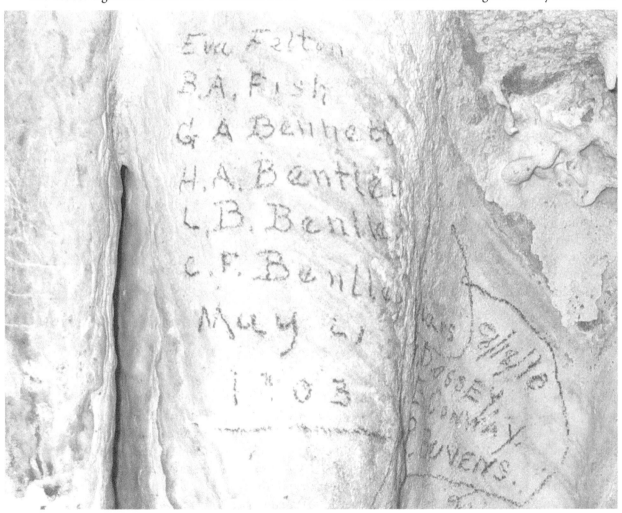

A closeup of a cave formation with names of a Bentley group that visited in May 1903. Photo by the author.

took place and says the source of the story appears to be old L.B. himself.

But Bentley can be credited with taking many great photographs of the local area. His collection is in the Rio Grande Historical Collections at the New Mexico State University library. Since he visited the cave many times, I called the library and asked them to check if there was a cave photo in the collection. They could only find one dim photo that appears to have been taken in the cave. Years later, in searching their on-line data base, I found several photos that are probably Teagarden.

A spelunker from the Mesilla Valley Grotto struggles to exit the opening that leads down to the water pool room. Note, just above his head are the stubs from broken stalactites that once hung down over the opening. Many of the cave formations are damaged like this as explorers in the late 19th century and early 20th century broke off formations to gain access to other parts of the cave or as souvenirs to take home. Photo by the author.

How many names are on the cave formations? On Oct. 25, 1997, I escorted a group of cavers from the Mesilla Valley Grotto to Teagarden so they could survey it, photograph it, and record any historic information available. Dave Belski was with the group and went around recording all the names he could find on the cave formations. The number was close to 200 names with many undated. The most recent dated one was 1956.

When Osborne first came to me hunting for this cave, he referred to it as "Tiergarten" Cave. At the time, the Mesilla Valley Grotto had it documented under that name instead of "Teagarden." Other sources show it as "Tiergarten" as well.

So, which is correct? The word "tiergarten" means animal garden or zoo in German but doesn't make too much sense for this cave. I suppose you could stretch things a bit and look at the formations as a display or zoo of fantastical shapes.

What about the Teagarden version? One old-timer said he assumed the cave was named after G.H. Teagarden of Las Cruces.

That gave me a clue and off I went looking for a "Teagarden" in the old *Rio Grande Republican*, a Las Cruces newspaper from the 1880s. I found him. In the paper there were display ads plugging "The Organ Mountain Coach Line, G.H. Teagarden, Proprietor."

He ran four-horse coaches to "The Organs and San Augustin three times a week on Mondays, Wednesdays and Fridays." The fare was $2 one-way and $3 for a round-trip. Express material could be sent at the rate of one cent per pound.

His name also popped up in lists of businessmen who contributed to one cause or another in Las Cruces.

This doesn't prove the cave should be called "Teagarden," but in my mind that name has a lot more going for it than "Tiergarten."

In 1990, I visited the cave with Jim and Andrea Goodbar. Jim was a Lands and Cave Specialist with the Bureau of Land Management. At the time he had completed two and a half years of graduate schoolwork in geography and cave/karst studies at Western Kentucky University. The school is only 20 miles from Mammoth Cave which has over 350 miles of cave - the longest in the world.

Goodbar theorized that the void of Teagarden Cave was formed by fracturing as opposed to being hollowed out by the action of water. The passages in the cave are all at right angles which is typical for limestone that has broken under stress. This means the void was made by rock movements (faulting) and the decorative materials were added later.

In fact, the formation building process is still ongoing in Teagarden. Rainwater and snow melt soak into the ground above the cave. The water becomes laden with carbon dioxide from decaying plant and animal material in the ground's topsoil and forms dilute carbonic acid. As this water seeps through the limestone forming Bear Peak, it dissolves some of limestone's main component, calcium carbonate. This solution drips into Teagarden and carbon dioxide bubbles away. Then the calcium carbonate precipitates and slowly adds calcite to the cave formations - crystal by crystal.

At one time Teagarden must have been a very wet cave because almost every surface is covered with formations. Goodbar felt many of the formations could have been deposited during glacial periods when this area was much wetter.

Evidence of Goodbar's theory was found during the late 1990s when I visited the cave again. This was in the middle of a run of drought years. The pond was dry and very few formations had water dripping from them. The cave is close to the surface, so water seeping into it may be directly related to seasonal rain and snowfall.

According to Goodbar, this cycle of wet and dry years makes it impossible to tell how old the cave is. When caves are dry they do not produce formations and the rate of formation growth during wet periods depends on a great many variables.

In our tour of the cave, Goodbar pointed out stalactites, stalagmites, columns (the joining of a stalactite and stalagmite), popcorn, coral (a jagged version of popcorn), dams, draperies and helictites. Helictites are small twisted straw-like formations that tend to randomly corkscrew from the wall or ceiling. Goodbar said the Europeans call them "eccentrics" which seems appropriate and is easy to remember.

In one part of the cave is a series of draperies that chime when they are gently tapped. Each sounds a different note because of their differing sizes. One is very impressive because of its deep, dignified ring.

During our visit we found evidence of wildlife at the cave entrance and inside. At the mouth of the cave we found a pile of mountain lion scat that included pieces of bone almost the size of my thumb.

Inside we found a couple of bats hanging from the low ceilings.

Although the cave has a lot of damage, Goodbar said it wasn't so bad. He said he is used to seeing caves on BLM land that are unprotected from the public and are spray painted, sledge hammered, and completely trashed. He also pointed out that many of the signatures, because of their dates, now have historic significance.

Teagarden is the best of the known caves on White Sands Missile Range. There are some gypsum caves such as Craven Cave and Craven Pit in the northeast portion of the range, but they do not have the formations found in Teagarden.

There probably are other caves in the San Andres and Oscura Mountains. The limestone is there, the area has been very wet at times in the past and Teagarden proves it is possible. If these other caves exist, more than likely their entrances are buried and may never be found.

But who knows, someday a young soldier on a missile recovery team may wander into some bushes and discover the opening to a another Carlsbad Caverns - a virgin world to explore.

Texas Canyon

It looks like a jagged scar that angles up the mountain from the golf course at White Sands and then disappears as it jogs toward Texas Canyon. The trail is visible from most places on the main post, but few people know it was once a road to the mines hidden deep in Texas Canyon.

In many places the trail is little more than a deep rut rapidly developing into a ravine. But through the middle of the 20th century it was a nasty little road that determined miners used to haul heavy equipment up to their operation. Part of one of their trucks is still on site along with several rock-crushing devices and a diesel engine to power them.

According to a New Mexico School of Mines bulletin published in 1935, two gold deposits were discovered in Texas Canyon between 1890 and 1900. John Dodd and his brother were the first to work the canyon's mines.

To crush the ore the brothers used an arrastre until 1898. Used for centuries all over the world, an arrastre is a crude but effective way of crushing ore to free the valuable mineral. It consists of a large rock or slab being pulled over another rock with the ore in between. The weight and motion effectively smash the ore to bits and can reduce it to flour if done correctly.

In 1898, the Dodd's reportedly erected a more modern two-stamp mill to crush ore.

In 1910, a company known as the Texas Canyon Mining and Milling Company was organized and acquired the property. They brought in an aerial tramway that had previously been used at the Modoc mine in Fillmore Canyon on the west side of the Organ Mountains.

The mining bulletin states that the tram was never used. However, the tram may have been used after 1935. In a visit to the canyon in 2005, I found one of the tramway towers was still standing between two of the mine adits. It could be that the tram was used to move ore from the upper adits to the road in order to haul it to the crushers.

The road into the canyon was constructed in 1917 and, according to the School of Mines bulletin, the last full-scale mining was done in 1927. It also states that by 1935 the road was impassable but could be made adequate for small trucks without great expense.

Enter Fred Schneider. Schneider came from Germany and kept a family, a wife and seven children, in El Paso while he and partner George Hohenberger prospected throughout the Organ and southern San Andres Mountains. Individually and together they filed and worked many claims around what is now White Sands Missile Range and Fort Bliss.

Before WWII, Schneider settled in Texas Canyon to work the vein at the end of the canyon. He was assisted by his sons George and Pete and partner Hohenberger.

Son George is quoted remembering how hard the work was – drilling holes by hand in solid rock to tamp explosives in and then mucking out the broken rock to haul it to the crushers after the blasts. Moving the rock down a steep slope to the crusher was no picnic either. The days were described as physically exhausting.

One history describes the reward as "meager." A perfect description came from one of the sons when he said, "they made enough to keep on going but not enough to leave."

It was White Sands Proving Ground that made him leave after 1948. Before he went, however, Schneider befriended a young soldier named Tom

Grosch who was stationed at White Sands in the machine shop.

In 1979 I met Grosch and his wife Polly when they showed up at Public Affairs asking if they could visit Texas Canyon. When I heard he knew Schneider and used to spend his weekends in 1948 helping to work the mine, I agreed to take them up to the operation.

According to Grosch, he didn't fit in very well at White Sands so he started hiking up into Texas Canyon. At first Schneider wasn't very friendly because GIs often vandalized his cabin and equipment. But after a few trips Schneider warmed up to young Grosch and became a second father to him for that one year.

Grosch said that some of the German V-2 scientists used to visit Schneider. Apparently, it was a way for them to get away from their military overseers and relax. He said they would speak in German and drink schnapps provided by Schneider. Von Braun supposedly made at least one visit.

Eventually, Grosch spent whole weekends at the mine. They found him a place to sleep in the cabin, although in the summer it was more comfortable out under the stars.

The cabin had two rooms (some of the walls are still standing) with the walls covered with shelving. The shelves held ore samples, notebooks and chemicals. Every morning Hohenberger sprinkled the dirt floor with water and tamped it down. It was spotless – for dirt.

Grosch related that one summer night they were sleeping inside with the door open for ventilation. In the middle of the night a skunk walked in. Grosch said he was awakened by the roar of gunfire and the overpowering stench of a skunk spraying the room. Schneider was shooting at the skunk as it jumped from shelf to shelf. He only managed to make it mad.

All three men were sprayed so they fled the house and spent the rest of the night sleeping outside wherever they could curl up around a rock.

Sleeping outdoors wasn't like sleeping in your

The ruin of Schneider's cabin in Texas Canyon. Photo by the author.

backyard because rattlesnakes were common. Grosch said Schneider didn't like snakes and always walked with a stick, tapping the ground ahead like a blind man.

Grosch had one encounter with a rattlesnake that almost forced him to jump off a cliff. He said he took a break one day on the edge of a rock looking down on the canyon bottom. After a while he noticed a rattlesnake had crawled up behind him. He said he was tempted to jump off the rock, but it looked like a 40-foot drop and that was as scary as the snake. Instead, he stayed very still and the snake eventually slithered away.

As a young man Grosch said he was a bit of a romantic and Schneider was good at telling a story. When Grosch was bored, Schneider told him stories from books. When not telling stories, Schneider would read Voltaire.

To feed Grosch's dreams, Schneider pointed out the old cross vein that is on the north wall of Texas Canyon. The opening was covered over, as it is now, but Schneider told Grosch it was his to work and anything he found would be his. He added that he didn't know who originally made the tunnel.

Grosch attacked the entrance with enthusiasm and, once he gained entrance to the adit, he cautiously entered. He said his head was full of stories of Spanish conquistadors and lost treasure as he explored it. Of course, the vein was played out long before, but Grosch got to work his own "claim."

On our hike into Texas Canyon, Grosch explained in some detail how the mining operation worked when he was there. From the cabin there was a road to the northwest that climbed to the base of the saddle at the end of Texas Canyon. From the mine dump, another road looped back south and to the cabin and milling equipment. Evidence of the roads is still there in many neat lines of rocks that were pushed aside for the roadway.

In 1948, Schneider had an old truck he called Hitler. It had very large wheels and tires on the rear with regular wheels on the front. When going up steep slopes, the difference made the truck almost level.

Grosch said Schneider had to drive the truck wearing a gas mask. There was no exhaust system on the vehicle and no cab or firewall. The exhaust blew right into the driver's face. At one steep spot on the ascent, both Hohenberger and their dog Mica would get out and walk because it was just too scary.

They would load the back of the truck with ore from a day's dynamite blasting and haul it down the other road. The brakes on the truck were not up to this task, so they hooked chains and logs to the back end to provide drag and help brake the truck.

They would then mill the ore once a week. The crushers were run by the diesel engine that still sits in the canyon.

Grosch said getting the diesel going was a real trick. One of his jobs was to preheat the single cylinder using a blowtorch. Then he would crank the flywheel while Schneider primed the thing with gasoline.

Once the engine was chugging along, they didn't run it with diesel fuel. Instead, there was a hopper mounted on top of the cylinder that contained either sawdust or coal dust. It was cheaper than diesel.

The engine drove a flat belt coming off a fixed pulley on one flywheel that, in turn, drove an axle with a variety of pulleys on it. Belts from this single axle and the different pulleys would be moved to engage the various crushing devices to smash the ore into smaller and smaller bits.

The "one-lung" diesel engine in Texas Canyon that powered the crushing equipment used by Schneider. It and the other metal machinery survived the fire that burned through the canyon years ago. No one has ever tried to steal it. Photo by the author.

The first device opened and closed to crush rock between two plates like a set of jaws. Then the small pieces were run between two metal wheels that broke it down further. Finally, the small pieces were placed under two stamps that rose and fell like big hammers to pulverize the rock into powder.

From the crushing equipment, the flour was flushed over a shaker table located in the bottom of the canyon. The shaker table was lined with copper plates coated with mercury. The gold pieces would stick to the mercury and the rest was washed into the canyon bottom. It was then a matter of cooking off the mercury to leave a small blob of gold behind.

This small tower with its support pulleys proves a tram system was once installed to carry buckets of ore from the upper adits, near the top of Texas Canyon, down to a point where a vehicle could haul it down to the milling machinery. Photo by the author.

The shaker table was driven by a belt from the diesel engine as well. Also, water for the process came from a deep pool upstream. The diesel engine turned a generator that powered an electric pump to suck the water out of the "well," as Grosch called it, down to the table.

The pool had a cover over it and also supplied their drinking water. He said they once noticed a bad smell coming from the canyon bottom. They followed their noses to the pool to find one of Jim Cox's cows dead in the water. Grosch said Schneider, after removing the cow, pumped the pool dry and went to town for a few days.

As we toured the canyon, Grosch still was dreaming of Spanish explorers and the possibility they had visited the canyon centuries ago. He said Schneider used to show him a dagger that had Moorish symbols on the handle. Schneider supposedly found it in the sand down at the mouth of Texas Canyon. They used to imagine a Spanish miner or conquistador losing it in the canyon.

There is no doubt that gold and silver exist in the vein in Texas Canyon. I once escorted Fred Potter, a geologist with the Bureau of Land Management, into the canyon. He told me the ore contains small amounts of gold, silver, copper and iron. The iron appears as iron pyrite or "fool's gold" while the copper is often seen as green copper oxide.

I was at the mines once and found Boy Scouts breaking apart rocks for the copper oxide on the surface. They were sure they had found turquoise and were taking it home to show their moms.

According to Potter, the vein fills a vertical gap in the saddle at the end of the canyon. The fault that created the gap runs to the northwest and causes a similar saddle north of Sugarloaf Peak and between the Rabbit Ears and Needles in the Organs.

There are several adits into the vein starting where the main dump is at 5,670 feet. Some of the track used for running ore cars in and out of the adit is still on the dump. The top entrance is at 5,925 feet.

Today the trail up into the canyon is rocky and rough. It is used frequently, at least to the remains of an old communications reflector. Only the supports are left as the billboard-like panel was removed years ago.

From the reflector the trail loops south to the stream draining the canyon. In good wet years there is usually a flow of water here with many pools and falls. When it is really wet or there is a huge thunderstorm dumping inches of rain above the canyon, the runoff can reach the WSMR golf course and end up running under the El Paso road into the main post.

In the upper canyon the trail is overgrown with acacia or "catclaw" which tears at your skin and clothing. In some places the trail has almost disappeared.

The canyon is also interesting as far as land ownership goes. If the 7.5-minute topographical maps are halfway accurate (the disclaimer on the map says boundaries are approximate), the canyon floor is part of White Sands. The south wall belongs to Fort Bliss and the mines themselves are on BLM land. The land to the west of the saddle is part of the Cox ranch and is a mix of private and leased federal land.

Even if the trail into Texas Canyon was once some sort of road, it must have taken a great deal of sweat and ingenuity to move the mining equipment to its present location. Dreams certainly push people to do the most astonishing things.

The Silver King Mine

In 1990, I met with Jack and Marjorie Jones so I could take them onto the missile range to visit the Silver King Mine just north of U.S. Highway 70 at the northeastern base of San Augustin Peak. Jack wanted to visit the place where he spent five years of his youth helping his father try to make a living by mining silver. It was a small-time operation.

Jack was born in Las Cruces. His father Samuel and his mother divorced when Jack was nine. Samuel took Jack and Jack's little brother Robert out to the Silver King Mine in 1933. They lived in a two-room shack at the mine until 1938 when Samuel sold the property to Henry Heuer.

Heuer held the claim until the government acquired the property. The annual rent paid by the government for the claim was $218.35 per year.

Also helping at the mine was Evert Jones, Jack's grandfather.

The men built a clapboard shack near the mine. They lined the inside with cardboard from boxes to keep the wind out and provide a bit of insulation. Jack said the wind always seemed to be howling through their place.

At night during summer months, they could hear scorpions and other things crawling between the cardboard layer and the outside wooden walls.

Other critters visited as well. Jack said one morning they awoke to find a skunk in the doorway to the shack. Every time they made a move, the skunk would turn and raise its tail as if it was getting ready to spray them. They figured it would eventually go away and they settled back into bed. However, after an hour or so, Jack said his father couldn't take it anymore. He crawled out a window, snuck around the shack, and clubbed the skunk with a rock. Unlike Tom Grosch in Texas Canyon, Jack was saved from a long day or two of smelling bad.

Their property was dry so they had to haul water from a tunnel near the highway. Jack said they put a bucket at the rear of an old mine adit where water dripped continually down one wall. It was good and cold.

The two Jones boys made a little spending money during the summer by taking a jug of water out on the highway and selling it to drivers whose cars overheated climbing up San Augustin Pass. Jack said they sold it for 10 cents a gallon.

Like many places in America, it was even drier in the area during the 1930s. Jack remembered it raining only a couple of times. He was surprised in 1990 by the amount of vegetation at their old place. He said there was no grass then, just rocks and cactus on the slopes.

For meals the four men ate a lot of rabbit, beans with bacon, and biscuits with gravy. When Jack got older, his father bought him a single-shot .22 rifle. Jack remembered it cost $5.61. Then Jack's job was to hunt rabbits for meals and he became a major provider for the family.

Once in a while they would have venison, but since they worked around the mine most all the time they saw very few deer.

Jack and his brother regularly attended school in Organ by walking over the pass. If they were late, they hiked straight over the ridge north of San Augustin Peak and cut some distance off the trek. Their father was very strict about school and made sure they went every day.

When not in school Jack had other jobs. Since they worked the mine totally by hand, there was always something to do. To extract the ore they drilled holes in the rock face with hammers and rock bits. They started with a short bit and hammers weighing about four pounds.

As the holes deepened, they switched to longer bits, eventually drilling four to six holes several feet into the rock. Samuel mated a little scoop to the end of an engine rod they used to scoop the powdered rock out of the holes as they progressed.

The holes were then filled with dynamite and blasted in the late afternoon. They would let the dust settle overnight before going back in the morning to muck out their broken rock.

Since this was a mine with a shaft instead of an adit or tunnel, they were always working up and down. They had to haul the rock straight up using a windlass. Samuel would go into the hole and load a bucket with rock. Jack and his grandfather would then crank it to the top.

When they got a pile of ore on the ground, Evert would take the pieces and, using a hammer, break them apart to get the silver-bearing chunks that were about the size of your thumb. The waste was tossed down the hill. The good stuff was bagged and stored at the shack. When they had collected enough, Samuel would call the smelter in El Paso and they would send a truck to pick it up.

Jack's family was like many others trying to mine in the surrounding mountains. They made enough money to live on but never much more.

To help tote those bags of ore to the shack, Samuel purchased a burro in El Paso for $5 and brought him home. They named him Shaggs. Jack said it was easy to tell when Shaggs was fully loaded because if the weight grew too heavy his lower lip would quiver.

When the family sold the mine to Henry Heuer in 1938 and moved to California, they simply turned Shaggs loose with the cattle in the area and left him to his own devices. Jack had fond memories of Shaggs and still wondered whatever happened to the little guy.

Jack said the thing he remembered about his grandfather during that time was that he always, every minute, had a plug of tobacco in his mouth. When he got up in the morning, he pulled on his pants and reached for his tin of tobacco to cut a new plug to chew. Every night, as Evert undressed and got into bed, he threw the wad of tobacco out the open door opposite his bed.

After the family left, Jack missed the place so much he returned to New Mexico to work for Heuer at the mine. He said he traded being around one form of tobacco user for another. Heuer never did anything without a pipe in his mouth.

Jack went on to serve 20 years in the military and then nine years in civil service. When I met him he was retired and had the time to reconnect to places from his past.

Estey City

"It (Estey City) is today the most important mining proposition in this territory, and is exceeded by few in the entire country."

"The Company owns one of the most valuable pieces of mining property in the Southwest--rich in copper, lead, gold and silver ores."

The above quotes are taken from the 1905 prospectus issued by the Dividend Mining and Milling Company of Boston concerning its Estey City, New Mexico holdings.

On the other hand, in 1904 Fayette Alexander Jones wrote this in *New Mexico Mines and Minerals* about Estey City, "If a success is made working these low grade ores, it will require the greatest metallurgical skill and the strictest economy." The Jones book was written as a history of New Mexico mining for the Louisiana Purchase Expo in St. Louis in 1904. It was meant to portray New Mexico in a rosey light but he didn't seem too enthused about Estey City.

Estey City is the only sizeable ghost town on White Sands Missile Range. At the very beginning of the 20th century, Estey City claimed several hun-

David Estey from the Dividend Mining Prospectus.

dred hardy souls and existed long enough to have its own post office. It was a typical mining boomtown where hope, expectations and grinding hard work far exceeded any riches.

Estey City is located in the northeast part of the range near the Oscura Bombing and Gunnery Range. In 1910, a U.S. Geological Survey Professional Paper stated it was "located about 15 miles slightly north of west from Oscura station on the El Paso and Southwestern Railroad." The easiest way to get to this isolated spot now is by helicopter.

Information about Estey City is sketchy at best. We do know that copper deposits in the foothills of the Oscura Mountains were known in the 19th century. It is estimated the first copper mining efforts in the Estey area started about 1900.

The Estey City general store and post office from the Dividend Mining and Milling Company's prospectus. Nothing is left of this building but its outline on the ground where a rock foundation supported the structure.

The town was named after David M. Estey, a furniture manufacturer from Owosso, Michigan. He came from the Vermont family that made the Estey organ, but David struck out on his own. He started a lumber business back East but ended up in Michigan where he built a large furniture business and had interests in banking, lumber extraction, farming, cart manufacturing and mining.

His furniture business shipped to every state in the union and many countries overseas. This successful business gave him the where-with-all to enter the mining industry as a recreational owner. Also, he got to name the place after himself.

He started his mining development in 1901, but it quickly ran into difficulties; he died in September 1903 before it completely fell apart. The Dividend Mining and Milling Company, run by his son-in-law, purchased the property toward the end of David's life and carried on.

In the July 25, 1903 issue of *The Mining World* it was reported, "One of the largest copper deals ever made in New Mexico was consummated recently. J.M. Bryson purchased for the Dividend Mining and Smelting Company the entire property of Estey, N.M. The purchase price has not been made public … the new owners will erect a 500-ton concentrator and make other extensive improvements." The purchase included over 2,000 acres of land and 93 mining claims.

About the new owners, Fayette Jones wrote, "a new organization has recently been effected and is now rehabilitating the wreckage and mistakes of its predecessor."

According to James and Barbara Sherman in *Ghost Towns and Mining Camps in New Mexico*, the Estey City post office was in operation from 1901 through 1903 and then again from 1904 through 1910. The town boasted about 50 dwellings, a general merchandise store, one saloon, a church, a school and a hotel. At its peak, the town's population may have reached 500.

At Estey City the company erected a stone building to house its reduction plant for crushing and storing ore. The structure measured 50 by 88 feet and the reduction plant supposedly could handle 250 tons of ore per day. From what we know now, the trick was to find that much ore each day.

A 60-by 112-foot, two-story stone structure was called the precipitating building and was used for the special process the company invested in for separating the copper from the waste. Also, there were stone boiler and engine rooms and a stone assay office.

The equipment included a variety of boilers, engines, dynamos (generators), pumps, crushers, tanks, a smelter and a 90,000-gallon water tank. It was huge. Some folks estimate Estey and his son-in-law spent close to $200,000 in developing the place.

The company prospectus is so glowing and so

promising, it is hard to believe the mining district produced almost nothing. The prospectus says, "No industry known to the human race affords the profit for the investor, nor has so bright a future, as copper and lead mines have furnished for the last few years."

Of course, incredible hype was typical of mining operations across the West whether the riches were real or just hoped for. In this case, there was very little ore to begin with and the difficulties of getting it proved overwhelming.

New Mexico was often portrayed as a territory awash in mineral wealth. After all, this was the prime hunting ground for the Spanish search for the legendary seven cities of gold. Almost every county in New Mexico has at least one lost gold mine or lost treasure story.

But was the reputation warranted? *U.S. Geological Survey Bulletin #285*, dated 1905, reported on the minerals produced in New Mexico for 1904. The territory produced a measly $2,186,287 worth of gold, silver, copper, lead and zinc. In the same period, New Mexico produced 1,500,000 tons of lowly coal with a value of $1,900,000. Coal just about overwhelmed all the metals put together. So much for Estey City being "one of the most valuable pieces of mining property in the Southwest."

In the end, very little ore was milled at Estey City, and only a few carloads were shipped from the site. In fact, Bureau of Land Management mining engineers, who were asked to study the area in 1973, were reluctant to use the word "ore" in describing the material that was worked at the mill. They also cited other reports in 1903, 1910, 1916, 1959 and 1968 which all concluded the copper deposits in the Estey City district have no economic value.

The writer for Volume IX of *The Copper Handbook* published in 1909 wrote a summary of the operation. He said, "The company has been very pro-

---

Pop-Up: *When I examined an actual copy of the prospectus, it was obvious many of the photographs had been doctored or touched up. In numerous photos, light-colored objects such as faces are washed out and lacking in details. To fix this the people who produced it penned in the features – eyeglasses, facial hair, eyes, etc. In one photo of the company's office it looks like whole people may have been inserted in the background.*

Also, many of the same people appear in photo after photo. They are identifiable by their clothing and hats. However, their facial features were sometimes changed to make it look like different people.

The pictures of the machinery were probably taken before the mill was in actual operation because everything is clean, almost pristine. A photo of the inside of the store does show shelves stacked with cans and other goods. There are even children in some of the photos.

---

lific of 'estimates' and promises, demonstrating – on paper – how, by merely producing 14,400,000 lbs. of copper yearly, profits of millions of dollars could be earned. Company's advertising is indefensible." He summed it up by saying, "The promoters of the company are sadly lacking either in sense or truth. Property is considered one of fair promise but the management is not well regarded."

The prospectus, on the other hand, went to some lengths to extol the experienced and successful men on the board of directors who "are gentlemen fully capable of handling the affairs of the enterprise."

In the prospectus, President John M. Bryson is not identified as Estey's son-in-law but as someone associated with the development from the beginning and that "it has been largely through his untiring efforts on behalf of the Company that it has met with such signal (sic) success." Also, no one mentions that much earlier Estey had to step in to pay some of his son-in-law's debts to keep the creditors away.

B.F. Coburn was the company's secretary and treasurer and came from a background in making boots and shoes. The prospectus states, "His business training and experience were therefore along the lines that made him fully competent to become one of the officials of a large company . . ."

J. William Rice, a board member, was president of the Gutta Percha Paint Company. Samuel Porter was president of the Florence Savings Bank and ran the Nanatuck Silk Company. A.G. Spear was in the lumber business and James Putnam was in the streetcar business. Other board members were in real estate and groceries.

If I'm not mistaken, there is not a single person on the board who knew anything about mining or the milling of minerals.

Couple this group of obvious wannabe miners

with the lack of any significant amount of copper ore at the site and the inability to get reliable water, and you have some researchers who feel the mining operation may have been a scam from day one. They say it was started to swindle investors - a time-honored profession in New Mexico.

However, I agree with Bob Eveleth, the New Mexico mining official in Socorro, who once wondered if the developers didn't simply convince themselves of their own sales pitch. People can and will believe absolutely anything These men may have been sure they had found the proverbial pot of gold. As humans we are suckers for a little enthusiasm, especially if we wish something to be true.

I think the thing that argues against the fraud case is the amount of money and work put into developing Estey City. If you were going to sell shares to investors intending to swindle them and keep the money, why bother spending most of it on building very substantial structures and equipping them with expensive machinery? That would be money out of your own pocket – not exactly what criminals do.

On top of everything else, copper prices crashed just when they had finished their "modern" facility. They didn't stand a chance. By 1910, no one was hanging around.

In the 1918 Volume XIII of *The Mines Handbook*, an enlargement of *The Copper Handbook*, the author's stated, "At last account (Dividend Mining and Milling) was endeavoring to settle with bondholders by giving them the property."

Today, some of the stone walls to the mill and the assay office at Estey City are still standing. Photo by the author.

Today, only a few of the walls to the mill complex and assay office still stand. The foundations to the general store and a few other buildings are still visible. Rusted tin cans and other trash can be found in many dumps around the area. Many of the cans have neat little square holes punched in them as if some miner used his pick to knock a quick hole in the can so he could pour out the contents.

Some people today play the lottery and some play the stock market. Like the investors in Estey City, they are looking for that lightening strike of fortune to give them a life of ease.

Capitol Peak Tunnels

Near the north end of the San Andres Mountains on White Sands is Capitol Peak standing at 7,098 feet. From certain angles its pointed top does look something like the dome of a typical state capitol.

On the north side of the peak, near its base, there are some very modern holes. In 2002, White Sands allowed the Defense Threat Reduction Agency (DTRA) to bore several tunnels into the mountain's granite roots. The tunnels are equipped with portals and are used to simulate the tunnels and caves found around the planet.

One mission of DTRA is to defeat weapons of mass destruction. These threats could be nuclear, biological or chemical weapons. In places like Korea, Afghanistan and other countries, such weapons could be manufactured or stored in caves or tunnels. In DTRA's lingo, they were running a "hard and deeply buried target defeat program."

At the Capitol Peak Tunnel Complex, DTRA can attack the tunnels and their contents with old and new weapon systems to see how well they work at destroying the contents. They can also test various tactics to see how well they work.

Since these are tests, they employ a large array of instrumentation to measure the relevant variables like blast pressures and temperatures. They can use simulants to mimic real biological, chemical and nuclear weapons. The realistic tests allow them to measure how much of the hazardous material is destroyed in the attack or if some of it leaks out and still poses a threat.

This testing is very current and very

relevant to threats found all around the world today. Therefore, it is a very secure place when they test. The results of such tests are closely guarded secrets. As a nation we certainly don't want some bad guys with nerve agent stored in a cave to know what they have to do to protect their weapons from being destroyed.

In 2006 I was lucky to see one test at Capitol Peak from a high vantage point miles away. The test consisted of exploding a MOAB (Massive Ordnance Air Blast) bomb at the entrance to one of the tunnels. The bomb was not dropped on the site but was placed on a stand in front of the portal.

At the time MOAB was all the talk because it was such a large item. According to the Air Force, MOAB or GBU-43/B is a 21,500-pound GPS guided bomb delivered by a C-130 cargo plane. In one report, officials said, "The huge size of the MOAB will make it effective against hardened structures, caves and bunkers." The thing is 31 feet long and just over three feet in diameter.

By conventional standards it is a very large bomb.

But to put it in perspective with nuclear weapons, MOAB is equal to 11 tons of TNT. The Trinity Site bomb was equal to about 20,000 tons of TNT or 1,800 times more powerful than MOAB.

For us it was still a very big explosion, larger than most things that explode on the missile range. For safety and security reasons, we were positioned over five miles away at an old instrumentation site. We couldn't really see the bomb sitting in front of the tunnel.

When it was detonated there was an orange-red fireball that quickly faded to a cloud of dust and debris. What impressed us most was the quickly approaching shock wave. We could see it as it bumped and jumped along the mountain and canyon ridges below us, kicking up dust and blowing bushes like the short, but powerful gust of wind it was. Then, in a few seconds, it hit us with a resounding thud in our chests and a boom to our ears. And it was over.

Of course, we were never told what happened to the entrance to the tunnel or its contents and we were smart enough to never ask.

Tom Berard, on Feb. 16, 2007, when he was director of White Sands, He is surveying the ruins of Estey City from one of the mining company's walled terraces. The Estey milling operation was built into the side of a hill so the flow of ore through the various processes was downhill. Photo by the author.

21

Gold In That Thar Peak

Believing Doesn't Seem To Make It True

I met Ova Noss in early 1979 when I was the missile range's Public Affairs escort for a group of family members and supporters taking pictures of her on Victorio Peak. It was my first serious brush with the legendary 100 tons of gold supposedly hidden in the peak and some of the characters who have proven more interesting than the elusive treasure.

My job was to observe and control the photogra-

Ova Noss on Victorio Peak in 1979 to be interviewed by KENW-TV. Photo by the author.

phy. I took a few pictures as well and heard her say, as she posed, "Like they say, there's gold in them thar hills." Wearing a big Cheshire grin, she pointed up at the peak as she said it.

I sometimes tell about that day and what Ova said. I have been accused of making it up or making fun of Mrs. Noss. I didn't imagine it. It is what she said.

The missile range was told the photo session was necessary for a forthcoming book about the Noss family's pursuit of the treasure. In addition to taking still photos, Keith Kolb with KENW-TV of Eastern New Mexico University in Portales, New Mexico, shot motion picture film of Ova as background for a feature movie they said would be produced soon.

Along with Ova were her daughter Dorothy Delonas and Dorothy's son Terry, Dan Portwood, a self-described "advisor," and Les Smith, a mining engineer who was involved in many of the digs into Victorio Peak.

Two White Sands range riders were along to help escort, and they turned out to be as entertaining as the Noss group. These old-time cowboys just laughed at the whole idea of a cavern full of gold in Victorio Peak.

Tom Dayberry pointed out the Henderson family had a ranch house at the foot of Victorio Peak and if there was anything to find, "they certainly would have found it." Bill Bates, the other range rider, pointed to the gold tooth in his smile and said he had more gold in his mouth than was ever found in Victorio Peak.

In 1977, Norman Scott, president of Expeditions Unlimited, led an unsuccessful attempt to find the treasure at Victorio Peak. In 1974, the Associated Press quoted him as saying, "You make your money to a great extent on the marketability of the media rights as opposed to the actual find. The real money in many of these stories is the pursuit of the project as opposed to the end result."

At 83, Ova Noss was mining some of the treasure left to her by her husband Doc in the form of a little media action. She didn't enjoy it much longer as she died later in the year. Almost 20 years later, her grandson Terry took up his birthright to continue the family's claims of a fabulous fortune squirreled away in a most unlikely spot.

Gold Bars Stacked Like Cordwood

Details about how Doc Noss supposedly found a gigantic stack of gold bars and Spanish treasure in Victorio Peak are pretty much only available as second-hand information. As far as we know, Doc never left a diary or journal with his account. If one exists, the family hasn't shared it with the rest of the world. What we have are stories from family members, supporters, believers and others.

The essentials are that in November 1937, Milton "Doc" Noss went deer hunting in the Hembrillo Basin of the San Andres Mountains. He climbed the 400-foot-tall Victorio Peak in the center of the basin to take a look around.

As it started to rain (some say it was a sunny day), he found shelter in a natural opening in the peak. While sitting in this crack, he felt air moving past him and out the opening. He moved some rocks and later claimed he found a dark fissure heading down into the peak.

Some accounts say he encountered pictographs or hieroglyphics or rock art in this initial room near the surface of the peak. Those symbols have never been found.

Some time later he returned to the peak with his wife Ova and some basic equipment, a rope and light, and descended into the crack. According to Ova, he was gone quite some time and she worried for his safety.

When he came back to the surface, Doc had a tale to tell. He said he made his way via a torturous route of ledges, cracks and tight squeeze points to a large tunnel and then to caverns and rooms. Most of the storytellers describe the tunnel as being big enough to hold a freight train or a large house. In

fact, on Oct. 25, 1999, Terry Delonas described the tunnel in those terms to Judge Horn who was visiting the peak as part of a lawsuit before her in the U.S. Court of Claims. I was very surprised he was still hanging onto that part of the story.

Part of the yarn involves a stream of cold water Doc had to cross to get to the cavern and rooms. Apparently this was quite a flow of water. One author says Doc had to "ford" the stream. Fording a stream implies wading through a significant flow of water as opposed to simply stepping over a trickle, which is what you might expect to find in the San Andres Mountains.

That's a lot of water for an area where the springs below Victorio Peak are no more than trickles during wet years. It is even more remarkable given the fact that Victorio Peak is cut off from all surrounding higher ground by the drainages on the east, west and north. Even in this "magical" tale water still has to flow downhill, so the only place the stream could originate is the ridge to the southeast. It is the only ground higher than Doc's tunnel leading to the treasure.

It would probably have to rain just about every day for enough water to soak into such a small surface area to maintain a steady supply of water for the stream. Of course, that just doesn't happen in this part of the world.

When Doc got to the cavern and side rooms, he was greeted by more than two dozen human skeletons. These poor characters were tied up and chained to the floor and walls to slowly die in the dark. The implication is that these were the workers who hid the treasure and were killed to guarantee their silence by whoever was in charge. The number of skeletons shifts depending on who tells the account. One author had the number at 75 or so.

In the rooms, Doc found a riot of loot that would have made Long John Silver's heart skip a beat. There were chests filled with Spanish coins, jewelry, uncut precious stones, religious artifacts and documents. Also, a side room contained metal bars stacked like "cordwood."

At first Doc thought the bars were iron or lead, depending on which story you hear. Later, Doc or Ova or both (again depending on who is telling the story) discover the bars are gold. Doc estimated there were thousands of bars.

The bars were not a uniform size or weight

and are described as being anywhere from 30 to 80 pounds each. Given the number and general size of the bars, many people estimated the stash contained about 100 tons of gold. This is the logic behind the title to David Chandler's book, *100 Tons of Gold*, published after the 1977 gold search at Victorio Peak. This is the same author who proposed in 1994, in his last book, that President Thomas Jefferson had explorer Meriwether Lewis murdered.

Soon after the discovery inside the peak, Doc and Ova proceeded to mine the treasure. Doc went down repeatedly through 1939 and brought back dozens of gold bars and valuable artifacts. As proof, the family proudly shows off a sword, napkin rings and stirrups as evidence of these valuable artifacts.

Most skeptics don't consider these items rare or particularly valuable. Given the original claims, they want to see something more along the lines of a gold bar, a pair of gold earrings, an old Spanish document, or a single jewel.

For some reason the pile of gold bars draws most of the attention as if it was the only thing of value in the peak. Everyone seems to have blinders on and fails to see the possibility of centuries-old jewelry, coins and religious artifacts being worth much. Even when valuable gems are mentioned reporters seem to be struck dumb.

For example, in a January 1990 interview with local reporters, Letha Guthrie, one of Doc's stepdaughters, claimed Doc once brought out a canning jar half filled with uncut rubies. None of the wide-eyed reporters bothered to ask what uncut rubies looked like or where they might have come from.

In this case Doc may simply have picked up some small chunks of the purplish-red fluorspar found in the old Bohnstedt fluorspar mine in Hole-in-the-Wall Canyon, an arm of Sulphur Canyon. It is just a few miles north of Victorio Peak and has some nice crystals. I once took representatives of the New Mexico Bureau of Geology and Mineral Resources Museum in Socorro to the mine to collect samples for display.

Such crystals might suffice to fool people who have never seen rubies or fluorspar in the raw, especially a teenager during the 1930s. After all, how many of us today could identify an uncut ruby?

Avoiding the artifact issue is a huge hole in the whole Noss saga. The family always said Doc tried to turn the gold bars into cash and had great difficulty

because it was illegal to own gold in those days. If that was the case, the obvious question is why not take some of the jewelry, artifacts, coins and other material to dealers in Southwest cities? He would have been rich.

During the two years after the discovery, Noss supposedly buried his liberated gold bars around the Hembrillo Basin because he didn't trust anyone. Some say not even Ova.

Also, family members tend to portray him as a poor, uneducated Indian who just didn't have the wherewithal to turn the gold into cash. This argument looks really flakey. Such a meek person stands in stark contrast to the Doc Noss who was arrested in Texas for practicing medicine without a license.

Then there is the photo of Doc and Ova Noss standing in front of the "Noss Foot Clinic" in Hot Springs, New Mexico. They are decked out in classic white nurse and doctor outfits. A Las Cruces reporter digging into the story even found ads in a couple of newspapers for the clinic.

That photo never shows up on websites or in publications associated with the Noss family. It is such a negative spotlight on the couple's character, it seems to have been hidden away.

I think to run a medical scam requires someone who is a little shrewd and very devious. You have to know the jargon, how to use it, and be able to act like a real doctor. It seems more likely Doc was a fast-talking, scheming sort of person who could smile and be very convincing. He was probably the kind of person who fit the old cliché that he could talk an Eskimo into buying a freezer. This is supported by many of the local ranchers and business people who met Noss and later commented on his character.

I met Anna Lee (Bruton) Gaume in 1990. Her family ranched just west of the Victorio Peak area. She stated Doc Noss was a smooth talker who could sell you something you really didn't need or want. She characterized Ova as "hard and shrewd."

Anna's husband Paul added that Doc would salt the spring by Victorio Peak with gold flakes. Then, when potential backers arrived, he'd be panning the silt at the spring to show them bits of gold. They claim many backers provided money or support to Noss and he always lived well.

According to the myth, in 1939 Doc decided to hire a mining engineer to blast one of the choke points inside the mountain to make it easier for him

This aerial view of Victorio Peak was taken in the mid 1970s in preparation for "Operation Goldfinder" that eventually took place in March 1977. You are looking north. At the top of the photo, the line crossing from near the top-right corner down to the southwest is the main road through the Hembrillo Basin. It is very tiny, but the T-shaped Henderson home is visible just on the south side of the road near the middle of the photo. Hembrillo Pass is to the west and Rock Art Spring is to the east on that main road. The roads and scarring on the peak are the result of the 1963 Gaddis dig. The Gaddis tunnel is on the west side of the peak, in the shadow. The natural crack that Doc entered is on the north end of the peak. WSMR photo.

to come and go. Too much dynamite was used and part of the route caved in, sealing Doc out and the booty inside. Skeptics say it really wasn't an accident but merely the next step to seal the peak, so paying suckers couldn't demand to see the "treasure" rooms.

A Little Geography

Victorio Peak is a small, rocky mound at the end of a low ridge that protrudes into the Hembrillo Basin. The peak is only 400 feet high and its base on the floor of the basin is about a mile in diameter. In other words, if you plucked it up and dropped it onto a large parking lot, you could walk around its base in 20 minutes. It is not very big.

Hembrillo Basin is in the San Andres Mountains about 45 miles north of U.S. Highway 70 and due west of the White Sands Space Harbor. One of the most frequently asked questions by people visiting White Sands is, "Can I see Victorio Peak from here?" Unfortunately for them, the ridge of peaks east of Victorio towers 2,000 feet above it and the other sides of the bowl are hundreds of feet higher than the treasure peak. The bottom line is that you have to be on the basin's edge or in it to see Victorio Peak.

What water falls into the basin when it rains (probably about 10 inches during a good year) drains down Hembrillo Canyon that runs to the east out into the Tularosa Basin. Some of it soaks into the sandy and gravelly ground and feeds a few springs. For instance, the Hendersons developed a spring near their ranch house by digging it out and lining the hole. This made it easy to dip a bucket into the spring box and extract water. Just west of the house were other known intermittent springs that were used by the Apache at times.

Down in the canyon is another intermittent spring now called "Rock Art Spring" that creates a small oasis that has obviously attracted humans for centuries. The underground water keeps a stand of large cottonwood trees alive even when there is no water on the surface. On the cliff faces above the spring are the best Indian pictographs and petroglyphs on the missile range. Several images depict braves on horseback, which means the images are post-Spanish arrival and, therefore, Apache in origin. Other small, red pictographs nearby depict many wild animals and are believed to be from the Mogollon culture that preceded the Apache.

Also at the spring are the remains of a ranch out-post or "line shack." Some of the corral fences and a low rock wall are still visible but most of the ruins are covered in dense brush so most visitors have no idea it is there.

The shack was owned by the Ritch family whose ranch headquarters was in the Tularosa Basin to the east. The story from other ranchers is that the shack burned down one night when a log fell out of the wood stove. Evidence on site supports this story. The concrete foundation to the shack can be found in the brush along with a couple of metal bed frames, nails and other metal artifacts. There are no wooden beams or supports typical of a ruined shack. Scattered on the ground are several blobs of glass – probably bottles or jars that melted during the fire.

During the 1980s, there was a tiny trickle of water on the surface here, but it disappeared in the dry1990s and hasn't been seen yet in the 21st century.

Now, A Little Geology

To fully understand the Victorio Peak story and some of what's possible and what's not, it is necessary to learn a wee bit of the local geology.

The San Andres Mountains are made mostly of uplifted layers of sedimentary rock like limestone, sandstone, gypsum and shale. The rock itself was formed over a period of a couple of hundred million years, give or take a couple of years, when the area was under a shallow sea – back when New Mexico was part of Pangaea, the supercontinent. Because the sea was so shallow, Victorio Peak and other knobs in the area are topped with reef material that rests on soft shales and limestone.

Things have changed dramatically as the top of Victorio Peak is now just over 5,500 feet above sea level.

During the push to raise this rock a mile above the sea, it was cracked and fractured as stresses broke it here and there. In this mess of smaller cracks is a big one running on an east to west line that now bisects Victorio Peak. This fault is very visible from the air as it forms a small gap or saddle at the top of the peak; a depression can be seen in places running along the crack through the basin. The line appears on the satellite image at Google Maps as a nice straight line running almost perfectly east and west.

The crack was deep and eventually filled with oozing igneous rock from below, forming a cookie filling. The rock is characterized by its greenish grey color and can be found on the slopes of Victorio Peak along the fault line. Called a dike, this rock filling acts as a solid wall internally dividing the north and south sides of the peak.

Later, as material eroded away little by little to scratch out the Hembrillo Basin, the harder reef limestone was left to form Victorio Peak. Somewhere in the process, the limestone section of the peak north of the dike cracked and slumped several feet away from the main peak. Erosion and cave-ins mostly filled the new crack to some extent. There was an opening visible on top and tiny ones down the sides of the peak.

This secondary crack or fault in the limestone reef is what Doc Noss climbed into in 1937. Apparently, he worked his way down finding voids in the debris created by some of the larger rocks wedged in the crack.

In addition to this major crack, there are dozens, maybe hundreds, of smaller ones scattered all around the peak as a result of movement. Many have claimed the voids in the peak were caused by acidic water eating away the limestone, like Carlsbad Caverns. They point out the cave-like formations in a few spots. The reality is that these small mineral deposits were laid down afterward and are simply decorations Nature has left on the open surfaces.

A key fact about the mountain is that the limestone crack stops when it hits the shale layer underneath. The softer shale simply flexed and did not break under the stresses that fractured the limestone. That means Noss could only go so far down into the peak before he was blocked by the shale below and the igneous dike or wall to the south.

Where Did It Come From?

By most people's standards, 100 tons of gold is a whole lot of gold. When its price is quoted on the commodity markets in ounces, it is sometimes hard to relate to 100 tons. If we assume most people are talking about a standard ton at 2,000 pounds, the simple math solution says there would be 3,200,000 ounces in the pile.

We can all relate to a pound since dumbbells and bags of green chile are sold by the pound. Doing the math, it totals 200,000 pounds of metal bars in the peak.

Of course, the odds are it couldn't be pure, 24-karat gold. Nevertheless, it would certainly be worth hundreds of millions or billions of dollars depending on the price of gold.

In the beginning, Noss and the family connected the gold with the Padre LaRue legend. There is a family photo supposedly showing three gold bars from the peak, and one clearly has "LaRue" stamped on the top.

The LaRue legend is an old southern New Mexico story and is pretty typical *Boy's Life* or *True West* magazine stuff. It made perfect sense for Noss to try and tie his discovery to this legend because many people would jump right in to believe it.

In the story, a French priest named LaRue came to Spain's American territories to work with poor Indians further south in what is now Mexico. The Indians were starving and not doing very well.

One day, a sick and dying Spanish soldier stumbled into the village. LaRue tried to help him but couldn't save him. On his deathbed, the soldier told the padre about a fabulous gold find just two days north of Paso del Norte (El Paso) and to the east in the mountains.

Actually, in most retellings of this story the language used is very romanticized just like in a pulp fiction piece. It is not a turn to the east but a turn "into the rising sun." And, of course, the directions call for you to be there at sunrise or sunset on the longest or shortest day of the year and to look for the point of the shadow cast by some peak or promontory.

After the soldier died and the villagers buried him, LaRue decided to lead his Indian followers in search of the gold. They found it. They spent some time mining the gold and casting it into ingots.

Of course, when people dream these stories up, they fail to fill in really important details like what these folks ate while they mined and processed the gold. There is no farming in the San Andres Mountains and very little game. They could have used some of the gold to buy supplies from the Spanish, but that would have set off alarm bells all the way back to Madrid. One has to assume they ate, but what it was remains a mystery.

One way or another, the Spanish grew suspicious of the padre and sent soldiers out to see what he was up to. He was warned of their coming and had the Indians hide the gold and all evidence of their hard work.

They were found, incarcerated and interrogated. This happened about the same time as the Spanish Inquisition, so one has to assume the questioning was very thorough. The padre and his followers refused to tell the soldiers about the mine. All died while being tortured.

With their deaths, the location of the fabulous mine and its bullion died as well. That is, until Doc said he stumbled into Victorio Peak.

The LaRue story provided the kind of legend Doc needed to hook backers. He embellished the story with details about the cavern and rooms being part of a rich mine with several outside entrances, now blocked with timbers and rock. He said there was equipment in the peak for the smelting of gold. His descendants even pointed out how rocks on the peak's surface were stained black with soot from the smoking furnaces below.

This soot story was shot full of holes in 1990 and 1991 when the environmental assessment was done at the peak in preparation for the last gold hunt. All kinds of specialists, to include geologists, archaeologists and biologists, descended on the peak to survey the search area.

The soot turned out to be simply the same grayish to black limestone found throughout the San Andres Mountains. It turns out the more plant debris (carbon-based material) caught in the process of forming the limestone millions of years ago, the darker it will be. Some is almost jet-black.

One very big problem with the LaRue story and Doc's claims about Victorio Peak being home to the mine is the total absence of rock debris from the mining and then milling. Even a small prospect hole a few feet deep, like those found throughout the San Andres Mountains, leaves a pile of broken rock behind.

Believers counter by saying the padre and his Indians skillfully hid the tailings. I looked into this once by doing some simple math.

An assay was completed in the 1970s on some of the sandstone found in Victorio Peak. It came back showing one tenth of an ounce of gold in each ton of rock. That means, to get 100 tons of gold, the Padre's Indians needed to mine, crush and process about 32 million tons of rock. The broken rock left behind would easily cover a square mile of real estate to a depth of over 20 feet. Imagine trying to mine that much rock, process, and hide it using burros and hand tools. Even if you suppose the ore to be dozens of times richer than the richest mines ever found on

earth, the pile of tailings would be impossible to hide in such open desert.

When faced with such numbers, some believers turn to a little magical thinking. They say the Padre found veins of pure gold and simply cut out 100 tons of the soft stuff with saws. There was no rock residue to hide.

Apparently they got it all, every last finger or hair of pure gold, because no one has ever found anything like it in the area or in any of the fissures or adits in the peak.

Another obvious problem with the smelting idea is the almost total lack of fuel for the process. The melting point for gold is almost 2,000 degrees F. It would take a small forest of hardwood turned into charcoal to keep the furnaces going long enough to smelt 100 tons of gold. In the immediate area of Victorio Peak, there are occasional juniper bushes and some cottonwood trees near the springs. No one has gone so far as to claim the slopes were once covered with maples and oaks that were harvested for the mining furnaces.

When all this became clear, the backers and believers found themselves supporting a laughable explanation. It didn't bother them in the least. In 1990, they simply shifted to a new tale - no more gold bars with LaRue stamped on them. In the new version, they say Doc discovered the loot Maximilian was trying to escape with from Mexico.

Maximilian was born in Austria and declared emperor of Mexico in 1864 by a group of Mexican monarchists and Napoleon III. Most Mexicans and many foreign governments didn't support the scheme, and the whole enterprise crumbled in 1867. Maximilian was placed in front of a firing squad and shot.

Some people say Maximilian was trying to escape the country before his reign fell apart. Obviously Maximilian died, but the riches of Mexico he plundered were sent north by burro train and made it to the United States. Either the handlers found Victorio Peak and hid the treasure inside, or Apaches attacked the train and hid the booty there. Either way, Doc Noss accidentally found it in 1937.

If you remember the La Rue version the Noss family peddled, there was all that mining and smelting equipment found with the gold. This new explanation doesn't try to explain why that material was there. Surely Maximilian wasn't trying to escape with some everyday, worthless equipment? Surely the Apache weren't dumb enough to steal and hide heavy mining gear inside Victorio Peak?

I put pen to paper to do some simple math on this story as well. It turns out the burros could have carried 80 to 110 pounds and stayed healthy if they had plenty of water and feed while crossing the deserts and mountains of Mexico. If Maximilian had 100 tons of gold bars in the animal train, it would have required about 2,000 burros just to carry the gold.

Of course, this would have required a small army of handlers to lead the burros, unload them at night and load them again in the morning, feed them, and find water along the route. Since they couldn't count on finding water or grass along the way, hundreds more burros would have been required to carry food and water. As you stack on the problems it just gets to be one crazy explanation. It seems about as likely as getting struck by a meteorite as you read this.

In 2011, faced with this kind of factual information, believers shifted the source of the gold once again. Now the family is talking about Montezuma, the Aztec emperor. At least, in this version, we actually have a starting place that was known to have lots of gold. I wonder why the Aztecs poured it into European style ingots and put "LaRue" on some of the bars?

Although the family seems to stand behind these explanations, there are others. One is that the gold is all Apache plunder from raids on the many gold-producing areas of New Mexico. The state does have a number of mining districts that were fairly successful at one time or another.

Noss also claimed there was a Wells Fargo chest or two in the stash. Believers cite this Apache plunder story to explain the company's property being found in the peak.

Supporters of this story say when Apache chief Victorio fought U. S. Army buffalo soldiers at the base of Victorio Peak in April 1880, he was defending the stash of gold.

One problem with the Victorio angle is that most of the larger mining activities in New Mexico didn't start producing gold until 1879 or later. It would have been impossible for the Apache to collect a huge pot of gold before the battle if the mines didn't exist yet – unless they had a magical time machine.

Another story, one I am very familiar with, is that the gold is 20th century German gold sent to support Pancho Villa. In early 1916, Villa's forces attacked Columbus, New Mexico, provoking a U.S. punitive expedition under the leadership of General Pershing.

The basic idea here is that Germany shipped gold to the Southwest in order to provide Villa with military equipment and logistical support so he could openly engage the United States. Supposedly the Germans did this to draw America into another war with Mexico and distract them from joining Britain and France in World War I.

When you read about the raid on Columbus there are accounts of a "mysterious" train on the tracks there. When the shooting starts, the train backs down the track back toward El Paso. The idea here is that the train was carrying the gold.

The story vaguely suggests the gold was waylaid and hidden in Victorio Peak by unknown persons. In the end, Pershing's expeditionary force never found Villa and the U.S. was free to enter World War I in 1917.

The problem with this account is that it is a fairy tale concocted by Jim Bryant and myself when we rewrote the Victorio Peak factsheet decades ago for the missile range's Public Affairs Office. We based it on another story that sometimes floats about involving German gold but makes no sense whatsoever. Apparently, there are some who actually suggest Doc Noss found the gold captured by General Patton at the end of World War II and secreted it away to New Mexico for later use – hidden on a secure military base like White Sands.

How this would work with Noss finding the gold in 1937, I have no idea. Add to that the fact that Victorio Peak didn't fall within the missile range's boundary until 1955 and you have a fable Hollywood probably couldn't even use. Bryant and I thought our story was much more believable.

Salesmanship

Once the Noss mining engineer managed to close off the crack leading into Victorio Peak in 1939, Doc was freed from pesky backers and customers wanting to see the treasure room. Instead he could simply offer for sale a metal bar that looked like gold or a sword with some 19th century engraving.

But more important than selling bars (a bit risky when they are fake), the blast gave Doc the opportunity to solicit money to reopen the mountain. For this moneymaking stroke of genius he never had to actually produce anything – just a place to dig.

In 1939, one of the Noss gold bars made a public appearance. A "gold brick" was submitted to the U.S. Mint for assay by Charles Ussher of Santa Monica, California. Supposedly he paid $200 for the bar and got it from someone named Grogan. The assay revealed the bar contained 97 cents of gold. In other words, it was probably made of copper or some other metal and electroplated with a very thin (97 cents worth) layer of gold.

The Secret Service then conducted an investigation and Grogan alleged he obtained the bar from Doc Noss in New Mexico.

During the gold hunt in the 1990s, I used to receive calls from an old gentleman in El Paso who identified himself as Plez. He said he once had mining claims in the San Andres Mountains before the military took the land to form the missile range and, by the way, he knew Doc Noss. The news of the Victorio Peak treasure search had gotten his attention and prompted him to call.

Plez said Noss used to buy copper bars and have them electroplated with gold in El Paso. These could then be shown to prospective investors as evidence that his tale was true. According to Plez and others I have met, Doc rarely let other people handle the bars and never let anyone examine them closely or take a sample.

By 1941, Noss had a group of about 20 support-

ers who pooled money and muscle to form a company to clean out the crack in Victorio Peak and shore it up. Then the war started and Doc disappeared for a while from the public record.

We do know he divorced his wife Ova during the war and eventually married Violet Yancy.

Shot In The back

Doc turned up again in November 1948 in Alice, Texas when he was hired to make pickups and deliveries for Charley Ryan whose shop repaired oil field equipment. Very quickly the smooth-talking Noss convinced Ryan to accompany him to New Mexico to check on his "mine" in the San Andres Mountains. He said he needed Ryan's backing because people in New Mexico were out to cheat him and maybe kill him.

Charley Ryan had to be either one of the nicest people on the planet or a born sucker. When Ryan hired Noss, it was with the understanding Noss provide his own truck to make the runs to the oil fields. When Noss showed up in an old rundown pickup, Ryan offered to loan him the money for a newer one. Then, almost immediately, Noss was arrested for passing bad checks during the weeks before he was hired. Ryan paid off most of those checks, amounting to several hundred dollars, and still kept Noss on.

While helping Noss, supposedly Ryan hadn't heard about any mines in New Mexico or Victorio Peak yet. At his trial he painted himself as someone who felt sorry for Noss and then got sucked into the rest of it.

When Noss and Ryan arrived at Victorio Peak, they were stymied by Ova Noss who had her own group of backers and a New Mexico state permit to prospect there. It was still state property at the time. Noss checked in Santa Fe and found out Ova rightfully controlled the peak.

Noss told Ryan there were other opportunities and showed him an area just north of Victorio Peak that Doc said would yield valuable lead ore. In fact, Noss said he knew someone who would pay $55,000 for the valuable veins. Ryan and his helpers filed a legitimate mining claim on the ridge and dug several prospect holes.

The remains of the Noss cabin, an easy walk just northwest of Victorio Peak and next to some old springs. Photo by the author.

According to later trial testimony, Ryan finally realized he was being scammed. He talked to people in Hot Springs, Socorro and Hatch and got an earful about the silver-tongued Noss. Also, he found out the lead ore was basically worthless. It would have cost more to dig it out and process than it could be sold for.

On March 4, 1949, Ryan decided he'd had enough and ordered his operation to shut down so he could go home. In Hatch on March 5, he told Noss he was leaving New Mexico as soon as he called the sheriff to report Noss for fraud.

They argued in the small house Ryan was renting. According to the court record, Noss grew very angry, pushed Ryan down and rushed from the house shouting he was going to kill them all.

Ryan testified everyone knew Noss carried a gun in his truck and he was afraid Doc meant what he said. So he stepped out on the porch and fired his own pistol twice. The second shot hit Noss in the back of the head and killed him instantly. Ryan calmly walked back into the house and told one of his men to call the sheriff.

Ryan's murder trial was held in Las Cruces on May 25 and 26. It was obvious that Ryan had shot Noss in the back. The trick for his lawyers, J.B. Newell from Las Cruces and James Martin from Corpus Christi, Texas, was to convince the jury that Ryan's fear of Noss was reasonable, and he had every right to shoot Noss to protect his family and friends.

The defense accomplished this by calling witness after witness, more than a dozen, who testified that Noss usually carried a gun, was typically drunk, and often violent. They all concurred that Noss was a liar and cheat and not someone you'd invite home for dinner with the family.

And these were not just witnesses off the street. There were sheriffs, deputy sheriffs, state policemen, district attorneys, and other lawyers. As these men testified one after another, singing the same song, Lawrence Murray went to the stand and surprised everyone - at first.

Murray was sheriff of Socorro County from 1941 to 1945. He was asked if he knew what Noss' general reputation in Socorro was for being a peaceable and law-abiding citizen. Murray said, "During the time he was in Socorro it was pretty good."

Murray must have said it with a half grin because when the lawyer immediately jumped in and said,

"What do you mean by that?" Murray stated, "Well, he was in jail all the time."

Clay Hooker, a former deputy sheriff of Dona Ana County and a former New Mexico state policeman, took the stand and was asked to recount incidents he had with Noss. He said, "He tried to get my gun two or three times. I had to arrest him several times and he didn't want me to search him. I had to hit him over the head several times with a black jack to search him."

Also, Hooker was asked about a Noss incident when Hooker was in Santa Fe for refresher training. Hooker said, "I was called out by Chief Summers in training school and he said, "Doc Noss is on a big rampage." He said, "You might as well go down there and kill him, you are going to have to anyway." Hooker went on to state he went down and arrested Noss that time without incident.

Although Charley Ryan shot Doc Noss in the back, the defense attorneys successfully put Noss on trial instead. The jury was quick to bring in a verdict of not guilty based on self-defense.

Today, many of the Noss faithful talk about the trial in terms of a conspiracy much like UFO believers do. Fantastic claims and beliefs are often kept burning simply by adding more gasoline. In this case, some supporters claim there was a conspiracy at the trial to cover up the treasure angle, and the lawyers, judge and witnesses were really after the gold. They say Noss was really a pretty good person and over the years the law enforcement officers were simply abusing their power in order to search Doc for any gold bars or uncut rubies hidden in his clothing.

This idea of a general conspiracy against Doc or the rest of the family is the most recurring theme in this story. Decade after decade, the family is usually within inches of finding the gold when the government, and it usually is the big faceless federal bureaucracy, steps in to somehow thwart their efforts.

Picking Up The Baton

After Doc's death Ova took ownership of the treasure story. She had her backers energetically digging into the peak at a number of points.

What is not clear is whether or not Ova believed Doc really found treasure. Doc would never let her into the peak so she never saw the treasure room.

As you move further from Doc Noss into the cloud of family members and apparent supporters, skeptics are left to wonder if these descendants were working their own scams, or were they fooled into believing there was a real treasure in Victorio Peak.

I often talk about this story in terms of a huge oak tree growing from a tiny acorn. The acorn is the Noss discovery story. Now it has grown into a huge tree with branches running in all directions and branches running off of those. When discussing this story, people will want to argue about some tale that, in our analogy, is a small branch out on the edge of the tree someplace.

The bottom line is that the trunk, branches and leaves all depend on the acorn actually existing in the first place. Until that is determined to be true, the rest of it is an illusion or cartoon and not worth arguing over. But it is human nature to grasp onto this later information as if it was fact.

Given the issues surrounding Victorio Peak, there seems to be a steady but small stream of believers ready to carry on. Of course, as these investors dug year after year and uncovered absolutely nothing, the promoters – the Noss family - had to keep expanding their base of support because some people got tired or went broke or just headed home. Ova did this in the early 50s by selling shares of the treasure that were in turn sold by others.

On January 5, 1953, Ova assigned four percent of her Victorio Peak interests to J.L. Fowler of Enid, Oklahoma who turned around and sold shares to at least 10 people in Oklahoma and Kansas.

In the 1990s, during the last big gold search at Victorio Peak, a gentleman from Kansas contacted the missile range Public Affairs Office. He produced a document showing he had purchased three shares of the treasure back in the early 1950s. One share was equal to one twentieth of one percent. The selling price was hidden as the shares were recorded in the county clerk's office as a transaction with a value of one dollar and other considerations.

The man told us he paid $350 for each share. That was a lot of money in the early 50s. In the long run, however, his earnings would have been $150,000 if the gold was really found and turned out to be worth a minimum of $100,000,000. Many people have valued the treasure in the billions, not millions.

As the base of investors grew, the Noss group lost control of their small, local scenario and found themselves on the radar screens of people concerned about fraud. People like Mrs. Miller from Caldwell,

Texas asked the U.S. Mint about gold mining stock from Ova Noss.

Queries like this and the one in 1939 alerted the Treasury Department to possible fraud in the quiet New Mexico desert. Letters and memos in the missile range files mention Treasury fears of bunko and scam operations in New Mexico relating to Noss.

In fact, in 1952, the commissioner of lands in New Mexico wrote to the Mint asking about the delivery of gold bars to the mint by Noss. Mrs. Nellie Tayloe Ross, Director of the Mint, wrote back saying there was only one bar submitted and its value was 97 cents.

The director's letter further states, "The files of the Bureau of the Mint contain several investigative reports concerning the activities of Dr. Noss, and his widow, Mrs. Noss, who appeared to have originated various gold schemes involving alleged gold hoards, although to our knowledge they have never actually produced any gold. On the basis of information available, it appears that a number of persons in recent years have been victimized by investing in nonexistent gold hoards."

By the way, before being appointed to head the Mint, Ross was the first woman elected as governor of a state. In 1924 she ran for the office in Wyoming in a special election after her husband died in the office. She served from 1925 to 1927.

White Sands Stumbles Into The Story

In the early 1950s, Ova lost access to Victorio Peak. The missile range called an end to co-use of its property and smoothed its western boundary to make it easier to manage. The new "hard" boundary pretty much included all of the San Andres Mountains and is just over six miles west of the peak.

Following this action, there was a fierce legal attack against White Sands by lawyers for Noss and several other individuals and groups interested in the treasure. Their actions brought queries from senators and congressmen as well as investors throughout Texas, New Mexico, Kansas and Oklahoma. There was even correspondence from Senator Milton R. Young, North Dakota, pleading a constituent's case.

It lasted a few years but proved to be mostly a nuisance since research showed the various claimants had no legal standing. Noss supporters often held up a state permit signed in the 50s as their license, but it turned out to have been issued after New

Mexico relinquished all rights to the land to the U.S. Army. Also, when New Mexico turned over the land to the Army, there were no legal claims on file for Victorio Peak. Of course, the Noss supporters claim this was just part of the government conspiracy to steal the gold.

Because of its remote location on the missile range's west boundary, not much testing has ever occurred in the Victorio Peak area. However, it was perfect for training. White Sands and the Air Force defined a large rectangular box of airspace over the mountain range and dubbed it "Yonder Area." It was a place where Air Force pilots could practice aerial gunnery.

One airplane would take off next door from Holloman Air Force Base and, as it entered the box, unreel an aluminum tow dart behind it on a long cable. Another airplane, piloted by a trainee, would engage the towed dart with his guns and try to shoot it down. No missiles were used.

During decades of this training, dozens of square miles around Victorio Peak were littered with the cables and darts that broke loose or couldn't be hauled back to a designated drop point. The Air Force picked up much of it, but an observant visitor can still spot shiny sheets of aluminum high on the mountains or canyon walls.

Being inside White Sands Missile Range (White Sands Proving Ground until the name change in 1958) did not stop people from continuing to look for treasure in Victorio Peak. It seems everyone in the region knew about the Noss treasure claims. This included the military and civilian personnel working at White Sands and Holloman.

I've talked to many people who illegally spent time exploring Victorio Peak or actively digging there. My favorite is Lou Blundell.

I met Lou in 2007 during a talk I gave in Alamogordo about the Victorio Peak legends. He told me his story and it turns out, because of his experiences, the White Sands commander put Victorio Peak off limits to all personnel.

Blundell spent several weekends in 1960 with a friend, Hal Gregory, looking for the Padre La Rue mine on the western edges of White Sands Missile Range. They were both civilian employees at Holloman. Their inspiration was the book *The Curse of the San Andres* by Henry James.

Published in 1953 the book was the first one to cover the Victorio Peak/Doc Noss story in detail. James wrote about meeting with the Noss family and getting much of his information from them. In the preface to the book, he says, "I wish to give credit here to Mrs. Noss for accompanying me on these trips to verify her story of Doc Noss's adventures."

On May 20, 1960, Blundell and Gregory drove into Hembrillo Basin at nightfall. They camped at the foot of Victorio Peak and set off to explore it the next morning. Near the top they discovered a crack with a wooden ladder. Once inside the crack, Blundell said they could see light above from a narrow fissure.

They then climbed back out and went to the top of the peak and found the same fault or crack that allowed light to penetrate into the peak. To enter here required rope, which they had brought with them, and they let themselves down to explore the space.

After not finding any gold bars there, they went back down the west side a bit to an actual hand-dug shaft, not a fissure, with scaffolding around it. While Gregory returned to the top to retrieve their rope, Blundell impatiently climbed out onto the wood to get a better look. It collapsed and down he went with much of the scaffolding.

He fell about 75 feet and was knocked unconscious. He woke up hearing his named being called by his friend.

Once Gregory found out what had happened, he arranged to lower himself, very gingerly, down into the shaft. Some of the scaffolding was still intact but ready to fall at the slightest touch.

When Gregory got to the bottom, he found Blundell in an awkward position with his knees up under his chin. Blundell was paralyzed from the waist down and had suffered a concussion.

Gregory scrambled out of the hole and went for help. Blundell was left all alone in the dim light wondering when help would arrive. He said his watch was stopped at 9:50 indicating when he fell. It wasn't until 7 that evening that Gregory returned with help.

A small group of volunteers led by a New Mexico State Police officer, along with search and rescue folks from Las Cruces, managed to haul Blundell out. They then had to transport him out of the mountains, across the desert and down to Las Cruces.

Blundell was very, very lucky. It turned out he had broken his back, fractured his skull, broken an ankle, and his legs were paralyzed. He spent 110 days in the hospital and underwent surgery to fix his back. Eventually he regained full use of his legs.

While in the hospital, the White Sands military police visited him to issue a citation for trespassing.

Leonard Fiege, Another Holloman Explorer

A better-known story that runs through this same period is about the Leonard Fiege group and their trip to the peak. Leonard Fiege was an Air Force captain assigned to Holloman AFB in 1958. He later claimed in 1961 that he and three men--Berclett, Prather and Wessel--went hunting in the Hembrillo Basin in 1958 and stumbled upon a tunnel in Victorio Peak. Fiege and Berclett said they crawled through it into a room containing a small stack of gold bars.

Decades later, Berclett admitted in a press interview they were hunting gold to begin with and not wildlife.

Many people have used the cover story of being hunters to explore the missile range. Almost from the beginning of White Sands, military personnel and some civilian personnel were given the freedom to travel uprange on weekends to hunt birds, varmints and deer.

During the 1960s and 70s, even the general public was allowed in for limited deer hunts during a few weekends each year. These were hunts in specific areas but hundreds were permitted to enter and they were even allowed to camp in a few designated spots.

I conducted a geological tour of the San Andres Mountains once that was hosted by a professor from the University of Texas at El Paso. In my vehicle were two petroleum geologists who talked about how their companies used to take advantage of the deer hunts to survey the mountains for likely drilling sites. They obtained hunting permits and carried rifles, but their job was to walk specific areas studying the rock formations.

This was important to their companies because the rock strata of the San Andres Mountains are pretty much the same as the Permian Basin, a huge oil-producing area in Texas. The companies wanted to be prepared in case the military ever gave up the land or allowed oil exploration.

So Fiege and company did much the same thing, except they headed for Hembrillo and the legendary treasure. Later, when asked if they had a gold bar to prove their story, they had nothing. They said they didn't want to jeopardize their positions with the military, so they did not remove anything. Most of us scratch our heads in wonder at their wonderful principles.

Berclett claimed he did scratch his initials on one of the bars. The men supposedly then spent several hours caving in the entrance to the little room so no one would find it.

In May 1961, the missile range commander received a letter from the Holloman commanding general requesting Fiege and partners, under a "Col. Garman's supervision," be allowed to enter Victorio Peak to "get evidence which they will then provide to U.S. Treasury activities." On May 29, Fiege and group met with Major General Shinkle, the WSMR commanding general, and Fiege stated it would be a simple matter to recover a few bars of gold. Shinkle denied the request.

Most people don't realize Shinkle was well acquainted with the Victorio Peak story when he took command in 1960. In January 1951, he was a colonel and was assigned to run technical operations at White Sands. During that time he put in some time as acting commander and his name appears on some of the paperwork dealing with Ova Noss and her attempts to regain access to Victorio Peak.

At the end of June, a group that included Fiege, Berclett and Colonels Garman and Gasiewicz from Holloman visited the director of the Mint in Washington to plead their case. As a result of that meeting, the director sent a letter to the Secretary of the Army stating: "Our files show that back in the Thirties there was a doctor who duped many people on a gold hoard scheme from an operation near the location of this so-called hoard. Since the Thirties, we have had hundreds of inquiries concerning a large hoard of gold in this area. I am of the opinion that the doctor, in his efforts to defraud, may have stored some non-gold bars in a cave so that he could show his prospective buyers the so-called gold cache. I am interested in your granting permission to enter the cave because I should like to put an end to this rumor. I have not gone into the question of ownership as I am positive the bars will not contain gold."

When the Department of Army received the letter from the Mint, officials asked for Shinkle's comments on allowing Fiege onto the range. He said, "My stand has been that I shall deny entry . . . unless I obtain such permission. I desire this permission... and would like these rumors laid to rest." On July 30,

1961, Shinkle received permission from the Department of Army to allow the investigation.

On August 5, a group including Shinkle, Garman, Fiege, Berclett, Prather, Wessel, Major Robert Kelly, a number of WSMR military police and Special Agent L.E. Boggs of Treasury went to Victorio Peak. They didn't find anything. For four more days Fiege and his three partners worked to enter the tunnel but failed. At that point Shinkle told them to go away.

The Fiege group came back to Shinkle later in August and September stating they would like to continue and were willing to work on weekends only. On September 20, Shinkle notified the Secret Service he was going to give Fiege more time, but they would be restricted to the same tunnel. No new excavations would be allowed. In other words, he was not going to allow them to turn the permit into an open-ended hunt for treasure on the peak.

Work then continued on an intermittent basis for about five weeks under the surveillance of Captain Swanner. In late October, WSMR records indicate two men named Bradley and Gray entered the basin and approached the workers. Swanner supposedly ordered them to leave the missile range since they were trespassing. They demanded a piece of the action or they said they would tell Mrs. Noss. Swanner told them to leave.

On November 1, the state land commissioner notified the Army that Mrs. Noss was accusing them of mining her treasure. Things came quickly to a head and Shinkle ordered all work to stop on November 3.

Shinkle communicated with the Secretary of the Army and local officials that work was stopped and the Fiege group had found

nothing. The Secret Service already knew it since they had a man on site. The Noss lawyers pushed for access for Mrs. Noss. On December 6, with advice from a long list of other agencies, Shinkle excluded all persons from the range not directly engaged in conducting missile tests.

One can choose to believe that Fiege and his crew found a bunch of gold bars deposited in a crack in Victorio Peak. But a more likely explanation, and much simpler, is that these men were simply exploit-

In September 1990, I received a letter from retired Colonel Richard Wade that included this photo. Wade was the WSMR provost marshal during the Gaddis gold search and was told by the commanding general he was being held personally responsible for the operation. Wade is in the center. To his right is Les Smith, mining engineer with Gaddis. To his left is Chester Johnson, the archaeologist representing New Mexico during the search. They are standing in front of the Gaddis tunnel. WSMR photo.

ing their positions with the military to gain official access and use it to explore for treasure.

What better arrangement could you ask for? Unlike Lou Blundell, no military policemen were going to issue them citations. The MPs were there with them, so they were free to just dig away. Shinkle must have feared this possibility; it explains why he limited their activity to the single spot they said was their tunnel.

A New Mexico Search

In late 1962, the Gaddis Mining Company and the New Mexico Museum approached the missile range seeking permission to enter and dig at Victorio Peak. The state of New Mexico sponsored the request and the Army recognized the state's interest in a possible historical find – all those manmade artifacts. On June 20, 1963, a license was granted by the Army for a 30-day exploration.

The work began with simultaneous archaeological, seismic and gravity surveys. According to Chester Johnson, a museum rep on site, "a D7 caterpillar was used to cut and build roads wherever they were needed, even on top of the peak." Most of the scars on the peak people see today are a result of this activity, not any Army work at the site.

The roads and platforms were necessary for placing a drilling rig. According to Johnson, the rig, "using a 4.5 inch rock bit and drilling with air, was used to test the anomalies (those places indicated by survey that might be caverns). Drill holes varied from 18 to 175 feet in depth, depending on location . . . There were about 80 holes drilled during the project."

In addition to this work Gaddis Mining drove their own tunnel 218 feet into the side of Victorio Peak in an attempt to gain access to the lower regions. This failed.

The missile range has the proposal document

This old briefing photo points out the location of the Gaddis tunnel on the west side of Victorio Peak. All of those roads and platforms were dug into the side of the peak during the two months of the search. In the 1990s, the Ova Noss Family Partnership excavated their tunnel not that far from the Gaddis adit. WSMR photo.

from the Gaddis Mining Company which is dated November 1962. It was prepared by Loren Smith, a character who appears in most subsequent gold searches in association with the Noss family. In this proposal there is an aerial photo of "Victoria Peak" and a topographical map, both overlaid with the "proposed area of exploration." It clearly shows the area being south of the top of the peak and the diorite dike.

This is often the problem with these claimants and searchers. They say they know where to look but usually can't find their landmarks, or say they "need to move over there." Smith started with one area and when the digging began his diggers moved on to an area north of their proposal.

To accomplish all of this digging, New Mexico had to request an extension that was granted. The 30-day extension made the exploration period July 19 through September 17.

In the end Johnson stated they found nothing. The press reported Gaddis spent $250,000 on the effort. As part of it White Sands filed a claim with the state for reimbursement for support during the quest. The claim for $7,640.54 was filed in October 1963 and finally paid in November 1964.

Treasure Seekers Are Everywhere

What do you do if you are a Noss supporter and a hard rock mining company spends two months thoroughly exploring tiny Victorio Peak without result? You press on of course. In fact, other claimants start coming out of the woodwork, and you have to start defending your turf.

In 1964 and 1965, the Museum of New Mexico and Gaddis Mining were both back at the Army's door seeking permission to reenter the range. In the same period, D. Richardson and R. Tyler visited White Sands requesting permission to locate "lost treasure."

Also, Violet Yancy, Doc Noss' second wife, showed up asking to get onto the range. Violet popped up again in 1969 making headlines in Texas and New Mexico. She hired two Fort Worth lawyers and was trying to establish her right to the treasure. She indicated there was documentation showing Doc left her 76 percent of the treasure and Ova the other 24 percent.

One person conspicuously missing from the recorded requests during the sixties is Ova Noss.

More than likely she was operating through various backers at this time. A hot rumor during the Gaddis search was that Harold Beckwith, Ova's son, was financing the Gaddis operation. Reporters pressed the question at the time but could not confirm it. It was later confirmed during the 1990s' search that Beckwith was behind Gaddis.

In 1968, E. F. Atkins and party started a series of requests and petitions that carried on for years. This persistent group pulled out all the stops in trying to gain access.

They convinced Senator Barry Goldwater, Arizona, to write requesting permission for the Birdcage Museum of Arizona to explore for treasure. It was determined the museum and Atkins were one in the same. They supposedly also sought entrance through the cooperation of a man named Gill with ABC-TV.

Then the range received a letter from the Great Plains Historical Association of Lawton, Oklahoma stating they had accepted scientific sponsorship of a treasure project at WSMR as outlined by an E.F. Atkins.

When all this was denied, Atkins asked for reconsideration and stated to White Sands officials that several Washington Army authorities, senators and representatives had recommended approval. On checking with the Department of Army, WSMR learned the Secretary of Army had made no commitment and would back WSMR's decision 100 percent.

You'll note that many of these people, after seeing the success of Gaddis linked to the state of New Mexico's historical museum, tied themselves to quasi-official historical organizations to improve their own chances of gaining access.

This cat and mouse game went on for years. In August 1971, The Department of Army indicated it had already received 55 Congressional inquiries that year on behalf of Atkins alone and his request to search for gold. In a 1972 memo for record, one range official noted he had received another request from Atkins to explore for gold. He indicated Atkins wanted to get together on a "friendly" basis and maybe something could be worked out, so Atkins did not have to exert Congressional pressure on the Department of Army to gain access to WSMR. It didn't help. His request was denied again.

Eventually, the trickle of regional interest grew into a gusher that burst onto the national scene during the Watergate hearings, thanks to the likes of nationally syndicated columnist Jack Anderson and attorney F. Lee Bailey.

On June 2, 1973, Jack Anderson reported in his syndicated column the story of noted attorney F. Lee Bailey's involvement with gold bars in New Mexico and, specifically, White Sands Missile Range. According to Anderson, Bailey was retained by a consortium to gain legal possession of the gold treasure at WSMR. The group promised to pay taxes and then sell the rest of the gold at a profit for themselves.

Bailey was supposedly skeptical at first so he asked for proof. The group came up with a gold bar about four inches long and promised hundreds more to prove their claim. Bailey sent it to the Treasury Department and had it assayed. It proved to be basically 60 percent gold and 40 percent copper. Anderson's article pointed out ancient gold ingots often were not pure either, and this percentage shouldn't be viewed as significant.

A Bailey spokesman later stated the consortium knew the location of 292 gold bars, each weighing about 80 pounds. However, the Departments of Treasury and Army expressed no interest in Bailey's proposals.

Just a few numbers at this point because they are significant. The bar given to Bailey was obviously not one of the alleged 80 pounders. An 80-pound bar with the stated proportion of gold and copper would be about 12 inches long, five inches wide and three inches thick. Much bigger than a candy bar even back when they were full size.

Interestingly, modern 14-karat gold jewelry is about 58 percent gold and 42 percent other metals to include copper and a few other metals like tin. The other metals used in the alloy vary depending on what color you want the gold to be. Baily's bar is beginning to look modern and suspicious.

In 1974, New Mexico Governor Bruce King had the same small bar examined by Los Alamos scientists who came to the same conclusion that the bar was a 60/40 split. The press dutifully reported experts saying the Bailey bar was basically the same as modern jewelers gold. However, they actually went a step further, did some research and were able to point out that gold found in New Mexico doesn't naturally occur with some of the other metals found in this bar. It didn't seem likely that the gold could have been mined in New Mexico.

People were left to draw their own conclusions,

but it looks fairly obvious that someone had melted down a pot of modern gold jewelry to make the bar.

At the time, Baily was a famous lawyer representing one high-profile client after another. For example, he was involved in the Patty Hearst and Boston Strangler trials. He was very well connected and figured he knew how to overcome the Army's objections.

Bailey took his problem to U.S. Attorney General John Mitchell. Mitchell then repeated much of it at a lunch with H.R. Haldeman, Nixon's White House Chief of Staff, and John Dean, the White House Counsel. In the course of events, Dean, during his Senate Watergate Investigation testimony, mentioned Mitchell and Bailey, gold bars in New Mexico, and a request for a deal for Bailey's client to avoid prosecution for possessing gold.

After the testimony there was a storm of Watergate headlines linking the Victorio Peak treasure to the investigation; at the center was the headline-seeking Bailey. At one point in all the babble, he was quoted as saying that given a helicopter and access to White Sands, he could produce gold bars in 30 minutes.

The Weirdness Grows

To quote Alice while in Wonderland, it just kept getting "curiouser and curiouser!" With so much publicity, letters and phone calls came into the missile range from all over. People offered their special ray gun/gold detectors, divining rods, ESP capabilities, and exclusive family maps. There was one person who claimed unique knowledge passed down from Jessie James and Belle Starr who really put the loot in the mountain after they faked their own deaths.

Some people were more brazen and found their way to White Sands Missile Range to sneak into Hembrillo Basin and have a look for themselves. One set of trespassers even set off dynamite charges. At Bloody Hands, a site down Hembrillo Canyon to the east, they supposedly blasted the Indian pictographs off of a rock wall.

The rumor mill went to work right away. Some people claimed if you knew how to read the drawings they would guide you to the treasure. In this scenario, the interlopers captured the images on film and removed the evidence for anyone else.

The dynamiters also dug a number of holes in the basin. Most everyone familiar with the basin's history assumes there were looking for bars supposedly stashed by Noss before he was killed.

The Provost Marshall files have numerous reports on incidents like these. They are great fun to read. For instance, on Feb. 28, 1975, range rider Bill Bates notified security they had evidence of a trespass in Hembrillo. The evidence was a "1973 light green GMC pickup truck" from Idaho that parked in a drainage on the missile range and was covered with camouflage netting. Footprints from the truck were headed east to Hembrillo Basin and Victorio Peak.

By 11:30 a.m. a helicopter and additional military police were dispatched to the basin. The police were posted and the helicopter flew back and forth searching. The report states, "All efforts to locate trespassers during daylight met with negative results."

They didn't give up. At 9 p.m. one of the patrols detected fresh footprints crossing the road west of Hembrillo Pass. At 3 a.m. three people were found walking to the vehicle and they were apprehended.

It turned out the trio was a husband and wife from Idaho and the other man was from Nevada. They were following a hand-drawn map given them by Tony Jolley who was living in Idaho at the time. Jolley is the guy who claimed he helped Doc Noss bury his gold bars the night before he was killed in Hatch.

Once they found the right area they were planning to use a metal detector and a "witching stick" to find the buried bullion. They said they heard about Jolley on a Paul Harvey report, so they thought the map and Jolley's story were real.

The map is in the report and is quite a joke. It is so vague and uncertain, they could have been off by miles and not known it. There are several "X"s on the map (what else would they be?) with the words "search this hill" penned on the sheet of tablet paper.

Also, the map indicates several stashes of bars. One burial site is miles north near the Floyd Crockett Ranch. Of course, when Noss supposedly buried his bars up there, the Crocketts were living in their place and might have noticed.

One interesting bit of trivia about this incident is that the trespassers reported the helicopter flew over them at least five times. They easily hid in a drainage under an overhang of brush and were invisible during the air search.

So what happened to these people? Were they prosecuted in federal court for trespassing? Nope.

Range officials did what they often do to avoid long and expensive court proceedings – they issued a bar letter. It is something that is almost instant and is issued locally. It is easy to do and usually scares most folks from pushing the Army's good humor.

The letter warns the person they will not be allowed back onto White Sands for any reason. If they are apprehended on the range again, they may be "subject to prosecution in the appropriate United States District Court under the provisions of Title 18, Section 1382, of the United States Code." These three letters were signed by Colonel Frank Schoen who was acting chief of staff at the time.

These intrusions became so frequent, security was beefed up and a house trailer was put in at HEL site just west of Hembrillo Pass. It was to give shelter to range riders and military police who patrolled the western border. Anyone trying to drive onto the range and down to the peak from the west would have passed the checkpoint. Also, from the pass it was easy to monitor most of the basin.

In July 1974, the range announced it was making more improvements to the site with the addition of a helicopter pad, a 30-foot radio antenna and portable generators. The additional work was done in anticipation of approval for another gold search that was brewing. The enhanced security also made it possible to catch trespassers like the folks from Idaho.

By now Victorio Peak was a hot conversation topic in America. Newspapers like the *New York Times* and *Washington Post* ran stories.

There was lots of maneuvering by various groups trying to gain entrance. The Bailey group signed a deal with the State of New Mexico where the state would get 25 percent and the group would get first crack at the peak. The Army didn't fall for it and New Mexico officials went to war with the Army in the courts and the press for quite a while.

At the time it must have been very serious for the two sides – lawyers facing each other at high noon in the dusty streets itching for a legal shootout. But looking back on it and seeing how it played out in the press, it looks laughable, especially when you consider no one ever came up with anything approaching a whole gold bar or a single valuable artifact proven to have come from the peak.

As the story grew in the mid 70s, a kind of gold fever or hysteria developed with it. The Bailey group started claiming there were thousands of bars of gold, not just 292. Maybe it was the oil crisis, but somehow inflation kicked in and some in the news media reported the treasure's worth at 225 billion dollars. The amount seemed to be a little excessive and the *Washington Post* put the story to rest when they called the U.S. Treasury to find out how much gold was stored at Fort Knox. They reported that the United States only held 6.2 billion dollars in gold reserves there.

Some supposedly legitimate claimants emerged during this period. In August 1973, White Sands received a letter from a lawyer named W. Doyle Elliott. It turned out he was retained by Roscoe Parr to get a piece of the action.

Elliott stated in his letter that Parr alone possessed all of the necessary information and instructions from Dr. Noss to settle the issue. The letter went on to say Noss had an insight he might die before gaining access into the peak again and gave Parr the secret to access the gold. Also, he supposedly told Parr how to divide the treasure and generously offered Parr the balance after it was divided. Elliott

solemnly pointed out Parr "accepted and agreed to fulfill the requests made of him by Dr. Noss" with his impending doom hanging over him. None of Parr's claims were apparently in writing.

By the end of 1974, the Army needed some sort of team roster to keep all the claimants straight.

Someone reported Fiege had gone into partnership with Violet Noss Yancy, Doc's second wife. News media reports mentioned the mysterious Bailey group, Ova Noss, Parr, the Shriver group, the "Goldfinder" group, and Expeditions Unlimited headed by Norm Scott. Ova Noss took the bull by the horns and sued the Army for one billion dollars. The case was dismissed.

This mess of claimants was exactly the Army's problem when officials were considering whether to even talk to the various groups. The Army was reluctant to deal with any one group for fear of showing favoritism and being sued by the others. No one had clear-cut, in writing, proof of any legitimate ownership of any real property. To grant access to one

Ova Noss (left) looks at the camera, as her daughter Letha Guthrie (right) explains to Norm Scott, the head of Expeditions Unlimited, how Doc Noss went down into Victorio Peak to find the fabulous treasure rooms. The photo was taken toward the end of the 1977 gold hunt. WSMR photo.

group ahead of another would smack of some sort of conspiratorial bias.

The Army was obviously receiving pressure to allow people in and was wasting a lot money and effort in the courts. To actually allow people onto White Sands and let the claimants prove to the world they didn't know what they were talking about, a number of solutions were proposed. They included a lottery drawing to determine order of entry and a free-for-all gold rush that probably would have ended in a blood bath. None of these approaches was deemed acceptable.

Then Norm Scott, a recognized successful gold hunter, was able to organize the various claimants and he proposed his outfit, Expeditions Unlimited, represent the groups and deal with exploring their claims.

The Army liked the idea of dealing with only one entity and accepted. The search was set to start in July 1976. This was postponed twice and, finally, "Operation Goldfinder" got underway in March 1977. It was put up or shut up time for most of the claimants.

In a letter from Scott to White Sands dated March 11, 1977, the claimants represented by Expe-

ditions Unlimited were listed. They included Harvey Snow; E.D. Patterson/F. Lee Bailey; Ova Noss; Joe Newman; Millard Shriver; and Jack London.

Before it even started the range had to battle the rumors. Just a few days before the start, word got around that the search was open to the public. Fearing a flood of spectators, the missile range Public Affairs Office scrambled to get the word out that only authorized searchers and press would be allowed in.

A press conference was held on March 18 and the actual search began the next day. Each day, press and searchers were registered at the peak and searched. At one point there was a report one of the claimant groups was going to try to salt the site. They were asked to leave by Scott.

On the peak the searchers went from site to site seeking the elusive gold bars. Eventually, an extension was granted to run the operation until April 1.

To say there was some press interest in the event would be an understatement. The *New York Times*, *Washington Post*, *Los Angeles Times*, *London Daily Mail*, *Newsweek*, *Time Magazine*, *Rolling Stone* and the *National Enquirer* were all there along with the local and regional print media. Of course, the televi-

When it became obvious the various treasure claimants weren't going to produce any gold bars during Operation Goldfinder, much of the media's attention focused on itself. In the middle of this photo, just to the right of the white cowboy hat, is CBS newsman Dan Rather. At the time Rather was with 60 Minutes. WSMR photo.

sion and radio stations showed up in force too. Probably the most notable, or, at least, most famous reporter attending was Dan Rather, then with the CBS news program *60 Minutes*. He attracted almost as much attention as the peak itself.

In the end, most of the claimants had their time on Victorio and failed to turn up any gold bars or anything of value. Instead of an hour, Baily's group had days at the peak and came up empty as well. Most whined they were not given enough time and accused the Army of running a token operation simply to quiet the rumors.

Dale Green was head of the missile range's Stallion Range Center engineering branch in 1977. He was on hand to help during the search. In fact, he drove Dan Rather to the saddle on Victorio Peak in a troop carrier so Rather didn't have to walk up and scuff his boots.

Green said one day he talked to a lawyer on site for F. Lee Bailey's group. Green said the lawyer shook his head at one point and said his firm believed these people - that they really had seen gold and knew where it was. But when they were let go to scramble up the peak to locate their gold, they scattered like a covey of spooked quail. They moved without purpose, moving a rock here and a rock there, wandering from spot to spot. At that point the lawyer said he knew they didn't know anything about any gold bars and were just trying to get in so they could explore and maybe find some. They were probably inspired by Fiege.

Immediately following the 1977 search, there was a flurry of requests to reenter the range. But the Department of Army emphatically stated, "that no exploration for lost treasure on WSMR will be permitted for the foreseeable future."

The Foreseeable Future Lasted 12 Years

In early 1989, the Ova Noss Family Partnership (ONFP) approached the Dept. of Army seeking permission to talk to White Sands about possible entry onto the missile range to explore Victorio Peak. The ONFP was headed by Terry Delonas, one of Ova Noss' grandsons.

Back in play was Norman Scott and his company Expeditions Unlimited out of Florida. He was introduced as the project manager for the ONFP.

The Dept. of Army granted Terry Delonas and Norman Scott permission to talk to Major General Thomas Jones, missile range commander at the time. Delonas and company pitched their proposal in terms they thought the Army would find appealing. He promised to end the speculation once and for all about treasure in Victorio Peak, that this would be a proper scientific expedition using the latest technologies, and it wouldn't take more than a few months.

After listening to the presentation, Jones told the group he would allow the exploration of Victorio Peak on two conditions. The first was that all the work be done on a noninterference basis. The second was that White Sands be directly reimbursed for any support it would provide.

The first condition was readily agreed to. The Air Force wasn't using Yonder Area much anymore, and evacuations of that area for other missions were not frequent.

The second condition was a little trickier. Suffice it to say the federal and military budget system did not allow the partnership to pay White Sands directly. Under the system, the check would be made out to the U.S. Treasury and the money would disappear back East. The system needed to be tweaked to allow the money to stay in New Mexico.

The partnership approached New Mexico Congressman Joe Skeen and he attached a rider to the

Terry Delonas, head of the Ova Noss Family Partnership, poses with a 1977 photo of his grandmother. WSMR photo.

Defense Authorization Act for 1990 that would allow direct reimbursement to the Army and WSMR. Victorio Peak was in Skeen's congressional district.

With the signing of the money bill, Norman Scott arranged to conduct an environmental and engineering survey of Victorio Peak. He arrived on Jan. 8, 1990 to present the missile range with a check for $54,000. The check was actually presented by Aaron Kin, a financial backer. The money was deposited and Scott went to work.

Some of the money was used to cover costs incurred by the range during the survey period. Some of this support included security at the peak by the military police, scheduling by National Range, blading the old road by the Directorate for Engineering, Housing and Logistics, and Public Affairs support for a press day at the peak.

During the two-week survey period, the group was trying to figure out the best places to dig and to conduct the required environmental work. To determine where the supposed treasure room might be, Lambert Dolphin was back taking ground radar readings of the peak. Dolphin had a similar function during the gold search of 1977 and was under contract to Expeditions Unlimited. They also made infrared images of the peak and brought in a number of witnesses to try to determine where to excavate.

This was important to do before writing the federally mandated environmental study because the study required all impacts be considered and addressed. The ONFP couldn't know what the impacts were until they devised a plan of action.

Les Smith showed up again to help. Smith accompanied Ova Noss to the peak in 1979 and was with the Gaddis Mining Company when it searched for the gold in 1963.

The environmental work was contracted out by the partnership. While that work went on, a license was negotiated between the partnership and the Army. It could not be signed until the required environmental documentation was satisfactorily completed.

Once the environmental work was completed and the license signed, the partnership would be allowed to work at the peak as long as they kept enough money in a White Sands fund to pay for range support. The amount was supposed to be kept at $200,000.

With the sluggish nature of the military billing system, the Army demanded the ONFP maintain this escrow account at White Sands so the range could pay the support bills out of the fund. It insured there would always be enough money to pay the immediate bills. Major General Jones had made it very clear he did not want the taxpayer to foot the bill for the search.

On Jan.18, 1990, the missile range cooperated with the family partnership to give the press an opportunity to see and photograph Victorio Peak. The press representatives were mostly local except for the *Denver Post* and the *Houston Chronicle*. Interest was way down after the dismal results of the 1977 hunt.

The day started with a press conference at the Hilton Hotel in Las Cruces where Delonas and Scott introduced their key employees and supporters. In questioning by the press, Delonas said the project would probably cost the partnership and its supporters from one to two million dollars.

Ground Penetrating Radar

Sometime in 1990, the ONFP put together a video about their undertaking. In the tape they were very upbeat and sounded like getting into the Victorio Peak cavern would not be as difficult as originally thought.

On the tape, Lambert Dolphin, the group's geophysicist, said he had identified a large cavern under the northwest side of the peak that might be accessible by digging a modest tunnel into the peak. He theorized there may have been an opening down on the side of the peak long ago which allowed people hiding the treasure to simply walk into the room. This made sense since they obviously didn't use the tortuous route Noss found to hide all that gold.

In May 1990, Dolphin used a new ground penetrating radar to make images of the peak's interior. He said the radar was 20 times more powerful than the one used in 1977 when he tested the mountain during Operation Goldfinder. After hundreds of readings from different angles, he said he had a definite picture of the room. The really good news was the room was only 200 feet below the old Gaddis tunnel completed in 1963.

He said this made sense because the family always claimed Doc, by his own estimate, went down 300 to 400 feet into the peak. The Gaddis tunnel is 200 feet below the chimney opening on top of the peak.

Dolphin concluded all of this was good news for the partnership and its backers. First of all, he said this was proof there is a cavern of some sort. Second, its location should eliminate the need for long and costly tunnels – they should be able to drill a hole directly into it on the first try. Third, he said, "I doubt that anybody has been in that cavern since Doc Noss was there."

He went on to assure backers that most of the gold was still there by saying, "If any artifacts or gold have been removed in recent years, these are probably secondary deposits and I would suspect not the main deposit."

Dolphin's pitch was interesting for two reasons. The obvious reason is that it was needed to keep the backers and volunteers coming. If the gold had already been removed, as many claimed, what was the point of digging into Victorio Peak? Dolphin soothed investor's worries and offered them riches beyond their wildest dreams in the very near future.

The second reason is that it let the Army off the hook. Some people accuse President Kennedy and later President Johnson of removing the gold. Most people accuse the Army. They say the Army removed it all in the 60s by helicopter or by trucks, depending on who tells the story.

The tape's narrator then asked if all this work is worth it. He went on to say that Doc Noss reported seeing more than 16,000 bars of gold in the cavern. This would be a total gross weight of 640,000 pounds (works out to be 40 lbs. per bar) which turns out to be 384,000 pounds of gold, if each bar is only 60 percent gold. He then multiplied that out at $350 per ounce and got a value of $2,150,000,000. That's right, more than two billion dollars at 1990s gold prices.

This was an obvious marketing tool as it helped quell the fears of investors and appealed to their greed by showing there was an astounding amount of money to be made.

Another intriguing aspect of the tape was how it twisted some basic information. This was something we at White Sands would run into again and again during the adventure.

When discussing the history of the project, the narrator stated they got the Congressional support demanded by the Army and it was now law that the partnership was authorized to dig at Victorio Peak.

In reality, the partnership was told by the Army it could not dig unless it could directly reimburse the Army for required support. This required Congressional intervention and they were directed to seek the necessary action on the Hill. It would have been inappropriate for the Army to solicit Congress on behalf of the ONFP.

If the Army was not concerned about direct reimbursement, it would not have required an act of Congress to approve the permit.

The rider on the 1990 Appropriations Bill said, "The Secretary of the Army may, subject to such terms and conditions as the Secretary considers appropriate to protect the interests of the United States, issue a revocable license to the Ova Noss Family Partnership . . . " The operative words in that sentence are "may" and "revocable." The secretary was certainly NOT directed to allow the search.

The key to the section followed: "The Secretary of the Army shall require the Ova Noss Family Partnership to reimburse the Department of Army . . ." and that "Reimbursements for such costs shall be credited to the Department of the Army appropriation from which the costs were paid." This allowed the partnership to reimburse WSMR directly for support costs.

This may sound like a fine distinction, but it was important because contrary to what the partnership implied, there was no law passed directing the Army to allow them onto WSMR. The ONFP twisted this because their version gave the appearance of a strong position in dealing with the Army. That would be important in keeping various supporters and financial backers happy.

Environmental Studies And The License

The 200-plus-page draft environmental assessment for the gold search arrived at White Sands on June 14, 1990. It was called "An Environmental Assessment of The Ova Noss Family Partnership Expedition into Victorio Peak" and was prepared by ECoPlan, Inc. of Albuquerque with the archaeological work done by Human Systems Research, Inc. of Mesilla, New Mexico.

In the general description of the document, the ONFP simplistically outlined their effort. It sounded so easy.

To find the cavern they proposed drilling some holes and placing ground radar sensors in them. This would allow them to triangulate the room and then bore a tunnel to it. The tunneling could be done with traditional blast and mucking procedures, or they could hire a huge machine that would bore a 42-inch hole straight through the mountain to the cavern. They estimated that if they ran the boring rig 24 hours a day with an estimated progress of eight to 16 feet per day, it would take 20 to 50 days to penetrate 400 feet into Victorio. It would be a snap.

Before drilling they planned to open seven existing holes to see if any could be used to shorten the distance to the cavern and reduce the amount of work needed.

The seven holes they planned to look at were Porter-McDonald Tunnel, Soldiers Hole, Gaddis Tunnel, Upper Noss Shaft, Ova Noss Intercept, the West Lower Entry, and Trench 1 Entry. These are all on the west and north sides of the peak.

This all sounded very straightforward and is why Delonas told the Army the search would only require three months.

In addition to the proposed "how to" informa-

tion in the environmental assessment, there was a great deal of data on the natural and cultural background of the area. Some of it debunked a few of the peak's old myths, like the soot-coated rocks.

Another story was about a cross-like figure about four feet high and three feet wide on the east side of the peak in a rock outcropping. A few people feel the cross is a manmade marker for the treasure. The scientists said in the report the cross was simply formed by water eroding one line and water staining the rock to form the other line.

Once the report was turned over to White Sands to be evaluated there, it was also sent to interested agencies like the New Mexico Department of Game and Fish for their comments.

Finalizing the environmental assessment and hammering out the final license took until the spring of 1991. On April 4, 1991, the licensing agreement was signed by Terry Delonas and Brigadier General Ronald Hite, commander of WSMR. The license was

The Noss family at Victorio Peak during the news media day held at the peak in January 1990. From left to right are: Terry Delonas, Letha Guthrie, Dorothy Delonas (mother of Terry and Jim) and Jim Delonas. At this time, the partnership publicly said they should find the treasure room in a matter of weeks. WSMR photo.

for a period of one year (the Army suggested the longer period) that was to begin on May 15.

In addition to the timeframe, the 16-page document limited the search area to a one-mile radius of Victorio Peak.

The agreement went to some length to make a distinction between what constitutes treasure versus artifacts. Paragraph 12 stated, "All archeological resources, antiquities, or items of historical or cultural interest . . . whenever located on WSMR shall remain the property of the Government."

After this statement there was a long laundry list of what might be considered an artifact. It included such common items as mortars, baskets, pottery, rock carvings, arrowheads and jewelry – the stuff that could be studied to learn about a culture.

The list was obviously lifted from a generic license because it included, "all portions of shipwrecks." It seemed unlikely a shipwreck would be found within Victorio Peak, but there were a lot of bureaucrats and lawyers involved who probably wanted to cover all bases.

Then there is "treasure." The paragraph went on to define "treasure" as "coins, gold or silver bullion, precious metals (not including metals with radioactive value), precious cut and uncut gems (not including jewelry or gems set in valuable ornaments), unset and loose jewels, and related valuables."

So, what would have happened if anything of value had been found? The agreement said the partnership would cease operations immediately. Together, representatives of WSMR and the partnership would make a written and photographic inventory. The two parties would then categorize items as "artifacts" or "treasure" or neither with WSMR having the final determination in the matter.

The artifacts would then have been dealt with by WSMR according to federal law. Any treasure would have been removed by the partnership under the direction of WSMR personnel.

At the signing, Delonas said they were checking on vault storage with several banks in the area.

After removing the treasure, if any was found, the Department of Army would take custody of it. Following another inventory, the Army was, through the Department of Justice, to go to the United States District Court for the District of New Mexico and request a determination as to the ownership of the treasure part of the material found.

This requirement was necessary as far as the Army was concerned because there were so many claimants. The Noss family didn't like it because they say Doc was the first to see and claim the treasure.

However, from the Army's point of view none of it was that simple. For instance, in the 70s, representatives of the nearby Apaches claimed it was their loot. Their ancestors had stolen it and merely stored it in Victorio Peak. Their claim easily predated the Noss claim by a century.

Another interesting requirement of the license was that "neither the Licensee nor any individual or company shall sell participation interests in the project contemplated by this license or in any manner utilize this license to promote the sale of stock or other securities or effect the financing of such project without first disclosing such transaction(s) to the Secretary of the Army." This portion of the license was intended to prevent anyone from implying that the Army endorsed or backed the search.

To control the site and prevent any possible misrepresentation or fraud, all representatives of the partnership had to consent "to a thorough search of their persons, vehicles, equipment, and any other personal property by Government security personnel." This included a search prior to entry to the area or entry into any cavern or tunnel and a search on returning or emerging.

Of course, this was done to prevent anyone from "salting" the site with anything of value like Doc Noss used to do. If one of the believers planted a gold bar or religious statue and then "found" it, some people might have been led to believe there really was something in the peak.

After the signing, Delonas said their first efforts would be directed at drilling small holes into the peak and then lowering cameras down the shafts.

He said they had developed a very sophisticated camera apparatus containing video and still cameras and the lights needed to illuminate any void. They would be able to lower one device and control it from the surface to obtain live television video and 35-millimeter still photos.

After the signing some of us had lunch with Delonas. He was very likeable and sincere. He also revealed his sense of humor. He said he was happy the end of the search was finally in sight because all of his efforts during the past years had basically ruined his life.

Laughingly, he went on to say one of their financial backers was connected with the movie industry. This backer told Delonas the story of the search would make a better movie if nothing was found. The movie could then portray a man who had wasted his life on a wild goose chase. It would be a tragedy and, after all, most of the greatest stories ever written were tragedies.

It is remarkable how that thought became a reality during the next decade.

Wasted Time And Money

On July 20, 1991, the Ova Noss Family Partnership finally began its search at Victorio Peak.

While they waited for the arrival of their drilling rig to punch small bore holes into the peak to locate the cavern, the partnership expanded its original request and asked for permission to do a metal detector sweep of the area. Their intent was to try to find some of the gold bars that Doc Noss supposedly buried the night before he was killed in March 1949.

Tony Jolley visited the site the first day to give the searchers an idea of where to run their metal detectors. Jolley said he helped Noss bury about 110 bars that night. The newspapers have reported Jolley came back years later, dug up 10 of the golden bars, and sold them for $65,000. He indicated they should concentrate on the ridges and flat areas northwest and northeast of Victorio Peak.

This is a typical example of the questionable decisions made by ONFP throughout the search that wasted their time and burned up volunteers and money. Jolley's story is that he was just a kid who Doc hired to help dig up and rebury a bunch of bars. According to Jolley, this was necessary because Doc didn't trust Charley Ryan and wanted to make sure his bars were well hidden.

Let's think about this story a minute. These were bars that had been buried by Doc years before and only he knew their locations. All evidence of the original digging would have disappeared long before due to weathering and plant growth. The desert patina of loose rocks and blown sand would have returned to the disturbed area. It probably would have taken an army of men with metal detectors to find those hidden bars back in 1949.

Also, why would the secretive Doc tell a hired kid this story and let him see all the bars? It certainly doesn't sound like the Doc we know.

To rebury the bars meant digging new holes for them. That meant leaving a very fresh scar on the ground at every hole that any city slicker or third grader could have found. Depending on the desert winds and rains, those scars would have taken months to years to disappear into the background. Charley Ryan and his cronies would have had no trouble finding them in a couple of hours.

Surely we've seen that Doc wasn't as dumb as Jolley made him out. Doc would have known that the news holes would be very visible – after he was a pro at burying bars.

Because the area the metal detectors were searching was right in the middle of the Hembrillo battle site, all work was observed by an archaeologist representing the Army. Any time they got an indication of a metal object, the spot was marked. Most of the things they found were related to the battle and included things like rifle cartridges.

If they felt the item might be larger, like a gold bar, it was exposed. No gold bars were found but an anvil was discovered.

On July 28, the partnership and the missile range conducted a press briefing at the range´s Countdown Rec Center. Terry Delonas briefed on the history of the treasure and what they were doing at that time.

Also, they proudly displayed their $100,000 down-hole probe. Originally, they were going to lower the special probe into the holes they bored that ended up punching through to empty spaces.

Unfortunately, on their first try the hole had a bend in it and the probe, which is almost five feet long, could not flex to make the turn. This turned out to be a major problem; the fancy probe proved rather useless except as a prop for investors, reporters, and the curious.

Different Approaches

The ONFP had several different approaches for their almost five-year treasure hunt. That's right, five years. The ONFP had permission to work at Victorio Peak from May 15, 1991 until March 15, 1996, when the missile range finally suspended their operations. At the end of every year they asked that the license be renewed and it was.

They were sometimes evacuated for military test missions in the area, but if they had wanted to they could have easily worked over 1,500 days at the peak. As it was, they took big chunks of time off and worked only between 400 and 500 days at the peak. Doesn't seem very dedicated when the gold was always "just inches away."

The promised scientific approach to exploring the peak quickly turned into a bust. The infrared imaging, three-dimensional images, ground penetrating radar, special down-hole probe, aerial views, and acoustic soundings all came up empty.

The second and most promising approach was to simply dig into the peak by removing the debris in the crack that Doc said he followed. The logic was impeccable.

They knew Noss claimed to have entered the peak via the huge crack that bisects the mountain. He worked his way in and around the debris in the crack and came out in the monstrous tunnel and caverns. In 1939 that route was blocked when the fateful dynamite explosion caused the debris route to collapse.

The ONFP plan was simple. By cleaning out the debris from the west end to the east end of the crack, eventually you would work your way down to the elusive tunnel unless, of course, it was protected by a magical cloak of invisibility.

They worked for months on this and, with the help of some modern technology, it went faster than employing buckets to haul the debris out of the peak. They worked in the crack with hand tools like picks, shovels and sledge hammers to break free the rocks and dirt, and shoved it to the mouth of a huge vacuum hose that sucked the debris outside.

The vacuum cleaner was something called a "Guzzler," a large, truck-mounted industrial vacuum system most of us associate with city crews cleaning storm sewer lines under streets. But the truck's system can be used to move solids, powders, liquids and slurries up to a thousand feet and suck it right into the truck's holding tank. The truck can then be moved to simply dump the material elsewhere.

The volunteers broke rocks in the dimly lit crack, exposing themselves to continuous clouds of dust, week after week. The only good things about working in the fissure were the cooler temperatures in summer and the respite from howling winds in the spring.

Eventually they got to the bottom of the crack where they ran into the solid layer of shale. They encountered no tunnels, no treasure, no stream, no skeletons, and absolutely no valuable artifacts.

They didn't come up empty-handed, however. Early on, near the top of the debris fill, they found evidence of the many past trespassers who snuck in to dig for glory and wealth. It was mostly tools and buckets. They also found materials from the days when Ova watched over the backers she sold percentages to as they tried to dig out the fill material to get to the original route.

The only thing they found pointing to Doc Noss was a board with the letter "T" and a five-pointed star carved into it. When they presented the board to backers and government officials, the family suddenly remembered one of Doc's aliases was Tom Star. They said this was a clear indication they were on the right track.

Dorothy Webb was the government's contract archaeologist on the peak the day the diggers "found" the board. When I talked to Dorothy in 2013, she said the board itself was old but the carvings appeared very fresh with sharp edges and no dirt in the lines. Not at all like something buried for more than 50 years.

Also, she noted they disobeyed all of their established protocols to follow when a discovery was made. Whenever they found anything, they were supposed to notify Dorothy so she could enter the peak to examine it in place and help dig it up. That happened regularly with other material but not the board – they just showed up with the Tom Starr board claiming it came from the peak.

More than likely the board was needed to boost the morale of workers and backers. They did the same thing in their newsletter, *Peak of the News*, by periodically saying things like, "The unobstructed continuation of Doc's path may be only 20 feet away" and "By the time this newsletter is mailed we hope to have our discovery."

The lack of finding Doc's huge tunnel didn't deter the ONFP. They surmised the tunnel must be hidden behind the single large rock wedged in the excavated crack quite a ways above the bottom.

They decided not to simply break the rock apart and see what was behind it. I imagine the ancient Egyptians could have managed it with hand tools in just a couple of weeks. In little time, the great search could have ended when the rock was demolished. There would be a tunnel or there wouldn't.

Of course, that was exactly the problem. The search would have ended and the whole enterprise would have come to a screeching halt when there was no tunnel. It would have proven that Doc Noss did nothing more than wiggle his way through the broken debris and then hatch a scheme to make some easy money.

Claiming that removing the rock was too hard or too dangerous, the partnership moved outside to bore a tunnel to intercept Doc's path.

This operation was a classic mining action. Holes were drilled into the rock face at the end of the tunnel. Explosives were placed in the holes and detonated. Several feet of the rock face would be shattered and after the dust cleared, a low-slung vehicle with a scoop (a mucker) would move in to remove the busted rock. Once it was gone, they repeated the process. This way they worked their way through mostly solid rock a few feet at a time.

This tunnel was south of the cleared crack where the Guzzler was used and north of the lava-filled fault bisecting the peak. Eventually, it went back into the peak several hundred feet. When I visited, there was at least one branch tunnel that went north and intercepted the crack.

We didn't spend much time in the tunnels because the rock was rather unstable. Again, the limestone is riddled with cracks and is crumbling in many places – not exactly stable material for walls and a ceiling. Bob Burton, missile range archaeologist, grew up in Colorado where his father was a mining engineer. Burton had spent a lot of time in hard-rock mines and he said this one scared him.

During these fairly straight-forward efforts to clear the crack and tunnel into the peak, the ONFP looked to a third methodology to chase their treasure – magic. They wasted time, manpower and money on such mumbo jumbo as dousing for tunnels and the stashes of metal.

For instance, in 1993 a supposedly famous douser named Young visited the peak and surveyed the area. Young came up with a map of underground tunnels that made the place look like Swiss cheese. There were tunnels everywhere. When you saw it you had to wonder why previous searchers who put down those dozens and dozens of holes never accidentally hit one.

Crews from ONFP went off to dutifully dig at these sites and found nothing. Young told them that one site had a tunnel only one to five feet below the surface. They dug but nothing was found.

Young claimed he could find more than tunnels. In one area he said he detected six piles of precious metals. Nothing was found.

Finally, Young doused the drainage or canyon bottom around Victorio Peak. He said there were several tunnels present and no water, so they might lead to the treasure rooms.

The volunteers took their boring machine onto the road in the drainage and drilled a few holes to penetrate the tunnels. They never found the tunnels but they hit water. Later they put a small submersible pump down one hole to pump water up to a tank to be used during the tunneling process.

Later the ONFP claimed no one predicted there was water where they found it. I guess they were using the douser's information for that claim.

Some believers now describe it as a "pool" of water like it was some sort of underground lake. I think they are trying to make a case that this is somehow related to Doc's underground stream.

This whole issue is not an issue. It is the ONFP trying to drum up more support. Any hydrologist or old cowboy or city boy like myself would have predicted there was underground water in the drainage. The evidence is all around in the form of springs running down the canyon. Chief Victorio used the springs in 1880 and the Henderson family dug out a spring box for their use in the 1930s. In addition, the Henderson family had a windmill to pull ground water out for their livestock. Further down canyon are more springs.

This is not a magical or unusual phenomenon. The San Andres canyons are littered with springs. The gravel and sand washed into the drainage bottoms, as well as the fractured rock beneath it, act as a sponge every time it rains. In some places the water is right at the surface and in others it is down several feet or further. In some places it flows onto the surface and then back into the sand. It is a classic situation found in mountainous terrain everywhere on the planet – where they get some rain.

Another magical device was the Omnitron used in November 1993. This was supposed to be some sort of electrical dousing system that could detect different kinds of metal buried below it.

At least ONFP only wasted about five days on this tomfoolery. Wherever it was tried, it pointed to all kinds of materials. Not even ONFP volunteers believed it after a while.

This kind of folly was presented to the Public Affairs Office as well. We received one query from a gentleman who wanted to know if he could get permission to enter White Sands to look for a couple of gold stashes. When asked how he knew where they were located, he replied that he doused maps for precious metals.

He started by dousing a general map of New Mexico on his kitchen table. That pointed him to some general areas. The next step was to refine his search with larger-scale maps. The final step was to acquire the topographical maps for those hot spots and douse them. That, in turn, gave him very specific places in canyons and on mountainsides – within a mile or so supposedly.

To say the least, he was not granted permission to enter White Sands.

End Game

The ONFP search ended when they stopped putting money into the escrow account for paying the WSMR bills. The account gradually ran dry and eventually White Sands officials asked ONFP if they were going to replenish the account. ONFP said no.

Finally, on March 15, 1996, White Sands suspended ONFP operations at the peak and ordered them off the missile range. In May, the yearly license expired and was not renewed.

Many people claim ONFP finally ran out of money from backers who were getting sucked dry. Terry Delonas was adamant that was not case. He accused the missile range of overcharging them and they were going to do the "right thing" to end the thievery.

This generated some press coverage and members of ONFP actually said the Army shut them down just as they were about to make the final discovery. They said somehow the Army knew they were only a few feet from the mother lode and made them stop before they broke into it.

However, most thinking people wondered why any smart person who was just about to find a billion dollars in gold would jeopardize their access to it by failing to pay the monthly rent. There is stupid and then there is insane stupid.

In April 1997, the ONFP sued White Sands in the U.S. Court of Claims for overcharging them. In 1999, the Army filed a counter claim against ONFP for back payments.

The case went to Judge Horn who visited the site on Oct. 25, 1999. I drove her to Victorio Peak in the office Suburban. Also in the vehicle were Terry Delonas and various lawyers from both sides.

The thing that sticks in my mind during the trip was Delonas telling her the same old origin story about how Doc Noss found the gold and the fabulous tunnel, rooms, stream etc. Even after all the probing, digging and tunneling he was still hooked on those worn-out pulp magazine clichés for a treasure story. They seem amazing in a magazine. In the cold light of day, knowing what we know, they are too absurd to be even mildly believable.

Judge Horn returned to Washington to encourage both sides to settle. She wanted no part of a long court battle.

In November 2000, the two sides ended the lawsuit and by mid-February 2001 all the ONFP equipment was removed from the peak. In return the ONFP did not have to restore the peak to its original condition as stipulated in the license.

More Sure To Come

Has all this activity ended the legend of treasure in Victorio Peak? No way. In the years since the peak was buttoned up, the missile range has received requests for a copy of the license used for ONFP. Several others have indicated they have that special map or special knowledge and they would like to share with the Army and White Sands. All they need is permission to enter the area to prove their claims.

Most of us involved in the last gold hunt feel if the Army allowed gold hunters to completely bulldoze the peak flat and they found nothing, they would simply pull a Delonas. They would slightly alter the story and say, "We were misled. It is really in Geronimo Peak next door."

In 2013, a three-part series of books about the gold story was published. I haven't read them yet, but a blurb on the Victorio Peak website I saw last year claimed three different presidents got rich by stealing from the Victorio Peak vault. In another couple of decades, the supporters will need an encyclopedia of books to flesh out the ever bigger story.

And what about Terry Delonas? The movie producer got his wish for a tragedy. Delonas has probably wasted decades of his delicate life on this zany chase. It was revealed a few years after the search, in the book *What Men Call Treasure* by David Schweidel and Robert Boswell, that Delonas was suffering from AIDS during the whole fiasco.

Also, the process seems to have changed him from that sincere and smiling individual I had lunch with into a typical bitter treasure hunter. He seems a bit grim and angry as he points an accusing finger at likely targets and blames others for his inability to find the family inheritance.

These hand print pictographs down Hembrillo Canyon from Victorio Peak are done with red pigment. There are many other images on the walls but "Bloody Hands" is the name that has stuck. In the arroyo bottom there are many bedrock mortars used at one time by native people to grind mesquite beans and other seeds. Speculation swirls around the site because it is so near the treasure peak. One legend is that if you can correctly interpret the images, you will have directions to the gold. Another tale is that there is a tunnel entrance in the cliff that leads back to Victorio Peak and the treasure room. Because of these myths, for years the missile range has had trouble with trespassers stricken with gold fever. During the sanctioned gold hunts, searchers always requested permission to dig here. The trespass gold hunters have often left evidence of their activities here. In fact, just a few years ago WSMR personnel escorting a TV crew to the site caught some diggers at Bloody Hands. They said they were digging for artifacts. Even though the trespassers were caught on video by the TV crew, federal officials did not prosecute. Photo by the author

The Adobe Bismarck

How A Myth Is Hatched

After flying over the missile range many, many times in helicopters and seeing what I thought was most of the ground, I was startled to discover in 2012 there is supposed to be an adobe battleship on White Sands. This isn't just any battleship either. The buzz on the web says there is a dirt and sand mockup of the infamous German battleship Bismarck still out there. This mockup is even equipped with large logs to simulate the Bismarck's massive 15-inch guns.

Most web entries claim the target was to be used by bombing crews from Britain's Royal Air Force. They often say the target was built in May 1941.

The evidence of this battleship comes from a *Google Earth* satellite image of a spot at: 33 04' 38"N, 106 10' 59"W. Type in the coordinates on *Google Earth* and you can see what they are talking about.

Since the internet is a huge jumble of useful data, fact, fiction, rumor, lies and stupidity, this story is quickly growing, taking on a life of its own as one version shoots off from another, and may soon be one of our local loony legends. In February 2013, I found that the *Wikipedia* entry for the village of Tularosa, New Mexico mentions the battleship as a local attraction.

Some bloggers are saying it is not the Bismarck but is really a mockup of the Tirpitz, the Bismarck's sister ship. The Tirpitz survived until 1944 whereas the Bismarck was sunk on May 27, 1941, a half a year before the United States entered World War II. In fact, it was sunk about the time this target Bismarck was supposedly being built.

Again, on the web, anything goes and people are putting other spins on the *Google* image. One blogger thinks the United States actually built it to train bombing crews in preparation to destroy the Japanese navy. Given the construction date, that's pretty incredible by most any standard.

The bottom line is that people are arguing about something that doesn't exist. Amazing.

The construction date of May 1941 is a big, big problem for all of these theories. At that time, the United States was half a year from entering World War II, and local livestock owners were busy trying to make a living. No one had voluntarily or involuntarily given the government use of their land.

It is true that goat ranchers in the mountains were upset with Roosevelt because his administration bought all of Turkey's wool to keep it out of the hands of the Germans. That move was designed to deny the Nazis warm blankets and uniforms but sent U.S. wool demand into the tank. If local ranchers could sell their wool at all, it was at rock bottom prices.

In talking to these folks over the decades, I have never heard any scuttlebutt from them that one or more of them rented their land to the military prior to Pearl Harbor.

When I first went to *Google Earth* and found the image, I saw the very nice outline suggesting a battleship. But it is completely lacking in detail. Remember, these photos are taken from several hundred miles away.

It turns out, the battleship is one of those association tricks we humans are good at – connecting a vague shape with something we are familiar with. It is called pareidolia. We are very good at seeing puppies in clouds, famous people in rocks and the Virgin Mary in tortilla burn marks.

The first thing I did was zoom out to find exactly where the ship was on White Sands. That was easy as it is just west of the Tularosa Gate and a few yards directly south of the Tula-G launch area.

I have been by there many times and have watched MLRS rocket shots from Tula-G. Tula-G is a typical MLRS launch site. They are scattered all over the missile range to provide various ranges and azimuths for weapon testing while restricting the scatter of munitions to just a few areas on White Sands.

These launch sites are pretty simple with the main feature being a large berm or hill of earth making a safety barrier between the MLRS launch vehicle and the equipment and people on the other side.

When I zoomed closer to the outline of the Bismarck at Tula-G site, the reality was obvious. The thing that looks vaguely like a battleship is really the borrow pit for the berm. The engineers had to get the sand/dirt from somewhere to build the large berm and it was easy to dig it up on site and pile it up just a few yards away.

When I looked at the shadows cast by the sun on the small building at Tula-G and the other 3-D structures, it was clear the shadows for the battleship were for a hole, a negative space, not something sticking up in the air.

In late 2012, the White Sands Public Affairs Office received a couple of inquiries about this Bismarck. One was a request to go visit the old target.

At least one of these people has posted on the web the Public Affairs response pointing out the thing is a hole. We are now wondering if the posted response will kill further speculation, or if a German television network will call sometime in the future with a request to film the Bismarck.

Then, in 2013, there was a request from the Travel Channel to do a story on the Bismarck target. The network was starting a new show about out-of-the-way and mysterious places to visit. Their working title was *Destination Mystery*. When they went into final production, according to producer/director Seth Isler with Indigo Films (the company producing the series), the title was changed to *America Declassified*.

I worked with them when they visited Trinity Site during the April 6, 2013 open house. Trinity Site offered them the "mystery" of only being open to the public twice a year and being a place still radioactive – possibly still dangerous. Cue the *Twilight Zone* music.

I have to say they were very good about recording their expert and talking with me about how radiation at the site was not dangerous in the end. Who knows if our points will actually air as a counterbalance to the hype.

On hearing about other places on the missile range, they then requested trips to the Space Harbor and the Bismarck. Although the public can't visit them, both places are very visible to people using *Google Earth* to search the missile range for things of interest, maybe even something "secret."

On April 22 the network returned. I went along when Monte Marlin, Public Affairs Officer, escorted a new film crew and their "investigator" Ben McGee out to the site. McGee is an honest-to-god scientist who gingerly tries to straddle the fence between the show's need for a theme of mystery and intrigue with the realities of ordinary explanations for things – like a borrow pit's shape that suggests a battleship to some people. I was along to provide a little history.

We spent most of the day out at the site shooting video of the Bismarck, McGee explaining the scene and me providing the humdrum reality of the place. In the end, no matter how the crew approached the Bismarck, it was still just a hole.

When I first heard about the Bismarck, I spent some time trying to track down the origin of the story. It is pretty rare when you can find the origins of one of these Internet tales, but I think I found the source in the form of a local writer who specializes in history articles. Over the years, his articles have appeared in area newspapers. They are well-written and informative pieces.

In January 2007, his story about a B-17 crashing during a training flight in World War II might have triggered everything. The article is about how the big plane crashed west of Socorro. He was able to get the Air Force accident report and he documents the flight in great detail.

As part of the article he mentions all the targets and bombing ranges scattered around southern New Mexico during the war. For instance, between Las Cruces and Deming, the ground is littered with targets that are easily identified from the air.

He wrote, "In early 1941, another interesting target was constructed southeast of Socorro. It was a scale model of the German battleship Bismarck, and was made of dirt with wooden logs for the gun turrets. This was built to train pilots from the Royal Air

Force in identifying the famous battleship at night. However, the Bismarck was sunk in May 1941 — before the 'adobe' Bismarck saw much use. It is still there today."

This seems to be the source for all the current interest because most everyone uses this description with verbatim quotes.

When I talked to the author, he admitted he had never been to the battleship site and said he got the information from a man who is now dead who got it from someone else.

When I explained the borrow pit reality, he was genuinely concerned about his article. He said he has gone to great pains to be as accurate as possible and doesn't want misinformation floating around.

As I publish this, he is somewhere between wanting to believe his oral history source and admitting it is impossible given the time problems and physical reality on the ground. He recently wrote, "I have tried, but never found any documentation on this story, only oral testimony, so I remain lukewarm and confused on what this was all about."

I think it will be fascinating to see what happens next. Travel Channel's McGee agrees the Bismarck is nothing but a hole in the ground. However, the next step in the Internet tall-tale generator might be the idea that WSMR used the adobe battleship to build the berm and ended up having to dig into the basin floor to get enough sand. Eventually the blogosphere will fabricate its own "truth" in this matter.

While the satellite image of this area certainly suggests a battleship in our minds, this is the reality when you go to the spot - a big hole in the ground. David Soules and Monte Marlin are seen boarding the battleship and looking for those pesky logs used as guns. Photo by the author.

23

Wildlife

Lions And Oryx And Bears, Oh My!

People who visit the missile range are usually impressed by the wildlife they stumble upon in the Uprange areas. Just driving up the main internal roads, visitors have a chance of seeing horses, oryx, mule deer, pronghorn, coyotes, pupfish (in Salt Creek or one of the springs), golden eagles, all kinds of hawks, and a variety of snakes looking for a little early morning heat on the pavement.

Drive into the San Andres or Oscura Mountains and there is some prospect of seeing elk, mountain lions and javelina. When I worked at White Sands, every once in a while a bear would wander onto the missile range from the Sacramento Mountains looking for a good home.

In the first decade of the 21st century, there have been more sightings of elk and bear than ever before. In fact, the folks at the San Andres National Wildlife Refuge saw the same bear two years in a row indicating he might have been trying to make a living in the local mountains. They have also sighted elk on the refuge itself, which is a first.

Bear numbers are well beyond what anyone expected. In 2012, ECO Inc., an ecological consultant at White Sands, surveyed for bears. They put out game cameras and bait buckets to see how many were wandering around the missile range's mountains. From April through December they recorded 29 individual black bears.

With this many bears, devising an actual management plan takes on more importance than it did in the past when only an occasional transient bear was seen. The next step is to track bears and see how close they come to human activities. This will be essential in preventing future conflicts between bears and people who are out on the missile range training or testing.

Elk normally drift down from the Sacramento Mountains in the winter and cross over to the missile range's Oscura range. From there, they occasionally travel south into the north end of the San Andres Mountains. One of the missile range biologists once took a photo of an elk happily chomping on spring yucca blossoms.

For an elk to travel miles south of Rhodes Canyon to the refuge is rather remarkable. On the other

Mara Weisenberger, wildlife biologist for the San Andres Wildlife Refuge, snapped this photo of a black bear in the southern San Andres Mountains in the fall of 2010. She speculated it was so blond because of its exposure to the sun. Courtesy Mara Weisenberger.

hand, it may not have been an unusual occurrence 200 years ago, before ranching expanded from Texas into this region.

Some of these creatures travel from even further away. On a trip to Alaska in 2009, I took in the visitors center at Denali National Park. Amongst the wildlife displays was a golden eagle stuffed and mounted, along with a story of how biologists once tracked three nesting eagles from Denali to see where they went in the winter.

These true "snowbirds" headed south during the harsh Alaskan winter. One ended up in our own Tularosa Basin, which means it probably spent time hunting on the missile range. Every summer it flew all the way back to Alaska to nest in the same area where it was born.

This partial list of animals is pretty impressive given most outsiders have written off the missile range as a desolate desert, bombed out by the military. From what many visitors told me, they expected the place to look like a World War I battlefield.

"Uprange" is that area of White Sands north of U.S. Highway 70 all the way to the northern boundary near U.S. Highway 380. It is normally off-limits to the public because of safety concerns and security requirements.

Those limitations have kept the general public out since 1945. In addition, most WSMR employees never venture Uprange either – they have no need to be there. The most frequent travelers Uprange are people working on the various test programs, providing some sort of data collection for a test or doing maintenance.

When you spread that small number of personnel over a couple of thousand square miles and factor in that these missions don't occur every day, the impact of people Uprange is pretty low. In the mountainous areas, the San Andres and Oscuras, many roads may go weeks without seeing a vehicle.

It is true dangerous missions take place Uprange with missiles and targets frequently falling out of the sky. But those kinds of impacts tend to be out in the flats of the Tularosa Basin where much of the land is old lakebed or dry grasslands. Also, many impacts are restricted to just a handful of target areas scattered up the center of the range. All of this limits the impacts on the majority of the missile range's acreage.

The bottom line, and something that has been said by many professional biologists, is that White Sands Missile Range is a bit of a de facto wildlife refuge. During my 30 years in the Public Affairs Office, I was lucky enough to escort all kinds of television crews, newspaper and magazine photographers, wildlife writers, tour groups, and others Uprange and got to see the animals firsthand. Those days were always better than piloting a desk in the office or attending another meeting.

Who Owns the Animals

Before we examine some of these fascinating creatures, we need to talk about who owns or controls them and who makes decisions about their wellbeing.

Some people think that since the animals are on White Sands Missile Range, the U.S. Army decides what do with deer, oryx and the rest. Not true.

Some might think that the San Andres National Wildlife Refuge (SANWR) that belongs to the U. S. Fish and Wildlife Service, Dept. of Interior, might have jurisdiction over the desert bighorn sheep and deer residing in the refuge. Wrong.

In fact, the State of New Mexico, Department of Game and Fish (NMDGF) claims responsibility and ownership of all wildlife in the state no matter where the animals are located. That includes oryx on White Sands and bighorn sheep on the refuge.

This is how it appears on the surface. Privately, however, federal officials will tell you that the animals found on federal property like San Andres Wildlife refuge belong to the federal government, and when challenged in court states making such claims of ownership have never won a case.

Through the early part of the 20th century, states usually held absolute jurisdiction over wildlife anywhere within their borders. The pendulum has been swinging the other way for decades as the federal government exerted its constitutional authority of ownership of all things on the federal lands.

Another issue pushing the pendulum to the federal side was the need to protect species that crossed state lines. The Migratory Bird Treaty Act was necessary because the many species of birds going extinct in the early 20th century weren't found in just one state. They needed to be protected in whole regions if they were to survive. Only the overriding protection provided by the federal system could accomplish such a feat.

So, at White Sands we have two claims that appear to be polar opposites. However, instead of going to war over who decides what to do with any of the species found on White Sands or the wildlife refuge, the different agencies simply work together. Most of the time they see eye to eye and the process flows smoothly as they plan and coordinate with each other.

Sometimes serious discussions are needed to hammer out agreements on how to proceed. These discussions and negotiations can slow down the process but the parties, so far, have avoided going to court to settle their differences.

When there are differences of opinion, the compromises are often reached at high levels of management and not by the employees who actually work with the animals day to day. When this happens, the new players bring different priorities to the table. After all, some are political appointees while others have no biology backgrounds.

These upper level managers will probably look more closely at factors such as cost, the wishes of special interest groups, and the perceived reaction of the public. The subsequent compromises sometimes bother the specialists in the field but they rarely air their concerns in public.

An excellent example concerns the interaction of the first two species I will cover – desert bighorn sheep and mountain lions. On the question of killing lions to protect recovering populations of bighorn sheep, there are deep differences of opinion. And they are "opinion" since all the characters involved have the same folder of facts. The data isn't different. Instead, each biologist and manager has his or her own unique set of colored glasses to look through.

Desert Bighorn Sheep

One animal the missile range visitor rarely sees is the desert bighorn sheep. They live in the cliff tops of the San Andres Mountains, places most of us rarely get to. Also, there are not a lot of these critters and they are very elusive. However, their presence has driven a great deal of interesting wildlife work done on White Sands, to include studies of how other species impact the bighorns.

Bighorn sheep are native to North America and were once found in every western state to include places like Nebraska and Texas. They have a block-ish body with short legs and are covered with brown to gray hair. Males (rams) can weigh as much as 300 pounds while females (ewes) are smaller. Offspring are called lambs.

Not all bighorn sheep are the same. There are three subspecies – very close cousins. In New Mexico, the northern part of the state is home to Rocky Mountain bighorns and the south is populated with desert bighorns.

The Rocky Mountain bighorns are found all the way up into Canada, so they have adapted to very cold temperatures. They tend to be larger than their desert cousins and have a thicker coat. In addition to being smaller (a ram may only weigh 200 pounds), the desert version has coping mechanisms for dealing with very hot and dry weather. They have a digestive system that can extract almost every drop of moisture from the plants they eat.

Rams are characterized by their massive horns that curl back, then down and then forward and up past their cheeks. An older ram can have a full curl in his horns.

These horns are used by the rams against each other in head-butting contests when competing for mating rights. A large set of horns can weigh as much as 30 pounds. That is a lot of weight to carry around on your head, but the size of the horns and their structure help dissipate the impact forces when the rams head butt each other. Unlike humans playing football, bighorn sheep are built so they don't suffer concussions when engaged in these macho contests.

The ewes have small horns with a bit of a back curve to them.

Bighorn sheep have fascinated humans for centuries with their ability to bound about on the sheer rocky cliffs. Agile and at home in the high cliffs just like mountain goats, the bighorn easily climb vertical rock by using tiny ridges and edges that would scare most of us.

This ability, along with their keen eyesight, gives bighorns the advantage they need to elude natural predators such as mountain lions and wolves. Lambs are most susceptible and are also preyed on by smaller predators like bobcats, coyotes and eagles. The day after they are born, lambs need to be able to get up and follow mom to safety.

Estimates on numbers of all bighorn sheep vary. Some experts say there may have been one to two million animals in North America before European man overran the West. By the early 20th century, they had disappeared from Nebraska, the Dakotas, Washington, Oregon, Texas and some of Mexico. Some say the total population is now less than 70,000 individuals.

In the Southwest, desert bighorn numbers are just as dire. As populations shrank or disappeared, conservationists, hunters and others took notice and lobbied for government protection. In 1939, the Kofa National Wildlife Refuge was founded in Arizona just north of Yuma. It was established to protect desert bighorn sheep and their habitat.

In 1941, the SANWR was added to the system and joined others to protect bighorns. It is just northeast of Las Cruces, New Mexico and sits like an island in the tops of the San Andres Mountains north of San Augustin Pass. The SANWR was overlaid on a mixture of lands belonging to the Jornada Experimental Range, the Bureau of Land Management, and various private holdings. Also, there was a state refuge already in place. During WWII, the Department of Defense stepped in as a player as well.

In 1945, when White Sands Proving Ground was established, SANWR's 57,215 acres were further isolated as it was surrounded by military property. That situation continues today. The refuge manager and employees have to pass through the missile range to get to their property. They are issued White Sands passes and must coordinate their entries with mission control to make sure they are not in any danger from a test mission.

As these newer refuges scattered throughout the Southwest geared up to try and reverse the trend of disappearing desert bighorns, population estimates were at rock bottom. In 1960, the total desert bighorn population in the United States was estimated at less than 8,000 animals.

When you look at the numbers, there is strong evidence the refuges have been doing their job. By 1993, the population was estimated at close to 19,000 for desert bighorn sheep. As we will see, the trend did not hold in New Mexico where 400-500 desert bighorns were reported in 1960.

Since SANWR was established, there has been a great deal of effort put into managing the sheep to increase their numbers. In the 1940s, Arthur Halloran, the first refuge manager, wrote several short pieces about the new refuge and the bighorns. He cited many recorded instances of bighorn sheep spotted in the Organ and San Andres Mountains from the mid 1800s to 1941.

In one piece he said, "Our assignment was to restore the numbers of the few remaining sheep on this refuge so that this magnificent big game animal would not disappear from another southwestern range. First, however, we had to locate this pitifully small remnant band, estimated at less than forty survivors."

He thought most sheep were within the boundaries of the refuge with some probability of a few scattered animals both north and south. Early missile range personnel confirmed that belief as many reported seeing bighorn sheep north of the refuge boundary.

Halloran stated, "Under protection on the refuge the bighorns are slowly increasing. Ten lambs were reported in 1942 and the 1943 crop of lambs also numbers at least 10. The total present (1943) population is more than 60."

When he wrote his summary, Halloran had already taken steps to actively manage the conditions surrounding this native group of bighorns. He said, "Some water supplies have been developed and present plans call for more." Also, the refuge held public hunts to reduce the mule deer population. He said, "Preliminary food studies based on browse utilization and field observations indicate competition between the sheep and the numerous mule deer."

Then there was livestock grazing. He said he worked with the U.S. Grazing Service (now Bureau of Land Management) and local ranchers to make sure cattle and horses were "kept within the grazing capacity of the area." Since bighorn sheep are very susceptible to diseases carried by domestic sheep and goats, these animals were prohibited in the refuge.

Another negative impact on the San Andres sheep was predation by mountain lions. Halloran started a program to remove lions from the refuge.

Lastly, Halloran blamed some of the problem on local and transient poachers. He instituted active patrols to reduce this threat.

It seemed to be working. Halloran wrote, "As of the last of December 1946, it is reported that the sheep of the area number at least 85."

Since then, the bighorn population in SANWR has had its ups and downs with a dramatic crash in the late 1970s. According to SANWR's records, the population was up to 140 animals in 1950. Just five years later the numbers dipped to 70 because of severe drought and the subsequent lack of plants for food.

The herd continued to slowly recover and by the 1970s there were about 200 sheep in the San Andres. They were doing so well, the refuge and NMDGF were allowing limited hunting of bighorns.

That came to a screeching halt in 1978 when five of the rams harvested during the hunt proved to have scabies. Suddenly there was a new threat to add to Halloran's list of agents – disease. This menace, it turned out, was the worst of all and one that man just couldn't stop.

Scabies is a skin disease caused by parasitic mites that burrow under the skin to lay their eggs. They cause intense itching, welts, oozing sores and scabbing over of the skin. It is easily spread from one individual to another through contact.

Different mites infest different animals. For instance, humans have been bugged by Sarcoptes scabiei for thousands of years. It is commonly called the itch mite. Your dog or cat can get scabies, but it is from a different mite – a parasite that cannot survive on a human.

Domestic sheep and wild ones like bighorns have to deal with the psoroptic mite. It causes intense itching and can cause hair loss. This is critical during the winter because the cold will kill the sheep if they lose enough coat – they die from hypothermia. For instance, the cold snap of February 2011 would have killed many infected animals as temperatures hovered around zero for three nights in a row. It was a time where sheep needed to be as healthy as possible to survive.

Secondary bacterial infections are dangerous for scabies-infested sheep and can kill sheep weakened by the mites.

Also, the mites get into their ears and the resulting ooze and crusting effectively plugs them. Being almost deaf is not good when trying to stay away from hungry predators.

Since bighorn sheep are gregarious animals, the mites are easily spread throughout a herd.

When scabies was detected in the five rams, the NMDGF and SANWR went into overdrive to fix the problem. White Sands had no environmental office or wildlife biologist yet, so the range offered its support in the form of access and logistics.

Observation for several months showed many

of the sheep were infected and were dying fast. In 1979, game officials erected dust bags containing a mite insecticide. The idea was that the sheep would rub against the bags and transfer the mite killer onto their coats. Didn't work. They also tried ballistic implants and injections. They didn't work either.

By 1980, the population was estimated to be down to 70 animals statewide and New Mexico listed desert bighorns as a state endangered species. At this point the cooperating agencies, according to former SANWR manager Patty Hoban, decided to "initiate a salvage/treatment operation."

I escorted news media to observe the endeavor and photographed it for the WSMR post newspaper. Helicopters were used to fly "gunners" into the mountains and fire tranquillizer darts at sheep. "Muggers" would then jump out of a chopper, put a blindfold and hobbles on the sheep, and load it into a sling. The sleepy sheep was then flown back to a collection point where personnel treated the animal by dipping it into a solution designed to kill mites.

Some of the sheep were in bad shape. I photographed veterinarians scooping crust and other gunk out of their ears. In moving the animals around, the men sometimes came up with handfuls of hair as the skin underneath was so infected the hair wouldn't hold.

The whole effort turned out to be marginally successful, and that depends on your point of view. During the capture, 49 sheep were removed from SANWR. Only 35 animals survived the capture and initial treatments.

Seven rams were then given to New Mexico State University for study with the remaining 28 (23 ewes and 5 rams) sent to the state's bighorn sheep breeding facility at Red Rock out near Lordsburg.

According to Patty Hoban, "While in captivity, the San Andres sheep contacted blue-tongue, a disease endemic to that area." Half the animals died.

In January 1981, the remaining 14 sheep were radio collared and returned to WSMR to be released on the SANWR. Unfortunately, two rams died in transport, so only 12 sheep from the original 49 were actually released back into the wild.

After the release, the population in the refuge was estimated at 40 sheep. By 1990, Hoban reported the population was down to 23 animals. In Hoban's 1990 bleak assessment, she stated, "Based on recent information regarding minimum viable population

During the 1980 attempt to rescue desert bighorn sheep many were captured, treated and moved to Red Rock. Here, a ewe has her ears swabbed because they are probably full of mites and solidified ooze. The men are wearing respirators, goggles and rain gear because they are preparing to dip her in a vat of special insecticide designed to kill mites. Photo by author.

size, extinction is the anticipated outcome for San Andres sheep at their current population level."

According to biologists, you need a certain number of animals from which the population can actually grow. It doesn't matter if they are humans, bighorn sheep or frogs. The initial population has to be able to withstand normal deaths, individuals who can't reproduce, and unusual circumstances. A certain number is also needed to provide some genetic diversity. For the desert bighorn sheep in the San Andres Mountains, that minimum number is estimated to be 100 animals. That is why Hoban predicted extinction.

As the number of sheep continued to dwindle, some died from scabies while others showed some resistance to the mites. However, mountain lion predation and other agents were still killing sheep.

During this time, everyone was very aware of the plight of bighorns on White Sands. I remember

when one of our helicopter crews spotted a barbary sheep north of the refuge in the San Andres Mountains. The information was quickly relayed to the WSMR environmental office – by this time there was an office staffed with wildlife biologists and others to handle all kinds of environmental issues at WSMR. Initially, Daisan Taylor coordinated bighorn issues and planning. Most recently, Patrick Morrow has been the White Sands interface.

The barbary sheep info was passed on to the New Mexico Dept. of Game and Fish. The next day, personnel showed up from NMDGF and were flown to the area in a WSMR helicopter. Once the animal was spotted, it was shot by a New Mexico game warden. That animal was mounted and is on display in the WSMR Museum.

The quick response was brought on by fear the barbary ram would interfere with the normal reproduction cycle of the bighorns. The barbary ram could not successfully mate with a bighorn ewe, but he could tie her up while she was in estrus (in heat) and prevent a bighorn ram from coupling with her. At a time when every lamb counted in trying to bring back the population, the biologists couldn't afford to let the barbary go about having his horny way.

By 1997, there was only one indigenous bighorn sheep left, a ewe. She was captured several times and treated for scabies. Eventually she proved to be mite free.

At that point, biologists from the involved agencies started to plan on how to reestablish the San Andres sheep. After surveying other species for mites (mule deer, barbary sheep, elk, oryx and pronghorn) and mulling it over, experts decided the refuge could very well be free of scabies mites. The three agencies went to work to test that hypothesis.

In 1999, six bighorn rams from New Mexico's Red Rock Wildlife Area were released in the San Andres. The rams served two purposes. The first was to see if there were any undetected bighorn sheep left in the mountain range. Under normal conditions, the rams would find or be found by other sheep. None turned up.

The second purpose was to see if they remained scabies free in the couple of years they were to spend in the mountains. After being recaptured several times, the rams tested negative for scabies with each subsequent capture.

After the first few captures, the single surviving ewe apparently grew weary of helicopters and sought shelter under overhangs to avoid being harassed again. It became quite a challenge for the capture crews to get her into the open so they could get a net on her.

In a 2005 article in the *Journal of Wildlife Diseases*, authors Walter Boyce and Mara Weisenberger concluded, "Thus, the near extinction of the native bighorn sheep population finally accomplished what humans could not – the apparent elimination of Psoroptes spp. mites from the SAM (San Andres Mountains) herd."

With the San Andres bighorns effectively gone, the statewide population was estimated to be a paltry 220 animals in the wild in 1999. It was time to bring

sheep back to the best habitat in the state which was on White Sands Missile Range.

With the mountain range mite free, the three agencies started their efforts to resurrect the bighorns. Although New Mexico has a large bighorn sheep captive-breeding program, there were not enough animals there to satisfy the need at SANWR and other places in the state.

In anticipation of this issue, SANWR manager Kevin Cobble began talks with his brother refuge manager, Ray Varney, at the Kofa refuge near Yuma, Arizona. Cobble wondered about getting some sheep from Kofa where numbers were relatively high compared to New Mexico. Varney didn't see why not since he estimated they had 800 sheep.

According to Gary Montoya, U.S. Fish and Wildlife Service refuge supervisor for Arizona and New Mexico, the two refuges then went to their respective state game departments to work out the deal.

The deal turned out to be simple given the needs of the two states. Arizona had a large population of desert bighorn sheep subspecies but they were short on Rocky Mountain bighorns. New Mexico, on the other hand, had fairly large numbers of Rocky Mountain sheep and a decimated desert population.

The arrangement was for Arizona to donate desert sheep to New Mexico in exchange for Rocky

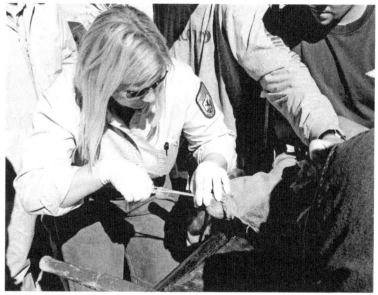

Mara Weisenberger, San Andres Wildlife Refuge biologist, takes a throat swab from a bighorn ewe at Kofa Wildlife Refuge in Arizona during the 2002 bighorn sheep exchange. Once the Arizona sheep were examined and treated, they were trucked to WSMR as quickly as possible. Photo by the author.

Mountain sheep. Once the paperwork was approved by all involved, a large team of personnel from all the agencies and facilities went to work in November 2002 to actually make it happen.

Patrick Morrow, a wildlife biologist with White Sands Missile Range, examines a vial of debris from a bighorn sheep's ear during the Kofa roundup of animals. He then assisted the San Andres Refuge personnel in getting the sheep from Arizona and onto the missile range. Photo by author.

I went to Kofa with the team from SANWR, WSMR and NMDGF to take photos and write about the operation. Also on hand were volunteers such as Las Cruces veterinarian Nancy Soules.

A large team of professionals was needed to capture, treat and move the sheep as quickly as possible from Kofa to White Sands. Biologists learned from the problems in the 1980 rescue attempt that they needed to keep drugs and handling to a minimum if the animals were going to survive.

On November 21, helicopter teams found the sheep in the Kofa Mountains and then swooped in on the animals. A gunner would fire a net from a gun that would entangle the sheep and bring it to the ground. Muggers quickly followed to wrap up the sheep and equip it with a blindfold and hobbles. No sedatives were used.

The sheep were then flown back to a central point where each one went through an assembly line examination. As sheep were unloaded, they were quickly surrounded by a cloud of people doing a very precise dance - each had a job to do and was expected to do

it quickly. Veterinarians and scientists collected ticks, others took throat swabs, extracted blood samples, injected drugs to kill mites and bacteria, put on ear tags, and affixed radio collars. All the while someone monitored the animal's core temperature and prepared to flood it with cold water if the temperature indicated shock.

It was masterfully done. In a matter of minutes each sheep was processed and placed in a crate for transport. The speed lessened the time each animal was handled which, in turn, lessened the stress each had to endure.

When darkness fell and the choppers couldn't fly anymore, the New Mexico team headed east to White Sands. Driving through the night, the team timed it to arrive on White Sands early in the morning for the release. The idea was to have the animals in captivity no more than 24 hours.

So early in the morning on Nov. 22, the trailers loaded with their precious wild cargo were driven to the missile range's Zebra instrumentation site, just below Bennett Peak. There, missile range commander Brigadier General Bill Engel and Kevin Cobble, SANWR manager, opened the first crate and a couple of Arizona ewes bounded out. A total of 20 sheep from Arizona were released that morning.

The next day, 31 bighorn sheep were released on White Sands from the New Mexico Red Rock facility. Of the 51 sheep released, 31 were ewes and 20 were rams.

Excitement about the reintroduction was palpable. Biologist Elise Goldstein, NMDGF, said, "The San Andres is the largest and best piece of habitat in the state, and we feel it can support a large herd. We know it's had up to 200 sheep in the past, and there's room for more than 600 animals." Time will tell if her enthusiasm was realistic.

One positive result the biologists, like Mara Weisenberger of SANWR, have talked about is the genetic diversity provided by the Arizona animals. In Arizona, bighorns are sometimes infected with scabies, but it doesn't seem to be the life-threatening situation it was for the San Andres herd.

In November 2005, we went back to Kofa and

did it all over again. This time 20 sheep were captured and transported on day one and 10 more were caught and shipped the next day. The breakdown was five rams and 25 ewes added to the San Andres herd. At that point SANWR officials estimated the herd size at just over 100 sheep.

During the decade since the first reintroductions, the agencies have been very proactive in creating enhanced conditions for the herd to flourish. The goal is to establish a healthy population capable of sustaining itself without much aid from man.

The introduced sheep had radio collars that allowed SANWR staffers to monitor them. Just watching the sheep they could count lambs and make observations about their health. When a radio-collared sheep died, biologists could pinpoint it and find out what killed it.

Over the years, SANWR officials have torched areas of the refuge with prescribed burns to create more natural habitat for the sheep. The San Andres Mountains experience large numbers of lightning strikes during thunderstorm season. Before WWII, these strikes occasionally led to fires that burned off the large juniper trees and other large bushes leaving grasses behind.

Those open mountaintops gave the bighorns an advantage when trying to elude stalking mountain lions. They have great eyesight and, with no cover for the lions, the sheep could often be away before a lion got close enough to strike.

Also, the burns created more forage for the sheep.

Since WWII, most fires on the missile range and the refuge have been put out as much as possible. Such misguided vigilance allowed the junipers to flourish and take over some of the sheep habitat. It gave lions the cover they needed for a completely hidden sneak.

These prescribed burns have been closely coordinated and supported by White Sands. The missile range has also altered its old philosophy on fighting wildfire and lets many of them die out naturally. On the other hand, the range has to be concerned about a fire possibly escaping the refuge and finding one of the few buildings nearby.

A very aggressive action taken by NMDGF to support the sheep has been the control of mountain lions. After disease, mountain lions are blamed for most bighorn deaths. Although mountain lions are part of the natural food chain in the San Andres, over the last 10 years, some 30 cougars have been removed by NMDFG.

Another management decision has been to allow oryx hunters onto the refuge to kill oryx during special hunts. Oryx is a non-native species of antelope from Africa and is covered later in this chapter. No extensive study has been done to see if oryx consume the same vegetation eaten by sheep, but observations put the two animals in the same areas.

Like other Department of Interior lands (national parks and monuments), the refuge has a directive to manage native species, not foreign interlopers. Refuge wildlife biologist Mara Weisenberger said, "We will never eliminate oryx but we can control their impact on the refuge."

A bighorn ram is released on the missile range in 2002 to make his way into the San Andres Mountains and the San Andres Wildlife Refuge. Photo by the author.

All of these actions have proved very successful. At the beginning of 2011, Weisenberger estimated there were around 120 bighorns in or around the refuge. In early 2011, the NMDGF said they were going to consider taking desert bighorn sheep off the state's threatened listing as the statewide population was estimated at 630 animals.

For several years, many WSMR employees were lucky enough to see a bighorn ram right along U.S. Highway 70 as they drove to and from work. Two of the introduced animals somehow made their way south across the highway where they took up residence on Antelope Hill. Seeing one of these magnificent animals on the drive into the office certainly introduced a new topic during the morning coffee break.

The two sheep are gone now. Weisenberger said they first lost radio contact with the animals when their collars' batteries died. Then they lost visual contact with the animals as well. One possibility is that one or both moved elsewhere, or that one or both died in the vicinity of Antelope Hill.

Mountain Lions - Top of the Food Chain

In December 1990, I found myself hiking about two hours north of Deadman Canyon in the San Andres Mountains on WSMR. We were staying in the bottoms in an attempt to be as elusive as our prey, a female mountain lion and her three, six-month-old kittens (also called cubs).

We were putting the "sneak" on her for *National Geographic* magazine photographer George Mobley. He was taking pictures to illustrate an article for the magazine that focused on lions in the United States. Leading us was Kenny Logan, the chief researcher for Maurice Hornocker's Wildlife Research Institute in Idaho. Hornocker was hired by the New Mexico Department of Game and Fish to study lions throughout the San Andres, work essential to understanding the complex relationship between a top predator and all the prey species below it. I was along to escort Mobley while he took pictures on White Sands.

Periodically, Logan would scramble up a ridge with his directional radio antenna to pinpoint the cat's location ahead of us. Mom had been captured before by Logan's team and was equipped with a collar containing a miniature radio transmitter. In the rugged terrain it was evident such technology was absolutely necessary if we were going to find her.

Logan would return each time and whisper what he found and what our next move was going to be. Logan hoped we would find the mother and kittens on a recent deer kill and Mobley would be able to photograph them having lunch.

We were putting in the long hike on a nasty, cold and windy day because Mobley insisted on grabbing photos of real mountain lions really in the wild. He and Logan both said most of the photos and videos of lions we see in magazines and on television are of trained lions or lions in huge outdoor enclosures.

Kevin Cobble, manager of the San Andres National Wildlife Refuge, shows reporters the little white spheres (think ping-pong balls) that they use to start fires for prescribed burns. The balls are filled with a highly flammable material and can be dispensed in remote areas by helicopter. Behind Cobble, San Andres Peak is smoking from a prescribed burn to get rid of junipers and other brush. Photo by the author.

Mobley, being a 30-year veteran of *National Geographic*, wanted the real deal.

And this was his second round at White Sands. Mobley visited in September 1990 to photograph three-week-old kittens in their den. Using the same technique of homing in on the radio signal from the mother lion's collar, we were led close to a den by Logan and his wife and co-researcher Linda Sweanor.

When the mother left the den we moved in on the three little kittens, two females and one male. They were so young they couldn't walk yet. Instead, they crawled about, hissed at us and generally were not happy to see us. Their fur was marked with spots and rings around the tail. Remarkably, they had bright blue eyes that wouldn't change to yellow until maturity.

Mobley photographed them in their immaculately clean den as the team took basic information about each kitten. As they were handled, both Sweanor and Logan wore good leather gloves. They said it helped keep their smell off the animals and protected their hands from the kittens' needle-like claws and teeth.

According to Logan, they never had a problem with mothers returning to the den and rejecting their young after handling by a human visitor. Typically, the mothers would return and simply move the kittens to a new den site.

The final step was to place an ear tag on each kitten for later identification. Radio collars were reserved for mature adults who were done growing.

North of Deadman Canyon we finally got close to our targets. Logan led us up a ridge and indicated the mother lion was just downhill from us. In anticipation, Mobley put a huge telephoto lens on his camera and screwed it to a tripod. I stood back to make sure I didn't block any lines of sight.

We didn't get far down the ridge when Logan hissed, "There she is." We all froze and searched for her. I caught sight of her about 50 yards down slope as she stopped and looked back at us. She held that pose for a second or two and bolted downhill.

Just as she sprang, I heard Mobley's camera shutter fire once. It was a long walk for a single photo of a lion's backside.

We hiked down the hill to a flat area where we had spotted her. There, I saw one of the kittens when I spooked it. He bounded away in a flash of

Mountain lion researcher Linda Sweanor holds a three-week old cub for National Geographic photographer George Mobley. Photo by the author.

blurred tan – not long enough to really appreciate what I was seeing.

The long day's trek didn't yield a single usable photo. But the researchers were able to confirm, by looking at prints, that all three kittens were still with mom.

Then we found the deer carcass. Logan estimated the lions had killed the deer the day before and were feeding on it when we ambushed them. Kittens usually stay with the mother for at least 12 months, so they are protected while they mature and can learn the trade secrets of stalking and killing prey.

This extraordinary opportunity for the *National Geographic* and myself was made possible because of the New Mexico lion study on the missile range. The study was one of the few large-scale efforts to look at the largest wild cat regularly found in the United States. Land and wildlife managers thought the study was necessary to finally gather some hard scientific facts about these animals instead of relying on old wives' tales.

Attitudes toward the lions on White Sands run from one extreme to the other. Many ranchers view lions or "cougars" or "puma" as some sort of evil incarnate, like the convenient Nazi villains in many movies. Like in the movies, many ranchers would say, "The only good lion is a dead one."

On the other hand, people at the other end of the spectrum see pumas as overgrown housecats that are cute and cuddly.

Most people are probably more in the middle, although there seems to be an unwarranted fear of lions. When lion tracks have been seen in the desert around the main post at White Sands, some people get nervous and call for officials to take action.

In reality, there have only been a handful of deaths and full-out attacks by lions in this country during the last 20 years. You are much more likely to die from a lightning strike or from falling down in your bathroom or from choking on a piece of steak.

It turned out a study of lions on the missile range made a lot of sense. The big cats have come and gone about their

business in the missile range's two mountain ranges without much notice. It is a huge rugged area with only intermittent human population. Like most people who have seen them, I was lucky enough to see one as it bounded across the road in Rhodes Canyon one morning.

The lion study started in 1985 and was originally advertised as a five-year effort. It was expanded to a total of 10 years in 1990.

The missile range cooperated in the study by making the mountainous areas available to the study team on condition they not interfere with range missions, and by providing support where needed. Also involved was the San Andres Wildlife Refuge because of the debated impact of lions on bighorn sheep populations.

According to Maurice Hornocker, the "dean" of mountain lion researchers, the goal of the study was to find out "what makes them tick." By getting to know the species, he said they would be better able to predict lion behavior and develop management strategies. This was and is very important as humans encroach more and more into cougar habitat.

Hornocker said White Sands was a perfect place for the study. Because of its isolation, there were few

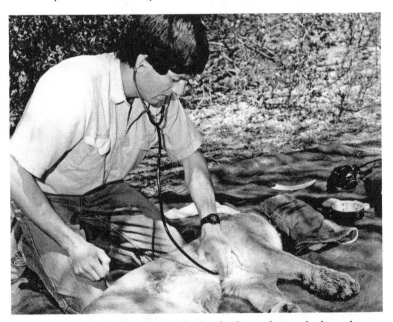

Lion researcher Kenny Logan checks the heart beat of a lion the team has snared and tranquilized. He covers the head of the lion with a cloth to protect the cat's eyes - while unconcious it won't blink and can be blinded by the sun. The lion is given a collar containing a radio transmitter so the researchers can follow it as it moved through the mountains. WSMR photo.

outside variables to interfere with gathering data; it was relatively easy to keep track of all the animals.

Joining Logan and Sweanor on the study team was Frank Smith. Smith was the most experienced of any of the team members in dealing with mountain lions. He retired in 1986 from the New Mexico Department of Game and Fish after 31 years. He was their chief lion catcher when he left.

He taught Logan and Sweanor how to track and trap the cougars for the study. He estimated in 1987 that he had tracked and trapped or shot close to 200 lions in his lifetime.

The basic idea for the study was to trap all the resident lions in the study area, radio collar them, and then keep track of each one throughout its life. On paper it looked easy, but the rugged and often road-less terrain made it was tough. Logan estimated after the study that he and his teammates walked almost 40,000 miles.

First of all, safely trapping lions at White Sands was difficult. The usual method used throughout most of North America is to find fresh lion sign and let loose the dogs to run down the cats. Typically the lions seek haven in a tree where researchers can easily find them, tranquilize them and then release them. However, in most of the San Andres Mountains study area, there are no trees.

Instead, Smith taught Logan and Sweanor how to set and use bear snares. The snare is a piece of steel cable with a loop at one end that will draw tight just like a lasso. The snares were set with a spring attached to one end and a trigger mechanism under the loop. When a cat stepped onto the trigger pad, the spring would be released and jerk the loop closed around the cat's leg.

In most cases the cat is captured and cannot get away. The cable had an anchor at the end so the lion couldn't walk away dragging the contraption with it.

According to Logan, the snares were a great improvement over regular jaw-type traps. The jaw traps often injure their captives and also allow some animals to escape with probable injuries.

After capturing almost 250 lions during the study, Logan said the method was very humane for the lions. When snared the lions quickly accepted their lot and did not fight the noose. Logan said some had a swollen foot but most showed no injury at all.

There was one serious injury during the study

when a lion broke her leg in the snare. She was tranquilized and ended up at the zoo in Albuquerque. Veterinarians performed surgery, bolting the leg, then nursed her back to health.

I was with the study team and representatives of the New Mexico Department of Game and Fish when they released "Lefty" back into the wild near Mockingbird Gap on the north end of the missile range. The zoo stint didn't seem to slow her down as Sweanor later reported the lion was making kills and gave birth to a litter of kittens.

This passive method of using snares was slow. Only a small number of snares were set on any given day. The number had to be such that team members could get to each trap every day to check it. If a lion was caught, they did not want it sitting out in the sun for extended periods and dying of dehydration. According to Logan, it required about 200 trap days for every capture they made. A "trap day" was one snare set for one day.

The snare method was fairly dependable for the team because of certain lion behaviors. One is that they like to walk along arroyo or drainage bottoms as opposed to ridgelines. This meant it was pretty easy to check the sandy bottoms and find lion tracks.

If the tracks were fresh, a snare was deployed in some narrow point in the arroyo. The trick was to funnel the cat to a point where it would be stepping over or on the snare trigger. Sometimes this meant "rearranging the furniture" a bit and using branches and other debris to artificially squeeze the walkway. It was an art to disguise the trap so the cats saw nothing out of the ordinary.

When a lion was caught, it was tranquilized so the team could collect data and possibly equip it with a radio collar. Injecting the drug was a bit of a heart-pounding drama. On the one hand it was fairly easy to stand back from the growling lion and shoot a tranquilizer dart into it with an air rifle.

On the other hand, it took some nerve to get close enough to the snarling cat to poke it in the haunches with a hypodermic needle-like device attached on the end of a pole that never seemed long enough.

Statistics were taken on each lion captured and included sex, age, color, size, weight, etc. Each was assigned a number and color-coded ear tag that made it possible to identify an individual lion, even kittens, from some distance using a spotting scope.

Logan and Sweanor were often asked by reporters about giving the lions names. They usually responded that as scientists they needed to try to be as unemotional as possible about their study animals. Most farm kids understand giving livestock names personalizes it too much when you have to eventually send the animals to slaughter. For Logan and Sweanor, their charges were probably going to meet pretty nasty deaths during the study.

However, as human beings they couldn't help it at times, plus everyone around them found it much easier to talk about "Lefty" instead of lion number 124. So, for instance, the first female lion captured in the study was number two but also went by "Eve." A cat captured in Good Fortune Canyon eventually was dubbed "Lucky."

Of the total captured, 77 females and 49 males were fitted with transmitter collars. Each collar emitted a signal on a unique frequency that pulsed as a beep-beep tone. The team members could always tell which lion they were remotely tracking by the frequency they were receiving.

The collar was also capable of sending out a "death" signal. If the collar remained motionless for something like 12 or 13 hours, i.e. the lion was dead, the beep-beep signal quickened making it distinctly different from the regular tone. This allowed the team to go looking for the animal and determine how it died.

One interesting finding in the study was that most lions don't die from old age. Also, these lions were free from injury at the hands of hunters and motor vehicles. It turns out the old saying "live by the sword, die by the sword" is very appropriate here.

During the study more than 50 percent of lion deaths were from other lions. Once you understand a bit of cougar psychology, it is perfectly understandable.

First of all, lions are very territorial – especially the males. They stake out a hunting territory and then, in many cases, protect it to the death. Logan and Sweanor found the males (between 120 and 160 pounds) with territories averaging 122 square miles.

Females (between 60 and 90 pounds) are not nearly as aggressive since they don't have the size to back up the threat. Instead, they try to avoid confrontation and establish home ranges averaging 44 square miles on WSMR.

Within that territory each lion expects to find his or her breakfast, lunch and dinner forever. When another lion moves in and proposes taking a share of the scant offerings, the home-cat is not going to take it lying down. Sometimes one cat will yield to the other and move on. If they fight, the chances are one will die.

Early on in the study, Logan and Sweanor came across a dead lion where the cause of death was such a battle. When they did an autopsy on the animal, they found a perfect canine tooth puncture through the skull into the brain. It was probably over in the first round.

The thing that complicates this territory business is the teenager. Male and female lions only get together to mate. Once the act is done, the male takes off leaving the female to give birth to a litter of kittens about 90 days later. By the way, during the 10-year WSMR study, the team documented 211 kittens being born.

After the birth the kittens are totally dependent on the mother for their survival. Initially, she has to nurse them, next is to feed them from her kills, and then teach them the skills they need to hunt and kill their own meals. Also during this time she has to protect them from any big tom that might come along – even their own father.

The logic here is the youngsters will later become competitors for territory, so a male has no compunction about killing kittens, even his own. After all, he left the female and has no idea if the cubs are his or not.

With all those kittens being born in the San Andres during the study, one might conclude WSMR is overrun with lions. Many ranchers will advance such a theory. In some versions of this theory, the lions are so smart they act like Robin Hood, knowingly hiding on the safe missile range and then raiding the surrounding flats to make their kills.

In reality, the researchers estimate there were only 35 to 45 breeding adults in the WSMR mountains at the end of the study.

Those kittens born during the study, if they reached adulthood, had only a few choices. One was to take over the territory of an older lion through intimidation or a fight. Another choice was to carve out a niche somewhere and live under the radar, so to speak. The third choice was for the lion to move on to someplace new and find a life there.

Individuals moving on are the ones people see

out in the desert or on the outskirts of towns and cities. They are looking for a better place where their neighbor is not a constant threat.

When I asked Logan about the percentage of lions that reach maturity, he said it was hard to pin down. He did estimate, "about 50 percent of female offspring and about 90 percent of male offspring either die or leave the population in which they were born." So much for close family ties.

In the summer of 2011, a mountain lion was struck and killed by a car in Connecticut. Lions in such an urban state are very rare, so state officials dug into the cat's background by doing DNA analysis. As the result of a great deal of sleuthing, they determined their lion came from the Black Hills of South Dakota.

Most people were amazed when the findings went public in July 2011, but some of us close to the study at WSMR thought it sounded very plausible.

During the second half of the White Sands study, the team captured and removed as many lions as they could get their hands on in the area around the San Andres Wildlife Refuge. The idea was to create a "power vacuum" with the top predator suddenly missing. Then they would study the lions that moved into the area, see what kind of territories they established, and study how it played out.

The captured lions were mostly relocated to the northern part of New Mexico near the Colorado line. Since they were radio-collared, it was possible to keep track of them.

One female in the bunch took it upon herself to go home. For weeks, researchers followed her progress down the spine of the Rocky Mountains in New Mexico until she returned home hundreds of miles later in the San Andres Range. How she knew exactly which way to go and how far is a remarkable mystery – especially to those of us that get lost in the shopping mall.

Other lion deaths on White Sands were the result of living in the wild and having to kill animals bigger than themselves. Logan and Sweanor found one dead cat that apparently bit off a little too much.

They found the lion's corpse on a piece of ground all torn up with hoof prints. When they cut the cougar open they found all kinds of broken bones and internal bleeding. They guessed the lion jumped on the back of a big buck deer and failed to get hold of its neck. The deer proceeded to thrash about and smash the lion against rocks and trees until it was too injured to hang on.

In another instance, they found a dead lion under a bush with no apparent injuries. They did notice one leg was swollen so they cut into it. There they found two small puncture holes and muscle tissue that was turning to jelly. The lion had been bitten by a rattlesnake and died from the venom.

Finally, some deaths were just odd. They found one dead male lion at the base of a power pole on the missile range. They surmise the young cat was chased by a bigger lion and climbed the pole to get away. At the top, the youngster stretched its body across two of the wires and was electrocuted.

Mountain lions are at the top of the food chain. When available, they will eat deer but will also munch lots of other critters as well. During the study, the team collected lion scat or droppings whenever they came across it. The samples were sent to a lab to determine what the lions were eating.

In addition to deer, WSMR lions were sometimes eating bighorn sheep and pronghorn. They also ate

This three-week old mountain lion kitten is still helpless. When the researchers entered the den, he and his two sisters were unable to run away. Note the spots which disappear as the lion matures. Photo by the author.

small prey such as badgers, skunks, rabbits, coyotes and porcupines – some scat samples had porcupine quills present. Gives a whole new meaning to the idea of fiber in one's diet.

In order to determine lion territories and how mobile they were, it was necessary to place lion locations on big maps and plot their movements over time. Since it was impossible to keep track of many cats from the ground on a frequent basis, the team relied on aerial observations.

Every week Sweaner spent about four hours flying up and down the San Andres Mountain range in a small plane, homing in on each lion's radio collar. This way, they were able to put each lion's location on the map at a given day and time. Over a period of months and years, this data was translated into lion territories.

It also gave them a chance to check and see if any of the collars were transmitting a "death" signal and later hike in to find the carcass.

From flying over lion territory and getting a quick lock on a radio signal, Sweanor also spent time just observing lions in the wild. She said she would often sneak near a lion den so she could watch the mother and kittens interact. Sometimes she was able to watch for hours at a time.

Two things that struck her when doing this were the cat's behavior and their vocalizations. She said that many of the things our pet housecats do are pretty much what lions do too – how they walk, run, jump, bathe, eat and play.

If you have a pet cat, you might notice the different vocal sounds they make. We have no idea what they mean but they most definitely mean something. Sweanor observed mothers and kittens making a number of different sounds. She related how well the communication worked because when the mother gave the danger signal, the kittens all stopped dead and quietly stayed still until she gave some sort of "all-clear" signal.

Given that mountain lions are very powerful killers, one would think they could easily dispatch coyotes and dogs. And they can. However, there is still something there between dogs and cats with the cats often giving way to the smaller canine. I saw it first hand when we put another sneak on a lion at a deer kill.

I was escorting a crew from WCCO-TV in Minneapolis that was shooting for their station and for the children's science show on PBS called *Newton's Apple*. Like Mobley from the *National Geographic*, they wanted footage of real lions in the real wild.

We camped out on the missile range at Hardin Ranch near Rhodes Pass and went looking for lions for a couple of days. As with Mobley, Logan found a lion's signal nearby that seemed to be fairly stationary, as though she had made a kill and was feasting.

We got up early in the morning to try and creep up to its location and film it. As we got out of the vehicles to proceed on foot, we heard a coyote barking in the direction we needed to go.

Logan and Sweanor led us out using their radio antenna to pinpoint the lion. In this area the hillside was covered with juniper bushes, so sneaking along was pretty easy – one bush to the next.

Eventually we got to a point where we could look into a little clearing and we peeked out. In clear view was the anticipated dead mule deer, but instead of a lion having breakfast there was a coyote eating away.

Using his radio receiver, Logan determined the lion was still here too. We looked and looked and finally Logan located it in a juniper not 50 yards from the coyote stealing its kill.

Logan surmised that after the lion killed the deer, the coyote came along and was brash enough to chase the lion away, even though the lion could easily have knocked the coyote's head off. Eventually we left since the story was about cats and not dogs, but it was an interesting insight into lion behavior.

When the study was completed, Logan and Sweanor took a year to write up their results. Also, they assisted the New Mexico Department of Game and Fish in preparing its statewide lion management plan.

What about all those lions wearing the latest in fashionable radio collars? They wore the collars until they died. There was no way to recapture all the lions and remove the collars. Some had their load lightened earlier as they were equipped with breakaway units that would eventually fall off.

One question people asked the team was what to do when attacked by a mountain lion. First of all, during the 10 years of following lions very closely, the team members were charged only three times by lions.

All the cats were females protecting cubs. In all three cases, when the lion realized she was looking at a human, she broke off the charge, turned and fled.

Logan and Sweanor suggested the following techniques when encountering a lion:

1. Remain calm. Don't run. Don't turn your back on the cat. If you run, you will trigger the lion's chase reflex – just like your pet cat at home chasing a fuzzy ball on the end of a string.

2. Stand tall and try to appear bigger than you are. Link arms with your friends and wave packs and other items. Shout.

3. Fight back if attacked. Throw your pack at the cat or use a stick to ward it off. If you have to, use your hands - punch and kick. These have all proved successful in the past.

Oryx, The Antelope That Really Are Antelope

Probably the most sighted animal on the missile range – at least the one people really notice – has to be the African oryx. Not only do people see them while traveling almost any road on White Sands, folks driving the highways and back roads outside the Range also see them. They have been spotted on Fort Bliss and down into Texas; I have seen them on the lands belonging to the Jornada Experimental Range just northeast of Las Cruces. To the north they have been seen as far as the Sevilleta National Wildlife Refuge.

It is hard to miss these big, powerful antelope. And they are true antelope, unlike the pronghorn here in the United States that everyone calls an antelope. The word antelope is a broad term that includes almost 100 species of ungulates found mostly in Africa. It includes such critters as oryx, gazelles, kudu, springbok, eland, Klipspringer, and gnus.

Pronghorn, on the other hand, are unique. They have evolved independently on North America and are not in the antelope family.

Unlike many native North American mammals that blend in with their surroundings, oryx stand out. They came from the Kalahari Desert in South Africa where there is little cover. In the Kalahari, there wasn't much reason to evolve camouflage since there was nothing to hide behind.

In addition, the oryx is a herding animal, and it is very hard to hide from a stalking lion when there are a dozen or more friends and family members clustered nearby. I have seen herds approaching 100 animals on the missile range so it is pretty hard to hide.

However, as an individual it is easy to hide in the group itself. If you can keep up with the herd and stay in the mix, only the old, sick, or slow ones get eaten by the lions or packs of dogs.

In South Africa oryx are called gemsbok, a word from the Afrikaans language. These animals have an obvious attraction for Africans as evidenced by their incorporating the animal's name into their wildlife park names. The "Gemsbok" National Park in Botswana is tied to the Kalahari "Gemsbok" National Park in South Africa to provide thousands of square miles of wilderness for all kinds of wildlife, not just gemsbok.

Oryx are very distinctive with their black and white facial markings looking very much like a painted mask. They are equipped with long rapier-like, jet-black horns that generally run about three feet in length. And these are horns, not antlers. Antlers are shed every year to be replaced in the next – like deer and elk. An oryx, with lions constantly coming around looking for dinner, can't afford to be without this primary defensive tool for months on end.

Their hide is tan colored but there is a black racing stripe circling the bottom of the chest and belly. At the back end is a tail with a large cluster of hair at the conclusion that makes a fine flyswatter. They have cloven hooves and leave a large footprint that looks a bit like a heart.

Oryx are big with a large male weighing well over 400 pounds. A few have been recorded at the 500-pound level.

Both males and females have identical markings. In fact, it is difficult to tell them apart at any distance. Males do tend to be larger with the horns more massive or thicker than a female's. However, seeing a smaller oryx doesn't guarantee it is a female. It could be a subadult male who just hasn't reached maturity yet.

This made the early oryx hunts at WSMR interesting. In typical American fashion, officials were planning to sell sex specific permits like they do for elk and other big game. It turned out hunters couldn't tell the difference. Since then, hunting permits have not been based on sex but on other factors like a trophy animal versus non-trophy and geographical location.

The oryx African homeland is a tough landscape. At White Sands Missile Range they roam the flats and foothills characterized as Chihuahuan Desert habitat. By our standards it is hot and dry, but for

Oryx out in the snow in Rhodes Canyon. Photo by the author.

the oryx it is probably an oasis with great variety.

To survive the Kalahari, they evolved strategies to stay cool, conserve moisture, and go long periods without drinking freestanding water. Scientists say they are so good at extracting every drop of water from the vegetation they eat and then conserving it so that they can go weeks without a drink.

The obvious question asked by many visitors is why there is such an exotic beast on an Army installation. The credit, or blame, depending on your point of view, has to go to Dr. Frank Hibben.

Actually, oryx were not the first exotic big game introduced to New Mexico. In 1950, the state released barbary sheep in the Canadian River Wilderness according to a 1963 article in *Sports Illustrated* magazine.

In a New Mexico Department of Game and Fish pamphlet from the 1960s, called "new mexico new game," many other animals were being studied for introduction within the state. In addition to oryx and barbary sheep, they were looking at markhor, Persian gazelle, Siberian ibex, greater kudu, elburz red sheep and Iranian ibex.

Hibben was not your average hunter or average anything. He was an archaeology professor at the University of New Mexico who supposedly earned his PhD from Harvard in just a year. Also he was an anthropologist, big-game hunter, author, and philanthropist. As a hunter he had the money to travel the world seeking a variety of prey. Ultimately, he wanted to bring that experience to New Mexico.

As an archaeologist, he created a major controversy when he wrote he found 25,000 year-old man-made artifacts in a cave in the Sandia Mountains. This was thousands of years earlier than any other expert estimated humans arriving in North America. The idea is largely discredited today.

Hibben served as the chairman of the state's game commission for 10 years and was chairman of the Albuquerque Zoological Board for 10 years. He gave his own money to UNM to build an anthropology facility. In other words, he was no lightweight college professor.

In the 1960s, the New Mexico Department of Game and Fish, with Hibben at the head, was looking at "filling niches" in the state with exotic game for hunters. They ended up releasing Persian ibex in the Florida Mountains near Deming and oryx on White Sands Missile Range.

In addition to hunting opportunities, Hibben always talked about rescuing many of these species that were rapidly disappearing in their native Africa. He told *Sports Illustrated* in 1963, "Would it not be ironic, if some future African businessman had to come to New Mexico to go on a safari?"

In the case of oryx, Hibben's dream probably won't happen anytime soon. In 2011, the International Union for Conservation of Nature estimated there were well over 300,000 oryx in South Africa.

The introduction of these exotics did not happen in a vacuum. At the time, there was much discussion and some criticism of the effort. Dr. James Findley, a biology professor at the University of New Mexico, objected saying the introduced animals would probably simply die out or explode across the landscape as rabbits did in Australia. He said it was unlikely the new animals would become really useful.

I have never seen any missile range documents about the introduction. However, in those days many of the key staff would have been hunters and would have looked favorably on the idea. They were already allowing hundreds of deer hunters onto White Sands each year, so a few oryx hunters probably didn't seem like any big deal.

In 1962, New Mexico acquired six oryx from Africa. They were housed at the Albuquerque Zoo since federal law banned the direct release of foreign species into the wild. The law allows only the next generations to be released. In 1966, the oryx offspring were taken from the zoo to the state's Red Rock Wildlife enclosure near Lordsburg.

The first release of oryx onto White Sands Missile Range was in 1969 with seven animals set free. From then until 1973, an additional 51 animals were released at WSMR.

The first hunt on White Sands was in 1973 when six permits for bulls were issued. During the next few years, all the remaining oryx (an estimated 50 individuals) at Red Rock were transported to WSMR and released. At the time, game and fish officials showed their lack of information about oryx when they said the population would climb to about 500 animals and stabilize.

What followed was a few decades of benign neglect. It was obvious the oryx did well at White Sands with their numbers increasing steadily. In response, the number of hunting permits was increased as well. By the mid-80s, 60 permits were being issued each year.

These early hunts were once-in-a-lifetime hunts. If you received a permit, you were allowed onto WSMR to shoot an animal during that one hunt and that was it. Whether you got an oryx or not, you weren't coming back for a regular oryx hunt.

The state devised a lottery system because there were many more applicants than permits. Every year they randomly drew applications out of the hat for the hunt.

To minimize the impact on the missile range, the hunts were held during the annual range shutdown period over the Christmas and New Year holidays. Not much happened during the holidays, so the shutdown period was always a time when WSMR employees could take annual leave and maintenance could be performed on equipment.

Hunters were allowed onto the range for four days to find and kill their oryx. They were even allowed to camp at Rhodes Canyon Range Center in the middle of WSMR.

Hunters were allowed out on their own and warned to stay within the designated hunt areas. When they killed an oryx they were required to check in with the state and WSMR officials before they were allowed to leave.

I arrived at WSMR in 1977 just as the oryx hunting boom started. Many reporters came to cover the hunts and I was lucky enough to escort many of them. In particular, I remember Bill Dyroff, an outdoor writer with the *Albuquerque Journal*.

Dyroff came in a beat-up old car that he camped in. I showed up every morning to take him out to photograph oryx and interview hunters while they were out doing their thing. At night I'd leave him as he made a home for himself in his car on those cold December nights.

To run the hunts, assist hunters and maintain security, there was always a combination of state and federal officials on hand. On one hunt I'd taken a reporter to interview some of these officials at their trailer/check station. It was a nasty day. It was cold with a low cloud cover and fog forming in the lowlands. In addition, it had snowed before the hunt and the flats were muddy bogs.

About an hour before sunset, a husband and wife

walked into the trailer looking for help. The wife had shot an oryx about a mile south of the paved range road. It was too muddy to drive their truck down to retrieve it and with the afternoon light rapidly fading, they weren't sure they could get it out before dark. They did not want to leave the carcass out over night because the coyotes would probably get to it.

So everyone in the trailer jumped up, the reporter and me included, and we followed the couple. Also tagging along was a contract trapper who happened to overhear the conversation and he brought his three-wheeled ATV.

Once gathered, we all slogged through the mud to the animal. The couple had already gutted the animal but the question was how to get it to the road. After a quick discussion with the game wardens, they decided to cut the animal in half to make it more manageable.

Once this was done, we were still faced with two heavy and very awkward pieces of oryx to handle. That's when the trapper came to the rescue. He drove his ATV with its big balloon tires out to the site. We then placed the rear end of the oryx in his lap with the legs over his shoulders so he could balance it.

The trapper left, driving slowly toward the road. He was out of sight in a hundred yards. The rest of us then took turns half carrying and dragging the front end of the oryx. We set up with one of us on each side of the oryx and grabbed a horn to lift the head off the ground. We then headed north following our own tracks. It was hard work.

Eventually, the trapper came back and we were able to place the front end in his lap. He had one horn under his left arm and the other over his right shoulder. This end of the oryx was bigger and heavier so we walked beside the ATV and helped balance the animal as the vehicle slowly squished through the muck.

We loaded up the animal in the dark.

As the years passed, officials would survey the oryx population on WSMR. As numbers quickly climbed past 500, so did the number of permits allowed each year. Also it was obvious oryx were pushing out way beyond what was originally expected.

These facts led to the addition of some different kinds of hunts on WSMR. One was a depredation hunt.

Occasionally, oryx hung around missile range or Holloman AFB facilities where people were working or, eventually, all the way to the WSMR main post where people lived. The easiest way to deal with these nuisance animals is to have them taken by a hunter. However, you can't wait until the next hunt when the animals are there right now.

New Mexico Game and Fish and WSMR developed a list that hunters could put their names on. The arrangement is for a New Mexico game warden to sanction a special hunt for a specific individual or small population. Once that is done, they call the first name on the list and say something like, "We've got an animal that is a safety hazard and needs to be eliminated. Can you be at White Sands tomorrow morning with your rifle?"

If he or she is unavailable, they call the next person on the list until they find the number of hunters they need for the situation. The advantages for these hunters are that they are pretty much guaranteed they will get an oryx and it doesn't count against them in the draw for a once-in-a-lifetime permit.

The disadvantages are that the hunter has to show up without much planning and then a game warden may dictate which animal to shoot.

Another kind of hunt officials developed was the broken horn variety. Most hunters want that trophy head with those graceful horns. That means they ignore the oryx out on the range with broken or malformed horns.

There are a lot of oryx with irregular horns and they are called non-trophy oryx. They often spar as youngsters and break or damage their horns.

So, every year a small number of permits are issued for broken-horned oryx. These permits do not count against a hunter in the once-in-a-lifetime lottery. With these kinds of hunts, a hunter has a chance to eat more than one oryx in his or her lifetime.

I was out with a photographer on one of the hunts when a man came into the check station with his oryx. Everyone gathered around as he told his tale of woe.

He had a broken-horn permit and had found an animal with only one intact horn. He shot the animal. It went down but was still struggling to get up so he said he thought he should shoot it again. He wanted to put it out of its misery and he certainly didn't want it running off.

He said he shot again but was too excited. The bullet hit the oryx's good horn and broke it off so he was left with a no-horn oryx.

He had the piece that was shot off and it was interesting to examine. The horn was fairly hollow with blood vessels running along the inner walls. Someone compared it to our fingernails as far as the structure and process.

By the 1990s, quite frankly, there were oryx everywhere. Driving up to Trinity Site to conduct a tour, I would often see oryx in a dozen different places near the road along that 75-mile stretch of Range Road 7.

Officials were seeing oryx in the canyons of San Andres National Wildlife Refuge, on the sand dunes in White Sands National Monument, on Fort Bliss, and on most of the ranches around WSMR. The national monument was the first to really sound the alarm.

Being part of the National Park Service, the monument has very strict regulations and policies concerning non-native species and their potential impact on flora and fauna in parks. The rangers in the monument were seeing more and more oryx and more and more negative impact to their fragile ecosystem.

As a remedy, they tried erecting a very expensive oryx fence along the monument's western boundary with WSMR. They were trying to be friendly to the oryx so they built a multi-strand fence with smooth wire that was spring loaded. The idea was that an oryx encountering the fence wouldn't be harmed by it even if the animal decided to charge it – he'd just bounce off.

It didn't work very well. We all witnessed oryx go up to the fence, put their noses between two strands with their horns laid on their backs, and simply step through using a lot of muscle to spread the wire.

The monument fixed this by putting stays on the wire between posts so the oryx couldn't spread the stands. Learning from this, they used regular stock fence to finish closing off the other three sides of the monument in 1996. The fence measures 67 miles.

When they closed the fence, they trapped an estimated 150-200 oryx inside the monument. The Park Service did an environmental evaluation and decided shooting the animals would be the cheapest and quickest way to remove the trapped oryx.

That didn't sit too well with many people and there was a public outcry against the idea. The monument re-examined their options. Eventually they enlisted the help of the New Mexico Game and Fish Department and the missile range. From 1999

Oryx portrait taken by Patrick Morrow.

to 2001, the organizations tried several non-lethal methods to extract the oryx.

One method was an attempt to drive large groups of oryx to openings in the fence and then close it behind them. It was supposed to be like a Western cattle drive but didn't work so well. Using horses, ATVs and helicopters they tried to move groups of oryx west to the fence. But as they moved the groups, oryx were constantly slipping away and refusing to go where the "oryxboys" pushed them.

Another method, using Army helicopters, was more successful but very expensive. For these round-ups, WSMR helicopters were used to find oryx and then tranquilize them with darts fired from a special rifle. Once the drugged animal went down, it was wrapped in a sling and then flown over to the missile range side of the fence to be released.

A completely different approach was passive and cheap. However, no one knows if it worked. A number of one-way gates were installed in the west boundary fence. A tank of water was placed on the WSMR side of the fence to lure oryx through the gate to get a drink. Once on the WSMR side, they were stuck.

In the end, the monument was able to move at least 174 oryx from their property. One criticism of this expensive process was that the animals were simply being moved a few miles so they could be shot during a hunt on WSMR.

Also, they didn't get them all. After 2001, monument officials quietly shot any more oryx they found within their boundaries. Years ago that number stood at 25.

Even the San Andres Wildlife Refuge with its rugged peaks, big cliffs and deep canyons wasn't off limits for oryx. They were found in the canyons and the foothills.

The refuge biologist didn't see much overlap between desert bighorn sheep habitat and the oryx, but there was some. And that was critical in deciding on a course of action. The bighorn were an endangered species; every effort was being made to make sure they recovered.

To eliminate any possibility of oryx depriving bighorns of forage, the decision was made to allow oryx hunts inside the refuge. The idea is to keep the numbers so low there is no real impact on refuge flora from the exotics.

However, in all this activity generated by the large number of oryx, someone was smart enough to ask if oryx could act as a disease vector. In other words, could oryx play host to some virus that didn't affect oryx, but might be deadly if passed along to some other species.

So, in the 1990s there were some very big questions and concerns about oryx. Oryx were obviously doing more than filling a small hunting niche. Patrick Morrow, a wildlife biologist at WSMR, was thrust into the job of becoming the Range's oryx specialist. Morrow, a hunter, relished the challenge.

He faced a number of problems. No one really knew how many oryx there were. There was no coordinated management plan on how to deal with them and there were no studies of oryx behavior on which to hang a plan.

The population estimates were off. The usual method for estimating the numbers was to do an aerial count and put the numbers into a computer model and let it spit out an answer. The only problem was there was no off-the-shelf model for oryx in a place like WSMR.

It was all new research, so they tweaked the models tying to get a more reliable figure. In 1996, based on new estimates, I told a reporter the number was estimated at 2,000 animals. In 2001, the estimate was 3,000 oryx. Estimates kept going up.

To get an idea of how oryx moved around the missile range, Morrow was able to put satellite radio collars on a number of bulls and cows. The location signals were bounced off a satellite to Boise State University and then back to White Sands. Using the data, Morrow could see how far oryx moved day to day and then over a year's time.

In 2011, I asked Morrow how many oryx were probably out on the range at the peak of their population. He said, looking back on it, there may have been at least 7,000 oryx. That's why harvesting a few hundred each year wasn't making a dent in the population. The models weren't working.

But to make a good model you have to have good information about the animals. Morrow pushed for more studies, and by 2000 work was well underway to learn what makes an oryx tick in New Mexico.

As an aside, Morrow was able to pay for the studies by using fees collected from oryx hunters. Initially, the missile range received no compensation for hosting hunts and providing all kinds of personnel to support them. Using the Sikes Act, White Sands was able to impose a user fee that can only be used to support wildlife work – like oryx studies and offsetting the expenses of supporting hunts.

One important fact gleaned from the studies was that the birthrate for oryx is 1.2 offspring per year. When this all started, everyone assumed it was one calf per cow per year. It turns out WSMR oryx are very productive reproductive machines. They mate all year round and cows can get pregnant while they are still nursing a calf.

Another finding was that oryx may carry a couple of diseases that might have a negative impact on native fauna. For instance, oryx have shown signs of malignant catarrhal fever that would affect deer. It is a deadly disease but is not considered contagious.

However, Louis Bender, the study's author, stated the virus might be shed into the environment by a host animal and then accidentally picked up by another species, like a deer. Morrow says they don't know if this is happening in the San Andres Mountains. There is no clear evidence it is happening and to do the necessary work to check it out would be incredibly expensive and difficult.

The other disease found in oryx by Bender is bovine respiratory syncytial virus. This virus, if picked up by bighorn sheep, could make them susceptible to pneumonia. Again, Morrow said they have no idea if this is happening.

When the studies were done, the agencies wrote an oryx management plan that calls for an oryx population of around 1,500 animals. To get to that number, Morrow suggested increased hunting permits and then more again and more again.

During the years after 2000, hunters were taking out over 1,000 oryx each year. The pinnacle was 2007 when some 1,400 oryx were killed within WSMR. Morrow keeps track of the surveys each year and how many oryx are taken in hunts, so he can recommend the number of permits for the next year.

I say "within WSMR" because as oryx spread, hunts were instituted elsewhere to control the expanding population. For instance, in 2011, hundreds of permits were offered by the state on public lands surrounding WSMR. Also, permits were offered for hunts on private lands and on Fort Bliss to include Otero Mesa and McGregor Range.

In addition, to get to oryx in remote areas on White Sands, Morrow got approval for "WSMR Security Badge Hunts." Applicants for these hunts must possess a White Sands security badge or be escorted by someone with such a badge.

Basically, with the cooperation of many government agencies and some landowners, a program has evolved to control the number of oryx pretty much everywhere they inhabit the local landscape.

Of course this all adds up to big money. In 2011, the fees for a resident license were $163 going to the state and $150 to WSMR. For nonresidents, the fee was $1,637 going to the state and $150 to WSMR.

To accommodate increasing numbers of hunters on White Sands, the agencies abandoned the once-a-year December hunts and started spreading out the crowds with several weekend hunts at many different locations. As of 2011, for most hunts, the hunters got two days instead of four to get an oryx. Also, they were assigned a specific area on the missile range to hunt in – could be the Stallion area or the Rhodes Canyon area or, for a few, the Red Canyon area.

At the beginning of this serious push to control oryx, the 9/11 attacks happened and hunting was temporarily shut down. New security restrictions were put in place and suddenly the whole hunt program was called into question.

Going into the 2001/2002 hunting season, 895 people had licenses to hunt on WSMR. The state had already collected over $150,000 in fees and WSMR was paid $85,000 by hunters. The aspect of losing the opportunity to reduce the population by almost 900 animals and lose all the associated revenue was daunting.

A compromise was finally reached to save the hunting season. It boiled down to treating every hunter as a potential terrorist by requiring he or she be escorted every minute they were on WSMR by a state or federal official. That meant lots of escorts.

With only so many escorts to go around, the strategy was to offer a number of one-day hunts over many weekends. The problem was the escorts were working every weekend. But it was successful.

The removal of oryx continued with just that one hiccup. In 2011, Morrow said they were making a significant dent in the oryx population. In fact, the number of permits was cut back to 985 that year.

The reduction has made finding oryx harder on WSMR. In the beginning, hunters simply drove up and down the range roads until they spotted a group close to the road. If the animals were too far out, they just drove on until they ran into more.

When I escorted media types wanting to photograph oryx, we ignored everything more than a hundred yards out. I told them we would see more, and most of the time we were able to roll up to some right along the road. The photographers were able to just film out the window.

Morrow said it isn't like that anymore. In the 90s, the hunter success rate was in the 96 percent range. By 2011, it was sliding back to around 80 percent.

One explanation for the lower success rate is that fewer animals are spread over the same area. Now the chance of running into one on a random basis is lower – simple probability. Morrow also thinks oryx have certain behaviors with each individual having his or her own proclivities. He theorizes that some animals might congregate close to roads for some reason and they were easy targets. For instance, rainwater runs off roads creating lush little strips of vegetation along the edges. That easy salad might appeal to some oryx and not others.

It could be most of those road users are gone and the more wary ones are left – the ones that start running as soon as something foreign like a hunter pops up on the environment.

Instead of stepping out of a vehicle to shoot an oryx, the hunts are much more challenging now. Hunters have to actually search for animals out in the greasewood and then try to put the sneak on them. It can be hard work but is probably more rewarding than the old easy days.

Another factor in the lower success rate is in the quality of hunters. The added difficulty is separating the men from the boys, so to speak.

Because oryx are so popular, hunters of all possible backgrounds have shown up on the missile range. Everyone has drawn permits from the world-class professional to your average working Joe to some bumbling fools to a few outright criminals. Some aren't even hunters.

Morrow said he ran into a man on one hunt who did not have a rifle or any kind of weapon. The "hunter" explained he thought oryx were neat animals and he wanted the chance to see them in the wild. When his application was drawn in the lottery, he paid the fee and came on out. He spent the hunt period driving around observing oryx wherever he could find them.

The idiots and fools probably provide the most head-shaking stories. One hunter arrived wearing flip-flops expecting the game wardens to carry her animal to her truck for her.

Another hunter shot at an oryx in a group of them. When it didn't drop dead right away, he shot at another animal. When it didn't drop right away, he shot at another. When queried, he didn't know if he had hit any or all of them. Game wardens were called to the scene to follow the blood trails and try to find the wounded oryx.

Having been on site when something like this happens, I can tell you there is not much that angers a game warden more than such carelessness. As a rule, they do not like to see animals suffer. I could see steam coming out of their ears as they geared up to track the wounded animals.

Finally, we need to dispatch one oryx myth. In general conversations about oryx, there is always someone in the crowd who knows someone, who knows someone, who heard oryx were terribly aggressive and would charge trucks and cars. The animals are portrayed as regular musketeers slashing their way around the range with those big horns.

In my chasing oryx with photographers, we never ran across an aggressive oryx. Of course, we never trapped one against a fence with our vehicle or tried to wave it through a gate by standing out in the open. Just the opposite. If we rolled up to oryx along the road, every time I let a photographer out of the car to film, the oryx invariably were spooked and took off sooner than later.

While this myth is pretty much an exaggeration of the normal behavior of most wild animals, there is another anecdote often passed along to clearly point out how hostile an oryx can be. In this tall tale, an oryx has supposedly been seen with a dead coyote or mountain lion stuck on its horns. The poor oryx has survived an attack by killing the predator but is stuck with a crown of decaying carcass.

When asked by WSMR or NM game officials where this person saw the oryx, they all say they heard it from someone who saw it or heard it from someone else. The game wardens and missile range personnel on hunts have never seen this. In fact, they all dismiss it as an urban legend.

It is true oryx in Africa defend themselves from lions and other predators with those horns, but getting a coyote stuck on them is probably as likely as me winning the lottery this weekend. One has to assume that any good headshake by the oryx would send a coyote carcass flying off the ends of the horns even if it was completely impaled.

Now, I have seen and photographed other things, wire and plastic fencing, stuck on oryx horns. In fact, back in the early 80s, I went with Daisan Taylor to photograph the bodies of two oryx wired together head-to-head. Taylor was the first wildlife biologist to work at the missile range's fledging environmental office.

This was a little southeast of the main post just off a back road. Taylor surmised someone had gathered up a bunch of wire, kind of wadded it together and never removed it. Somehow one oryx stuck his horns in the mass and came away with the whole bundle. Then another oryx tried to spar with the first one and got its horns hooked in the mess as well. In fact, the first one may have picked up the wire while sparring with the other animal.

The result was the two were locked together nose to nose and eye to eye. The ground around the death scene was all chewed up from them pushing and pulling at each other. When the oryx were found, the bodies were already badly decomposed, so Taylor and others had no way to determine if the two animals died of dehydration, starvation or stress.

It was a sad sight and one that called out for better policing of the desert after missions were completed on WSMR.

Here is my take on the character of oryx. It is easier to photograph or put the sneak on an individual oryx than a small group of them. They are used to being in groups, taking their danger cues from each other. You can see them thinking, "If old Charlie takes off running, there must be danger and I'd better head that way." With that instinct in place, one animal streaking away can cause a hundred to move.

On the other hand, if the oryx is all by itself, it has to make that "stay or flee" decision based on the perceived threat. Many aren't too alarmed – they'll hang around for a minute or two and let photographers or hunters take a shot. Of course, Morrow may be right and all those oryx are gone from the gene pool now.

Sometimes photographers have trouble with the hunters instead of the oryx. During one hunt, I was escorting a television crew filming a young woman on her two-day hunt. The story angle was "women big game hunters."

It was the normal weekend hunt and the woman did not get her animal on Saturday. The TV crew got lots of footage of oryx at a distance and of the hunting party sneaking through the brush, but no shots of her shooting.

Then on Sunday, the morning went by with no results. In such a situation, hunters start to lower their standards as the minutes tick by and sunset rapidly approaches. Suddenly, a broken horned animal will do just fine instead of a trophy animal.

In this case, in the middle of the afternoon, we spotted an oryx fairly close to the road. The caravan stopped and the woman jumped out with her rifle. The cameraman was in my vehicle and he was struggling to get himself and his gear out to photograph her taking the shot. As he fumbled around, he tried to call to her to wait, but he couldn't shout for fear of spooking the oryx. That would have been the ultimate black eye for a film crew from a hunting show – to scare off an animal and ruin a hunter's hunt.

The woman didn't hear him or chose to ignore him because she set up off the shoulder of the road and took the shot before the cameraman was ready. She killed her oryx and was quite happy – with a sigh of relief. There was no happiness amongst the TV crew members.

Mule Deer Ups And Downs

For an animal so ubiquitous throughout the West, mule deer do have an unusual story when it comes to White Sands Missile Range. Like many parts of the country, people living and working at WSMR regularly saw mule deer. In fact, deer have been a problem on the golf course as they browsed on the shrubs and gouged hoof prints into the greens.

At the Cox ranch, just west of the White Sands main post, I once came across a sizable herd of deer. I was driving down the alluvial fan above the ranch headquarters when I saw the deer in the distance. There was a large yucca that they passed by in almost single-file fashion enabling me to easily count them. I quit at 75.

During that same time, my office periodically posted articles in the *Missile Ranger*, the WSMR newspaper, and local papers warning of the possibility of deer being on U.S. Highway 70 on both sides of San Augustin Pass. For several years motorists were hitting deer right and left. One missile range employee lost his life in a one-vehicle crash when it was assumed he veered to avoid hitting one on the road.

In our warnings, we tried to tell drivers it was safer to go ahead and hit the animal if it was on the road instead of trying to suddenly swerve. This was especially true at highway speeds. Yanking the steering wheel to one side or the other at high speed often caused the driver to leave the road or head into oncoming traffic or, worse yet, cause a top-heavy vehicle to roll. Safety experts told us it was far better to take your chances with simply braking and keeping the car going in a straight line. If you hit it, you were probably going to be fine.

Mule deer can be found in all the mountain ranges on and around White Sands. They are big with bucks often weighing over 300 pounds. Unlike their whitetail cousins back East, mule deer tails are tipped with black hair.

Mule deer get their name from the big, mule-like ears they use to detect danger. Their eyesight isn't very good, so the big-dish ears provide a keen early warning system. In watching them, I find it fascinating that they can move the ears independently. One can be pointed at you listening for you to move while the other is rotated in another direction trying to detect any other sounds.

At White Sands, the muley population used to be tremendous. We know this because of the deer hunting that was allowed on the range beginning in the 1950s.

Like other hunts, these were done in coordination with the New Mexico Department of Game and Fish. The state would issue the licenses and then White Sands would allow the hunters in for short periods. Range officials would also help control the hunters.

The *Wind and Sand* reported on Dec. 21, 1956 that, "During the New Mexico big game hunting season, Nov. 10-12, the range was thrown open to a total of 1,681 deer hunters who checked in and out through checkpoints set by the Provost Marshal's Office. In a special season Nov. 30 through Dec. 2, permits to hunt on the range were issued by the PMO to 1,000 more hunters."

In an article in the Oct. 25, 1957 issue of *Wind and Sand,* the numbers were growing. The article stated 4,000 hunters were expected for a hunt in the San Andres unit from Nov. 9 through Nov. 11 and the Oscura unit from Nov. 30 through Dec. 2.

During the 50s and 60s, these hunters were allowed to camp on White Sands near the boundaries.

The 1957 article said there were 10 campsites located in the San Andres with hunt headquarters at Hardin Ranch on the west boundary.

At the north end of the Oscura Mountains, White Sands threw up an old building to house state and range personnel who supervised the hunters there. The building was dubbed "hunter's lodge" because it provided basic shelter to the support staff. The place has been turned into an urban legend and is now described as a special luxury hunting lodge on White Sands for the commanding general and VIPs.

In 1957, the resident fee for a deer permit was $6.50 and for non-residents it was $50.25.

Deer hunters on White Sands never had the success rates that oryx hunters enjoy today. However, the post newspaper did sometimes report on how many animals were taken during these hunts. It was usually over 500 each year.

Based on the number of deer harvested each year, one has to assume there were thousands out on the range during these years.

It all started to change in the 1990s. Most people talk about the deer population "crashing" at White Sands starting at that time. Patrick Morrow said in 2011, they estimate the current population of mule deer was only five percent of what it was in 1990. There haven't been any deer hunts on White Sands in years.

Eyewitness accounts reinforce this dramatic reduction. I used to go Uprange quite frequently escorting ranch families, news media, and others. Whenever I drove through the mountains, I usually saw deer every trip. By the time I retired in 2007, it was a special event to see deer.

Generally, the public and hunters were troubled at the deer decline. Depending on their backgrounds, people weighed in with their opinions on what caused it. Many wildlife experts said it was the corresponding drought in Southern New Mexico. Some said that taking so many animals during the hunts killed the goose that laid the golden egg. A few said the mountain lions were eating all the deer. Finally, some blamed disease on taking out much of the population.

In 2002, the disease theory got a big boost when a deer suffering from chronic wasting disease (CWD) was shot near the WSMR housing area. The stumbling, sick-looking animal was reported by a resident. Ben Archuleta, a Range game warden, was given permission to kill the animal but with instructions to get the animal to the Department of Game and Fish as quickly as possible. It turned out to be the first proven case of CWD in New Mexico.

Chronic wasting disease is a "transmissible spongiform encephalopathy or TSE" according to the New Mexico Department of Game and Fish. It is a rare disease found in elk and deer and is more prevalent on wildlife farms where the animals are in very close proximity to each other. A form can be found in cattle that we all know as "mad-cow disease." It has a human counterpart called Creuzfeldt-Jacob disease.

It is a nasty disease because it destroys parts of the brain, turning it into Swiss cheese. It is always fatal.

Chronic wasting disease in deer and elk was not a new story nationally in 2002. States like Colorado and Wyoming had seen the disease for decades. Officials in New Mexico were expecting CWD to pop up eventually in the northern part of the state, near an area already hosting the disease.

When it showed up, New Mexico Wildlife Disease Specialist Kerry Mower said, "We simply don't know how chronic wasting disease got to White Sands." Lots of guesses have been made. One theory is that CWD may spontaneously arise in some individuals.

Since then more deer have been found with CWD on and around WSMR. To assure hunters and the general public, the state looked at all the other states with their longer history of CWD and found no cases where the disease was passed on to humans.

The idea that CWD was responsible for the decline of mule deer at WSMR took a body slam when a five-year study found very few individuals with the disease. The biologists captured more than 500 deer and found the incidence of CWD at less than one percent. There is no way such a small infection rate could decimate such a large population.

So what happened to all those thousands of deer? In 2011, Morrow advanced an interesting theory. He told me it might be the current muley population is really closer to the norm, that the big numbers everyone saw at the beginning of White Sands were an oddity.

He said the Oscura and San Andres Mountains, before 1945, were picked bare by the thousands and thousands of angora goats run by ranchers. The

goats, being browsers, ate almost everything deer eat and they were everywhere – canyons, mountainsides and peaks – picking it all clean.

When White Sands was established all the livestock was removed. The vegetation immediately started to grow back. When it did, there was lots of very nutritious new growth on bushes, forbs and trees. It was Eden for the deer population and they flourished.

In Morrow's theory, the vegetation gradually matured and more and more of the nutritious new growth was too high for deer to reach. To complicate it, there was no natural fire anymore to clean out the old growth and promote new growth.

Gradually the deer numbers simply started dropping because of a dwindling source of high quality food. It was a slow process. He said you then pile on the mountain lions and drought and the numbers drop a bit faster.

So, it may be that the current deer population is closer to what might have been seen in 1900, before white man introduced large numbers of livestock into the area. The huge numbers of deer taken by hunters early on in the history of WSMR may go down as a manmade hiccup on the population graph.

Pupfish – Yes, Fish In The Desert

White Sands is as large as Delaware and Rhode Island combined but has no lakes, rivers or real streams. Yet there are fish found in several wet spots on the floor of the Tularosa Basin. These little guys live in some of the harshest conditions imaginable. Yet they have adapted and survived in their tiny niches for thousands of years.

Pupfish are very small and often described as "guppy-like." They are about two inches long. During breeding times, the males break out in bright, almost fluorescent colors like blue and orange to mark their presence.

Pupfish are the only fish to survive from the end of the Pleistocene Epoch in the Tularosa Basin when a huge lake, now called Lake Otero, dominated the bottom. This was a time of glaciers in the north. Several times most of Canada was almost completely covered with ice with some of it crossing into what is now the northern United States.

Further south much of the planet was dry and cold, but all across the western United States it rained and snowed, filling rivers and streams that drained into large, freshwater lakes. At its peak, Utah's Lake Bonneville was supposedly close to the size of Lake Michigan and about 1,000 feet deep. California's Death Valley, one of the most forbidding places on the planet today, once held a huge lake 175 miles long and about 600 feet deep.

John Pittenger and Craig Springer, in their June 1999 article about White Sands pupfish in *The Southwestern Naturalist*, report they found evidence Lake Otero probably maxed out with its surface at 1,250 meters above sea level. Its depth would have been at least 60 meters or close to 200 feet. One estimate is the lake covered at least 1,600 square miles.

As the weather changed during the past 10-12,000 years many of these lakes in the West dried up. As they shrank in size, the water became harder because salts were dissolved in smaller and smaller amounts of water. Fish died out at different times depending on how resilient they were to water that was getting saltier and warmer.

Eventually, all the fish died because the lakes completely went away. In a few places like the Tularosa Basin and Death Valley, there are some little holes and springs where water has been available the whole time. In some of those spots pupfish have survived.

Because these fish have been isolated from other pupfish for thousands of years, they are inbred and each population propagates different sets of gene mutations. In other words, they are slowing drifting apart from each other. Because of those differences, White Sands pupfish are technically called "Cyprinodon tularosa" while those in Death Valley's Devil's Hole are called "Cyprinodon diabolis."

They are all hardy creatures. At the missile range, pupfish have been found in pools of water over 90 degrees F and a salt concentration many times greater than ocean water.

What may be more impressive is their ability to survive in this water as it fluctuates dramatically

A pupfish researcher with the New Mexico Department of Game and Fish kicks her way across the pool at Mound Spring to collect samples of the fish for study. With no more horses to foul the spring, the water is crystal clear again. Photo by the author.

from time to time. At White Sands, pupfish are found in Salt Creek, the only "stream" on the missile range. The creek arises from springs at the north end of the basin, flows sluggishly south, and then disappears in the playas around Range Road 6. It is less than 20 miles in length and when it is really dry, it is reduced to a series of shallow pools.

This water is shallow, warm and salty. However, when a large summer rainstorm dumps a lot of water in the drainage, the creek is suddenly flushed with fresh water. Water levels can go from a few inches to a few feet in a matter of minutes. The stream temperature immediately drops and the alkalinity swings suddenly back toward neutral.

Pupfish live off algae, detritus, and small organisms like mosquito larvae. It's their mosquito larvae appetite that has attracted the attention of some researchers. Experiments have been conducted to introduce pupfish into mosquito breeding areas as a way to control the pests without pesticides.

White Sands pupfish can be found on the missile range in Malpais Spring, Salt Creek and Mound Spring. Also, they are found in Lost River, a small drainage from Holloman Air Force Base into White Sands National Monument.

Malpais Spring is a remarkable artesian phenomenon at the southwest corner of the lava flow on the eastern boundary of the missile range. Water just pops out of the ground and flows out into a large marshy area. According to the United States Geological Survey, the flow rate varies from 220 gallons per minute to as high as 1,500 gallons per minute. The water quality isn't too bad but does qualify as "brackish" according to the USGS.

When I first saw Malpais Spring, there was a manmade channel taking the water in a straight line south. It shows up today on *Google Earth* images. Word-of-mouth had it the waterway was dug by a farmer who used the outflow to irrigate crops he planted on the flats. The story goes that the plants sprouted fine but the brackish water coupled with the very alkaline soil caused them to wither and die in a matter of weeks.

Personnel from the WSMR environmental office eventually blocked the farmer's canal and returned the spring's flow to the marsh area. It is an area where passersby can see ducks, geese, heron, cranes and other water birds roosting for the night.

Pupfish found in Malpais Spring and Salt Creek

are thought to be native, according to Pittenger and Springer. Pupfish found in the other two spots were probably introduced by locals. In fact, the two researchers found a document saying that Ralph Charles planted pupfish in Lost River in 1970.

The Mound Spring population exists in a very unusual habitat. Mound Spring is just one of many "mound" springs at the north end of the Tularosa Basin. Some still flow while many more are dead.

This is an area where water flows out of the ground in small springs. Around the edges of the pool that is formed, material starts to build up. As the water evaporates it leaves behind gypsum and other minerals on the edges. Also, blowing sand sticks on the wet shoreline and builds up layer upon layer.

Given enough time, a mound starts to build with a pool of water in the center - kind of a mini Crater Lake. If everything goes right, the mound can reach a height of several feet. Eventually, the spring will get clogged or there isn't enough pressure to push water up into the pool and the process dies.

Around Mound Spring there is a collection of dead mounds with the pool filled in with blown sands. A couple of springs still flow water and are struggling to grow.

Mound Spring itself is a highly modified pool of water. According to Pittenger and Springer, the missile range dredged the spring pool in 1967 to deepen and enlarge it so water could be pumped for road construction. Currently its maximum depth is about 10 feet.

The area to the west and below the pool was dug out and surrounded with a dike to create a second pool from overflow. Before this work there were no reports of fish in the spring.

Pittenger and Springer found reports of pupfish in the pools in 1973 and concluded they were probably introduced by some local. I have heard some biologists speculate a bird might have dropped a fish or two accidentally into Mound Spring. It seems more likely that Ralph Charles put them there as well as Lost River.

Although there are literally hundreds of pupfish in the Tularosa Basin, the New Mexico Department of Game and Fish has listed them as a "threatened species." The reasoning is that they are only found in four places. Some sort of calamity at one or more of the sites could suddenly reduce the population by 25 to 50 percent or more. In other words, a small change in habitat could threaten a whole line of pupfish.

When the state raised this warning flag on pupfish, officials at the U.S. Fish and Wildlife Service were alerted to pupfish issues. When that happened, the plight of pupfish (so out of sight and out of mind for military officials) became a topic of concern for the missile range. If the USFWS listed *Cyprinodon tularosa* as a threatened and endangered species, bigtime federal laws and regulations would kick in and just might put some of the range off limits for military use. That is enough to make any military manager sit up and pay attention.

To preclude such a listing, a cooperative agreement and conservation plan was signed in 1994 and updated in 2006. The signers were White Sands Missile Range, White Sands National Monument, Holloman Air Force Base, New Mexico Department of Game and Fish, and the U.S. Fish and Wildlife Service. In a nutshell, the cooperators are all the landowners with pupfish on their property and the two agencies responsible for protecting native species of wildlife.

For the missile range, it means avoiding pupfish habitat to prevent water contamination or causing disruption to the flow of water in the springs or Salt Creek. Plans for missile and target impacts are made to avoid the small sensitive areas. Also, efforts are periodically made to educate White Sands personnel and their need to protect pupfish habitat. Signs are posted forbidding the removal of any water from the springs as well.

One negative impact on pupfish habitat, especially at Mound Spring, was not the responsibility of the missile range. Since water in Mound and Malpais Springs is not too salty, animals such the wild horses would drink there when fresh water sources dried up.

At Mound Spring, because of the steep banks, the horses used to wade into the water to drink. They broke down the banks and the subsequent erosion was threatening the integrity of the pond itself. Also, the horses urinated and defecated into the water. It got to the point the water looked like pea soup instead of the almost pristine clear water we saw in the 70s and 80s. It was tough on pupfish, no matter how resilient they were.

The solution was to fence off the spring in 1994. Although horses have been removed from WSMR, the old corral fence around the spring is still in place and the water is crystal clear again.

Horses – Looking For Grass In The Desert

The horses mentioned above used to freely roam the middle part of White Sands. I almost called it the "grasslands" north of Lake Otero, but there is so little grass most observers would think I was joking. But it is true. The lakebed is almost completely devoid of any vegetation. In contrast, the basin floor north of the lake is sparsely populated with mesquite and creosote bushes and clumps of grass in between. There is grazing, just not much.

When I arrived at White Sands, I knew nothing about horses. Right away another person in my office suckered me into a Saturday guided ride in the Sacramento Mountains. The idea was that I would get a free horseback excursion if I wrote a story about the experience.

The trip was billed as a ride up Dog Canyon to Frenchy's old stone cabin. Although the facts were liberally interpreted and misrepresented by our local guide, for me the day was an introduction to horses and some of the Old West history in New Mexico.

We rode several miles up what is today the bottom part of the Dog Canyon and Eyebrow Trail. Now access is through Oliver Lee State Park. In 1978, there was no park yet and the site was undeveloped.

The stone cabin we rode to was not Frenchy's cabin but was probably a later line shack for Oliver Lee. Frenchy's home was actually at the mouth of the canyon, near where we parked. It was where Frenchman Francois-Jean Rochas gardened and tended an orchard made possible by water flowing out of Dog Canyon. But a ride to that structure wouldn't have been much of an outing.

According to C.L. Sonnichsen, in his landmark history of the area called *Tularosa: Last of the Frontier West*, Rochas was murdered just after Christmas in 1894. Sonnichsen claims three men rode up and shot Frenchy.

A few years later, prominent Tularosa Basin resident Oliver Lee filed a claim on the water and land that were once controlled by Rochas. Lee built a house near the mouth of the canyon to take advantage of the water. Now, Lee's ruined house has been rebuilt by the State of New Mexico and is part of the state park.

Since my visit to Dog Canyon in late 1978, more

information has been gathered about Rochas. Mary J. Straw Cook, in her updated narrative *Loretto: The Sisters and Their Santa Fe Chapel* writes that before moving to Dog Canyon, Rochas appeared in Santa Fe to build the chapel staircase at Loretto.

Soon after the Loretto sisters' chapel was completed in 1878, the good sisters were faced with the fact they had no gentile access to the choir loft just over 20 feet above the floor of the church. The nuns rejected the idea of simply using a ladder and spent days praying for guidance. At the end of their prayers, a French master carpenter mysteriously appeared. He built the present spiral staircase using no nails or other metal fasteners.

Many have proclaimed it a miracle with the work done by an angel or the oldest master carpenter of them all, Joseph, the patron saint of carpenters.

Instead, Cook found evidence the work was done by the same Francois-Jean Rochas who was killed at Dog Canyon. Whether he built it from scratch or reassembled a custom-ordered staircase built elsewhere and shipped to Santa Fe remains unknown.

By the end of my ride up Dog Canyon I was hurting. I was intrigued by the history of the Frenchman making an oasis from the canyon's trickle of water, but my knees were so sore I swore I'd never get on another horse. It has been an easy promise to keep.

Although it was a painful experience, I saw how people could fall in love with these big, brown-eyed creatures while others just saw them, more-or-less, as tools for their work on the ranch.

Those attitudes and opinions about horses were frequently displayed when I took visitors and tour groups Uprange. When we saw horses, we would usually slow down or stop and allow folks to take photos. Some people gushed about what beautiful animals we had roaming the range. Others belittled the stock, saying they were nothing but a bunch of sway-backed animals and were sorry excuses for horses. It was another case of the same data resulting in totally opposed points of view.

Only knowing that horses are not kind to my knees or backside, I just listened and went about my business. I certainly had no knowledge or experience that could be brought to bear in the argument. I can say I always enjoyed seeing them near the roads except at night. That was a whole different story.

During my time at White Sands, the range's roads were probably some of the most dangerous

in New Mexico – all because of wildlife. Oryx and horse populations were peaking. There were thousands of these big mammals freely roaming the range and many of them hung around the paved roads.

When it rains on the pavement, most of the water flows to the sides and irrigates the plants within a few feet of the road. That means the desert can be fairly dry and barren while a thin strip of lush green plants brightens the immediate roadside.

The wildlife take advantage of those little garden areas and, during the summer, they come out to graze in the cool of the night. I remember one night driving from Stallion Range Center at the north boundary back through the range to my office on the main post, a distance of about 118 miles. That night I slowed for pronghorn up north, for horses in the middle of the range, oryx in a half dozen places, and a mule deer just north of the Small Missile Range gate. It was like driving through a minefield where the mines could jump out in front of you from almost anywhere.

Hitting any of those animals would have been a serious accident. But the horses were especially scary because they were tall, and if you hit one with a low riding vehicle a thousand pounds of horse just might slide down the hood right into your lap. Not good for horses or drivers.

Dodging horses was made harder because of their light-absorbing dark coats. If you wanted to live you couldn't afford to overdrive your headlights.

Many people assume the White Sands horses are like the wild "mustangs" found on public lands in places like Nevada, which are the descendants of those first Spanish horses brought to America centuries ago. They are not.

The WSMR horses are considered "feral" animals. The word means they were once domesticated livestock but have escaped and are living on their own. The definition applies even to horses born wild on the missile range. They still have the genes and demeanor to return to domestic duty.

This was proven to us during the White Sands horse adoption program. A soldier stationed at the missile range bought a mare at one of the adoptions. Within a week or so he had her gentle enough to carry his young daughter. He even walked the horse carrying the girl by our office to show us.

The original population of horses was established on White Sands during the turmoil of World

War II and the confusion following the war. Many horses were simply left behind when ranchers were forced to leave the property.

Since horses are social animals they quickly found each other. Herds or groups were formed where a dominant stallion controlled a harem of mares. Some of these groups were small and others were large, depending on how many mares a stallion could attract and defend. While he wasn't looking, another stallion might be trying to steal one or more of the females. Vigilance and strength gave a stallion more opportunities to mate.

Adding diversity to the stock of horses roaming White Sands was the occasional escapee from a neighboring ranch. Sometimes the animal was never found or the rancher never tried looking because of having to coordinate with White Sands.

Over the years the horse population would increase because mares can produce about one offspring per year. The numbers would quickly grow into the hundreds. Missile range officials knew they had to do something to manage the horses, otherwise the population would explode.

Very quickly a simple system evolved utilizing the New Mexico Livestock Board (or its predecessor organization, the New Mexico Cattle Sanitary Board – the name was changed in 1967). One of the missions of the board is to retrieve trespass livestock and return the animals to their rightful owners. If the owners cannot be found, the animals can be sold at public auction with the board pocketing the money to use in future endeavors.

For decades, this was how the horse population was controlled. When the numbers were deemed too high, a roundup was held, conducted by the Army, and the board would haul the animals away.

A White Sands news release from Oct. 14, 1957 detailed how Army "cowboys" rounded up horses in the middle of the range and "turned them over to the New Mexico Cattle Sanitary Board in Truth or Consequences, New Mexico for sale." An article in the July 29, 1971 issue of the *Albuquerque Tribune* announced 56 horses from the missile range would be sold at auction at the Alamogordo Fair Grounds.

For the Alamogordo sale, L. S. Garner who was head of the Livestock Board said the horses, "Are not even wild horses as far as I'm concerned…they are no more wilder than a ranch mare."

In 1989, the state received much criticism from horse advocacy groups for how it ran its end of the program. The groups accused New Mexico of allowing the WSMR horses to be purchased by slaughterhouses. The accusation was that horses were going for feed gourmands in France or being turned into dog food. The controversy was quite emotional for some people and we probably should have seen what was going to follow.

With the criticism came a decision by New Mexico not to cooperate with White Sands anymore. They wanted to avoid the bad publicity, and an easy way out was to say the horses were the missile range's problem. This was the case even though the New Mexico Attorney General's Office issued an opinion in January 1990, saying the state was responsible for the horses if the landowner, WSMR, wanted the animals removed.

At the same time, the missile range dragged its feet in finding a solution. There were a lot of horses but they were doing fine. Government agencies have difficulty in making preemptive strikes to prevent long-range future problems. There is always someone at the meetings who points out that spending money on just a potential or perceived problem could get them all in trouble. It is how bureaucrats think.

In the early 90s, the horse population was reaching record levels. When we traveled Uprange we saw horses all the time. I can remember seeing herds with close to a hundred animals in them. They ranged from the north end of Alkali Flats (Lake Otero) to Mockingbird Gap, where a low ridge connects the north end of the San Andres Mountains to the south end of the Oscura Mountains. To the east they were hemmed in by the boundary fence and to the west stood the eastern wall of the San Andres Mountains.

Normally the horses grazed wherever they could find food and drank from the few salty springs on the basin floor or from ditches and dirt tanks holding rainwater after storms. It was wet in the early 90s and there was plenty of water and grass.

By the summer of 1994, there were about 1,500 horses in the mid-range area. That year it was hot and dry all spring and into early summer. It meant the water spots filled by rainfall were bone-dry by June.

The requirement for a drink everyday drove the horses to those few perennial springs in the basin – Malpais Spring, Mound Spring, Oscura Range Camp

Spring, and the few springs feeding Salt Creek.

Since there was no other water, the horses stayed close to these water points. They had to eat so they ventured out from the springs and ate every desiccated, shriveled blade of grass to be found within a day's walk from the water. Given their record numbers, that grass didn't last long.

On July 5 and 6, 1994, missile range biologists discovered about 20 dead horses in the Mound Spring area while conducting their annual aerial horse survey. Going in on the ground during the next several days, WSMR's wildlife biologist and veterinarian plus personnel from New Mexico Department of Game and Fish discovered many more dead or dying horses. Some were so far gone they had to be put down in the field.

By the end of the month, 122 dead animals were found near water holes or actually in them. They had died from starvation and dehydration. Disease was ruled out in the first few few days when lab tests came back negative.

The missile range's response was prompt but too limited to accomplish much. In the Ropes Springs area, where most of the deaths occurred, range personnel set out water tanks on July 8 to provide good supplemental water.

However, based on advice from wildlife biologists, range management specialists and several wildlife activist groups, the missile range commander chose not to provide supplemental feed for the horses.

By July 10 and 11, the news media were picking up on the story. The response from some members of the public was quick and emotional. In fact, I experienced nothing else like it. Some people called our office in apoplectic rages, threatening us personally for letting the horses starve. Some damned us to hell and some cried into the phone. Many demanded we go out and rescue the animals.

On the other hand, many people called to offer whatever support they could provide. People were willing to donate money and feed, some were willing to help round up horses and haul them elsewhere, many wanted to adopt an animal, and some were willing to come out to build corrals or anything else needed. There was even a country-western radio station offering free advertisement for anything White Sands might need to help the horses.

What to do about the situation was a burning question for a few days. Everyone had the same set of facts, but what to do split the various advisors and experts.

Believe it not, one of the first questions that needed an answer was who owned the horses. No cautious bureaucrat was going to commit to any action if his or her agency wasn't actually responsible for the horses. Missile range officials thought it was a no-brainer since they had a working arrangement with New Mexico dating back more than 40 years. New Mexico countered, saying the horses were no longer considered livestock and not subject to the state's estray law.

While officials tossed the horse hand grenade back and forth, the missile range went out to bury dead horses so the carcasses didn't rot in the sun. It was a dismal job done by employees who volunteered for the work. The bodies were hauled to a mass grave for burial.

Often machinery was used to pick up the carcasses but, in some cases, horses were in or next to the water holes. This complicated the situation because the influx of decaying flesh and bacteria could have been a real threat to the state endangered pupfish found in the waters.

In some instances the body was so decayed it was impossible to simply drag the horse out. The body literally came apart when disturbed. So men had to go in and pull the animals out, putrid piece by putrid piece. It was appalling work.

On July 15, the New Mexico summer monsoon finally started in the Tularosa Basin. There were substantial rains in the Ropes Springs areas. It rained again the next day and then again.

The rains created puddles, check dams and ditches full of good fresh water. The horses quickly dispersed to the new water points and new grazing possibilities. In fact, by July 23 White Sands stopped hauling water to its tanks.

The immediate problem, in just 10 days, suddenly went away. Personnel out on the range stopped seeing dead horses. Of course, fixing the root problem of too many horses on such miserable land was only postponed. Now, everyone clearly saw the issue and the bureaucrats from the various agencies were motivated to fix it.

Karen Sussman, then president of the International Association for the Protection of Mustangs and Burros, weighed in with her energy and clout.

The missile range's position was that the horses were still feral animals and technically belonged to the State of New Mexico. The status of the horses hadn't changed just because of some public inconvenience for the state.

Sussman convinced New Mexico to form the White Sands Feral Horse Task Force. New Mexico Lt. Gov. Casey Luna headed the task force. The missile range was represented by the commanding general and many from his staff. Other task force members included Sussman, representatives of the Bureau of Land Management, the New Mexico Livestock Board, the New Mexico Correctional Facility, plus members of animal rights groups and other citizens.

One of the first things Luna did was ask the New Mexico Attorney General for an update on the horse ownership issue. In a letter to Governor Bruce King dated Aug. 2, 1994, the attorney general's office stated, "The horses at White Sands are not 'livestock' within the meaning of the New Mexico Livestock Code and, therefore, the Livestock Board does not have jurisdiction or authority to treat them as estrays. Consequently, the Livestock Board is not authorized to take custody of the horses and has no authority to sell them at auction or otherwise."

The opinion goes on to clarify this interpretation. It states, "It should be noted at this point in the analysis that although Attorney General Opinion 90-01 issued Jan. 30, 1990 comes to a conclusion opposite the one just given regarding the status of the White Sands horses, this difference results from statutory change that occurred between the time when that opinion was written and the present." The statute was changed in 1993 and conveniently lets New Mexico off the hook.

Although the opening of the opinion allowed New Mexico to wash its hands of the horse issue, the lawyers went on to keep New Mexico in play. Later in the opinion, the attorney general basically concluded the horses were not wildlife either but were a kind of quasi wildlife. Since New Mexico sees itself as the caretaker of all wildlife in the state, they had some responsibility for the horses.

At the same time, the opinion concluded the horses were on federal property so the state shared that quasi responsibility with the Army.

Luna's task force met four times, the first time on Aug. 2, and talked about solutions such as adoption programs involving state prisoners gentling horses.

New Mexico liked this idea because it would resurrect the state's old horses in prison program. The idea was that the federal government would contract with the New Mexico prison system to take horses, gentle them for adoption, and run public adoptions. The program was supposed to make prisoners better people.

Initially, White Sands liked the idea but federal lawyers pointed out the Army couldn't enter into a contractual agreement where convict labor was used. It was a major roadblock that was never lifted.

Luna grew frustrated and disbanded his task force by the end of the year when he and Governor King were leaving office to make way for the new Gary Johnson administration. In his letter ending the task force, Luna, being a political animal, absolved the state of any fault and laid the blame at WSMR's doorstep. He wrote, "There are a multitude of problems and obstacles that cannot be overcome by the Task Force, brought on by the decisions of the U.S. Army (WSMR). I also do not see the possibility of WSMR entering into a contract with the New Mexico Corrections Industries any time in the near future."

That was Luna's lead. He concluded with, "Sadly, it appears that the Task Force was unable to win the trust, faith and confidence of the U.S. Army at WSMR in entering into a simple and timely solution to resolve the future of these horses for the benefit of all. We New Mexicans tried to be good neighbors, with positive solutions. Instead, the Army chose to take the route of worst case scenario."

Although the task force did come up with several good ideas, there was always one ever-present problem with any proposal - funding. New Mexico wasn't going to fire up its prison program for the welfare of horses. They wanted to get on the federal gravy train and have the Army fund a whole program for them. It was a win-win situation for them if the Army agreed.

New Mexico Congressman Joe Skeen fixed the funding problem in November 1994 when Congress appropriated $1.5 million to round up horses from White Sands and run a public adoption program to reduce the numbers.

To show how you can never win, this appropriation was condemned by Senators John McCain, Arizona, and John Warner, Virginia, as "pork barrel" politics.

Of course, actually removing and adopting out

horses was not as easy as it sounds. As they say, "the devil is in the details." Sussman and her groups wanted to make sure no slaughter houses got horses. That meant strict rules had to be written on who could adopt and how many horses they could have. They wanted followup to ensure horses were still owned by the original adopters. Also, they were concerned about the health of the animals, so more rules were written about things like the kind and size of trailer an adopter could use to transport the animal.

It meant rejecting, for instance, the fool who showed up at an adoption wanting to put a colt in his convertible. He said he'd put the top down.

In 1995, White Sands signed a contract with the Tadpole Cattle Company of Bartlesville, Oklahoma to remove and adopt out missile range horses. The roundups began in February and ran through the end of the year. Adoptions for some 1,500 horses were held in New Mexico, Oklahoma, Tennessee, Texas and California.

White Sands continued horse adoptions for several years after this, trying to keep herd numbers low and to give locals a chance to acquire a horse. Some 200 horses were adopted out locally through 1998.

In 1997, the missile range finished and published an environmental assessment on feral horses. It stated White Sands management was going with the proposed alternative to remove all feral horses from the range. It seemed the sane solution after years of watching horses suffer and die, fighting bureaucratic battles for solutions, spending millions of taxpayer dollars, and wanting to never experience it again.

In the summer of 1998, the process began with 120 animals going to a ranch in Missouri specializing in horse gentling techniques. Some were sent to a working youth ranch near El Paso to help troubled youth.

In the fall of 1998, with still more than 100 horses left on White Sands, the International Society for the Protection of Mustangs and Burros came forward to take the rest of the horses. They planned to keep the herd intact on a ranch in South Dakota.

The first shipment to South Dakota occurred in April 1999 with the last group leaving on May 27, 1999.

They didn't get them all, however. As of 2012, there were still a few old stallions left on White Sands. Since there are no mares, there is no fear the population will come back. The decision was made to let

the stallions just finish their lives on White Sands. This means travelers Uprange sometimes still see a horse or two on their drive.

In 2006, Don Hoglund, a veterinarian who advised WSMR on horse issues, published a book called, *Nobody's Horses – The Dramatic Rescue of the Wild Herd of White Sands.* It received good reviews and was selected as one of the 100 best books in New Mexico by the New Mexico Book Co-op.

First of all, this book is sold as a true story, a nonfiction account of the horse die off and later rescue at White Sands Missile Range. It says so right on the dust jacket. As I read the book, that idea bothered me. I'm afraid that people not associated with that chapter in the range's history will swallow Hoglund's story hook, line and sinker.

Don't get me wrong here. The book tells a good story and gives a great deal of credit to White Sands and its people. However, it has to be viewed with a bit of skepticism as Hoglund portrays himself as the white knight riding to the rescue.

This book is very much a slick blend of nonfiction, fiction, romanticism, lots of exaggeration, and myth sold as gospel.

There are lots of errors, like having Pat Garrett killed near Chalk Hill. Then there is made-up stuff that is more interesting. At the very beginning of the book, Hoglund claims he first saw White Sands horses in the 1980s while driving U.S. Highway 54 between Carrizozo and Tularosa. He said he saw them on the west side of the road near a missile range sign warning against trespassing and "high levels of radiation." As he watched the horses, MPs in a Humvee, came up on the other side of the fence and waved him away.

Of course, this is a total fabrication since the White Sands boundary and fence is miles west of Highway 54. If he saw horses, they belonged to some rancher living along the highway. Also, no MPs had Humvees at WSMR in the 80s.

At one point in the book he visits the range's main post. He says "small groups of MPs led scientists in guarded caravans." That one is just laughable at best.

On the other hand, he sometimes got things just right. On the same visit he said, "I had expected brand-new buildings, super duper gadgets everywhere, and all the business-world amenities, but the 1940s, drab green barracks-like, prefab offices spoke of a barebones, make-do command…" That hits the nail on the head.

A lot of the fictional material is there to add an air of importance to the story by associating it with famous people and events. It is the "George Washington slept here" ploy. The missile range does it all the time using Wernher von Braun instead of Washington.

In one case, Hoglund states some of the horse bands on White Sands were direct descendants of horses owned by Eugene Rhodes and Pat Garrett. This is a lot of poppycock. Rhodes left New Mexico for New York just at the beginning of the 20th century. When Garrett was shot and killed outside of Las Cruces in 1908, he left a large family back on the ranch to deal with their assets. Besides, the Garrett place is almost 50 miles from the grasslands of WSMR where our horse herds roamed.

Hoglund could be claiming Rhodes and Garrett horses were sold to other New Mexican ranchers and, many generation later, some of those descendants might have escaped to White Sands from other ranches. He might as well go all the way and say they were descendants of George Washington's horses.

In another instance, he says General Douglas McArthur was responsible for having ranch families escorted from their places in World War II. It is unbelievably hard to imagine the War Department diverted McArthur from planning the war in the Pacific to something as mundane as establishing Army Air Corps training ranges.

Another ploy used by the author is the so-called "mystery" of what really killed the horses. This is truly unconscionable. Instead of saying upfront that the scientists, within a week, discovered the cause of death was dehydration and starvation, Hoglund hints at sinister causes all through the book. He repeatedly raises this question of secret poisonous experiments as he portrays himself as some sort of detective hero determined to solve the case – another nice literary device used for effect.

He cheaply brings into play the cliché that maybe the Army secretly did something to the horses and is covering it up. He wonders if the Army didn't spray nerve agent near the horses or maybe run an anthrax experiment that went wrong or maybe some sort of radiation got them. It is right out of some shoddy, mindless television offering.

He strings the reader along through the book and in the end he concludes they died because of drought and starvation.

One of the key indicators this is fiction is a three-page segment near the end of the book where Hoglund appears as a third-person omniscient narrator. It is a year after he left White Sands and he describes in great detail, as only an "all knowing" fiction writer can, what Les Gililland did after he received news that the range was going to remove all the horses.

So why did he make up these things? I suspect it was an effort to create a complete "literary" package. This is not an ordinary journalistic account of the horse rescue like you might read in a newspaper or magazine. It is striving to be literature, so it doesn't matter if it is true as long as it's a good tale.

Unfortunately, for this story, many dedicated people who worked their tails off are not mentioned in the book. That is a shame.

Books like this help perpetuate much of the misinformation that flows through our society. My office dealt with it all the time. Sometimes it was funny. Sometimes it was sad.

During the horse roundups, the *El Paso Times* published a letter to the editor on Feb. 19, 1995 from someone who probably read Hoglund's book with glee when it came out years later. The letter said, "Regarding the Army's round up of wild horses: I would be willing to bet that every one of those horses are taken to a slaughterhouse rather than adopted out.

"After all, the Army also conducts 'canned hunts' on the oryx on White Sands Missile Range. These oryx are herded by helicopter (paid for by taxpayers, by the way) into a holding area where 'sportsmen' can slaughter them and then have their pictures taken with their trophy."

I have always found it amazing what people can and will believe.

Camels and Radioactive Goats

We now get to the strange stuff.

In the case of the camel, they actually started out as a species in North America around 50 million years ago and eventually spread to Asia. The last camels found locally were in the Tularosa Basin at the end of the Pleistocene era about 10,000 years ago. They disappeared along with many other large mammals such as horses, mammoths, cave bears, and saber-toothed cats. Scientists are still arguing about why they disappeared. Many say it was the climate;

others say it was the influx of the greatest predator of all, man, moving from Asia to America.

In 2012, a group of scientists announced, after much study of wooly mammoth remains, that the big beasts probably disappeared because of a combination of circumstances. Surprise, surprise. Unlike so many people looking for black and white answers, these researchers said the climate changes, habitat changes, and influx of human hunters combined to create a perfect storm of extinctions. Although the article I read only mentioned wooly mammoths, I suspect mammoth contemporaries, like camels, suffered the same fate.

I once took a professor from UTEP and several of his students to look for bones on the north shore of old Lake Otero. At the end of the last ice age, this would have been a large body of water that attracted wildlife.

On the bluffs at the north end, they found various bones and numerous teeth. Their on-the-spot evaluation was that they were the remains of prehistoric horses and camels.

Also, along the west shore of the lake, between Range Road 7 and the lakebed just south of Brillo Site, is an area with pedestalled footprints. When these were originally found in the 1930s by an official from White Sands National Monument, he interpreted them as the footprints of a huge human being. There was talk of a tribe of giants who once lived in the Tularosa Basin.

I escorted a group of university and state scientists out to the site and they concluded the raised footprints were either mammoth or camel in origin, or both. They explained that the animals came down to the reed-covered shore of the lake and walked in the mud. Where they stepped, the mud was compressed and eventually was harder than the surrounding material. Eventually, the prints were covered with fill material.

Now the softer material has eroded away, leaving the footprints as mounds or pedestals several inches tall. In some of the best areas, 20 to 30 feet of track was exposed and you could easily see a trail of 3-D tracks.

For a time there was some talk at White Sands about trying to preserve the footprints by erecting a shelter over them. Of course, no one had the money to actually build it. Also contributing to a decision to do nothing but rope off the area was an assurance from the scientists that there would be lots of prints. As the ones we saw disappeared because of rain and wind, others would be exposed for later generations to see.

Finally, historically there were some modern camels in the Southwest in the second half of the 19th century. Before the Civil War, a few Army officers championed the idea of using camels for freighting and other work traditionally done by horses and mules. The argument was that in Africa camels carried huge weights, could move quickly in sandy conditions, needed less water, and could get along on pretty marginal browse.

In Congress, Jefferson Davis (future president of the Confederacy) supported the idea. Eventually, in the 1850s, Congress funded the military to purchase camels and experiment with them in West Texas, New Mexico, Arizona and Southern California.

The camels were shipped to Texas along with some "Arab" handlers. They were then walked west.

There are a few examples of the camels doing great work. However, the Civil War interrupted the experiment and personnel and money disappeared. Eventually the animals were turned loose.

Interestingly, there were camel sightings in the Southwest until the beginning of the 20th century. Many sightings are thought to be questionable but some were proven, as when a train hit one and killed it.

Now, fast forward to the 1980s. White Sands is bordered on its southwest corner by the Jornada Experimental Range. In fact, the eastern section of the 300-square-mile Jornada overlaps the western edge of White Sands. This Department of Agriculture facility was established in 1912 to do research on livestock grazing in the Southwest.

The facility, in conjunction with New Mexico State University, runs experiments and studies on their desert lands to try and improve production. During the 1980s, one interesting study was to introduce camels on some of their pastures to see if they might reduce weed populations.

The logic was that since camels survive in other lands much harsher than the local Chihuahuan Desert, maybe they would eat the nasty weeds that cattle, goats and sheep won't touch. It was thought camels just might be an ecologically friendly way of improving grazing conditions for more valuable animals.

The camels were deployed and observed. It

turned out camels are not dumb. They ate the grasses and other good stuff before resorting to the thorny stuff.

The radioactive goats are the result of another experiment conducted by the folks at the Jornada Experimental Range in the spring of 1991. This one involved trying to track which coyotes killed which angora goats.

Actually, I must clarify what I just said so I do not make the same mistake made by so many reporters when dealing with White Sands. The experiment was not conducted by personnel running the Jornada. The researchers were from organizations such as the Denver Wildlife Research Center and Utah State University. They were using the Jornada as their test bed.

Apparently, there is debate about coyote predation on livestock. It is an open question as to what percentage of coyotes will take advantage of the easy pickings offered by ranchers in the form of goats, lambs and calves. Will they all go for the domestic livestock or will some stick with the rabbits and rodents offered naturally by the neighborhood?

To find out, baits were set out on the range containing radioactive iodine. Also, goats were equipped with collars holding small reservoirs of radioactive elements. The adults got cesium and the kids got zinc.

The idea was to then capture and sacrifice the coyotes in the area and see which isotopes they were exposed to, if any.

Two things happened. Some of the goats escaped across the boundary onto White Sands Missile Range along with possibly contaminated coyotes that just wandered east. The second thing was the experiment became public knowledge.

Once the public got wind of the test, it was doomed. Folks living around the Jornada howled about radiation and claimed they were all going to get cancer and die. The Associated Press called the experiment "bizarre" which actually might be pretty accurate.

Officials couldn't stand the awful publicity and quickly ended the study and destroying all the animals.

When some of the goats made its way onto White Sands, the researchers had to notify the missile range because they couldn't just barge onto restricted military property to conduct a massive goat hunt. Their were other hazards to take into consideration at WSMR. With the help of White Sands personnel, all but one of the wayward goats was recovered.

According to a letter dated July 5, 1991 from Russell F. Reidinger, the Director of the Denver Wildlife Research Center, to Brigadier General Ronald Hite, White Sands Commander, they couldn't find one goat. Reidinger said, "One isotope collar has not been recovered. The radio transmitter attached to that collar was identified as being on White Sands Missile Range on 25 April 1991 but 7 aerial searches since that time failed to locate the signal in that vicinity. Whether that collar remains on White Sands Missile Range is not known."

Reidinger also pointed out that as many as four coyotes ingested radioactive materials and were unaccounted for. One or some of them may have travelled to WSMR.

In the end, the Nuclear Regulatory Commission was investigating the experiment to see if all laws, regulations and rules had been followed.

If it wasn't already in such common use, I'd say this is where the term "goat rope" originated.

24

Kaboom!

Many areas of the missile range are pockmarked with impact and explosion craters. In the early days, when missiles were liquid propelled, the fuselages were quite large to house the tanks and pumps. When these massive objects crashed to the ground, they were sometimes traveling at supersonic speeds. The kinetic energy released at impact was tremendous and gouged out some sizeable holes.

Like the V-2/Hermes II that crashed near Juarez, one V-2 smacked the desert floor and blew a big hole in the ground. There is a series of photos of the crater with men scrambling down into it to look at the debris. The only thing recognizable in the hole is the heavy steel rocket motor.

Judging from the size of the men in the photos, the crater was probably about 30 feet deep.

Some craters were created from explosions set on the ground. For instance, during the late 1970s and 80s, the old Defense Nuclear Agency (later the Defense Threat Reduction Agency) conducted a series of tests on the north end of White Sands to expose hardware, vehicles and shelters to blast effects and ground vibration found during a nuclear explosion.

They used ammonium nitrate and fuel oil (ANFO) to simulate small nuclear explosions. A total of five tests had yields larger than a one-kiloton blast. Two of them, Minor Scale (1985) and Misty Picture (1987), were huge, using over 4,600 tons of ANFO. That amount of ANFO gave the testers the equivalent of an eight-kiloton burst.

The ANFO pellets were placed inside a 44-foot diameter hemisphere that rested on the ground. For one of these huge blasts we escorted guests onto the test bed soon afterwards to see the damage. The crater was about 50 feet deep and about a hundred feet across.

These two photos capture DNA's Dice Throw test at the first few moments as the blast wave moves out. This was the first of the DNA tests using ammonium nitrate and fuel oil. It used about 600 tons of ANFO in the form of bagged pellets stacked in a tall column. The test took place on Oct. 6, 1976. WSMR photos.

An interesting piece of trivia about the crater is that it was much deeper and larger than the atomic bomb explosion at nearby Trinity Site on July 16, 1945. The bomb tested at Trinity had a yield of almost 20 kilotons, or about two and a half times stronger than either ANFO explosion, but it had a much, much smaller crater.

This is simply due to the fact that the Trinity Site bomb was exploded on top of a 100-foot tall tower. The 100 feet of air under the much bigger bomb changed the dynamic enough to prevent it from scooping out hundreds of feet of desert sand and digging a huge crater.

The old DNA craters were all filled in after the tests so there is little evidence they ever took place..

Testing around Trinity Site then continued as the DTRA shifted gears and started conducting explosive tests for law enforcement. They simulated car and truck bombs and other potential terrorist threats against different structures and vehicles.

I visited one day just after they had conducted a test using a propane tank as the bomb. It was a small tank, much like you would find around many homes in America.

The tank was placed in a tight area next to a concrete structure, like in an alley, and rigged to leak gas and then explode. The cars placed in the alley for realism were pretty beat up. They didn't show us all of the results.

Law enforcement agencies participated in these tests. We were told by a DTRA official that after the Oklahoma City courthouse bombing in 1995, one of the first FBI officials on site was able to identify the explosive material used as ANFO based on his experience at White Sands.

DTRA also reached out to look at bunkers and weapons designed to penetrate those hardened structures. Over the years they built a series of bunkers in the Trinity Site area to different standards and then allowed the various military services to attack the bunkers with their new weapons.

On another tour of the DTRA facilities, I saw a concrete roof, several feet thick and heavily reinforced with thick steel rebar, that had a neat hole punched clean through it. The hole was about the size of a manhole cover. It was the result of a penetrator bomb designed to slice through the protecting concrete and then explode inside.

If an enemy had biological or chemical weapons stored in the bunker, the resulting explosion would probably have destroyed the material before it could be used.

Railcar Explosions

Some explosions on the missile range were not military-based tests. In 1973, two tests were conducted on railroad tank cars filled with liquefied petroleum gas (LPG). The gas is usually a combination of propane and butane. The tests were dubbed the Liquified Petroleum Gas Railcar Cook-Off Test Program.

The idea was to expose real tanker railcars to fire and see if insulation coatings could protect the tank longer. The tests were sponsored by the Department of Transportation, several railroad organizations, the American Petroleum Institute, and some of the manufacturers of tankers.

After testing many coatings on subscale tanks, officials ran a test with the best performing substance on a full-scale tank at White Sands. First, however, they ran the test on a tank without any insulation to set a baseline.

The baseline test was conducted in the missile range's Hazardous Test Area on July 28, 1973. The railcar was a standard 33,000-gallon capacity tanker. The tank was 10 feet in diameter, 60 feet long and made of 5/8-inch thick steel.

The railcar was placed in a huge pit with a plastic liner under it. The plastic liner was filled with JP4 jet fuel and ignited.

According to one report, "The internal pressure of the tank car reached the safety valve actuation pressure of 280 PSI in 1 minute and 40 seconds into the test. The pressure peaked out at 357 PSI and the car exploded after 23 1/2 minutes of testing. The car disintegrated into 128 identifiable pieces. The farthest was located approximately 1,300 feet from the test pit. Very few pieces remained in the pit but all pieces were recovered. The tank contained about 15,000 gallons of propane at the time of the explosion. The rest had vented through the relief valve during the test."

The second test took place in the HTA on Dec. 6, 1973 using a railcar with a 1/8-inch thermal coating. The coating delayed the opening of the relief valve. It opened 15 1/2 minutes after the test start so there was a significant difference when compared to the first test. In addition, the tank didn't explode until more than 93 minutes into the test. It was a marked improvement over the baseline.

When the tank finally exploded it only held 1,200 gallons of propane, so there was a much smaller explosion. The railcar was broken into just a few pieces and only two pieces left the pit.

Distant Runner

In 1981, White Sands was home to the Distant Runner Aircraft Shelter Test Program involving the Air Force and a dozen other agencies. The Defense Nuclear Agency was the sponsoring agency for these five tests conducted near SW 70 just off of Range Road 7. The test site was called Queen 15.

The Air Force has hardened aircraft shelters they use all around the world. The shelters are designed to protect valuable aircraft and explosives from outside explosions – think enemy or terrorist attack. At the same time, the shelters are meant to lessen the effects of an explosion from inside

Pop-Up: *The term "SW 70" refers to the southwest corner of the 70-mile impact area. In the early days of the missile range, the land was divided into impact areas based on their distance from the launch complexes on the south end. So, through the heart of the range, there were 30-mile, 50-mile and 70-mile areas that were basically rectangular in shape. Since these were impact areas, it would have been dumb to put camera sites in the middle of them. Instead you stayed on the edges or on the corners. At SW 70 there is an abandoned optics site that includes an old building.*

the hangar – maybe an accident or attack detonating stored munitions.

Based on earlier tests using a completely different shelter, the Air Force was restricted on how close these shelters could be placed to each other. Officials felt the new shelters, third generation, were much better and could be moved closer together.

The Air Force was interested in this because space at many of its bases was getting tighter and tighter. There wasn't enough room to scatter the shelters out over a large area. Also it was a way for the Air Force to deal with other encroachment. As populations have grown, bases that were once on the edge of town or out in the country are being surrounded by golf courses, shopping malls, and neighborhoods filled with houses.

Tests using real shelters and various-sized explosions were needed to gather enough data to see what the restrictions should be. For the test series, DNA leveled a small piece of land to build two of the Air Force third-generation hardened shelters.

The first three events were explosions outside

the shelters in different locations. The first was composed of four Sidewinder missile warheads – equal to about 42 pounds of explosives. The next two were each 120 tons of ANFO.

After the first of these large ANFO explosions, the missile range newspaper reported the blast left a crater 160 feet across and 15 feet deep. The crater was deep enough that it broke through to the water table. Witnesses said the water and sand mixed in the crater to create a "giant bowl of chocolate pudding."

The fourth event was the placement of 12 MK-82 bombs inside one of the shelters. The structure was destroyed in the explosion as debris distances were carefully measured.

The finale was to explode pallets of 500-lb. bombs and a fighter in the hangar to measure surrounding damages. There were 48 MK-82 bombs in the shelter for the test.

For this test on Nov. 18, 1981, the Air Force invited the news media to watch.

It was impressive. We were located over a mile away but could clearly see the remaining concrete hangar. They gave us a countdown and at zero the building disappeared in a cloud of fire, smoke and dust. Even from our distant vantage point we could see some large chunks of concrete fly out of the cloud.

When the smoke cleared the building was gone. We then bused the media down to the hangar to look at the remains. The only thing left standing was a reinforced concrete doorway that was extra heavy. The floor of the hanger was intact except where the two pallets of bombs sat. On those spots there were neat rectangular holes punched through the concrete to the desert sand underneath. Nothing remained of the fighter.

In the end, the results supported the Air Force reducing the distances between shelters in uninhabited areas but would not support any reduction in distances involving inhabited buildings.

Large Blast Thermal Simulator (LBTS)

After almost 20 years of outdoor high-explosive

tests, the Defense Nuclear Agency switched to a more controlled, laboratory-type method for conducting such experiments. They built the world's largest "shock tube" on the northern fringe of the missile range near Stallion Range Center.

Called the Large Blast Thermal Simulator (LBTS), it is big – very, very big. When it became operational in 1995, the $6.5-million LBTS doubled the size of any similar facility in the world.

The LBTS was not a new concept. It is a shock tube in which experimenters can simulate the blast and thermal effects of a nuclear explosion without any radiation. At LBTS compressed gas is explosively released at one end of a concrete tube. It rushes down the tube striking a tank, aircraft, or some other object with tremendous force.

According to Major Dave Swann, a DNA official during construction, the LBTS is capable of simulating the shock wave from a 600-kiloton nuclear blast. By comparison, the yield of the Trinity Site nuclear test was a mere 20 kilotons.

In addition to the shock effects, powdered aluminum and liquid oxygen could be sprayed into the air and burned near the test item to simulate some heat effects of a nuclear explosion. This burn usually took place for a short duration just before the shock wave struck the test item. It is similar to the initial heating from a nuclear fireball which is followed by the collision of the blast wave.

This capability was eventually removed when the facility turned more toward simulating smaller conventional explosions.

In the 1970s and 80s, DNA conducted large outdoor explosions to get these kinds of large blast effects. With LBTS they planned to schedule up to 150 separate tests a year. Since the tests are conducted indoors in a very controlled, repeatable environment, testers are able to collect precise data on the survivability and vulnerability of a variety of military systems.

Basically, LBTS is a semi-circular tube or tunnel about two football fields long and 32 feet high in the center. It is oriented on a north/south axis with the driver section at the north end and the exit on the south. Toward the south end is a test chamber where hardware is placed for the experiments.

The driver section or business end of LBTS consists of nine driver tubes that store and then suddenly release highly pressurized gas. The tubes are essentially storage tanks of varying lengths with the longest one being 145 feet. Each is six feet in diameter and has walls two inches thick.

The driver tubes are filled with pressurized hot nitrogen. Liquid nitrogen from a cryogenic storage system is passed through a heated pebble bed that raises its temperature to a maximum of 700 degrees F. and turns it to a gas.

The gas is pumped into the tubes. A maximum blast requires a total of about 25,000 gallons of liquid nitrogen. The pressure inside the tubes can reach 2,250 pounds per square inch (PSI).

The trick is then to release the nitrogen from all nine tubes simultaneously to form the appropriate shock wave. To do this, the diaphragms on the ends of the tubes are opened instantly with explosives.

These diaphragms are not simply blown apart with the explosives. Instead, each diaphragm is cut or scored from the center to the edges so there are lines of weakened steel radiating to the edge. They are a bit like the perforations in paper that makes it possible to cleanly tear a sheet from a tablet.

When the small explosive charges are detonated, the diaphragm splits along the scored lines and simply peels open like the petals on a flower. By doing this, the diaphragm opens but remains intact, and no debris flies down the tunnel to strike the test item.

After its release, the nitrogen rapidly expands down the reinforced concrete tunnel until it strikes the test item in the test section. This section of the tube is not concrete but is constructed of three-quarter-inch steel plate.

Test items can be subjected to pressures ranging from two to 35 PSI, depending on the test parameters. To put that in perspective, most wooden structures like frame houses would be destroyed when subjected to pressures between two and three PSI. When built, DNA reported typical tests would require operating pressures in the 12 to 15 PSI range.

In the test section, because of the old thermal radiation source, there are 454 ejectors in the steel walls. These vents were used to clear the smoke from the burning aluminum as quickly as possible from a burn.

Beyond the test chamber, the blast of nitrogen continues down another 100 feet of tunnel to the end of the shock tube. As the gas exits into the open atmosphere, it can create a vacuum in the tube that wants to suck air back into the tunnel. When this happens, the experiment can be ruined. To prevent this, a "rarefaction wave eliminator" can be rolled across the exit for each test.

It lets the blast wave out but prevents a return wave from entering. This device looks and acts like a giant Venetian blind. To withstand the forces involved, it is made of heavy-duty steel and weighs more than 400 tons. It has louvers that are open when the test begins. As the shock wave passes through the open louvers, they can be closed in 30 milliseconds to block any large amount of air headed back in.

An entire test is over in a matter of seconds. One of the BIG things about the LBTS is the amount of energy being safely handled. When the compressed nitrogen is released, gigantic forces are unleashed which are contained in the massive structure of LBTS.

In simple terms, there is a recoil in the system just like when firing a shotgun. The nitrogen bursts out the end of the shock tubes just like the pellets in a shotgun. Like the shotgun jolting against a hunter's shoulder, the LBTS driver tubes push north in their frames. But the force is so great here, it is more appropriate to talk in terms of rocket engines - big engines.

According to design calculations, the driver tubes can generate about 33 million pounds of thrust when opened for a maximum shot. This is equivalent, just for a second, to the thrust at liftoff of five space shuttles blasting away from Cape Canaveral.

With forces of such magnitude, the designers had to insure the driver tubes and their framework would stay put. The tubes are anchored in a massive concrete reaction pier. The pier contains 860,000 pounds of steel reinforcement alone and enough concrete for a building one-half block long and five stories tall.

As the nitrogen exits the driver tubes, it also exerts tremendous pressure on the floor and walls of the semicircular shock tube. The floor at that point is about 12 feet of solid reinforced concrete. Initially the tube walls are about 10 feet of reinforced concrete and taper down to a thickness of three feet for most of the tube's length. The thick floor and great mass of the reaction pier transfers much of the energy to the ground.

It all adds up to a lot of building material. It is estimated it took almost 47,000 cubic yards of concrete and seven million pounds of steel rebar for the massive structures of LBTS.

The only problem with the state-of-the-art facility has been a decided lack of customers. When LBTS was first envisioned there was still a Cold War. By the time funding was acquired, environmental work done, and the actual construction completed, the Cold War was passé. Most defense organizations haven't been interested or don't have the funding to see how their equipment would fare on a nuclear battlefield.

Some testing was completed in the first few years, but the facility was essentially mothballed for a time. In the meantime, DNA was reinvented and evolved into the Defense Threat Reduction Agency (DTRA). This organization deals with the threat of weapons of mass destruction and the menace of terrorism.

The LBTS can still be used to simulate a nuclear or large-scale conventional explosion, but it is also used to simulate terrorist attacks. For instance, specially designed, blast-resistant walls and windows have been exposed to blast effects in the tunnel. Many organizations are concerned with protecting people inside buildings from explosions on the outside. Before constructing a building based on theory and intuition, it would be better to actually test the components to see how they hold up.

A section of wall and its windows can be erected inside the tunnel. Strands of detonation cord (det cord) can be hung nearby as the explosive source.

Det cord is simply a long skinny tube filled with explosives. It can be wound around trees to cut them down or it can be used to trigger larger explosives. When strands are hung in a frame and all the strands detonated simultaneously, a nice even shock wave is created to hit the test item in the LBTS. It is much cheaper and easier to use than the nitrogen-charged tubes.

With a few simple tests, a customer can evaluate the survivability and vulnerability of their design.

Nike Hercules Tests

On May 22, 1958, a team was making modifications to the Nike Ajax missiles on station near Leonardo, New Jersey. As they worked on one of the missiles something horrible went wrong and it exploded. This set off a chain reaction causing the warheads in several other nearby missiles to explode which ignited many of the missile boosters. At the time of the accident most of the station's missiles were out of their magazines and sitting on the surface.

When the explosions were done and the fires out, six soldiers and four civilians were dead. Homes and vehicles in the neighborhoods surrounding the site suffered damage. The Army ended up paying thousands of dollars for broken windows and other more serious damage.

Concerns about such an accident at a Nike site were voiced early in the 1950s by community leaders across America when the plans for the missile sites were released. On June 2, 1958, *Newsweek* magazine reported the Army had claimed in 1953 that such an accident was impossible. The article noted an Army brochure on the Nike system that said the missile site "is as safe as a gas station." *Time* magazine cited the promise and mockingly said, "Last week the gas station blew up."

Given that Nike Ajax was soon to be replaced with Nike Hercules and its capability to carry nuclear warheads, *Time* magazine said, "In the wake of Leonardo's explosive afternoon, it is going to be hard to convince the neighbors in New Jersey – or around Nikes guarding 22 other U.S. industrial complexes – that living alongside atomic warheads was still like living beside a gas station." The Army was suddenly on the spot to make sure neighbors were safe.

Initially, when developing the Ajax, each missile site was supposed to occupy 119 acres. It gave military planners the safety cushion they calculated they needed. But was that enough? *Time* reported debris from the New Jersey explosion raining down three miles away.

In urban areas like Brooklyn, New York and Chicago, a hundred acres was simply impossible. The real estate was too valuable and in some cases not even available.

Designers came up with a compromise idea of storing the Ajax missiles and warheads underground, in magazines, and taking them to the surface using an elevator system for actual launches. This reduced the safety area needed for each site to just 40 acres – a number much more acceptable to community leaders.

To test this new design, an underground magazine and elevator system was constructed and tested at White Sands in 1953. Successful testing allowed the Army to start deploying the Nike defensive system in 1954 with the first site located at Fort Meade, Maryland. Eventually several hundred sites were established to protect military targets, population centers, and industrial areas.

The underground magazine used in the concept tests at WSMR still exists on the west edge of LC-33.

The system didn't work in New Jersey because the missiles were all up on the surface.

A Nike Hercules missile on its launcher at WSMR's LC-37 in July 1971. Some of the concern about the safety of these missiles was linked to their size. The vehicle was 41 feet tall and its conventional warhead contained hundreds of pounds of high explosive. Couple that with rocket motors filled with a few thousand pounds of propellant and you have the makings for a pretty sizable accidental explosion and fire. WSMR photo.

At the time of the accident, the Army was starting the process of replacing the Nike Ajax with the new Nike Hercules. The Hercules was a totally new missile. It was much larger than the Ajax giving it a significantly greater range. In addition to carrying a conventional high explosive warhead, it could be equipped with a nuclear warhead as well.

It was obvious from the May 1958 incident that accidents can happen. Officials decided they needed new tests to determine what the standoff distance should be for the Hercules sites. Two full-scale tests were conducted at White Sands to collect data for making the plans.

In an area now occupied by the Electromagnetic Radiation Effects facility north of U.S. Highway 70, the project built three underground magazines to each hold a normal complement of six Hercules missiles. The magazines were constructed of reinforced concrete and included an adjoining crew shelter.

Although the site was set up for three tests, only two were conducted.

At the time of the tests, the calculated standoff distance for neighboring inhabited buildings was 528 feet. For each test, eight houses were constructed around each magazine at a distance of 528 feet. The houses were arranged in pairs on cardinal points, one brick and one frame building in each pair.

Only 20 houses were actually constructed because the second magazine, sitting between the other two, was to share two pairs of houses with the other sites.

Each house was two stories tall and had a full basement. All houses had four rooms on each floor and each living room had a brick fireplace.

The first test was conducted on March 23, 1959, the second one on April 20. In both tests, the missile warheads exploded and the booster motors exploded or burned. Both magazines were totally destroyed basically leaving nothing but a crater filled with shattered concrete and debris. The crew shelter was flattened as well. It was surmised that no one underground in the shelter would have survived.

The houses suffered varying degrees of damage, none of it serious. Windows facing the magazine were blown in as well as the front doors. Some of the roof rafters were broken from the shock wave and from impacts by flying debris. Some chunks of debris were found well beyond the houses.

The conclusion about damage to the houses,

however, did not speculate on possible injuries to people living in the homes. Glass in the windows was blasted clear across the rooms. What would have happened if some unsuspecting soldier was looking out a window at walkers passing by when the explosion had occurred? The person probably would have been sliced and diced.

The testers concluded that at a distance of 1,500 feet, the houses would have suffered no significant damage from blast or debris, probably not even window breakage. They estimated the magazine and its heavy walls and ceiling absorbed 60 percent of the energy from the explosion.

Later, two of the houses left standing were incorporated into the Electromagnetic Radiation Effects site and used as office space. Those houses, one brick and one frame, are still there today.

Project Banshee

Over the years most explosion tests at White Sands involved placing the explosives on the ground or atop towers. Another example was a series of TNT explosions sponsored by the Air Force Special Weapons Center in Albuquerque. These tests started on April 6, 1961 and ran through the year. They involved charges ranging in size from 10,000 to 15,000 lbs. of TNT. The tests were conducted to measure "blast wave phenomenon."

However, sometimes the military researchers wanted data about explosions that are difficult to measure. For instance, at the beginning of the 60s all the military services and the Defense Atomic Support Agency were interested in explosions at very high altitudes, the kind of altitudes one might encounter with a missile intercepting another missile - somewhere in the 100,000-foot range.

The bottom line was finding out how destructive the explosives would be in a rarified atmosphere against enemy vehicles and what might be needed to improve U.S. weapons used in such situations.

Making something explode at 20 miles up in the sky was fairly easy to accomplish, but they had to figure out how to get sensitive instruments close enough to accurately measure the shockwave, photograph the fireball, and gather other data. The obvious answer was to use high altitude balloons to suspend everything.

A series of tests dubbed "Project BANSHEE" in 1961 and 1962 was the result. "BANSHEE" was an acronym for Balloon and Nike Scaled High Explosive Experiments.

The basic idea was a series of balloon flights originating from off-range sites like Hobbs and Artesia, New Mexico and some on the missile range itself. The balloons carried 200-foot-long trains of control equipment, instrumentation to measure the blast effects, cameras, and a sphere containing 500 pounds of high explosive. Pentolite was the explosive used because it is not too sensitive nor is it that difficult to detonate. As Goldilocks might say, "It was just right."

In the first tests, the explosive charge was the last item on the train of equipment hanging down from the balloon. In other tests, the explosive charge was rapidly moving because it was delivered to a spot in space near the balloon's instruments by a Nike Hercules missile.

Looking at the summary, this looks like a pretty simple test. However, like most tests at White Sands, when you look at the details you see all kinds of preparatory planning, testing and safety issues to overcome. To the engineers the checklist and its challenges can be daunting.

For instance, the safety issues on these tests proved interesting. To begin with, the testers needed a place for their launches that met the regulatory requirement for safely storing and handling 500-lb. explosive charges.

Since the balloons were launched outside the missile range and travelled through public airspace over ranches and communities, the testers needed permission from the Federal Aviation Administration. Before they launched balloons loaded with explosives, they had to conduct a number of flights using ballast to demonstrate their designs were sound.

The explosives hanging from the balloons were to be set off with a radio command. That meant designing a communication and control system that would not allow premature detonation with the broadcast from a neighboring HAM radio operator.

Launching the balloon train turned out to be quite a challenge as well. Getting balloon payloads safely off the ground has always required special techniques, but this one was exacerbated by the 500 lbs. of pentolite at the bottom. When Joe Kittinger lifted off under a balloon, his gondola had to be protected so it wasn't damaged. It certainly didn't pose the same threat to the support team as having a bomb dangling in front of them.

When everything was laid out on the ground, testers had an empty balloon on one end and a cable stretched for 200 feet with the equipment and explosive attached along it. The problem was that when they inflated the balloon it started to rise, straight up if there was no wind. As the balloon went up, the cable would be dragged along the ground to catch up with the balloon. That meant all that sensitive gear and the explosive sphere would be bounding along the desert floor before getting airborne. Not good.

Early on, balloon launch teams figured out how to deal with this problem. They developed launch racks where much of the balloon train could be folded or coiled up under the balloon. When the balloon lifted, the train would unfold and follow.

They held the balloon until it was filled with the appropriate amount of helium. Then they let it slowly rise a bit to get the top part of the instrumentation train out of the rack and up in the air.

The rest of the train was held in the air by its tail by a crane with a tall boom on it. When the balloon was finally released, the crane would be driven toward the balloon at the right speed and, if successful, keep the rest of the equipment off the ground. The crane operator would release the end of the train as he got directly under the balloon.

When you watch video of balloon launches, this is how Joe Kittinger got off the ground. For Project BANSHEE, the question arose concerning the 500-lb. bomb being next to the crane and the guys operating it.

Testers put their heads together and came up with the idea of using an old modified M-48 Army tank as the launch vehicle instead of a crane. Testing proved men inside could survive an accidental detonation of the explosives, so the tank was used for the launches.

Two full-scale dry run flights, reaching an altitude of 78,000 feet, were conducted out of Hobbs in July 1961. The first successful test flight was Bravo 4 which flew on July 24, 1961 and terminated over WSMR after reaching an altitude of 78,000 feet.

After two more launches from Hobbs, the program moved to Artesia to be closer to WSMR and to launch bigger balloons. On Sept. 11, 1961, a 200-foot-diameter balloon called Bravo 7 reached an altitude of 101,500 feet. However, it never reached WSMR and was detonated 12.5 miles northwest of Artesia. The program then established a launch site on White

Sands, since upper level winds weren't cooperating and were blowing the balloons back to the east.

A total of 11 Banshee tests were considered successful with some detonations occurring 15 miles above the desert floor. According to a published "preliminary report" from the Defense Atomic Support Agency called, "Project BANSHEE Field Operations, 1961 and 1962" dated May 1963, the results of the tests were being used "to determine scaling laws for detonations in a rarefied atmosphere."

Flagpole

Finally, here is another kind of explosion – the kind delivered by Zeus. In the middle of the afternoon on April 16, 1958, a Wednesday, the flagpole in front of the headquarters building at White Sands was struck by lightning and destroyed.

The post newspaper said hundreds of workers in Bldg. 100 and the surrounding buildings were shaken by the flash and immediate explosion of thunder. Many thought a missile had malfunctioned and crashed in front of the building. Actually, because of the approaching storm, missions on the range were postponed.

Electrical power was knocked out in headquarters and several other structures in the immediate area. Bldg. 100, however, had backup generators and was able to keep the lights on.

The newspaper reported the top third of the 90-foot pole was splintered. Chunks of wood from the pole were recovered over 100 feet away.

April is an odd time to get a thunderstorm in southern New Mexico since most are generated by the heat and humidity found here in July and August.

A month later, in May, a new 100-foot telescoping flagpole was installed and ready to use.

25

Rocketing Into Space

The Birthplace Of America's Space Activity

For almost 2,000 years, Western Man was stuck with Aristotle's vision of how the universe was constructed and what made it tick. It was a philosophy rather devoid of any science.

Aristotle reasoned that the earth was the center of the universe and it was surrounded by a series of spheres - perfect ones no less. On these spheres the sun, the moon, the planets and the star field were mounted. The spheres continuously rotated which is why the sun and moon came up in the east, traveled across our sky and set in the west.

This arrangement made the ancient Greek story about Icarus possible. In the myth, Daedulus and his son Icarus were held captive by Minos on the island of Crete. To escape, Daedulus fashioned two sets of wings that attached to their bodies with wax.

Before they flew away, Daedulus warned his son not to fly to close to the sun. Icarus, however, being a typical youth, ignored the wide advice of his elder when he discovered the joy of flight. He went too high, got too close to the fiery sun, the wax melted, the wings fell off, and he crashed into the sea and drowned. In Aristotle's world this made perfect sense because the sun was mounted on a sphere not very far away - you could get too close simply flying up like a bird.

In addition, Aristotle said there were four elements and that everything was composed of these. The elements were fire, air, water and earth. The heavier an item, the more earth it contained and the more fire in an item, the warmer it was. Supposedly the human body contained all four elements; we are all different because of the many possible mixtures using more or less of each element.

There was a fifth element called aether which was a perfect substance making up the spheres around the earth.

To make it all go, he posited there was a prime mover outside the last sphere energizing the system. When Christianity rediscovered the Greeks, religious leaders latched onto Aristotle's scheme and made god, with a capital G, the prime mover.

By the time Copernicus and Galileo came along in the 16th century, not only was there no science in this Rube Goldberg arrangement, it was absolute Church doctrine backed up by the muscle of the Inquisition.

Toward the end of Galileo's life, he discovered what would happen to suggest Aristotle was wrong. Using the observations from his telescope and his mathematical calculations, he demonstrated that the sun was actually the center of the solar system. Of course, he could not convince the Church which had a thousand years invested in Aristotle.

His fame saved his life, but he was required to recant his ideas and suffer house arrest for the remainder of his life.

Isaac Newton eventually annihilated Aristotle's ideas. It left curious people wondering what was up there, in the sky. Unfortunately, they didn't have many tools for finding out.

Early on scientists climbed mountains to measure temperature and barometric pressure, and to gather gas samples at altitude. Then some clever people devised ways to send the instruments even higher using balloons. By the end of the 19th century, scientists were launching "sounding" balloons with these instruments and attaining altitudes of 50,000 feet. It was a pretty good effort but it was a long way from reaching Space.

Sounding Rockets

Thanks to the U.S. Army's Colonel Toftoy and others, the German V-2 rocket at White Sands was turned into a "sounding" rocket. Just like the balloons, the rockets carried sensitive instruments to take measurements in the upper atmosphere, much higher than ever dreamed possible.

The word "sounding" was used to describe this type of balloon or rocket because it is an old nautical term meaning to measure water depth. In this case, the term was broadened a bit to simply mean taking measurements of all kinds, deeper and deeper into Space.

This idea of using rockets to take measurements in the upper atmosphere continues today at White Sands. Because it is such a simple and solid idea, the sounding rocket program at White Sands has continued since its V-2 days and is the longest running program at the Range.

In fact, the rockets have taken on new uses within the program. For example, the testing of materials in microgravity can be done in a sounding rocket. Also, astronomy packages have been sent aloft to gather data about the sun or other stars light years in the distance. It is a tool limited only by the imagination of the experimenter.

Relative to other methods of putting a payload up, like the old space shuttle, the rockets are a fairly inexpensive and quick way to send a package to altitudes ranging from 75 miles to hundreds of miles straight up. In addition, the packages can be recovered within the hour and the analysis started.

Aerobees

James Van Allen was one of the scientists involved with V-2 payloads who realized the limitations of using the old German rocket. During World War II, Van Allen joined the Applied Physics Labo-

Pop-Up: One of America's greatest authors was familiar with sounding water depth and stole some of the terminology. When steamboats plied the Mississippi River, the leadsman would drop a knotted and weighted rope into the water to measure its depth. The info was used to avoid running aground. The depth was measured in fathoms (about six feet per) and he would call out the depth as "mark one," or "mark two" and so on. Sometimes older words crept into the process and instead of two, "twain" was substituted. So a depth of 12 feet or two fathoms would be called out, "By the mark, twain."

Samuel Clemens, a former riverboat pilot, took one of these calls for his pen name – Mark Twain.

ratory at Johns Hopkins University where after the war he organized and directed some of the scientific experiments flown on V-2s. Eventually, he chaired the government's research panel for some time that divvied up the V-2s to various experimenters.

Early in the program he suggested a smaller rocket be designed specifically to carry experiments aloft. He was familiar with the Navy's Bumblebee missile development and Aerojet's WAC Corporal, so he drew up a proposal to the Navy to marry the two designs.

Van Allen went on to scientific fame when his rocket-launched payloads discovered the radiation belts surrounding the earth that now bear his name. Also, he and his students built a cosmic ray detector that flew on America's first satellite, Explorer I. During the 1950s, his stature rivaled that of Wernher von Braun in the United States.

Van Allen's rocket was dubbed the Aerobee – a portmanteau using the words Aerojet and Bumblebee. It was about 25 feet tall, weighed in at about 1,600 pounds, burned liquid propellants, and was built to carry a 100-pound payload to an altitude of 75 miles. It required a booster and a tall tower to keep it stable at launch. The first full-up flight was conducted at White Sands on Nov. 24, 1947.

The Aerobee turned into a great success with hundreds launched. In addition to the Navy, the Air Force and Army used them as well as NASA later on. Foreign countries bought them too for conducting their own experiments. It was the primary sounding rocket in the 1950s and wasn't completely retired until well into the 1980s.

According to George Helfrich, who worked for the Applied Physics Lab from Johns Hopkins University in support of the Navy at White Sands, the Aerobee totals were just over 1,250 flights worldwide with 675 of them sent aloft at White Sands.

In addition to its great reliability, the Aerobee was successful because it was constantly being improved and modified to meet the needs of experimenters. There was a whole series of Aerobees starting with the basic model followed by the first variant, the Aerobee Hi. With the Aerobee Hi, payloads could be boosted to altitudes around 150 miles. In fact, it was later called the Aerobee 150. These were followed by the Aerobee 170, Aerobee 200 and Aerobee 350.

Earlier, the Air Force had no luck bringing back mice and monkeys from high altitude flights using V-2 rockets. In 1951, they finally succeeded using an Aerobee rocket launched at Holloman Air Force Base with the payload landing on White Sands. It was the first time biological experiments were recovered alive after a flight into "Space."

The Aerobee was so successful it put another Navy sounding rocket development out of business. In the same timeframe, the Naval Research Laboratory was developing a sounding rocket called the Viking that was designed to carry a payload larger than 100 pounds, more like 500 pounds each time.

Originally it was going to be called Neptune but was changed to Viking when the project discovered the Navy already had an airplane called Neptune.

The rocket started out as a tall, pencil-like vehicle standing over 48 feet high and only 32 inches in diameter. Later it was reworked into a shorter, squat-looking vehicle only 41 feet tall but 45 inches in diameter.

One of the great innovations incorporated into the Viking was the use of a gimbaled rocket motor for stability instead of using the graphite vanes mounted in the exhaust like a V-2.

Viking flights started at White Sands in 1949 and ended in 1954. Some successfully carried large payloads but only a dozen or so were actually flown.

At White Sands each Viking propulsion system was static fired before an actual launch. To do this, the vehicle was bolted down over the flame bucket at Launch Complex 33, the Army's launch area, or at Launch Complex 35, the Navy's copy of the Army's arrangement.

On June 6, 1952, Viking 8 was being static tested when the rocket broke away from its mooring. Since it was a static test, the vehicle had no nose cone and there was no radar or other Army instrumentation running to keep track of the Viking as it lifted off the pad.

The personnel inside the blockhouse were safe and were smart enough to remain there because they had no idea where the Viking was headed. After many seconds, they felt a thump as the rocket crashed harmlessly to the desert floor about five miles away.

When I gave tours to the launch complex, I would often joke that the Navy might still hold the world altitude record for a "static" firing.

Even after the close call with the V-2 fired from the deck of the U.S.S. Midway, the Navy tried another sea launch using the Viking. The firing took place from the deck of the U.S.S. Norton Sound on May 11, 1950, off the coast of California. Great care was taken to factor in the ship's movement at the instant of liftoff. It was very successful as the Viking reached an altitude of 105 miles over the Pacific.

In the end, the Viking was too expensive and too complicated to be competitive. Also, experimenters learned to design smaller packages for the Aerobee as it kept going higher and higher. However, the Viking did have another life as it was chosen to be the first-stage motor for the Vanguard program later in the 1950s.

As the sounding rocket program evolved, the Navy kept its finger in the pie. Early on, the Navy became the missile range's sponsor for programs wanting to launch a payload. It continues that role today.

Over the years, quite a variety of rockets have been built to launch payloads, so many we could take several chapters on just the vehicles, but the process and its goals are pretty much the same as they always were. After the Aerobee there was a succession of rockets ranging from the Astrobee, Viking, Nike Apache, Super Arcas, and Aries to the vehicles of choice today, different versions of the Black Brant and Orion.

Sometimes the military will have packages for sounding rockets like the time an Aries lofted a target and kill vehicle into the upper atmosphere, so they could be tested in the microgravity of Space. Most of the time the payloads and rockets are sponsored by NASA. The payloads themselves are often built by students at various universities or researchers at institutions with ties to NASA.

So, in the end, you might see a payload built by graduate students that will look at the sun's corona at noon. NASA sponsors the rocket and the Navy sponsors them onto White Sands, an Army installation. On top of that are various contractors hired to provide support. So it turns into a truly collaborative scientific effort.

A Black Brant 9 sounding rocket is launched off of a rail at the Navy's LC-36 on Dec. 5, 2003. The Terrier booster accelerates it quickly, burning for only a few seconds. It then falls away as the Black Brant's motor ignites. The rocket was launched about 1 p.m. and carried a solar ultraviolet mission. This configuration of a Black Brant and Terrier booster stands 40 feet tall on the rail and can reach an altitude of 180 miles. NASA photo.

Comet Hale-Bopp

What kind of science? Comet Hale-Bopp grew into big news after it was discovered on July 23, 1995. Given its orbit around the sun, astronomers realized it would be bright and very visible for a long time. In fact, in the first part of 1997, observers in the northern hemisphere enjoyed it for months as it outshined everything in the night sky except the moon.

The comet was discovered the same night by independent "local" observers. Dr. Alan Hale observed the comet using a telescope from his home in the Sacramento Mountains just above Alamogordo, New Mexico. Thomas Bopp, an amateur enthusiast, observed the comet using a borrowed telescope while out with friends in Stanfield, Arizona. They were declared co-discoverers by the International Astronomical Union and both of their names were affixed to the comet.

The unexpected comet gave scientists a great opportunity to study its makeup. One way to glean more information was to send up instruments using sounding rockets launched from places like White Sands Missile Range.

The light coming from the comet was much more extensive than just what was visible to the naked eye while standing on the earth's surface. Our atmosphere filters out most of the ultraviolet light, not enough to prevent a sunburn but enough to keep us from being fried. That filtering robs us of valuable information about the comet's makeup.

A way around this issue was to send up the instruments in rockets so they were above the atmosphere where they could catch all the incoming ultraviolet light. At White Sands, NASA sponsored four sounding rocket launches in the spring of 1997 as the comet passed only 85 million miles from the sun. This was the comet's "perihelion," its closest approach to the sun.

The first White Sands launch was on the night of March 24 with a payload from the University of Colorado. The next night, a rocket was fired with instruments from the University of Wisconsin. The third launch was on March 29 with a package from the Southwest Research Institute in San Antonio, Texas. The final shot was April 5 with a payload from Johns Hopkins University.

The experiments were launched shortly after sunset on two-stage Black Brant sounding rockets.

The payloads reached altitudes from 175 to 240 miles and landed back on the missile range following a parachute descent.

Specifically, the instruments were looking at the ultraviolet light from the coma and tail of Hale-Bopp. Each experiment had about five minutes for data collection.

The experimenters were trying to determine the origin of the comet and, possibly, the early composition of the universe. What they learned complements information gathered from other sources such as the Hubble Space Telescope (HST).

As an example, according to Dr. Alan Stern of the Southwest Research Institute, they were looking for the emissions of noble gases like argon and neon. At the time he said no one had ever seen these gases before in a comet. If found they might provide clues as to the origin of Hale-Bopp.

In the summer of 2000, after a careful analysis of the data, Stern and his associates announced they had detected argon in the comet. In fact, they found an "abundance" of argon.

In a news release from Southwest Research Institute on June 5, 2000, Stern is quoted as saying, "Our results indicate that Hale-Bopp was likely formed in the Uranus-Neptune zone" of our solar system. The release concludes, "The high argon abundance of Hale-Bopp may also explain the unexpected findings by the Galileo Jupiter probe, which found that Jupiter has an argon abundance similar to Hale Bopp." Stern then surmised Jupiter was seeded with extra argon by the impact of many comets like Hale-Bopp early in the history of the solar system.

In addition to this kind of scientific research, the sounding rocket program has created opportunities for the science and military communities to reach out to school children and the public. For the Hale-Bopp launches, the missile range hosted visits by several groups of school kids. They were able to visit with the scientists beforehand and then watch the launches from just a few miles away.

Both Hale and Bopp showed up for some of the flights, talked to kids, signed autographs, and were generally treated as rock stars.

Also, the general public was invited out each night to watch the launches from the safety of the main post on White Sands. A briefer was on hand to provide background information and a countdown so visitors knew what was going on.

A curious person might ask how an instrument flying 200 miles above the earth gets focused on a comet or any other light source in the big sky. With computers and the appropriate sensing devices, the onboard system can point the instrument in the general direction of the target. After that, it still takes a human being to find the one you want.

I once escorted a film crew to a University of Colorado shot at White Sands and got to see how that final bit of aiming is done. The payload was built by Colorado graduate students under the direction of their professor. They were looking to collect information from a single star with the data going into the lead student's PhD thesis.

When you think about it, this is a tricky proposition. When you look into the dark sky above the earth's filtering atmosphere, there are millions of stars visible in that huge umbrella that hangs over us.

For a human, the only way to recognize the target is to recognize the stars and their patterns around it. But that is impossible if you consider the whole sky.

For this reason, scientists and engineers have developed an onboard aiming system that points the instrument in the right direction as the rocket drifts to its apogee. Once the camera is pointed in the right area, it is up to a controller on the ground, running a joystick, to maneuver the

> *Pop-Up: These visits by the kids were desperately needed. After receiving a briefing about the comet and what the rockets, with their payloads, would be doing, one teacher actually asked a scientist if the rocket would be able to bring back a sample of dust or gas from the comet's tail.*
>
> *Now, we always liked to say there are no dumb questions but the questions sometimes illuminate the reasoning ability of the asker. In this case the teacher just heard a briefing about a comet tens of millions of miles away and how our rockets would go about 200 miles up and come back down a few minutes later.*
>
> *Her question was probably akin to asking a kicker in football if he could kick a field goal through the posts in New York from Los Angeles. With such ragged thinking on the part of teachers, no wonder many American kids are way behind their foreign contemporaries.*

payload so it points exactly at the target. This takes much practice in a simulator because there is no time for learning on the job. The controller only has about five minutes to acquire the target and gather the data because what goes up is shortly coming down.

For the University of Colorado grad student it was crunch time. He was locked away in a dark room with his professor looking over his shoulder. There were to be no distractions from friends or family.

In the end he did fine. He quickly acquired the target and they were able to collect data for several minutes. Afterward it was time to pop the corks on the champagne.

Calibrating Satellites

Also, sounding rockets are still used to measure the gases in the atmosphere. Years ago, the ozone layer of our atmosphere was in the news as measurements showed this protective layer was thinning. It is a major filter protecting us from that ultraviolet light that is capable of blistering our skin in a very short time.

Data about the concentrations of ozone in the atmosphere came from satellites looking down through the air from orbits high above. The satellites were not directly sampling the gas but were using other passive methods.

The average American just assumes the instruments work and they don't sweat the details. However, the question arises about how to calibrate these instruments. Any instrument has to be calibrated when it is built. You have to know that when your bathroom scale says you weigh 155 pounds, you really do weigh that and not 185 pounds. You have to make sure it is measuring what it is supposed to measure.

An instrument can fall out of adjustment after it is used frequently or if it is just left sitting around for a long period. This leads to incorrect readings. So, to make sure your readings are correct, you frequently measure some known quantity and make appropriate adjustments. For our bathroom scale example, you might calibrate it using a piece of iron you know weighs exactly 100 lbs.

For a satellite spinning high above the earth measuring something as fluid as a layer of gas, calibration is a bit of a difficulty. The problem has been solved by using sounding rockets launched from places like White Sands.

It's a pretty simple idea. At the time a satellite measuring the ozone layer is directly overhead, a sounding rocket is shot through the ozone layer to take actual measurements of the gas's concentration. The scientists then compare the results. If there is a discrepancy, it is probably the fault of the satellite since the rocket's instrument was calibrated just before launch.

The controllers can then reset the satellite's equipment to correctly read what it is seeing.

We know from the many Space shots since the 1960s that objects orbiting earth are subjected to just a fraction of the gravity we feel at the surface. Astronauts have spoken about it as one of the wonders of going into Space - effortlessly floating from point to point.

Scientists and engineers have been interested in the effects of microgravity for decades. Medical researchers have wondered if drugs or cell cultures might be different when manufactured or grown in a microgravity atmosphere.

When President Ronald Reagan's administration pushed for the commercialization of Space in the 1980s, engineers wondered if you could manufacture perfect spheres and beams in the microgravity of Space. Some sounding rockets were launched at White Sands during this time to find out.

Fire in Space

After the Space Shuttle program began, NASA had questions about what would happen if there was a fire onboard the spacecraft. Most people's reaction was that it would be catastrophic due to all the oxygen on board. What made it worse was that the astronauts would have no place to go.

Initially, NASA couldn't conduct live fire tests on the shuttle itself as that was considered just foolishly dangerous. Instead, NASA launched a series of payloads on sounding rockets at White Sands to see what happens if there is a fire in Space.

I was at the Navy launch complex for one of these launches and chatted up one of the experimenters. What he said surprised me because it is something we don't ordinarily think about. Yet it is so incredibly simple, it calls for a self-inflicted head slap.

For their tests, the engineers mounted pieces of plexiglas in the payload and provided a way to light it on fire. Cameras and other devises were in place to capture the resulting conflagration.

He explained they used plexiglas because it was a much studied material with lots of test data behind it. It had been studied and repeatedly analyzed so they didn't have to do much background work.

During the first flight, they learned the plexiglas wouldn't burn. It would initially ignite and then go out when in Space.

My fire tutor then went on to explain that gravity really is the fourth requirement for fire as we understand it. As kids we all learned that fire required fuel, heat and oxygen. These were all present in this payload, but the plexiglas wouldn't burn.

It turns out gravity is needed to create the air currents that whisk away the exhaust gases and allow oxygen in to keep the proces going. This is obvious when you light a match or a candle. You get a nice teardrop-shaped flame with the hot exhaust gases rising and the cool air containing oxygen coming in from below.

This mechanism needs gravity to work. Because of gravity we have an up and a down. Down is the source of gravity's pull and up is away from it. Smoke and carbon dioxide bubbles in Pepsi go up. Bowling balls and glaciers go down.

In Space there is no up or down because gravity has little or no influence. When you light a match in Space, you get ignition and very quickly the flame will be snuffed out. This is because the off-gases like carbon dioxide and smoke from the initial flame don't have an up. They spread out equally in all directions and cut off the flow of oxygen to the fuel. They form a cloud around the ignition spot and, presto, the fire is self-extinguishing.

To overcome this, the NASA testers resorted to mounting a fan in their payload to blow the exhaust gases away and move oxygen in.

Measuring Shock Waves

Finally, some sounding rocket payloads don't carry any sensitive payload at all. Toward the end of my time at White Sands (2005 and 2006), a series of launches was conducted to simply carry a known amount of explosives (70 lbs. TNT) to a given altitude (about 20 miles) and explode it.

Of course this wasn't just for the fun of it. A group of scientists was studying infrasound and trying to calibrate their ground listening stations with an explosion with a known yield, known location in three dimensions, at a known time. As the scientists develop their sensing stations, they should be able to calculate position and size of an explosion from the signals they receive.

Infrasound consists of the very low frequency waves generated in the atmosphere by explosions or similar events. The audible part of an explosion disappears pretty quickly, but the infrasound can travel huge distances. In the case of a volcanic eruption or nuclear test, delicate instruments can detect it halfway around the planet.

Picking up these sounds, recording them and then analyzing them can get difficult because of the many possible sound sources and the obvious variability of the atmosphere itself with different winds, temperatures and pressures. Early on, for example, scientists realized their equipment in Hawaii was detecting the regular impact of waves crashing against the island's cliffs. They need a baseline to be used in measuring other noise.

With an array of sensitive microphones spread throughout the Southwest, scientists were able to create their own controlled explosions over White Sands and then compare the data to natural events like meteorites exploding in the atmosphere and volcanoes spewing rock and ash.

The Launch Facility

Most of these rockets are launched by the Navy at its Launch Complex 36. The facility is equipped with support buildings for assembling rockets and payloads, a concrete blockhouse, and a number of launch towers and rails.

One old structure is the Aerobee 350 tower that was used for launching other sounding rockets in addition to the Aerobee series. What makes it interesting is that the launch tower is completely enclosed by a building. The structure acted as an environmental shelter for the rockets, their payloads and the crews assembling everything. When it came time to fire the rocket, large doors were opened around the building to allow the sudden buildup of hot gases to escape as the rocket left the pad.

Currently, sounding rockets are mostly launched off of rails. The rocket bodies are equipped with lugs that protrude just a bit and fit into a channel on the rail launcher. The rocket is assembled by simply sliding the pieces together, in order, on the rail and bolting them together – often, the second stage simply rests on top of the booster. This is done with the rail in the horizontal position so everything just slides on while the rail is just a few feet off the ground. Everything is very accessible.

The whole contraption is covered with an environmental building that can be rolled out of the way on launch day. The building provides protection for personnel and equipment from the wind, sun and rain.

The old launch tower and the current rails are adjustable because rockets are rarely launched in a perfect 90-degree, straight-up angle. First of all, range officials want the payloads to come down toward the middle of White Sands where there is no one to injure and very little infrastructure to damage. Depending on winds, the tower or rail can be tipped toward the north and the middle of WSMR.

Secondly, the launchers have to be tilted to take into account the cross winds at various levels, especially near the surface. Since a sounding rocket is unguided, crosswinds can greatly affect where it goes. When the rocket is at its slowest speed as it leaves the tower, the winds can cause the rocket to tip into the wind, and it will actually fly off-course against the wind. This may sound counterintuitive, but the fins at the bottom of the rocket have a much larger surface area than the rest of vehicle. That means the winds will push the bottom further to one side than the top – it tips to one side. The tipping points the rocket into the wind and possibly off course.

Using a special computer program, the launch crew plugs wind data from a nearby "met" tower and upper level balloons to calculate the wind direction and speed at many altitudes. The computer then spits out how many degrees to tilt the tower to make sure the parts and pieces stay on the range.

The met tower at LC-36 is 500 feet tall. Most people assume it is some sort of radio tower. Actually, it is there to provide a platform for a series of anemometers from the ground to the top. Its data feeds into the blockhouse for the crew's use.

Apollo and Orion

In 1963, NASA constructed a research facility on the western edge of White Sands Missile Range. It is a few miles north of the little town of Organ and sits at the western base of the San Andres Mountains.

Prior to this, White Sands had a small play in the first American manned space flights. For the Mercury flights where Glenn, Carpenter, Schirra and Coo-

per orbited the earth, White Sands provided radar tracking when the capsule passed nearby. The vehicle was acquired using its telemetry signals. A position was then calculated and a FPS-16 tracking radar was pointed to that spot in space. About 75 White Sands personnel were involved in each mission.

The same support was then provided for Gemini flights. For all these missions, the post newspaper ran a short article announcing the mission and the range's role.

The NASA facility is called the White Sands Test Facility (WSTF) and is part of the Johnson Space Center. It was built to provide laboratory facilities for the testing of Apollo program propulsion systems and the materials used in the spacecraft. It has grown over the decades supporting programs such as Viking Lander, Cassini, the space shuttle, the International Space Station and many more.

Over the years, the facility has tested hundreds of different rockets motors with millions of firings. To simulate the lack of an atmosphere in Space, NASA built vacuum chambers for the testing of rocket engines in conditions their vehicles might encounter in orbit or on the way to the moon.

These large vacuum chambers are driven by nothing more than steam. The high-pressure steam is channeled out a nozzle. Connected to the nozzle is a pipe connected to the test chamber. As the steam blasts by the opening, it sucks the air out of the pipe and, in turn, out of the test chamber.

Besides being a simple system, the setup also vents the chamber of the rocket's exhaust gases as it fires.

The materials testing at the facility gets into the nitty-gritty of what goes into space. On one tour I took of the facility, we were told of an early example of why everything, and they mean everything, has to be tested before it is launched.

The example involved something as mundane as the ink used to label all the switches and lights in a Space capsule. In one instance, the manufacturer of the ink changed the formula, apparently in an attempt to make it more readable.

When the newly printed labels were tested in a vacuum chamber, researchers found the ink gave off significant amounts of a gas that would be noxious to astronauts. It was not a fatal situation but one that could cause membrane irritation for humans breathing in the fumes.

As a result, NASA notified the manufacturer who went back to another formula that proved more stable in a vacuum.

Sometimes, NASA's WSTF has sponsored programs requiring space or facilities on the missile range. One of those programs was the testing of the Apollo Launch Escape System (LES).

The Apollo program was dedicated to landing Americans on the moon and was the culmination of President Kennedy's challenge to do it by 1970. Preparation for the Apollo flights progressed in the 1960s through a series of programs, Mercury and Gemini, that put Americans into Space longer and longer and with more complicated requirements.

One of the riskiest parts of any space flight is the launch. Rockets have been known to malfunction, break apart or just blow up. For the Apollo launches, because of the size of the crew capsule, a bigger and better LES needed to be built and tested.

The LES consisted of a tower attached to the top of the crew capsule. Solid-propellant rocket motors were mounted on the tower which could be quickly fired in an emergency. The rockets were designed to lift the capsule away from the main vehicle and boost it to the side and out of the way. Then parachutes were to be deployed for a soft landing back near the launch point.

The NASA WSTF was too small for the planned tests of the LES, so they were conducted on the missile range at what is now LC-36. One remnant of the test series is a large assembly building at the launch complex with the big red NASA letters on the side.

There were seven firings at White Sands for this program. There is sometimes a bit of confusion when referring to it because of the different scenarios. Also, some people will talk about it as NASA's Little Joe II launches at White Sands but that is only part of the picture.

Basically NASA wanted to test the LES under the various possible conditions that might require its use. That meant firing the LES before the booster rockets ever left the ground and also firing it during various stages of flight.

For the first condition, the LES with a mockup of the capsule was fired while it sat on the launch pad. There was no rocket under it. These were dubbed the Apollo pad abort tests and were conducted in November 1963 and June 1965.

For the second condition, NASA jury-rigged a booster from a bunch of smaller engines, tying them all together into one unit. They called it Little Joe II and it stood in for the mighty Saturn rocket.

Before the Little Joe II could be used in a test of the LES, NASA launched one at White Sands to make sure it performed as advertised. This successful flight was performed in August 1963 and confuses things a bit because it was the seventh test in the program.

There were then four tests of the LES utilizing the Little Joe II vehicle to simulate Saturn liftoff conditions. These took place on May 13, 1964; Dec. 8, 1964; May 19, 1965; and Jan. 20, 1966. The last one went the highest as the abort system wasn't activated

The first Little Joe II launch at White Sands on May 13, 1964. WSMR photo.

until 73 seconds into the climb. In fact, for this flight, the Little Joe was equipped with additional rocket motors to provide a second-stage lift.

Now, fast-forward 45 years to an almost identical test by NASA at the missile range. On May 6, 2010, the Orion Launch Abort System was successfully tested at White Sands from a pad at Launch Complex 32. From a distance it looked very much like the Apollo escape system tests.

At the end of the 20th century, NASA was looking for a replacement for the space shuttle. The shuttle vehicles were old and had outlived their usefulness. Something new was needed.

In the first decade of the 21st century, NASA selected its next crew launch vehicle system and dubbed it "Ares 1." The plan was to return to having the astronauts ride atop a rocket, much like in the days of Apollo, in a capsule named "Orion."

In other words, NASA was returning to the simple days of putting a manned vehicle atop a big, expendable rocket and propelling the crew or payload (depending on the mission) into space. The Orion capsule could be configured to deliver crews to the space station and bring them back to earth using a parachute system or provide the setup to send crews to the moon or Mars.

Like the old Apollo system, Orion was to have a launch abort system. In its simplest terms the Orion was to have a tower mounted on top of it equipped with rocket motors and a parachute package. In the event of an emergency, the rockets could be used to pull the capsule away from the Ares booster and then safely parachute the crew back to earth.

The first test of this system was like the first pad abort test for Apollo where the system was activated as it rested on the concrete pad and not atop a booster. However, the Orion test involved three different rocket motors. According to a NASA news release after the test, the "abort motor produced a momentary half-million pounds of thrust to propel the crew module away from the pad. It burned for approximately six seconds."

Simultaneously with the abort motor, the attitude-control motor was fired to keep the capsule on a controlled flight path away from disaster.

Finally, a "jettison motor" was activated to pull the entire abort system off of and away from the capsule so the parachutes could be deployed.

Since then, the whole Orion project was put on hold by President Obama as he proposed using commercial vehicles to lift men and material into Space.

The Space Shuttle

Lamentably, 30 years of space exploration using the world's first reusable spacecraft ended on July 21, 2011, when the space shuttle Atlantis touched down in Florida. It also marked the end of nearly four decades of shuttle support by White Sands Missile Range, the birthplace of America's space activity.

Many people are aware that the space shuttle Columbia landed at White Sands on March 30, 1982 on just the third flight for the program. However, the missile range's involvement in the shuttle program long preceded the system's first launch in 1981.

As early as 1976, White Sands agreed to allow NASA to use Northrup Strip, in the middle of the old Lake Otero lakebed, as a shuttle pilot training site. The Northrup runway was originally used to launch and recover drones. In preparation for the shuttle pilot training, the strip was lengthened to 15,000 feet. A second runway was added and training began in Oct. 1978.

Yes, the name of the strip is misspelled. Apparently Northrop Corp. used the runway but somewhere along the line the company name was misspelled in a news release and on maps. Maps are really hard to change so the misspelling stuck.

In 1979, the two runways were designated an alternative landing site for actual shuttle missions. To accommodate this move, the runways were stretched to 35,000 feet. That's right, seven miles. They started life being 100 yards wide but were widened to 300 yards later.

In 1970, NASA conducted the first of a series of one-tenth-size scale model drop tests of the shuttle over the Northrup area. The 13-foot-long models were dropped from an Army CH-54 "Sky Crane" at an altitude of 12,000 feet above sea level. According to NASA, the aerodynamic tests were "designed to demonstrate the vehicle's transition from a steep re-entry angle of attack to a level cruise attitude and its stability in stalled conditions."

In 1989, a third runway was added to the system. This was a short, narrow runway to simulate an emergency landing in Morocco.

The scenario for such an event was called "Trans-Atlantic Abort Landing" and was based on the shuttle having engine failure during launch and not being able to reach orbit. There were a number of these launch failure possibilities and subsequent emergency procedures. If the shuttle wasn't very high and was still intact, it was supposed to separate from the fuel tank and boosters and land back in Florida.

If the shuttle was high enough and had enough energy, it was to glide across the Atlantic to reach the Morocco site.

Finally, if the shuttle was just short of orbit, the protocol was for an "Abort Once Around" landing. For an AOA, the shuttle would have enough energy to circle the earth once and land back in the United States. Because of the launch angle and lack of maneuvering possible in such a situation, White Sands was frequently designated the prime AOA site. Both NASA and WSMR often had people on call or on site ready to respond.

Early on in the program when shuttle flights still attracted the public's attention, our Public Affairs Office sometimes had news media camped at our door ready to go just in case there was an AOA situation.

The shuttle landing strip was managed by NASA's White Sands Test Facility located on the western edge of WSMR. The range's NASA tenant was responsible for much more shuttle work than just the landing strips.

For instance, each shuttle was equipped with small thrusters that were tested at WSTF. These little guys were part of the Reaction Control System and were scattered around the body of the shuttle to turn and move it just a bit when docking with other vehicles or retrieving something like a satellite.

Also, at the back of each shuttle were two "Orbital Maneuvering System" rockets that were tested at WSTF. When you look at the back of the shuttle you see the three large rocket engines that are used at launch. Just above them are the OMS rocket pods.

The OMS engines had enough juice to move the shuttle to a higher orbit. Also, on every mission they were used as big brakes to slow the shuttle down so it would fall out of orbit and begin its descent through the atmosphere.

To understand why the shuttle Columbia landed at White Sands, you need to go back to catch a little historical perspective. Its a case where NASA was answering critics who said space exploration was burning up money with its boosters and other throw-away equipment.

NASA came back by advertising that the very expensive space shuttle was to used as a "space truck." They said they would be hauling cargo into space for all kinds of organizations and nations and they would run it on schedule just like a trucking company.

You have to remember this was early on in Ronald Reagan's presidency and one of his major themes was to make government more efficient, more like private enterprise. NASA was trying to fit in by comparing itself to United Parcel Service.

The other major factor was that the program was still testing these new vehicles and managers wanted to land on the dirt of dry lakebeds instead of unforgiving short, hard concrete runways. So, the first series of missions was scheduled to land on Lake Rogers at Edwards Air Force Base in California.

At the time, the public was excited by the shuttle program. This was the next great thing after going to the moon. For instance, after the early shuttle missions, NASA announced when and where the Boeing 747 would be as it hauled the shuttle back to Florida. People all along the route would step outside their homes and offices hoping to catch a glimpse of it as it went by. In the Las Cruces/El Paso area we were sometimes lucky to have the 747 actually land in El Paso to spend the night before flying on to Florida.

When it came time for the third mission, NASA ran into a problem. Seasonal rains soaked the lakebed at Edwards making it way too soft for a shuttle landing. They could have opted for a concrete runway landing but that was completely outside their safety directives.

At the same time, their "trucking" schedule was looming. The public needed to see they could keep to the schedule. So instead of delaying, they decided to launch on time and land at their backup dirt runway, Northrup Strip at WSMR.

The announcement about the new landing site was made by NASA on March 18, 1982 – four days before the launch on the 22nd.

Almost immediately phones started ringing in my office and other places on range. Most of our calls were from news media wanting to know where White Sands was and how they could get onto the facility to report on the landing.

The public called as well, wanting to know if they could come and watch. The Air Force and NASA had already set a precedent to allow public viewing with the first two landings at Edwards. On the first mission, when John Young and Bob Crippin landed

Columbia on Rogers Lake on April 14, 1981, over 200,000 people were on hand to watch. Some estimate the crowd was closer to 300,000.

At first, the shuttle program was hugely popular. Witnesses raved about the double sonic boom that accompanied the shuttle as it glided out of the clear desert sky headed for Edwards AFB. The California landings were huge "geek" festivals. Eventually, the effort to go and see a "truck" land lost its luster.

Our office immediately went into overdrive working with NASA and just about every major WSMR organization to figure out how we were going to take care of the reporters. We had to get them registered, keep control of them, move them about, and provide all kinds of support.

Of course, Public Affairs was only one organization. Gary Lindsey, a National Range engineer, estimated about 1,000 missile range employees were busy at one time or another supporting the shuttle mission. The school kids even got involved. Their moms and dads baked cookies and brought boxes of them to our building for the news media.

One of the major problems for us in Public Affairs was the early announcement. On March 18, they announced Columbia was coming to WSMR, but the landing wasn't scheduled until the 29th. That meant just about every news agency and outlet in the U.S. and the free world had the opportunity to get themselves to New Mexico.

In the end, close to 900 people registered as "media" types. A lot of these were support personnel and not reporters. Why all the support? For instance, the three networks each brought in a huge house trailer and planted it at Northrup. They built wooden platforms on top to mount cameras and have a place for their reporters to report from.

Public Affairs allowed Associated Press into our building (Bldg. 122) to construct a dark room in the back where the old Officer's Club kitchen was located. Running water was the key ingredient.

So we had all these people descending on WSMR from all over and it was days before the landing. They needed to file stories daily with their newspapers, news services and radio/television stations about what was going on. They needed to justify their existence in New Mexico.

It was perfect as it turned into an ideal opportunity for WSMR to tell its story. NASA didn't seem

Space Shuttle Columbia touching down at Northrup Strip on White Sands on March 30, 1982. Afterward the landing facility would be renamed the White Sands Space Harbor. WSMR photo.

to care what we did with all the local and regional reporters. Because they were only interested in the three broadcast networks, it fell to us to keep all the other folks busy and informed.

We were not NASA spokespeople, so we arranged for the reporters to visit and interview missile range personnel on our preparations for the landing. We escorted groups of reporters to watch the commo guys setting up radios and landlines out at the site, to get a demonstration by the meteorology guys of weather balloons being launched, to record the explosives ordnance disposal teams recover and dispose of ammo, to talk to the engineers blading and smoothing the runways, and to visit the WSMR test nerve center, Range Control, Bldg. 300.

There was so much time to kill, we even took loads of people to Trinity Site and Launch Complex 33 to show them the range's two National Historic Landmarks.

Most of the reporters were thankful and loaded us up with souvenir pens, hats, t-shirts, etc. Afterwards, for a couple of years, I jogged in a t-shirt from a radio station in Portland.

My favorite story about a reporter was a woman from the *Los Angeles Times* who showed up at our office to register about a week before the landing. I happened to be in the office that morning when she reported to Debbie Bingham.

Debbie explained there were Army buses running from our office out to the site, about 40 miles, and they ran from early in the morning until well past sunset. The reporter asked when the next one would leave.

Taking a look at the woman's nice dress, stockings, high heels and expensive leather briefcase, Debbie suggested she might want to change her clothes and come back later in the day – after all, nothing was going to change in a couple of hours.

The woman became a little agitated and said she needed to see the site immediately and would take the next bus. She left in a huff.

In the afternoon I was back out at Northrup and ran into Ms. LA Times. She was carrying her shoes because the heels sank into the sandy soft spots. Her stockings were all frayed and coming apart because of the gypsum abrasion. Also, the breeze was picking up the dust and her makeup seemed to be a magnet. Her cheeks looked like the cracked mud at the bottom of a dried puddle.

I didn't see her again until landing day. Someone said she returned to Los Angeles to write an obituary for someone famous. On landing morning I saw her again and was surprised. She must have been a horse person. She was wearing those jodhpur riding pants that balloon out above the knee and are tight below the knee so they can be tucked into tall riding boots. The boots were an improvement over the high heels.

She wore a matching shirt and topped it off with a real, honest-to-God pith helmet. It looked silly, but I'm sure it was more comfortable than her previous outfit.

One of the neat historical artifacts from the event we displayed in the White Sands Museum was a model of the space shuttle created by local artist Bob Diven. Diven still lives in Las Cruces and is known as a painter, writer, performer, editorial cartoonist, musician and street artist.

He was helping one of the TV stations at the site. During his down time, he built the model using manila folders, foam coffee cups, and other debris he found.

While all this media babysitting was going on, the decision was made to allow the public in to watch the landing. Major General Alan Nord, White Sands commander, made the announcement at a news conference in our conference room on March 24.

I distinctly remember the news conference because our office prepared Nord for the event. It was my first close encounter with a general where we gathered rather informally and talked about formats and what to expect.

We hashed out details and told him we would prepare a list of 10 to 12 questions with appropriate answers for the conference. He came by our office the night before and we went through the Qs and As. He seemed a bit nervous as he had never done anything like it before. We reassured him and told him to study the answers.

At the news conference, when the general opened it up for questions, we all listened to see if we had calculated correctly on what reporters wanted to know. It was amazing. The first four or five questions were right off our list. As Nord fielded them you could see him visibly relax. He had the answers and it was easy. I think they asked eight out of ten on our list.

Adding the public to the landing created a whole new level of complication. Folks were allowed to drive to the northwest corner of Lake Otero where they were seven miles northwest of where the landing strips crossed. An instrumentation site on the edge of the lakebed was the focal point.

In preparation, the Explosive Ordnance Disposal (EOD) personnel walked and cleared a square mile of lakebed to make sure it was safe. One of my days escorting reporters involved taking a van full of them to record the soldiers doing their job.

As we drove across the lakebed to get to the EOD guys, we drove by a belt of cartridges sticking out of the dirt. I left the CBS television crew there so they could photograph while I got a couple of EOD techs to come look at it. Before I left, I hammered home the warning about the explosive dangers on the missile range and they were not to touch anything. We'd been hitting them with that day after day.

I came back to the site with a couple of soldiers who made a nice show of delicately lifting the belt a bit so they could make an identification. The CBS cameraman was all over it, right down in the dirt with the tech.

The reporters were told what it was and how it probably got there. Finally, one of the techs gently pulled the belt out of the moist ground and carried it over to his pickup truck.

In the meantime, all the reporters were focused on one of the guys talking about EOD. I kept my eye on the soldier with the belt and about fell over laughing when he pivoted and made an over-the-head hook shot with the belt into the back of the truck. It crashed and rattled home but was never recorded on any camera.

To get to this viewing site, the public was told they could enter through the Tularosa gate, drive west to Rhodes Canyon Range Center and then south down Range Road 7 to the site. Security was a big, big deal. To make sure no one took off cross country from the paved road, soldiers and vehicles from Fort Bliss were positioned every few miles. They weren't just jeeps and trucks either. There were armored personnel carriers and other heavy vehicles mixed in the lot.

Reporters claimed that since the shuttle was a national asset, the security people had license to "shoot to kill" if anyone came too close to it.

The news outlets were given a much closer vantage point. They were located just east of the point where the two runways intersected. It was thought this maximized the possibility of seeing the shuttle no matter which runway was used or which direction it landed.

In addition to the news media watching from this sweet spot, VIPs were thrown into the mix - hundreds of them. Bleachers, more portable toilets and shelter tents had to be erected. Workers soon found out why Northrup Strip is the perfect natural surface for a runway.

The lakebed is gypsum-based with some sand, clay and other materials. Over the centuries the wet gypsum compacts and hardens to a density close to concrete. To make a runway you just have to wet it and blade it smooth.

Teams needing to erect tents or drive stakes for poles or dig holes soon found it was just about impossible. Jackhammers and drills were used to punch holes in the ground so the stakes could be driven home.

Having said that, the runways could be a little temperamental. When the gypsum dried out it began to flake away. When the winds blew, the gypsum sand went with it creating a blow-out or pothole.

That is exactly what happened on the scheduled landing day, March 29. By mid-morning the wind was howling. It was more than a typical spring day. The winds picked up the gypsum sands on the lakebed and lifted them to form a low-hanging fog bank.

Being from Nebraska, I experienced my share of blizzards. As I sat in a trailer at Northrup Strip I was reminded of January back home. The trailer rocked back and forth. The noise of the wind screaming around the windows was nonstop. Out the windows all you could see was white, not even the trailer next door.

The big difference, of course, was that when I went outside the wind was warm and gritty - no moisture, no biting cold. When I drove in it, I sometimes couldn't see the front end of my car and I opened the door to check road markings to see if I was on track.

Personnel everywhere scrambled for goggles to protect their eyes and dust masks to protect their lungs.

Because of the sand blizzard, the landing was postponed a day. The wind blew potholes in the runways and sand was drifting like snow across them in other places. The engineers went to work after the wind died down to move sand and fix the holes.

One requirement for blading the sand was to get it wet. Tankers hauled in water from a tiny well on Range Road 7 just north of Pony Site. The water had one remarkable trait. Because of its high sulfur content it smelled like rotten eggs.

Everyone was aware of the smelly water because we'd all been stuck, at one time or another, behind the tankers as the runways were initially prepared. It was pretty foul.

After the landing was postponed, the news media immediately started a joke saying they didn't see any reason to postpone the landing. Certainly, the pilot would be able to smell the runway even if he couldn't see it.

At the public viewing area, visitors suffered through the winds. Camper tops were blown off of trucks and people lost chairs and other light items as they flew toward Tularosa.

Everyone reloaded then and we tried again the next day, March 30. Since the weather forecast was for high winds again, NASA brought Columbia in earlier in the morning to make sure they got it on the ground before the dust storms cranked up. The shuttle successfully touched down at 9:04 a.m.

The mission commander was Jack Lousma and the pilot was Gordon Fullerton. They completed 130 orbits and traveled 3.3 million miles while circling the earth.

The WSMR landing was a bit different than all the other landings in the program. We were told Columbia would come from the west, we would hear a double sonic boom, it would make a big swooping loop turn to bleed energy, and then it would touch down on the north/south runway heading south.

We saw and heard most of that except for the big loop at the north end of the runway. Instead, Columbia came from the west and made a big right turn and shot for the runway. As a result, according to Al Paczynski, NASA's manager at Northrup Strip, the shuttle came in hotter than planned. When it touched down it was going close to 50 miles per hour faster than intended.

As Columbia rolled down the runway on its rear wheels, the nose started to drop. Suddenly we all saw the nose rise back up as if it was going to do a back flip. However, it quickly stopped going up and dropped back down hard onto the runway.

You can always distinguish the WSMR landing from all the others because of that little hiccup.

Fullerton later said he thought the nose was dropping too fast so he pulled back on the controls and brought it up but went too far.

We also learned the landing gear deployed at just 150 feet off the ground and locked in place only five seconds before touchdown. That was cutting it close.

Paczynski said the two rear shuttle tires left a great deal of burned rubber embedded in the runway where they initially touched down. He said he had workers cut out those blackened areas of the runway and gave small pieces to employees as souvenirs.

Once on the ground, the two astronauts were removed from the shuttle, given a quick health check, and then whisked to a ceremony near the media/VIP viewing area. Soon after that concluded, the winds started to blow again. By noon, we couldn't see the shuttle out on the runway from the press viewing area.

The winds continued for days. They plagued all operations at the site.

Public Affairs and other organizations didn't end their involvement with the landing. Columbia was towed to a "de-service" area to prepare it for its piggyback ride back to Florida. While this work was being done, NASA and WSMR allowed the public and WSMR personnel and their families the chance to ride a bus to Northrup Strip and look at the shuttle.

WSMR devised a schedule to run long caravans of buses from the main post out to the strip and back. Then we made up color-coded tickets for the different days and times and distributed them.

So the missile range's labors in supporting the mission of STS-3 didn't really end until Columbia flew away on the back of a 747 on April 6. It was a long few weeks and we were tired.

As a result of the flight, Major General Nord proclaimed the spot where Lousma and Fullerton rejoined their wives out on the strip as "Columbia Site." Also, New Mexico Senator Harrison Schmitt, a former astronaut who walked on the moon, introduced a bill that Congress passed renaming the old Northrup Strip as the "White Sands Space Harbor."

Lousma and Fullerton, along with their wives, flew into WSMR again on May 17, 1982 to thank White Sands for its support. They visited the school to talk to students, gave a slide presentation about their mission at the post theater, and shared their experiences again at a luncheon attended by 450 people.

Locally, people were quite excited about the Columbia landing. They eagerly looked forward to future landings at WSMR. Unfortunately, that was it.

There was a persistent rumor around WSMR that NASA never wanted to land at WSMR again because of the blowing dust. Apparently, when Columbia got back to Florida, the maid found gypsum in just about every nook and cranny in the shuttle. The rumor took on more urgency when it expanded to include NASA throwing away the engines from Columbia.

Sand was certainly a factor, but more important might have been the cost and time delay of landing at WSMR. The expense of moving a great deal of specialized equipment to New Mexico was huge plus getting two cranes to lift the shuttle onto the 747 became a major issue. The scuttlebutt was that it might take weeks to get the necessary cranes which would really put a crimp in NASA's scheduling.

However, the Space Harbor did serve as a backup landing site throughout the program. Improvements were continually made to keep it up-to-date.

For instance, lights were added so a night landing could be accomplished. This was a simple system that used huge xenon spotlights with a total of more than 11 billion candlepower.

The lights were mounted at one end of the runway and were tilted to shine parallel to the ground, down the runway. Along the edge of the runway were small stakes with reflective tape at the top. If a shuttle came into the runway at night, the pilot would see a long area at the beginning of the runway fairly well lit and then the edges lit by the reflectors, probably all the way to the end.

Also, the de-service area was moved west to the edge of the lakebed. In 1982, the blowing gypsum got into everything on the shuttle. By moving the preparation area to the edge of the runway there would be much less dust to contend with in the event of high winds.

The closest White Sands ever again came to hosting another landing was on Dec. 22, 2006. Bad weather at Edwards and in Florida made it necessary for NASA to activate the Space Harbor. We were told

The 747 carrying Columbia lifts off from Northrup Strip at White Sands on April 6, 1982. Columbia's landing at the missile range was the one and only landing of a shuttle at White Sands. WSMR photo.

it was landing on the 22ⁿᵈ come hell or high water because it couldn't stay up another day.

Our office notified the media and after lunch we took two buses of local and regional press out to our viewing area. At that point it was looking pretty good for a landing at WSMR.

As I got off the bus, my cell phone rang. It was my boss Larry Furrow who was at the NASA Ops center. He said Discovery had just completed a de-orbit burn for Florida. I said "damn" and went to tell the reporters to get back on the buses.

The value of the White Sands Space Harbor to America's space program certainly can't be measured in actual shuttle landings. In the end it was the training of the shuttle pilots that made the site important.

All the pilots trained to fly one of the shuttles in trainer aircraft that simulated the controls and actions of the shuttle. When the trainee sat in the pilot's seat, the controls were exactly like those found on the shuttle. They went so far as to cover parts of the cockpit windows to simulate the limited visibility found up front in a shuttle. They also modified the plane, a Grumman executive jet, to behave like a shuttle falling much like a rock out of the sky.

Over 85 percent of that training was done at WSMR. The pilots trained in all kinds of conditions – day, night, cloudy, head winds, tail winds, cross winds, calm – using the runways. According to NASA, the pilots "logged in more than 100,000 training runway approaches."

The pilots liked the Space Harbor. The runways were so long and wide, they were very forgiving. They said the old lakebed surrounding the Space Harbor was visible from an orbiting shuttle as a large white spot on the ground.

Even though the shuttle never landed at the Space Harbor again, it became a handy emergency landing site for military aircraft. Probably the most memorable one occurred in 1994 when a KC-135 lost a landing gear assembly on takeoff at Holloman AFB. The whole thing fell off leaving just a strut sticking down.

The pilot and crew spent hours flying around WSMR's airspace burning fuel and then finally landed at the Space Harbor. The pilot was able to keep the plane off the strut for sometime before she lost enough speed and had to set the plane down all the way. The strut plowed into the gypsum, acting as a huge brake on one side, and spun the plane around.

Not only did the crew survive but there was no serious damage to the plane.

On June 13, 2011, NASA held a farewell ceremony out at WSSH. Brigadier General John Regan, WSMR commander, was on hand to accept a commemorative plaque from NASA administrators for WSMR's support.

So what is the future for the Space Harbor? As of early 2012, it is up in the air. My guess is it will return to being a lakebed with the runways disappearing very quickly. NASA offered the facility to the missile range but WSMR had no money and no hot projects needing such a capability.

Lights out.

The Delta Clipper

By 1990, everyone realized there were two shortcomings to the space shuttle – it was fast becoming old and worn out and scheduling was unreliable. At the same time, the Department of Defense's Strategic Defense Initiative (SDIO) was interested in finding a new vehicle to replace the shuttle for servicing space-based weapons and other assets.

In 1991, McDonnell Douglas started building a demonstration vehicle for SDIO, calling it the DC-X (Delta Clipper-Experimental). The vehicle was the first of several planned vehicles designed to progressively work out the bugs of building something relatively inexpensive, compared to the shuttle, with a turnaround time of only hours for a return flight to Space.

The project tried to accomplish many firsts. The vehicle looked something like an obelisk sitting on its fat end (tail) which housed the rocket engines. It was launched in the vertical position, like most rockets, but also landed in the vertical position using retro rockets to set down. Although a very familiar idea from 1950's science fiction movies, this was a first in the real world.

Another goal was to eventually make Delta Clipper a single-stage-to-orbit vehicle. This meant there were to be no boosters in the final design. Nothing would fall off at launch, so when it returned from orbit and landed at its launch site, it could be refueled, restocked, recrewed and be ready to go again in a day or so.

This second goal has been a dream for decades but has been impossible to reach. The basic problem is the strong gravitational force of the earth. To put a reasonably sized payload into orbit requires a lot of thrust to overcome gravity's pull, which in turn requires a lot of fuel and a large heavy structure to hold it all together. During launches, by jettisoning pieces of that structure (spent boosters, empty fuel tanks, etc.) and burning fuel, the vehicle gets lighter every second and is able to eventually reach the speed needed for orbit.

In the 1990s, the dream was that materials technology, rocket engine systems and new fuels might be advanced enough to make the total package sufficiently light so nothing would need to be discarded.

In addition, the prototype was cheap. For instance, McDonnell Douglas used the avionics package from one of its jet fighters to control the Delta Clipper. It was much cheaper and faster to jury-rig an off-the-shelf system than design and build one from the basement up.

Testing of the vehicle at White Sands Missile Range began on Aug. 18, 1993 when the DC-X launched, climbed a short distance, hovered and then landed next to its launch stand. The total flight time was just under a minute.

The Delta Clipper generated a great deal of interest, especially among amateur Space enthusiasts. As a group they were called "Trekkies" after the popular television show *Star Trek*. They saw these tests as the next great thing after the shuttle, especially as it took off and landed on its tail. Calls came to the missile range Public Affairs Office from all over the world as Trekkies wanted to attend the launches.

Eventually some of them were invited – if they knew someone important or were representing a news media outlet. We were surprised at how many news outlets there could be.

After the third flight in 1993, funding from SDIO dried up. NASA stepped in and provided more money and made some changes. Eventually, they used Delta Clipper to test some new alloy components to make the vehicle lighter. For example, toward the end of the series the hydrogen tank was replaced with a McDonnell Douglas-built one made of graphite composite, and the oxygen tank was replaced with a Russian-built aluminum-lithium one. This series of tests changed the name to Delta Clipper Experimental Advanced (DC-XA)

Testing at White Sands resumed with the vehicle staying aloft longer, going higher, demonstrating its ability to move horizontally, and even rolling over on its side in one maneuver. On July 31, 1996 on its 12th flight, the Delta Clipper suffered a failure that doomed the vehicle.

When Delta Clipper was launched, it lifted off from a stool. When it landed, so it could put down

The Delta Clipper comes to a firey end on its last flight. In the photo on the left, the ship has toppled because one of the landing legs failed to deploy. It was a perfect landing, but the vehicle fell over after coming to a standstill. At right, the Clipper is just beginning to explode and burn. WSMR photos.

on any pad, it deployed four legs or landing struts – one from each corner. The McDonnell Douglas people who built the thing, being from an aviation background, sometimes called the legs "landing gears." On its last flight, one of those legs failed to deploy.

You can watch a video of the landing on *YouTube*. Just be sure you get one that includes the mission audio. As the vehicle descends, you hear one of the engineers call out "missing a gear." Pete Conrad, who was McDonnell Douglas's project manager, continues to call out the progress of the vehicle until it lands and the engine shuts down. It was a perfect flight and landing. Then as the Delta Clipper starts to fall over toward the corner missing its leg, another voice can be heard saying, "she's coming over." That is followed by a crash and explosion of fire.

The resulting fire was a conflagration of hydrogen and oxygen incinerating the vehicle. Afterward it was just a pile of charred metal.

How White Sands Got Its Own Flying Saucer

Back in the 1960s, in addition to taking a trip to the moon, NASA was making plans to send unmanned, exploratory spacecraft to Mars. Initially this program was dubbed "Voyager" but morphed into a smaller lander and was called the "Viking" program. Voyager was the term later applied to the flyby vehicles exploring the outer planets.

The NASA team planned to have their vehicle parachute to the surface of Mars after the 460-million-mile flight. Since Mars has a much thinner atmosphere than Earth, they couldn't slap some regular Earth-tested parachutes on the vehicle and call it good. They needed to design a different system and then test it.

For the test, they chose White Sands Missile Range. They built a "Planetary Entry Parachute Program (PEPP) Aeroshell to carry their parachute system. It was disk shaped and looked very much like the flying saucers portrayed in science fiction movies from the 1950s and 60s. Under it were several small rocket motors.

The lander simulator was carried aloft, starting in Roswell, under a huge, helium-inflated balloon. Upper level winds carried the package to the west over White Sands where teams of range employees were busy collecting data.

When the balloon reached an altitude of about 150,000 feet, the PEPP Aeroshell was dropped and the rocket engines ignited to push it even higher. It was at this point the parachute system was tested in the very thin atmosphere some 30 miles above the missile range.

The first test was conducted on Aug. 30, 1966. The other three were done in the summer of 1967.

The White Sands Museum has one of these PEPP Aeroshells on display in its Missile Park. Visitors usually refer to it as the "flying saucer" in the park.

A few years later, after the Mars lander program had evolved into the Viking program, NASA returned to White Sands to basically conduct the same tests with a different vehicle and parachute system. Four successful tests were conducted during the summer of 1972.

It all started to come together when Viking 1 was launched on Aug. 20, 1975 and Viking 2 on Sept. 9. Viking 1 entered Martian orbit on June 19, 1976 and Viking 2 followed on Aug. 7. Then, on July 20, 1976, the tests at White Sands were proven useful as Viking 1 successfully landed on Mars. On Sept. 3, Viking 2 landed as well.

Gil Moore's Satellites

Right now, three aluminum spheres containing a small amount of historical White Sands Missile Range are zooming around the earth going thousands of miles per hour. The spheres are part of an experiment to measure fluctuations in the density of the earth's upper atmosphere in response to blasts of energy and particles from the sun.

The aluminum balls are all 10 cm (4 inches) in diameter but each has a different mass: 1 kg (2.2 lbs.), 1.5 kg (3.3 lbs.) and 2 kg (4.4 lbs.). The spheres are hollow and use ballast that is a mixture of bismuth shot (the same stuff put in some shotgun shells) and sand from three significant historical spots. They were launched on Sept. 29, 2013 from California.

Gil Moore, the driving force behind this effort, put together the balls and paid for their launch into orbit. He collected sand from where Robert Goddard first launched his amateur rockets back in Massachusetts and from Goddard's launch area near Roswell. Also, through the efforts of some WSMR pioneers, sand from Launch Complex 33 and an up-range rocket impact area was collected for the effort.

Moore included sand from White Sands for the obvious reason that it is where America's missile and space activity began with WAC Corporal and V-2 firings. Also, Moore has past connections to the missile range - when it was still a "proving ground."

Moore was an engineering student at what is now New Mexico State University when the V-2 flights began at White Sands. He has said he was fascinated by the contrails left by the V-2s. The idea of big powerful rockets was a kick and the idea that the atmosphere was doing a variety of things at different altitudes was intriguing.

In April 1947, he went to work for the school's Physical Science Laboratory (PSL) and providentially he got to work the V-2 program. He reduced V-2 telemetry data (this means transforming the raw numbers and squiggly lines of measurements into concise and meaningful information), photographed the V-2 vapor trails to measure upper-level winds and got to install instruments and cameras in the rockets.

After graduating with a degree in chemical engineering, Moore signed on at PSL fulltime continuing his work with V-2s. Of course, the V-2 program ended soon but Moore continued to work with research rockets such as the Viking and Aerobee and was eventually supervising teams launching his own Pogo and Speedball rockets.

In the fall of 1953, Moore served on a panel of local experts to talk about rocketry, jet propulsion and space travel during a forum in Las Cruces. The meeting was sponsored by the New Mexico-West Texas Section of the American Rocket Society and included others from White Sands. Gushing about the event and possible Space travel, the *Wind and Sand* newspaper reported, "Mankind is on the verge of the most exciting, adventuresome and rewarding journeys he has ever made into the unknown."

Also on the panel were G. Harry Stine and Edward Franciso, Jr., both with the White Sands Electro-Mechanical Laboratories; Herb Karsch, special assistant to the White Sands commander; and Major D.G. Simons from the Space Biology Lab at Holloman.

Stine went on to become a prominent science and science fiction writer. Simons went on to direct the Air Force's Man High balloon project out of Holloman. In fact, he piloted the second Man High balloon flight that reached an altitude of 101,500 feet in August 1957. The balloon was launched near Crosby, Minnesota and came down near Frederick, South Dakota more than 32 hours later.

While at PSL, Moore continued his education with an emphasis in physics and astronomy. In 1962, he left Las Cruces to start a division of Thiokol Corporation in Utah. Since then he has served as an adjunct professor of physics at Utah State University and taught astronautics at the Air Force Academy in Colorado Springs.

After Moore retired in 1997, he and his wife Phyllis set up an all-volunteer space education effort. This is where Moore's years in the rocket and space business paid off with contacts all over the country.

Moore has become a bit of a wheeler-dealer using those contacts to develop educational programs that universities, small corporations and government

Gil Moore holding one of his three satellites. The aluminum spheres were launched into Space on Sept. 29, 2013. They should start falling back to earth in 10 years. Photo by the author.

432

agencies are willing to participate in, for free. For instance, the mechanism to deploy the spheres from the Falcon 9v1.1 rocket for this current mission was donated by a company founded by one of Moore's students from 20 years ago.

Prior to this, he was able to get NASA to launch a couple of his satellites from the Space Shuttle and one from an unmanned vehicle launched from Kodiak, Alaska, as part of his Project Starshine. Kids and volunteers from all over the world helped build the satellites by grinding and polishing the array of mirrors mounted on the satellites. Then observers on earth were able to track the satellites at sunset as they orbited overhead.

The orbit for the current spheres is 80 degrees off the equator so it not a true polar one that would pass directly over the poles. Also, the orbit is very elliptical. That means it is not a circle but a very lopsided oval. At the closest point to the earth (the perigee) the spheres are about 200 miles overhead. At their furthest point (the apogee), they are more than 900 miles out.

These distances are only true at the beginning of the experiment. Because there is some atmosphere out there at distances of even 200 miles, those gas molecules provide drag on orbiting objects and shrink their orbits.

In addition, most of us probably think of the atmosphere as pretty consistent, especially as you get away from the surface weather manifestations. But it isn't. Because of blasts of energetic particles from the sun, called coronal mass ejections, those upper levels compress and expand (dense and less-dense) and swirl.

If the sun is particularly active during the peak of its eleven-year sunspot cycle, the earth's atmospheric gas molecules are closer together. That, in turn, affects the orbit of a satellite or a piece of space junk more than during "average" times.

The Air Force is very interested in this phenomenon because they are charged with keeping track of all the stuff in orbit – everything from the junk nuts and bolts to the Space Station. This is critical to the health and welfare of manned vehicles like the Space Station and other valuable satellites. Using their radar observations and computer modeling, the Air Force is able to notify users like NASA that

they might have to use on-board thrusters to move the Space Station a tad just to guarantee its safety. It is simple collision avoidance but involves valuable assets travelling at high speeds.

To make sure these computer models are as perfect as possible, the scientists need to understand the sun's effect on things in orbit, especially as the sun's output shifts.

Moore's spheres are helping. During most of their orbit, the balls are outside the atmosphere and only dip into it on the approach to perigee. Powerful and precise Air Force radars are tracking the spheres over the next decade. The total time for each orbit will be well established.

Then, as the density of the atmosphere changes during the approaching peak of sunspot cycle #24, researchers will be able to see how that changes the speed of the small satellites and in turn the actual orbit.

In addition to the Air Force's radar tracking, students and amateur observers using "Go To" telescopes are being asked to provide optical tracking data. When married together, these many extra data points will provide an even better picture of what is happening.

Moore says over the years the balls will separate from each other because of their different masses. After about 10 years, depending on changes in the atmosphere, the lighter sphere should come out of orbit. The heavy one could stay up as long as 15 years.

According to Moore, the new rule for manmade objects going into low Earth orbit is that they have to come down and burn up in 25 years. He says it is called "design for demise." Since each of his spheres has a thin aluminum wall, they and the bismuth shot will burn up on reentry leaving a light scatter of sand to be spread over hundreds of square miles.

In 2013, those interested in the project could see and hear Moore talk about it in a short *YouTube* video called, "POPACS: Cooperative science of collision avoidance in space."

White Sands Missile Range has never been a major player in America's space programs. However, since 1946 the range has been a very active participant in this area and continues to make crucial contributions to learn more about the universe we inhabit.

26

Aliens, Balloons And John Stapp

The Real Story Is Better Than The Myth

Some might consider a chapter about the Roswell incident inappropriate for a history of White Sands Missile Range. However, having answered to the public and news media for 30 years, I can tell you the public considers White Sands part of the alien visitors mythology.

I don't know how many times I've been asked where we kept the alien bodies on ice, where we tested reverse-engineered spacecraft, did the White Sands radars track the Roswell UFO, or did a V-2 rocket get away and crash outside of Roswell.

Here's an example. A few years before I retired I received a series of emails from a young man asking why the government didn't release the records about UFOs and alien visits. He said the American people had a right to know.

Being busy with real work, I think I gave him some glib answer about having never seen such a record and I was, therefore, not interested. Eventually he sent me a link to a website with a video supposedly showing a UFO being tested at White Sands. He wanted my comments on this reverse engineering project.

I went and looked. What I saw was a shimmery white object, looking like a traditional movie-prop, oval-shaped UFO, flying toward the ground. The thing strikes the ground on its flat side and bounces into the air continuing from right to left as the camera pans to track it. Power poles appear as the camera follows it. Soon the saucer hits the ground nose on and breaks apart into a shower of white sparkling pieces.

I said, "That sure looks like some infrared footage of a test out here." I called the guys in Optics.

I asked them to take a look and see if they recognized the footage since they probably shot it. Their response was that they were not allowed to stream video from the web.

This was a basic missile range restriction to discourage employees from wasting their time looking at *YouTube* or porn videos and to keep the bandwidth uncluttered. I told them to consider it an official request since I was responding to a member of the public and to go ahead and look.

The response was quick. They were familiar with the video as it was shot on White Sands by Audio Visual and was from a missile test. Since it was infrared or thermal photography, the hot stuff, like a missile body and the hot air around it, appeared white. The heat made the missile body, which was mostly rocket motor, look like a flying saucer on the video because the whole thing was hot and glowing.

The object had no hard lines because the heat radiating from the missile body heats the air around it. That hot air shows up on the image and blurs the hard edge of the fuselage.

For data collection this setup makes a lot of sense. With a big telephoto lens on a camera, it can sometimes be difficult tracking a distant object, especially with lots of distractions in the background. Using thermal imaging, the object of interest, the missile, is hundreds of degrees warmer than anything else. Its stands out like a beacon. When this missile broke apart on impact, it was almost possible to count how many pieces of hot debris went airborne.

I emailed the young man the explanation without telling him which missile was involved. It didn't help. I got the same response I usually received from people who are fully involved in such things. He didn't believe me and simply accused me of being part of the government cover-up - case closed.

I find the story of a crashed UFO at Roswell fascinating for two very different reasons. The first reason is that most of the story can be traced back to military testing at the Holloman/White Sands complex. Most of the accounts, sightings and testimonials are based on ordinary people catching a glimpse of some of the cutting-edge work done here from 1947 to 1960.

The second reason is the wonderful insight into human behavior the legend provides. We are more sophisticated now than we were in the 50s and better understand how unreliable humans are as witnesses. Investigators have demonstrated over and over how easy it is to ask leading questions to get almost any response they want. Studies are showing that eyewitnesses are about as reliable as casting bones to read the future.

Understanding this doesn't make anyone a better witness, but it sure gives officials and all of us more ammunition when we want better proof than someone's simple say so.

An excellent example of this came to light a few years ago when we had a rash of news stories across the country about children being tortured and sacrificed to Satan at several daycare centers. What an uproar.

Of course law enforcement found no children missing, no children molested, no bodies, and no Satan worshippers running amok. It turned out that one or two people believed these stories and then asked kids and their parents some leading questions about the atrocities. Bingo, all of a sudden others swore they had seen these suspicious activities.

In a more alarming example, research in the past few decades is dramatically showing how unreliable eyewitnesses are in identifying criminals. It seems like every week we read or hear about some person convicted of a felony being released because DNA evidence proved they couldn't have done it or someone else confesses to the crime. Some studies are showing close to 50 percent of those falsely convicted were put in prison based on eyewitness accounts. To say that is scary is an understatement.

Balloons At The Beginning

One common thread running through my sum-

mary of what actually happened at Roswell is the use of balloons at the White Sands/Holloman complex to accomplish all kinds of experiments. In fact, for decades the high altitude balloon has been a workhorse for all the military services because the huge box of airspace over White Sands provides the perfect place to conduct inquiries.

The Roswell story begins with early balloons in June and July of 1947, less than two years after the end of World War II. It was a time when everyone was trying to get on with their lives after the war, to start anew with families, homes, schools and jobs. But life still had an edge to it. The Soviets were threatening and some people actually feared an invasion or, at least, waves of Russian bombers blasting northern cities.

In June 1947, a pilot in the air near Mt. Rainer in Washington spotted a formation of "saucer-like" vehicles flying near his airplane. He reported his sighting and it made national news. There was much speculation as to what he saw. Some of the leading theories were clouds, secret Soviet aircraft spying on us, and secret U.S. airplanes being tested. The idea he saw alien spacecraft was not a leading theory.

Meanwhile in southern New Mexico, rancher W.W. Brazel found some bright materials scattered across one of the pastures of the J.B. Foster ranch that he managed. He didn't think much of it but gathered up some of the material. In a July 9, 1947 article in the *Roswell Daily Record*, he was quoted describing the debris as "rubber strips, tinfoil, a rather tough paper and sticks."

In the article he described finding the material weeks before on June 14 and then bundling it together on July 4. The next day, he heard talk about the Washington "flying disks" while he was in Corona, New Mexico.

He dutifully went to the county sheriff in Roswell and reported he might have found one of the disks. The sheriff promptly contacted the Roswell Army Air Field and got Major Jesse Marcel involved. (From now on I'll attribute all Army Air Force activity to the "Air Force" since they broke away from the Army and became independent in 1947.)

Together, Brazel, Marcel and the sheriff went to the ranch to examine the debris. The Roswell paper reported, "When the debris was gathered up the tinfoil, paper, tape and sticks made a bundle about three feet long and 7 or 8 inches thick, while the rubber made a bundle about 18 or 20 inches long and about 8 inches thick. In all, he (Brazel) estimated, the entire lot would have weighed maybe five pounds." They put it in the backseat of one of the cars and drove it back to town.

Based on this initial report, they obviously didn't find the Starship Enterprise or even a WAC Corporal rocket for that matter. In fact, the article said they took the material and tried to reconstruct the "vehicle" as a kite but had no success.

The Roswell Air Force officials put the material on a plane and flew it to the Eighth Air Force headquarters in Fort Worth, Texas. There, according to another article in the July 9 issue of the *Roswell Daily Record*, Brigadier General Roger Romey, commander, explained the debris material was from a "harmless high-altitude weather balloon."

This is where the story gets interesting and where the UFO believers like to jump up and down, get red in the face and point out that the government lied. Yes, it did. It was just a little white lie – the kind we tell all the time to cover some sensitive activity that is exposed to the public.

In this case the material was not from a weather balloon but similar balloon materials and associated debris from Project Mogul. The similarity in the kinds of materials and the amount was considered close enough that a weather balloon story would provide the necessary disguise for the sensitive project. At the time, this ploy was used consistently to provide a reasonable cover story when classified programs popped up.

White Sands did the same thing just weeks before when a modified V-2, built up by Werhner von Braun's German scientists at Fort Bliss to test ramjet technology, went astray and crashed outside Juarez. The vehicle was called a Hermes II and was part of a sensitive project.

When it crashed it looked like a V-2 because it basically was one, just like a Mogul balloon train looked like a weather balloon with just more stuff. In the case of the V-2, it could hit the ground with the force of a 2,000-pound bomb, so not much was left but little pieces. It made perfect sense that the cover story released from White Sands was that a V-2 crashed in Mexico. It was simple and straightforward without getting deep into some sort of extravagant *X-Files* lie.

Two years before that, the military did the same

thing for the Trinity Site atomic bomb test on July 16, 1945. For this cover story, the news release stated a "remotely located ammunition magazine containing a considerable amount of high explosives and pyrotechnics exploded." No extravagant claims, just a fairly reasonable explanation for a bright light and a big boom.

So what was Project Mogul? If you are a little geeky or have a sciencey focus, this is probably more interesting than the UFO story. It was an attempt by scientists to detect the test of the first Soviet atomic bomb whenever that might be. Everyone knew the Soviets were working on the bomb, and U.S. officials were anxious to know when they would actually accomplish it. It would make a big difference in how America dealt with the Eastern Bloc, politically and militarily. In other words, the stakes were high, very high.

Scientists looked around for all kinds of ways to detect the big explosion from the outside since it was unlikely any Western observers would get an invitation to the test. One idea surfaced that is still being pursued by scientists today.

During the war, scientists learned they could "hear" loud noises like explosions through hundreds, if not thousands of miles, of water. Somebody said, "why not listen in a less dense fluid like the upper atmosphere and see if we can 'hear' that bomb test." Today the research is called infrasound and experts find they can detect the non-audible, low frequency sound waves created by volcanoes and nuclear explosions half a world away.

So the Air Force set about making it happen. Unfortunately, they greatly lacked the technology we have today to really accomplish it. But they marshaled on.

They devised ways to string a batch of weather balloons together and from them dangle radar reflectors (foil) for tracking and a sensitive microphone to gather sound. The foil reflectors were used on the early balloon launches in June 1947 because they didn't want to use radiosondes yet. They were going to depend on White Sands Proving Ground radars to track the balloons.

The idea was to get the balloon train up into a level of the atmosphere where it could stay suspended for days if not a week or two at a time. And, of course, not blow to Sweden on some river of fast-moving air.

These things, like the many research-balloon launches later, generated UFO reports all by themselves because they shone bright in the early and late sun. The Mogul balloons were sometimes reported as UFOs in formation because there were several balloons uniformly spaced out on one line.

Later, other military groups took the balloon idea further, hoping to put up balloons with spy cameras to provide look-down photographs. This, of course, was years before the U-2 spy planes and satellites, so intelligence folks were scratching for any advantage they could find.

Mogul balloon trains were launched in June 1947 from Holloman and proved not very unsuccessful. They blew all over the place and strong winds and storms brought them down prematurely.

From published interviews with some of the personnel associated with Project Mogul, we know all the material found by Brazel northwest of Roswell matches up perfectly with what went into their research balloon trains. In fact, the balloon train launched on June 4, 1947 from Holloman was never accounted for and used the foil reflectors. Plus, it fits the timeframe for Brazel's discovery.

After the Air Force announced that Brazel had found a weather balloon, the whole thing pretty much died away - died away for decades! There were a few people who brought it up, but for mainstream America it didn't exist.

No one said anything about aliens and Roswell until the late 1970s and beyond – 30 years after the fact. So, you might ask, "where did the story about a big spacecraft, alien bodies and a military recovery come from?"

Blame It On John Paul Stapp

This is where another interesting military project associated with the Holloman/White Sands complex comes dramatically into play. It is safe to say this part of the legend comes mostly from the work of Air Force Colonel John Stapp. A plane crash and a few other events probably added details to the legend but Stapp's work in the 1950s takes center stage.

Some people living in the Alamogordo area know a little about Stapp because they remember he rode one of the rocket-propelled sleds at the Holloman track to a speed of 632 miles per hour on Dec. 10, 1954. It put him on the cover of *Time* magazine and he was declared the "fastest man on earth." But

today most people have no idea who he was or what incredible things he did. Holloman AFB seems to have forgotten him as well as they don't have any streets or buildings named after him.

In 1946 Dr. John Stapp, with the Army's Air Forces Medical Corps, was assigned to the Aero Medical Laboratory at Wright Field in Ohio. In addition to medicine, Stapp became an expert in biophysics. His interest took him to Muroc Field in California in 1947.

Stapp was initially interested in why some pilots died in plane crashes and some didn't. In scientific terms it meant finding out what happens to human bodies during high rates of acceleration and deceleration.

One obvious observation was that if not properly restrained in a crash, the human body flies all over the place and hits all kinds of hard objects. This bashing and gashing of soft tissues was often fatal.

This led to looking at ways to perfect aircraft crewmembers' safety harnesses so the occupants stayed in one place during a "rapid deceleration." For some of his early testing of restraint systems, Stapp himself rode sleds on a track at Muroc. On this track he was once accelerated to 150 miles per hour and then stopped in just 19 feet. He experienced forces 35 times greater than gravity, or 35 Gs.

Colonel John Stapp's official portrait. Air Force photo.

At the time, he remarked that the leading experts thought humans couldn't survive 18 Gs and yet he was walking proof that if properly restrained they could easily survive twice that.

At the same time, the Air Force was moving to jet aircraft and then to supersonic aircraft. In turn, the survival game took a quantum leap as the speeds and altitudes were suddenly breathtaking.

Stapp moved to Holloman after more than four years in California. He and his fellow researchers had new questions to answer. Can a pilot survive an explosive ejection-seat exit? What happens when the ejected pilot hits the airstream outside the cockpit? What should said pilot be wearing? Does the flight suit need to be pressurized? What kind of breathing system should be on board these high-flying airplanes? What kind of parachutes will work at both low and high altitudes? And on and on.

To find answers to these and many other questions, Stapp led an extensive set of investigative tests during the 1950s. This is why he rode the sled at Holloman to a supersonic speed followed by an abrupt stop. He wanted to show that pilots just might be able to eject from planes travelling faster than the speed of sound.

Stapp wrote about his experience on Dec. 10, 1954 in a very detached, observational tone. He said, "I was the subject. I had been sitting there during an hour and a half of lashing my helmet to the head rest and putting on double thickness of 6,300-pound-test nylon shoulder straps 3 inches wide, attached to the seat buckle, from which similar straps passed downward around my thighs to the rear corners of the seat. The chest strap had been drawn too tight for comfort, but I could not speak while gripping the protective rubber bite block between my teeth." In addition his wrists were strapped to his knees so his arms wouldn't flap about.

When the countdown for his ride hit zero, he wrote, "It took only 0.067 second for the nine rockets to leap to life on the propulsion sled, ramming a pusher plate on the back of my sled. An instantaneous acceleration of 15 times gravity slammed into my back, as the 3 tons of sled and rockets reacted to 40,000 pounds of thrust."

As he started down the track, he said, "I could see the ditch between the rails blur then blackout in 1.5 seconds as the blood was drained backward from my retinas by the forward surge of the sled."

The sled reached a speed of 632 miles an hour and then hit the braking section of the track. Blood in his eyes rushed the other way and for a moment he saw a brilliant flash of light. This was followed by his eyeballs trying to fly out of their sockets "with a searing pain like a dental extraction without anesthetic."

His summation was, "In 5 seconds, I had gone from standstill to 632 miles an hour, and in 1.4 seconds I had crashed to a stop – a crash lasting 18 times longer than that of a car hitting a wall at 60 mph."

After that, Stapp liked to point out that at its top speed his sled was going 927 feet per second while a .45 caliber bullet traveled around 900 feet per second.

Stapp immediately saw that restraining the human body in a car crash would prevent the same kind of injuries suffered in a plane wreck. Heads bashing against metal dashboards and windows while chests were crushed on steering wheels could be minimized with seatbelts.

So Stapp set about, in the 1950s, to demonstrate to police and safety officials what kind of forces were at work in car crashes. He offered rides on a simple seat that slid down a short ramp and was stopped abruptly. A seat belt kept the rider from flying off the end. It was a simple and effective demonstration of how much energy is involved in a very, very low-speed crash.

At one point the Air Force objected to his promotion of restraints in cars saying it was outside their scope of work. Stapp won continued support for the program when he pointed out more Air Force pilots were killed in car wrecks than in plane crashes. In 1966, after overcoming the objections of the car companies and many other powerful lobbies, Stapp got to see the Federal law signed mandating seatbelts in automobiles.

In the early 1980s, Stapp was introduced as someone who had probably saved more than 100,000 lives because of seatbelts.

Most of the time Stapp didn't use humans as guinea pigs for his tests. For the dangerous stuff he used animals and dummies. In fact, Stapp revolutionized the science of using dummies in this kind of research.

Early dummies used to test parachutes weren't much more than sandbags tied together to have the general shape of a human. Stapp demanded much more realistic subjects and came up with the requirements for anthropomorphic dummies – those crash-test dummies we've seen in television safety spots. These dummies were much more realistic, resembling men in weight and articulation. They had heads, faces, hands, the whole package because Stapp wanted them to wear helmets, oxygen masks, goggles, and flight suits complete with gloves and boots. They also had to bend at their joints just like a human.

He then went about flinging these dummies from the rocket sleds to test ejection seats and the parachute mechanism. To get high altitude data, he launched dozens of big balloons carrying dummies to be ejected or dropped from various heights.

The dummies were carried to altitudes from 30,000 feet to 98,000 feet under balloons. Sometimes they were housed in gondolas and sometimes they were simply hung from racks hanging from the balloon. Instruments such as accelerometers, pressure gauges and cameras were used to collect data.

Most of the balloon launches took place from Holloman, but other New Mexico launch locations included White Sands Proving Ground, Hatch, Truth or Consequences, Nutt, Lake Valley, and Fort Craig. The idea was to have them land on White Sands for fast and easy recovery but that was rare. Instead Stapp's crews chased balloon payloads all over southern New Mexico.

The caravan of vehicles used to chase down the balloons was fairly extensive. To handle the dummies, and several times there were many, an old military ambulance was used. It was convenient to go out into the desert, put the dummies into body bags to keep the arms and legs from flopping all over the place, put each one on a stretcher and then load the stretchers onto racks in the ambulance.

Accompanying the group would be trucks for personnel, recovery equipment like a wrecker or some sort of crane to lift the payload onto a big truck, and a truck to collect all the balloon material. The polyethylene balloons Stapp used could carry hundreds of pounds of payload and could be inflated to millions of cubic feet. They were huge. Clean-up of all this material was a major part of the mission.

According to the Air Force, in their narrative *The*

Stapp's Project High Dive prepares to launch a large, high-altitude balloon over the WSMR/Holloman complex. Dangling below the balloon will be two anthropomorphic dummies equipped with the latest designs in high-altitude parachutes. Air Force photo.

Roswell Report: Case Closed, Stapp's team launched 43 high-altitude balloons carrying 67 dummies between June 1954 and February 1959.

The point here is the Air Force was able to track their balloons and sent a convoy of vehicles out quickly to run down each one, recover the equipment and valuable data, and smooth relations with any rancher or farmer who was distressed at having his property trampled. To maintain positive relationships with ranchers, Air Force personnel usually sought the cooperation of the families involved and tried to clean up after themselves so little trace was left.

Some UFO believers claim that when the alien spacecraft crashed near Roswell, local civilians always found the Air Force already on the spot, cleaning up the situation before they could get to it. It sounds remarkably like Stapp's work but with a different headline.

Also, if you have worked for the military as long as I have in southern New Mexico, you know a military unit could not have been mustered, the object found and recovery started in just a few hours unless the event had a pre-planned impact area with the teams assembled and waiting to go. That is how we did it at White Sands. If an unplanned event occurred in the middle of the night, like a plane crash, it took a lot of time to get organized and start looking for the site.

Instead of this magical event and a magical military response described by a few, could "witnesses" be misremembering Stapp's operations decades after the fact? Could witnesses be substituting aliens for the test dummies at the suggestion of the investigators/believers? Given what we know now about the reliability of witnesses, no matter who they are, it seems millions of times more probable that the aliens and the spaceships were really Stapp's equipment and his men rounding it all up.

Joe Kittinger Drops In

At the end of the decade the Air Force upped the stakes by putting some of the new-fangled clothing and innovations to more realistic tests. In the meantime Stapp had already outgrown his time as a guinea pig with 29 rocket sled rides. Instead, he enlisted others to give it a try by riding in gondolas below some of the big balloons.

The first three tests were dubbed "Project Man

High" and consisted of "pilots" riding balloons to altitudes from 96,000 feet to 101,500 feet. They then descended with the balloons. The pilots were Captain Joe Kittinger, Lieutenant Colonel David Simons and First Lieutenant Clifton McClure.

Next, the researchers went all in with a series of three flights where Kittinger actually jumped from his gondola to test the new parachute systems. These were the legendary Project Excelsior tests.

Or maybe they are not so legendary. It could be that all the publicity surrounding UFOs has buried Kittinger's accomplishments.

On Nov. 16, 1959, Kittinger jumped from an altitude of 76,400 feet. Unfortunately, his stabilizer parachute deployed early, wrapped around his neck and rendered him unconscious. He missed the show and his main chute had to deploy automatically to deliver him safely to terra firma.

The next mission was on Dec. 11, 1959 with Kittinger jumping from 74,700 feet. He free-fell for 55,000 feet (that's just over 10 miles) before opening his parachute for a safe landing on White Sands.

His final flight was on Aug. 16, 1960 when the balloon reached an altitude of 102,800 feet – 19.4 miles above White Sands Missile Range. After he

Captain Joe Kittinger's official photo. Air Force photo.

jumped he dropped like a rock for 4 minutes and 36 seconds before triggering his parachute.

The altitude Kittinger reached in the balloon, the altitude for his jump and the length of his free-fall were world records until Felix Baumgartner jumped from 127,000 feet (24 miles) on Oct. 14, 2012. Baumgartner jumped from a capsule under a balloon that was launched from Roswell.

In his free-fall Kittinger reached a speed of just over 600 miles per hour. Baumgartner hit 843 miles per hour in his jump.

Baumgartner did not break Kittinger's time for free-fall as he was going faster and popped his parachute earlier.

I once head Kittinger say he did not experience or sense he was traveling "faster than a speeding bullet." There was no air rushing past and he was so far up, the cloud cover below did not rush up at him as he approached. It was quite leisurely until he got much closer to the ground.

Kittinger is still justifiably famous because of that jump. He was enlisted as an advisor to Baumgartner for his endeavor. Over the years, news and documen-tary people have interviewed Kittinger about his exploits. Some brought Kittinger back to New Mexico so he could be interviewed at Holloman and on the spot he touched down on the missile range.

Debbie Bingham, from Public Affairs, coordinated these visits and helped Kittinger find the "spot." Basically it was an impossible task because there are no landmarks out in the desert close to the "spot." Plus, Kittinger was in no condition to notice exactly where he was at the time.

So, Bingham and Kittinger drove out into the up-range areas and found a likely spot in the middle of nowhere but very close to a good road, easy to get to, and called it the "spot." From then on, they always took crews to the same area for interviews.

Kittinger followed this with a job as project engineer for Project StarGazer. This was another balloon-based program attempting to put a manned laboratory aloft for hours at a time to do astronomical research.

Putting the telescope, cameras and other instruments at the edge of the atmosphere provided unique viewing opportunities at the time. Rockets obviously

Joe Kittinger, left, and Navy astronomer Bill White photograph the preparation going on around them as they get ready to button up the hatch of their capsule for the Stargazer mission on Dec. 13, 1962. Air Force photo.

could get to these altitudes, but the useful time for gathering data was only minutes long.

The system consisted of a two-person gondola or capsule suspended from a 280-foot-diameter mylar balloon. The gondola was only partially pressurized, so the men had to wear quasi-spacesuits which gave them some protection while allowing them to move about freely to complete their tasks.

There was supposed to be a series of four launches, but the first one on Dec. 13, 1962 was the only successful one. The pilot/engineer on the flight was Kittinger. His job was to operate communications, control the balloon, and monitor the life-support system.

The astronomer was Bill White, a civilian Navy scientist. With Kittinger taking care of the infrastructure, White's job was to run the telescope and other instruments.

The balloon was launched at 11:30 a.m. on the 13th. During the night, Kittinger was able to keep the balloon at 82,000 feet to provide stable observation conditions for White.

Kittinger ended the flight early the next morning because the balloon was beginning to drift toward Mexico. The total flight time for the experiment was 18.5 hours.

The flight was put together by a consortium of institutions that included the Smithsonian Astrophysical Observatory, the Experimental Astronomy Lab of MIT, and the Air Force's Office of Scientific Research. In 1966 the project was formally cancelled.

So, what does all this testing in the 50s around White Sands have to do with the Roswell incident? Well, it looks like just about everything.

First I have to mention an incident that adds a twist to the Roswell story. On June 26, 1956, a fully fueled KC-97G aircraft took off from Walker AFB (Roswell) on a refueling training mission. Just four minutes after takeoff, there was a propeller failure with the blade slicing into one of the fuel tanks. The plane burst into flame and crashed about nine miles from the base. All 11 personnel were killed by the impact and incinerated in the resulting fuel fire.

The bodies were moved back to Walker for identification which required an expert from Wright-Patterson AFB. In addition, three bodies were taken into Roswell where they were autopsied by a local pathologist.

Beginning in the late 1970s and through the

80s, UFO researchers looked at the Roswell incident trying to prove aliens actually crashed there. There were no records of alien spacecraft so they assumed a cover-up and called for help. They advertised in the local papers asking for people to come forward who might have seen the Air Force working at the spacecraft crash site, who might have seen them extracting the alien bodies, who might have seen them hauling the debris away, etc.

A few people did come forward with rather vague stories about seeing something along the lines of what was suggested by the investigators. Most of them were unsure or vague about the actual dates because this was decades after the event.

It turns out these witnesses usually gave very nice descriptions of Stapp's crews and vehicles out in the countryside recovering their equipment. When they described the alien bodies they saw, they were almost perfect matches with Stapp's dummies down to the grey color and webbed fingers.

The dummy designers knew the dummies couldn't have individual fingers because they would be too fragile and would just break off on most impacts. So they stuck the fingers together to provide needed strength.

In another case a civilian witness described the alien bodies arriving at a morgue in a burned condition and base officials performing autopsies on them. He complained about the smell. Also, he said an officer told him to mind his own business.

Most folks assume the witness saw some of the aircrew from the KC-97 crash being brought in – many of the victims were charred beyond recognition and everything was soaked in jet fuel. The smell must have been incredibly awful.

As for the Air Force officer telling the civilian to go away, it seems a reasonable reaction when he had just lost 11 of his mates in a terrible crash. He might have been a tad upset. That he and the other military personnel would close ranks against the outside world is perfectly normal.

At this point in time it seems rather pointless to go chasing down all the little stories in an attempt to explain every niggling detail. Believers are always wanting to argue far-flung details or accounts from someone who knew someone who was related to someone at Roswell. These are usually events way down the line from the original action.

This grasping at little, individual events to prove

the big hypothesis is something we humans do very well. One person says it was cold last winter so global warming is nonsense and his neighbor says July was hot last summer so global warming is fact.

Also, we are suckers for a "trusted" eyewitness. We grab their story, caress it, feed it, and maybe even expand it.

Roswell certainly is a big myth – so big I doubt if it can die. The people of Roswell certainly don't want it to go away, since they have built a tourist industry around aliens and it helps keep the city afloat.

In the end you are left with a choice. One choice is to believe a series of pulp fiction-like fantastic stories: that aliens travelling across the galaxy with fuel and life support in a spaceship smaller than a Winnebego somehow managed to crash at Roswell; that the military somehow detected it, found it at night, assembled a crack response team and rushed to the site to retrieve the vehicle and bodies in less time than it takes to play a round of golf; that the government managed to keep it all a secret with tens of thousands of people involved over a period of decades; and finally, that it took the reverse engineering of the alien technology to get us transistors and many of the other post World War II technologies. That last one is much like the argument that the Egyptians were too stupid to build the pyramids and needed alien help to make a neat pile of stones.

The second choice is much simpler and brings into play facts and artifacts – the kind of real things you find in an honest-to-god museum. This choice involves understanding that the really neat and quite real (with "true facts") military research being done at Holloman/White Sands was simply misremembered years later. With the pump primed by the suggestive questions of investigators, it is easy to see how a few witnesses jumbled their memories and misidentified what they saw.

Of course, the choice is yours.

WSMR's UFO

There are lots of word-of-mouth stories about WSMR employees seeing UFOs while going about their duties. Most of the ones I have heard came along with an explanation.

For instance, in the 1950s a pilot flying over the missile range reported seeing a flying saucer parked on the ground near the salt flats. He radioed in to report and then circled the spacecraft until a detail of military police could drive to the site. When they arrived, they found one of those big round metal water tanks used for cattle. It had been turned over years before to discourage ranchers from trying to run cattle on White Sands soon after they had been evicted.

In another instance, a camera operator told me about sitting at his camera at a site just northwest of the main post and preparing to film a missile shot from one of the launch complexes. As the countdown neared zero, he was looking through his tracking scope and saw a white glowing ball pass across his vision. In fact, it was between his position and the launch complex.

He called his partner over to look through the scope and confirm there really was something floating above the basin. They then filmed the missile shot assuming their UFO was captured on the film as well.

They did not report what they had seen because they wanted to view the film first. When the footage was developed they eagerly looked at it. There wasn't a glowing ball on a single frame of film.

Kind of disappointed and kind of relieved, they went back to the same site to photograph another test the next day. When setting up the camera and looking through the tracking lens, low and behold, there was another glowing ball and then another one.

This time they got off the camera mount and looked out over the basin. Then they noticed fluffy bits of vegetation, like the feathery seeds from a cottonwood tree and some bushes, floating near them. The proverbial light bulb went on.

They realized they could see the fluff because it was just the right distance when viewed in their lower-powered tracking lens and it got their attention because it kind of looked like those stereotyped images of flying saucers. It was a true unidentified flying object, for a short time.

Most UFO stories coming out of White Sands are like this. But not all. One man wrote a whole book about his encounter with aliens at the Range.

The White Sands Incident by Dr. Daniel Fry was originally published in 1954. Right up front, I have to say Fry is either a lunatic or a well-meaning hoaxer.

In the book's introduction Fry says, "Believe it or not, on the evening of July 4, 1950, I had the experience of seeing, touching and riding in an unmanned, remotely controlled space capsule which landed near the White Sands Proving Grounds outside the city of

Las Cruces, New Mexico." Actually, as he describes it later, the space ship landed just south of the main post area about where the golf course is now.

According to Fry, he worked for Aerojet at White Sands. On July 4 he missed the bus into town to watch the fireworks. The sun had already set when he decided to take a walk down toward the 100K static test stand. On his way he detoured to the west and was surprised to see "an oblate spheroid about thirty feet in diameter at the equator or largest part" land just 100 feet from him.

As he approached the ship and tried to touch it, a voice rang in his head, "Better not touch the hull, pal, it's still hot!" I love it when space aliens communicate with us. The human imagination really is very limited and tends to stay close to what the mind already knows. That line sounds like it came right out of a B movie from the early 1950s.

In fact, the premise for this book may have come from the classic science fiction movie *The Day the Earth Stood Still* which opened in 1951. The themes are very similar. Fry goes on to tell about his ride in the spaceship and his conversations with the alien controller of it. But most of the book is a preachy message about how the world must reform itself or nuclear destruction is inevitable.

In the famous movie starring Michael Rennie and the wonderful Patricia Neal, the alien robot Gort will do the annihilating if earth doesn't change its ways and find peace. Fry's alien says we'll naturally blow ourselves up if we don't change.

The bottom line here is that Fry wrote an allegorical tale using such best-selling models as the Bible. In fact, much of his message is rehashed biblical wisdom.

Fry even sets himself up as a modern-day prophet. The clearly superior and wise alien tells Fry, "your conduct has pleased me" and "your mind is of the type we hoped to find."

The alien, whose name is A-Lan, eventually tells Fry he can't "hide his light under a bushel." He urges Fry to get out there and spread the word. Sounds kind of familiar doesn't it? Fry certainly sets himself up as the chosen one.

A-Lan then goes on to explain that there are three kinds of science - material, social and spiritual. He urges Fry to tell people "the importance and eternal truth of spiritual science remains ever-dependable since the very dawn of human intelligence. This

is why it must always be regarded as the primary branch of science."

This is all well and good but dressing up the old Christian themes in new space garb can only be interesting for a while. But Fry presents this material in the context that he really met an alien and that he really flew in a space ship. In fact, there are people out there today who cite his adventure as proof that aliens have actually been visiting earth.

Fry claims that A-Lan gave him all kinds of advanced technical knowledge. It is now decades later, so where is it? Instead we get the same kind of mumbo jumbo you hear on *Star Trek* episodes. Fry talks about a "differential accumulator" and projecting gravitational force fields so the spacecraft is pulled toward the artificial gravity point - a "gravitational field mechanism."

It is just the kind of techno babble people fall for with health supplements, diets, miracle cures and perpetual motion machines.

But, like so many kooks, Fry can't leave well enough alone. He had to spice things up with the Atlantis legend as an allegory tale. According to Fry's alien, Atlantis existed 30,000 years ago in the Atlantic Ocean and a rival continent, Lemuria, existed in the Pacific Ocean.

These two peoples couldn't get along and so they eventually destroyed each other (sound familiar again) with weapons that make our hydrogen bombs look puny. The radiation levels were so high after the war that very few humans survived. Some chose to leave and colonize Mars. Others stayed and de-evolved into primitive creatures.

Of course, some of us have questions. Like, why didn't the radiation affect the rest of life on the planet - like apes, camels, lions and tigers and bears, oh my?? Why haven't we detected the radiation layer in our soil?? After all, we have detected dust layers which are millions of years old from other events, but nothing this recent.

The obvious answer is that Fry was an electronics guy and didn't know a thing about radiation except for what he had read in the newspaper. We know how accurate that is. He made up the story and his facts don't work.

There are other problems. Fry predicted in his book that we would be flying in ships using anti-gravity devices within eight years and be walking on Mars and Venus in just 14 years. Oops. These things don't help his credibility.

So, if you are interested in Daniel Fry's personal proposal on how to save the world, this might be a book for you. After all the dust jacket proclaims "This is a significant book."

It Continues

In August 2012, the *Huffington Post*, an Internet newspaper, reported the claims of retired Air Force Lieutenant Colonel Richard French who said there were really two crashes of alien spacecraft at Roswell.

What makes French's story stupendous is his claim that the first Roswell UFO "was shot down by an experimental U.S. airplane that was flying out of White Sands, New Mexico, and it shot what was effectively an electronic pulse-type weapon that disabled and took away all the controls of the UFO, and that's why it crashed."

French stated he was told this story by a "confidential" informant from White Sands.

The story goes on to explain that a second UFO crashed near the first one. French was quoted as saying, "We think that the reason they were in there at that time was to try and recover parts and any survivors of the first crash. I'm [referring to] the people from outer space -- the guys whose UFO it was."

French is supposed to be some sort of very experienced Air Force pilot who investigated UFO sightings later. Here we go again with the age-old and totally bogus assumption that someone with a responsible position is by definition an honest, reliable, competent and truthful person. They really are just as loony as the rest of us.

Some people probably believe his story because they really want to. But his claim we had an electromagnetic pulse weapon mounted on an airplane in 1947 is a magical claim because it is not supported by any science or technology from the time. In fact, it is similar to Fry's claim about us flying around using anti-gravity devices in the 1960s. Pure movie fodder.

Another one of these self-proclaimed insiders, and much better known, was Phillip Corso. The cover of *The Day After Roswell* by Lieutenant Colonel Philip J. Corso (Ret.) asserts that "A former Pentagon official reveals the U.S. Government's shocking UFO cover-up" and "the truth exposed after fifty years!" It may sound exciting but it is rather tedious.

The premise behind the book is the same story we have seen elsewhere. He said that an alien space-craft crashed near Roswell on the night of July 3 or 4 and that the military got to it in a matter of hours by going to coordinates provided by radar from Roswell Army Air Field. This is the same old magical idea about the capabilities of radar and military preparedness in 1947.

The military picked up the vehicle and the aliens and within minutes had the place cleaned up. All the stuff was secreted away for study.

Corso said he personally entered the picture when he was put in charge of Roswell artifacts by Lieutenant General Arthur Trudeau, head of Army Research and Development in 1961 and 1962. Corso's job was to farm the artifacts out to industry and research labs so the technology could be reverse engineered to benefit the United States.

Instead of *Men in Black* we had Corso in Army green being a techno-hero by spreading the goodies around to all kinds of patriotic American companies.

According to Corso the following technologies benefitted or were a direct result of this effort:

> *Image intensifiers for night vision*
> *Fiber optics*
> *'Supertenacity' fibers like Kevlar*
> *Lasers*
> *Integrated circuits - computers*
> *Portable atomic generators*
> *Irradiated food*
> *Particle beams*

Corso's science is a little movie-like in most of the book. For instance, the spacecraft they supposedly recovered had no engine, no fuel, no controls, etc. He said that by looking at it they deduced it was somehow equipped with "electromagnetic antigravity propulsion" and "brain-wave-directed navigational controls."

On the other hand, he and his ghostwriter, William Birnes, wove a great deal of real techno history into the story to provide a bit of non-fiction heft. For example, they went into great detail about the history of the computer by explaining everything from Charles Babbage's efforts to make a mechanical thinking machine to the military's ENIAC.

Corso went on to claim we have been secretly battling aliens since 1947. He said the cold war was a battle to outdo the Soviets but it also served to disguise our advances against the aliens. For instance,

U2 spy planes not only took pictures of Soviet installations but they were also equipped to photograph alien activity in space.

He claimed we have particle beam weapons deployed in space ready to take on the aliens, that we have mined the alien technology, and are now using it against them. I imagine French read Corso's book but somehow didn't realize he couldn't have had an electromagnetic pulse gun reverse-engineered from the aliens if the aliens hadn't crashed yet.

Corso said the reason we are so hyper about these aliens is that they are not friendly. He said the cattle mutilations and human abductions are all real and they prove the aliens are doing something dastardly to the human race.

By the way, did you know that the CIA was controlled by the KGB in the 1950s or that the aliens had a base on the moon? That's Corso's take on reality.

This is Corso's Achilles heel. He loved being in the spotlight and went to great lengths to portray himself as a Pentagon insider pulling the strings on all kinds of secrets, not just the Roswell story. His time in the bright lights for one item just whet his appetite for more. He just kept churning out the nonsense.

One of his claims was that President Eisenhower abandoned hundreds of POWs in Korea at the end of that war. He got himself a great deal of publicity with this one and testified before Congress. Senator John McCain, someone who knows about being a POW, blasted Corso and his totally unsubstantiated claims.

It really isn't much different than those poor souls who claim military service or combat when they had none or those retired service members who show up wearing medals they never earned. Our culture puts great value on being in the spotlight and some people will do just about anything to get there. Pride and shame are missing in action.

The consequences are that we lose track of the real heroes. John Stapp and Joe Kittinger were more important than any of these folks, but they don't get much attention. In Roswell, there is an excellent city museum with a tribute to the early pioneering rocket work of Robert Goddard, another unsung hero. Not many know it exists but they sure know about the UFO museums in town.

Balloons Again

In the meantime, balloons have continued to demonstrate their value for all kinds of research. In the late 1960s, the Air Force and Army atmospheric researchers at White Sands put up monster balloons to take ozone-measuring instruments ever higher for longer periods.

The first launch from WSMR's Pony Site on Sept. 11, 1968, used what was then the world's largest balloon with a capacity of 28.6 million cubic feet of helium. Its diameter, when fully inflated as it rose, was 410 feet. It would have been easy to stack several 747 jetliners on top of each other in such a space.

The balloon was launched at 6 a.m. carrying an instrument package weighing 85 pounds. It quickly rose to its peak altitude, a world's record of 158,300 feet. Then for just over 10 hours as it drifted west over Arizona to California, the instruments collected information about the concentration of ozone and how it changed with the change in sunlight.

Data from the instruments was telemetered (radioed) to ground stations at White Sands; Lordsburg, New Mexico; Fort Huachuca and Eager, Arizona.

Like the Mogul balloons back in the 1940s, this payload was difficult to find. The instruments were parachuted from the balloon as it drifted into California. They were not found and White Sands soon posted $200 reward notices for anyone finding the payload.

I couldn't find any record of it ever being found. It may still be sitting in some remote spot just waiting for someone to come along and find the next alien spacecraft.

27

Killing The SST

Why The U.S. Never Built A Supersonic Transport

During the first couple of years I worked at White Sands, I experienced my first sonic boom. I was driving uprange in our office station wagon when, out of the blue, I heard and felt a loud boom.

My immediate reaction was to grab the steering wheel and hang on because the sound was very much like the time I blew a tire while driving down the highway. As my heart raced, I waited for the car to veer to one side or the other as the tire would go flat almost instantly – long before I would be able to slow down.

But nothing happened. I stopped and got out to inspect the tires. They were fine.

However, in the distance I could hear a jet flying away. It then dawned on me what had happened. I got back in the car and said to myself, "That was pretty neat."

Since then I experienced many sonic booms over White Sands. Most were in association with Air Force training flights in the airspace over the missile range. Over the years it was common to see two or more jet fighters engaged in mock dogfights high above us. Sometimes these engagements would produce a whole series of booms spread out over several minutes.

Sonic booms continue to be heard over the missile range, still mostly during Air Force training. There is an area in the heart of White Sands where low-level (down to 300 feet off the ground) supersonic flight is permitted. Higher altitude sonic booms are allowed outside this area all the way into blocks of airspace off the missile range to the west and east. Here the jets are supposed to be at least 10,000 feet above sea level for breaking the sound barrier.

For the communities around the missile range, residents don't normally experience that sudden jolt provided by a supersonic plane directly overhead. Instead, windows may rattle but it is often more of a distant rumble, like an approaching summer thunderstorm that may or may not make it to your backyard.

Such blocks of air for supersonic training are relatively rare inside the United States. Restrictions drive much supersonic flight out over the oceans so there is little impact on communities.

Sonic Boom Studies

Young people today might well ask, "Why did the French and British have the Concorde, a supersonic airliner, and the U.S. nothing similar?" Part of the answer happened at White Sands Missile Range.

In the mid 20th century, commercial aviation transitioned from piston-driven airplanes to jets. It was an age of rapid technological advances when many people assumed the next step for the airline industry was supersonic flight.

During the 1950s and 60s, our country's ego and self-esteem were tied to our technology and industrial might. When the Soviets were first to launch an earth-orbiting satellite in 1957, Americans ran into the streets with their hair on fire. In reality it meant very little. It certainly didn't prove the Soviet's crude efforts were superior to Western developments, but the perception was grim. And, of course, government and industry leaders sounded the alarm to keep the money flowing.

In the early 60s, airplane companies and government agencies were proposing various designs and strategies for what became known as the Supersonic Transport or SST. Most of the buzz was positive as people speculated on how short the flight from New York to Los Angeles would be.

The U.S. government held a competition with three manufacturers to select the best design. The Boeing 2707 won. When the program was finally scuttled in 1971, Boeing had over 100 orders on the books for the new airliner.

Of course, one of the side effects of any SST is the sonic boom created whenever the plane is flying in excess of Mach one. Based on experience with supersonic military aircraft, proponents knew they had to address a couple of sonic boom issues. One was the possibility of property damage; the other was the impact on humans experiencing repeated sonic booms.

To answer some of the questions, the FAA, NASA and DOD teamed up to run two significant tests in 1964 and 1965. At White Sands Missile Range, a study was conducted to examine structural response to sonic booms.

Booming Oscura Range Camp

The study area was the Oscura Range Camp on the east boundary of White Sands, a little over 20 miles southwest of Carrizozo. According to a paper entitled "Sonic Boom Research and Design Considerations in the Development of a Commercial Supersonic Transport (SST)" by Thomas Higgins, 21 structures were observed during the study. Nine of the buildings were already at Oscura and seven new ones were constructed at the site. The other five were older ranch houses and other missile range buildings located nearby.

A couple of the ranch houses were off the missile range and occupied. The government met with these people and wanted to evacuate them for the tests. The ranchers refused and, instead, a deal was struck to monitor their houses for damage with the residents in place.

The old Oscura structures included a barracks, a warehouse, a radar building, a radar shop, and a communications building. On one side of the sheet metal warehouse, they installed "three representative glass store fronts having nine panes of glass. Included were two 8-foot by 10-foot glass show windows." Also a greenhouse was constructed on site.

In addition to the real estate and some of the buildings for these tests, White Sands provided communications, meteorology, photography and utilities support.

The Oscura flights were done in two phases: from Nov. 18 to Dec. 15, 1964 and from Jan. 15 to Feb. 15, 1965.

Higgins reported two kinds of aircraft flew the sonic boom missions over Oscura. They were an Air Force F-104 stationed at Holloman Air Force Base and a B-58 stationed at Edwards Air Force Base in California. The F-104 flew 1,433 runs and the B-58 flew 61 runs over the small, simulated town. On average about 30 flights a day were conducted during six-hour periods.

At Oscura, in addition to numerous instruments to measure the strength of each sonic boom and the stresses exerted on the structures, observation teams visually monitored the buildings each day. According to Higgins, the observers were "from the National Bureau of Standards, Boeing and Lockheed aircraft companies, USAF, England, France, Federal Aviation Agency and the technical contractor." He added that, "All of the cracks, even those which required a magnifying glass for identification, were observed daily, marked as appropriate, and recorded."

During the scheduled flights most of the sonic boom overpressures were between 1.6 and 19 pounds per square foot (psf). The maximum overpressure recorded during daily operations was 23.4 psf.

The results of the test were probably reassuring to SST proponents. Generally, low pressures caused little damage. As the pressures went up there was more chance for glass breakage, plaster cracking, nails popping in gypsum board, and damage to bric-a-brac. Since the SST was projected to create sonic booms with overpressures in the

---

Pop-Up: Sonic booms and how they are created was intensely studied during these years as well. One thing learned was that a larger airplane like the B-58 creates less intense sonic booms than the small fighters. Also, a jet maneuvering creates isolated intense booms where the shock wave is focused over a small area. On the other hand, a high-flying plane traveling in a straight line creates a sound wave that can be audible for dozens of miles on either side of the flight path. The intensity of the sound diminishes the farther the listener is from the flight path.

neighborhood of 1.5 to 2.0 psf, officials generalized the impact as insignificant.

Of course, this wouldn't be reassuring to those few who actually had windows broken because of the sonic boom. Because the government had generalized the impact as insignificant there would be a built-in bias to make victims absolutely prove that a sonic boom broke their window. How do you do that?

There was one slight hiccup. On Dec. 2, the FAA brought the news media to Oscura to watch the day's series of flights. *Time* magazine was there and filed a story in their Dec. 11, 1964 issue.

The magazine said, "In all, the FAA put their manufactured desert town through 15 sonic booms over a three-hour stretch. So well did the buildings bear the booms that a disappointed CBS camera crew left before the show was over."

What CBS missed was a final, low-level flight at subsonic speeds to provide a photo opportunity for the media. Somehow the pilot miscalculated and came over very hot.

Time said, "A heavy ruby-glass ashtray flew off a desk and sprayed shards over the floor. Outside, both panes of a mock-up storefront were smashed, a glass window in a trailer caved in, and 16 out of 90 panes in a small greenhouse were shattered."

Years later in the April 1970 issue of *American Heritage* magazine, a very negative article appeared about the SST. Describing the White Sands incident, the author said, "Gordon Bains, then director of the S.S.T. program, is at White Sands Missile Range explaining to reporters that persons who claimed their property was damaged by sonic booms often were victims of their own imaginations. 'I believe,' he is saying, 'that there's a great deal of psychology in this.' Suddenly, five hundred feet overhead, an F-104 punctures the sound barrier. Two plate-glass windows blow out, canceling Bains's banter."

The tests at White Sands certainly didn't kill the SST, but they did demonstrate that sonic booms can cause damage. It just depends on their intensity.

Booming Oklahoma City

But how do people respond? Military aircraft had been producing sonic booms in some areas of the country for over a decade already. In fact, military and airplane companies, probably because of their isolated experience, were fairly cocky.

The same article in *American Heritage* mockingly summarized, "Yet the Air Force has called the boom 'the sound of progress,' just as early industrial air polluters announced that 'smoke means jobs.' The Boeing Company, manufacturer of the S.S.T. airframe, has described the boom as the sound of the twentieth century. And Major General Jewell C. Maxwell, the Federal Aviation Administration's former director for S. S.T. development, once predicted that people could learn to live with the boom—and maybe even love it."

In hindsight, those attitudes were wishful thinking on the part of the Establishment. A series of tests conducted over Oklahoma City earlier in 1964 turned out to be an initial indicator of where citizens were headed on this issue.

The tests took place from February 1964 through July 1964. They were performed to see how people responded to sonic booms on a day-to-day basis over several months. In addition, a number of buildings were monitored to see if they incurred any damage.

Higgins stated in his report, "A total of 1,253 supersonic flights were made over the Oklahoma City metropolitan area at altitudes ranging from 21,000 to 50,000' and speeds with Mac number range of 1.2 to 2.0."

For these tests, Air Force F-104, F-101, F-106 and F-58 aircraft were used. Each flight was closely monitored for altitude and speed. Also, an assortment of atmospheric measurements was taken to see how they figured into the results.

On the human side, a large cross section of the local population was interviewed at the beginning, middle and end of the testing period to measure their reactions to the booms. Also, complaints and damage claims were tracked.

Flight International magazine, the world's oldest continuously published aviation news magazine, summarized the study in its May 6, 1965 issue. The article said, "Up to early March 1965, 15,116 telephone calls and letters of complaint or inquiry were made about the Oklahoma City tests. Of this total, 9,594 alleged damage to property. A total of 4,629 formal damage claims had been filed and processed. Following investigation and adjudication under established Air Force procedures for sonic-boom claims, the number of claims approved for payment was 229 at a total cost of $12,845." It was mostly plaster and glass damage.

The results of the study were very informative, especially since the test was heavily stacked in favor of the FAA. You couldn't have asked for a more pro-military, pro-industry and patriotic group. The counter-culture attitudes of the 60s had not yet reached Oklahoma City and much of the city was tied to the Air Force and airplane industries. In fact, almost 30 percent of the original study group had to be disqualified because the respondents felt it was improper for a citizen to complain when annoyed by such noise. They were judged too biased to provide meaningful responses.

It is interesting how human beings gloss over details and can be easily led to agree to just about anything. When you start adding details and individuals see a personal impact, the attitude often quickly shifts to, "not in my backyard."

According to *Flight International,* over 90 percent of the survey group said, at the beginning, they could tolerate eight supersonic flights a day. At the mid point, the positive respondents dropped to 81 percent and in the end it was down to 73 percent. At the very end, 25 percent felt they could not learn to accept the booms.

While monitoring showed very little significant damage to any buildings in Oklahoma City and very few claims were paid, over 40 percent of the respondents believed their homes were being damaged.

Of the two studies, the White Sands tests probably had less of an effect on shooting down the SST. The data showed little damage was done at White Sands, but the Oklahoma City surveys showed people believed their homes were being damaged by the continuous rattling of their rafters. When it comes to dealing with the public, perception is reality.

Also, it looks like residents of Oklahoma City initially had no idea what eight booms a day, every day, really meant. As the test progressed, their agreeableness diminished. One has to wonder what the approval rating would have dropped to after a year, especially if night flights were added.

Major Richard M. Roberds in his paper "Sonic Boom and the Supersonic Transport" summarized the question when he wrote, "The sonic boom from the SST looms as a possibly serious intruder into the nation's justifiably deserved peace and quiet. The persistent lay question is simply whether the SST is worth the price of enduring its sonic boom."

Environmental concerns about the noise, the ozone layer, mounting costs, and the price of oil eventually terminated the SST in the United States. One of the Oklahoma senators started out as an enthusiastic backer, but as hundreds of noise complaints flooded his office, he eventually turned his back on the SST.

Then there was the economics of this new technology. Many pie-in-the-sky ideas are technologically possible but never show a penny of profit. For instance, two SST programs were eventually built and operated by foreign countries. The French and British (remember they were at the White Sands tests to look at structural damage) teamed to build the Concorde and the Russians built the Tu-144.

The Concorde did successfully fly for quite a while but was mostly a trans-Atlantic limo for the rich. It simply could not provide reasonably priced transportation compared with traditional jet travel. It certainly never made money.

The Tu-144 was a crude airplane that was built quickly and demonstrated the Soviet's serious lag in engineering behind the West. It was quickly grounded.

The bottom line is that the United States was probably very lucky it didn't build a SST. It could have bankrupted many an airline and required huge taxpayer subsidies. Also, the booms might have set off every barking dog from Los Angeles to New York. Imagine that several times a day, every day.

28

Lasers

Killing Targets With Light

At White Sands the use of lasers varies from pointers used in conference rooms to laser weapons capable of shooting down jets and missiles. My first encounter with lasers was an abandoned research facility in the Organ Mountains behind the main post.

Four thousand feet above the WSMR main post sits a moldering Atmospheric Sciences Lab (ASL) research station. It has no name and is situated on a high point south of Sugarloaf Peak and east-northeast of Organ Peak. In the 1970s, ASL scientists and technicians used the facility to monitor and study the atmosphere.

According to Alex Blomerth, a former ASL division chief, the site was abandoned in 1977. However, there are still two buildings, some debris and what appears to be miles of cable and wire left on the mountain.

For years, the old optics dome that was left behind was visible from the main post early in the morning. The white paint reflected the low sunlight and made it easy to see. The paint has peeled now, bushes have grown up around it, and most people need a pair of binoculars to pick it out.

The dome is eight feet in diameter and weighs about 4,000 pounds. It was airlifted to the mountaintop in May 1970 by a CH-54A helicopter, also known as a "skyhook."

The chopper was assigned to Fort Sill, Oklahoma and was flown in for the job because it had a payload capability at sea level of something like 20,000 lbs. and an operational ceiling of more than 18,000 feet. It easily handled the task at around 8,400 feet.

The researchers placed a larger 16-foot dome across the Tularosa Basin to the east on Mule Peak in the Sacramento Mountains. The domes sheltered helium-neon lasers and associated equipment. At night the scientists flashed laser beams back and forth across the 80 miles of desert air above the basin. The operation was done to study the effects of the atmosphere on lasers beams.

Specifically, they looked at how much the beam spread traveling 80 miles and the amount of scintillation. Scintillation refers to rapid changes in the brightness of a light source due to the atmosphere. Most people have seen this phenomenon at night when they see stars appear to flicker or blink.

A quarter of a mile from the dome in the Organs is the second building, a small shack once used to house instrumentation. When the site was not manned, recorders kept track of data for the scientists. The equipment was powered by a thermoelectric generator which converted the heat from burning propane directly into electricity without any moving parts. When manned, power came from a gasoline generator.

In addition to the laser research, Radon Loveland used the site to look at the flow of electrical current between the air and the ground during a storm. Four remote instrumentation sites were set up on the ridges radiating from the shack. Data was fed back to the recorders in the shack via cables.

The study came with a number of special problems. Lightning strikes often burned up equipment plus deer liked to nibble on the cables. The cable insulation was polyvinyl chloride that had a salty taste and was attractive to deer and rodents. Loveland said he always made sure there was a salt lick on the mountain to deter deer from eating his wiring.

Other studies on the mountain included cloud physics research and the effects of lightning on radio communications. The latter study was done by Oklahoma State University. Radio receivers set at different frequencies were placed in an airplane and then flown around thunderstorms when they were active over the Organs. Transmissions were made from the mountain sites through the storms to the airplane.

Some experiments never quite got off the ground. Personnel worked to put up a small wind-powered generator but it was blown down in the first storm.

As part of their lightning studies, Oklahoma State scientists wanted to build a ring of silver tipped brass rods on top of the mountain. They asked for a volunteer from ASL to sit in the middle of the ring during a thunderstorm and record lightning strikes. No one raised their hand.

Because there are no roads or trails within miles of the mountain facility and the slopes are incredibly steep in places, men and equipment were usually helicoptered back and forth. Skyhooks from Fort Sill carried the concrete for foundations and the heavy equipment to the site.

On one of those ferrying flights, one of the two engines that power a skyhook stalled. Luckily for the crew and passengers, the pilot was quickly able to restart the engine and get down safely.

The ASL personnel learned very quickly about one electrifying hazard involving the helicopters. As the helicopter blades churned through the dry air, they and the body of the chopper built up a large static electrical charge. If someone on the ground grabbed the cable hanging from the helicopter before it touched the ground, the electrical charge would

The old Atmospheric Sciences Lab's abandoned astrodome on top of the ridge south of Sugarloaf Peak in the Organ Mountains. During the 1970s, the lab's scientists studied the atmosphere by beaming laser light back and forth across the Tularosa Basin. In the 1980s the small building was very visible from main post in early morning light. Photo by the author.

travel through their body to the ground. It could be quite large - enough to knock a person on their rear end. It was a very rude awakening.

Sometimes the men had to walk off the mountain. Loveland hiked out once just to see if it was possible. Others walked down because weather grounded the helicopters.

It was a rough trip because of the steep slopes covered with loose rock in places and brush in others. Then there was always cholla and prickly pear cactus ready to stab ankles and legs, leaving whole clumps of cactus to be gingerly removed. It was the kind of trip that required care and caution to negotiate safely.

Eventually the high cost of airlifting men and materials and the difficulties in getting the needed equipment killed the mountaintop facility. Now, the only people who see the buildings and debris are those willing to make the long climb up from the BLM's Aguirre Springs Recreation Area.

Technically the site is just inside the northwest corner of Fort Bliss. Very few people at Bliss know about their boundary in the Organ Mountains. Years ago lightning struck in the vicinity of Organ Peak and started a brush fire.

The public assumes those peaks are on the missile range. When we got calls from the news media about fighting the fire, I pointed out that the land actually belonged to Bliss. Initially when called by reporters, Bliss officials denied it was their property or problem. Eventually, someone at the base found the right map and they began dealing with the fire and answering questions from the media.

Writing about this laser facility in the 1980s earned me a visit by someone from the WSMR security office. He wanted to know where I'd gotten the information about the laser site and what else I knew.

I asked why he was investigating and he explained the word "laser" was on their alert list and they were required to investigate anyone's use of it. It all seemed rather silly since ASL wasn't in the business of developing or testing some new laser technology, and by then the effort was ancient history. Certainly the data might have been sensitive but nobody was talking results.

I suspect security's interest was a result of the big push in the 1980s to actually develop laser weapons as part of the Strategic Defense Initiative (SDI), commonly referred to as the Star Wars effort. New weapons are normally kept under wraps for sometime until their bugs are worked out. That was the case with Star Wars.

Sometimes there are reasons to publicize a weapon's capabilities, especially if it is doing well in testing. In my experience, that is done mostly when the program needs more money or is in some danger of being cancelled. The Pentagon is hoping to gather enough positive publicity to make it unpopular to cut the funding.

Of course, there can be other reasons like strategic political ones. However, when you think about what happened, the Stars Wars programs were calculated to be a very public effort. At our level at White Sands, most things were classified, but there was a steady stream of information gushing out of Washington about these fantastic new weapons America would soon have to defend against Soviet missiles.

It turned into one of the great examples of "perception equals reality." The great publicity that surrounded the various laser and missile programs that made up SDI basically pushed the Soviets to the point they had to cry "uncle." Their perception may have been that if only some of these new weapons were real possibilities, they didn't have the money or science or engineering to possibly keep up.

White Sands Missile Range played a role in testing SDI weapons, some of which continue today. The biggest Star Wars system slated for WSMR was the multi-billion-dollar Ground-Based, Free-Electron Laser facility. This was going to be a mammoth undertaking.

The basic idea behind this facility was a huge plant built out near the Orogrande Gate where energy could be stored off the grid and then, when needed, turned into a huge laser beam. The beam was to be shot up through the atmosphere to a satellite that would send the energy to other "fighting" satellites that, in turn, would aim the light at Soviet-launched missiles and destroy them.

One major problem was getting the nice, coherent beam of energy through the atmosphere that was going to bend and distort it. To take care of this problem, the system was supposed to analyze the atmosphere and then bend and distort the beam on the ground so the atmosphere would act to refocus it before it arrived in Space. A special computer-controlled deformable mirror was required to make this happen.

Of course, to get a powerful beam of light out of a laser device requires a great deal of power going in to be transformed into light. This thing was going to be so potent it needed more electricity than the regular power grid could provide. So in addition to the laser, mirrors, satellites, and who knows how much computing power, this monster required a huge electrical storage area nearby. The plan called for a titanic, cryogenic battery buried in the desert floor south of Nike Ave.

The plan was quickly abandoned but the cluster of administrative buildings did get put up and, like so many other buildings at WSMR, is being used by another program.

Apparently this is still an incredibly ambitious idea that would eat up the DoD budget and still take decades to accomplish. The military spent over a billion dollars just in studies before anything was actually built. Some of the needed technologies existed on a small scale but when you looked into ramping them up to industrial strength, the challenges were tremendous.

Although the ground based laser never materialized, White Sands was tagged as the site for a multiservice laser test facility known as the High Energy Laser Systems Test Facility (HELSTF). It was intended for use by all the military services and others who might need its capabilities for testing high-energy lasers.

Instead of starting from scratch, the Department of Defense picked the old Multi-Function Array Radar (MAR) site on White Sands to house HELSTF. The MAR site was the Army's first phased array radar (a radar without moving parts) and was built as part of the Nike X program in the early 1960s.

At the time Nike Zeus, a big missile system designed to shoot down incoming intercontinental ballistic missiles (ICBMs), was changing as the threat shifted and technology improved to develop new countermeasures. Nike Zeus morphed into the Nike X and the old mechanical spinning radar was replaced with the phased array radar. The MAR was capable of scanning a huge volume of sky, detecting targets, discriminating one from another, tracking the targets, and then tracking the defensive missile when it was launched.

The MAR site, now HELSTF, is located just north of U.S. Highway 70 midway in the missile range. The radar was housed in the white domed building that is visible from the highway. It is a steel building, heavily reinforced, with control rooms and vital equipment buried several floors underground.

Eventually, Nike X morphed into Sentinel and then finally into Safeguard, a scaled-down version of Sentinel using the same missiles. Finally, when the Anti-Ballistic Missile Treaty was signed with the Soviets in 1972, the ICBM interceptor programs died. Both sides were dedicated to MAD – mutually assured destruction.

So, the MAR was sitting unused when site selection for HELSTF started. The main MAR building proved to be a major draw as personnel and equipment could be housed underground when the projected lasers shot down all kinds of targets overhead.

The first major laser weapon actually tested at HELSTF proved to be powerful enough to destroy airplanes and ballistic missiles. It was the Navy's Mid-Infrared Advanced Chemical Laser (MIRACL). At first it was called transportable but that was a bit of a misrepresentation since moving it required a large ship to house all the components.

On Sept. 6, 1985, the second-stage to a Titan I missile was tied down in the target area of HELSTF and lit up using MIRACL. The booster had no fuel but was pressurized to simulate a missile in flight with the rocket motor burning. The powerful laser beam quickly burned a hole in the outer skin and motor casing which caused the chamber to burst like a balloon.

The SDI Office capitalized on the test by sending out press releases and color photos of the experiment. Soon the news media came calling.

Before I relate what happened with the CBS news crew, you have to understand how the MIRACL worked. It was a chemical laser which means it burned a fuel and oxidizer in a combustion chamber just like a rocket engine. These and other compounds were piped in from storage tanks.

The process generated excited atoms that, when returning to a stable state, emitted light. These photons were collected and extracted from the combustion chamber using mirrors and directed elsewhere.

As long as the combustion fuels held out, the laser would pump out energy. At HELSTF the MIRACL had a runtime of less than two minutes. At that point they were out of gas.

The exhaust from the process was toxic, so it was treated and washed before being vented to the open atmosphere. This required a huge multi-million dollar system attached to the laser building that, of course, would not have been required if the laser had actually been installed in a ship and used in the middle of the ocean.

When site officials took a visiting CBS television crew on a tour of the facility, they were shown the large building where the combustion chamber was located. The place was a web of pipes, big and small, valves and gauges. It looked like it could have been a coffee maker in a Rube Goldberg cartoon - a plumber's nightmare.

That was the laser and the television people didn't like it for a number of reasons – nothing moved, it was a hazardous place to be, and it just wasn't sexy.

Officials then took the crew up onto the building's roof to show them the beam director. This was a sophisticated aiming devise that could track targets and paint them with the laser beam. With its big mirror and ability to move, it was much more interesting. The CBS director said something like, "Now that's a laser."

When the piece aired on CBS News, viewers saw the beam director in action but not the MIRACL. The audience was left with the impression that the laser light somehow magically came out of the beam director.

By 1987, MIRACL had shot down subsonic targets like jet-propelled drones. On Feb. 23, 1989, the big laser, using the beam director, shot down a Vandal missile traveling at supersonic speed.

By the way, Vandal supersonic targets were refurbished Navy Talos missiles. Talos was a shipboard air defense system dating from the late 1950s that was used through the 70s. It was capable of carrying a conventional or nuclear warhead. Early Talos testing took place at the Navy's desert ship launch complex.

For Vandal's use as a target, the Navy established a launch point just southwest of NASA's Space Harbor along Range Road 7.

Other tactical lasers, much smaller in scale, have been tested at HELSTF. One idea was to use lasers to clear minefields. Of course, if the mine or other device was not right at the surface, the laser didn't work very well.

Some impressive tests were conducted at HELSTF from 2000 to 2004 using a joint Israeli/United States system called the Tactical High-Energy Laser or THEL and its more transportable version,

the Mobile THEL or MTHEL. Early on, the laser was used to shoot down Katyusha rockets and artillery shells. Later it was used to destroy mortar rounds.

What makes the THEL results so impressive was not the laser beam but the entire system. First of all, the system was able to track relatively cold targets like mortar rounds coming in from very short ranges. Then, the computers and machinery were able to keep the laser beam focused on the rounds long enough to kill them. Pretty good shooting.

An added capability at HELSTF is a huge vacuum chamber. It is 50 feet in diameter and capable of simulating an altitude of 120 miles. The air is very thin up there - you might require a yardstick to measure the distance between oxygen atoms. In addition, it was specially built so, at vacuum, a high-energy laser beam could be shot into the chamber. Some might assume such a capability could be used in testing lasers against satellites, or ICBMs at lift-off, or as they re-enter the atmosphere.

Other weapons systems tested at White Sands in the past few decades are more traditional missiles or projectiles but which used lasers for guidance. An excellent example is the Army's Copperhead. This was an anti-tank artillery round that was guided to its target by reflected laser light.

The basic scenario was for an observer on the ground or in the air to ask an artillery unit for a Copperhead to be fired against a tank target. The unit would fire a Copperhead in the direction of the indicated target. Once the Copperhead left the canon, stubby fins would spring out from the projectile. The nose of the Copperhead was covered with a glass dome that sheltered a laser seeker.

The observer would shine a laser designator on the tank target. As this light scattered off the target, the Copperhead seeker would detect it and home in. The projectile's processor would adjust the fins and basically fly the armor-piercing warhead into the laser-painted tank.

The special warhead drove a dense metal rod into the tank and, because of the kinetic energy released, burned its way into the interior of the tank. When examining the outside of the tank, there would be a small hole in the armor with little other outside damage. The rod and other molten metals would be sprayed inside the tank and disable it.

One obvious problem with the system was the fact the observer had to keep the laser beam focused on the tank during the entire flight of the Copperhead. That made him a very detectable target.

The missile range uses lasers for many applications that aren't just for military purposes. For instance, laser rangefinders have been commonly used for exactly measuring the distance between two points. These kinds of devices are very common in the civilian world now with hunters measuring the distance to their target and golfers finding the exact yardage to the next green.

When I got to White Sands the Instrumentation Directorate (ID) was still a major organization and a major player with the other DoD test ranges. The ID scientists and engineers were busy developing new instrumentation systems not only for the missile range but other military test ranges. They also tested and fixed stuff.

In the basement of Bldg. 1506, ID has an optical test facility with an air-isolated test bench to isolate it from any kind of vibration. The bench is over 100 feet long and weighs 130 tons.

One way to test an optical lens to make sure it has no imperfections is to split a laser beam in half, sending one half through the lens and the other half around it. On the other side of the lens, they put the beam back together and examine it to see if the two halves still match up. If not, some fault in the lens probably caused the distortion.

Handily, ID has the capability to grind and polish lenses and mirrors.

Letting People Be Creative

Safety considerations have certainly taken some of the adventure out of life. Sometimes it is for the best and other times we just seem to have gone overboard.

In 1957, the Navy at White Sands came up with a novel solution to a problem that just wouldn't fly in today's world – literally and figuratively.

At the Desert Ship, Launch Complex 35, the Navy was faced with a damaged weather instrument atop a 135-foot tower. It was a problem because there was no way to climb the tower (no built-in ladder) and the aviation people said it was too risky for a helicopter to hover beside the tower.

What do you do? Someone suggested having a volunteer ride under a helium-filled weather balloon to the top of the tower and replace the instrument. Today, such a solution sounds a little farfetched, but it is exactly what the Navy did.

According to the Feb. 7, 1958 issue of *Wind and Sand* newspaper, Paul Sullenberger was the brains behind the idea. At the time Sullenberger worked for the Navy's Public Works organization that was the same as the Army's facilities engineers. He was responsible for estimating and engineering for the office.

Sullenberger had helped put up the tower which sat beside the Navy Aerobee launch tower. The damaged instrument was an anemometer used to measure wind speed and direction at the same height as the top of the Aerobee tower.

A taller wind tower is currently located at Launch Complex 36 where the Navy launches NASA sounding rockets. It has anemometers spaced incrementally all the way to the top. Since a rocket launched

vertically is most susceptible to cross winds at lift off, when it is going the slowest speed, it is important to know what those winds are before launch. Real-time wind measurements on the spot make it possible for controllers to know whether or not it is safe to push the firing button.

When I interviewed Sullenberger in 1984, he said the logical and traditional solution to the tower problem was to put up scaffolding. This is how the tower was erected in the first place, but it was estimated the job would require 900 man-hours.

It was after watching weather observers use balloons that Sullenberger got his brainstorm. He arranged to borrow a balloon from the weathermen at Holloman Air Force Base and rigged a boatswain's chair under it. A boatswain's chair is a seat consisting of a board and a rope and is used while working aloft or over the side of a ship. It is very minimal and, therefore, very light.

As one might imagine, the safety office was not crazy about the idea but didn't reject it outright. Safety officials wanted Sullenberger to wear a parachute just in case the balloon got away and he started drifting to Alamogordo or the Texas Panhandle. They also required the balloon be tethered with a steel cable. This was to be in addition to the nylon straps held by a ground crew and used to guide the balloon to the tower top.

Before Sullenberger strapped himself onto the seat, the safety officer talked to him about using the parachute if the balloon got away. He assured Sullenberger that it would not be a problem. If it got away, he was supposed to let the balloon rise. The safety people would then yell instructions to him and let him know when it would be safe to jump. All he had to do was drop and pull the ripcord.

After this briefing, the Air Force officer in charge of the balloon talked to Sullenberger on the side. He assured Sullenberger he did not want to jump, especially since he had never used a parachute before. Instead, he advised Sullenberger to stay with the balloon and gradually let the gas out. Doing this he would save himself and the balloon.

As Sullenberger later found out, the officer may have had other motives for his advice. It turned out the weathermen had borrowed the balloon without their colonel knowing about it. They very much wanted to get the balloon back without incident and intact.

With all his briefings complete, Sullenberger got onto the chair and slowly started the ascent. He didn't get very far. As the ground crew played out more steel cable and more nylon strapping, the balloon had to lift more and more weight. When it became evident Sullenberger wasn't going to make it, they pulled him back down and tried to lighten the load.

They tried again and again without any luck. On his last try, Sullenberger had stripped down to his underwear and had tossed the parachute aside. Still no luck. He made it about three quarters of the way.

Drastic action was required. Harry Green, a "skinny little guy" who worked for Sullenberger, was coaxed into going aloft. Green wsa just right and easily made it to the top. In less than 10 minutes he fixed the anemometer.

Pictures of the escapade were published in the *Wind and Sand* and in the June 1958 issue of *Popular Mechanics* magazine. From all the publicity, Sullenberger said he received queries from California, England and Australia. They all had "high work" to do and wanted more information to see if the method would work for them.

According to Sullenberger, the Navy duplicated the effort about six weeks later. Green went up again to help replace the transmission cable to the anemometer. This time he was afloat for about one hour.

Unfortunately, the tower has been torn down. If it was still still there, it could have been turned into a monument to White Sands creativity. For decades, the WSMR workforce has shown the right stuff for coping with any kind of problem. That capability made the range a great place for customers and workers alike.

A White Sands Chronology

I created this chronology of dates connected to White Sands Missile Range years ago when I was working in Public Affairs. We posted it on the WSMR website. I quit actively building it in 2007 when I retired although I still occasionally add an event here and there.

The chronology includes events relating to White Sands Missile Range, the technology used or tested there and the local area itself. There is no particular criterion for any event listed except the author's interest and opinion.

10,000,000 BC - Tularosa Basin formed

10,000 BC - Lake Otero open for water skiing

3,000 BC - Malapais or lava flow forms in Tularosa Basin

1,000 AD - Indians raise various crops in the area

1232 - Chinese propel arrows with small gunpowder rockets

1536 - Cabeza de Vaca walks through the area on way to Calif.

1598 - Onate leads colonists over Camino Real to northern N.M.

1812 - The British use Congreve rockets to attack Ft. McHenry

1838 - Albert Fountain born in N.Y.

1850 - Pat Garrett born in Ala.

1859 - Butterfield Trail passes through Ft. Filmore, Mesilla and Picacho

1861 July - Confederates led by Col. Baylor capture Ft. Fillmore forces

1869 Jan. 19 - Eugene Manlove Rhodes born in Tecumseh, Nebr.

1880 - Billy the Kid captured by Pat Garrett

April 6 & 7 - Apache Chief Victorio battles Buffalo Soldiers in Hembrillo Basin

1881 - The parents of Eugene Manlove Rhodes move to N.M.

April 15 - Billy the Kid, after Mesilla trial, ordered to hang for killing Sheriff Brady

April 28 - Billy escapes killing deputies Bell and Olinger

July 14 - Pat Garrett kills Billy at Fort Sumner

1882 - Robert Goddard born in Mass.

1886 July 1 - Ozanne & Company start mail and passenger service from Socorro to White Oaks. They use the Mountain Station Ranch in Oscura Mtns. as a break spot and stopover for passengers

1893 - WW Cox acquires the San Augustin ranch

1894 June 30 - Urbain Ozanne's mail service ends after 2 four-year contracts. The Mountain Station eventually becomes part of the Bursum ranch in the 20th century

Dec. 26 - Francois Jean Rochas (Frenchie) is murdered at mouth of Dog Canyon

1895 - Wilhelm Roentgen discovers X-rays

1896 Feb. 1 - Albert Fountain and son, Henry, disappear at Chalk Hill

April - Pat Garrett becomes sheriff of Dona Ana County

1897 - J.J. Thomson discovers electrons

1899 March - Gene Rhodes shelters Lee & Gilliland at his ranch in San Andres Mtns.

May - Lee and Gilliland stand trial in Hillsboro for murder of Fountains – not guilty

1901 - Post Office established at Estey City, N.M. -- copper mining town on NE WSMR

Dec. 20 - Pat Garrett appointed El Paso Customs Collector by President Roosevelt

1904 - N.M. Territory produces $2.1 million in metals (gold, silver, copper, lead, etc.)

1906 - Eugene Rhodes moves to N.Y. to live and write

1908 Feb. 29 - Pat Garrett shot and killed outside Las Cruces by Wayne Brazil

March 5 - Garrett is buried in the Las Cruces Odd Fellows Cemetery

1909 April 19 - Wayne Brazil tried for murder of Pat Garrett - jury takes 15 minutes to declare self-defense

1910 - Post Office at Estey City closes and town becomes a ghost town

1912 - Wernher von Braun born in Germany

Goddard develops and patents idea of multistage rockets

1914 - General John J. Pershing takes command of Ft. Bliss in El Paso

1919 - Goddard publishes A Method of Reaching Extreme Altitudes

1926 - Robert Goddard flies first liquid-fueled rocket on March 16

Feb. 2-27 - Gene Rhodes' *Paso Por Aqui* published serially in Saturday Evening Post

1929 - Hermann Oberth publishes The Road to Space Travel

1931 - Ellis Wright discovers giant pedestal footprints (mammoth & camel) on alkali flats

1932 - Sir James Chadwick discovers the neutron

1933 - White Sands National Monument established

1934 June 27 - Eugene Rhodes dies in Calif. but is buried in San Andres Mtns.

Enrico Fermi splits atoms (including uranium) using neutrons

1937 Nov. - Doc Noss enters Victorio Peak & supposedly finds room filled with gold

1938 - Enrico Fermi is awarded the Nobel Prize & flees to the U.S.

1939 - Doc Noss accidently seals entrance to the peak using too much dynamite

Jan. - Enrico Fermi and Neils Bohr meet to discuss possibilities of nuclear chain reaction

Aug. 2 - Einstein signs letter to President Roosevelt warning about atomic bombs

Sept. - Hitler invades Poland

1940 Sept. 7 - *Saturday Evening Post* publishes William Laurence's article about atomic bombs

1941 - San Andres Wildlife Refuge established in San Andres Mtns.

Dec. 6 - President Roosevelt approves program to develop atomic bomb

1942 - William Laurence's article is classified and the *Post* is asked to remove magazine

Alamogordo Bombing Range established

Range ranchers leave their homes for first time

92 square miles of Tenn. acquired at cost of $2.6M to build Oak Ridge nuclear facility

Sept. 18 - Leslie Groves placed in charge of Manhattan Project

Oct. - First successful V-2 flight in Germany

Nov. 25 - Approval granted to acquire Los Alamos Boys Ranch at cost of $415,000

Dec. 2 - Nuclear reaction sustained in Enrico Fermi's atomic reactor at U of Chicago

1943 Jan. 1 - University of California is notified it will run Los Alamos

Feb. 28 - Commandos destroy 3,000 pounds of heavy water at Norway's Norsk Hydro Hydrogen Electrolysis plant to put a hole in Nazi atomic bomb efforts

June 7 - Construction begins on the Hanford nuclear facility to house reactors

1944 - More than 850 buses needed at Oak Ridge to move personnel to and from work & around facilities

Jan. 27 - First operations at Oak Ridge to separate U235 from its more common form of U238

Aug. - Babcock and Wilcox tasked to build Jumbo for Trinity test

Sept. - Plutonium producing reactor at Hanford put into operation

Sept. 7 - A 18x24 mile area at the Alamogordo Bombing Range is Selected for Trinity Site

1945 Feb. 17 - Carl Rudder arrives at Trinity Site

April 1-13 - JPL's Private "F" rockets (17 rounds) fired at Ft. Bliss Hueco Range just south of WSPG

May 7 - 100 tons of TNT exploded at Trinity for rehearsal & calibration

July 9 - White Sands Proving Ground is established

July 16 - First atomic bomb (plutonium fueled) exploded at Trinity Site at 5:30 a.m.

Aug. 9 - Fat Man atomic bomb (identical to Trinity bomb) dropped on Nagasaki

Sept. - Blockhouse completed at Launch Complex 33 at cost of $95,000

Sept. 11 - News media reps visit Trinity Site, ground zero

Sept. 26 - Tiny Tim booster fired from tower at LC33

Oct. 11 - Full up WAC Corporal with Tiny Tim goes to 43 miles altitude

1946 - *Dawn Over Zero* by NY Times reporter William Laurence is published (only reporter allowed inside the Manhattan Project during WWII)

Jan. - Army Signal Corps bounces radio signal off the moon

Mar. 15 - Static firing of V-2 at 100K Static Test Stand. Red-hot steel plates fly

Apr. 16 - First V-2 fired from LC33 -- only reaches 3.4 miles in altitude

May 10 - V-2, with VIPs watching, successfully reaches 70 miles altitude

June 14 - Navy establishes a presence at White Sands

July 9 & 19 - V-2 carries corn seeds and fruit flies aloft to expose to cosmic rays

July 30 - Explosives used to separate nose cone from V-2

Oct. 24 - Motion pictures taken from V-2 showing 40,000 square miles of earth

1947 Jan. 23 - First auto pilot system used on a rocket. Also, all performance data successfully telemetered to ground recorders

March 7 - Naval Research Lab team led by John Mengel puts camera onboard V-2 that achieved 100-mile altitude and brings back first "space" photos of earth

March 16 - GAPA (toothpick maker) missile launched at Holloman

May 15 - V-2 goes astray and crashes in foothills northeast of Alamogordo

May 22 - First Corporal "E" flight from LC33. This is first American ballistic missile

May 29 - Missile 0 of Hermes series (modified V-2) crashes outside Juarez. Testing halted temporarily

June 4 - First balloon launch from Holloman AFB

July 2 - Secret Air Force balloon (Mogul project) crashes near Roswell, N.M. -- mistaken for UFO

Nov. 24 - First of Navy's Aerobee rockets launched -- reaches 34.7 miles altitude

1948 - Gene Rhodes' *Paso Por Aqui* appears on film as *Four Faces West* starring Joel McCrea as Ross McEwen and Charles Bickford as Pat Garrett

Jan. 13 - Alamogordo Army Air Field changed to Holloman Air Force Base

May 13 - First Bumper firing -- 1st stage was V-2, 2nd was WAC Corporal

May 21 - Launch of JB-2 Loon (American V-1) at Holloman AFB

June 11 - First Blossom flight with Albert, a rhesus monkey, aboard

July 26 - Negatives pieced to make one photo covering 800,000 miles

Nov. 15 - Letter from New Mexico allowing military roadblocks on U.S. 70

1949 Feb. 24 - Bumper reaches 250 miles altitude and 5,000 miles per hour

March 5 - Doc Noss shot and killed by Charlie Ryan

May 3 - Navy's first Viking missile fired

May 26 - Charlie Ryan found innocent of Noss murder based on self-defense

Sept. - Soviets test their first atomic bomb

1950 - Range fields football team which plays freshman college teams and other installations.

Army Ballistic Missile Agency (ABMA) formed in Huntsville, Ala.

March 2 - Weather research balloon launched at Holloman. Lands March 4 in Myrdal, Norway

May - First of five Hermes A-1 firings

June 23 - Test of first launch sled on Holloman test track

Aug. 31 - Fifth and final Blossom flight photographed mouse in flight

Sept. 28 - First successful animal balloon from Holloman. Reaches 97,000 ft. with 8 mice aboard

Oct. - *National Geographic* magazine features photos from their cameras aboard a V-2

Dec. 3 - Range football team (Red Devils) plays Nellis AFB Mustangs in "Silver Bowl" - lose 53-6. White Sands newspaper reported the score as 53-8

Dec. 21 – First test flight of Air Force's SNARK missile

1951 - Hermes C-1 missile with range of 500 miles becomes the Redstone

July 10 – First Navy TALOS missile flight. Later, range personnel would joke the missile's name was an acronym for "Try And Launch On Schedule"

Aug. 22 - V-2 reaches altitude of 132 miles over the range (highest in series)

Sept. 20 - One monkey & 11 mice survive Air Force Aerobee flight to 45 miles

Nov. 6 - New post theater is dedicated and opened

Nov. - Nike destroys B-17 for first intercept of plane by a guided missile

Dec. 25 – Comedian Jack Benny & actress Ann Blyth entertain at new theater at 4 p.m.

1952 - "Integrated Range" put under control of the Army

April 5 - *Collier's* magazine highlights Whiz Kids and wonder weapons at WSMR

June 6 - Navy Viking rocket sets world's altitude record for a static test when rocket breaks free during motor test and reaches an estimated 4 miles

1953 May 1 - First anthropomorphic dummy jump from balloon at 85,000 ft.

Sept. 12 - Navy pool renamed "Holland Pool" in honor of Gunner's Mate First Class George Holland who was killed in a motorcycle accident earlier in the year

Oct. - Red Canyon Range Camp opens for Nike Ajax training shots

Contractor scrapes up Trinitite and top one inch of soil at Ground Zero and deposits in mounds around GZ

1954 - According to David Martin, in *Wilderness of Mirrors,* sixteen handpicked Army sergeants dig 450-foot tunnel at WSPG in preparation for doing it in Berlin for CIA. Nobody at WSMR knows where this was done, if it was at all

Mar. 19 - LTC John Stapp rides rocket sled at track for first time

Oct. 5 - Viking rocket from WSPG takes pictures of a hurricane for the first time from altitudes beyond 100 miles. The photos show an area greater than 1000 miles in diameter

Dec. 10 - Stapp experiences 43 Gs on a rocket sled at Holloman and is labeled in *Time* magazine as the "fastest man in the world"

1955 - Ova Noss evicted from Victorio Peak because it becomes part of WSMR

Boston Celtic great Sam Jones plays basketball with WSMR team during 55/56 season.

Dec. - First successful firing of a U.S. developed ballistic missile (Redstone) with inertial guidance

1956 Mar. - Movie producer Michael Todd films Corporal launch for the opening of his film *Around the World in 80 Days* that goes on to win best picture at the Oscars

Mar. 2 - Todd's friends Eddie Fisher and Debbie Reynolds put on benefit show on post

May - DoD refuses Army's offer to put a satellite in orbit by 1957

June - Hawk missile successfully destroys F-80 jet drone

Nov. - Nike renamed the Nike Ajax to distinguish it from other Nikes

WSPG crews run into polar bears while installing equipment at Fort Churchill, Manitoba for International Geophysical Year rocket launches there

1957 Feb. – Lois Laidlaw, daughter of the CG, marries the CG's aide, First Lieutenant Robert Mackintosh

Mar. 3 – Television show *Wide, Wide World* hosted by Dave Garroway, broadcast live show featuring the launch of 9 missiles

Aug. - Manned MANHIGH balloon attains record 102,000 ft. & 32 hours aloft

Oct. 4 - Soviets launch world's first manmade satellite, Sputnik I

Oct. - Range personnel track & photograph Sputnik for Naval Research Lab

Nov. 3 - Soviets really shock the world with Sputnik II launch - 1,100 lb. satellite carries dog

1958 - Leonard Fiege and 3 men supposedly find gold bars in side tunnel of Victorio Peak

The Navy turned Holland Pool over to the Army at WSMR

Jan. 31 - U.S. Explorer I put into orbit - led to discovery of Van Allen radiation belts

April 6 – Volunteer-built chapel at Red Canyon Range Camp open for Easter services

May 1 - White Sands Proving Ground is changed to White Sands Missile Range

July 1 - 75 generals, 100 reporters & hundreds of industry leaders visit WSMR for PROJECT AMMO and see 6 missile launches (Talos, Hercules, Hawk, Dart, Little John, Lacrosse)

Oct. 1 - National Aeronautics and Space Administration (NASA) formed

Oct. 8 - Lt. Clifton McClure reaches 99,900 feet aboard Manhigh balloon over WSMR

Dec. 6 - Army's Juno II (Sergeant motor atop Jupiter first stage) launches Pioneer 3 for NASA

1959 Feb. - WSMR converts to direct-dial system so personnel can dial places themselves

March - New Post Exchange opens

March 16 - Armed Forces Day open house attracts 10,000 visitors

Aug. - Red Canyon Range Camp closed as functions move to McGregor Range

Aug. – Last of B-17 targets flown in missile test. Over 600 were used as targets since WWII

Construction completed making Highway 70 a 4-lane highway from WSMR to Cruces

1960 - *Tularosa, Last of the Frontier West* by C.L. Sonnichsen is published

Jan. 29 - HAWK intercepts Honest John missile for first supersonic missile kill ever. Film released to the news media

Jan. 31 - WSMR reports there are 10,286 military, civilian and contractor personnel working at the range

Feb. 3 - First evacuation of ranchers in the FIX – two separate missions run, Nike Hercules and Nike Zeus. A total of 130 people evacuated

March - NASA's 7 Mercury astronauts train over WSMR for a week in a special C-131, dubbed "How High The Moon." It provides several seconds of weightlessness

March 15 - Crown Prince Muhammad bin Talal of Jordan watches Redstone launch

June – Stallion Range Center, with its 200 military and civilian personnel hosts an open house

June 27 - Socorro County Chamber of Commerce requests the donation of Jumbo for a Trinity Site monument in a tourist park at the intersection of U.S. Highways 85 and 60

July - California Institute of Technology Jet Propulsion Lab closes WSMR office

Aug. 12 - A Nike Hercules shoots down another Nike Hercules at 11-mile altitude

Aug. 16 - Capt. Joe Kittinger jumps from balloon at 102,800 ft. altitude. New record

Sep. 23 & 24 - WWII hero and movie star Audie Murphy visits WSMR to film documentary

Oct. 30 - About 600 people visit Trinity Site

1961 Jan. 23 - HAWK shoots down Corporal ballistic missile

Jan. 31 - HAM, chimp trained at Holloman, does 155-mile-high flight for Project Mercury

March 1 - Commissary annex opens at Stallion to serve 60 families

March 26 - First services in new post chapel

April 12 - Cosmonaut Yuri Gagarin becomes first man in space as he orbits earth once

May 5 - Astronaut Alan Shepard flies short 15-minute flight into space

June 1 - Construction begins on 9-hole golf course at White Sands -- cost is $150,000

Aug. 5 - Fiege and crew start work at Victorio Peak to recover gold

Sep. - Post school enrollment for new school year at 791 students

Nov. 3 - MG Shinkle orders Fiege off the range and bars all gold searches

Dec. 14 - Nike Zeus successfully intercepts a Nike Hercules missile high over WSMR

1962 - NASA White Sands Test Facility established on July 6

WSMR FPS-16 radar track Mercury manned flights as their orbits pass nearby

Fire on the Mountain by Edward Abbey is published. It is a fictional account of John Prather's battle with Ft. Bliss over his ranch. Abbey places it at White Sands Missile Range instead of Bliss

May 26 - The nine-hole golf course was officially opened

July 27 - Successful Banshee (Bravo 20) explosive test 15 miles above WSMR

Nov. – "Missile Rangers" choral group wins 4th Army small chorus competition

Dec. 13 - Only successful StarGazer high-altitude balloon launch with Joe Kittinger as pilot/engineer and Bill White, Navy astronomer, collecting data. They worked all night above 80,000 feet from their capsule. Total flight just over 18 hours. It was meant to demonstrate the ability to take a laboratory to very high altitudes for extended periods

1963 - Huge RAMPART radar installed at WSMR for Athena shots. Could track a basketball 1,000 miles out

Feb. – Flying Club boasts of acquiring a twin-engine C-45 to join their eight other planes

April - Off-range firing of Sergeant missile to WSMR from Old Horse Springs on the Plains of San Augustin

June 5 - President Kennedy visits to view launches at White Sands

July 19 - Gaddis Mining starts 60-day dig at Victorio Peak

August - First overland flight of Pershing missile, Bliss to WSMR

Sept. - Pershing launch from Black Mesa (near Blanding), Utah to WSMR

Oct. - Pershing launch from Fort Wingate to WSMR

Nov. 12 - Radio commentator Paul Harvey visits WSMR

1964 Feb. - Wadsworth Blvd. is renamed Headquarters Blvd. on WSMR. Wadsworth was first Chief of Ordnance, 1812-1821

April - Science exhibit consisting of 5 modules, contained in semi-trailer, is sent to New Mexico Bldg. at New York World's Fair until Oct. In Nov. it went to the Ariz. State Fair which started bookings for other fairs and events through the early 1980s. Modules eventually serve as basis for first Visitors Center in Public Affairs

July 8 - First Air Force successful flight of Athena from Green River, Utah

Aug. 27 - Informal activation of Nuclear Effects Lab

Sept. - First engine tests at NASA´s WSTF

Oct. 4 - Trinity Site open house draws 706 visitors

Oct. 23 - WSMR newspaper *Wind and Sand* runs photo of LPGA member Mickey Wright teeing off from V-2 rocket lying on its side in Missile Park. Wright was in Las Cruces to play in Las Cruces Open. In the 1960s Wright was leading money winner on LPGA and won 13 titles in 1963

Nov. 19 - Pershing missile overshoots target and ends up near Creede, Col.

Dec. 2 - Sonic boom tests are demonstrated for news media at Oscura Range Camp. F-104 accidently generates estimated 40 lbs. psi shock wave and shatters many windows

1965 - Sprint missile first flight at White Sands

Range spruces up Trinity Site by destroying manned bunkers in spring and erecting lava obelisk at GZ

The Air Force's Aerobee tower at Holloman is moved to the Navy launch complex

Jan. 3 – Start of direct in and out dialing tying WSMR to other military and government facilities throughout the world. Dubbed Automatic Voice Network or AUTOVON

March - Major Vincent D'Angelo, Army radio correspondent interviews range rider Floyd Adams, mathematician Lucille Graham and electronics engineer Joy Arthur. Graham and Arthur went on to be elected to WSMR Hall of Fame

April 30 - Target missile crashes into Highway 70 and gouges hole in pavement

May - SP4 Melvin Hueston and PFC Stanley Stenner, performing as the Shakers, take second place in the vocal group competition at the 4th Army's entertainment contest

July 16 - *Wind and Sand* newspaper runs photo showing the recently completed Trinity Site obelisk marking ground zero

Sep. - Some Pershing debris found 12 miles north of Creede, Co. by Maurice Chaffee. Missile was lost after launch from Hueco Range, Ft. Bliss in Nov. 1964. In 1982 hunters found the second stage, guidance package and reentry vehicle

Oct. 6 - Wayward Pershing is destroyed after Utah launch with debris then found north of Blanding during the next week. Later in month Germans perform first "annual training firings" from Utah at Gilson Butte

Oct. 31 - Vonda Kay Van Dyke, Miss America for 1965, visits – gives talk at chapel and performs at theater

Nov-Dec - Two, two-day deer hunts on WSMR yield 700 deer to 1,645 hunters

1966 - NASA completes Little Joe II test program for Apollo

Feb. - First launch of Navy´s Tartar missile

March 9 - First launch of Navy´s Terrier missile

March 30 - MG John Cone, WSMR Commander, dies while helping motorist

April 14 - First dual Aerobee rocket launch by the Navy. University of Colorado students built the payloads. Rocket #1 hit 114 miles while rocket #2 reached 120 miles

May 10 - First launch of Navy´s Standard missile

June - normally dry and hot, the month turned freakish with 6.94 inches of rain recorded

Sept. - Project Gunfighter at range as Army and Navy artillery pieces fire 20-lb. payloads straight up to an altitude of 50 miles

1967 - Henry Kerbow finds 1919 military ID in desert near C Station. Belonged to MSGT Thomas Wooten who trained recruits from Ft. Bliss in that area

March - First dual launch of Pershing from off range (Blanding, Utah) at 5:30 p.m.

Sept. 11 - Pershing missile fired from Blanding, Utah crashes just over Mexican border near Van Horn, Texas

Three underground bunkers at Trinity Site are made safe by Los Alamos to include "Sleeping Beauty." Los Alamos conducts radiological survey of Trinity. WSMR constructs inner fence at Ground Zero. Los Alamos removed 10 garbage cans filled with Trinitite from buried bunker south of GZ and "trucked to the contaminated dump at Los Alamos"

1968 Apr. 27 - Ceremony in Green River, Utah park dedicating Athena missile donated by the Air Force. About 90% of the display missile's components actually flew on missions

May - Thirteenth annual Armed Forces Day at WSMR draws estimated 15,000 people Five hot rocket and missile shots. Simultaneous open house at Stallion

May 31 - Last issue of the *Wind and Sand* newspaper for White Sands after 1950 start

June 21 - First issue of the *Missile Ranger* newspaper for White Sands, published by Wendell Faught and the Deming Headlight. Uses new offset presses

Sept 11 - A 28.7 million-cubic-foot Air Force research balloon reaches 158,300 feet – world's largest balloon and world's altitude record

1969 - Oryx introduced on White Sands by N.M. Dept. of Game and Fish

Aguirre Springs recreation area is developed by the BLM just west of WSMR

July 1 - General Schedule civilian employees receive, on average, a 9.1% pay raise

Sept. - Nike Javelin used to release barium creating multi-color cloud visible in Miss.

Oct. - NASA's WSTF completes Apollo Lunar Module landing radar and rendezvous radar test program

Dec. - Clutter fence (105' tall) around RAM radar at RAMPART is completed by the Air Force

1970 - Annual Armed Forces Day activities moved to July to coincide with 25th anniversary of WSMR

July 11 - Athena crashes in Mexico after launch from Green River, Utah. Incident is made worse because it is carrying radioactive Cobalt 57

Installed in 1964, the Fast Burst Reactor records its 4,000th test

1972 July - First test of Viking Mars lander after being boosted to 150,000 feet

1973 June 1 - First launch of a Navy Talos missile to be used as a low-altitude supersonic target

June 2 - Jack Anderson mentions F. Lee Bailey and Victorio Peak in column

July 28 - First in series of propane railcar cook-off tests. Unprotected tank explodes in 23.5 seconds

1974 March - Solar Furnace opens at WSMR -- capable of 5,000 degrees F.

July - WSMR Nuclear Effects Lab dedicated

Congress appropriates money for purchase of ranch lands on WSMR

1975 May - Germans successfully fire 300th Pershing from Green River, Utah to WSMR

1976 Oct. - 600 tons of ammonium nitrate & fuel oil exploded (= to 1 kiloton) in Dice Throw test

1977 March – Trident missile destruct test. Burning missile creates green glass almost identical to the glass at Trinity Site except it isn't radioactive

March - Operation Goldfinder starts at Victorio Peak

Jim Eckles and Debbie Bingham begin work in WSMR Public Affairs

Dec. - First test round of Multiple Launch Rocket System successfully fired

1978 June 21 – Demonstration for national news media of the Navy Tomahawk cruise missile. Secretary of Defense Harold Brown brought the reporters

Aug. 19 - Ten inches of rain fall in two hours, five killed in flash floods

Oct. - Shuttle astronaut training begins at Northrup Strip

Oct. 21 – CBS anchorman Walter Cronkite visits Trinity Site to do standup by obelisk

Dec. - Press demonstration of 5 precision guided munitions (Copperhead, TOW, GBU-15, Walleye, laser-guided bombs)

1979 - Northrup Strip identified as possible shuttle landing strip

Ben Burtt, soundman for George Lucas films, visits to collect sounds

1980 - NASA WSTF tests on shuttle maneuvering engine and landing system

The Roswell Incident by Berlitz & Moore is published

Congress appropriates more money for purchase of ranch lands

July 4 - First induction into newly formed WSMR Hall of Fame - 6 inductees were Tombaugh, von Braun, Turner, Brillante, Hemingway and Billups

1981 Feb. 18 - General of the Army Omar Bradley speaks at WSMR Patriotism Luncheon

1982 March 30 - Shuttle Columbia lands at Northrup Strip. 8-day mission

April 6 - Columbia leaves Northrup Strip on back of 747

July - Air Force's Ground Based Electro-optical Deep-Space Surveillance System opens at Stallion

Oct. - Dave McDonald enters missile range to protest rancher payments, demands his ranch back

Nov 19 - First successful Pershing II launch from McGregor Range to WSMR

1983 Jan. 18 - Ribbon cutting for the new High Energy Laser System Test Facility

June - Tracking Data Satellite Relay System put into operation by NASA at WSTF

Oct. 26 - Direct Course explosion using 600 tons of ammonium nitrate and fuel oil

1985 - Ten-year mountain lion study begins on missile range

1986 - *The Zone of Silence* by Gerry Hunt is published in paperback. The author claims the "zone of silence" in Mexico sucked the Athena missile off course in 1970 where it crashed

1989 - Ova Noss Family Partnership proposes new search at Victorio Peak

March - First commercial rocket launch at WSMR

1992 - Digging actually starts at Victorio Peak by ONFP

1993 Aug. 18 - First flight of Delta Clipper at White Sands

1995 - Writer Doug Preston visits for several days for article in *New Mexico* magazine. He was just getting famous for his horror/thriller book *Relic*

July 16 - Trinity Site open house on 50th anniversary --biggest crowd ever (5,400)

Missile range rounds up 1,530 horses and adopts them out

USFWS proposes White Sands for possible release of Mexican wolves

1996 March 23 - First annual Tumbleweed 25 mountain bike ride hosted by WSMR

July 31 - Delta Clipper tips over on landing, explodes and burns

October 17 - Army TACMS missile successfully fired from Ft. Wingate to White Sands

1997 March 24 - Media Day prior to 4 rockets launches to look at Comet Hale-Bopp

March 24 - April 7 - Public invited to watch the 4 launches from the parade field

April 24 - International Astronomers Union happens to visit Trinity Site on day UFOs are predicted to land and aliens to officially meet with earthlings

Nov. 17 - First Hera launch from Ft. Wingate, N.M. 2nd stage did not ignite

Nov. 20 - Konrad Dannenberg, German V-2 scientist, visits WSMR

1998 April 4 - largest crowd ever for regular Trinity Site tour (4,200)

April 19 - 1,700 run/walk in the annual Bataan Memorial Death March at WSMR

1999 - New cruise missile (JASSM) - joint Air Force & Navy program - is tested

March 15 - Patriot Advanced Capabilities (PAC-3) intercepts Hera ballistic target

April - Very windy Spring. Average wind speed for month was 10.5 mph (that's 24/7) Peak wind on Salinas Peak was 122 mph.

April 24 - Hembrillo Battlefield ceremony honors those who fought in the 1880 battle

June 10 & Aug. 2 - First intercepts of ballistic targets by THAAD (shooting bullets w/bullets)

2000 May 31 - New Cox Range Control Center Bldg. is dedicated

June 6 & Aug. 28 - Tactical High Energy Laser (THEL) shoots down Katyusha rockets

2001 Oct. 6 - Trinity Site open house cancelled for first time in decades because of 9/11 attacks

2002 June - Tests confirm first NM case of chronic wasting disease found in a WSMR deer

Nov. 5 - Army's Mobile Tactical High-Energy Laser destroys artillery projectile in flight

Nov. 21-23 - Desert bighorn sheep roundup in Ariz. & N.M. with release of 51 animals at San Andres National Wildlife Refuge on WSMR

2003 Jan. - More cases of chronic wasting disease are confirmed in deer from WSMR

Feb. 1 - Space Shuttle Columbia breaks apart and is destroyed on re-entry

Feb. 7 - First ever SCUD missile fired at WSMR - successful

March 30 - Bataan Memorial Death March cancelled because of lack of medical support. Military personnel were deployed overseas

2004 Oct. 1 - IMA (Installation Management Agency) funding begins

Nov. - Dedication of the V-2 Annex at the Museum to house refurbished V-2

2005 July 13-16 - The range celebrates its 60th anniversary with tours and Hall of Fame induction (Joy Arthur and Paul Arthur - first husband and wife to be inducted), history seminars and a Trinity Site open house

Nov. 30 - BG Bob Reese retires and Mr. Tom Berard (civilian) takes over as first "Director" of WSMR

2006 May-June - DreamWorks movie company films several scenes for a feature motion picture based on the Transformer cartoons and toys. They built a desert village in the dunes along Range Road 10

May 25 - Photographer Roland Miller shoots LC-33 and the 500K Static Test Stand.

June 14 - Navy celebrates 60th anniversary at WSMR. They donate 5-inch gun and missile launcher to the museum's missile park

Informational Lists

White Sands Commanders

This is a straight-forward list of the past commanders at White Sands Missile Range. Occasionally there are breaks of a month or two between commanders. These are the result of gaps between one commander leaving and the replacement actually taking the official reins.

Photos of each commander can be seen on the White Sands Museum's website.

Colonel Harold Turner
July 1945 - August 1947

Brigadier General Philip Blackmore
August 1947 - January 1950

Brigadier General George Eddy
January 1950 - June 1954

Major General William Bell
August 1954 - January 1956

Major General Waldo Laidlaw
February 1956 - June 1960

Major General John Shinkle
July 1960 - June 1962

Major General Frederick Thorlin
July 1962 - July 1965

Major General John Cone – died while on duty at WSMR
August 1965 - March 1966

Colonel Karl Eklund – served as acting commander after Cone's death
March 1966 - October 1966

Major General Horace Davisson
October 1966 - March 1970

Major General Edward deSaussure
April 1970 - May 1972

Major General Arthur Sweeny
June 1972 - July 1974

Major General Robert Proudfoot
July 1974 - July 1975

Major General Orville Tobiason
September 1975 - February 1979

Major General Duard Ball
March 1979 - July 1980

Major General Alan Nord
July 1980 - September 1982

Major General Niles Fulwyler
September 1982 - June 1986

Major General Joe Owens
June 1986 - October 1987

Major General Thomas Jones
October 1987 - August 1990

Brigadier General Ronald Hite
August 1990 - July 1991

Brigadier General Richard Wharton
July 1991 - June 1994

Brigadier General Jerry Laws
June 1994 - April 1998

Brigadier General Harry Gatanas
April 1998 - November 1999

Brigadier General Steven Flohr
November 1999 - October 2001

Brigadier General William Engel
October 2001 - May 2003

Colonel Lawrence Sowa
May 2003 - July 2003

Brigadier General Robert Reese
July 2003 - November 2005

Mr. Thomas Berard – first "Director" of White Sands
November 2005 - October 2007

Brigadier General Richard McCabe
October 2007 - October 2008

Brigadier General David Mann
October 2008 - August 2009

Brigadier General John Regan
August 2009 - August 2011

Brigadier General John Ferrari
August 2011 - September 2012

Brigadier General Gwen Bingham – first woman commander of White Sands
September 2012 -

WSMR Hall Of Fame Members

The White Sands Hall of Fame was created in 1980 by Range Commander Brigadier General Duard Ball to recognize and honor WSMRites who made significant and lasting contributions to the range's mission. Nominations are taken annually and then reviewed by a special committee of the range's leadership. They make recommendations to the commander who actually makes the selection.

There have been a few years where no one was inducted. As of 2013, 50 individuals have been chosen for the Hall of Fame.

The first induction took place during the White Sands 35th anniversary celebration in July 1980. Six were inducted that day, the most at any one time. It was also the cream of the crop since it included Wernher von Braun, Clyde Tombaugh and some big names from the Range's earliest years.

The inclusion of von Braun occasionally stirs some controversy because of his background in Hitler's Germany. Since he was a member of the Nazi Party, some say he doesn't belong. Others say it was the only way he could have survived the war years.

Also, some point out he did very little at White Sands when he got to America. His personal work focused on activities at Fort Bliss.

On the other hand, he was the face of rocket science in the 20th century and including him was a way to kick-start the program.

According to Austin Vick, who is in the Hall of Fame himself and who helped the general set up the system, Ball intended it to be a little more inclusive and not quite so exclusive. Still, it is the highest honor the missile range can bestow on one of its own.

While General Ball may have thought it would include more folks, I once heard a senior retired Army officer say there were too many low-ranking civilians in the Hall of Fame. So Hall of Fame inductees come from all walks of life at WSMR and often generate some debate as everyone has an opinion about an honoree's worthiness.

Over the years, the commander's review panel has struggled with defining what "significant" means when they review the nominations. This toil and trouble seems appropriate given the diversity of the WSMR workforce. The vast range of contributions possible at White Sands should not be judged by some sort of a nifty Army 10-point checklist. With the rather vague guidelines set down in the Hall of Fame Pamphlet, the review committee gets to make that tough decision - after all they are the top managers at the missile range.

Below is a diagram of the Hall of Fame medal. Each inductee receives a medal and certificate. His or her photo, along with a copy of the certificate, then hangs in the Hall of Fame.

Hall of Fame Members
By Year of Induction

1980

Colonel Harold Turner
First Range Commander
Served 1945 – 1947

Dr. Werhner von Braun
Rocket Scientist
Served 1945 – 1950

Clyde Tombaugh
Chief of Optical Measurements
Served 1946 – 1955

Benjamin Billups
Chief of the Plans Office
Served 1951 – 1973

Frank Hemingway
Technical Director of National Range
Served 1947 – 1977

Gabriel Brillante
Public Affairs Officer
Served 1953 – 1974

1981

Joseph Franczak
Civil Engineering Technician
Served 1952 – 1973

1982

Brigadier General George Eddy
Range Commander
Served 1950 – 1954

1983

Herbert Karsch
Range Technical Director
Served 1945 – 1956

Robert Lechtenberg
Technical Director
Army Material Test & Evaluation Directorate
Served 1950 – 1972

1984

Dr. Ernst Steinhoff
Rocket Scientist
Served 1945 – 1972

Nathan Wagner
Father of Missile Flight Safety
Served 1950 – 1973

1985

Ozro Covington
Tech Director, Army Signal Missile Support Agency
Served 1946 – 1961

Gabriel Galos
Chief of Optics in Instrumentation
Served 1952 – 1977

Glenn Elder
Chief of Nuclear Effects Lab
Served 1955 – 1974

1986

Alice Lucile Graham
Chief of Computer Operations
Served 1951 – 1969

Dr. George Gardiner
Founder of NMSU's Physical Science Lab
Served 1946 – 1961

Roy Autry
Civilian Personnel Officer
Served 1960 – 1974

1987

Wayne Roemersberger
Range Instrumentation Developer
Served 1946 – 1956

1988

Patrick Higgins
Chief, Data Sciences Division
Served 1950 – 1981

Samuel Teitelbaum
Range Comptroller
Served 1952 – 1971

1989

Major General Duard Ball
Commanding General
Served 1979 – 1980

1990

Major General John Shinkle
Range Commander
Served 1960 – 1962

1991

Leon Goode
Ballistic Missile Defense pioneer
Served 1956 -1988

1992

Edward Noble
Pioneer in Development of Range Optics
Served 1952 – 1979

1994

Major General Alan Nord
Range Commander
Served 1980 – 1982

1995

Frances Williams
Chief of Equal Employment Opportunity Programs
Served 1969 – 1987

1996

Major General Niles Fulwyler
Range Commander
Served 1982 – 1986

1999

William McCool
Father of Real Time Data Processing
Served 1959 – 1973

2000

John Bayer
Test Conductor
Served 1955 – 2000

Alex Paczynski
Space Harbor Project Manager
Served 1964 – 1995

2001

Austin Vick
Manager and Engineer, National Range Operations
Served 1950 – 1984

2002

Father Paul Betowski, SJ
Catholic Chaplain
Served 1970 – 2002

Carlos Bustamante
Test Facility Design Engineer
Served 1952 – 1997

2004

James (Scotty) Scott
Operations Manager
Served 1952 – 2003

Lloyd (Gunner) Briggs
Director, Navy Research Rockets
Served 1966 – 1986

Jed Durrenberger
Photo-Optical Engineer
Served 1951 – 1981

2005

Joy Arthur
Research Electronic Engineer
Served 1958 – 2005

Paul Arthur
Tester - Director - Mentor
Served 1956 – 2004

2006

Joseph Gold
Optics Pioneer/Program Manager
Served 1949 – 1979

Moises Pedroza
Telemetry Pioneer
Served 1968 - 2005

Melvin Lux
Manager, Land-Air Range Operations.
Served 1950 – 1987

2007

Joaquin Provencio
Operations and Signal Security Pioneer
Served 1951 – 1985

2008

Richard W. Benfer
Director - Bell Labs, White Sands
Served 1946 – 1969

2009

Mary Beth Reinhart
Chief of the Community Recreation Division
Served 1982 – 2005

Dale Green
Chief of the Engineers Uprange Division
Served 1951 – 1983

2012

Colonel Daniel E. Duggan
Deputy Commander and Director, National Range
Operations
Served 1961 – 1965 and 1980 – 1985

Dr. Gene Dirk
Physicist and Electrical Engineer
Served 1963 – 2011

2013

Andres Portillo
Optics Systems Manager
Served 1958 – 2001

Jim Eckles
Public Affairs Factotum and Historian
Served 1977 – 2007

Some Sources

Books

100 Tons of Gold by David Leon Chandler

Buried Treasures Of The American Southwest by W.C. Jameson

City Of Fire – Los Alamos and the Atomic Age, 1943-1945 by James W. Kunetka

Clyde Tombaugh – Discoverer Of Planet Pluto by David H. Levy

Day of Trinity by Lansing Lamont

Day One – Before Hiroshima And After by Peter Wyden

Fire On The Mountain by Edward Abbey

German Guided Missiles of WWII by Rowland F. Pocock

Ghost Towns And Mining Camps of New Mexico by James and Barbara Sherman

Hombrecito's War by W. Michael Farmer

Incident at San Augustine Springs by Richard Wadsworth

Leo White – Mountain Rocket Man by Ralph Roberts

Lost Gold & Buried Treasure by Kevin D. Randle

Lost Treasure, A Guide To Buried Riches by Bill Yenne

Manhattan: The Army And The Atomic Bomb by Vincent C. Jones

Men And Atoms by William L. Laurence

Mount Dragon by Doug Preston and Lincoln Child

New Mexico Mines and Minerals by Fayette Alexander Jones, 1904.

Nobody's Horses, The Dramatic Rescue of the Wild Herd of White Sands by Don Hoglund

Now It Can Be Told by Lieutenant General Leslie R. Groves

Paso Por Aqui by Eugene Manlove Rhodes

Pat Garrett, The Story of a Western Lawman by Leon C. Metz.

Relic by Doug Preston and Lincoln Child

Rockets And Missiles Of World War III by Robert Berman and Bill Gunston.

Rockets of the World by Peter Alway.

Science With a Vengeance, by David DeVorkin.

Stallion Gate by Martin Cruz Smith

Tales of Tomorrow #1: Invaders at Ground Zero by David Houston

The Authentic Life of Billy the Kid by Pat Garrett. Scholars say it was ghostwritten by Ash Upton.

The Best Novels and Stories of Eugene Manlove Rhodes edited by Frank Dearing

The Curse of the San Andres by Henry James

The Day The Sun Rose Twice by Ferenc Morton Szasz

The Executioner #35: Wednesday's Wrath by Don Pendleton

Some Sources

The Illustrated Encyclopedia of the World's Rockets & Missiles by Bill Gunston

The Life and Death of Colonel Albert Jennings Fountain by A.M. Gibson

The Making Of The Atomic Bomb by Richard Rhodes

The Malpais Missiles by Master Sergeant Jean-Paul Moore, USAF Retired

The Rocket Team by Frederick Ordway III and Mitchell R. Sharpe

The Rocketmakers by Harry Wulforst

The Rockets and Missiles of White Sands Proving Ground 1945-1958 by Gregory Kennedy

The Roswell Incident by Charles Berlitz and William L. Moore

The Roswell Report, Case Closed by Captain James McAndrew, U.S. Air Force.

The Roswell Report, Fact Versua Fiction in the New Mexico Desert by U.S. Air Force.

The Trinity Factor by Sean Flannery

The Two Alberts by Gordon Owen

The Zone of Silence by Gerry Hunt

These Hallowed Grounds. A Pursuit Of American History by Deborah Busenkell and Richard Busenkell.

Treasure of Victoria Peak by Phil A. Koury

Trinity's Children: Living Along America's Nuclear Highway by Scott McCartney

Tularosa, Last of the Frontier West by C. L. Sonnichsen

V-2 by Walter Dornberger

What Men Call Treasure, The Search for Gold at Victorio Peak by David Schweidel & Robert Boswell

Wilderness of Mirrors by David C. Martin. CIA had Army sergeants dig 450-foot tunnel at WSPG in 1954 as practice before doing it in Berlin.

Newspapers

Albuquerque Journal

DARCOM News

El Paso Times

Las Cruces Sun-News

Las Vegas Review Journal

Rio Grande Republican

Roswell Daily Record

Valencia County News-Bulletin

Wind and Sand (1950-1968) & *Missile Ranger* (1968-present) -White Sands Missile Range newspapers

Magazines and Journals

Air and Space Magazine

Air Defense Artillery

American Heritage

American Heritage Of Invention & Technology

Archaeology

Army – Army Missiles in June 1973

Army Information Digest

Army R, D & A, Vol. 25, No. 1

Army Times

Battlefields Review – issue 20

Collier's

GPS World

Health Physics

National Geographic Magazine

New Mexico Magazine
New Mexico Space Journal
New Mexico Stockman
New Mexico Wildlife
New Yorker Magazine
Nuclear Weapons Journal
Polo: Players' Edition Magazine
Popular Mechanics Magazine
Relics Magazine
Sky and Telescope
Soldiers Magazine
Sports Illustrated
The American Magazine
The Friends Journal
The Western Horseman
Time
True West
Wild West

Newsletters

Hands Across History. Joint newsletter for White Sands Missile Range Historical Foundation and White
        Sands Pioneer Group
MSD News. Publication from Atlantic Research Corporation.
Peak of the News. Produced by the Ova Noss Family Partnership
The Broomstick Scientist, A Journal/Newsletter. Quarterly newsletter for broomstick scientists veterans and
        published by Arnie Crouch for almost a decade.
The Good Old Days. Newsletter for White Sands Pioneer Group for first year - 1984.
Whispering Sands Pioneer Gazette. Newsletter for the pioneer group, starting in 1985.

Reports

500,000-Pound Rocket Static Test Facility At White Sands Proving Ground, New Mexico, Special Report, Feb
        ruary 1957, signed by Lieutenant Colonel James Hamill, Chief of the Ordnance Mission.
A Cultural Resource Inventory and Assessment of Dona Ana Range by Skelton, Freeman, Smiley, Pigott.
An Environmental Assessment of the Ova Noss Family Partnership Expedition Into Victorio Peak by ECoPlan,
        Inc. and Human Systems Research, Inc.
Athena Flight Test Matrix. Atlantic Research, Missile Systems Division.
Atmospheric Phenomena At High Altitudes, Final Progress Report for the period July 15, 1946 to August 31,
        1950, Engineering Research Institute, University of Michigan.
Conline's Skirmish: An Episode Of The Victorio Peak War, December 2005. Archaeology Report No. 481 by
        Human Systems Research, Inc.
Final Report, Project Hermes V-2 Missile Program by General Electric (Report No. R52A0510 under contract
        DA-30-115-ORD-23)
Findings of Disease Screening of Gemsbok on White Sands Missile Range by Louis Bender, USGS
First American Showing of the V-2, by R.W. Porter, General Electric.
Geology and Minint History of Good Fortune Camp, San Andres Mining District by Robert Eveleth,
        NMBM&MR, 2001.
Geology of Organ Mountains and southern San Andres Mountains, New Mexico by William Seager, New
        Mexico Bureau of Mines and Mineral Resources.

Health Physics Survey of Trinity Site by Frederic Fey, Los Alamos Scintific Laboratory, 1967

High Altitude Research At The Applied Physics Laboratory In The 1940s, Johns Hopkins APL Technical Digest, Vol. 6

Los Alamos 1943-1945: The Beginning of an Era. Los Alamos publication LASL-79-78

LPG Railcar Cook-Off Test Program.

Missile I by Guenther Hintze, a special report from the Ordnance Research and Development Division, Sub office (Rocket) at Fort Bliss, Texas (Hermes II).

Native Range And Conservation Of The White Sands Pupfish (Cyprinodon Tularosa) by John Pittenger and Craig Springer, *The Southwestern Naturalist.*

Preliminary Report and Interpretation of Investigations Concerning the "Big Footprints" Alleged Camel Tracks on White Sands Missile Range by Peter Eidenbach, HSR, June 18, 1981.

Project Trinity 1945-1946 by Carl Maag and Steve Rohrer for the U.S. Defense Nuclear Agency.

Radiological Survey and Evaluation of the Fallout Area from the Trinity Test: Chupadera Mesa and White Sands Missile Range, New Mexico. Los Alamos.

Reintroduction Of The Mexican Wolf Within Its Historic Range In The Southwestern United States – Summary of Final Environmental Impact Statement, November 1996 by Fish and Wildlife Service.

Reopening S.R. 52 For Public Use. A study report prepared in accordance with House Memorial 6, State of New Mexico, 33rd Legislature, 2nd Special Session, 1978.

San Andres Desert Bighorn Sheep: A Review Of Population Dynamics And Associated Management Concern by Patricia A. Hoban, April 1990.

Status Report For The Mexican Wolf Recovery Program – several years of these.

Technical Data On The Development Of The A4/V-2 by Heinrich Schulze for Dr. Von Braun's birthday in 1965, NASA's Historical Archives.

The Story of White Sands Proving Ground, April 30, 1946. I have a photocopy of the report with no other information except on the edge of each page it says, "Reproduced at the National Archives."

Trinity by Kenneth Barinbridge. Los Alamos publication LA-6300-H.

Upper Atmospheric Research Report No. XXI, Summary of Upper Atmospheric Rocket Research Firings, by Charles P. Smith, Jr. dated February 1954 and supplemented February 1958 and January 1959, U.S. Naval Research Laboratory.

Use of V-2 Rocket To Convey Primate To Upper Atmosphere by Captain D.G. Simons, May 1949. AF Technical Report 5821.

Miscellaneous

1948 United States Military Academy Visit to 1st AAA Guided Missile Battalion, White Sands Proving Ground on 12 June 1947.

A Brief History of White Sands Proving Ground, 1941-1965 by Peter Eidenbach.

A Discussion Of Overland Missile Flights In The United States by Major Guy O. King, U.S. Air Force. A thesis submitted to the Air War College, November 1963.

A History of Land Use of the San Andres National Wildlife Refuge, New Mexico by Arthur F. Halloran, Refuge Manager, August 1944.

A History of White Sands Proving Ground, 30 September 1947.

A Number of Things by Peter Eidenbach and Robert Hart.

Alleged Treasure Trove, White Sands Missile Range, June 13, 1973.

An Evaluation Of The Ecological Potential Of White Sands Missile Range To Support A Reintroduced Population Of Mexican Wolves by James Bednarz, 22 June 1989.

An Introduction To White Sands Missile Range, Birthplace of American Missilery, 1 April 1968.

Army Ordnance Department Guided Missiles Program, 1 January 1948.

Army Technical Manual 4-236. March 7, 1942. Instructions for the use of Rocket Targets by Antiaircraft Units, dated March 7, 1942.

Biographical Data: Dr. Wernher von Braun from Alabama Space and Rocket Center.

Capabilities, White Sands Test Complex, 1975.

Congressional Recognition of Goddard Rocket and Space Museum with Tributes to Dr. Robert H. Goddard. U.S. Congress.

Design And Fabrication Of The WAC Corporal Missile, Booster, Launcher, And Handling Facilities by W.A. Sandberg and W.B. Barry. JPL Report No. 4-21.

Development And Flight Performance Of A High Altitude Sounding Rocket The 'WAC Corporal' by F.J. Malina. JPL Report No. 4-18.

Dividend Mining And Milling Company's Mines and Mills At Estey City, New Mexico. A company prospectus.

Dorothy Knipe's Extracts From Correspondence, With Photos.

Flight Requirements Plan for Black Brant IX 36.087 US (July 1991) and others like it from NASA, Goddard Space Flight Center.

Green River Launch Complex Public Information Plan, February 2000

Hearing Before The Subcommittee On Public Lands And Reserved Water of the Committee on Energy And Natural Resources United States Senate Ninety-Eighth Congress, First Session on Acquisition of Land, and Acquisition and Termination of Grazing Permits or Licenses by the Bureau of Land Management Pursuant to the Taylor Grazing Act at White Sands Missile Range, New Mexico, Nov. 15, 1983.

Hembrillo Battlefield Briefing by Karl W. Laumbach, April 24, 1999.

Hembrillo, An Apache Battlefield of the Victorio War by Karl W. Laumbach

Historic White Sands Missile Range by Joel Powell and Keith Scala in *Journal of the British Interplanetary Society*, Vol. 47, 1994.

History Of Space And Missile Systems Organization, Deputy For Reentry Sytems, 1 July 1970 – 30 June 1971 by Harry C. Jordan. SAMSO History Office.

Homes On The Range, edited by Peter Eidenbach and Beth Morgan. Oral recollections of early ranch life on the U.S. Army White Sands Missile Range, New Mexico.

Integration of the Holloman – White Sands Missile Test Ranges 1947 – 1952. An Air Research and Development Command Historical Monogaph.

Introduction to White Sands Proving Ground – Post Guide, 1952.

Life at Trinity Base Camp by Thomas Merlan

Major Achievements in Space Biology at the Air Force Missile Development Center, Holloman Air Force Base, New Mexico 1953-1957.

NASA Sounding Rockets, 1958-1968, A Historical Summary.

National Register of Historic Places Registration Form for "Estey City Historic Mining District" by National Park Service. Laboratory of Anthropology – LA 50095.

New Mexico Archaeological Council Tour, White Sands Missile Range, June 9, 1984.

New Mexico Mines, A Storehouse of Precious and Base Ores and Metals, 1906 by the Bureau of Immigration. NMSU Library, RGHC. Transcript of Tape No. RG79-80

Nuclear Files Archive – a website at: http://www.nuclearfiles.org/docs

Off-Range Corridor System Plan by National Range Operations, White Sands Missile Range, NM 27 August 1993

Operation Goldfinder (19 Mar thru 1 Apr 77) After Action Report

Origin And Construction of White Sands Proving Ground, 1945 – 1954.

Outward Bound! by Willy Ley in *Air Trails Pictorial*, November 1946.

Pershing Launch Configuration Summary, February 1960 Through October 1988, An Historical Record from Martin Marietta Missile Systems, December 1988.

Pioneer, Vol. 5 Nos. 3 & 4 – The Basin of Tears, Tularosa Basin Historical Society.

Pit Assembly Crew Interviews by Alice Buck, September 1983. Department of Energy McDonald Ranch House Project.

Pre-1963 Designations of U.S. Missile And Drones by Andreas Parsch

Prelude To The Space Age, speech by James Van Allen for George Gardiner Memorial Lecture at New Mexico
    State University, March 26, 1986.

Preparation and Firing Schedule for V-2 Rocket No. 45. Memo dated 24 January 1949.

Project MEWS (Missile Exercise White Sands) – Your Guide to Project Mews. Captain Dan Duggan's copy.

Proposal And General Plan for An Experimental release Of The Mexican Wolf by David Parsons,
    February 19, 1991.

Proposed Exploration Program, Victoria Peak, White Sands Missile Range by Loren Smith, Gaddis Mining
    Company, November 1962.

School Days, edited by Peter Eidenbach and Linda Hart. Education during the ranching era on The U.S.
    Army White Sands Missile Range, New Mexico.

Sonic Boom and the Supersonic Transport by Major Richard M. Roberds in the Air University Review,
    July-August 1971.

*Sonic Boom Research And Design Considerations In The Development Of A Commercial Supersonic Trans
port (SST)* by Thomas H. Higgins. Presented at the Seventh Meeting of the Acoustical Society of
    America, November 3, 1965.

System Introduction, Brief of this Instructional Unit. Nike system info covering 1954-1964 from the U.S.
    Army Air Defense School at Fort Bliss, Texas. File No. HA1.12003.

The Aeromedical Field Laboratory, Space Medicine at Holloman Air Force Base by Gregory Kennedy when he
    was at the Space Center in Alamogordo.

The Athena Story – WSMR. A brochure about the Athena/Abres project and its operation. No date but
    appears to be prior to first firings from Green River.

The Beginnings of Research in Space Biology at the Air Force Missile Development Center, Holloman Air
    Force Base, New Mexico 1946-1952.

The Culmination: Creation of the WAC Corporal. Chapter 13 of Benjamin Zibit's Ph.D. dissertation.

The Guided Missile, July 1946 – a technical journal from the Guided Missiles Committee under the Joint
    Chiefs of Staff.

The Man Behind the Rocket – The Story of Robert Goddard – Unsung Father of the Space Age by
    Leonard M. Fanning.

The Mission of White Sands Proving Ground and You, a briefing prepared by the Post TI&E Branch, 1953.

The Rise And Fall Of Psoroptic Scabies In Bighorn Sheep In The San Andres Mountains, New Mexico by Walter
    M. Boyce and Mara E. Weisenberger. In the *Journal of Wildlife Diseases,* 2005.

The Trinity Experiments by Thomas Merlan.

Theater Missile Defense Extended Test Range, draft Environmental Impact Statement, 6 January 1994.

Thermal Effects Of Atomic bomb Explosions On Soils At Trinity And Eniwetok by Eugene Staritzky,
    June 13, 1950. LA-1126.

U.S. Army Missile and Rockets from the U.S. Army Missile Command, Redstone Arsenal, Alabama.

U.S. Geological Survey Bulletin #285. 1905.

U.S. Geological Survey Professional Paper #68. 1910.

U.S. Naval Ordnance Missile Test Facility, A History by James Glynn.

White Sands History, Range Beginnings and Early Missile Testing, Public Affairs WSMR – reproduction of the
    first section of the White Sands 1959 historical report on the first 10 years of the range.

White Sands Missile Range Capabilities Handbook, 2000.

White Sands Missile Range Technical Capabilities, circa 1986.

White Sands Missile Range, Range Customer Handbook, 2011.

WSPG Diary 1957, 1958, 1959

WSPG In Retrospect On Eighth Anniversary by Eve E. Simmons. Undated.

Fact Sheets

Acquisition of Land for White Sands Missile Range

Aerobee-Hi

Athena

Beech C-45B

Birds Of The San Andres National Wildlife Refuge

Bumper Project - Part of G.E.'s Decade of Guided Missile Progress

Copperhead

DC-XA Flight Test and Operations

First Firings At WSPG – released by JPL

Flying Saucer, Voyager Balloon

G.E. Reveals Missile Milestones

Geology of the Organ Mountains, BLM

GMLRS

Guided Missiles – Modern Weapons For The Modern Army, by General Electric

Hawk Surface-to-Air Missile System

High Energy Laser Systems Test Facility

HIMARS

Historical Background of White Sands Missile Range Area

Introducing The Aerial Cable Range

Large Blast/Thermal Simulator

Launch Complex 33

Launch Complex 33, National Historic Landmark Dedication, May 27, 1986

Lichtenberg Figures

Loki-Dart

Mammals Of The San Andres National Wildlife Refuge

Matador, Surface-to-Surface Guided Missile

Media Information Package – Media Day For LINEAR Program. MIT Lincoln Labs November 18, 1998.

Missile Fact Sheets by WSMR in one package: Aerobee, Dragon, HAWK, Lance, Little John, Nike Hercules, Pershing, Redeye, SAM-D, Sergeant, Standard, Talos.

Missile Park

Multiple Launch Rocket System (MLRS)

NASA fact sheets for Comet Hale-Bopp sounding rocket missions: 36.155, 36.156, 36.157 and 36.158

Nike

Nike

Patriot Air Defense Guided Missile System

Pogo-Hi

Project Bumper

Redstone

Rockets: History and Theory

Roland

Safeguard BMD: The Spartan Missile

Significant Events, 1945 – 1983

Skyscreen (West) Fact Sheet

Solar Furnace

Space Shuttle And White Sands Missile Range

Statistics – annual fact sheet published by WSMR

The Hermes Project

The Mexican Wolf

The Road To Stallion – A Guide to RR7

The Von Braun House

Tomahawk Cruise Missile

US Army White Sands Missile Range Utah Launch Complex, Green River, Utah

V-2 Project – Part of G.E.'s Decade of Guided Missile Progress

V-2 Story

Viking

White Sands Missile Range At A Glance

White Sands Missile Range Fauna

White Sands Missile Range Hall of Fame

White Sands Pupfish - *Wildlife Notes,* New Mexico Game and Fish

White Sands Space Harbor

Index

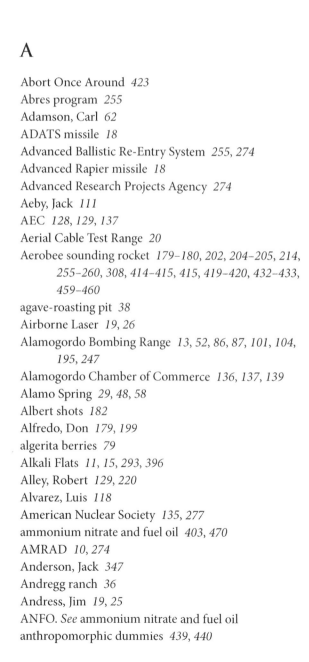

Made in the USA
Middletown, DE
01 November 2024

63515244R00285